AF600079

THE RIGHTS AND OBLIGATIONS OF METROPOLITANS

THE CATHOLIC UNIVERSITY OF AMERICA
CANON LAW STUDIES
No. 260

The Rights and Obligations of Metropolitans

A HISTORICAL SYNOPSIS AND COMMENTARY

BY THE

REV. ALPHONSE SYLVESTER POPEK, M.A., J.C.L.
Priest of the Archdiocese of Milwaukee

A DISSERTATION

Submitted to the Faculty of the School of Canon Law of the Catholic University of America in Partial Fulfillment of the Requirements for the Degree of Doctor of Canon Law

THE CATHOLIC UNIVERSITY OF AMERICA PRESS
WASHINGTON, D. C.
1947

NIHIL OBSTAT:
CLEMENS V. BASTNAGEL, J.U.D.
Censor Deputatus

Washingtonii, D. C., die 3 maii, 1948

IMPRIMATUR:
✠ MOSES E. KILEY, S.T.D.
Archiepiscopus Milwaukiensis

Milwaukiæ, Wis., die 8 maii, 1948

PRINTED IN THE UNITED STATES OF AMERICA
BY THE SERAPHIC PRESS, MILWAUKEE, WIS.

DEO
UNI TRINOQUE

TABLE OF CONTENTS

Chapter III

Chapter IV

PAGE

CHAPTER V

Chapter VII

Chapter VIII

Chapter IX

CHAPTER X

CHAPTER XI

FOREWORD

The present study is a delineation, along historical and canonical lines, of the metropolitan institution from the earliest times to the present day.

Although the exact historical date of the beginning of this ecclesiastical institution is shrouded by the lack of pertinent data in the sources of Christian antiquity, the canons of the I Council of Nicæa (325) give us the first precise historical note implying its existence even before the holding of the Council. From that date forward the sources are most generous in their contributions toward a rather complete picture of the growth and development of the institution.

In spite of an early breakdown of the metropolitan system in the Western World, the institution was re-born, especially through the efforts of the Popes who saw the utility of this intermediary hierarchical grade between the papacy and the episcopate. After a few centuries the system was all but broken again by the combination of civil and ecclesiastical forces. The one great factor at this time which sought the dissolution of the metropolitan system were the False Decretals. It is to the credit of the Council of Trent (1545-1563) that the institution was not only salvaged from a possible disappearance, but was stabilized in the scope of its powers. The growth of the metropolitan institution in the East was concurrent with that in the West until a little after the IV Council of Constantinople (869-870). At that time the growth of the power of the patriarchs and the frequent invasions of the infidels so weakened the metropolitan institute that it has not altogether recovered all of its power even to the present day.

The portrayal of the metropolitan institution is developed in this dissertation with an eye to the various rights and obligations which the metropolitans enjoyed in the divergent phases of the checkered history of the institute.

Beginning with a bare modicum of power, through canonical legislation the rights and duties of metropolitans grew to such tremendous proportions in the Latin Discipline that there was a danger that these would weaken papal and episcopal power. The struggle against metropolitans, which is evidenced in the ecclesiastical legislation of the early Middle Ages, reduced their stature to that in which they found themselves prior to the publication of the Church's Code of Canon Law. In the Oriental Discipline the weakened condition of the office of the metropolitan precluded a struggle against the patriarchs, so much so that the latter absorbed the rights and obligations of the former without much difficulty. The publication of the Oriental Code of Canon Law should do much to stabilize the rights and duties of the Oriental metropolitans within and outside the patriarchates. The insertion of rich material on metropolitans into the *Fonti* seems to indicate the Church's desire to renew and re-strengthen metropolitan rights and obligations.

In the historical section of this study the writer does not pretend to have exhausted the many possibilities which the sources provide. He simply has dug along one vein of material in a veritable mine of information. He has attempted to present an over-all view of the growth and decline of metropolitan rights and obligations rather than to exhaust any of the many details which still call for deeper and wider study. Such phases of the metropolitan institute as the accumulation of privileges and the history of the pallium have been omitted for the sake of brevity. Another feature which could have been developed is the history of the rights and obligations of the Oriental metropolitans from the time of the IV Council of Constantinople to the present date. This too was forsaken lest the study take on major proportions not intended by the writer.

In the canonical commentary, the chief concern of the writer were the canons which deal with metropolitan rights and obligations, namely canons 271-280. It may be true that the above-mentioned canons are not the most practical canons of the Code, yet there are so many laws which can be collated with them, that the full strength of the metropolitan institution can never be realized unless a sincere effort is made to study and to understand them in these relations. The whole gamut of metropolitan rights and obligations, if carried out in the spirit of the Code, cannot but help advance the observance of Church discipline. In the drawing up of a commentary on the rights and obligations of the Oriental metropolitans the project was difficult in view of the lack of a Code and commentaries. Here, too, it is to be hoped that the metropolitan institution will return to its deserved place in the Oriental hierarchy. Its result will be to bring the hierarchical arrangement of the Oriental Discipline closer to that of the Latin Discipline and to knit together the faithful and the clergy within each of the various Rites.

The greatest difficulty encountered by the writer in dealing with the extent of ecclesiastical provinces was the unsettled territorial condition of the war-torn world. The condition of flux with regard to civil boundaries in many corners of the world will inevitably bring about changes in the geographical status of ecclesiastical provinces. A similar difficulty arose from the status of concordats which also find themselves in not too happy a situation during these times.

Finally, at this point, the writer wishes to express his sincere gratitude to his Ordinary, the Most Reverend Moses Elias Kiley, Archbishop of Milwaukee, for the opportunity he has given the writer to continue the study of Canon Law at the Catholic University of America. Then, too, appreciation must be tendered to all the members of the Faculty of the School of Canon Law at the Catholic University of America for their kind assistance and priceless inspiration. The many priest students who assisted in the translations, as well as the librarians of the Mullen Library deserve the writer's heartfelt gratitude.

Historical Conspectus

CHAPTER I

THE METROPOLITAN INSTITUTION IN THE EARLIEST TIMES

SECTION A

ETYMOLOGY OF THE TERM "METROPOLITAN"

The name *metropolitan* is almost a complete transliteration of the Greek word μητροπολίτης, which in turn is derived from another Greek word, namely, μητρόπολις. Gratian, in one of the canons of his *Concordia Discordantium Canonum* (c. 1140), which he ascribed to Isidore of Seville (+636) (*Ethimologiæ*, Liber VII, Caput 12), noted that the name as such may have been derived from the combination of μέτρον and πόλις.[1] The two words give the meaning of measure, boundary or limits of a city, which, when applied to a metropolitan, would signify that as such he was one who was at the head of the territory within the limits of his own city, and nothing more. In support of this derivation the gloss turned to a letter written by Pope Pelagius II (578-590), in which the Pope spoke of the number of cities an ecclesiastical province included in order to insure proper judicial procedure in the court of its ecclesiastical metropolitan.[2]

---

[1] "...metropolitani autem a mensura civitatum vocantur..."; "... metropolitanus a mensura civitatum [vocatur]..."—c. 1, D. XXI—*Corpus Iuris Canonici* (editio Lipsiensis secunda post Aemilii Ludovici Richteri curas ad librorum manu scriptorum et editionis Romanæ fidem recognovit et adnotatione critica instruxit Aemilius Friedberg, 2 vols., Lipsiæ: Ex Officina Bernhardi Tauchnitz, 1879-1881. Editio anastatice repetita, Lipsiæ: Tauchnitz, 1928). (This edition will be used exclusively, except for citations from the *Glossæ*, which will be taken from the Roman edition).

[2] "Scitote certam provinciam esse, quæ habet decem, aut undecim civitates...et unum metropolitanum, aliosque suffraganeos x vel xi episcopos iudices: ad quorum iudicium omnes causæ episcoporum, et reliquorum sacerdotum, ac civitatum referantur, ut ab his omnibus iusta consona voce discernantur..."—*Glossa Ord.* ad c. 2, C. VI, q. 3. Jaffé, *Regesta Pontificum Romanorum, ab condita Ecclesia ad annum*

It hardly seems likely that μητροπολίτης should be derived from a μέτρον root, although the meaning of the combination is not altogether incongruous. However, Gratian included another possible derivation, as given by Isidore of Seville, from the combination of μητρός (the genitive of μήτηρ) and πόλις.[3] This union of words gives the combined word *metropolis* the meaning of mother-city. The name *metropolitan* would then mean, if this derivation is followed, that he was the head of a mother-church from which a foundation of new churches went out, which daughter-churches stood in a relation of dependence on him as the head of the mother-church. The gloss turned to canon 3 of the XI Council of Toledo (675) in support of this derivation. The canon in question prescribed that in the provinces everyone hold to the same manner of reciting the psalms as observed in the metropolitan see, because the metropolis is the mother of the sacerdotal dignity of its filial cities.[4] Many authors accept this derivation

---

post Christum natum MCXCVIII (2. ed., correctam et auctam auspiciis Gulielmi Wattenbach curaverunt F. Kaltenbrunner [ad annum DXC], P. Ewald [DXC-DCCCLXXXII], S. Loewenfeld [DCCCLXXXII-MCXCVIII], 2 vols. in 1, Lipsiæ, 1885-1888), n. + 1051 (hereafter cited as Jaffé); Hinschius (*Decretales Pseudo-Isidorianæ et Capitula Angilramni* [Lipsiæ: Ex Officina Bernhardi Tauchnitz, 1863], p. 724), claimed that this letter was spurious (hereafter cited as *Decretales Pseudo-Isidorianæ*). Cf. Mansi, *Sacrorum Conciliorum Nova et Amplissima Collectio* (53 vols. in 60, Paris, Arnhem, Leipzig, 1901-1927), IX, 900 (hereafter cited as Mansi); Migne, *Patrologiæ Cursus Completus — Series Latina* (221 vols., Parisiis, 1844-1855), LXXII, 738 (hereafter cited as *MPL*).

[3] "...vel dicitur a metros, quod est mater, et polis, quod est civitas, quia est mater aliarum civitatum." — *Glossa Ord.* ad c. 1, D. XXI.

[4] "...placuit huic sancto concilio, ut metropolitanæ sedis auctoritate coacti uniuscuiusque provinciæ cives, rectoresque ecclesiarum unum eumdemque in psallendo teneant modum, quem in metropolitana sede cognoverint institutum.... Sic enim iustum est, ut inde unusquisque sumat regulas magisterii, unde honoris consecrationem accipit, ut iuxta maiorum decreta sedes, que [quæ] uniuscuiusque sacerdotalis dignitatis est mater, sit ecclesiasticæ magistra rationis...." — c. 13, D. XII; cf. Bruns, *Canones Apostolorum et Conciliorum Sæculorum IV-VII* (2 vols., Berolini, 1839), I, 309. Note use of "pontifices" instead of "cives" in the Bruns text. (Hereafter cited as Bruns.)

without even alluding to the other possibility of origin.[5] The II Provincial Council of Baltimore (1866), in drawing up its decrees on metropolitans also accepted this derivation.[6]

Section B

Relation of Ecclesiastical Provinces to Civil Provinces

Article 1. The Roman Provincial System

The civil metropolis was an important feature in the plan of Roman government. At the time of the liberation of the Church from the catacombs, the Empire was divided into districts called provinces (ἐπαρχίαι). To maintain a uniform system of government throughout the Empire there

---

[5] Badii, *Institutiones Iuris Canonici* (3. ed., 2 vols., Florentiæ: Libreria Editrice Florentina, 1921-1922) I, 187 (hereafter cited as *Institutiones*); De Meester, *Juris Canonici et Juris Canonico-civilis Compendium* (nova ed., 3 vols. in 4, Brugis: Desclée, 1921-1928), II, 104 (hereafter cited as *Compendium*); Coronata, *Institutiones Iuris Canonici* (5 vols., Vols. I-II, 2. ed., 1939; Vol. III, 2. ed., 1941; Vol. IV, 2. ed., 1945; Vol. V, 1936; Taurini: Marietti), I, 432 (hereafter cited as *Institutiones*); *Haring, Grundzüge des katholischen Kirchenrechts* (3. ed., 1 vol. in 2, Graz: Ulrich Moser-J. Mayerhoff, 1924), I, 264 (hereafter cited as *Kirchenrecht*); Prümmer, *Manuale Iuris Canonici in Usum Scholarum* (6. ed., Friburgi Brisgoviæ: Herder, 1933), p. 151 (hereafter cited as *Manuale*); Raus, *Institutiones Canonicæ iuxta Novum Codicem Iuris* (ed. altera, Lugduni-Parisiis: Typis Emmanuelis Vitte, 1931), p. 173 (hereafter cited as *Institutiones*); Sipos, *Enchiridion Iuris Canonici* (4. ed., Pécs: Ex Typographia "Haladás R. T.," 1940), p. 204 (hereafter cited as *Enchiridion*); Thomassinus, *Vetus et Nova Ecclesiæ disciplina circa beneficia et beneficiarios* (10 vols., Magontiaci, 1787), Pars I, Lib. I, cap. xxxix, n. 3 (hereafter cited as *Ecclesiæ Disciplina*); Van Espen, *Ius Ecclesiasticum Universum* (5 vols., Lovanii, 1753), Pars I, Tit. XIX, c. 1, nn. 3, 4 (hereafter cited as *Ius Universum*); Icard, *Prælectiones Iuris Canonici Habitæ in Seminario Sancti Sulpitii* (6. ed., 3 vols., Parisiis: apud Lecoffre Filium et Socios, 1886), I, 235 (hereafter cited as *Prælectiones*).

[6] "Metropolitæ nomen originem ducit a principaliori provinciæ civitate, quæ metropolis, quasi cæterarum urbium mater, vocabatur." — *Concilii Plenarii Baltimorensis II, in Ecclesia Metropolitana Baltimorensi, a die VII ad diem XXI Octobris, A.D. MDCCCLXVI, Habiti, et a Sede Apostolica Recogniti, Acta et Decreta* (2. ed., Baltimoræ: John Murphy, 1880), n. 78, p. 59 (hereafter cited as *Acta et Decreta Concilii Plenarii Baltimorensis II*).

was in each of these eparchies a mother city (μητρόπολις), which served as a clearing-house for all the administrative and judicial matters pertaining to Rome, and later to Constantinople, the civil capitals of the Empire. From the metropolis in each province, the outlying cities, villages and rural regions, felt the influence of the imperial cities, and through it the inhabitants of each eparchy made their contact with the imperial cities.[7]

Article 2. Adoption and Adaptation of the Roman System

With the Edict of Milan (313) under Constantine the Great (c. 272-337), when the Church began its civilly authorized existence in the open, there was a serious necessity to expand to the full its latent governmental powers, which had been held back from normal development during the period of civil persecution. It was not strange that the Church found it convenient, as a rule, to adopt the civil boundaries as ecclesiastical territorial divisions as well.[8] By divine institution, the papacy, over the whole Church, and the episcopate, aiding the Pope in each episcopal see, were intended to be the nucleus of legislative, administrative and judicial power, and as such were capable of directing the Church to the fulfillment of its divine mission.[9] Yet, the Church, to become more efficient in handling such matters, adopted and adapted the Roman provincial system. This is particularly true in the Orient. Hefele (1809-1893)-Leclercq

---

[7] *Cambridge Ancient History* (12 vols., Cambridge: University Press, 1928-1939, Vol. X, ed. Cook, Adcock, Charlesworth, 1934), Vol. X; Bury, *History of the later Roman Empire from the death of Theodosius I to the death of Justinian (A.D. 395 to A.D. 565)* (2 vols., London: Macmillan and Co., 1923).

[8] Hefele-Leclercq, *Histoire des Conciles* (10 vols. in 19, Paris: Letouzey et Ané, 1907-1938), I, 540 (hereafter cited as Hefele-Leclercq); Hinschius, *Das Kirchenrecht der Katholiken und Protestanten in Deutschland* (6 vols., Berlin, 1869-1897. Vols. I-IV, *System des katholischen Kirchenrechts, 1869-1888*), I, 539 (hereafter cited as *Kirchenrecht*).

[9] Ottaviani, *Institutiones Iuris Publici Ecclesiastici* (2. ed., 2 vols., Romæ: Typis Polyglottis Vaticanis, 1935-1936), I, 233-434 (hereafter cited as *Institutiones*).

(1869-1945) remarked that, if the Church often accepted these civil divisions as models for its own, it was to facilitate the transaction of business, and to prevent the abandonment of traditional customs. Along with the adoption of these civil provinces as ecclesiastical provinces came the adoption of the great network of metropolitan cities, again for the sake of facilitating the conduct of administrative and judicial matters, and also to continue the Apostolic tradition.[10]

The Council of Nicæa (325) ordered in its 4th canon that a bishop be chosen by the other bishops of the whole eparchy, and that the metropolitan in each eparchy had the right to confirm the bishop's election.[11] The word *eparchy* here most certainly designated the civil province; and evidently the Council simply accepted the civil division as the basis of the ecclesiastical division. In the 5th canon of the same Council, where the legislation concerned the convocation of synods in each province, the Fathers of the Council simply took the civil division in the sense of an ecclesiastical division.[12] It was especially the importance of the political province that the Council of Antioch *in Encæniis* (341) had in view when it said in its 9th canon: the bishops of each eparchy must understand that it is the bishop of the metropolis who has charge of the business of the eparchy, because all must meet at the metropolis to transact their business.[13]

---

[10] Hefele-Leclercq, I, 540.

[11] The expression occurs twice in this canon: "...ἐν τῇ ἐπαρχίᾳ...."; "...καθ' ἑκάστην ἐπαρχίαν...." — C. 1, D. LXIV; Bruns, I, 15; Hardouin, *Conciliorum Collectio Regia Maxima* (12 vols., Parisiis, 1714-1715), I, 323-324 (hereafter cited as Hardouin); Mansi, II, 670; Schroeder, *Disciplinary Decrees of the General Councils: Text, Translation and Commentary* (St. Louis: Herder, 1937), p. 513; p. 26 (hereafter cited as *Decrees*).

[12] The expression occurs three times: "...καθ' ἑκάστην ἐπαρχίαν ..."; "...καθ' ἑκάστην ἐπαρχίαν..."; "ἵνα κοινῇ...τῆς ἐπαρχίας..."; Bruns, I, 15; Hardouin, I, 325-326; Mansi, II, 669-670; Schroeder, *Decrees*, p. 513; p. 28.

[13] C. 2, C. IX, q. 3; Bruns, I, 82-83; Hardouin, I, 595-598; Mansi, II, 1311-1312. Cf. *infra*, p. 16, footnote 48, for discussion of the date of the Council.

It sometimes happened that a civil province was divided into two. This generally had the result that the city which was elevated to the position of a civil metropolis also rose to the dignity of an ecclesiastical metropolis. Not infrequently a bishop, for the sole purpose of exalting himself to the rank of a metropolitan, would induce the emperor to raise his see, contrary to the canons, to the rank of an ecclesiastical metropolis, the rank of civil metropolis, however, being withheld from the city; or the title of civil metropolis was granted to the city, and the bishop from motives of ambition would arrogate to himself all the rights and privileges of an ecclesiastical metropolitan and cut the province into two, though there was no intention on the part of the emperor to divide the province for civil, and much less for ecclesiastical, purposes. The Council of Chalcedon (451) was concerned with such cases in two of its canons.

The controversy between Tyre and Berythus probably gave occasion for the drawing up of canon 12.[14] During the fourth session of the Council, held on the 20th of October, Bishop Photius of Tyre came before the Council with a complaint against Bishop Eusthathius of Berythus. Photius had appealed to the emperor for a solution of his problem, and the emperor directed his case to the Council. According to the complaint of Photius, Eusthathius violated the rights of the Church of Tyre by procuring a decree from Emperor Theodosius II (418-450) permitting him to consecrate bishops in the cities of Biblus, Botrys, Tripolis, Orthosias, Arcas and Antaradon, which cities were situated in the ecclesiastical province of Tyre. Photius begged that the Council restore the ancient privileges to the Church of Tyre.

Eusthathius, on the other hand, leaned heavily on the above-mentioned decree of Emperor Theodosius II in making his defense, but the imperial commissioners and the Fathers of the Council declared that not a decree of the

---

[14] C. un., D. CI; Bruns, I, 28-29; Mansi, VII, 376-377; Schroeder, *Decrees*, p. 521; p. 104.

emperor but the canons of the Church were the standard in such matters. In answer to this Eusthathius declared that the emperor had raised Berythus to the rank of a metropolis, and at a Synod of Constantinople under Bishop Anatolius had assigned the six cities to his new metropolis.[15]

Photius complained that from the very beginning he had not accepted the arrangement made by the emperor. After some further discussion it was decided, in virtue of the 4th canon of the Council of Nicæa (325), that in the whole ecclesiastical province of Phœnicia I there should be but one ecclesiastical metropolis, Tyre, and that only the bishop of Tyre should consecrate the bishops of the province. The bishop of Berythus was told that he could no longer appeal to the rights which Emperor Theodosius II had accorded him, since the Fathers of the Council agreed with the papal legates that all imperial decrees which were in opposition to the canons had to be considered void.[16]

Canon 17 of the same Council settled the strife between Nicomedia and Nicæa with regard to metropolitan rights.[17] At the 13th session, held on the 30th of October, Archbishop Eunomius of Nicomedia appealed to the emperor, petitioning him to protect and to restore the privileges of his see which had been forcibly violated by Bishop Anastasius of Nicæa. The emperor decided that the case should be settled by the Council. During the Council Anastasius denied that

[15] Hefele-Leclercq, II, footnote on pp. 714-715. There is no question that the emperor had the power to raise Berythus, which had previously belonged to the civil and ecclesiastical province of Tyre, to the rank of civil metropolis, which in time might have led to its becoming an ecclesiastical metropolis. But it appears that in this case the emperor had by his own authority declared the city of Berythus an ecclesiastical metropolis without at the same time raising its civil rank. It is clear that he intruded improperly into the ecclesiastical sphere. There is no doubt that the Synod of Constantinople, in true Byzantine fashion, had lent a helping hand to give practical effect to the assumption of the emperor.

[16] Hardouin, II, 435-446; Mansi, VII, 85-98; Hefele-Leclercq, II, 713-715; Thomassinus, *Ecclesiæ Disciplina*, Pars I, Lib. I, cap. xxxix, n. 5.

[17] Bruns, I, 30; Mansi, VII, 378; Schroeder, *Decrees*, pp. 521-522; p. 116.

he was guilty of any offense, and asserted that it was rather the bishop of Nicomedia who made encroachments on his province. Eunomius in response to this declared that Anastasius excommunicated clerics of Basilinopolis, a city which was situated in the eparchy of Bithynia, subject to him as metropolitan of Nicomedia. Anastasius stated that Basilinopolis belonged to the Church of Nicæa because: first, Emperor Julian (361-363) had raised it to the position of a city while it was still a village belonging to Nicæa, and second, after it became a city, the bishop of Nicæa went there to consecrate on the invitation of John Chrysostom, Bishop of Constantinople. Eunomius answered this by saying that many more consecrations took place in Basilinopolis from Nicomedia than from Nicæa.

Again the 4th canon of the Council of Nicæa (325) was invoked as the determining standard. Anastasius claimed that this canon was in his favor inasmuch as he was a metropolitan, and he based this contention on the decrees of Emperor Valentinian I (364-375) and Emperor Valens (364-378). Eunomius then appealed to a still later decree of Emperor Valentinian I, which stated that the honor given to Nicæa could in no way interfere with the rights of the Church of Nicomedia. The imperial commissioners remarked that in both imperial decrees nothing was said of the ecclesiastical position of the two cities, but only of the civil honors which were to be given to both of them. Since, according to the canons of the Church there could be only one ecclesiastical metropolis in each province, the Council asserted that Nicomedia was the ecclesiastical metropolis of Bithynia, and that the bishop of Nicomedia was the one to consecrate all the bishops of that province. The bishop of Nicæa had only the right of precedence over all the other comprovincial bishops of the province because of the civil rank given to his city.[18]

[18] Bruns, I, 30; Hardouin, II, 563-571; Mansi, VII, 301-314; Hefele-Leclercq, II, 761-763; Thomassinus, *Ecclesiæ Disciplina*, Pars I, Lib. I, cap. xxxix, n. 8.

These are but two cases from among many concerning the conformity of ecclesiastical provinces with civil provinces.[19] The policy of the East was to maintain this conformity. Rome gave its sanction to this mode of action sometime between the Councils of Nicæa (325) and Chalcedon (451). Already Pope Innocent I (401-417), in a letter to an Antiochian bishop, declared that whenever the emperor changed the boundaries of provinces, either by diminishing or enlarging them, the churches were not to recede from the old division, thereby showing that ecclesiastical provinces followed the plan of civil divisions.[20]

Egypt in 325 numbered four civil and ecclesiastical provinces, namely: Egypt, Thebaid, Libya and Pentapolis.[21] Canon 6 of the Council of Nicæa (325) in giving the supervision of these provinces to the bishop of Alexandria made no allusions to any distinction between the civil and the ecclesiastical eparchies.[22]

Northern Africa was divided into three great civil provinces: Proconsular Africa, Numidia and Mauretania. The early legislation of the African Church seems to point to an identity between the civil and the ecclesiastical provinces. Canon 1 of the Council of Hippo (393) declared that all African provinces were to be guided by the Church of Carthage with regard to the celebration of Easter; the canon simply took for granted that the political division into provinces was the same as the church division.

Since canon 3 of the same Council stated that Mauretania Sitifensis was to have a primate of its own and did not need to consider itself a part of the Numidian primacy

[19] Thomassinus (*Ecclesiæ Disciplina*, Pars I, Lib. I, cap. xxxix, n. 9) mentions a few more solutions of such disputes along the same line.

[20] "Nam quod sciscitaris, utrum divisis Imperiali iudicio Provinciis, ut duæ Metropoles fiant, sic duo Metropolitani Episcopi debeant nominari: non vere visum est ad mobilitatem mundanarum necessitatem, Dei ecclesiam commutari, honoresque aut divisiones perpeti, quas pro suis causis faciendas duxerit Imperator." — Jaffé, n. 310; Mansi, III, 1055; *MPL*, XX, 547.

[21] Hefele-Leclerq, I, 558; Schroeder, *Decrees*, p. 30.

[22] Bruns, I, 15-16; Hardouin, I, 325-326; Mansi, II, 669-672; Schroeder, *Decrees*, p. 520; pp. 29-30.

any longer, it appears that the African Church was making an attempt to adjust the ecclesiastical territorial boundaries to the already existing civil ones. Further, canon 4 of the Council of Hippo distinguished between the primates of the first sees and the bishops of other sees, which distinction can be justified only on the grounds that the former headed the larger districts mentioned above, while the latter were restricted to their small episcopal sees.

In corroboration of this, canon 9, which insisted that all ecclesiastical provinces send their deputies to the General Councils held every year, specifically exempted Tripolis, a lesser district within one of the provinces, from sending more than one deputy on account of the poverty of its bishops. Finally, canon 10 ordered that any accusation against a bishop had to be lodged before the primate of the province. Since every one of the lesser bishops was always called a bishop only, the Fathers of the Council made this bit of legislation clearer by deliberately calling the bishop heading the greater territorial district the primate of the province.[23]

The great synodal activity, both in the provinces and in the entire country as such, is a strong argument that Africa followed suit in the matter of adopting the civil provinces as ecclesiastical provinces. It was decided in the 5th canon of the VI Council of Carthage (401) that the primates of the several provinces were so to arrange their provincial councils that they would not interfere with the General Councils of the country. The canon did not speak of many provinces but only of several; hence there must have been a division along the line of the three great civil provinces. Canon 11 of this Council advised every primate to divide his province into two or three districts in order to have deputies from each of them at the General African Councils. These divisions were not to be understood as permanent

[23] Hefele-Leclercq, II, 84-85; Hardouin, I, 954; Mansi, III, 849-850. Bruns in his collection (I, 136) labels cc. 1, 3 and 4, which are cc. 2, 4 and 5 respectively in the collections of Hefele-Leclercq, Hardouin and Mansi.

political districts, but simply as discretionary boundaries in order to assure every part of the province some form of representation at the General Councils.[24]

Nevertheless, what is more certain of Africa is this, that so-called metropolitan rights were not attached to any particular cities, as was done in the Orient. It was always the oldest bishop in consecration in each province who was the primate of the ecclesiastical eparchy.[25] His bishopric was called the *prima sedes* of the province.[26] As early as 305, at the Council of Cirta in Numidia, Secundus, the Bishop of Tigisium, the oldest of the eleven bishops present, presided at the meeting.[27]

Carthage alone was the exception to this rule. It was a primatial see by reason of place, and not by reason of episcopal authority. In this Carthage can be compared, not to the ordinary metropoles of the Orient, but rather to the extraordinary metropolitan sees of Alexandria and Antioch, which were mentioned in canon 6 of the Council of Nicæa (325). The bishop of Carthage stood on a higher plane than all the bishops of the *primæ sedis* variety and the simple bishops within the several provinces of Africa. He was a primate, and of the three primates over the great civil divisions he was the chief primate. Perhaps one could call him an archprimate, but to avoid confusion it is proper to refrain from using a name which was never given to him in history. In the course of time he would probably have

---

[24] Hefele-Leclercq, II, 127-128; Hardouin, I, 986.

[25] Hefele-Leclercq, I, 85, footnote 1; Coronata, *Institutiones*, I, 432; Haring, *Kirchenrecht*, p. 263, note 7; Hinschius, *Kirchenrecht*, II, 2; Saegmüller, *Lehrbuch des katholischen Kirchenrechts* (4. ed., Freiburg im Breisgau: Herder, 1925-1934) p. 304 (hereafter cited as *Kirchenrecht*); Sipos, *Enchiridion*, p. 224; Thomassinus, *Ecclesiæ Disciplina*, Pars I, Lib. I, cap. xl, n. 17; Wernz-Vidal, *Ius Canonicum ad Codicis Normam Exactum* (7 vols. in 8, 1923-1938; Vol. II, *Ius de Personis*, 3. ed., 1943, Vol. VI, *De Processibus*, 1. ed., 1927-1928, Romæ: Apud Aedes Universitatis Gregorianæ), II, 647-648 (hereafter cited as *Ius Canonicum*); Van Espen, *Ius Universum*, Pars I, Tit. xix, c. 2, n. 7.

[26] Canon 29 of the Council of Hippo (393): "The bishop of the *prima sedes* shall not be called *princeps sacerdotum* or *summus sacerdos*, but simply *primæ sedis episcopus*." — Hefele-Leclercq, II, 88.

[27] Hefele-Leclercq, I, 209.

become a patriarch. It was Aurelius of Carthage who opened the long series of councils which began with the one of Hippo in 393. During his term of office this first Council was followed by twenty more, and almost all of them were held at Carthage itself.[28] But even before 393 it was another Bishop of Carthage, Genethlius by name, who presided at a Council held in 387.[29]

The condition of Christianity in Spain before the time of Constantine (272-337) was none too fair. The Catholic religion was widespread in the south, but sparse in the north and east. Great ravages were committed in the southern part by the persecution of Decius (250-253) and his successors.[30] During the time of Augustus Imperator (c. 27) Spain was divided into three civil provinces: Terragona, Baetica and Lusitania. According to Flórez (1702-1773), a new division took place under Constantine the Great, when he divided the civil province of Tarragona into three sections: Tarragona, Carthagina and Galicia. This subdivision partitioned Spain into five civil provinces.[31]

As far as the relation between the civil and ecclesiastical provinces was concerned, Garcia-Villada (1879-1936) stated that there was an attempt to arrange the ecclesiastical organization according to the civil organization from the time of Diocletian (284-305) onward. According to this author, Diocletian was responsible for the division of Spain into the above-mentioned five provinces and for assigning to each of the five their respective capitals: Tarragona for Tarragona, Braga for Galicia, Merida for Lusitania, Seville for Baetica, and Carthagina for Carthagina. Garcia-Villada declared that the Church adopted this provincial division

---

[28] Hefele-Leclercq, II, 88.

[29] Hefele-Leclercq, II, 76.

[30] Poulet, *A History of the Catholic Church* (trans. and adapt. from the 4. French ed. by Raemers, 2 vols., St. Louis, Mo.: Herder Book Co., Vol. I, 1945), I, 133 (hereafter cited as *History of the Catholic Church*).

[31] *España Sagrada. Theatro Geographico-Historico de la Iglesia de España* (54 vols., Madrid, Vol. IV, 1749), IV, p. 70, n. 125 (hereafter cited as *España Sagrada*). A map of the provincial division may be found in this volume on pp. 106-107.

and metropolitan arrangement; the only ecclesiastical capital which did not coincide with the civil capital was in the case of Carthagina, where the Church chose Toledo as the metropolis.[32] Flórez, in keeping with his contention that Constantine the Great divided Spain into five provinces, pushed back the attempt of ecclesiastical and civil provincial coincidence to the times of Constantine.[33]

However, as in Africa, no metropolitan rights were attached to any particular cities in the very beginning. These rights were most probably given to the bishop who was senior by reason of consecration.[34] This may be the reason why the Bishop of Acci presided at the Council of Elvira (c. 300-306). Most probably he was the oldest of all the bishops present from the standpoint of episcopal consecration.[35] In examining canon 58 of this Council, one must note that what was called the *prima sedes* in Africa was known as the *prima cathedra* in Spain.[36]

But once the provincial system was consolidated, metropolitan rights were given to the bishops residing in the ecclesiastical metropoles according to the model of the Oriental metropoles. According to the division, five metropolitans should have been active in Church affairs, and yet Hefele-Leclercq mention six metropolitans in reporting on two Councils. At the X Council of Toledo (656) only three metropolitans were present, namely: Eugene of Toledo, Fugitivus of Seville and Fructuosus of Braga, while the metropolitans of Merida, Tarragona and Narbonne were absent.[37] And again, at the XIII Council of Toledo (683),

---

[32] *Historia Eclesiastica de España* (1 vol. in 2, Madrid: Compañía Ibero-Americana de Publicaciones S. A. Libreria Fernando Fe, 1929), I, 206 (hereafter cited as *Historia de España*).

[33] *España Sagrada*, IV, p. 129, n. 38.

[34] Hefele-Leclercq, I, 253-254; Garcia-Villada, *Historia de España*, IV, 206; Wernz-Vidal, *Ius Canonicum*, II, 647-648; Coronata, *Institutiones*, I, 432.

[35] Hefele-Leclercq, I, 253-254; Hinschius, *Kirchenrecht*, II, 2-3.

[36] "Placuit ubique et maxime in eo loco in quo prima cathedra constituta est episcopatus..." — Bruns, II, 9; cf. Hinschius, *Kirchenrecht*, II, 3, footnote 1.

[37] Hefele-Leclercq, III, 294.

the archbishops of Toledo, Braga, Merida, Seville, Tarragona and Narbonne were present.[38] The metropolitan of Narbonne is mentioned in both cases as the sixth metropolitan. Flórez called the division of Spain into five provinces Constantinian, and insisted that the addition of Narbonne was not of Roman but of Gothic institution. Hence from the times of the Goths, chiefly from the death of Liuva (Hermano de Leovigildo), the Church of Narbonne was added to the five metropolitan sees of the kingdom of Spain.[39]

Saegmüller (1860-1942) admitted that in the Occident there was a partial lack of political divisions before the fourth century.[40] So also Sipos.[41] The truth of this statement is borne out by what has been said of Spain before the time of Constantine. Italy fared badly in this respect, and yet the country as a whole could be considered as one vast church province. Gaul, of all the Occidental territories, was the least settled in the matter of provinces, until a semblance of political divisions came into the land with the end of the fourth and the beginning of the fifth century.

In recapitulation it must be said that even prior to the fourth century the Church in the East almost generally accepted the boundaries of the civil provinces as the limits of the ecclesiastical provinces. The Church of the Orient did not change these boundaries, not so much because of the material changes involved in such transactions, but because of imperial interference in matters purely ecclesiastical. However, before the time of Constantine the Great the Church in the West lacked the provincial division of territory for the most part, but, because of the practicability of such a division, it began to adopt the net-work of provinces and metropoles after the beginning of the fourth century.

---

[38] *Ibid.*, p. 547. Evidently the statement that Constantine the Great divided Spain into seven political provinces is an error. Cf. *ibid.*, I, 254.

[39] *España Sagrada*, IV, p. 130, n. 40.

[40] *Kirchenrecht*, p. 341.

[41] *Enchiridion*, p. 224.

The ecclesiastical territorial division along the lines of the civil territorial division was not an iron-bound rule. Hefele-Leclercq insisted that the Church was not obliged in principle to conform itself to these divisions of the states and of the provinces in establishing its own territorial divisions. The inference is clear, namely that the Church was free to accept or reject the entire plan, and free to adapt the system to its needs.[42] Wernz (1842-1914)-Vidal (1867-1938), in defending the hierarchical order of the Church, strongly protested against the false theory that the Church slavishly followed the civil provincial system in establishing its own.[43]

SECTION C

EARLIEST BEGINNINGS OF THE METROPOLITAN INSTITUTION

Article 1. Canonical Proof

The beginnings of the metropolitan institution are most obscure. The very first time the term *metropolitan* appeared in ecclesiastical legislation was at the beginning of the fourth century in the 4th canon of the Council of Nicæa (325).[44] The same Council employed the name again in its 6th canon.[45] The canons show that in the Oriental Church, even at this early date, the metropolitan institution was a highly developed organization, which embraced several episcopal sees and had already assumed the position of a link between the simple bishops on the one hand and the higher bishops, later exarchs and patriarchs, on the

[42] I, 540.

[43] *Ius Canonicum*, II, 541.

[44] 'Επίσκοπον προσήκει μάλιστα μὲν ὑπὸ πάντων τῶν ἐν τῇ ἐπαρχίᾳ καθίστασθαι...τὸ δὲ κῦρος τῶν γινομένων δίδοσθαι καθ' ἑκάστην ἐπαρχίαν τῷ μητροπολίτῃ." —C. 1, D. LXIV; Bruns, I, 15; Hardouin, I, 323-324; Mansi, II, 669-670; Schroeder, *Decrees*, p. 513; p. 26.

[45] "...Καθόλου δὲ πρόδηλον ἐκεῖνο, ὅτι εἴ τις χωρὶς γνώμης τοῦ μητροπολίτου γένοιτο ἐπίσκοπος, τὸν τοιοῦτον ἡ μεγάλη σύνοδος ὥρισε μὴ δεῖν εἶναι ἐπίσκοπον." Bruns, I, 16; Hardouin, I, 325-326; Mansi, II, 671-672; Schroeder, *Decrees*, p. 514; pp. 29-30.

other. Further, the canons make it rather clear that the Oriental metropolitans were already at the head of districts known as provinces, and that their sees were situated in cities which were important both politically and ecclesiastically. Finally, they give evidence that the metropolitans already formed a higher instance over the individual bishops under them in the common ecclesiastical affairs of their own entire district.[46]

Because of the high development of the institution at so early a time, it cannot be denied that metropolitans assumed power even before the Council of Nicæa (325).[47] The beginnings, therefore, must be pushed back into the period of the persecutions, but how far back it is difficult to say. Sixteen years after the Council of Nicæa (325), a Council was held at Antioch in 341.[48] The bishops, gathered together in this Council, drew up canon 9, which seems to shed some light in this regard. The canon approved the prerogatives of authority and honor which the bishop residing in the metropolis of the civil province had throughout the entire eparchy, safeguarding, however, the rights of all the comprovincial bishops in their parishes.

---

[46] Hinschius, *Kirchenrecht*, II, p. 1; Saegmüller, *Kirchenrecht*, p. 340; Sipos, *Enchiridion*, p. 224; De Meester, *Compendium*, II, 105; Makée, *Institutiones Juris Ecclesiasticæ tum Publici tum Privati* (2 vols., Parisiis: apud Roger et Chernovitz, 1897), I, 292 (hereafter cited as *Institutiones*); Prümmer, *Manuale*, p. 151; Raus, *Institutiones*, p. 173; Van Espen, *Ius Universum*, Pars I, Tit. XIX, c. 1, n. 2; Vermeersch-Creusen, *Epitome Iuris Canonici* (3 vols., Mechliniæ-Romæ: H. Dessain, Vol. I, 6. ed., 1937; Vol. II, 6. ed., 1940; Vol. III, 6. ed., 1946), I, 309 (hereafter cited as *Epitome*); Wernz-Vidal, *Ius Canonicum*, II, 647.

[47] Coronata, *Institutiones*, I, 416; Wernz-Vidal, *Ius Canonicum*, II, 547; Hinschius, *Kirchenrecht*, II, 2.

[48] There is a controversy concerning this Council. Some authors hold that it was held in 341 in Antioch *in Encæniis*. Cf. Hefele-Leclercq, I, 702-733. Some hold that the canons of this Council must be attributed to another Council held in Antioch about the year 332, e.g., P. and H. Ballerini, Alexander Natalis, Bardy. Some there are who hold the opinion that it was held in or close to the year 427. Cf. Van Hove, *Commentarium Lovaniense in Codicem Iuris Canonici*, Vol. I, Tom. I, *Prolegomena ad Codicem Iuris Canonici* (2. ed., Mechlinæ-Romæ: H. Dessain, 1945), 143-144, footnote 3 (hereafter cited as *Commentarium*). The writer will use the traditional date.

This canon, according to Wernz-Vidal, seems to hearken back to the 35th canon (33) of the *Canons of the Apostles*.[49] Although this so-called Apostolic Canon vouches for the existence of a higher organ of direction over the single bishops, it does not prove much, for the date of this collection of Canons is not definitely set, having been pushed back to the fifth century by certain authorities. Something which is a bit more definite is the existence of the so-called topical or particular councils held in the second century, at which more outstanding bishops presided.[50] But even this argument does not satisfactorily bring the beginnings of the metropolitan institution to a more definite date than does the 4th canon of Nicæa (325).

Article 2. Foreshadowing of the Institution in Apostolic Times

A dim foreshadowing of the metropolitan system can be found in Apostolic times. The Apostles often passed through the principal cities of one province for the purpose of preaching the Gospel there before entering another, and afterwards treated the faithful of that province as if they formed one community. For instance, when St. Paul wrote to the Church of Corinth, and to all the faithful of Achaia, he united all the Christians of the province of Achaia and at the head of that province he placed Corinth, which was its principal city or capital.[51]

He addressed in the same manner another of his letters "to the churches of Galatia," again uniting in his mind all

---

[49] "Τοὺς ἐπισκόπους ἑκάστου ἔθνους εἰδέναι χρὴ τὸν ἐν αὐτοῖς πρῶτον." Cf. *Ius Canonicum*, II, 647.

[50] Hefele-Leclercq, I, 125 ff., 141; Wernz-Vidal, *Ius Canonicum*, II, 547. One such Council held at Pontus near the end of the second century points out the importance of the presiding bishop. Eusebius in his *Historia Ecclesiastica* (V, 23) recorded this fact. "τῶν τε κατὰ πόντον ἐπισκόπων ὧν πάλμας ὡς ἀρχαιότατος προὐτέτακτο." — Migne, *Patrologiæ Cursus Completus — Series Græca* (161 vols., Parisiis, 1857-1866), XX, 495 (hereafter cited as *MPG*).

[51] II Corinthians, I, 1.

the communities of that civil province.[52] In writing to the Churches of Macedonia and Achaia, he spoke of them separately, indicating that the provinces of which Phillipi and Corinth were metropolitan cities were really distinct.[53]

The Apocalypse was addressed to the seven Churches forming a part of the province of Asia, of which Ephesus was the metropolis. For that reason St. John gave first place to the bishop of Ephesus.[54]

St. Peter began his First Epistle with the words: "Peter, an apostle of Jesus Christ, to the strangers dispersed through Pontus, Galatia, Cappadocia, Asia, and Bithynia, elect."[55] These were certainly territorial divisions in the provincial system of the Roman Empire.[56]

According to Hefele-Leclercq, the result of this procedure could have brought about the condition that bishops of the same region soon considered that there was a bond between them, and the bishop of the capital thus gained implicitly a sort of pre-eminence over his colleagues in the province. This pre-eminence could only be based in some cases on the civil importance of the capital.

Yet it must not be forgotten that the civil capitals were often also the ecclesiastical capitals, inasmuch as they were the first cities in the province in which a Christian Church was founded and from which the Gospel was made known to the other cities in the province.[57] Coronata adds the note that the Roman Pontiffs consented to the growth of the metropolitan institution either tacitly or explicitly during the early centuries, for they must have been conscious of the power which the bishops in these metropolitan cities

---

[52] Galatians, I, 2.

[53] Romans, XV, 26.

[54] Apocalypse, II, 1.

[55] I, 1.

[56] Cf. *Cambridge Ancient History* for general reference; also Bury, *History of the later Roman Empire*. Both of these works are cited *supra*, p. 4, footnote 7.

[57] I, 540-542; cf. Schroeder, *Decrees*, p. 26, footnote 63.

were assuming over the bishops within their civil provinces.[58]

Other authors, though they agree to this general Apostolic procedure as a possible explanation of the development of the metropolitan institution, appeal to the specific action on the part of St. Paul, who appointed Timothy over the province of Asia (I Timothy, I, 3; III, 1-16), and Titus over the Island of Crete (Titus I, 5-6). Timothy and Titus were to constitute bishops and priests in the individual cities, and to watch and preside over the bishops of their particular provinces of Asia and Crete respectively.[59]

The Fathers of the II Provincial Council of Baltimore (1866) referred to the appointment of Titus and Timothy as the beginning of the metropolitan institution without making any allusion to the canonical insecurity of their stand.[60]

Oesterle does not appeal to Apostolic times for the possible beginning of the institution as such, but goes back to the second and third centuries for its origin. He says that in these two centuries, when the Church was besieged by heretical and schismatic tendencies, the bishops were forced, as it were, to gather their strength into a unity, and thus

---

[58] *Institutiones*, I, 432.

[59] Badii, *Institutiones*, p. 187; Bargilliat, *Prælectiones Juris Canonici* (2 vols. Parisiis: apud Baston, Berche et Pagis, Vol. I, 37. ed. 1923), I, 140 (hereafter cited as *Prælectiones*); Cocchi, *Commentarium in Codicem Iuris Canonici ad Usum Scholarum* (8 vols. in 5, Taurinorum Augustæ: Marietti, Vol. II, 4. ed., 1937, Vol. III, 4. ed., 1940, Vol. VII, 3. ed., 1940, Vol. VIII, 4. ed., 1938), III, 117 (hereafter cited as *Commentarium*); De Meester, *Compendium*, II, 105; Makée, *Institutiones*, I, 292; Prümmer, *Manuale*, p. 151; Icard, *Prælectiones*, I, 223.

[60] "Officium autem Metropolitæ vel ab ipsis temporibus repeti potest Apostolorum, qui latiorem Episcopo in insigniori urbe constituto jurisdictionem tribuebant. Quod ex verbis D. Pauli ad Titum scribentis satis liquet: 'Hujus rei gratia reliqui te Cretæ, ut ea quæ desunt corrigas, et constituas per civitates presbyteros, sicut et ego disposui tibi.' Sic etiam, ut ex historiæ ecclesiasticæ monumentis apparet, Timotheus Ephesi, aliique aliis in locis constituti sunt, qui cæteros earum regionum Episcopos et dignitate anteirent, et in eos jurisdictionem ecclesiasticam exercerent." — *Acta et Decreta Concilii Plenarii Baltimorensis II*, n. 78, p. 59.

it is not at all surprising to find, in the third century, and perhaps in the second century, bishops who were closely situated to one another gathering together into councils. The president, so to speak, of these gatherings, was the bishop of the metropolis, that is to say, the bishop of that city which was the head of the respective province of the Roman Empire.[61]

Perhaps the best theory for the possible beginning of the metropolitan institution is that which is offered by Wernz-Vidal, who combine many possibilities into one. They said no one can deny that from the earliest times not all bishops had the same jurisdiction and honor. Apart from the prerogative of the Roman Pontiff, authority was delegated to certain bishops by the very ordination of the Apostles, as to Timothy in Proconsular Asia, and to Titus over the Island of Crete. But these bishops were still subject to the Apostles. In his letters St. Paul seemed to insinuate that certain churches, such as those of Corinth, of Phillipi and of Ephesus, were the centers toward which the other churches of the provinces were drawn, e.g., of Achaia, Macedonia and Proconsular Asia. These prerogatives of jurisdiction and honor were easily noticeable in those cities in which the Apostles themselves held their episcopal see or which they founded, such as Antioch and Jerusalem. Besides the example of the Apostles, the very spread of the Church, by which particular churches founded new filial churches which did not break away from their mother-church; the frequent celebration of Councils in different civil provinces; the reasonable custom adopted by the Church whereby the civil boundaries of provinces were approved as the limits of the ecclesiastical ones; in a word, all these combined, brought about the effect that already in the first centuries authority was given to certain sees either because of the importance of the see itself or because of the one who founded or governed it.[62]

---

[61] *Prælectiones Iuris Canonici* (Vol. I, Romæ: In Collegio Sancti Anselmi, 1931), p. 150 (hereafter cited as *Prælectiones*).

[62] Wernz-Vidal, *Ius Canonicum*, II, 647-648.

CHAPTER II

THE METROPOLITAN INSTITUTION TO THE EIGHTH CENTURY

SECTION A

DEVELOPMENT OF METROPOLITAN POWERS

Article 1. The Oriental Church

The powers and privileges of metropolitans in the Orient were determined by the various councils held there. The singular rights were the following: (a) the direction of elections which were conducted to fill vacant episcopal sees of the province, as well as the confirmation and consecration of the newly elected bishop; (b) the convocation of the bishops of the province to meetings held during the year, and the right to preside at these so-called provincial councils; (c) the granting of permissions to bishops of the province should they wish to travel; and finally, (d) the right of higher instance over the individual bishops for the direction of the common ecclesiastical affairs of the district.[1]

Should an episcopal vacancy occur in one of the minor cities of an eparchy, the comprovincial bishops were to gather for the election of a new bishop.[2] The much quoted

---

[1] Hinschius, *Kirchenrecht*, II, 1-2.

[2] This electoral procedure raises a problem. How is this mode of election to be reconciled with the older method? In apostolic times the Apostles themselves chose bishops. In the period immediately following apostolic times, the disciples of the Apostles ἐλλόγιμοι ἄνδρες chose bishops, but the election had to be approved by the whole community συνευδοκησάσης τῆς ἐκκλησίας πάσης (St. Clement, *Epist. I ad Corinth.*, c. 44). After the death of the disciples of the Apostles, according to St. Cyprian (+ 258), still another change came in. In almost all the provinces the nearest bishops in the province met in the city where the election was to be held. The bishop was elected *plebe præsente*. The episcopal dignity was conferred *universæ fraternitatis suffragio et episcoporum iudicio*. The people had the right of voting *(suffragium)*, whereas the right of decision *(iudicium)* was reserved to the bishops of

canon 4 of the Council of Nicæa (325) did not grant the metropolitan the exclusive right of choosing the new bishop, but insisted that the latter must be chosen by the bishops of the whole eparchy, and defined, by precise rules, the duties of the comprovincial bishops in the episcopal election. The metropolitan was given only the right either of confirming or of rejecting the elected candidate.[3]

From the canon itself it does not seem that the metropolitan was expected to summon the comprovincial bishops, or to be present at the electoral synod. Yet, somehow the spirit of this legislation seems to demand both of these duties to be fulfilled by the metropolitan. The occasion for the enactment of this canon was most probably given by Meletius, Bishop of Lycopolis in Egypt, who without the participation of the bishops of the province, and without the approval of the metropolitan, chose and consecrated bishops and thus brought about the Meletian Schism.[4]

The 6th canon of the same Council was chiefly concerned with the prerogatives of the greater metropolitans (later patriarchs) of Alexandria and Antioch, who received pre-eminence or higher jurisdiction over a number of ecclesiastical provinces. The lesser metropolitans, who are the subject of this study, were ruled by these greater metro-

---

the provinces. In certain cases the bishops elected and consecrated a candidate *sine prævia plebis electione*, for instance, when the people would undoubtedly have made a bad choice. The Council of Nicæa thought it necessary to define by precise rules the duties of the bishops who took part in the elections. The Greeks interpret this canon in the sense that it took away the right of voting from the people and confined the nomination exclusively to the bishops of the province. The Latins interpret the canon as though it said nothing of the rights of the bishops of the province in the election of other new colleagues, but determined that: (1) three bishops were necessary for consecration, and (2) episcopal confirmation rested with the metropolitan. In the West the people were removed from episcopal elections somewhere in the 11th century; and not only the people, but the bishops of the province as well, for the elections were conducted by the clergy of the cathedral chapters.— Hefele-Leclercq, I, 543-547.

[3] C. 1, D. LXIV. Bruns, I, 15; Hardouin, I, 323-324; Mansi, II, 669-670; Schroeder, *Decrees*, p. 513; p. 26. Nothing more was allowed.

[4] Hefele-Leclercq, I, 546; Schroeder, *Decrees*, pp. 27-28.

politans. Nevertheless, the canon clearly re-emphasized the legislation of canon 4 when it stated that if anyone was made bishop without the approval of the metropolitan, the Council did not permit him to exercise the office of bishop.[5] This repetition was made to safeguard the rights of the lesser metropolitans against the possible encroachments on the part of the greater metropolitans. The meaning, therefore, was this: no one may be consecrated a bishop, not even by the chief metropolitans or patriarchs, without the approval of the metropolitan under whose jurisdiction the candidate resided.[6]

The Synod of Antioch *in Encæniis* (341), which enjoyed great authority in the Church of the East, in its 19th canon clarified and extended the meaning of the 4th Nicene canon. It stated that the metropolitan was to summon by letter all of his colleagues to attend a synod which had as its burden the election of a bishop. If all of the comprovincial bishops were present, so much the better, but if there were some difficulty which held them from attending, there was to be a majority present at the meeting, and those who were absent had to send their consent in writing. Only then could the appointment of the new bishop take place in the presence or with the consent of the majority. This canon, though it extended the power of the metropolitan, did not give him the exclusive right to choose the new bishop.[7]

Canon 16 of the same Council re-asserted the ruling of canon 4 of the Council of Nicæa (325) when it took up the case of a bishop who had usurped a vacant see. The canon stated that a regular synod was one at which a metropolitan was present, and then insisted that, if the consent of a regular synod had not been obtained, the intruding bishop

---

[5] Bruns, I, 15-16; Hardouin, I, 325-326; Mansi, II, 669-670; Schroeder, *Decrees*, p. 520; pp. 29-30.

[6] C. 8, D. LXIV; cc. 1, 2, D. LXV. For an exhaustive commentary on this canon see Hefele-Leclercq, I, Appendix VIII.

[7] Hefele-Leclercq, I, 720; Bruns, I, 85; Hardouin, I, 601-602; Mansi, II, 1315-1316.

was to be deposed, even if he had been chosen by the whole diocese into which he intruded.[8]

At the Council of Sardica (343 or 344) the same legislation on the matter of episcopal elections was drawn up in canon 6. The question was asked whether an episcopal assembly of a province could appoint a new bishop without waiting for the arrival of an absent comprovincial bishop. The Council forbade such a step. In order that the right of the absent bishop be not prejudiced, the Council ordered that the bishop of the metropolis intimate by letter to the absent bishop that the people of a certain town desired a pastor. If the latter upon the lapse of a certain fixed time did not answer the letter, or failed to appear, the wishes of the people were to be complied with, and the new bishop was to be chosen without the vote of the absent bishop.[9]

Connected with the prerogative of confirming the election of the future bishops of his province was the metropolitan's right to consecrate them. In keeping with canon 19 of the Council of Antioch (341), a newly elected bishop could not be consecrated without a synod and without the presence of the metropolitan of the eparchy.[10] Canon 4 of the Council of Nicæa (325) seems to imply that the consecration of the new bishop was to take place immediately after the election.[11] This canon demanded that all the comprovincial bishops be present at the electoral synod, and that at least three bishops take part in the consecration of the new bishop. The deduction follows that all the comprovincial bishops could participate in the consecration service; no maximum was set, but the minimum of three was strictly to be observed.

---

[8] Hefele-Leclercq, I, 719; Bruns, I, 84-85; Hardouin, I, 599-600; Mansi, II, 1315-1316.

[9] C. 9, D. LXV. Hefele-Leclercq, I, 777-778; Bruns, I, 90-93; Hardouin, I, 639-642; Mansi, III, 24.

[10] C. 7, D. LXIV. Hefele-Leclercq, I, 720; Bruns, I, 85; Hardouin, I, 601-602; Mansi, II, 1315-1316.

[11] C. 1, D. LXIV. Bruns, I, 15; Hardouin, I, 323-324; Mansi, II, 669-670; Schroeder, *Decrees*, p. 513; p. 26; Van Espen, *Ius Universum*, Pars I, Tit. xix, c. 2, n. 4.

With these two canons properly collated, all that can be said is that the metropolitan was one of the number of consecrators. Hinschius (1835-1898) and Saegmüller (1860-1942) claimed that the metropolitan had the right of consecrating the new bishop, but they did not state how exclusive his right to the conferring of the consecration actually was. Both quoted c. 1, D. LXIV, but this excerpt from Gratian states nothing concerning the metropolitan's exclusive right to consecrate.[12]

The first direct statement came in the much disputed canon 28 of the Council of Chalcedon (451). There was inserted in the canon the following prescription: "Of course, each metropolitan...shall ordain the bishops of his province in union with the other bishops of the same province, as is prescribed by the holy canons."[13] An indirect indication of this prerogative is to be found in canon 25 of the same Council.[14] This canon threatened metropolitans with a canonical penalty if the consecration of a bishop did not take place within three months. There was no clear declaration that the metropolitan was the one who had to consecrate the bishop, but it can be argued that, if the consecration had been left to the decision of the comprovincial bishops, they certainly would have been the ones who should have been punished rather than the metropolitan.

Two later pieces of legislation show this prerogative in a clearer light. Pope Gelasius (492-496) wrote to all the bishops of Dardania (Upper Mœsia, the modern Servia) that it was the metropolitan who had the right to consecrate his comprovincial bishops.[15] Canon 2 of the II Council of Nicæa (787) required that everyone who was to be raised to the rank of a bishop was to know the Psalter by heart.

---

[12] Hinschius, *Kirchenrecht*, II, n. 1; Saegmüller, *Kirchenrecht*, p. 340.

[13] Hefele-Leclercq, II, 815; Bruns, I, 32-33; Mansi, VII, 369-370; Schroeder, *Decrees*, p. 523; pp. 125-126.

[14] C. 2, D. LXXV. Hefele-Leclercq, II, 811; Bruns, I, 32; Mansi, VII, 367-368; Schroeder, *Decrees*, p. 523; pp. 122-123.

[15] C. 6, D. LXIV. Jaffé, n. 716; Mansi, VIII, 134; Thiel, *Epistolæ Romanorum Pontificum Genuinæ a S. Hilario usque ad Pelagium II*, Vol. I (Brunsbergæ, 1868), p. 145 (hereafter cited as *Epistolæ*).

It was the duty of the metropolitan to inquire whether the candidate was inclined to read the sacred canons and Sacred Scriptures diligently, whether he lived according to the commandments of God, and also if he taught the same to the people. If such was not the case, the metropolitan was not to consecrate the candidate.[16]

The next great prerogative of metropolitans was that of calling the bishops of his province to the so-called provincial councils, and the right to preside at them. It is undoubtedly correct to state that metropolitans exercised these rights earlier than the year 325, yet the sources are not unmistakably clear or generous. Even canon 5 of the Council of Nicæa (325), which decreed that two councils be held annually in each eparchy, one before Lent, and the other in the autumn of the year, did not state that it was the sole duty of the metropolitan to preside over them.[17] It was the Council of Antioch *in Encæniis* (341) which stated in its 16th canon that a regular council was one which was held in the presence of the metropolitan.[18]

In its 20th canon the same Council of Antioch ordered that for the good of the Church and the settling of disputes a meeting of the bishops was to be held twice a year in each eparchy: "the first, after the third week after Easter. . . . It was the duty of the metropolitan to summon his colleagues of the eparchy to this meeting. The second was to be held on the Ides of October. . . . It was not allowed for bishops to hold meetings without their metropolitan."[19] This enactment not only changed the times when the meet-

---

[16] Hefele-Leclercq, III, 777; Hardouin, IV, 487-488; Mansi, XIII, 748; Schroeder, *Decrees*, p. 524; pp. 145-146.

[17] C. 3, D. XVIII. Hefele-Leclercq, I, 551; Bruns, I, 15; Hardouin, I, 325-326; Mansi, II, 669-670; Schroeder, *Decrees*, pp. 513-514; pp. 28-29. Cf. Hinschius, *Kirchenrecht*, II, 1; Saegmüller, *Kirchenrecht*, p. 340.

[18] Hefele-Leclercq, I, 719; Bruns, I, 84; Hardouin, I, 599-600; Mansi, II, 1315-1316.

[19] Hefele-Leclercq, I, 720; Bruns, I, 85-86; Hardouin, I, 601-602; Mansi, II, 1317-1318. Cf. Kober, *Kirchenbann nach den Grundsätzen des canonischen Rechts* (Tübingen, 1863), p. 222 (hereafter cited as *Kirchenbann*).

ings were to be held, but specified that it was the metropolitan's duty to summon the comprovincial bishops to attend and to be present himself.

The I Council of Constantinople (381), some forty years later, restated the Nicene decisions on the observance of eparchal synods in its canon 2, but did not add any of the specifications given in the 20th canon of the Council of Antioch (341).[20] The Ecumenical Council of Chalcedon (451) in its 1st canon accepted the enactments of five preceding councils: Ancyra (314), Neocæsarea (315), Nicæa (325), Gangra (340) and Antioch (341), giving them a character of universally and unconditionally valid ecclesiastical rules.[21] It was this general canon which incorporated the specifications concerning the eparchal synod as made in canon 20 of the Council of Antioch (341) and canon 5 of the Council of Nicæa (325). Yet in its 19th canon the Council, inasmuch as the practice of holding these synods had fallen into desuetude, prescribed that the bishops assemble twice a year whenever the metropolitan thought it to be suitable.[22]

As late as 787, when the VII Ecumenical Council (II General Council of Nicæa) was held, the matter of the provincial synod received legislative attention. Canon 6 of this Council renewed one of the canons of the VI Ecumenical Council (III General Council of Constantinople, 680-681), in which it was decided that synods should be held in each province but once a year. It further decreed that if any metropolitan, without a reasonable excuse, failed to observe this ruling, he would be subject to canonical penalties. The Council likewise forbade the metropolitan to demand any of the possessions which a bishop had brought with him. If

---

[20] Hefele-Leclercq, II, 21; Bruns, I, 20-21; Hardouin, I, 809-810; Mansi, III, 559-560; Schroeder, *Decrees*, p. 517; pp. 64-65.

[21] C. 14, C. XXXV, q. 1. Hefele-Leclercq, II, 770-772; Bruns, I, 25; Hardouin, II, 602; Mansi, VII, 357-358; Schroeder, *Decrees*, p. 519; pp. 85-86.

[22] Hefele-Leclercq, II, 807; Bruns, I, 30; Mansi, VII, 365-366; Schroeder, *Decrees*, p. 522; pp. 117-118.

he was found guilty of making such a demand, he was to be forced to restore the matter fourfold.[23]

Among the affairs treated in these provincial synods or councils were: the legality of excommunications from the ecclesiastical community made by the individual bishops; the exercise of penal jurisdiction over bishops; the decision of disputes between the bishops themselves and with their subjects; in fine, the administration of any ecclesiastical matter which needed correction.[24] In delineating the purpose of the provincial council or synod, canon 5 of the Council of Nicæa (325) declared that at such a gathering an investigation of the excommunications of the clergy or of the laity was in order for determining whether or not the imposed censures were inspired by narrow-mindedness, quarrelsomeness, or any spirit of animosity on the part of the bishops throughout the province. The investigations were to prove that those who were guilty were justly excommunicated and were to remain in that condition unless the assembly of bishops modified or abrogated the sentence.[25]

Canon 6 of the Council of Antioch (341) treated such a case. It stated that if a man when excommunicated by his own bishop was not received into the Church by the latter, he could not be received by any other bishop until, upon the celebration of the synod, he had appeared before it to defend himself and had succeeded in convincing the synod to grant him a new decision. This rule included laymen, priests, deacons and all ecclesiastics.[26]

At the Council of Sardica (343 or 344) Hosius proposed that if a bishop in consequence of an unduly passionate temperament, or as a result of his anger against a priest or

---

[23] Hefele-Leclercq, III, 780-781; Hardouin, IV, 489-492; Mansi, XIII, 750-751; Schroeder, *Decrees*, p. 526; pp. 147-148.

[24] Hinschius, *Kirchenrecht*, II, 1-2; Saegmüller, *Kirchenrecht*, p. 340.

[25] C. 3, D. XVIII. Hefele-Leclercq, I, 548-549; Bruns, I, 15; Hardouin, I, 325-326; Mansi, II, 669-670; Schroeder, *Decrees*, pp. 513-514; pp. 28-29.

[26] C. 2, C. XI, q. 3. Hefele-Leclercq, I, 716; Bruns, I, 82; Hardouin, I, 595-596; Mansi, II, 1311-1312.

a deacon, wanted to cast him out of the Church, care was to be taken that such a one was not hastily condemned and thereupon deprived of communion. The Fathers responded that he who had been excommunicated would be allowed to have recourse to the metropolitan.[27] Since even in the absence of the metropolitan no petitioner was to be refused a hearing, the one who was excommunicated could approach the nearest bishop and ask him to investigate his cause thoroughly. The bishop who had decreed the excommunication could not take it amiss that the cause was being investigated, and that his sentence was being confirmed or amended. Until all was thoroughly and faithfully investigated and a decision given, the excommunicated person could not demand communion *(in suspensivo)*. If, however, the clerics who were assembled for judgment observed in the one who was excommunicated a pride or a haughtiness, they were to reprimand him sharply and severely, in order that the reasonable demands of the bishop would be obeyed.[28]

As regards the exercise of penal measures against bishops, canon 14 of the Council of Antioch (341) indicated the power which rested with the synod. If a bishop was to be condemned for certain offenses, and the bishops of the eparchy were divided in opinion concerning the matter, the Council decreed that the metropolitan of a neighboring

[27] Here the Latin text uses the phrase "*ut finitimos interpellet*" instead of the text "*ut metropolitanos interpellet.*" Most probably this was done because the metropolitan institution was not so developed and so universal in the West as in the East. Canon 11: "...si episcopus quis forte iracundus (quod esse non debet) cito aspere commoveatur adversus presbyterum sive diaconum suum et exterminare eum de ecclesia voluerit, providendum est ne innocens damnetur aut perdat communionem; habeat potestatem eiectus ut finitimos interpellet ut causa eius audiatur et diligentius tractetur, quia non oportet ei negari audientiam roganti...."—Turner, *Ecclesiæ Occidentalis Monumenta Iuris Antiquissima Canonum et Conciliorum Græcorum Interpretationes Latinæ* (2 vols. in 6, Oxonii: e Typographeo Clarendoniano, 1899-1930; Tomus I, 1930), Tomus I, Fasciculus II, Pars III, 480. Cf. *op. cit.*, *ibid.*, pp. 522-523, for the variant readings (hereafter cited as *Monumenta*).

[28] Hefele-Leclercq, I, 796; Bruns, I, 102-103; Hardouin, I, 649-650; Mansi, III, 17-18.

eparchy was to summon other bishops to try the matter, clear the doubt, and with the bishops of the province confirm the decision. The text of the canon did not specify which of the neighboring metropolitans had the right to accept the appeal.[29] The canon spoke of an extraordinary case and delegated it to a court of second instance, so to speak, and gave the neighboring metropolitan and his bishops the right to settle the doubt. This procedure shows that the metropolitan's own court was not as yet in existence to serve as a higher court than that of the provincial synod or council.

Canon 15 of the same Council took the ordinary case into consideration. If a bishop upon being accused of certain offenses had been tried by all the bishops of the eparchy, and all had unanimously given sentence against him, he could not be tried again by others, but the unanimous decision of the bishops of the eparchy held good.[30] This canon proves that the metropolitan as yet did not have the exclusive right to judge any case which involved a brother bishop; that he was simply one of the episcopal body when it came to trials. He did not have power to punish a bishop who refused to take occupation of his episcopal see. The power of excommunication still rested with the body of comprovincial bishops according to canon 17 of this same Council.[31]

In cases which involved church property, the episcopal body made the decision of guilt, and not the metropolitan. Canon 25, the last of the Antiochian canons, declared that

---

[29] *Prisca:* "...et metropolitanum episcopum et qui ex vicina est provincia convocarentur..."; *Isidori:* "...metropolitanum alterius vicinæ provinciæ advocari et aliquantos cum eo episcopos alios...."; *Dionysii I:* "...ut metropolitanus episcopus a vicina provincia iudices alios convocet..."; *Dionysii II:* "...ut metropolitanus episcopus a vicina provincia iudices alios convocet...." — Turner, *Monumenta,* Tomus I, Fasciculus II, Pars altera, 276-279. Cf. Hefele-Leclercq, I, 71; Bruns, I, 84; Hardouin, I, 599-600; Mansi, II, 1313-1314.

[30] Hefele-Leclercq, I, 719; Bruns, I, 84; Hardouin, I, 599-600; Mansi, II, 1313-1316.

[31] C. 7, D. CXII. Hefele-Leclercq, I, 719; Bruns, I, 85; Hardouin, I, 599-602; Mansi, II, 1315-1316.

if a bishop used church property for private purposes, and not according to the wishes of the priests and deacons, he was held accountable to the synod of the eparchy. If a bishop or priest misused landed property or any other goods, he was also held responsible before the synod. The metropolitan could in no way reserve the right of punishment to himself.[32]

The decision of disputes between bishops among themselves and with their subjects was also part of the business of the eparchal synod. In demanding the holding of synods, canon 20 of the Council of Antioch (341) prefaced the legislation with the remark that synods were convoked for the settling of disputes.[33] The Council of Chalcedon (451) in its 9th canon clarified this point. If any cleric had a cause against another cleric, he was not to disregard his bishop by turning to a secular court, but was to lay his case first of all before his bishop, or, with the consent of the bishop, before persons by whom both parties agreed to have their claims adjudicated. Again, if a cleric had a cause against his own or some other bishop, it was to be decided by the synod of the province.[34]

The list of synodal matters which were to be treated under the presidency of the metropolitan is exhausted with the prescription of canon 19 of the Council of Chalcedon (451). The wording of the law begins with a complaint that the provincial synods were not being held, and that on this account many ecclesiastical matters which needed correction were being neglected. After renewing the decision on these assemblies, the canon declared that the synod was competent to settle whatever matters arose within the province.[35] Not only did canon 6 of the II Council of Nicæa

---

[32] C. 23, C. XIII, q. 1. Hefele-Leclercq, I, 722; Bruns, I, 87; Hardouin, I, 603-606; Mansi, II, 1319-1320.

[33] C. 4, D. XVIII. Hefele-Leclercq, I, 720; Bruns, I, 85-86; Hardouin, I, 601-602; Mansi, II, 1315-1316.

[34] Hefele-Leclercq, II, 796-797; Bruns, I, 28; Mansi, VII, 361-362; Schroeder, *Decrees*, p. 520; pp. 98-101.

[35] C. 6, D. XVIII. Hefele-Leclercq, II, 807; Bruns, I, 30; Mansi, VII, 365-366; Schroeder, *Decrees*, p. 522; pp. 117-118.

(787) legislate as to the change in the holding of synods from twice to once a year, but it decreed that it was the duty of the assembled bishops to be solicitous for the observance of the commandments of God.[36] As in the election of a new bishop in a province the metropolitan had no more rights than the other comprovincial bishops, except that of confirmation and only later that of consecration, so in all these matters which were taken up by the provincial synods the word or the vote of the majority prevailed, and not the exclusive vote or decree of the metropolitan. From the canonical standpoint at least, if not also in practice, the procedure at these synods was altogether democratic.[37]

The third prerogative of metropolitans was that of giving to comprovincial bishops the necessary permission to travel. Canon 15 of the I Council of Nicæa prohibited bishops, priests and deacons to pass from one church to another, and legislated that if they attempted to do so they were to be sent back to the church for which they were ordained.[38] Nothing was said of the metropolitan power to grant permissions in this early canon. It was canon 13 of the Council of Antioch (341) which initiated the list of laws giving the metropolitan the right to issue permission for travel. No bishop was permitted to travel from one eparchy to another for the purpose of consecrating anyone, even if he was accompanied by other bishops, unless he was summoned by letters from the metropolitan and the other bishops in connection with him into whose district he went. If contrary to the rule he went without being summoned to ordain someone, or to meddle with church affairs which did not concern him, all his acts were to be considered invalid and the synod of bishops was to punish him with deposi-

---

[36] Hefele-Leclercq, III, 780-781; Hardouin, IV, 489-492; Mansi, XIII, 750-751; Schroeder, *Decrees*, p. 526; pp. 147-148.

[37] Cf. c. 5 of the I Council of Nicæa (325); c. 20 of the Council of Antioch (341); cc. 9, 19 of the Council of Chalcedon (451), and c. 6 of the II Council of Nicæa (787).

[38] Hefele-Leclercq, I, 597; Bruns, I, 18; Hardouin, I, 329-330; Mansi, II, 673-676; Schroeder, *Decrees*, p. 515; pp. 44-46.

tion.[39] It is not clear from the canon whether the metropolitan was the one who was the bishops's own metropolitan or the one of the neighboring province.

Canon 3 of the Council of Sardica (343 or 344) is a repetition of the 13th Antiochian canon, but at the same time is both clearer and more detailed. It stated that no bishop could rightfully go to another province for the performance of any spiritual office unless he was called to do so by the metropolitan and the bishops of that province.[40] Canon 5 of the Council of Chalcedon (451) simply stated that the canons enacted by the Fathers in regard to bishops and clerics moving from one city to another would have their proper force.[41] These canons did not give the metropolitan any power with reference to the travel of his own comprovincial bishops, but rather in relation to the travel of the comprovincial bishops of another province.

There are two canons, however, which gave every metropolitan the right to issue letters of travel to his own bishops, namely, canon 11 of the Council of Antioch (341) and canon 9 of the Council of Sardica (343 or 344). The first mentioned canon dealt with a bishop, priest or any other ecclesiastic who wished to travel to the emperor's court. If any cleric presumed to go without the consent of, and letters from, the bishops of the eparchy, and especially from the metropolitan, he was to be excluded from communion and deprived of his rank, inasmuch as he acted contrary to the canons. If such a one was impelled by necessity to approach the emperor, he could do so only with the consent of the metropolitan or of the bishops of the eparchy, and he had to take their letters with him.[42]

The next-mentioned canon dealt with a similar situation.

---

[39] C. 4, C. IX, q. 2. Hefele-Leclercq, I, 718; Bruns, I, 84; Hardouin, I, 603-604; Mansi, II, 1313-1314.

[40] C. 17, C. VI, q. 4. Hefele-Leclercq, I, 762-763; Bruns, I, 90-91; Hardouin, I, 637-640; Mansi, III, 23.

[41] Hefele-Leclercq, II, 783-784; Bruns, I, 27; Mansi, VII, 375; Schroeder, *Decrees*, p. 520; pp. 94-95.

[42] Hefele-Leclercq, I, 717-718; Bruns, I, 83; Hardouin, I, 597-598; Mansi, II, 1313-1314.

After a bishop sent his petition to the metropolitan, the latter was to dispatch a deacon with the petition to the emperor, and give him at the same time letters of recommendation to those bishops who were at the emperor's court.[43] The affair was probably to go through the hands of the metropolitan, in order, on the one hand, that he would be informed of what was happening in his province, and at the same time that he could reject unfit petitions which any of his comprovincial bishops might desire to bring to the emperor; and, on the other hand, that he might use his position to give more weight to the just petitions presented at the imperial court.[44]

In the first mentioned canon the power of the metropolitan was checked by the comprovincial bishops who together with him issued the letters. It was not the metropolitan who punished the presumptuous bishop, but the comprovincial bishops when assembled in a synod. The canon of the Council of Sardica, however, seems to give the metropolitan the exclusive right to permit, not the bishop personally, but the deacon, to present a bishop's petition to the emperor.

The fourth and last prerogative of metropolitans was their right to direct the common ecclesiastical affairs of the entire district. So already canon 9 of the Council of Antioch (341) decreed. It read as follows:

> The bishops of every province must be aware that the bishop presiding in the metropolis has charge of the whole province; for all who have business come together from all quarters to the metropolis. For this reason it is decided that the metropolis should hold also the foremost rank, and that without the metro-

---

[43] Hefele-Leclercq, I, 788-789, footnote. According to the Latin text, it was expressly ordered that every bishop should send his petition through the metropolitan. Yet the Greek text does not express this. The Greek Scholiasts, however, found much in it, because the 11th Antiochian canon had already ordered the same, namely that everything was to pass through the hands of the metropolitan.

[44] Hefele-Leclercq, I, 788; Bruns, I, 95-97; Hardouin, I, 643-644; Mansi, III, 25-26.

politan the other bishops should, according to the ancient and recognized canon of our Fathers, do nothing beyond what concerns their respective sees and the districts belonging thereto; for every bishop has authority over his own see and must govern it according to his own conscience, and take charge of the whole region surrounding his episcopal city, ordaining priests and deacons, and discharging all his duties with circumspection. Further than this he may not venture without the metropolitan, nor the latter without consulting other bishops.[45]

Again, there was for the metropolitan a countercheck in the last ruling of the canon: he could not direct any matter in the sees of any of his comprovincial bishops unless he consulted them beforehand.

Throughout the first eight centuries the metropolitans of the Orient steadily grew in power through the legislation of the synods and councils, but at their every advancing step the checking influence of the comprovincial bishops can be seen very noticeably.

Article 2. The African Church

The hierarchical organization in the Church of Africa reached its complete development early in the fourth century, and therefore, as in the Orient, its origin must go back at least to the third century. The strongest argument

---

[45] C. 1, C. IX, q. 2; C. IX, q. 3. Τοὺς καθ' ἑκάστην ἐπαρχίαν ἐπισκόπους εἰδέναι χρῆ τὸν ἐν τῇ μητροπόλει προεστῶτα ἐπίσκοπον καὶ τὴν φροντίδα ἀναδεχέσθαι πάσης τῆς ἐπαρχίας διὰ τὸ ἐν τῇ μητροπόλει πανταχόθεν συντρέχειν πάντας τοὺς τὰ πράγματα ἔχοντας· ὅθεν ἔδοξε καὶ τῇ τιμῇ προηγεῖσθαι αὐτὸν, μηδέν τε πράττειν περιττὸν τοὺς λοιποὺς ἐπισκόπους ἄνευ αὐτοῦ κατὰ τὸν ἀρχαῖον κρατήσαντα τῶν πατέρων ἡμῶν κανόνα ἢ ταῦτα μόνα ὅσα τῇ ἑκάστου ἐπιβάλλει παροικίᾳ καὶ ταῖς ὑπ' αὐτὴν χώραις· ἕκαστον γὰρ ἐπίσκοπον ἐξουσίαν ἔχειν τῆς ἑαυτοῦ παροικίας διοικεῖν τε κατὰ τὴν ἑκάστῳ ἐπιβάλλουσαν εὐλάβειαν καὶ πρόνοιαν ποιεῖσθαι πάσης τῆς χώρας τῆς ὑπὸ τὴν ἑαυτοῦ πόλιν, ὡς καὶ χειροτονεῖν πρέσβυτέρους καὶ διακόνους καὶ μετὰ κρίσεως ἕκαστα διαλαμβάνειν, περαιτέρω δὲ μηδὲν πράττειν ἐπιχειρεῖν δίχα τοῦ τῆς μητροπόλεως ἐπισκόπου μηδὲ αὐτὸν ἄνευ τῆς τῶν λοιπῶν γνώμης· Bruns, I, 82-83; Hardouin, I, 595-598; Mansi, II, 1311, 1323, 1331.

in support of this contention is the active synodal life of this Church in the early centuries.[46] The rights of the African primates were essentially the same as those of the Oriental metropolitans, namely: (a) the right of confirming the election of provincial bishops and the right of consecrating them; (b) the right to convoke synods and to preside at them; (c) the right to give bishops the necessary permission to travel abroad. They had other rights which the Oriental metropolitans did not enjoy, namely: (d) that of ordering the formation of electoral bodies, called *turmæ*, for the election of deputies to the general synods; and (e) the right to give consent for the erection of new dioceses.[47]

The earliest legislation concerning the primatial right to confirm the election of a new bishop is found in canon 12 of the Council held at Carthage (387 or 390). The canon declared that no new bishop could be appointed without the consent of the primate.[48] Nothing was said of the consecration of the new bishop by the primate in this canon, but if the ceremony took place immediately after the election, as in the Orient, he most probably participated in the service. The ruling of canon 4 of the Council of Nicæa (325), which insisted that at least three bishops participate in the consecration of a new bishop, was renewed for the African Church in canon 2 of the III Council of Carthage (397).[49]

Already in 305, the year in which the Council of Cirta was held, it was the Primate Secundus, Bishop of Tigisium, senior of the eleven bishops present, who presided over the assembly. It is very probable that he convoked the synod in order to fill the vacant see of Cirta.[50] Almost a century later, legislation giving the primate the right to convoke

---

[46] De Meester, *Compendium*, II, 105; Hinschius, *Kirchenrecht*, II, 2; Van Espen, *Ius Universum*, Pars I, Tit. xix, c. 2, n. 7.

[47] Hinschius, *Kirchenrecht*, II, 2.

[48] Hefele-Leclercq, II, 78; Bruns, I, 121-122; Hardouin, I, 954; Mansi, III, 696, 872.

[49] Hefele-Leclercq, II, 101; Bruns, I, 15; Hardouin, I, 323-324.

[50] Hefele-Leclercq, I, 209-210.

synods, and to preside at them, came into being at the VI Council of Carthage (401). Canon 8 dealt with the convocation of the General African Synods and decreed that the primates of the several provinces should so arrange their provincial synods that they would not interfere with the holding of the General Synods.[51] Again the canon said nothing concerning the right of the primate to preside, but it may be taken for granted that the rule of seniority held as much as it did a century before.

Among the matters treated in these synods were the trials of bishops. As in the Orient, so here the primates had but a limited power at first. Canon 10 of the Council of Carthage (387 or 390), stated that a bishop could be judged and deposed solely by a committee of twelve bishops.[52] Some years later, in the Council held at Hippo (393), there was drawn up in canon 10 a ruling which extended the judicial power of the primate and limited that of the bishops. This canon stated that a bishop was to be accused before the primate of the province, and that the accused bishop was not to be suspended without a judicial trial, unless, after being summoned by the primate, he did not appear before him within a month.[53] This was a much greater power than the Eastern metropolitans had in the trials of bishops.[54]

The prerogative of granting bishops permission to travel abroad was also enjoyed by the African primates. Canon 15 of the Council of Hippo (393) warned bishops, priests and deacons not to be agents or procurators for others, and not to undertake any office which might oblige them to travel and keep them from their ecclesiastical duties.[55] Among the decrees of this same Council there is canon 30, which explicitly stated that bishops were not to travel across the

---

[51] C. 10, D. XVIII. Canon 73 of the *Codex Canonum Ecclesiæ Africanæ:* Hefele-Leclercq, II, 127; Bruns, I, 174-175; Hardouin, c. x, I, 980.

[52] Hefele-Leclercq, II, 78; Hardouin, I, 953; Mansi, III, 695-696.

[53] Hefele-Leclercq, II, 86; Hardouin, I, 953-954; Mansi, III, 921.

[54] Cf. *supra*, pp. 29-31.

[55] Hefele-Leclercq, II, 87; Hardouin, I, 953-954; Mansi, III, 850.

sea to Europe without the consent of the bishop of the *prima sedes,* from whom they were also to obtain their *litteræ formatæ.*[56] The African Codex records the ruling of the III Council of Carthage (397) between numbers 56 and 57. According to this ruling no bishop was allowed to make a sea voyage without *litteræ formatæ.*[57] In comparing this power of the African primates with that of the Oriental metropolitans, one will note that this one was much wider, for the primates issued the letters alone without the necessity of waiting for the decision of the comprovincial bishops.[58]

A power which the Oriental metropolitans did not possess was that of forming electoral bodies for the election of deputies to the General Synods. It was decided at the Council of Hippo (393) that every year there should take place a council to which all ecclesiastical provinces were to send their delegates.[59] The VI Council of Carthage (401) prescribed in its 11th canon that every primate should divide his province into two or three districts, and should send deputies from each of them to the General Council.[60]

Still another power which the African primates had, and which the Eastern ones did not possess, was that of issuing consent for the erection of new dioceses. Canon 4 of the XI Council of Carthage (407), declared that communities which never had a bishop could not get one in the future except with the consent of the plenary council of each province, of the primate, and of the bishop to whose diocese the church in question had hitherto belonged.[61] All in all, the prerogatives of the African primates were an extention of the powers enjoyed by the Oriental metropolitans.

---

[56] Hefele-Leclercq, II, 88; Hardouin, I, 953-954; Mansi, III, 850.

[57] Hefele-Leclercq, II, 99-100; Bruns, I, 168; Mansi, III, 747-766.

[58] *Supra,* pp. 32-34.

[59] Hefele-Leclercq, II, 86; Hardouin, I, 953-954; Mansi, III, 850.

[60] Canon 76 of the *Codex Canonum Ecclesiæ Africanæ:* Hefele-Leclercq, II, 127-128; Bruns, I, 174-175.

[61] Hefele-Leclercq, II, 157.

Article 3. The Spanish Church

From the fourth century onward the metropolitan institution began to flourish in the Occident. The institution in Spain, however, must be projected into the third century in view of the evidence presented in the Council of Elvira (c. 300-306). Canon 58 of this Council argued for the existence of a higher organ of direction over the individual bishops of the Spanish Church. The canon gave the bishop of the *prima sedes* the right to question Christians who were coming into the country about their respective dioceses from which they made their departure, and these travelers were to present their commendatory letters to him and were to answer if they could affirm that all specifications mentioned in the letters were satisfactorily fulfilled.[62] After the political and ecclesiastical division of the country into provinces, and the assigning of definite cities as metropoles of these districts, the institution began to settle into a definite pattern. Already in the following century, Pope Hilary (461-468) in writing to Ascanius, Bishop of the province of Tarragona, not only called him a metropolitan, but reserved the right of episcopal consecration to him.[63] The letter is dated the 30th of October, 465, and was addressed not only to Bishop Ascanius but to all the bishops of the province of Tarragona.

In reading the signatures attached to the canons of the Council of Tarragona (516), one notes the following names: Metropolitan John of Tarragona, the presiding officer, and his comprovincial bishops, Paul of Impuria (Emporias), Frontinian of Gerona, Argutius (Agrocius) of Barcelona,

---

[62] Hefele-Leclercq, III, 253-254; Hinschius, *Kirchenrecht*, I, 152. Part of the canon is quoted *supra*, p. 13, footnote 36.

[63] "Hoc autem primum juxta eorumdem patrum regulas volumus custodiri, ut nullus præter notitiam atque consensum fratris Ascanii metropolitani aliquatenus consecretur antistes, quia hoc vetus ordo tenuit, hoc trecentorum decem et octo sanctorum patrum definivit auctoritas; cui quisquis obvias tetenderit manus, eorum se consortio fatetur indignum, quorum preceptionibus resultarit."—Thiel, *Epistolæ*, p. 166; Mansi, VII, 927; *MPL*, LVIII, 17; Jaffé, n. 560; Hinschius, *Decretales Pseudo-Isidorianæ*, p. 631.

Ursus of Tortosa, Camidius (Einidius) of Ansona, and Nibridius of Egara. Besides these there are named from other ecclesiastical provinces, Orontius of Elvira (perhaps it should be Lerida, which lay in the province of Tarragona), Vincentius of Cæsar-Augusta (Saragossa), and Hector of Carthagina, which is mentioned as a metropolis (by which is meant only its dignity as a civil metropolis of the *Provincia Carthaginiensis* established in Spain by Diocletian; in its ecclesiastical position Carthagina belonged to the province of Toledo).[64] This listing brings into light the process of development which the institution was undergoing at the time. By the next century the process was complete, for at the X Council of Toledo (656) and the XIII Council of Toledo (683) the list of metropolitans is drawn up in both cases.[65]

The sources show that the prerogatives of the Spanish metropolitans were essentially the same as those of the Oriental metropolitans: (a) the privilege to co-operate in the filling of episcopal sees; (b) the right to convoke and to preside at the provincial synods; (c) the prerogative of being over the bishops of the province. The right to issue permissions to bishops for the purpose of travel is not mentioned in the sources. Some distinct Spanish rights were: (d) the highest competence in the matter of Easter, and, finally, (e) the rights over ecclesiastical property in certain instances.[66]

Concerning the right of episcopal confirmation and consecration, the reader needs but to turn to the letter written by Pope St. Hilary (461-468) to the metropolitan of Tarragona in the year 465. There it was very clearly stated that

[64] Hefele-Leclercq, II, 1027; Garcia-Villada, *Historia Eclesiástica*, I, 206-207. The latter says: "The fact that there was no coincidence between the ecclesiastical capital of the province of Carthagina with the civil capital is one exception, due undoubtedly to the geographical situation and the strategic importance of Toledo. Nevertheless the bishops of this province held to the name of Carthagina in the official documents in the same way that the other four bishops called themselves the bishops of the Tarragonians, Baeticans, Galicians and Lusitanians."

[65] Cf. *supra*, pp. 13-14.

[66] Hinschius, *Kirchenrecht*, II, 3.

no one could be consecrated a bishop without the knowledge and the consent of the metropolitan. The Pope strengthened his statement by insisting that the ruling was one of long standing and subscribed to by the Fathers of the Nicæan Council.[67] Some fifty years later, canon 5 of the Council of Tarragona (516) prescribed that if anyone were to be consecrated a bishop outside the metropolitan city, that is, not by the metropolitan himself but with his consent, he was to present himself before the metropolitan within the next two months in order to receive more personal directions from the latter.[68] The tone of the canon implied that at this time the metropolitan rights of confirmation and consecration were taken as a matter of course. Even the detail of the place of consecration was a matter decided by the metropolitan. Canon 19 of the IV Council of Toledo (633) decreed that the consecration was to take place on a Sunday at a place designated by the metropolitan, and it was to be administered by at least three bishops.[69]

The system of provincial synods must have been established quite some time before 516. This is said because canon 6 of the Council of Tarragona (516) took for granted its existence when it decreed that if a bishop, notwithstanding the admonition of the metropolitan, failed to attend a synod, he was to be excluded from the *communio charitatis* of his brother bishops until the next council.[70] The canon did not reveal whether the metropolitan was the one who convoked the synods, nor did it show that he presided at them. However, at the end of the II Council of Toledo (527 or 531), the king requested that the Metropolitan Montanus give the bishops an early notice of each new synod.[71] Whether this request was an innovation or a regular procedure is difficult to say. This suggestion took

---

[67] Cf. *supra*, pp. 39-40, and footnote 63 of this chapter.

[68] C. 8, D. LXV. Hefele-Leclercq, II, 1027; Bruns, II, 16.

[69] Hefele-Leclercq, III, 270; Bruns, I, 229-230; Hardouin, III, 584-585.

[70] C. 14, D. XVIII. Hefele-Leclercq, II, 1027-1028; Bruns, II, 16.

[71] Hefele-Leclercq, II, 1083.

on legal form in canon 18 of the III Council of Toledo (589) when it stated that at the end of each synod the time and the place of the next one should be announced, so that no further writings or invitations needed to be made by the metropolitan.[72]

Canon 5 of the Council of Merida (666) is interesting in this connection, for here the interference of the king is in full evidence. The canon decreed that if a provincial synod was announced by the will of the metropolitan and at the command of the king, all the bishops of the province were to appear.[73] A still stronger interference becomes evident in the 15th canon of the XI Council of Toledo (675), which legislated that the date of the annual synod was to be determined by the king and the metropolitan. The canon continues with a sanction. Anyone who did not appear was to be excommunicated for a year.[74]

Canon 20 of the III Council of Toledo (589), after deploring the fact that many bishops burdened their clergy with fees and taxes in a cruel manner, gave the burdened clergy the right to complain to their metropolitan.[75] It seems that such cases were settled extra-judicially, that is, outside the provincial synod. Canon 12 of the XIII Council of Toledo (683) renewed this legislation by granting any one who wished to take proceedings against his own bishop the right of recourse to his metropolitan.[76] But the power of correction belonged to the metropolitan, for the most part, in conjunction with the provincial synod.

In Spain this power of correction was checked not only by the comprovincial bishops but by the judges and officers of the king.[77] In keeping with this policy canon 3 of the IV Council of Toledo (633) decreed that anyone who wished

[72] Hefele-Leclercq, III, 227; Bruns, I, 217; Hardouin, III, 482.

[73] Hefele-Leclercq, III, 304; Bruns, II, 86; Hardouin, III, 1000.

[74] Hefele-Leclercq, III, 314; Bruns, I, 316; Hardouin, III, 1029.

[75] Hefele-Leclercq, III, 227; Bruns, I, 218; Hardouin, III, 483.

[76] Hefele-Leclercq, III, 549; Bruns, I, 346; Hardouin, III, 1746; Mansi, XI, 1074-1075.

[77] C. 18 of the III Council of Toledo (589); Hefele-Leclercq, III, 227; Bruns, I, 217; Hardouin, III, 482.

to make a complaint against bishops, judges, magnates or anyone whatever, had to do so before a provincial synod, and an *executor regius* was to give effect to the judgment of the synod. The *executor regius* was also the one to admonish judges and the lay folk to appear at the synod.[78] The Council of Merida (666), in its 7th canon, expressly granted the power of correction to the metropolitan, which power was to be exercised together with the synod. If a bishop did not appear at a provincial synod, he was to be shut out from communion until the next council, and was to be a penitent until that time at a place chosen by the metropolitan and the bishops present at the synod.[79] The same power was guaranteed the metropolitan in canon 15 of the XI Council of Toledo (675).[80]

The prerogative of precedence was granted to metropolitans in canon 6 of the I Council of Braga (561). Bishops were told to sit according to the time of their consecration, but metropolitans were assured first places.[81] The same Council decreed that throughout the provinces the same lessons were to be read during the Masses of vigils and feasts as were read in the metropolitan's church, that the Masses and the rites of baptism were to conform to the *ordo* which was sent from Rome by Pope Vigilius (537-555) to Profuturus, a former metropolitan of Braga.[82] The XI Council of Toledo (675) insisted in its 3rd canon that the services throughout the province were to conform to those of the metropolitan church.[83]

The Spanish metropolitans had the highest competence in the matter of dating the celebration of Easter. Canon 9

---

[78] Hefele-Leclercq, III, 268; Bruns, I, 222; Hardouin, III, 579-580.

[79] Hefele-Leclercq, III, 304.

[80] Hefele-Leclercq, III, 314; Bruns I, 316; Hardouin, III, 1029-1030.

[81] Hefele-Leclercq, III, 179; Bruns, II, 34; Hardouin, III, 351.

[82] *MPL*, LXIX, 15-19; Jaffé, n. 907. Cf. Archdale King, *Notes on the Catholic Liturgies* (London: Longmans, Green and Co., 1930), pp. 159-160. Chapter V of this work, entitled "Rite of Braga," pp. 153-207, affords a fine history and description of this liturgy. Cf. cc. 2, 4 and 5: Hefele-Leclercq, III, 179; Bruns, II, 34; Hardouin, III, 350-351.

[83] C. 13, D. XII; Hefele-Leclercq, III, 312; Bruns, I, 309; Hardouin, III, 1024-1025.

of the II Council of Braga (572) made it the duty of the metropolitan to announce the date of the feast, so that the bishops and the rest of the clergy might be able to advise their people in their churches when to begin the penances of the season of Lent.[84] Canon 5 of the IV Council of Toledo (633) gave metropolitans the power of deciding the date of Easter. Since the feast was being celebrated on different dates, due to the use of erroneous Easter-tables, the metropolitans were, upon counseling with one another by means of letters three months before Epiphany, to decide the time of Easter, and to make the right date known to their comprovincials.[85] Another indication of this power is shown in canon 2 of the III Council of Saragossa (691), wherein it was stated that bishops residing close to the metropolitan city were to have recourse to their primate at Easter time and to celebrate the feast with him.[86]

The rights which metropolitans enjoyed over ecclesiastical property were determined by certain conditions. As early as 524 the Council of Valencia prescribed a certain procedure in the case of the death of a bishop. Canon 2 forbade clerics to appropriate anything which the deceased left behind. The Council of Valencia cited an earlier ordinance of the Council of Riez (439), in which a neighboring bishop was, after the celebration of the obsequies, to superintend the orphaned church, and to make an accurate inventory of the late bishop's property. This inventory, once it was drawn up, was to be sent to the metropolitan. An administrator of the vacant diocese was then to be appointed. He was to pay the clerics their stipends, and in turn was to give an account of his transactions to the metropolitan. Canon 3 of the Council of Valencia warned that the relatives of the departed bishop could not appropriate anything he left, without the previous knowledge of the metropolitan or

---

[84] Hefele-Leclercq, III, 195; Bruns, II, 41-42; Hardouin, III, 387-388.

[85] Hefele-Leclercq, III, 268; Bruns, I, 223; Hardouin, III, 580.

[86] Hinschius notes the use of the word "primate" instead of "metropolitan" in this canon. Cf. *Kirchenrecht*, II, 3, footnote 3; Hefele-Leclercq, III, 557.

of the comprovincial bishops, so that church property might not be mixed with the private property of the testator.[87]

The IX Council of Toledo (655) similarly enacted two canons touching the metropolitan right over church property. In canon 1 it decreed that no one was allowed to encroach upon the property of another church in order to appropriate it to himself or to his church. The heirs of the founder had the right to watch over the property and to summon before the bishop anyone who encroached on it. Should it be a bishop who attempted to appropriate it, the metropolitan was to be informed. The canon made it clear that even a metropolitan could be reported to the king, if he were a guilty party.

Another restriction placed on the metropolitan was enacted in canon 9. The bishop who held the obsequies of a brother-bishop, and who made the inventory of his possessions could, if the church was rich, claim a pound of gold; if it was poor, half a pound; but the metropolitan could not lay claim to anything.[88] In case a bishop was excommunicated for non-attendance at a provincial synod, his house and his possessions were administered by the metropolitan while the former was doing penance. Such was the prescription of canon 7 of the Council of Merida (666).[89]

Although the rights of the Spanish metropolitans were much greater than those of either the Oriental metropolitans or the African primates, it must always be remembered that the Spanish kings interfered in ecclesiastical affairs to a point where these prerogatives were not fully enjoyed in practice. Especially in the matter of the occupation of episcopal sees, the kings proved to be an enormous obstacle. Metropolitan power was checked somewhat later by the primate of Spain once the archbishops of Toledo received that title of honor.

Hinschius (1835-1898) claimed that the great number of

---

[87] Hefele-Leclercq, II, 1067-1068; Bruns, II, 25.

[88] Hefele-Leclercq, III, c. 1, 291-292, c. 9, 293; Bruns, c. 1, 291-292, c. 9, 294-295; Hardouin, III, 973.

[89] Hefele-Leclercq, III, 304; Bruns, II, 87; Hardouin, III, 1000-1001.

provincial and national synods made the position of the Spanish metropolitans so important that in the development of the metropolitan institution they were hardly influenced by the Holy See.[90] This author stated additionally that this was clear from the small number of decretals which were directed to Spain after the conversion of the Visigoths to Catholicity (589). Yet the two decretals he himself mentioned are proof that the Spanish Church was influenced by Rome and the Popes. In 599, Pope Gregory (590-604) wrote to Leander, Archbishop of Seville, consoling him in the trials he was bearing. Near the end of the letter the Pope conferred the pallium upon him.[91] The Pope's letter was written in answer to Archbishop Leander's letter, in which, according to the decretal, the Spanish Archbishop acknowledged the great authority and position of the Pontiff.

The second decretal concerns the delegation of a certain John as papal *defensor* to settle negotiations in answer to the appeal of two Spanish Bishops, Januarius and Stephen. The letter was written in August of the year 603. It contained an accumulation of rules taken from the Novels and Constitutions of Roman Law, and also from the Capitularies, in order to teach John how to render a judgment in the case.[92] Hinschius declared this correspondence of the

---

[90] *Kirchenrecht*, II, 3.

[91] "Præterea ex benedictione beati Petri apostolorum principis pallium vobis transmisimus ad sola missarum sollemnia utendum."—*Monumenta Germaniæ Historica* (edidit Societas aperiendis fontibus rerum germanicarum medii ævi, Berlin: apud Weidmannos; Hannover: Hahn; Leipzig: Karl W. Hiersemann, 1824-), *Epistolæ*, Tom. I, pars 1, *Gregorii I Papæ registrum epistolarum*, Libri I-IV (ed. Paulus Ewald, Berolini: apud Weidmannos, 1887); Tom. I, pars 2, *Gregorii I Papæ registrum epistolarum*, Libri V-VII (post Pauli Ewaldi obitum ed. L. M. Hartmann, Berolini: apud Weidmannos, 1891); Tom. II, pars 1, *Gregorii I Papæ registrum epistolarum*, Libri VIII-IX (post Pauli Ewaldi obitum ed. L. M. Hartmann, Berolini: apud Weidmannos, 1893); Tom. II, pars 2, *Gregorii I Papæ registrum epistolarum*, Libri X-XIV (post Pauli Ewaldi obitum ed. L. M. Hartmann, Berolini: apud Weidmannos, 1895), Tom. II, pars 1, p. 220 (n. IX, 227) (hereafter cited *MGH: Epistolæ Gregorii I*); Jaffé, n. 1756.

[92] *MGH: Epistolæ Gregorii I*, Tom. II, pars 2, pp. 410-418 (n. XIII, 47, 49, 50); Jaffé, n. 1912.

Pope to be the only decisive interference *(Eingreifen)* throughout this period.[93] The word "interference" hardly seems proper in face of the appeals made by these two bishops. By their appeal to Rome these bishops acknowledged the supreme jurisdiction of the Pope. Furthermore, is it not likely that decretals may have been sent to the Spanish Church by the Popes, which decretals either have not been discovered, or have been permanently lost as a result of the ravages of time? There is a further consideration also. All the successors of Gregory I contributed relatively few decretals to the development of Canon Law up to the eighth century. When the flow of decretals began again in the eighth century, Spain was already conquered by the Arabs.[94]

Article 4. The Italian Church

The metropolitan institution began to exist in Italy sometime during the fourth century. The Pope as Bishop of Rome made his influence felt throughout the Roman province much earlier than this, however. During the fourth century the Pope began to be thought of as the metropolitan of the Roman province. As time went by, the more the concept of the metropolitan institution developed, the greater became the limitation of the Roman province, until in the sixth century it extended only to the nine suburbicarian regions: Latium and Campania, Tuscania and Umbria, Valeria, Picenum suburbicarium, Picenum annonarium, Samnium, Apulia and Calabria, Lucania and Brutii, and Corsica.[95]

As the restrictions of the limits of the Roman province were growing, the metropolitan institution began to appear

---

[93] *Kirchenrecht,* II, 3, footnote 6.

[94] Cf. Kehr, *Papsturkunden in Spanien* (2 vols., Berlin: Weidmann'sche Buchhandlung, 1928). This collection does not report any decretals for the time period here in question. It contains Post-Gregorian decretals from the twelfth century onward.

[95] Hinschius, *Kirchenrecht,* I, 213.

in the northern regions of Italy. The oldest metropoles there were Milan, Aquileia and Ravenna.[96]

In a report which is dated with the year 355, mention was made of a number of ecclesiastics who remained steadfast in the Faith in spite of the onslaughts of Arianism; the name of Dionysius, Bishop of the metropolis of Milan, is among them.[97] It seems then that Milan, already at the beginning of the fourth century, was a metropolitan province in the north, corresponding in its vast ecclesiastical territory to the vicariate of Italy to the south. It may be that the temporary residence of the Western emperor at Milan was responsible for this situation.

Aquileia appeared as a metropolitan city sometime near the end of the fourth century or at the beginning of the fifth. This can be surmised from a letter written by Pope Leo I (440-461) in 458 to Nicetus, Bishop of Aquileia, in which letter comprovincial bishops were mentioned.[98] The text which referred to them reads as follows: "We send this, our letter, in order to consult you, our brother, that you may call it to the attention of all our brethren and your comprovincial bishops, that in the observance of all things authority may prosper."

Baronius (1538-1607) reported that in 432 the direction of an ecclesiastical metropolis was given over to Ravenna in a decree of Valentinian III (425-455).[99] But this

---

[96] Hinschius, *Kirchenrecht*, II, 4.

[97] "Ex quorum numero clarissimæ sunt confessionis viri religiosi et episcopi boni, Pauli episcopi Treverorum, quæ Galliarum metropolis est (hic enim ex conciliabulo Arelatensi anno superiore exulaverat), Lucifer metropolitanus episcopus Sardiniæ, Eusebius Vercellis civitate Italiæ, Dionysius Mediolani, quod et ipsum est Italiæ metropolis." — Baronius, *Annales Ecclesiastici* (37 vols., ed. A. Theiner, Vols. I-XXVIII, Barri-Ducis, 1864-1875; Vols. XXIX-XXXVII, Parisiis, 1876-1883), IV, p. 537, n. 23 (hereafter cited as *Annales*).

[98] Jaffé, n. 536; Mansi, VI, 331-335; *MPL*, LIV, 1135.

[99] "...Flavius Valentinianus fidelis Iesu Christi maior imperator augustus Iohanni viro sanctissimo archiepiscopo Ravennæ civitatis.... Ac proinde imperiali auctoritate sancimus, sanctitatem tuam, et sanctam tuam Ravennatem ecclesiam, atque universos postea Deo...amabiles præsules archieratica dignitate evectam metropolitæ decore sublimandam seu archiepiscopali fastigio...præponendam. Constituimus sub

decree is spurious, having been composed sometime in the seventh century.[100]

Near the end of the sixth century (591), Pope Gregory I (590-604) wrote three letters in which Cagliari (in Sardinia) was called a metropolitan city. The first of these three letters was written upon the complaint of Ianuarius, whom the Pope called a metropolitan explicitly.[101] The second[102] and the third[103] were written to Ianuarius, and in both instances the Pope addressed him again as the metropolitan of Cagliari (in Sardinia). In the year 599, Gregory I (590-604) wrote to the bishops of Sardinia, advising them to observe the old custom of reporting to their metropolitan at Easter-time, and reminding them that they were not to leave the Island without the metropolitan's knowledge and letters of permission.[104] In view of the evidence given by these letters the metropolitan nature of Cagliari must be pushed back to a date earlier than 591.

Hinschius stated that there was no relationship of subjection on the part of Milan, Aquileia and Ravenna to Rome, such as was the case in the East, where the metropolitans were subject to their patriarchs. This author claimed that the Italian metropolitan sees stood in this independent

---

sacrosanctæ eius ecclesia editione ordinationem totius Aemiliæ nostræ provinciæ civitatum omnium Deo amabilium episcoporum creationis id est Sarsenæ, Cæsenæ, Forum Populi, Forum Livii, Faventiæ, Forum Cornelii, Bononiæ, Mutinæ, Regii, Parmæ, Placentiæ, Brixillii, Vicohabentiæ, Hadriæ omniumque monasteriorum sub eius dispositione reiacentium et in eis serventium monachorum." — *Annales*, VII, 429, n. 92.

[100] On the origins of the metropolitan jurisdiction of Ravenna see: Kehr, *Regesta Pontificum Romanorum, Italia Pontificia* (8 vols. in 10, Berolini apud Weidmannos, 1906-1925, Vol. V, 1911), V, 13-73; on this point see V, 13-14; Lanzoni, *Le Origini delle Diocesi Antiche d'Italia*, Studi e Testi, n. 35 (Romæ: Tipografia Poliglotta Vaticana, 1923), pp. 464-475; on this point see p. 465.

[101] *MGH: Epistolæ Gregorii I*, Tom. I, pars 1, p. 73 (n. I, 47); Jaffé, n. 1117.

[102] *MGH: Epistolæ Gregorii I*, Tom. I, pars 1, pp. 83-84 (n. I, 61); Jaffé, n. 1131.

[103] *MGH: Epistolæ Gregorii I*, Tom. I, pars 1, p. 84 (n. I, 62); Jaffé, n. 1130.

[104] *MGH: Epistolæ Gregorii I*, Tom. II, pars 1, p. 189 (n. IX, 202); Jaffé, n. 1729.

position until the sixth century.[105] In spite of the contention of Milan and Aquileia that their bishops were equal to the Bishop of Rome, which can be found in between canon 56 and 57 of the *Codex Canonum Ecclesiæ Africanæ*,[106] and the imperial edict of Constans II (642-668), given in 666, which declared Ravenna *"sui iuris"* and determined that it was not to be subject in any way to the patriarch of ancient Rome but was to remain autocephalous,[107] there is testimony that Ravenna was in a position of subjection even as early as 482.

In the fifth and sixth centuries the archbishops of Ravenna had to attend the Roman provincial synods. Milan and Aquileia were made conscious of their dependence on Rome perhaps sometime near the middle, but most certainly at the end, of the sixth century. Pope Simplicius (468-483) threatened to withdraw the right to consecrate the comprovincial bishops from John, the Archbishop of Ravenna, if the latter dared to consecrate anyone against the wish of the Pope. This letter is dated with the year 482.[108] It was Pope Pelagius I (556-561) who permitted (c. 558-560) the continuance of the custom which held that the archbishop of Milan was to consecrate the archbishop of Aquileia, and vice versa, thereby showing his authority over both these metropolitans.[109] The letters which Pope Gregory I (590-604) wrote to the bishops of the province of Aquileia during the years of 591, 592, 595, 602, certainly indicate the existence of a relationship of subjection on the part of Aquileia to Rome.[110]

Since the institution of metropolitans was in such a poor

---

[105] *Kirchenrecht,* II, 4.

[106] Bruns, I, 168-169.

[107] Muratori, *Rerum Italicarum Scriptores* (25 vols., Milan, 1723-1751), II, 124.

[108] Thiel, *Epistolæ,* pp. 201-202; Jaffé, n. 583; Mansi, VII, 972; *MPL,* LVIII, 35.

[109] C. 33, C. XXIV, q. 1; Jaffé, n. 983; Mansi, IX, 730; *MPL,* LXIX, 411.

[110] *MGH: Epistolæ Gregorii I,* Tom. I, pars 1, p. 16 (n. I, 16); Tom. I, pars 1, pp. 150-151 (n. II, 49); Tom. I, pars 1, p. 359 (n. V, 56); Tom. II, pars 2, p. 360 (n. XII, 13); Jaffé, nn. 1048, 1203, 1372, 1863.

state in Italy, it followed naturally that their rights and prerogatives were not clearly defined. The metropolitan of Milan had the right of consecrating his comprovincial bishops. This is known from one of the letters of St. Ambrose.[111] So likewise the metropolitan of Ravenna had the same right, as can be seen from the letter of Pope Simplicius (468-483) to John of Ravenna.[112] The only proof to be had concerning the metropolitan right to convoke and preside at a provincial synod is the fact that St. Ambrose held a synod at Milan in 381, and still another in 390.[113] The prerogative of holding a higher judicial position as far as the bishoprics of the province was concerned is clear from two letters of St. Ambrose.[114] Therefore it can be said, in general, that the Italian metropolitans had the same rights over their comprovincial bishops as the Oriental metropolitans.

Article 5. The Church of Gaul

The metropolitan institution is to be found in Gaul from the end of the fourth or the beginning of the fifth century. There was a shadow of the institution in the second century, but it is not sufficiently distinct to allow tracing the beginnings to that early date. Eusebius (c. 263-339) in his *Historia Ecclesiastica* (V, 23) is responsible for this intimation.[115] The passage in Eusebius' *Historia* declared only that Irenæus of Lyons (+ ca. 202) had a higher position in contrast to the other Gallic bishops, but it did not explicitly name him a metropolitan. The beginnings must be placed sometime before the Council held in Turin (401), for three metropolitans, i.e., of Marseilles, of Arles and of

---

[111] Ep. 63 — *MPL,* XVI, 1188-1219. St. Ambrose advised the Church of Vercelli to choose a bishop.

[112] Thiel, *Epistolæ,* pp. 201-202; Jaffé, n. 583; Mansi, VII, 972; *MPL,* LVIII, 35.

[113] Hefele-Leclercq, II, 52-53, 78-80; Mansi, III, 518, 664-667.

[114] Ep. 516 — *MPL,* XVI, 891-904. St. Ambrose wrote to Syagrius concerning a case decided by the latter, and reverses the latter's decision.

[115] "...γραφὴ...τῶν κατὰ Ταλλίαν δὲ παροικιῶν ἃς Εἰρηναῖος ἐπισκόπει" — *MPG,* XX, 495.

Vienne, attended it in order to have their respective jurisdictions settled.[116]

Unlike Italy, where the metropolitan subjection was rather tenuous, the metropolitan institution of Gaul leaned heavily on the Popes. The great quarrel over the eminent position of the primate of Arles drew Rome in to settle the argument.[117] That this dependence on the Papal See lasted for the greater part of the sixth century is clear from the evidence in the sources. Bishop Contumeliosus of Riez, having been deposed by the Council of Marseilles (533), appealed to the Pope for a decision in his case.[118] Pope Agapitus I (535-536), in a letter written in 535, decided that Bishop Contumeliosus be given proper revenue for his personal maintenance, but also decreed that the latter remain suspended from the administration of his ecclesiastical patrimony and from the celebration of Mass until a final decision be reached.[119] A little later, at the II Council of Lyons (567), the condemned Bishops Salonius of Embrun and Sagittarius of Gap appealed to Pope John III (560-573) with the consent of King Guntram of Burgundy (561-

---

[116] Hinschius, *Kirchenrecht*, I, 588.

[117] *Ibid.*, pp. 588-590.

[118] Hefele-Leclercq, II, 1125-1129; *MGH: Leges*, Sect. II, *Capitularia Regum Francorum*, Tom. I (ed. A. Boretius, 1883), Tom. II (ed. A. Boretius et Victor Krause, 1897); Sect. III, *Concilia*, Tom. I, *Concilia ævi Merovingici* (rec. F. Maassen, 1893), Tom. II, *Concilia ævi Karolini I* (rec. Albertus Werminghoff, pars 1, 1904-1906; pars 2, 1904-1908), *MGH: Legum Sectio III, Concilia*, I, 60-61 (hereafter *Capitularia Regum Francorum* will be cited as *Legum Sectio II, Capitularia; Concilia ævi Merovingici* and *Concilia ævi Karolini I* will be cited as *Legum Sectio III, Concilia*, each being identified by the volume number).

[119] "Delegaturi enim...sumus examen, ut secundum canonum venerabilium constituta, sub consideratione iustitiæ, omnia quæ apud fraternitatem tuam de huiusmodi negotio acta gestave sunt, diligentissima vestigatione flagitentur....Melius autem fecerat fraternitas tua, si posteaquam sedis apostolicæ appellatione interposita desideravit examen, circa personam eius a tempore sententiæ nihil permississet imminui; ut esset integrum negotium, quod interposita provocatione quæreretur. Nam si in executionem mittitur prima sententia, secunda non habet cognitio quod requirat." — Mansi, VIII, 856; *MPL*, LXVI, 46-47; Jaffé, n. 890.

592). In reply the Pope commanded the King to restore both Bishops to their sees.[120]

The dependence of suffragan bishops on metropolitans began to break down near the middle of the sixth century. Pope Pelagius I (556-561) complained, in a letter written sometime between the years 557 and 558, to King Childebert I that Sapaudus, the Bishop of Arles, was forced to undergo judgment contrary to the canons.[121]

With the passage of time the Popes were called less and less to form the first instance in those ecclesiastical affairs which concerned the metropolitans and their synods, and to reform their decrees and resolutions. Gregory I (590-604) tried to restore the influence which his predecessors had in the fifth and the first part of the sixth centuries, but met with little success.[122]

Dudden, speaking of the relations of Gregory with the Franks, remarked that

> there can be no doubt that Gregory failed in his efforts to bring about a reformation of abuses. The country was not yet ready for anything of that sort. Political confusion had bred moral disorder, and amid the general disorganization Gregory's attempts to enforce the observance of law were inevitably futile. It took nearly two hundred years for the

[120] "At illi, cum adhuc propitium sibi regem esse nossent, ad eum accedunt, implorantes se iniuste remotos, sibique tribui licentiam, ut ad papam urbis Romanæ accedere debeant. Rex vero annuens petitionibus eorum, datis epistolis, eos abire permisit. Qui accedentes coram papa Iohanne, exponunt se nullius rationis existentibus causis dimotos. Ille vero ad regem epistolas dirigit, in quibus locis suis eosdem restitui iubet. Quod rex sine mora...implevit." — *MGH: Scriptores rerum merovingicarum*, Tom. I: *Gregorii Turonensis opera* (ed. W. Arndt et B. Krusch, 1884), p. 217 (v, 20); *MPL*, LXXI, 341; Jaffé, n. 1040; *MGH: Legum Sectio III, Concilia*, I, 139-141.

[121] "...miramur, quia...passi estis subripi vobis, Sapaudum...Arelatensis civitatis antistitem, cuius ecclesia in regionibus Gallicanis primatus privilegio et sedis apostolicæ vicibus decoratur, ad petitionem episcopi ab ipso ordinati, in iudicium sequentis civitatis episcopi, quod nulla ecclesiastica lege vel ratione conceditur, iudicandum iuberetis occurrere...." — Mansi, IX, 726; *MPL*, LXIX, 406-407; Jaffé, n. 948.

[122] Hinschius, *Kirchenrecht*, I, 504, 509.

> Gallican Church to recover from the effects of the invasion of the Franks. Nevertheless, Gregory's work in Gaul was not in vain. He succeeded in establishing a regular intercourse between himself and the Church of Gaul, especially in the cities of the east and the south; he fixed a tradition of friendship between the Apostolic See and the Frank princes; he held up an ideal of Christianity before a savage and half-pagan people; and he caused the name of bishop to be once more reverenced in a land where it had grown to be almost synonymous with avarice, lawlessness, and corrupt ambition. If Gregory did no more than this, he accomplished enough. Though his work was not rich in definite results at the moment, yet afterwards, in the age of Charlemagne, its effects became manifest.[123]

In another place the same author stated:

> The relations which he [Gregory] succeeded in establishing with her [Gaul's] kings were not sustained after his death. For more than a century there appears to have been no intercourse between the Popes and the Frank rulers; at any rate, till the time of Gregory the Second no documents exist which can be quoted in proof of any intercommunication. Rome left the Merovingian princes to their fate. Yet, though communications between Gaul and Rome practically ceased with Gregory, the work of the great Pope was not thrown away.[124]

Because of the decline of the Merovingian Kingdom and the troubles which the Popes encountered in Italy with the Lombards during this century of silence, the connection between the Roman See and the Frankish metropolitans became very loose, so much so that their position became as

---

[123] *Gregory the Great, His Place in History and Thought* (2 vols., London: Longmans, Green and Co., 1905), II, 69.

[124] *Ibid.*, p. 98.

good as independent. From 613 onward to the beginning of the eighth century only three papal letters directed to the Frankish Kingdom have been found. The first is that of Pope Martin I (649-653) to Amandus, Bishop of Tangres, written in 649, in which the Pope dissuaded the Bishop from resigning his episcopal office. Nothing was mentioned about papal consent which was later required for such a resignation.[125] The second one, written in 668 by Pope Vitalianus (657-672) to Archbishop John of Arles (658-675), was given to Archbishop Theodore of Canterbury for delivery to the Frankish Archbishop. A record of this letter is had in Bede's *Historia Ecclesiastica*, IV, c. 1.[126] The final letter of this period was sent by Pope Adeodatus (672-676) sometime during his pontificate to all the bishops of Gaul. It treated of the exemption of the monastery of St. Martin from episcopal power.[127]

Within their districts the metropolitans of Gaul possessed the same prerogatives as the metropolitans in the countries already discussed.[128] They had the right to convoke and preside at provincial synods. Such an early synod as the one held at Riez in 439 decreed in canons 8 and 10 that two synods were to be held each year.[129] A trifle later, in the year 441, the I Council of Orange in its 29th canon not only blamed those who did not make their appearance at the Council, but declared that every future council was to be announced at the previous one, and commissioned

---

[125] Mansi, X, 1183; *MPL*, LXXXVII, 135-138; Jaffé, n. 2059.

[126] "Qui cum pariter per mare ad Massiliam, ac deinde per terram Arhelas pervenissent, et tradidissent Iohanni archiepiscopo civitatis illius scripta commendaticia Vitaliani pontificis. . . ." — Plummer, *Venerabilis Bædæ Opera Historica* (2 vols., Oxonii: e Typographeo Clarendoniano, 1896), I, 203; *MPL*, XCV, 171-173; Jaffé, n. 2094.

[127] Mansi, XI, 103-106; *MPL*, LXXXVII, 1141-1144; Jaffé, n. 2105. Two texts of this letter are extant, but differ from each other; both are suspect.

[128] Hinschius, *Kirchenrecht*, II, 5, footnote 4.

[129] Canon 8: Bruns, II, 120; Hardouin, I, 1750-1751; Hefele-Leclercq, II, 430; Mansi, V, 1094; Canon 10: Bruns, *ibid.*, p. 121; Hardouin, *ibid.*, p. 1751; Hefele-Leclercq, *ibid.*, p. 430; Mansi, *ibid.*, 1094.

Bishop Hilary, present at the Council, to give notice of the next council to those who were absent.[130]

Canon 35 of the I Council of Agde (506) clearly stated that it was the metropolitan who had the right to summon his comprovincial bishops to the provincial synod or council. The latter were to appear on the day appointed unless they were excused by serious illness or by the command of the king.[131] The same legislation is found in canon 1 of the Council of Epaon (517).[132] Canon I of the III Council of Orleans (538) strongly insisted that the metropolitan had to summon a provincial synod every year, and warned that, if he failed to do so for two years in spite of the requests made by his comprovincials, he would not be allowed to say Mass for a whole year.[133] The IV Council of Orleans (541), in canon 37, again stressed the metropolitan's duty to hold a provincial synod yearly in order to maintain discipline.[134]

These provincial synods, and not the metropolitans, had the power of correction. Canon 1 of the Council of Clermont in Auvergne (535) stated that the chief business of the provincial synods was the improvement of morals.[135] The III Council of Orleans (538) made it clear in its 21st canon that clerics who entered into a conspiracy against their bishops were to be punished by the latter assembled in synod.[136] Again, it was the provincial synod which was the instance of appeal, and not the metropolitans. According to canon 5 of the I Council of Vaison (442) anyone who was

---

[130] Bruns, II, 126; Hardouin, I, 1786; Hefele-Leclercq, II, 452-453; Mansi, VI, 440.

[131] C. 13, D. XVIII; Bruns, II, 153; Hefele-Leclercq, II, 996; Mansi, VIII, 330-331.

[132] Bruns, II, 167; *MGH: Legum Sectio III, Concilia*, I, 19; Hefele-Leclercq, II, 1036; Mansi, VIII, 559.

[133] Bruns, II, 191-192; *MGH: Legum Sectio III, Concilia*, I, 73; Hefele-Leclercq, II, 1157; Mansi, IX, 11-12.

[134] Bruns, II, 208; *MGH: Legum Sectio III, Concilia*, I, 95; Hefele-Leclercq, II, 1174; Mansi, IX, 119.

[135] Bruns, II, 185; *MGH: Legum Sectio III, Concilia*, I, 66; Hefele-Leclercq, II, 1140; Mansi, VIII, 860.

[136] Bruns, II, 198; *MGH: Legum Sectio III, Concilia*, I, 80; Hefele-Leclercq, II, 1161; Mansi, IX, 17.

unable to acquiesce to the judgment of his bishop could have recourse to the provincial synod.[137] Canon 48 of the II Council of Arles (443 or 452) repeated this legislation.[138] Should a cleric believe himself wronged by his bishop, then according to canon 20 of the III Council of Orleans (538) he had the right to appeal to the provincial synod.[139]

A power which metropolitans in Gaul enjoyed was that of presiding over the cases which involved bishops. The 17th canon of the V Council of Orleans (549) legislated that, if anyone had a dispute with a bishop or administrator of church property, he could have recourse to the metropolitan. If the accused bishop, after two admonitions of the metropolitan, neither satisfied his opponent nor appeared before the metropolitan, he was to be cut off from the communion with the metropolitan until he made satisfaction. If it was shown that the metropolitan had been approached twice by one of his comprovincial bishops in a case and the former had not given a hearing to the latter, the bishop could bring the case before the next provincial synod, and the decision of the comprovincials would stand.[140]

The II Council of Lyons (567) stated in its 1st canon that if bishops within an ecclesiastical province should have a controversy, they had to be content with the sentence of their metropolitan and comprovincials; that, if the quarrel took place between bishops of different provinces, their respective metropolitans were to meet to decide the matter.[141] This power over bishops became more exclusive when the legislation of canon 9 of the II Council of Mâcon (585) insisted that clergymen were not to be dragged from their

---

[137] Bruns, II, 128; Hardouin, I, 1788; Hefele-Leclercq, II, 457; Mansi, VI, 454.

[138] Bruns, II, 136; Hefele-Leclercq, II, 474; Mansi, VII, 884.

[139] Bruns, II, 198; *MGH: Legum Sectio III, Concilia*, I, 80; Hefele-Leclercq, II, 1161; Mansi, IX, 17.

[140] Bruns, II, 212-213; *MGH: Legum Sectio III, Concilia*, I, 106; Hefele-Leclercq, III, 162; Mansi, IX, 133.

[141] Bruns, II, 222-223; *MGH: Legum Sectio III, Concilia*, I, 139-140; Hardouin, III, 353-354; Hefele-Leclercq, III, 183-184; Mansi, IX, 786-787.

churches and thrown into public prisons by the secular powers, but that, if there were any charges against a bishop, these complaints were to be brought before the metropolitan who, if the matter was light, was to decide the matter himself, or if the matter was serious, was to bring it before a synod.[142] The V Council of Paris (614-615) declared in its 11th canon that if a bishop had a dispute with another bishop, he was to apply to the metropolitan for a decision, and not to a secular judge.[143]

The second prerogative of the metropolitans of Gaul was that of co-operation in the filling of episcopal sees and in the consecration of comprovincial bishops. The II Council of Arles (443 or 452) decided in its 5th canon that no bishop could be consecrated without the metropolitan, or without at least his written permission, or without three comprovincial bishops. In case of a controversy as to the election of a bishop, the metropolitan was to agree with the majority.[144] Canon 6 of the same Council declared that if anyone was consecrated without the consent of the metropolitan, the consecration was null and void.[145]

About a hundred years later, the Council of Clermont in Auvergne (535) decreed in canon 2 that a bishop, when chosen by the clergy and laity, could be elected only with the consent of the metropolitan.[146] The III Council of Orleans (538), besides specifying in canon 3 the manner in which a metropolitan was to be chosen, made it clear that a bishop was to be chosen by the clergy and the laity with the consent of the metropolitan.[147] Canon 10 of the V Coun-

---

[142] Bruns, II, 252; *MGH: Legum Sectio III, Concilia,* I, 168-169; Hardouin, III, 462-463; Hefele-Leclercq, III, 210; Mansi, IX, 953-954.

[143] Bruns, II, 258; *MGH: Legum Sectio III, Concilia,* I, 189 (canon 13); Hardouin, III, 553; Hefele-Leclercq, III (canon 13); Mansi, X, 542.

[144] Bruns, II, 131; Hefele-Leclercq, II, 464; Mansi, VII, 879.

[145] *Loc. cit.*

[146] Bruns, II, 188; *MGH: Legum Sectio III, Concilia,* I, 66-67; Hefele-Leclercq, II, 1140; Mansi, VIII, 860.

[147] Bruns, II, 192; *MGH: Legum Sectio III, Concilia,* I, 73-74; Hefele-Leclercq, II, 1157-1158; Mansi, IX, 12.

cil of Orleans (549) legislated that a new bishop was to be consecrated by the metropolitan or his representative in union with the comprovincials.[148]

In declaring that no one was to be forced upon a city as a bishop unless he had been elected with complete freedom by the clergy and the laity, canon 8 of the III Council of Paris (557) added that not even the command of the king could work against the will of the metropolitan and the comprovincials in the election of bishops.[149] The II Council of Tours (567) made a special provision in canon 9 for the Province of Aremorica (the region which covered Brittany inland to Tours). No one could consecrate a Breton or a Roman bishop without the consent of the metropolitan and his comprovincials under the penalty of exclusion from the communion of bishops until the next synod.[150] Canon 1 of the V Council of Paris (614-615) forbade bishops to choose their successors, and reiterated that an episcopal successor could, without simony, be chosen only by the metropolitan, comprovincials, clergy and laity of the city in question.[151]

The Gallic metropolitans also enjoyed the right of granting consent for the alienation of church property. According to canon 12 of the Council held at Epaon in 517 no bishop could sell any church property without the previous knowledge of his metropolitan.[152]

In Gaul also the ecclesiastical service of the metropolitan church was the pattern for the services held in the other cathedral churches. Already at the Council of Epaon (517) it was decided in canon 27 that the ordering of the divine

---

[148] Bruns, II, 211; *MGH: Legum Sectio III, Concilia,* I, 103-104; Hefele-Leclercq, III, 161; Mansi, IX, 131.

[149] Bruns, II, 221-222; *MGH: Legum Sectio III, Concilia,* I, 144-145; Hefele-Leclercq, III, 173; Mansi, IX, 746-747.

[150] Bruns, II, 226-227; *MGH: Legum Sectio III, Concilia,* I, 124; Hardouin, III, 359; Hefele-Leclercq, III, 186; Mansi, IX, 794.

[151] Bruns, II, 256; *MGH: Legum Sectio III, Concilia,* I, 186 (canon 2); Hardouin, III, 551; Hefele-Leclercq, III, 251; Mansi, X, 539-540.

[152] Bruns, II, 168; *MGH: Legum Sectio III, Concilia,* I, 22; Hefele-Leclercq, II, 1038; Mansi, VIII, 560.

services by the metropolitan was to be observed in his entire province.[153]

In retrospect it should be noted that in their authority the Gallic metropolitans were not superior to the provincial synods. Rather, the synods in their joint authority transcended the power of the metropolitans.

Article 6. The Church in Germany and Britain

Matter is too scarce and too doubtful to prove the existence of the metropolitan institution in Germany during the period here considered. For these reasons it is difficult to show that Trier and Cologne were metropoles during the Roman-Merovingian times.[154]

The first attempts of establishing metropoles in Britain took place in the beginning of the seventh century.[155]

Section B

Characteristic Features of the Early Metropolitan Institution

The metropolitan institution, which began in the Orient, brought about two distinct results in the most important countries of the Occident during these early centuries. The first worked for their common good, for it concentrated ecclesiastical power within the various provinces and developed to a high degree a new link in the system of church organization. In this feature metropolitans were bound in the exercise of their power to co-operate with their episcopal colleagues in every important provincial matter. The other result was not as fortunate for the Church. In relation to the Pope, the metropolitan system created a spirit of independence from Rome in matters regarding ecclesiastical legislation and administration. Nevertheless, the metro-

---

153 Bruns, II, 170; *MGH: Legum Sectio III, Concilia,* I, 25; Hefele-Leclercq, II, 1040; Mansi, VIII, 562.

154 Hinschius, *Kirchenrecht,* II, 6, footnote 1.

155 *Ibid.,* I, 616.

politans were checked by the Pope or his vicars.[156] Quite often they were checked in the exercise of their power by their own patriarchs or primates.[157]

SECTION C

USE OF TERMINOLOGY DURING THESE TIMES

During these centuries the expression μητροπολίτης or *metropolitanus* was by far the most common. The Latin form can be found in the papal decretals of the times, as in Pope Hilary's (461-468) letter to Ascanius, which was written in 465.[158] The same Latin form was employed in the various canons of the numerous Spanish and Gallican Councils which delineated the powers and prerogatives of the metropolitans.[159] The designation ἔξαρχος τῆς ἐπαρχίας appeared infrequently. The Greek version of the 6th canon of the Council of Sardica (343 or 344) made use of it.[160]

[156] For Illyricum see: Silva-Tarouca, *Textus et Documenta in usum exercitationum et prælectionum academicarum Epistolarum Romanorum Pontificum ad Vicarios per Illyricum Aliosque Episcopos Collectio Thessalonicensis*, Series Theologica, n. 23 (Romæ: apud ædes Pont. Universitatis Gregorianiæ, 1937); Duchesne, "L'Illyricum ecclesiastique," — *Byzantinische Zeitschrift* (Leipzig: Druck und Verlag von B. G. Traubner, 1892-), I (1892), 531-550; Greenslade, "The Illyrian Churches and the Vicariate of Thessalonica, 378-395," — *The Journal of Theological Studies* (Oxford: Clarendon Press, 1899-), XLVI (1945), 17-30; Streichhan, "Die Anfänge des Vikariates von Thessalonike" — *Zeitschrift der Savigny-Stiftung für Rechtsgeschichte* (Weimar: Herman Böhlaus Nachfolger), Kan. Abt., XII (1922), 330 ff.

[157] For limitations by the patriarchs see Hinschius, *Kirchenrecht*, I, 549 ff.; for the checking power of the primates see *ibid.*, 581 ff. for Africa, and 592 ff. for Spain.

[158] Thiel, *Epistolæ*, pp. 166-169; Mansi, VII, 927; *MPL*, LVIII, 17; Jaffé, n. 560. For the Latin text cf. *supra*, p. 39. Cf. Hinschius, *Kirchenrecht*, I, 596, footnote 4; Hinschius, *Decretales Pseudo-Isidorianæ*, p. 631.

[159] *Supra*, pp. 39-47, for the Spanish Councils, and pp. 51-60, for the Gallican Councils.

[160] Hefele-Leclercq, I, 777; Bruns, I, 90-92; Hinschius, *Kirchenrecht*, I, 577, footnote 9. The Latin versions designate the metropolitan variously; in the *Authenticum Latinum* he was called "episcopus qui in eadem provincia moratur." Evidently such a reading proved to be confusing, inasmuch as the canon as such spoke of the absence of all the bishops within a province; hence the "episcopus qui in eadem pro-

In the African Church the bishop who held the position of primate was called *senex, primas, episcopus primæ sedis.*[161] The designation of *primas* was also given to metropolitans of other countries. Canon 1 of the Council of Turin (401) referred to the metropolitans of Illyricum as primates.[162] Pope Innocent I (401-417), when writing to Rufus of Thessalonica in 412, called the metropolitans of Illyricum primates.[163] Canon 2 of the III Council of Saragossa (691) spoke of Spanish metropolitans as primates.[164] The 35th canon of the *Canones Apostolorum* called the metropolitan ὁ πρῶτος.[165] The designation *episcopus primæ sedis,* used by the African Church, was employed in the 58th canon of the Spanish Council of Elvira (ca. 300-306).[166]

The title ἀρχιεπίσκοπος, *archiepiscopus,* during these centuries was a designation given to those bishops who held important positions. Quite frequently it was given to patriarchs.[167] But from the sixth century onward it was also given to metropolitans. In 591 Pope Gregory I (590-604), in addressing a letter to Anastasius of Corinth, called him an archbishop.[168] The same Pope, writing in the same year

---

vincia moratur" had to be more than a simple bishop. *Codex* Θ called him "primatus episcopus provinciæ, hoc est, metropolitanus," while *Codex T* referred to him as "qui provinciæ illius sortitus est principatum, id est, qui iure metropolitano subnixus est." If the Latin version was composed at the Council, and the Greek version was a translation, it followed that the Greek version clarified the meaning of the phrase "episcopus qui in eadem provincia moratur" on the grounds that it really meant the metropolitan, who already held a recognized position in the East, though such was not the case in the West. — Turner, *Monumenta,* Tomus I, Fasciculus II, Pars III, canon 4, pp. 498-501.

[161] *Supra,* p. 11; Hinschius, *Kirchenrecht,* I, 581.

[162] Hefele-Leclercq, II, 133-134; Hinschius, *Kirchenrecht,* I, 558, footnote 3.

[163] Mansi, VIII, 751; *MPL,* XX, 515; Jaffé, n. 300.

[164] Hefele-Leclercq, III, 557; Hinschius, *Kirchenrecht,* II, 3, footnote 3. Cf. *supra,* p. 44.

[165] Cf. *supra,* p. 17.

[166] Hefele-Leclercq, III, 253-254; Hinschius, *Kirchenrecht,* I, 512. Cf. *supra,* p. 39.

[167] Hinschius, *Kirchenrecht,* I, 546.

[168] *MGH: Epistolæ Gregorii I,* Tom. I, pars 1, pp. 39-40 (n. I, 26); Jaffé, n. 1095.

to the metropolitan of Cagliari, addressed him an an archbishop.[169] The patriarch of Aquileia and the metropolitans of Gaul were interchangeably called metropolitans and archbishops in an instruction drawn up at the Council of Aquileia (591).[170] Isidore of Seville (+636) stated in his *Etymologiæ* that this interchange was no longer adapted to his times.[171]

The district over which the metropolitan exercised his rights was called an ἐπαρχία in the Orient.[172] In Africa, Spain and Gaul, the term which was employed was *provincia.*[173] Pope Hormisdas (514-523) called the metropolitan district a *parœcia* in his *Indiculus,* written in 516.[174] Again Pope Gregory I (590-604) designated the territory headed by a metropolitan as a *diœcesis.*[175] However, these latter two designations were exceptions to the general rule of the employment of the two former terms.

The bishops who resided under metropolitans were called *episcopi comprovinciales* or *episcopi provinciales* in the Spanish and Gallic Councils.[176] Pope Leo I (440-461), in writing to Nicetus of Aquileia in 458, had already made mention of comprovincial bishops.[177]

---

[169] *MGH: Epistolæ Gregorii I,* Tom. I, pars 1, pp. 83-84 (n. I, 60, 61); Jaffé, nn. 1130, 1131.

[170] Mansi, X, 463-466.

[171] Lib. VII, cap. 12: "Ordo episcoporum quadripartitus est; i.e. in patriarchis, archiepiscopis, metropolitanis atque episcopis....Archiepiscopus græco vocabulo, quod sit summus episcoporum: tenet enim vicem apostolicam, et præsidet tam metropolitanis quam ceteris episcopis." — c. 1, D. XXI.

[172] Cf. *supra,* pp. 3-4.

[173] Cf. *supra,* pp. 9-12 for Africa; pp. 12-14 for Spain; pp. 51-60 for Gaul.

[174] "...ut postquam episcopus [called a *metropolitanus* in another passage] Nicopolitanus acceperit litteras nostras, episcopos quod in sua parœcia habet colligat." — Thiel, *Epistolæ,* pp. 780-781; Mansi, VIII, 408; *MPL,* LXIII, 394; Jaffé, n. 783.

[175] *MGH: Epistolæ Gregorii I,* Tom. II, pars 1, p. 215 (n. IX, 223); Jaffé, n. 1752.

[176] C. 1, D. LXII. Cf. *supra,* pp. 12-14 for Spain; for Gaul, pp. 51-60.

[177] Cf. *supra,* p. 48.

CHAPTER III

METROPOLITAN INSTITUTION FROM THE EIGHTH CENTURY TO THE DECREE OF GRATIAN

SECTION A

DEVELOPMENT OF THE METROPOLITAN INSTITUTION IN THE EAST

Article 1. Old Rights According to the Canons of the IV Council of Constantinople

The metropolitan institution in the East was completely crystallized by the beginning of the eighth century. The powers and privileges of metropolitans had been definitely settled by the legislation of the provincial synods and the Ecumenical Councils held in the seven earlier centuries. The last General Council held in the East, the IV of Constantinople (869-870), added only a few touches to the completed picture of the institution.

The old right which metropolitans had, of directing the elections at which the bishops of the province provided for the filling of the vacant episcopal sees, was taken for granted in the 22nd canon of the Council. It decreed that all promotions and consecrations of bishops were to be made through the election and the decision of the college of bishops, in accordance with earlier canons. Nothing was said concerning the metropolitan's right of confirming the election, or of his right to consecrate the new bishop. The sole reason for this legislation was that of prohibiting the interference of secular rulers and other lay persons who possessed a potential influence in the elections and promotions of clerics.[1]

The Council made no new provisions concerning the provincial synods. It may accordingly be taken for granted that the metropolitan rights of convoking and presiding at

[1] Hardouin, V, 909; Hefele-Leclercq, IV, 529; Mansi, XVI, 174-175; Schroeder, *Decrees*, p. 172; p. 539.

them were well entrenched in the Eastern Church. The only change which took place with regard to the matters to be treated in these synods was a significant one. All the former legislation had checked the power of the metropolitan with regard to the excommunication of clerics by their individual bishops, and the settling of disputes between bishops and their subjects, by insisting that a cleric could appeal only to the bishops gathered in a provincial synod. Canon 26 of the IV General Council of Constantinople expanded the power of the metropolitan to a sort of appellate jurisdiction in such matters. If a priest or deacon, when deposed by his bishop on account of some crime, maintained that he had suffered injustice, and hence was dissatisfied with the judgment of his bishop, he was allowed to appeal to the metropolitan of the province who, with the bishops of the province, was to examine the matter in a provincial synod and to pronounce judgment in accordance with the results of their investigation.[2] This change is significant, not because of what actually was conceded to the Eastern metropolitans at the time, but because of what this actually led to in the West.

No new legislation touched the right of metropolitans relative to the granting of permission for travel.

Article 2. Limitations According to the Canons of the IV Council of Constantinople

But it seems that the East was being troubled with the difficulties which were taking place in the West, namely, the usurpation of still further power on the part of the metropolitans. The Council placed a number of checks on them.

The first one came in the form of canon 17, which declared that the patriarchs had the right to summon to their patriarchal synods, and to punish, if they were convicted of any misdemeanor, all metropolitans who had been elevated by them either through consecration or the bestowal

[2] Hardouin, V, 911; Hefele-Leclercq, IV, 530; Mansi, XVI, 177-178; Schroeder, *Decrees*, p. 175; p. 540.

of the pallium. The metropolitans were warned that they could not excuse themselves from these synods on the ground that they themselves held metropolitan synods, since, according to the canon itself, the patriarchal synods were far more important than the metropolitan ones. The canon concluded with another warning in the form of a penal sanction. Any metropolitan who without good reason failed to obey the summons of his patriarch within two months was to be suspended, and if he failed to obey within a year he was to be deposed. In fine, failure to comply with the decision of the canon under consideration meant anathema.[3] The canon, however, as can be seen from the historical events which followed, had a double effect. It had the benign result of checking the metropolitan institution from further usurpation of power, but it had the disastrous effect of increasing the authority of the patriarchs to a point where their dependence upon Rome was completely broken down.

If the metropolitans gained their limited appellate jurisdiction over the subjects of their comprovincials, they had to pay for it by a diminution of authority over their comprovincial bishops. Canon 26 insisted that a bishop could appeal to the patriarch against the decision of his metropolitan, so that then the patriarch together with the metropolitans subject to him would decide the matter. No metropolitan or bishop was to be judged by the neighboring metropolitans of his province; this was to be done by the patriarch. Again, anyone who did not submit to this decision was to be excommunicated.[4]

A further checking of the power of the metropolitans was introduced in canons 19 and 24. The first of these two

---

[3] Hardouin, V, 906-907; Hefele-Leclercq, IV, 528 (Greek Text); Mansi, XVI, 170-172; Schroeder, *Decrees*, p. 170; p. 537. A detailed discussion of the *Pallium* can be found in Hinschius, *Kirchenrecht*, II, 23-36; Eidenschink, *The Election of Bishops in the Letters of Gregory the Great*, The Catholic University of America Canon Law Studies, n. 215 (Washington, D. C.: The Catholic University of America Press, 1945), Appendix, pp. 101-143 (hereafter cited *Election of Bishops*).

[4] Hardouin, V, 911; Hefele-Leclercq, IV, 530; Mansi, XVI, 177-178; Schroeder, *Decrees*, p. 175; pp. 540-541.

prohibited any archbishop or metropolitan from leaving his own church, and, under the pretext of visitation, but really impelled by avarice, betaking himself to the churches of his suffragans to abuse his power by imposing heavy burdens on their subjects and squandering the money intended for the poor and other ecclesiastical purposes. The metropolitans were told to accept, with reverence and the fear of God, the hospitality and the other necessities of the journey which were extended to them, but were urged not to make other demands which might prove a burden to those churches or their bishops.[5] This canon is perhaps the first one which explicitly mentioned visitations made by metropolitans in their provinces. No legislation of the former Ecumenical Councils made this a specific right of duty of metropolitans. However, this prerogative, as will be shown later, became part of the metropolitan institution in the West.[6]

The other prohibitive canon (24) took severe steps to eradicate an evil which must have been growing during these times. The canon strongly lashed out against metropolitans who, contrary to ecclesiastical law, were so absorbed in secular pursuits and so utterly negligent and careless in their spiritual duties that they had all their divine

---

[5] Hefele-Leclercq, IV, 528; Hardouin, V, 908; Mansi, XVI, 172-173; Schroeder, *Decrees*, p. 172; p. 538. The interchange of the two words archbishop and metropolitan is to be noted here: "*nullum archiepiscopum, aut metropolitanum,*" as also the introduction of the term suffragan instead of comprovincial: "*coepiscopos et suffraganeos.*" Cf. *infra*, pp. 88-90. The acts of this Council have come down to these times in a twofold text, one in the Latin version of Anastasius, librarian of the Roman Church, who was present at the last session as a member of the Frankish embassy, the other in a shorter Greek account. The former gives all the acts *in extenso* and is regarded by scholars as a thoroughly reliable text. To this text scholars owe most of their documentary knowledge of the proceedings of the Council. The Greek text is evidently a synopsis or an epitomized presentation of the acts. The greatest divergence in these two texts is found in the canons, of which the Latin text gives twenty-seven, while the Greek contains only fourteen. For a detailed account of these two texts and also for the probable reasons for the omission of canons from the Greek text, the reader is referred to Hergenroether, *Photius, Patriarch von Constantinopel* (2 vols., Regensburg, 1867), II, 63-75.

[6] *Infra*, pp. 95-99.

services in their own churches conducted by one of their suffragan bishops, the latter being commanded to perform those services in their turn and at their own expense, thus forcibly employing those vested with episcopal dignity as clerics subject to them, a procedure which lacked all Apostolic sanction. Any metropolitan who employed his suffragans to perform the above-mentioned services was to be punished by his patriarch, and, if he did not amend, he was to be deposed.[7]

Section B

Development of the Metropolitan Institution in the West

Article 1. Initial Breakdown of the Institution

It seems that as early as in the second half of the seventh century in Gaul the metropolitan institution had lost much of its former importance. This decrease of prestige and power can be laid to the following causes: (a) the celebration of the provincial synods, which were so important for the exercise of metropolitan rights, no longer depended on the metropolitans, but on the Frankish kings; (b) there was constant interference on the part of the Frankish kings in the filling of vacant episcopal sees; and (c) there resulted a gradual decay of the metropolitan institute itself.[8]

Although canons 25 of the Council of Rheims (624 or 625),[9] 28 of the Council of Clichy (626)[10] and 10 of the

---

[7] Hefele-Leclercq, IV, 529-530; Hardouin, V, 910-911; Mansi, XVI, 176; Schroeder, *Decrees*, p. 540; pp. 174-175. Note again the use of the term: *"per suffraganeos episcopos."* Cf. *infra*, pp. 89-90.

[8] Hinschius, *Kirchenrecht*, II, 7, footnotes 1 and 2; De Clercq, *La Legislation Religieuse Franque de Clovis à Charlemagne (507-814)* (Paris: Librairie du Recueil Sirey S. A., 1936), p. 111 (hereafter cited as *Legislation*).

[9] "Ut decedente episcopo in locum eius non alius subrogetur, nisi loci illius indigena, quem universale et totius populi elegerit votum ac provincialium voluntas assenserit." — Hefele-Leclercq, III, 264; Hardouin, III, 574; Mansi, X, 597-598.

[10] De Clercq, *Legislation*, p. 64; Hefele-Leclercq, III, 264, footnote 2. On page 63 of the former work the author includes a map which shows the metropolitan and episcopal sees of Gaul at the time of this Council.

Council held at Chalon-sur-Sâone (649)[11] seem to revert to the old system of electing a bishop to a vacant see, it cannot be concluded that, inasmuch as the metropolitans were not mentioned in these Councils, the entire metropolitan system was completely dissolved even before the middle of the seventh century. What can be said is that the rights of the metropolitans were limited at these Councils by the Frankish kings. The Council of Bordeaux (663-675), held in the second half of the century,[12] still bears the signatures of three metropolitans. In consequence, however, of the above-mentioned factors, probably around the end of the seventh century or at the beginning of the eighth century, the metropolitan system of the previous centuries was completely dissolved.[13]

Article 2. Re-organization under Boniface

It was St. Boniface (672/73-754) who tried to reorganize the system. In a letter written to him in 744 by Pope Zachary (741-752), the Pope confirmed the three metropolitans: Grimon, Abel and Hartbert, whom Boniface chose to head the provinces of Rouen, Rheims and Sens, respectively.[14] Boniface himself received Maintz as a metropolitan see in 748. This is recorded in a letter written

---

[11] De Clercq, *Legislation*, p. 69; Hefele-Leclercq, III, 283.

[12] "Adus metropolitanus Bituricensis urbis episcopus, Johannes metropolitanus Burdigalensis urbis episcopus, Scupilio metropolitanus Elosane urbis episcopus..." —*MGH: Legum Sectio III, Concilia*, I, 216; Hefele-Leclercq, III, 298-300. Cf. De Clercq, *Legislation*, p. 70.

[13] Hinschius, *Kirchenrecht*, II, 7; De Clercq, *Legislation*, p. 111.

[14] "De episcopis vero metropolitanis, id est Grimone....Abel sive Hartbercto, quos per unamquamque metropolim per provincias constituisti, hos per tuum testimonium confirmamus...." —*MGH: Epistolæ Selectæ*, Tom. I, *S. Bonifatii et Lulli Epistolæ* (ed. M. Tangl, Berolini: apud Weidmannos, 1916), Tom. II, fasc. I, *Gregorii VII registrum* (ed. E. Caspar, pars 1, Libri I-IV, 1920; pars 2, Libri V-IX, 1923), Tom. II, fasc. 2, *Gregorii VII registrum* (ed. E. Caspar, 1923), I, 103 (hereafter cited as *MGH: Epistolæ Selectæ*); Jaffé, *Bibliotheca Rerum Germanicarum* (6 vols., Berolini: apud Weidmannos, Vol. III: *Monumenta Moguntina*, 1866, Vol. IV: *Monumenta Carolina*, 1867, Vol. V: *Monumenta Gregoriana*, 1868), III, 132 (hereafter cited as *BRG* with the proper designation of the volume used). "...idcirco constituemus super eos episcopos archiepiscopus [archiepiscopos?] Abel et Ardobertum,

to him by Pope Zachary in that year.[15] Since Boniface understood that the metropolitan system had definite advantages, the chief of these being its unifying force, he did not want to change any of the rights which the metropolitans had over their suffragans.[16] But he also saw the

---

ut ad ipsos vel iudicia eorum de omne necessitate ecclesiastica recurrant tam episcopi quam alius populus." —*MGH: Legum Sectio II, Capitularia*, I, 29. This second piece is taken from the *Capitulare Pippini Suessionis* (744). The absence of Grimon's name and the use of the term *archiepiscopus* are to be noted.

[15] "Nos vero adiutore Deo consilium prebemus tuæ reverende sanctitati, ut pro salute animarum rationabilium fautore Christo sedem, quam obtines, sanctæ Magontinæ æcclesiæ [ecclesiæ] nequaquam relinquas, ut impleatur in te dominicum preceptum: 'Qui perseveraverit usque in finem, hic salvus erit.' " —*MGH: Epistolæ Selectæ*, I, 180; Jaffé, n. 2286. This letter was written on the 1st of May, 748. "Igitur, dum in Germania provincia tua fraterna sanctitas ad prædicandum fuisset directa a sanctæ recordationis prædecessore nostro domno Gregorio papa et post inchoatum opus et aliqua ex parte spiritaliter ædificatum Roma reversus ab eo episcopus ordinatus et illic ad prædicandum denuo remissus es et elaborasti Deo prævio nunc usque per annos xxv in eadem prædicatione, ex quo episcopatum suscepisti. Sed in provincia Francorum nostra vice concilium habuisti....Et dum in his piis operibus occupata esset tua sancta fraternitas, nunc usque cathedralem sedem sibi minime vindicavit. At ubi vero Deus prædicationem tuam auxit, obtinere tibi cathedralem eclesiam [ecclesiam] vel successoribus tuis confirmare debemus iuxta eorundem filiorum Francorum petitionem. Et idcirco auctoritate beati Petri apostoli sancimus, ut supra dicta eclesia [ecclesia] (Mogontina) atque etiam perpetuis temporibus tibi et successoribus tuis metropolis sit confirmata...." —*MGH: Epistolæ Selectæ*, I, 201-202; Jaffé, n. 2292. This letter was reputedly written on the 4th of November, 751. It is to be considered spurious, however. Jaffé, *BRG*, III, *Monumenta Moguntina*, p. 227; cf. De Clercq, *Legislation*, pp. 128-129.

[16] Epistola Zachariæ ad Bonifacium (744): "...informantes eos metropolitanos ut sciant...ita ut nullus repperiri possit sacris deviare canonibus...." —*MGH: Epistolæ Selectæ*, I, 104; Jaffé, n. 2270; Jaffé, *BRG*, III, *Monumenta Moguntina*, p. 132; cf. *Capitulare Pippini Suessionis* (744), *supra*, pp. 69-70, footnote 14; C. 1 of the General Capitulary of Heristal (779): "De metropolitanis, ut suffraganei episcopi eis secundum canones subiecti sint, et ea quæ erga ministerium illorum emendanda cognoscunt, libenti animo emendent atque corrigant." —*MGH: Legum Sectio II, Capitularia*, I, 47; *Admonitio Caroli* (789), c. 8: "Episcopis. Item in eodem concilio [c. 9 of Antioch], ut ad metropolitanum episcopum suffragani episcopi respiciant, et nihil nove audeant facere in suis parrochiis sine conscientia et consilio sui metropolitani nec metropolitanus sine eorum consilio." —*MGH: Legum Sectio II, Capitularia*, I, 54. Note the use of the words "*suffragani episcopi.*"

dangers which might flow from their independence from the Roman See.

In order to reap the benefits of the metropolitan arrangement and to avert its dangers, he strove to bring the metropolitans into a closer relation and a more certain dependence on the Pope. The means he employed were twofold. He imposed the duty of getting the pallium from the Pope. In a letter written to Archbishop Cuthbert of Canterbury in the year 748, Boniface declared that this duty was imposed by the decrees drawn up in a Council at which he himself presided.[17] The other means he employed was the necessity on the part of the metropolitan to make the profession of faith before assuming jurisdiction over any province. This was insisted on by Pope Zachary in a letter to Boniface, written in 744.[18] However, not all the archbishops accepted these conditions. Boniface complained in a letter to Pope

---

[17] "Decrevimus autem in nostro sinodali conventu et confessi sumus fidem catholicam et unitatem et subiectionem Romanæ ecclesiæ fine tenus vitæ nostræ velle servare; sancto Petro et vicario eius velle subici; sinodum per omnes annos congregare; metropolitanos pallia ab illa sede querere et per omnia precepta sancti Petri canonice sequi desiderare....Decrevimus, ut metropolitanus, qui sit pallio sublimatus, hortetur ceteros et admoneat et investiget, quis sit inter eos curiosus de salute populi quisve neglegens....Statuimus, quod proprium sit metropolitani iuxta canonum statuta subiectorum sibi episcoporum investigare mores et sollicitudinem circa populos, qualis sit, et moneat, ut episcopi, a sinodo venientes in propria parrochia cum presbiteris et abbatibus conventum habentes precepta sinodi servare insinuando præcipiant. Et unusquisque episcopus, si quid in sua diocesi corrigere vel emendare nequiverit, id item in sinodo coram archiepiscopo et palam omnibus ad corrigendum insinuet, eodem modo quo Romana ecclesia nos ordinatos cum sacramento constrinxit, ut, si sacerdotes vel plebes a lege Dei deviasse viderim et corrigere non potuerim, fideliter semper sedi apostolicæ et vicario sancti Petri ad emendandum indicaverim. Sic enim, nisi fallor, omnes episcopi debent metropolitano et ipse Romano pontifici, si quid de corrigendis populis apud eos impossibile est, notum facere...." —*MGH: Epistolæ Selectæ*, I, 163-164; Jaffé, *BRG*, III, *Monumenta Moguntina*, pp. 201-202.

[18] "Qualiter enim mos pallii sit, vel quomodo fidem suam exponere debeant hi, qui pallium uti licentia conceduntur, eis direximus...." — Jaffé, *BRG*, III, *Monumenta Moguntina*, p. 132. *MGH: Epistolæ Selectæ*, I, 103-104; Jaffé, n. 2270.

Zachary, written in 751, that archbishops neglected to apply for the pallium.[19]

In spite of the great efforts on the part of Boniface, the organization of the metropolitan system was not quite complete in 754, the year of his death, for canon 2 of the Council of Verberie (753) speaks of bishops who served as vicars of the metropolitans.[20] Hinschius was of the opinion that these vicars were part of a provisionary institution, and explained that as such they were temporarily authorized to perform the functions of metropolitans because the incumbents of the old metropolitan sees were not capable of performing them.[21] De Clercq agrees with Hinschius that their institution was merely of a provisionary arrangement, but gives a different explanation for their institution. According to him, though none of these vicars were indicated as metropolitans by name, nevertheless they were made titular possessors of the metropolitan sees whose prerogatives the Council of Verberie wished to re-establish. This Council tried to renew an attempt to bring back the metropolitan system into being, which attempt had failed in the past.[22] Even as late as 769, when one of the Lateran Councils was held in Rome, the organization was still incomplete. Of all the Gallic bishops present at this Council, only Wilchaire of Sens was designated an Archbishop, while the metropolitans of Maintz, Tours, Lyons, Bourges, Narbonne, Bordeaux and Rheims were called bishops.[23]

---

[19] "De eo autem, quod iam præterito tempore de archiepiscopis et de palleis a Romana æcclesia [ecclesia] petendis iuxta promissa Francorum sanctitati vestræ notum feci, indulgentiam apostolicæ sedis flagito. Quia quod promiserunt tardantes non impleverunt; et adhuc differtur et ventilatur, quid inde perficere voluerint, ignoratur. Sed mea voluntate impleta esset promissio." — Jaffé, *BRG,* III, *Monumenta Moguntina,* p. 219; Hefele-Leclercq, IV, 847-850.

[20] "Episcopos quos in vicem metropolitanorum constituimus, ut ceteri episcopi ipsis in omnibus obœdiant secundum canonicam institutionem, interim quod secundum canonicam constitutionem hoc plenius emendamus." — *MGH: Legum Sectio II, Capitularia,* I, 33; Hefele-Leclercq, III, 935; Hardouin, III, 1995; Mansi, XII, 580.

[21] *Kirchenrecht,* II, 7, footnote 6.

[22] *Legislation,* pp. 134-135, also footnote 2 on p. 134.

[23] Hefele-Leclercq, III, 731-732.

Article 3. Re-organization Completed under Charlemagne

The system was completed only during the reign of Charlemagne (768-814). Canon 1 of the General Capitulary of Heristal (779) insisted that suffragan bishops be subject to their metropolitans as demanded by the canons of the Church.[24] Only in the year 798 was Salzburg elevated to the position of a metropolitan see by Pope Leo III (795-816) at the wish of Charlemagne.[25] An enumeration of metropolitan sees in existence at the end of Charlemagne's reign was given in his Testament (811).[26] At this time, as before, the dignity of metropolitan was connected with a definite province, and was not transferable as a personal favor from the bishop of one city to the bishop of still another city. Hinschius defended this opinion with two sound arguments: (a) the terms *metropolitanus* and *archiepiscopus* were not identical, and (b) the conferral of the pallium was separable from the metropolitan dignity.[27]

---

[24] *Forma communis:* "De metropolitanis, ut suffraganii episcopi eis secundum canones subiecti sint, et ea quæ erga ministerium illorum emendanda cognoscunt, libenti animo emendent atque corrigant." *Forma Langobardiis: supra,* p. 70, footnote 16—*MGH: Legum Sectio II, Capitularia,* I, 47: "De metropolitanis ut suffraganei episcopi eis secundum canones subiecti sint."—Hefele-Leclercq, III, 977; Hardouin, III, 2056; Mansi, XII, 894-895.

[25] Jaffé gives us three letters to this effect: nn. 2495, 2496, 2498; *MPL,* CXXIX, 970 reproduces n. 2495.

[26] "Nomina metropoleorum,...hæc sunt: Roma, Ravenna, Mediolanum, Forum Iulii, Gradus, Colonia, Mogontiacus, Iuvavia quæ et Saltzburc, Trevesi, Senones, Vesontio, Lugdunum, Ratumagus, Remi, Arelas, Vienna, Darantasia, Ebrodunum, Burdigala, Turones, Bituriges."—Jaffé, *BRG,* IV, *Monumenta Carolina,* p. 539.

[27] Hinschius, (*Kirchenrecht,* II, 7, footnote 7) called attention to the false interpretation of the text in the spurious letter of Hadrian I, which reputedly was written to Berthorius of Vienne in 775. "Unde placuit nobis, ut omnibus archiepiscopis et episcopis auctoritatem nostrarum literarum mitteremus, ut sicut antiquis privilegiis singulæ metropolitanæ urbes fundatæ sunt, ita maneant, ut habeat unaquæque metropolis civitates sibi subditas....Nec propterea ulla metropolis præiudicium patiatur, si alicui suffraganeorum aut nos aut prædecessor noster, rogantibus piis Francorum ducibus pallium largiti sumus."—Jaffé, n. 293 (CCCXVII); Mansi, XII, 847; *MPL,* XCVI, 1215-1216. The conferral of the pallium, according to Hinschius, was separable from the

But even under Charlemagne the metropolitan dignity had not yet taken the character of a solely higher instance of administration between the Roman See and the individual bishops, in which system the latter were to be bound to ask instructions from the former, and to feel obliged to follow their advice in all the more important matters of their dioceses. Charlemagne, himself, did not understand what Boniface understood; or if he did understand it, he was not willing to allow the dependence of the two types of ecclesiastics upon the Roman See to work itself out into action. This attitude can be seen in his great desire to direct ecclesiastical as well as civil affairs, and to limit the Pope to the purely spiritual side of the Church and the guardianship over the ecclesiastical canons.

This was evidenced by his letter written in 796 to Pope Leo.[28] The influence of the king's court even touched the provincial synods, which, though ordered several times during this period, were limited to the purpose of watching over the internal discipline of the Church, either to better it, or to execute the decrees approved by the emperor. In all important points the formation of law in these times was influenced not by the provincial synods, but by the so-called mixed synods in which both the ecclesiastical and the civil princes participated.[29] Nevertheless, though the provincial synods, which were so necessary for the exercise of metro-

---

metropolitan dignity, for in the Occident, even before the eighth century, the pallium had been given to simple bishops. Cf. *Kirchenrecht*, II, 23-36.

[28] "Nostrum est: secundum auxilium divinæ pietatis sanctam ubique Christi ecclesiam ab incursu paganorum et ab infidelium devastatione armis defendere foris, et intus Catholicæ fidei agnitione munire. Vestrum est, sanctissime pater: elevatis ad Deum cum Moyse manibus nostram adiuvare militiam; quatenus, vobis intercedentibus, Deo ductore et datore, populus Christianus super inimicos sui sancti nominis ubique semper habeat victoriam, et nomen domini nostri Iesu Christi toto clarificetur in orbe. Vestræ vero auctoritatis prudentia canonicis ubique inhæreat sanctionibus et sanctorum statuta patrum semper sequatur. . . ." — Jaffé, *BRG*, IV, *Monumenta Carolina*, p. 356.

[29] Hinschius, *Kirchenrecht*, II, 8, footnote 8; Hefele-Leclercq, III, 935.

politan rights, no longer had their original significance; and even though the old laws which required metropolitan co-operation in the filling of vacant episcopal sees gave way to the practice of royal appointments to these sees, the metropolitan dignity, though it did not rise to its pristine prominence, assured the metropolitans a certain higher position among the rest of the bishops.[30]

Article 4. Changes in the Metropolitan Institution

The situation began to change in the early ninth century, shortly after the death of Charlemagne (814). This change was effected by the following causes: (a) the efforts of an ecclesiastical reform favored by Louis the Pious (816-840); (b) the weakening of the royal power brought about by the division of the Empire and by wars; and (c) the increased power of the papacy. Through the interplay of these circumstances, the Pope, because of his recognized position as custodian of the *Canones*, began to exercise a greater and more direct influence on the metropolitans.

It was at this point in history that the Frankish metropolitans began to act only as an intermediary instance between the Roman See and the individual bishops in their provinces. This change began to take tremendous strides in the middle of the ninth century with the appearance of the Pseudo-Isidorian Decretals, the pronouncements of which, unwittingly however, favored the position of the Pope and the Roman See. The change did not take over without a struggle. In particular instances there were attempts to enhance the metropolitan institution and the system of provincial synods to the position of importance that both had held in the earlier centuries.

In the *Petitio* (canon 4) of the Capitulary held at Worms (829) there was an insistence that the system of provincial synods be restored according to the ruling of the old

---

[30] Concerning the use of the term *archiepiscopus* cf. *infra*, pp. 88-89.

canons.[31] The VI Council of Paris (829) in *Liber I, cap. 26*[32] and *Liber III, cap. 11*[33] insisted on holding provincial synods twice a year, and declared that if two could not be held, then at least one should take place yearly. The Council of Meaux-Paris (845-846) in its 31st and 32nd canons called for a return to the old discipline in the things touching the metropolitans and the provincial synods.[34] But neither the Pope nor the bishops were inclined to recognize the independence which the metropolitans wished to enjoy.

Article 5. Specific Efforts to Bring Metropolitans to Former Status

The famous case of Hincmar (ca. 806-882) and Rothad (+ ca. 869) brought out into the clearest light the fact that the metropolitans were not independent from Rome. At a provincial synod held in 861, Hincmar, the metropolitan of Rheims, excluded Bishop Rothad of Soissons from the community of bishops.[35] In spite of the exclusion, Rothad ap-

---

[31] "Cum sacri canones bis in anno concilia celebrari iubeant, illud obnixe vestram pietatem deposcimus, ut saltim [saltem] vel semel in anno libertas opportuni temporis concedatur, quo hæc ad honorem Dei et utilitatem sanctæ Dei ecclesiæ multorumque correctionem congruenter decenterque fieri possint. Quoniam si hæc semel, ut dictum est, in anno per unamquamque provinciam celebrata fuerint...."—*MGH: Legum Sectio II, Capitularia*, II, 37.

[32] *MGH: Legum Sectio III, Concilia*, II, 628-629; Mansi, XIV, 555-556; Hardouin, IV, 1313-1314.

[33] *MGH: Legum Sectio III, Concilia*, II, 674; Mansi, XIV, 599; Hardouin, IV, 1356.

[34] Canon 31: "Ut metropolitanis sedibus antiquitus statuta iura serventur, et a comprovincialibus episcopis iuxta regulas ecclesiasticas eis reverentia exhibeatur." Canon 32: "Ut principes, iuxta decreta canonum, per singulas provincias saltem bis aut semel in anno a metropolitanis et diocesanis episcopis synodice conveniri concedant: quia quælibet confusio rerum temporalium dissolvere non debet collegium sacerdotum."—Mansi, XIV, 826; Hardouin, IV, 1488-1489.

[35] Rothad presented the occasion of the dispute quite differently in his *Libellus Proclamationis* (Mansi, XV, 681-685) from that which Hincmar described in his second letter to Pope Nicholas I (*MPL*, CXXVI, 28-42). Cf. Hefele-Leclercq, IV, 296-297; Schrörs, *Hinkmar, Erzbischof von Reims* (Freiburg: Herder'sche Verlagshandlung, 1884), and also Dümmler, *Geschichte des ostfränkischen Reiches* (2. ed., Leipzig: Dunker und Humblot, 1887-1888), I, 530.

peared at the Empire-Synod of Pistres held in 862. When this Synod, at the plea of Hincmar, insisted on pronouncing his deposition, Rothad, before the sentence was rendered, in contradiction to the customary ecclesiastical law, appealed to the Pope. The Synod permitted the appeal.[36] When the bishops were later informed that Rothad had given up the prosecution of his appeal which he had raised at the Synod, they deposed him after the Synod moved to Soissons in the same year (862).

Although the details cannot be substantiated with utter preciseness, nevertheless, this much was certain, namely, that Hincmar of Rheims had proceeded too violently against Rothad. The latter again appealed to Rome. When Nicholas I (858-867) received word of the whole affair, he refused to confirm the deposition made at Soissons, and reserved judgment in the case until Rothad would make his appearance in Rome. Rothad was held in France, but, after pushing back all the obstacles placed in his path by the bishops, he eventually arrived in Rome. The West-Frankish bishops, realizing that the insistence of Nicholas I to draw the case to himself bore no promise of a decision favorable to themselves, did not reintroduce their accusation against Rothad. In 865 the Pope reinstated Rothad in the see which had been taken from him.[37]

It is remarkable that Hincmar, in defending his procedure, based his mode of action from the very beginning on the decrees of the Council of Sardica (343 or 344).[38]

---

[36] Mansi, XV, 681-685.

[37] Hefele-Leclercq, IV, 354, 358; Dümmler, *Geschichte des ostfränkischen Reiches*, I, 533, 535-537; Jaffé, n. 2785.

[38] Canon 3: "...Quodsi aliquis episcoporum iudicatus fuerit in aliqua causa, et putat se bonam causam habere, ut iterum concilium renovetur: si vobis placet, sancti Petri memoriam honoremus, ut scribatur ab his, qui causam examinarunt, Iulio Romano episcopo, et si iudicaverit renovandum esse iudicium, renovetur et det iudices; si autem probaverit, talem causam esse, ut non refricentur ea quæ acta sunt, quæ decreverit confirmata erunt. Si hoc omnibus placet? Synodus respondit: Placet." Canon 5: Osius episcopus dixit: "Placuit autem, ut si quis episcopus accusatus fuerit et iudicaverint congregati episcopi regionis ipsius et de gradu suo eum deiecerint, si appellaverit is qui deiectus est, et con-

Kober (1821-1897),[39] in using the Capitularies of Benedict the Levite and a letter of Hadrian I (772-795) to Tilpen, Archbishop of Rheims, claimed that these decrees had a practical recognition in early Carolingian times.[40] Hinschius claimed the opposite to be true by stating that the quotations from the *Capitula Benedicti Levitæ* and the *Epistola Hadriani* were not, on the one hand, the laws of

---

fugerit ad episcopum Romanæ ecclesiæ et voluerit se audiri; si iustum putaverit, ut renovetur iudicium vel discussionis examen, scribere his episcopis dignetur, qui in finitima et propinqua provincia sunt, ut ipsi diligenter omnia requirant et iuxta fidem veritatis definiant. Quod si is, qui rogat causam suam iterum audiri, deprecatione sua moverit episcopum Romanum, ut de latere suo presbyterum mittat, erit in potestate episcopi, quid velit et quid æstimet; et si decreverit mittendos esse, qui præsentes cum episcopis iudicent, habentes eius auctoritatem a quo destinati sunt, erit in suo arbitrio. Si vero crediderit episcopos sufficere, ut negotio terminum imponant, faciet quod sapientissimo consilio suo iudicaverit." — Bruns, I, 90-95; Hardouin, I, 637-640; Hefele-Leclercq, I, 762-770; Mansi, III, 7-10.

[39] *Deposition und Degradation* (Tübingen, 1867), p. 429.

[40] *Capitula Benedicti Levitæ* (Liber III, libellus 7), c. 314: "Nullus episcopus extra suam provinciam ad iudicium devocetur. Sed vocato eo canonice in loco omnibus congruo, tempore synodali, ab omnibus provincialibus episcopis audiatur, qui concordem super eum canonicamque proferre debent sententiam." c. 315: "Placuit, ut si episcopus accusatus appellaverit Romanum Pontificem, id statuendum, quod ipse censuerit." c. 412: "Ut iudicatus episcopus ad apostolicam sedem, si voluerit, appellet *Concilio Sardicensi titulo quinto.* Quod si appellaverit, in cathedram ipsius alter non ordinetur." — *MGH: Leges* (5 vols., ed. G. Pertz, G. Waitz, H. Brunner, Hannoveræ: Hahn, 1835-1889, 2. unveränderter Neudruck, Leipzig: Verlag K. W. Hiersemann, 1925), II (2), pp. 122, 128 (hereafter cited as *MGH: LL*); *Epistola Hadriani ad Tilpinum Archiepiscopum Remensem:* "Tua vero fraternitas nobis retulit, quia faciente discordia inter Francos archiepiscopus Remensis, nomine Rigobertus, a sede contra canones dejectus et expulsus fuit sine ullo crimine, et sine ullo Apostolicæ Sedis consensu vel interrogatione; sed solummodo quod antea non consensit in parte illius, qui postea partem illam de regno in sua potestate accepit, in qua parte Remensis civitas est.... Et te, aut futuris temporibus Remensem episcopum et primatem illius diœcesis, non præsumat neque valeat umquam aliquis de episcopatu dejicere sine canonis judicio: et neque ullo judicio sine consensu Romani pontificis, si ad hanc sanctam sedem Romanam, quæ caput esse dignoscitur orbis terræ, appellavit in ipso judicio." — Hardouin, III, 2026-2027; *MGH: Scriptores* (30 vols. in 31, ed. G. Pertz, G. Waitz, H. Brunner, Hannoveræ: Impensis Bibliopolii Hahniani, 1826-1892, unveränderter Neudruck, Leipzig: Verlag K. W. Hiersemann, Vol. VIII, 1925; Vol. XIII, 1925), XIII, 463 (hereafter cited as *MGH: SS*); Jaffé, n. 2411.

the Frankish Kingdom, and, on the other, that both of these pieces of proof were spurious.[41]

Hincmar himself had acknowledged the supreme right of papal jurisdiction inasmuch as he had obtained for Rheims the privilege of being judged solely by the Apostolic See.[42] However, he himself offended against the decrees of the Council of Sardica, since immediately after the deposition of Rothad a new bishop was installed at his instigation, and no suspending force was acknowledged in Rothad's sentence in the face of his appeal to Rome. Because of the interpolations within the canons, Hincmar interpreted the Sardican decrees in such a way that the Pope could permit a new examination of the case, not however by the Pope himself in Rome, but only in the province where the matter was of concern, and only by the bishops of the province under the supervision of the papal legate.[43] Over and above this exclusive reservation of the case to the provincial synod, he defended metropolitan rights with very strong language by calling attention to two possibilities fraught with danger: that ecclesiastical courts would be despised even more than they were, and that bishops would become bolder in their opposition to the *canones*, if the rights of archbishops were limited by papal action.[44]

---

[41] *Kirchenrecht*, II, 10, footnote 6; *Decretales Pseudo-Isidorianæ*, p. CXV.

[42] Hinschius, *Kirchenrecht*, I, 602-604.

[43] "Et hinc iuxta Sardicense concilium summus primæ et sanctæ sedis Romanæ Pontifex, pro examinis renovatione ad se reclamantis et confugientis cum sua clamatione dejecti provincialis episcopi, non statim singularitate privilegii et auctoritatis suæ restituit, sed remittens eum ad provinciam, ubi causa patrata fuerat, et in qua iuxta Carthaginenses canones, et jura legis Romanæ, causa potest diligenter inquiri et quod non sit difficile, testes producere, veritas inveniri, aut finitimis episcopis dignatur scribere, aut a latere suo mittit, qui habentes eius auctoritatem præsentes cum episcopis judicent, et diligenter causam inquisitam diffiniant, aut dignantur credere episcopos sufficere, ut negotio terminum possint imponere." —*MPL*, CXXVI, 36, cf. 28.

[44] "Credo tamen diligentissimam discretionem vestram provisuram contemptum ac contumaciam subiectorum erga prælatos suos, et libertatem impune delinquendi contra canones sacros, quæ hinc in nostris

Nicholas I, however, employed these very same Sardican decrees, and by a very courageous interpretation of them insisted that it was the duty of the provincial synod, which made its decision without appealing to the Pope, to repeat its procedure and to report to him concerning it. This he made clear in a letter written to the bishops of the Soissons Synod (863).[45] Furthermore, the Pope, basing his argumentation on the decrees of the Council of Chalcedon (451), declared that he was within his rights to judge the case of Rothad.[46] Nicholas I explained to Hincmar in a letter that it was a papal right to reserve to himself the case in which

---

regionibus poterunt, ut quibusdam videtur, noxias vires accipere.... Et quod non solum ab ecclesiasticis personis, verum et multo magis etiam a sæcularibus nostra iudicia contemnuntur et pro nihilo ducuntur....Si qui in provincia nostra, quorum querela illo [Rothado] restituto ad vos valeat pervenire, de maioribus causis de cætero quædam commiserint, sicut de quibusdam rebus frequentius quam in istis retroactis temporibus committuntur, ne a deo damner silentio, eos commonere studebo, et si corrigere se voluerint, congaudebo, sin autem, ad vestrum eos iudicium provocabo. Qui si ire voluerint, vestra sancta sapientia quid inde melius viderit decernere procurabit. Si autem ire noluerint, facient quod sibi utile iudicaverint....Ea propter, sicut vestræ discretioni providendum est, ne subiecti episcopi a metropolitanis irregulariter condemnentur, ita nihilominus providendum est, ut metropolitani a subditis suis episcopis non irregulariter contemnantur." — *MPL*, CXXVI, 37-40.

[45] "Maxime cum iuxta constitutionem sanctæ huius synodi, etiamsi nunquam reclamasset [Rothadus] nunquamque sedis apostolicæ mentionem fecisset, a vobis, qui causam eius examinastis, memoria sancti Petri honorari debuerit atque ei se perscribi, ut si iudicaret renovandum esse iudicium, renovaretur, et daret iudices." — Mansi, XV, 303; Jaffé, n. 2723. See also the five letters written by the Pope after the restitution of Rothad: (1) Rothad; (2) Carolus Calvus; (3) Hincmar; (4) the bishops of Gaul and (5) the clergy and people of Soissons — Mansi, XV, 688-703; Hefele-Leclercq, IV, 356-358; *MGH: Epistolæ*, Tom. VI, *Epistolæ Karolini Aevi* (6 vols., ed. Ernestus Perels, Vol. IV, 1925, Berolini: apud Weidmannos), IV, 382-401; Jaffé, nn. 2781, 2782, 2784, 2785, 2786.

[46] "Denique, ut pauca de multis commemorem, *si adversus provinciæ metropolitanum episcopus vel clericus habeat querelam*, iuxta Calcidonenses regulas iubetur, ut *petat primatem diœceseos aut sedem regiæ urbis Constantinopolitanæ et apud ipsum iudicetur*." — *MGH: Epistolæ Karolini Aevi*, IV, 358; Mansi, XV, 688; Jaffé, n. 2783. (Italics as found in text).

a bishop was accused, since it constituted a *negotium maius*.[47]

Finally, the Pope completely justified his mode of action on the grounds of the Pseudo-Isidorian Decretals by leaning heavily on two principles contained in them.[48] These principles defended the position that all the more important matters, such as the removal of a bishop, must be regulated in a decisive manner, not by provincial synods, but by the Popes, and further, that provincial synods could not be convened without the approving knowledge of the Popes.[49] In consequence of the favorable constellation of political and ecclesiastical conditions, the Pope exercised his superior juridical prerogative in a very delicate case, which the most

[47] "Si coram tuæ prudentiæ oculis ullus esset paternorum canonum vel reverentiæ apostolicæ sedis respectus, nunquam Rothadum...sine nostræ temptasses scientiæ notione deponere; præcipue cum tantum negotium, quod merito inter maiora connumeratur negotia, de persona scilicet episcopi iudicare, cuius in ecclesia ceteris ordo maior est, ventilanti et multipliciter rimanti tibi adeo de se difficiles exitus daret, ut octo circiter annis, ut deponeretur, elaboraveris et...in tanta intercapedine temporum nullam beati Petri memoriam prorsus habueris.... Et cum in suis opportunitatibus ad sedem apostolicam beatitudo tua scripserit et ab illa sibi manum porrigi contra falsos fratres poposcerit et quædam privilegia concedi petierit, in causa Rothadi solum, quasi eius solatii non indiga, sedis apostolicæ non memor fuit...." — *MGH: Epistolæ Karolini Aevi*, IV, 389; Mansi, XV, 691; Jaffé, n. 2784.

[48] It is probable that Nicholas I received knowledge of these from Rothad himself. Cf. Hinschius, *Decretales Pseudo-Isidorianæ*, pp. CCV-CCVII. This opinion is confirmed by Fournier-Le Bras, *Histoire des Collections Canoniques en Occident* (2 vols., Paris: Recueil Sirey, 1931-1932, Vol. I, 1931), I, 225 and 228. The authors say on p. 228: "The attitude of the Holy See with regard to the False Decretals was for a long time marked by an extreme reserve. One can see in two points, in both the writings and the action of Nicholas I, the influence of the Isidorian work, which the Pope was aware of most probably not in its entirety but by means of the fragments inserted in the procedural papers, such as those of Rothad." The letter of the Pope which considers them most explicitly is the one written to the bishops of Gaul. — *MGH: Epistolæ Karolini Aevi*, IV, 392-400; Jaffé, n. 2785; Mansi, XV, 693-700; cf. Hinschius, *Decretales Pseudo-Isidorianæ*, p. CCV.

[49] C. 6, C. IX, q. 3; cc. 3, 12, 16, C. II, q. 6; c. 9, C. III, q. 6; cc. 1, 2, 5, D. XVIII. Concerning the contradictions between the foregoing and the other citations which have a bearing on the same matter, see Hinschius, *Decretales Pseudo-Isidorianæ*, p. CCXIV.

ambitious metropolitan of the Frankish Empire had assumed for himself.[50]

Another opportunity to exercise this same right presented itself with the divorce case of King Lothair II (855-869) and Queen Teutberga (Dietburg). The queen appealed several times to the Holy See.[51] The case was taken up by Nicholas I. Both Archbishops, Teutgard (Dietand) of Treves and Günther of Cologne, creatures of Lothair, who presided at the Sy̆nod of Aix-la-Chapelle which granted the king his divorce from Teutberga, were deposed by the Roman Synod (863).[52] Even though the Church law in force up till then had been over-ruled, since the auxiliary bishops had not been present at the Synod, no voice was raised in defense of the deposed archbishops. Even Hincmar did not take up their cause.[53]

In the procedure against him at the Synod of Doucy (871), Hincmar, Bishop of Laon (858-870), appealed to Rome before sentence was passed on him. In spite of his objections, which he fortified by appealing to the Pseudo-Isidorian Decretals, chiefly in reference to the *exceptio spolii,* Hincmar was removed from office.[54] Hincmar, metropolitan of Rheims, to justify the bishop's removal turned about-face and spoke for the superior judicial rights of the

---

[50] Hinschius, *Kirchenrecht,* II, 11.

[51] Dümmler, *Geschichte des ostfränkischen Reiches,* I, 452, 461, 477, 503, 505; Poulet-Raemers, *History of the Catholic Church,* I, 363-364.

[52] C. 10, C. XI, q. 3; Dümmler, *Geschichte des ostfränkischen Reiches,* I, 510; *MGH: Epistolæ Karolini Aevi,* IV, 284-286; Jaffé, n. 2847; Mansi, XV, 649.

[53] Dümmler, *Geschichte des ostfränkischen Reiches,* I, 511-513: "The fatal and the immensely important element in this case did not lie only in this that the Roman Church simply rose up as a moral judge over the state, but also at the same time the Apostolic See, as the supreme ecclesiastical *instantia,* directed its rays of excommunication toward the negligent members of this church, who had sunk to be accomplices of the royal lust. The victory, which papal authority carried off, was therefore no less over the autonomy of the crown than over the independence of the bishops." — *Ibid.,* p. 504.

[54] Mansi, XVI, 662. Compare with Hefele-Leclercq, IV, 619-636; Dümmler, *Geschichte des ostfränkischen Reiches,* I, 767; Fournier-Le Bras, *Histoire des Collections Canonique en Occident,* I, 225; *MGH: Epistolæ Karolini Aevi,* IV, 738-746; Jaffé, nn. 2945, 2946, 2951.

Pope, declaring that these were based on the decrees of the Synod of Sardica (343 or 344).[55] Pope Hadrian II (867-872) declared the condemnation of the Bishop of Laon null on the grounds of the Pseudo-Isidorian Decretals.[56] King Charles the Bald (840-877) and the bishops protested strongly.[57] The Pope was forced by these protests to put himself on the grounds of the older rights which they defended.[58] The new trial of this affair, as ordered by him,

[55] "Tunc Hincmarus metropolitanus Rhemorum episcopus legens dixit...episcopali honore ac dignitate privatum iudico, et omni sacerdotali officio spoliatum decerno: reservato per omnia iuris privilegio domni et patris nostri Hadriani apostolicæ ac primæ sedis papæ: sicut sacri Sardicenses canones decreverunt et eiusdem apostolicæ sedis pontifices Innocentius, Bonifacius, Leo, ex eiusdem sacris canonibus promulgaverunt." — Mansi, XVI, 676-677.

[56] *Epistola ad Episcopos Duziacensis Synodi:* "Primo...respondemus...quia cum clamaret in synodo se ad sedem apostolicam velle incunctanter venire...damnationis in eum non erat proferenda sententia...volumus et auctoritate apostolica...iubemus ipsum Hincmarum Laudunensem episcopum vestra fretrum [fratrum] potentia ad limina sanctorum apostolorum nostramque venire præsentiam. Quo sane veniente, veniat pariter accusator idoneus, qui nulla possit auctoritate legitima respui. Et tunc in præsentia nostra et totius sedis Romanæ synodali collegio, causa illius prudenti ventilata examine...sine protelatione aliqua finietur...." — Mansi, XV, 853-854; Fournier-Le Bras, *Histoire des Collections Canonique en Occident*, I, 228; Jaffé, n. 2945.

[57] *Epistola episcoporum Synodi Duziacensis ad Hadrianum II* — Mansi, XVI, 569-571; *Epistola Caroli Calvi* — *MPL*, CXXIV, 881-896.

[58] *Epistola ad Carolum Calvum Regem:* "De pontifice Laudunensi Hincmaro a præsulibus decem provinciarum deposito, et a metropolitano suo...Hincmaro archiepiscopo, *reservato per omnia* huius primæ *sedis privilegii iudicio*...tanta dictu nefanda, tantaque exsecranda, et auctorem suum dampnantia referuntur, ut incredibilia ab ignorantibus videantur. Sed de his nihil audemus iudicare, quod possit Niceno [Nicæno] concilio et quinque ceterorum conciliorum regulis vel decretis nostrorum antecessorum obviare....Nec in ullo deviantes a tenore canonico servantes omnibus sua iura metropolitanis....Sed quia non satis idonea videntur et matura nostris, et huic sanctæ sedi condigna, donec ad hanc sanctissimam et apostolicam, quam appellavit, sedem spatium habeat veniendi, ideo veniat et ostensis sibi litteris, quas nobis misistis, et libello continenti seriem synodi, libellulo etiam cleri et plebis Laudunensis proclamationem... asserens se iniuste dampnatum: tunc electis iudicibus, non tamen eo prius in gradu restituto, aut ex latere nostro directis legatis cum auctoritate nostra refricentur quæ gesta sunt et negotia in qua orta sunt provintia [provincia] canonice terminentur." — *MGH: Epistolæ Karolini Aevi*, IV, 745-746; Mansi, XV, 858-859; Jaffé, n. 2951.

never took place. John VIII (872-882), the successor of Hadrian II, in 876 confirmed the removal of Hincmar of Laon which had been pronounced at Doucy. The new Pope gave orders to Hincmar of Rheims to have the see occupied by another bishop.[59] It was also John VIII who failed to get the vicarship of Ansegisus (+ 883) recognized by Hincmar of Rheims and by the rest of the bishops.[60]

Article 6. Former Independence of Metropolitans Lost Completely

In spite of these two successes on the part of the metropolitans, the former position which they enjoyed as independent directors of their provinces had been lost. The acknowledgment of the superior juridical rights which the Council of Sardica (343 or 344) attributed to the Pope, and his position according to the Carolingian concept of the state, as custodian of the *Canones*, placed the metropolitans in a position of an instance of administration over whose decrees the Pope exercised juridical cognizance *(cognitio)*. This situation was more firmly established when the duty to ask Rome for the pallium was imposed upon them.[61]

That this change of policy was brought about by the desire of the Popes for power, or because of their usurpations, is a prejudicial statement. There were many influences at work which brought about the change in the metropolitan position of independence. First, there were the great efforts in the West for the unification of the political empire, then there was the great missionary activity which worked in the interests of the unity and universality

---

[59] Mansi, XVII, 226; Jaffé, n. 3034.

[60] Hinschius, *Kirchenrecht*, I, 597. On this occasion of dispute with Ansegisus, Hincmar wrote his *De Iure Metropolitanorum* (876), which treated of the position of vicars with regard to the metropolitans. — *MPL*, CXXVI, 189-210. He treated more explicitly the rights of the metropolitans over their suffragans in his *Libellus Expostulationis* in his case against Hincmar of Laon. The latter writing was presented at the Synod of Doucy (871). — Mansi, XVI, 581-643.

[61] The duty of asking the Roman See for the pallium had become general at this time. Cf. Hinschius, *Kirchenrecht*, II, 23-36.

of the Catholic Church. But aside from these two concurrent movements there were the ambitions of the simple bishops as against their metropolitans, the lust for power on the part of the metropolitans themselves, the repeated appeals to Rome of the former against the latter, and, finally, the many changes in the political structure of the decaying Carolingian Empire. All of these working together were favorable to what Hinschius unfortunately calls interferences from the Pope.[62] In spite of this author's opinion, these must be designated as the main factors of the development of the metropolitan institution as an instance of administration between the Pope and the bishops of the province.

There can be no denial that the Popes encouraged this arrangement, but they did so, not for the acquisition of power, but rather for the unification of the Church's organization. Again, there can be no denial that when they employed and introduced into practice the principles of the Pseudo-Isidorian Decretals they only brought into clearer light their already latent authority over the universal Church. Hinschius, in all frankness, admits that he cannot wrestle with the facts of history to prove the contrary.[63] The Frankish episcopate, under the direction of Hincmar of Rheims, resisted papal control, but its opposition died after a short time.

Occasionally the old law of the canons of the Councils of Nicæa and of Sardica were appealed to. Canon 13 of the Synod of Hohenaltheim (916) reflects one such attempt to

---

[62] *Kirchenrecht,* II, 13.

[63] *Kirchenrecht,* II, 13, footnote 1: "Naturally, I must accept the decision of Mast [*Dogmatisch-historische Abhandlung über die rechtliche Stellung der Erzbischöfe in der katholischen Kirche* (Freiburg, 1847)], p. 61: 'It would be the greatest historical injustice to accept the view that it [the power of the Pope] had been deduced from the self-seeking interests of the great medieval Popes. Such an opinion, which in truth is real violence to history, is shared today only by the most prejudiced and narrow-minded.' "

reinforce the old law.[64] So also at the Synod conducted under Hugh Capet (991), which was convoked to condemn Arnulf of Rheims, an appeal to the ancient canons was invoked in opposition to the claims of Pseudo-Isidore, which claims the followers of the accused used to defend him. Bishop Arnulf of Orleans, the presiding officer at the Synod, was the one who interposed the old canons.[65] But the course which the Pseudo-Isidorian Decretals had set in motion continued along the lines of development. Bishop Theoduin of Liège (1048-1075), in writing to the King of France, Henry I (1031-1060), sometime about the year 1050, followed the False Decretal Law rather than the old canons.[66] This gradual reception of the False Decretals, which were not questioned in the matter of their authenticity, and their distribution through ecclesiastical collections of law, washed away the consciousness of the former importance of the

---

[64] "...constitutum liquet a tempore apostolorum et deinceps placuit, ut accusatus vel iudicatus a comprovincialibus in aliqua causa episcopis licenter appellat et adeat apostolicæ sedis pontificem." — *MGH: LL,* II, 556. Hinschius understands the "vel" in this passage as "et." *Kirchenrecht,* I, 317, footnote 2. So also Hefele-Leclercq, IV, 745-746.

[65] "Nos...Romanam ecclesiam propter beati Petri memoriam semper honorandam decernimus, nec decretis Romanorum pontificum obviare contendimus, salva tamen auctoritate Nicæni concilii....Nos autem Sardicense concilium, quod privilegio Romanæ ecclesiæ plurimum favet, ita ad hanc causam inflectimus, ut quod de solo episcopo in qualibet provincia relicto dicit, ad Romanum episcopum affectum esse credamus. Sic enim habetur in tit. sexto c. 6 Synodi Sardicensis....Iuxta huius sententiæ tenorem ad petitionem populorum ab episcopis et principe conventus est, ut sua auctoritate Arnulphus deponeretur....Videat autem, qui potest, quod non sine quodam scrupulo paulo ante lectum est: Ut nostis, inquit Damasus, synodum sine eius, id est Romanæ sedis, auctoritate fieri, non est catholicum. Quid ergo, si barbarorum gladiis circumsævientibus licentia commeandi Roman intercludatur...num interim aut nulla concilia erunt, aut orbis terrarum episcopi ad suorum regum damna, vel interitus ab hostibus disponendarum rerum consilia, et concilia expectabunt? Et certe Nicænus canon, qui ipsa Romana ecclesia teste omnia concilia, omnia decreta eminentia sui exuperat, bis in anno concilia debere fieri dicit, nihilque inde ad Romani episcopi auctoritatem spectare præscribit." — Mansi, XIX, 131-136; cf. Hefele-Leclercq, IV, 854-863; c. 9, D. LXV.

[66] "...cum Bruno existat episcopus [Andegavensis]: episcopum autem non oportet damnationis subire sententiam præter apostolicam auctoritatem." — Mansi, XIX, 784.

metropolitan power, and broke every attempt which was made to restore it on the foundations of the old law.

The restoration could have been effected, in part if not completely, if there had been put into practice the old custom of holding provincial synods, but neither the metropolitans nor the bishops, in their desire for political and ecclesiastical influence, were inclined to accept the limitations set upon them by this institution. This is why provincial synods were convoked rarely in the following centuries; if they were called, it was for urgent reasons and for the settling of pressing questions and affairs. The Council of Metz (888) complained in its 1st canon that no synods had been held for a long time.[67] Although the metropolitan institution was not destroyed during these times as it was at the end of the seventh century, nevertheless it no longer had the great importance it formerly enjoyed.

All affairs of great importance were handled either by civil princes, especially the emperor, or at larger synods, at which the archbishops and bishops of several provinces were united. It sometimes happened that such matters were taken care of at the councils arranged by the Popes and with the understanding of the Popes. The regular metropolitan administration lost its independence through the principle that the Pope had the unique right to decide the *causæ maiores*, and that the Roman See had the right of mediation, through its legates and vicars, whenever intended reforms were to be executed.[68] At this time, therefore, the position of the metropolitan changed from that of the highest rank of administration over the bishops of a province to that of bishops of special rank who had only certain rights over the bishops of certain districts. This concept appeared in the eleventh century, and thenceforth

[67] "Nos autem, qui tanto tempore transacto comprovincialem synodum non habuimus, et invicem quærere misericordiam Dei neglеximus. . . ." — Mansi, XVIII, 77-78. Hefele-Leclercq (IV, 688-1063) recount only thirty provincial councils from the Council of Metz (888) until 1050.

[68] Hinschius, *Kirchenrecht*, I, 154, 507.

was sanctioned by the decretals which were taken into the *Corpus Iuris Canonici.*[69]

Section C

Development of New Terminology

Within this period the designation *archiepiscopus* came into its own. As early as 716 Pope Gregory II (715-731) had used the expression.[70] Pope Zachary used the expression in his correspondence with Boniface.[71] Boniface, in turn, also used the designation a number of times.[72] In the Capitulary of Pepin, convened at Soissons in 744, reference was made to Abel and Hartbert, and both of them were called Archbishops.[73] Charlemagne addressed two letters

---

[69] *Dictatus Gregorii VII, Registrum II, 552 — MGH: Epistolæ Selectæ, Gregorii VII Registrum,* II, fasc. 1, 202-208; Jaffé, *BRG,* V, *Monumenta Gregoriana,* p. 174.

[70] *Capitulare Gregorii Papæ II datum Martiniano Episcopo:* c. 3: "Ut consideratis locorum spaciis, iuxta gubernationem uniuscuiusque ducis episcopia disponatis, et dyocesane [diœcesanæ] subiacentia singulis sedibus terminetis. Et si tres, aut quatuor vel maiores numeri visæ fuerint constitui sedes, reservato præcipue sedis loco pro *archiepiscopo* resedendo, adhibito trium episcoporum conventu probabiles fide ac boni testimonii et eruditos sana doctrina viros ordinetis antistites ex auctoritate beati Petri apostoli et nostra subsequentis vigoris tradita dispensatione locis eos traditis colocantes." c. 4: "Ut præviso propter *archiepiscopum* loco, si talem reperire potueritis virum qui possit doctrinis salutiferis et operum exemplis instruere sibi subditos sacerdotes ac regere prudentissime clerum ac plebem et amplificare congrue creditas oves, aut datis litteris vestris eum ad nos dirigatis, aut vobiscum venire faciatis. Si certe talem invenire non poteritis, hoc aut per vos aut per vestras litteras innotescatis; quatenus de hoc sacra præmissa sede prævidentes utilem cum Dei auxilio dirigamus." — *MGH: LL,* III, 452-453; Mansi, XII, 257-258; *MPL,* LXXXIX, 351; (Italics supplied by writer). Jaffé, n. 2153.

[71] In writing to Boniface (744) the Pope used the word metropolitan with regard to Grimon, Abel and Hartbert. Cf. *supra,* pp. 69-70, footnote 14. However, in another letter written to him that same year, the Pope calls the three candidates archbishops. Cf. Jaffé, *BRG,* III, *Monumenta Moguntina,* p. 134.

[72] A letter written in 748 to Cuthbert of Canterbury not only addressed the recipient as an archbishop, but spoke of archbishops within the text. Cf. *supra,* p. 71, footnote 17. In another letter, written in 751, Boniface complained about the Gallic archbishops to Pope Zachary. Cf. *supra,* pp. 71-72, footnote 19.

[73] Cf. *supra,* pp. 69-70, footnote 14.

(809-812) to Odibert of Milan, and in both cases called him an Archbishop.[74] In 817 Louis the Pious (814-840) addressed two Encyclicals to all the archbishops of Gaul.[75] Canon 6 of the Council of Aix-la-Chapelle (817) placed an obligation on archbishops.[76] This idiom maintained itself throughout the Middle Ages.[77] C. 23 of the *Gesta Treverorum* also made use of the title archbishop.[78]

The expressions *comprovinciales* or *provinciales* for the bishops subject to the metropolitan were still in use, but a new term began to make its appearance, namely *suffraganei*. Canon 1 of the Synod of Heristal (779) made use of the idiom, and from then onwards it appeared in many writings.[79] Amalarius, Bishop of Trier (809-816?) attempted to give the meaning of the word *suffraganeus* in a letter to Charlemagne.[80] To his mind a suffragan meant as

[74] Jaffé, *BRG*, IV, *Monumenta Carolina*, pp. 401, 403.

[75] *MGH: LL*, I, 219; Mansi, XIV, 147.

[76] "De ecclesiarum vero servis communi sententia decretum est, ut archiepiscopi per singulas provincias constituti nostram auctoritatem, suffraganei vero illarum exemplar illius penes se habeant." — *MGH: LL*, I, 207.

[77] C. 10, C. III, q. 6. Cf. Hinschius, *Kirchenrecht*, I, 583, footnote 3.

[78] "Sed non omnes qui palliis utuntur archiepiscopi sunt, nisi quorum sedes metropolis subiectis sibi aliis civitatibus et episcopis principatur...." — *MGH: SS*, VIII, 196.

[79] Canon 1 of Heristal, cf. *supra*, p. 70, footnote 16. See its use in the following: *Admonitio Caroli* (789), canon 8, cf. *supra*, p. 70, footnote 16; *Epistola Caroli Magni ad Trevirensem Episcopum* (809-812): "De episcopis suffraganeis ad ecclesiam Treforum, in qua Domino annuente te presulem esse voluimus, sicut anterius nostram ordinacionem et disposicionem atque iussionem expectasti, volumus: ut, interim quod ad nostrum veneris conloquium, ita expectes." — Jaffé, *BRG*, IV, *Monumenta Carolina*, p. 409; *Epistola Caroli Magni ad Odilbertum Archiepiscopum* (809-812): "Nosse itaque per tua scripta aut per te ipsum volumus, qualiter tu et suffraganei tui doceatis et instruatis sacerdotes Dei et plebem vobis commissam de baptismi sacramenti [sacramento]." — Jaffé, *BRG*, IV, *Monumenta Carolina*, p. 401; canon 6 of the Capitulary held at Aix-la-Chapelle (817), cf. *supra*, p. 89, footnote 76.

[80] "Suffraganeus est nomen mediæ significationis. Ideo nescimus, quale fixum ei aponere [apponere] debeamus: aut presbiterorum aut abbatum aut diaconorum aut ceterorum graduum inferiorum. Si forte episcoporum nomen, qui aliquando vestræ civitati [Trevirensi] subiecti erant, addere debemus...." — Jaffé, *BRG*, IV, *Monumenta Carolina*, p. 408.

much as an *adiutor*, a helper, a cleric who stood at the side of another to be of help or assistance. The use of the idiom in the East can be noted in canons 19 and 24 of the IV General Council of Constantinople (869-870).[81]

It must be stressed, however, that the terms *metropolitanus* and *archiepiscopus* were not absolutely identical.[82] Every metropolitan was an archbishop in the meaning of the word in those times, but, vice versa, not every archbishop was a metropolitan, that is to say, a bishop who had the higher direction of several episcopal districts. As already mentioned, the designation of archbishop signified only a bishop of superior importance. The bestowal of the pallium to a simple bishop was considered an honor.[83] In Carolingian times, simple bishops, upon receiving this decoration of honor from the Pope, were also called *archiepiscopi*.[84]

The term *provincia*, as the designation of the metropolitan's district, was still in use.[85] But the new idiom *diœcesis* was already occurring.[86]

---

[81] Cf. *supra*, pp. 66-68, footnotes 5-7.

[82] For the confusion caused by the documents containing these two idioms cf. *supra*, pp. 69-75.

[83] Hinschius, *Kirchenrecht*, II, 23-36.

[84] From this alone can it be understood why in the Middle Ages, which retained the old meaning of *archiepiscopus* for a bishop of eminent position, those bishops who were destined for the pagan missions where they would have no suffragans were called *archiepiscopi gentium*. We have a few examples of this in Peter Damian's *Vita Romualdi*, c. 39: "Deinde licentia ab Apostolica sede suscepta, et duobus de suis discipulis in archiepiscopos consecratis...iter arripuit."—*MPL*, CXLIV, 989; c. 33: "...dixit fratri nomine Ingelberto qui postea archiepiscopus in gentibus factus est."—*Ibid.*, p. 984; c. 36: "Hic autem Gregorius archiepiscopus in gentibus postmodum est."—*Ibid.*, p. 987.

[85] Cf. c. 6, of the Capitulary of Aix-la-Chapelle (817)—*supra*, p. 89, footnote 76.

[86] The *Encyclica ad Archiepiscopos* of Louis the Pious (817) employed the term *diocesis* or *diœcesis* about a dozen times, but did not use the word *provincia* at all. Cf. *supra*, p. 89, footnote 75. In the *Dictum* heading c. 1, C. IX, q. 3, the *Decretum Gratiani* makes use of *diocesis*. For a very early use of this idiom cf. *supra*, p. 63, footnote 175.

CHAPTER IV

METROPOLITAN RIGHTS IN THE DECRETALS AND GLOSSES

SECTION A

RIGHTS OVER SUFFRAGANS

The Decretal Collections of the *Corpus Iuris Canonici* attributed the following rights to metropolitans: (a) the right to confirm the elections of their suffragans and to consecrate them after the confirmation; (b) the right to convoke provincial synods and to preside at them; (c) the right to visit their provinces and to inflict censures and penalties in cases expressed by law; (d) the office of acting as judge in the second instance in judicial matters which were brought to them by appeals from the tribunals of their suffragans; (e) the right of devolution; and, finally, (f) the right to grant indulgences for their entire province within prescribed limits.[1]

Article 1. Confirmation of Episcopal Elections and Consecration of Suffragans

Pope Innocent III (1198-1216) wrote to the Patriarch of Antioch in 1198, notifying him that he was suspended from exercising the right of confirming the elected bishops, since he had transferred a certain metropolitan to an episcopal see, whereas this metropolitan had been confirmed for the metropolitan see of Tripoli. The Pope reported in passing that this metropolitan after his own confirmation, but before his own consecration, had confirmed the election of one of the bishops of his own province.[2] The Pope did not con-

[1] Hinschius, *Kirchenrecht*, II, 14-16; Wernz-Vidal, *Ius Canonicum*, II, 648-649.

[2] C. 1, X, *de translatione episcopi*, I, 7. Potthast, *Regesta Pontificum Romanorum inde ab anno post Christum natum MCXCVIII ad annum MCCCIV* (2 vols. in 1, Berolini, 1874-1875), n. 52 (hereafter cited as Potthast).

test the exercise of this right, but brought mention of it into his decision as proof that the said metropolitan had already exercised metropolitan jurisdiction in the see for which he had been confirmed, insofar as he was able.

The same Pope wrote to the dean and chapter of Anjou in the year 1199 that the transfer of those who had been elected and confirmed as bishops was reserved as a *maior causa* to the Holy See. This decision was occasioned by the case of the bishop of Avranches, who after his election was confirmed by his metropolitan and then transferred to the see of Anjou and there consecrated by the archbishop of Tours. The archbishop of Rouen absolved the new bishop without a mandate from the Pope, and gave him permission to be transferred to the see of Anjou. Because of these delicts both the metropolitans of Tours and of Rouen were suspended from the exercise of the right to confirm and consecrate bishops.[3] The action of suspension showed that the metropolitans had the right to confirm the elections of their suffragans and the right to consecrate only those bishops who were subject to them.

It was Pope Innocent again who, in a letter written in 1200 to the archbishop of Canterbury, spoke of the metropolitan right of episcopal confirmation. Both the metropolitan and the suffragan bishops of the Canterbury province had written to the Pope concerning the status of a certain archdeacon of York who had been unanimously elected bishop of Worcester. This election was presented to the metropolitan for confirmation, but he delayed the confirmation until the elected archdeacon, who had not been present at the election, approached him. When the archdeacon of York demonstrated by a secret confession that he was illegitimate, the metropolitan did not deem it expedient to confirm the election, and in consequence sent the matter to the Pope for decision. The chapter which presented the candidate for confirmation to the metropolitan, not knowing the reason of the delay of the confirmation, asked Rome for

[3] C. 2, X, *de translatione episcopi*, I, 7. Potthast, n. 575.

the confirmation of the election.[4] Although this passage referred to an extraordinary case, it clearly showed the procedure followed by the metropolitan in ordinary cases.

In still another letter written in 1208, Pope Innocent III reviewed the case of a certain John, Archdeacon of the Church of Therouanne,[5] who had been elected by three canons who served as *compromissarii.* The metropolitan, after examining both the form of the election and the qualities of the elected person, confirmed his election.[6]

It was the right of metropolitans not only to confirm the elections of their suffragans but also to consecrate them. Already Alexander III (1159-1181), in a decretal written sometime during his pontificate, declared that a metropolitan, once his own election was confirmed, even though he had not as yet received the pallium, could licitly permit his suffragan bishops to consecrate a new suffragan bishop who belonged to his jurisdiction. The fact that a metropolitan was impeded either by illness or by any other obstacle was reason enough to confer this power to his suffragans by mandate.[7] The proof is not positive but negative, for it must be argued that if the metropolitan could delegate the consecration of a new bishop to his own suffragans, it meant that he himself had the right of conferring the consecration.

Innocent III took the same position when he wrote to the archbishop of Tours in 1199 in answer to the latter's question concerning the delegation of the act of consecration to suffragans in case the metropolitan should be impeded by illness or some other just cause. When the metropolitan inquired whether the new suffragan who was to receive the consecration should be consecrated only by his own suffragans delegated for this duty, the Pope responded that the new bishop had to receive the consecration only

[4] C. 20, X, *de electione et electi potestate,* I, 6. Potthast, n. 953.

[5] T(h)erouanne: Tarvenna (civitas Morinorum), city of the Morini. It was formerly a bishopric in Flanders (Morinensis, Tarvenensis diœcesis), which was a suffragan see of Rheims.

[6] C. 32, X, *de electione et electi potestate,* I, 6.

[7] C. 11, X, *de electione et electi potestate,* I, 6. Jaffé, 14198.

from the properly delegated bishop who was in communion with the Apostolic See.[8]

Somewhat later Pope Gregory IX (1227-1241) in a decretal written to the patriarch of Grado sometime between 1227 and 1234 made passing reference to the right which metropolitans had of demanding the oath of obedience from their suffragans at the time of the latter's consecration.[9] The Pope forbade the patriarch to demand an oath which went beyond the canonical form approved by Rome. The *Glossa Ordinaria* extended this prohibition to all metropolitans. Hence, if a metropolitan demanded from any of his suffragans an oath whose demands exceeded those of the canonical form, the suffragans were not bound to observe any of the excessive demands.[10]

Article 2. Convocation of Provincial Synods and Right of Presiding at Them

The old right and duty of convoking synods was still retained by the metropolitans according to Decretal Law. Canon 6 of the IV General Council of the Lateran (1215) made the ruling that metropolitans, with their suffragans, must not neglect to hold annual provincial councils. The matters which the provincial councils were to take up were: the correction of abuses; the reformation of morals, especially those of the clergy; a renewed familiarity with the canons, especially those enacted by the Lateran Council itself; and the strict enforcement of these canons by the imposition of punishments on those who transgressed them. In order to bring about the observance of the canons, certain prudent and upright persons were to be appointed in each diocese who would, during the year, without having any jurisdiction however, investigate all matters which needed correction or reform, and the fruits of their investigations

---

[8] C. 10, X, *de officio iudicis ordinarii*, I, 31. Potthast, n. 703. Cf. c. 2, X, *de translatione episcopi*, I, 7, *supra*, p. 92, footnote 3.

[9] C. 13, X, *de maioritate et obedientia*, I, 33. Potthast, n. 9564.

[10] "Si metropolitanus a suffraganeo iuramentum exigit ultra formam statutam a canone, in eo, quod est ultra, suffraganeus non tenetur."

were to be presented to the metropolitan and the suffragans at the following synod. All this was to be done under the pain of suspension from office and benefice.[11]

Article 3. Visitation of Province and the Infliction of Penalties

In 1185 Pope Lucius III (1181-1185), in writing to the archbishop of Ravenna, insisted that the monasteries within his province had to provide him with procuration since they were without privilege or custom to exempt them from giving it.[12] This decision was occasioned by the refusal of the monks and nuns of Bologna to render procuration to the metropolitan of Ravenna. Since the metropolitan fortified his position with the avowal that the other monasteries in his province gave him procuration without any debate, and that he followed the custom of his predecessors, the Pope imposed the duty upon the recalcitrant monasteries and guaranteed the right of procuration to the metropolitan and his successors. Nothing in the decretal testified to the metropolitan's right of provincial visitation, yet it can be deduced that such was his right, for procuration was possible only in times of visitation.[13] The archbishop of Compostella was assured by Pope Innocent III in a letter written in 1207 that churches brought anew under a metropolitan's jurisdiction were expected to observe the custom of the neighboring provinces in the matter of rendering procuration. There is clear testimony in this decretal that it was the right of metropolitans to visit their entire province or a part of it.[14]

---

[11] C. 25, X, *de accusationibus, inquisitionibus et denunciationibus*, V, 1. Cf. Hardouin, VIII, 23-24; Hefele-Leclercq, V, 1334-1335; Mansi, XXII, 991-992; Schroeder, *Decrees*, p. 564; pp. 246-247.

[12] Procuration is the contribution in food and lodging which the parish or place visited must provide for the visitor and his retinue. Cf. Slafkosky, *The Canonical Episcopal Visitation of the Diocese*, The Catholic University of America Canon Law Studies, n. 142 (Washington D. C.: The Catholic University of America Press, 1941), p. 3.

[13] C. 14, X, *de censibus, exactionibus et procurationibus*, III, 39. Jaffé, n. 9723.

[14] C. 22, X, *de censibus, exactionibus et procurationibus*, III, 39. Potthast, n. 3124.

Gregory IX, in a decretal written some time in the period between 1227 and 1234, ordained that the archbishop of Benevento had the right to pass sentence on those within the province who refused to give him procuration during a provincial visitation, whether the visitation was made on his own authority or on the authority of the Pope.[15] This is an advanced step from the legislation of Lucius III and Innocent III. Gregory's decretal did not give the metropolitans power to punish those who refused them procuration, but simply presupposed that they already had the right to do so.

The most comprehensive legislation on the metropolitan visitation of his province was given in a decretal written in 1246 by Pope Innocent IV (1243-1254). The decretal placed the metropolitan under obligation to make a visitation of his own diocese before he could be allowed to visit his province.[16] Only after this condition was fulfilled could a metropolitan make a visitation of his province according to the norms set by the Pope in the same decretal. The metropolitan was permitted to visit all the cities and dioceses within his province, all his suffragans and their subjects, all chapters whether of the cathedral or of other churches, all monasteries, churches, places of worship, the

---

[15] C. 25, X, *de censibus, exactionibus et procurationibus*, III, 39. Potthast, n. 9656.

[16] C. 1, *de censibus, exactionibus et procurationibus*, III, 20, in VI°. This decretal is part of a long sentence passed by Innocent IV in the law-suit between the archbishop of Rheims and his suffragans. — Potthast, n. 12062. The following parts of this judicial sentence are distributed throughout the *Liber Sextus:* c. 1, *de supplenda negligentia prælatorum*, I, 8, in VI°; c. 1, *de officio et potestate iudicis delegati*, I, 13, in VI°; c. 1, *de officio ordinarii*, I, 16, in VI°; c. 1, *de foro competenti*, II, 2, in VI°; c. 3, *de testibus et attestationibus*, II, 10, in VI°; c. 3, *de appellationibus*, II, 15, in VI°; c. 1, *de censibus, exactionibus et procurationibus*, III, 20, in VI°; c. 1, *de pœnis*, V, 9, in VI°; c. 1, *de pœnitentiis et remissionibus*, V, 10, in VI°; c. 5, *de sententia excommunicationis, suspensionis et interdicti*, V, 11, in VI°. For a detailed study of this sentence see: Kuttner, "Decretalistica: Die Novellen Papst Innozenz' IV und die Literatur zu den Novellen Innozenz' IV" — *Zeitschrift der Savigny-Stiftung für Rechtsgeschichte* (Weimar: Hermann Böhlaus Nachfolger), Kan. Abt., XXVI (1937), 439-443.

clergy and the people, and to receive procuration from those whom he had visited.

If he made the visitation of one diocese and then moved to another, regardless of the fact that he had or had not completed the visitation, the metropolitan was not allowed to return to the first diocese unless he began to make a new visitation of his province. If it was absolutely necessary to re-visit a diocese already visited, the metropolitan needed the counsel and consent of all the suffragans, or the greater number of them, to conduct the visitation anew. If he encountered difficulty because of the malicious refusal of the bishops, he could request permission from the Apostolic See to over-rule the malicious decision of his suffragans. Once the metropolitan completed the visitation of his entire province, he could make the visitation again only after counsel with his suffragans, who had to give him their consent in writing. The renewed visitation was to proceed according to the norm given above, unless the metropolitan deemed it necessary to visit the churches, clerics and people of certain dioceses before the others inasmuch as he had not made a visitation of these before.

During the visitation the metropolitan had to inquire, without the use of force or the demand of an oath, about the life and habits of the ministers associated with the churches and other places designated for divine worship, and about those things which pertained to divine worship. If he found after this inquiry that infamy was connected with any of the clerics, he was to denounce these clerics to their ordinaries. If the delicts were notorious, and if the ordinaries had shown negligence in punishing them, the metropolitan could freely correct these by inflicting proper punishments. Neither the metropolitan nor his retinue was allowed to accept money as procuration under the pretext of an officially performed duty, or of usage, or of any other excuse. They were to be content with the payment that sufficed to cover the cost of the food. The Pope warned that no gifts were to be received under the pain of malediction, from which the guilty could be freed only after restitution of double the amount taken had been made.[17]

The important ruling that the metropolitan first had to make the visitation of his own diocese, and the further ruling concerning the punishment of clerics subject to his suffragans, were extensions of the former legislation. Within the same decretal Innocent IV declared that any notorious delict committed against the metropolitan, his retinue, or others to whom the metropolitan had given the right of visitation, could be punished by him if the delict implied an act of abuse against the jurisdiction of the one making the visitation.[18] The *Glossa Ordinaria* extended the right of punishment to cases which did not involve any abuse against the metropolitan jurisdiction.[19] The exercise of this right was limited by two conditions: the notorious delicts had to occur in connection with the visitation, and the punishment of the perpetrators had first to be in default on the part of the proper suffragan.

The metropolitan had the right to punish not only the clerics of his suffragans but his suffragans as well. Pope Honorius III (1216-1227) found some difficulty in deciding the true state of affairs in the case concerning the suspension of the bishop of Le Mans by the archbishop of Tours. In order to relieve the bishop of the suspension, the Pope, in a decretal issued sometime between 1216 and 1227, delegated a certain canon of Tours, who was the proxy of the metropolitan, to absolve the bishop from the suspension *ad cautelam* only after the latter had previously testified under oath whether or not he was guilty of the delict for which the metropolitan had punished him.[20] The Pope did not question the right of the metropolitan to punish his suffragan. His interest concerned the justice or injustice of the inflicted suspension.

At the time of the IV General Council of the Lateran

[17] C. 1, *de censibus, exactionibus et procurationibus*, III, 20, in VI°.

[18] C. 1, *de pœnis*, V, 9, in VI°. Cf. *supra*, p. 96, footnote 16.

[19] "Sed hodie tales iniurias tunc punit, etiamsi iurisdictionem non impediant."

[20] C. 52, X, *de sententia excommunicationis*, V, 39. Potthast, n. 7856.

(1215) the power of metropolitans was being checked in this regard. Canon 30 lashed out against all prelates of the Church who chose unworthy men to occupy ecclesiastical benefices, and demanded that these be rejected and worthy occupants be chosen in their stead. Yet the canon did not concede the right of withdrawing unworthy clerics from these benefices to metropolitans, but stated that such matters were to be investigated in the annual provincial councils and that the council was to concur with the metropolitan if a removal was to take place. The metropolitan's appointment of an unworthy cleric to a benefice was to be made known by the council to a higher superior.[21]

Innocent IV checked the metropolitans still more by limiting the power of their *officiales*. The Pope forbade the archbishop of Rheims to constitute officials forane in the dioceses of his suffragans, even in cases which, through future appeal, were to devolve to him, unless such a custom had already been entrenched. In the eventuality of an existing custom, these *officiales* were not to take these cases, but were to wait until an appeal was made. The *officiales* of the province of Rheims were not allowed to pass any sentence of interdict, suspension or excommunication on any of the suffragan bishops. The Pope extended this last piece of legislation to protect all suffragans.[22] But the metropolitan's power to inflict punishments and censures was still left intact. However, exceptions to the general rule were the depositions and reconciliations of bishops; these the Popes reserved to themselves. The *Dictatus Gregorii VII* contained two rules to this effect.[23]

---

[21] C. 29, X, *de præbendis et dignitatibus*, III, 5; Hardouin, VIII, 41-44; Hefele-Leclercq, V, 1358-1359; Mansi, XXII, 1017-1018; Schroeder, *Decrees*, pp. 572-573; pp. 268-269.

[22] C. 1, *de officio ordinarii*, I, 16, in VI°. Cf. Kober, *Kirchenbann*, pp. 69-70.

[23] III: "...quod ille [Papa] solus possit deponere episcopos vel reconciliare"; XXV: "...quod [Papa] absque synodali conventu possit episcopos deponere vel reconciliare."—*MGH: Epistolæ Selectæ Gregorii VII*, II, fasc. 1, pp. 202, 207; cf. Jaffé, *BRG*, V, *Monumenta Gregoriana*, pp. 174, 176; c. 2, X, *de translatione episcopi*, I, 7, *supra*, p. 92, footnote 3.

Article 4. Second Instance in Judicial Matters Brought in by Appeal

Alexander III wrote to all the suffragans of the Church of Canterbury that the archbishop of Canterbury was not only their metropolitan but a legate of the Pope, and as such he had the right to hear, not only those cases which were brought to his tribunal in appeal, but all cases which were brought to him by a simple complaint, not because of his metropolitan right but because of papal delegation.[24] But the prerogative of appeal grew during the hundred years which followed, for by the time of the pontificate of Innocent IV metropolitans considered that they had the right of adjudication in any and every case brought to their courts, for the reason that they were metropolitans, and not exclusively for the reason that they were delegates or legates of the Pope.

When Innocent IV prohibited the archbishop of Rheims from constituting *officiales foranei,* he took notice of custom in this matter and contested the abuses which were creeping in through the extension of the metropolitan's right to the officials.[25] The same Pope declared that appeals in cases adjudicated by the officials of suffragan bishops were to be made not to the suffragans but to the curia of the metropolitan of Rheims. With regard to decisions made by archdeacons and inferior prelates who were subject to the suffragans and their officials, the subjects of the suffragans were to appeal to their suffragan bishop and not to their metropolitan, unless another custom prevailed in the Church of Rheims.

Neither the metropolitan nor his official had the right to cite the parties of a trial or to commit to others a case given in appeal to them, until a definitive sentence had been passed

---

[24] C. 1, X, *de officio legati,* I, 30.

[25] C. 1, *de officio ordinarii,* I, 16, in VI°; cf. *supra,* p. 99, footnote 22.

by the court of the suffragan or his official when a probable or legitimate reason for the appeal had not been expressed. If, after the parties were cited, the case was not given in appeal to the metropolitan or his official within ten days after the passing of an interlocutory or definitive sentence by the suffragan or his official, neither the metropolitan nor his official was to prohibit the case from proceeding even to the execution of the sentence, unless the entire case belonged to the metropolitan by devolution.

If a case was appealed for some unjust reason, the metropolitan and his official could not prohibit the case from proceeding, unless they had accepted the appeal as probably legitimate and had begun to investigate the truth of the case. In cases in which appeals were forbidden by law, should a metropolitan begin an investigation, the case could be checked to prevent the sentence from being executed. The metropolitan, after refusing to accept a case turned over to him by means of an appeal could not recall it to himself. If a subject of one of the suffragans had appealed his case to the curia of Rheims, the subject still remained under the jurisdiction of his own suffragan bishop in all other cases, and could not be completely taken away from his own suffragan's jurisdiction by the metropolitan.

The subjects of the suffragans had to appeal to their metropolitan from the decision of their bishops in those cases in which the metropolitan exercised temporal jurisdiction, unless custom, privilege or special statute gave them the right to appeal to another. The metropolitan could not recall or declare null the sentence of interdict, suspension or excommunication inflicted upon the appellant by the first court unless the parties had been cited and unless he had taken legal cognizance of the case. If an appeal had been made to the metropolitan before the sentence was passed, the metropolitan was not to postpone the returning of the case to his suffragan once he had ascertained that the appeal was unjustly made.[26]

---

[26] C. 3, *de appellationibus*, II, 15, in VI°.

Article 5. Devolution

Metropolitans had the right to supply whatever their suffragans omitted to supply, and to do what their suffragans had neglected to do, only if the latter had neglected to supply or to do what was expected of them by law. This right was called devolution. Metropolitans were allowed to exercise the right derived by devolution when the suffragan bishops or other persons in authority in their provinces delayed the filling of certain offices beyond the prescribed time set in the law. Canon 8 of the III General Council of the Lateran (1179) specified that if a bishop or chapter neglected to fill an office, it was the duty of the metropolitan to take care of the matter. Benefices were to be filled with incumbents within six months after vacancy.[27]

Some years later Innocent III decided a case in which two clerics were involved in litigation over the archdeaconry of Richmond. When the Pope ascertained that neither of the two clerics was assigned to the benefice within the period specified by the III General Council of the Lateran, he assumed the right of bestowal to himself, and declared that any other bestowal by any other person or group of persons would be null and void. The original right of conferral belonged either to the archbishop of York as bishop of the diocese in which Richmond was situated, or to the chapter, but since there was no metropolitan superior to the archbishop of York and the chapter, the Pope assumed the right to himself.[28] The decretal in reporting this case argued for the metropolitan's right of devolution inasmuch as it settled a controversy in a situation where no metropolitan system was instituted. Had there been a metropolitan whose authority would have been superior to that of the metropolitan of York, he would have been the person to whom the right of conferral would have passed by devolu-

[27] C. 2, X, *de concessione præbendæ et ecclesiæ non vacantis*, III, 8. Cf. Hefele-Leclercq, V, 1094; Mansi, XXII, 222; Schroeder, *Decrees*, p. 553; p. 222.

[28] C. 3, X, *de supplenda negligentia prælatorum*, I, 10. Potthast, n. 5035.

tion. Canon 23 of the IV General Council of the Lateran (1215) reduced the time period from six to three months.[29]

The right derived by devolution was also available whenever the cathedral chapters proved negligent during the vacancy of the episcopal see. In such a case the metropolitan could appoint a visitator or administrator. If chapters acted in a negligent or disorderly fashion in the direction of the ecclesiastical affairs and the administration of church property, the metropolitan could interpose his authority by devolved right. Boniface VIII (1294-1303) stated in one of his decretals that only the Pope could depute visitators for vacant episcopal sees, but if a chapter administered the spiritualities or temporalities negligently or badly, the metropolitan could intervene even before a papal appointee was selected, and could depute a visitator or administrator after notifying the Pope of conditions in the vacant see.[30]

Phillips (1804-1872)[31] and Kober (1821-1897)[32] enumerated other actions which they considered expressions of the right derived by devolution, but Hinschius declared that these particular cases simply followed as corollaries upon the acknowledged metropolitan rights.[33] One such corollary was the right to absolve from excommunication anyone who had been unlawfully refused absolution by his suffragan. Three such cases will be treated in this connection. Innocent III, in a decretal sent to the archbishop of Rouen in 1198, ordered that the metropolitan, when approached by an unjustly excommunicated person who lodged an appeal with him, send the appellant back to the suffragan for absolution, and that only after the suffragan had refused to ab-

[29] C. 41, X, *de electione et electi potestate*, I, 6. Cf. Hardouin, VIII, 37-38; Hefele-Leclercq, V, 1352; Mansi, XXII, 1011-1012; Schroeder, *Decrees*, p. 570 and p. 264.

[30] C. 4, *de supplenda negligentia prælatorum*, I, 8, in VI°.

[31] *Kirchenrecht* (7 vols., Regensburg: Druck und Verlag von Georg Joseph Many, 1845-1872, Vol. VI, 1864), VI, 834 (hereafter cited as *Kirchenrecht*).

[32] *Kirchenbann*, p. 459.

[33] *Kirchenrecht*, II, 15.

solve him could the metropolitan annul the refusal by granting the desired absolution.[34]

The same Pope wrote to the archbishop of Sens in 1203 about the absolution given to the archpresbyter of Auxerre who had been excommunicated by his bishop. After declaring that certain canonists insisted that an excommunicated person had no right of appeal and that because of this no metropolitan had the power to absolve such a person whenever an unlawful appeal was made, the Pope cited a decretal which had been drawn up by his predecessor Pope Alexander III, and then he likewise adverted to the canons of the Council of Sardica in order to delineate a distinction between the justly and the unjustly excommunicated. The distinction warranted the conclusion that the one who was unjustly excommunicated could appeal to his metropolitan. The Pope then concluded his letter with the legislation just considered in the decretal which he had sent to the archbishop of Rouen.[35]

In one of his decretals to the metropolitan of Rouen, Innocent IV declared that metropolitans could not upon appeal absolve those who were excommunicated by the subjects of his suffragans, but only those who were excommunicated by his suffragans or their *officiales*.[36] If each of these three cases be examined closely, it can be noted that in each of them the metropolitan's right is not that of devolution, but rather a consequence of his right to take cognizance of a case in its second instance.

Phillips insisted in this connection that the metropolitan's right to punish notorious crimes which had not been tried by the suffragan bishops was also an expression of the metropolitan's devolved power.[37] He cited a text to support his view.[38] Though the text as such referred to the rights which the metropolitans had in connection with pro-

[34] C. 8, X, *de officio iudicis ordinarii*, I, 31. Potthast, n. 250.

[35] C. 40, X, *de sententia excommunicationis*, V, 39. Potthast, n. 1830.

[36] C. 7, *de sententia excommunicationis, suspensionis et interdicti*, V, 11, in VI°. Potthast, n. 15454.

[37] *Kirchenrecht, loc. cit.*

[38] C. 1, *de censibus, exactionibus et procurationibus*, III, 20, in VI°.

vincial visitations, it can be said that there was a connection between the rights deriving through the act of visitation or by way of devolution. The metropolitan's right of extraordinary visitation could not be exercised except for grave reasons. The neglect on the part of his suffragans to punish notorious crimes could serve as a sufficient reason for the visitation, and for the consequent employment of the devolved right to inflict proper punishments.

Another right which Phillips[39] connected with a metropolitan's devolved rights was that by which metropolitans were allowed to hold the goods of cathedrals during the vacancies of episcopal sees until such a time when bishops would be elected. This legislation was enacted by the Trullan Synod of 692.[40] But inasmuch as this legislation belonged to the earlier institution of metropolitan rights, and since no guilt was involved in the circumstances which the canon described, the predicated right cannot be considered a feature in the metropolitan's devolved rights.

It is incorrect to think that the metropolitan's devolved rights extended to all imaginable cases of negligence on the part of the suffragans, for in general metropolitans were forbidden to interfere in the jurisdiction of their suffragans. In a decretal written to the bishop of Ely in 1204 by Innocent III, the Pope made it clear that a metropolitan could not force an unwilling suffragan to assume a case which had been previously sent in appeal to the metropolitan.[41] The gloss of the words *exceptis quibusdam articulis* showed the limitations set to the jurisdiction in matters which were reserved to the jurisdiction of the metropolitan's suffragans. Furthermore, the concept that metropolitans could always intervene when the suffragans were handicapped must be specifically refuted. In a lengthy decretal issued by Innocent IV it was stated that the jurisdiction of an excommunicated bishop did not devolve to his metropoli-

---

[39] *Kirchenrecht,* VI, 835.
[40] C. 48, C. XII, q. 2.
[41] C. 11, X, *de officio iudicis ordinarii,* I, 31. Potthast, n. 2350.

tan.[42] The gloss to the word *culpis* specified the cases in which a metropolitan did not have ordinary power of jurisdiction.

Article 6. Granting of Indulgences

Within their entire provinces archbishops were allowed to grant indulgences according to prescribed rules. Honorius II re-affirmed the doctrine that metropolitans could grant indulgences within their provinces, and added the note that this was to be done according to the specific regulations set by one of the general councils.[43] The *Glossa ordinaria* employed the word *indulgentias* instead of *literas generales*.[44] So, too, Innocent IV re-iterated the same doctrine when writing to the archbishop of Rheims.[45]

SECTION B

RIGHTS OVER THE SUBJECTS OF THEIR SUFFRAGANS

Article 1. General Principle

All the afore-mentioned rights of metropolitans have some relation to the suffragan bishops. If the question is asked whether the metropolitans had any jurisdiction over the subjects of their suffragans, it must be answered that they had it only insofar as it was connected with the rights they actually possessed for exercise in accordance with law.[46] A further application of this principle can be found in one of the decretals of Pope Innocent IV. According to it a metropolitan could not assume any cases which concerned the subjects of his suffragans. If an appeal was not made, even though there might have been a complaint of some sort, a metropolitan could not hear the case of a subject of any of his suffragans, even though the suffragans

[42] C. 1, *de supplenda negligentia prælatorum*, I, 8, in VI°. Potthast, n. 12062; cf. *supra*, p. 96, footnote 16.

[43] C. 15, *de pœnitentiis et remissionibus*, V, 38. Potthast, n. 7853. Most probably the Pope referred to canon 62 of the IV Lateran Council (1215). Cf. Schroeder, *Decrees*, pp. 581-582, pp. 286-287.

[44] "Archiepiscopus infra provinciam suam potest concedere indulgentias secundum formam concilii generalis."

[45] C. 1, *de pœnitentiis et remissionibus*, V, 10, in VI°.

[46] Cf. c. 11, X, *de officio iudicis ordinarii*, I, 31.

themselves would have given their consent for such a hearing.

A metropolitan could not compel the subjects of his suffragans to take up causes by delegating these causes to them, nor could he force them to fulfill his sentences or counsels, nor could he insist that they give testimony in causes which had devolved to him, unless some custom had disposed otherwise. A metropolitan could not be a competent judge against the officials, archdeacons, archpresbyters and other inferior prelates subject to his suffragans, as long as custom did not dispose otherwise, nor against the other subjects of the suffragans, even whenever the dispute concerned the salaries of the advocates and procurators who were employed in the handling of cases tried in the curia of the metropolitan.

A metropolitan could not compel unwilling transactors of other dioceses in matters which concerned their own property to bring their case before him, unless they were actually present in the metropolitan's diocese. But if the cited transactors refused to appear or if they hid themselves maliciously in order not to be cited, the metropolitan was allowed to sequester their goods which were located in his diocese or to make other provisions by arrangement with their ordinaries.[47] A metropolitan was not allowed to send his own clerics into the dioceses of his suffragans in order to have contracts drawn up before these clerics, or, if the contracts were already drawn up, to have these clerics ap-

[47] The text of c. 1, *de foro competenti*, II, 2, in VI°, uses the expression "missionem facere" in this connection. The *Glossa ordinaria* uses the same phrase without giving the meaning of the clause. According to Roman procedural Law it has the same meaning as sequestration. Wenger (*Institutes of the Roman Law of Civil Procedure* [revised ed. translated by Otis Harrison Fisk, New York: Veritas Press, 1940], pp. 242-244) declares that a *missio in possessionem* "consists of putting one into possession of all of a person's property or of objects belonging to him....a means of coercion against the *iudicatus* who did not pay *(executio)*, and against the *indefensus*, with whom in consequence of his declining attitude no normal suit could be founded. This *missio* begins with a putting into possession *(rei servandæ causa)* and ends with a sale...the *missio in bona* is met with in the most varied forms: varied according to its provocation, to its aim, to its extent, to its outcome."

prove them. If a contract was made or approved by these clerics, he could not force the subjects of his suffragans to litigate concerning these contracts before him, nor could he excommunicate the officials or subjects of his suffragans if they refused to litigate before his court.[48]

Article 2. Appeals in Second Instance

In cases of second instance, the metropolitan could decide a matter only when brought to his cognizance in consequence of an appeal. He was not allowed to draw to himself any other matters which concerned the same party.[49] He was not permitted to institute in advance an *officialis* in the dioceses of his suffragans, so that he might eventually cite the subjects of his suffragans before his own court.[50] Nor was he allowed to set up his court except in his own city or diocese, and in those suffragan dioceses from which the appeal was made to him. This limitation was set by Boniface VIII.[51]

Article 3. Visitation Rights

In consequence of his right of visitation, the metropolitan had the right to hear the confessions of his suffragans' subjects and to impose penances. This he could do only during the visitation. Boniface VIII set forth these rules in one of his decretals.[52] The imposition of these penances was to follow the pattern of procedure he used in notorious cases, otherwise he had to leave to the suffragans the prosecution of crimes not yet brought to court.[53]

Article 4. Penalties for Crimes of Subjects

Finally, the metropolitan had penal power against all those who hindered him, his helpers or delegates, either

---

[48] C. 1, *de foro competenti*, II, 2, in VI°. Cf. c. 1, *de officio ordinarii*, I, 16, in VI°, *supra*, p. 99, footnote 22; c. 3, *de appellationibus*, II, 15, in VI°; *supra*, pp. 100-101.

[49] C. 3, *de appellationibus*, II, 15, in VI°.

[50] C. 1, *de officio ordinarii*, I, 16, in VI°; *supra*, p. 99, footnote 22.

[51] C. 5, *de officio ordinarii*, I, 16, in VI°.

[52] C. 5, *de censibus, exactionibus et procurationibus*, III, 20, in VI°.

[53] C. 1, *de censibus, exactionibus et procurationibus*, III, 20, in VI°.

during the visitation, or at a provincial synod, or also the while he prepared for it, as well also against those who refused him the necessary protection, or who insulted him on these occasions. He could punish these persons if their crimes were notorious. In a decretal written in 1202 to the bishop of Paris, Innocent III recounted the fact that the archbishop of Sens had suspended certain clerics when they refused him the procuration which was his due during the visitation of the province of Sens. When these suspended clerics refused to observe the suspension, the archbishop excommunicated them. The Pope commanded the bishop of Paris to carry the archbishop's punishments into effect and to hold the clerics excommunicated until they made fitting satisfaction.[54] Jurisdiction which went beyond these rights over the subjects of suffragans can be explained only by custom.

Article 5. Interpretation of Gloss-Verse on Metropolitan Rights over Suffragan Subjects

In the text given in connection with cc. 1-20, X, *de officio iudicis ordinarii,* I, 31, Hostiensis (1271) was clear on this matter.[55] He attempted to combine all the metropolitan's powers over the subjects of the suffragans into the following verse:

Officium varium, forus, appellatio, crimen,
Peccans, non parens, res, consultatio, deses
Præsul, canonici tumidi, sententia nequam:
Visitat, indulget, custos, quia papa dat, usus:
Permutat sociis, suspectus cumque remittat,
Casibus his primas subiectos præsulis arcet.

Officium varium concerned the chanting of the psalms in the province according to the mode used by the metropolitan cathedral. This metropolitan prerogative had already become antiquated at the time.[56] *Forus* referred to

[54] C. 16, X, de *præscriptionibus,* II, 26. Potthast, n. 1778. Cf. c. 1, *de pœnis,* V, 9, in VI°, *supra,* p. 98, footnote 18.
[55] *Summa Aurea* (Venetiis: Ad candentis Salmandræ Isigne, 1570).
[56] C. 13, D. XII; *supra,* p. 43, footnote 83.

the cases of absolving from unlawful excommunications.[57] *Appellatio* had reference to the metropolitan's right of judgment in second instance.[58] *Crimen* connoted a right already out of usage. It referred to the right of the metropolitan to accept an accusation against a bishop made at a synod by clerics and lay-folk.[59] *Peccans* referred to the right of a metropolitan to have the *forum delicti* in his own diocese. This right did not belong in this listing of metropolitan rights over the subjects of the suffragan. *Non parens* connoted the right of the metropolitan to again put under a ban those of their suffragans' subjects who had been absolved but who did not fulfill the conditions imposed for obtaining the full absolution.[60] *Res* pointed to the right of the metropolitan to have the *forum rei sitæ* in his own diocese. This like *peccans* did not belong in this listing. *Consultatio*, like *res*, had no place in this listing. This term referred to the privilege possessed by the suffragan, namely to turn to his metropolitan for advice. *Deses presul* had to do with the right of devolution.[61] *Canonici tumidi* bespoke the right which the metropolitan, as an apostolic delegate, had for instituting measures at the call of the bishop against obstinate clerics.[62] This right also did not belong in this listing. *Sententia nequam* designated the right which the metropolitans had in cases in which an appeal was made against the unjust sentence of a suffragan bishop.[63]

Visitat referred to the right of visitation.[64] *Indulget* had to do with the metropolitan's right to grant indulgences

---

[57] C. 40, X, *de sententia excommunicationis*, V, 39; *supra*, p. 104; c. 8, X, *de officio iudicis ordinarii*, I, 37; *supra*, p. 104; c. 7, *de sententia excommunicationis, suspensionis et interdicti*, V, 11, in VI°; *supra*, p. 104.

[58] *Supra*, pp. 100-101.

[59] C. 1, C. VI, q. 2.

[60] C. 8, X, *de officio iudicis ordinarii*, I, 31; *supra*, p. 104, footnote 34.

[61] The text of Hostiensis *(Summa Aurea)* made it clear that this right was not as extensive as many claimed it to be.

[62] C. 13, X, *de officio iudicis ordinarii*, I, 31. Cf. c. 7, of IV Lateran Council: Hardouin, VIII, 23-26; Hefele-Leclercq, V, 1335-1336; Mansi, XXII, 991-994; Schroeder, *Decrees*, pp. 564-565; pp. 247-248.

[63] C. 54, X, *de appellatione*, II, 26. Potthast, n. 3245.

[64] *Supra*, pp. 95-99.

in his province.[65] *Custos* implied the metropolitan's right to take care of the goods of vacant cathedral churches.[66] *Quia papa dat* referred to all the rights which could be increased for a metropolitan in virtue of privileges; *usus*, to those which could be enlarged through custom. *Permutat sociis* had to do with that sentence of law, abstracted from medieval doctrine as derived from a series of decretals, which provided that, should contracts of exchange be drawn up between a bishop and a chapter, the metropolitan had to give his consent as their superior. This rule was followed in the year 1203.[67] *Suspectus cumque remittat* dealt with the transfer of a case to the metropolitan when the suffragan was suspect.[68]

In comparison with the jurisdictional prestige that attached to his position in former times, the status of the metropolitan's position was now considerably reduced. To understand this correctly, one must attend to the significant fact that certain legal concepts were developed in the twelfth century. One of these was that only the Pope could dispense from the general laws of the Church. Another was that only he could accept, as *iudex ordinarius*, appeals and other legal matters from all parts of the world without having to pay attention to the intermediary instances.[69] Still another concept was that he could send his legates everywhere to exercise his rights.[70] The groundwork was laid in the eleventh century when the Popes insisted that only the pallium gave the full archiepiscopal power, and that therefore metropolitans possessed their rights only by participation in papal jurisdiction.[71]

---

[65] *Supra*, p. 106.

[66] C. 48, C. XII, q. 2; *supra*, p. 105, footnote 40.

[67] *Gallia Christiana in Provinciis Ecclesiasticis Distributa* (16 vols., Parisiis: Venit apud Firmin Didot Fratres, Filios Sociosque, Vol. XVI, ed. J. B. Haureau, 1865), XVI, 197-198.

[68] C. 61, X, *de appellatione*, II, 28; cf. c. 48 of IV Lateran Council, in Schroeder, *Decrees*, pp. 577-578; pp. 278-279.

[69] Hinschius, *Kirchenrecht*, I, 174.

[70] *Ibid.*, pp. 507 ff.; pp. 583 ff.

[71] C. 4, X, *de electione et electi potestate*, I, 6. Jaffé, n. 4851. Cf. Hinschius, *Kirchenrecht*, II, 23-36.

CHAPTER V

METROPOLITAN INSTITUTION FROM THE COUNCIL OF TRENT TO THE PUBLICATION OF THE CODE

SECTION A

THE ORDINARY POWER OF METROPOLITANS

Article 1. Terminology Used to Define This Power

Throughout the period following the Council of Trent (1545-1563) a metropolitan was considered not only as a bishop who had jurisdiction in his own diocese, but also as one who had authority to exercise certain rights of jurisdiction over the bishops of his province and over the subjects of these bishops. This right of jurisdiction was called *ius metropoliticum*,[1] *auctoritas metropolitana*[2] or *lex metropolitana*.[3] As such, this so-called *potestas ordinaria* was circumscribed by law, so that metropolitans could do only that which was expressly permitted them by law according to the existing discipline of the Church *(iuxta vigentem Ecclesiæ disciplinam)*.[4]

Article 2. Derivation of This Power

On the one hand, the office of metropolitan was not held to be absolutely necessary, since it was not introduced into the hierarchy of the Church by divine authority *(ius divi-*

---

[1] Cf. c. 1, X, *de officio legati*, I, 30; c. 13, X, *de arbitris*, I, 43.

[2] Cf. c. 54, X, *de appellationibus, recusationibus et relationibus*, II, 28.

[3] Cf. c. 11, X, *de officio iudicis ordinarii*, I, 31.

[4] Cf. c. 9, of the Council of Antioch (341); *supra*, pp. 34-35; c. 11, X, *de officio iudicis ordinarii*, I, 31; c. 7, *de sententia excommunicationis, suspensionis et interdicti*, V, 11, in VI°; c. 1, *de supplenda negligentia prælatorum*, I, 8, in VI°; c. 1, *de foro competenti*, II, 2, in VI°; c. 1, *de officio ordinarii*, I, 16, in VI°; Bouix, *Institutiones Juris Canonici in Varios Tractatus Divisæ: Tractatus de Episcopo ubi et de Synodo Diœcesana* (2. ed., 2 vols., Parisiis, 1873), I, 451-456 (hereafter cited as *De Episcopo*); Phillips, *Kirchenrecht*, II, 82-83, 90-91; VI, 811-817; Hinschius, *Kirchenrecht*, II, 18; Wernz, *Ius Decretalium* (2. ed., 6 vols., Romæ et Prati, 1906-1913), II, 850.

num), but, on the other hand, it was considered a useful office which had come into being in consequence of historical development, and therefore existed by authority of human law *(ius humanum)*. Hence it is that the power which in time had accrued as ordinary power for metropolitans was initially a delegated power which derived from the Popes.[5] Hinschius did not incline toward this opinion concerning the pristine nature of the metropolitan right of jurisdiction.[6] Nevertheless, historical proof in opposition to his opinion indicates that in their rights metropolitans were never independent of the Pope, but simply shared power as derived from the primacy in the Church. Phillips rightly claims that all metropolitan jurisdiction is but an outlet for power inherent in the papal primacy.

With the exception of Peter and his successors, no bishop, according to divine law, stands higher than any others in the episcopate. If one be higher than the others, this position of eminence rests merely and solely on the fact that the Head of the Church tacitly or expressly tolerated its occurrence. By his very nature, therefore, a metropolitan has no jurisdiction over another bishop except through the Pope, nor has he any such jurisdiction over the subjects of his suffragans except inasfar as the Pope, who rules all the members of God's Kingdom, has conferred it upon him for definite cases.[7] What earlier Church History reveals is the constant attempt on the part of metropolitans to assume more and more jurisdiction independently of the Pope. Certain metropolitan jurisdictional excesses grew up locally simply for the reason that the Popes were not cognizant of

---

[5] Thomassinus, *Ecclesiæ Disciplina*, Pars I, Lib. I, c. 26, n. 5; Berardi, *De rebus ad canonicam scientiam pertinentibus commentaria in ius ecclesiasticum universum* (4 vols., Taurini, 1766), Lib. I, pars II, diss. 3, c. 1 (hereafter cited as *Commentaria*); Phillips, *Kirchenrecht*, II, 80; Schulte, *Lehrbuch des katholischen und evangelischen Kirchenrechts* (4. Auflage des katholischen, 1. Auflage des evangelischen Kirchenrechts, 2 vols., Giesen: E. Roth, 1886), II, 207 (hereafter cited as *Kirchenrecht*).

[6] *Kirchenrecht*, I, 171-181.

[7] *Kirchenrecht*, II, 87-88.

them; when these were recognized, the Popes acted against them in a legislative manner. The only valid conclusion which can be drawn from what has been said above is that the metropolitan power of jurisdiction was a power which derived from the papal power itself.

SECTION B

THE LOSS OF CERTAIN METROPOLITAN RIGHTS

Article 1. Failure of Jansenistic and Gallican Efforts

The Jansenists and Gallicans strove to bring back the ancient discipline in which the metropolitans had held many rights which in the course of time were abrogated. But their efforts failed miserably.[8] One of the chief rights which metropolitans lost was that of intervening in the elections of their comprovincial bishops.[9] The rights to confirm the elections of their suffragans and to consecrate them were taken away from their jurisdiction even before the celebration of the Council of Trent. It is true that both these rights were assured them by Synodal and Decretal Law, but the Popes re-assumed them some time in the fourteenth century.

Article 2. Confirmation of Episcopal Elections in Papal Hands

The right of episcopal confirmation was vested in the Popes in such a way that they alone made the final appointments of all bishops throughout the world. Innocent III (1198-1216), in a decretal written in 1198 to the patriarch of Antioch, made it clear that the transfer of a bishop was a *causa maior* which belonged to the jurisdiction of the Apostolic See. Because the patriarch had dared to transfer

---

[8] Bouix, *De Episcopo*, I, 448-451, 457-473; Wernz, *Ius Decretalium*, II, 850.

[9] Cf. cc. 4, 6, of the I Council of Nicæa (325); *supra*, pp. 15-16; cc. 11, 20, 32, X, *de electione et electi potestate*, I, 6; c. 10, X, *de officio iudicis ordinarii*, I, 31; Wernz, *Ius Decretalium*, II, 850; Hinschius, *Kirchenrecht*, II, 17; Bouix, *De Episcopo*, I, 457.

a metropolitan from a metropolitan see to an episcopal see, he was suspended from the right of confirming bishops.[10] By issuing this suspension, Innocent III proved that it was within papal jurisdiction to transfer bishops, and implicitly resumed the right of confirmation when he withdrew it from the jurisdiction of the patriarch. The implicit resumption of episcopal confirmation by the Pope argued for the papal right to delegate it to those subordinate to himself.

In keeping with this position Clement IV (1265-1268) declared that the entire disposition of dignities pertained by right to the Roman Pontiffs and was by custom reserved to them. Nevertheless, Clement IV did not disturb the existing discipline entirely, but reserved to the Popes in a most special manner the bestowal of those dignities and benefices which pertained to the Roman Curia. If any election, provision or conferral in which these reserved dignities and benefices were concerned was not made by the Popes, it was to be considered null and void.[11] By this special reservation the Pope recalled to the Apostolic See the confirmation, if not also the entire nomination, of bishops. By the time of the Council of Trent the matter of episcopal confirmation was already in papal hands. The Council went so far as to anathematize anyone who contended that bishops chosen by the Roman Pontiffs were not legitimately and truly bishops.[12]

It was Benedict XIV (1740-1758) who in a clear fashion expressed the resumption of episcopal nomination and confirmation by the Popes. He insisted that the old discipline by which the Apostolic See nominated and appointed bishops was to replace the customary procedure of elections conducted by the canons of vacant sees, except in those coun-

---

[10] C. 1, X, *de translatione episcopi*, I, 7.

[11] C. 2, *de præbendis et dignitatibus*, III, 4, in VI°.

[12] Sess. XXIII, *de ordine*, c. 4, can. 8: "Si quis dixerit, episcopos, qui auctoritate Romani pontificis assumuntur, non esse legitimos et veros episcopos, sed figmentum humanum: anathema sit." — Schroeder, *Canons and Decrees of the Council of Trent* (St. Louis: Herder Book Co., 1941), pp. 435-436; p. 163 (hereafter cited as *Canons and Decrees*).

tries which through concordats with the Holy See retained the right of election. But even in the latter case the Pope expressly specified that the confirmation still belonged in every instance to the Roman Pontiff.[13]

Reiffenstuel (1642-1703), after declaring that it was the ruling of the common law that confirmations of elections belonged to the immediate superiors of those who were elected, stated that a bishop's election was to be confirmed by his metropolitan. The author alluded to a concordat drawn up between Germany and the Apostolic See, in which the confirmation of German bishops was reserved to the Supreme Pontiff. This concordat, drawn up between Nicholas V (1447-1455) and Frederick III (1440-1493) in 1448 referred to this right only indistinctly.[14] Schmalzgrueber (1663-1735) represented the very same view.[15] Both authors still held to the legislation that a metropolitan could confirm the election of his suffragans, inasmuch as that legislation existed before the time of Pope Benedict XIV.

Article 3. Episcopal Consecration Delegated to Metropolitans

The papal right to confer episcopal consecration could still be exercised by metropolitans, but only through special delegation. Although the Council of Trent made no specific provision concerning episcopal consecrations, the old rule that bishops were to be consecrated by no one else but their metropolitan fell into desuetude. When the bishops themselves gradually worked away from the ruling, the popes took the opportunity to reserve episcopal consecrations to themselves.

---

[13] Ep. "*In postremo,*" 20 oct. 1756, § 15 — *Codicis Iuris Canonici Fontes*, cura Emi Petri Card. Gasparri editi (9 vols., Romæ [postea Civitate Vaticana]: Typis Polyglottis Vaticanis, 1923-1939 [Vols. VII, VIII, et IX ed. cura et studio Emi. Iustiniani Card. Serédi]), n. 442 (hereafter cited as *Fontes*).

[14] *Jus Canonicum Universum* (5 vols., Parisiis, 1864-1870), Lib. I, tit. 6, nn. 321-322 (hereafter cited as *Jus Canonicum*).

[15] *Jus Ecclesiasticum Universum* (5 vols. in 12, Romæ, 1843-1845), Lib. I, tit. 6, n. 361, q. 78 (hereafter cited as *Jus Ecclesiasticum*).

Gonzalez-Tellez (ca. 1673) stated that episcopal consecrations followed the lines of the reservation of bishoprics to papal jurisdiction[16] for the appointment of their incumbents. F. Schmier (1680-1728) testified that episcopal consecration, according to the common teaching of his times, was reserved to the Pope in such a manner that only he could delegate the rightful use of this power to others.[17] In quoting from these two canonists, Benedict XIV not only accepted their opinion in the matter, but cited historical proof to strengthen their and his own position.[18] To avoid complications of one kind or another, the Supreme Pontiff conceded to all those who were promoted to the episcopacy the faculty of receiving consecration from any bishop they might choose, as long as the consecrator was in communion with the Holy See.[19]

---

[16] *Commentaria Perpetua in Singulos Textus Quinque Librorum Decretalium Gregorii IX* (5 vols., in 4, Venetiis, 1699), Lib. I, tit. 11, n. 7 (hereafter cited as *Commentaria*): "Hodie tamen consecratio Episcoporum non ex Metropolitani iussu, sed Pontificis mandato fit; cum enim Romanus Pontifex sibi reservasset Cathedralium Ecclesiarum collationem, similiter ab eius libito pendere voluit Episcoporum consecrationem."

[17] *Jurisprudentia canonico civilis seu ius canonicum universum iuxta quinque libros Decretalium* (Salisburgi, 1716), Lib. I, tract. 3, cap. 1, n. 569 (hereafter cited as *Jurisprudentia*): "Moderno iure consecratio Episcoporum et Archiepiscoporum Summo Pontifici reservata est; et ab eo specialiter delegandam esse, communiter dicitur."

[18] Ep. "*In postremo,*" 20 oct. 1756, § 15: "...in eumdem Romanum Pontificem quoque recidit ius consecrandi Episcopos, vel constituendi delegatos ad consecrationem peragendam; etsi superioribus sæculis Suffraganeorum consecratio esset Metropolitæ reservata, nec manus in ea apponeret Summus Pontifex, præterquam si quandoque Metropolita iniuste Suffraganeum consecrare abnueret, veluti noscitur ex *Rhemensi historia* Frodoardi, atque etiam ex *Annalibus* Cardinalis Baronii ad annum Christi 885, ubi cum Pontificem Stephanum VI appellasset electus ad Episcopatum Lingonensem, retulissetque, Lugdunensem Archiepiscopum Metropolitam suum detrectare, ipsi consecrationis munus impertiri, præmissis iteratis monitionibus, ut imploratam Consecrationem perageret, ipsoque Archiepiscopo in sua contumacia obfirmato, Pontifex, usus competenti sibi in universam Ecclesiam auctoritate, in Episcopum eumdem consecravit."—*Fontes*, n. 442.

[19] Ep. "*In postremo,*" 20 oct. 1756, § 16: "Verum tot tantæque excitatæ expostulationes, et querelæ, non solum propter incommoda, sed et ob sumptus necessario subeundos, si Suffraganeo adeundus fuisset suus

Upon asking by whom a bishop was to be consecrated, Schmalzgrueber answered by referring to the traditional law that the consecration be performed by the metropolitan with two of his comprovincial bishops, or by three bishops deputed to consecrate through a mandate issued by the metropolitan. However, when summarizing the law even of his time (early 18th century), Schmalzgrueber stated that the right of consecration was reserved to the Apostolic See in such a manner that, without a special mandate, bishops who were inferior to the metropolitan could not rightfully confer the consecration unless custom allowed them to act as consecrators.[20]

Article 4. Listing of Other Powers Lost by Metropolitans

Hinschius (1835-1898) contented himself by stating that the metropolitans retained for the most part that position which had been guaranteed to them by the decretals save for the loss of the right of episcopal confirmation and consecration.[21] Wernz (1842-1914), however, specified some of the other rights which metropolitans lost after the Council of Trent.[22] According to his opinion metropolitans no longer had the power: to demand the promise of canonical obedience from their suffragans;[23] to insist that suffragans visit the metropolitan church at stated times even outside the time of the celebration of the provincial council;[24] to judge the criminal and contentious trials involving suffra-

---

Metropolita, ut consecraretur, vel Metropolitæ Suffraganeus per ipsum consecrandus, ut quum Nos nullis licet Nostris suffragantibus meritis, ad Summum Pontificatum fuimus evecti, restitutam invenerimus veterem formulam, iuxta quam, uti prædictum est, Mandatum *de consecrando* ad eum dirigitur Episcopum, quem sibi consecrandus elegit." — *Fontes*, n. 442.

[20] *Jus Ecclesiasticum*, Lib. I, tit. 6, n. 8, q. 78.

[21] *Kirchenrecht*, II, 17.

[22] *Ius Decretalium*, II, 850-852.

[23] C. 13, X, *de maioritate et obedientia*, I, 33.

[24] C. 8 of the XIII Council of Toledo (683); c. 6, X, *de temporibus ordinationum et qualitate ordinandorum*, I, 11; Conc. Trident., sess. XXIV, *de ref.*, c. 2: "Nec episcopi comprovinciales prætextu cujuslibet

gans with their own subjects or with other bishops during the provincial council;[25] to grant their suffragans *litteræ formatæ* and permission to leave their diocese for purposes of travel;[26] to give his consent in the alienation of ecclesiastical property administered by the suffragans;[27] to order, at least indirectly, the liturgy and the celebration of feasts within the entire ecclesiastical province;[28] and, finally, to administer any diocese of his province during the vacancy of the episcopal see.[29]

Section C

Rights of Metropolitans over Suffragans

Article 1. Convocation and Direction of Provincial Councils

Among the rights retained by the metropolitans was that of holding and directing provincial councils. The Council of Trent not only recognized this right, but made it a duty incumbent upon them to convoke such councils at least once

---

consuetudinis ad metropolitanam ecclesiam in posterum accedere inviti compellantur." — Schroeder, *Canons and Decrees*, p. 463; pp. 192-193. Cf. S. C. C., in *Surrentina*, 23 mart. 1697 — Pallottini, *Collectio omnium Conclusionum et Resolutionum quæ apud Sacram Congregationem Cardinalium S. Concilii Tridentini Interpretum prodierunt ab eius institutione anno MDLXIV ad annum MDCCCLX, distinctis titulis alphabetico ordine per materias digestas* (18 vols., Romæ: Typis S. Congregationis De Propaganda Fide, 1868-1895), II, 397 (hereafter cited as Pallottini); Ferraris, *Prompta Bibliotheca Canonica, Iuridica, Moralis, Theologica, nec non Ascetica, Polemica, Rubricistica, Historica* (9 vols., Romæ, 1885-1899 [Vol. IX prepared by I. Bucceroni]), I, v. *archiepiscopus*, art. 2, n. 30 (hereafter cited as *Prompta Bibliotheca*); Bouix, *De Episcopo*, I, 464-466.

[25] Cc. 14, 15, 17, 20 of the Council of Antioch (341); c. 17 of the V Council of Arles (549); c. 12 of the XIII Council of Toledo (683).

[26] C. 11 of the Council of Antioch (341).

[27] C. 12 of the Council of Epaon (517); c. 7 of the XI Council of Toledo (655).

[28] C. 1 of the Council of Gerona (517); c. 27 of the Council of Epaon (517); c. 3 of the XI Council of Toledo (675).

[29] C. 25 of the Council of Chalcedon (451); Thomassinus, *Ecclesiæ Disciplina*, Pars II, Lib. II, c. 9, n. 8; Pars III, Lib. II, c. 51, n. 11.

every three years.[30] Though such was the demand of the Church's universal law, these councils were hardly ever held during the three centuries following the Council of Trent. No provincial councils were held in France, Germany and Spain. Even Italy was remiss in this regard, the only exceptions appearing in the province of Milan during the time of St. Charles Borromeo (1563-1584), and in the province of Beneventum under the rule of Cardinal Orsini (1686-1724).[31]

The situation was so bad that canonists could not but report on the general desuetude of the canon which had been so hopefully enacted by the Council of Trent.[32] It is difficult to determine the exact reasons for the neglect, but these could be enumerated among the causes: (a) the obstacles placed by civil rulers in certain regions to the summoning of bishops to councils; (b) the dissensions which arose between metropolitans, bishops and chapters; and (c) the negligence of bishops concerning the fulfillment of the conciliar decrees.[33] Whatever the reasons may have been, the law of the Council of Trent still held until the publication of the Code.

---

[30] Sess. XXIV, *de ref.*, c. 2: "Provincialia concilia, sicubi omissa sunt pro moderandis moribus, corrigendis excessibus, controversiis componendis, aliisque ex sacris canonibus permissis renoventur. Quare metropolitani per se ipsos, seu, illis legitime impeditis, coepiscopus antiquior, intra annum ad minus a fine præsentis concilii, et deinde quolibet saltem triennio post octavam Paschæ Resurrectionis Domini nostri Jesu Christi, seu alio commodiori tempore pro more provinciæ, non prætermittat synodum in provincia sua cogere, quo episcopi omnes et alii, qui de jure vel consuetudine interesse debent, exceptis iis, quibus cum imminenti periculo transfretandum esset, convenire, omnino teneantur." — Schroeder, *Canons and Decrees*, pp. 462-463; p. 192. Compare with c. 6 of the IV Lateran Council (1215); c. 25, X, *de accusationibus, inquisitionibus et denunciationibus*, V, 1; Hinschius, *Kirchenrecht*, II, 18; Wernz, *Ius Decretalium*, II, 852.

[31] Petra, *Commentaria ad Constitutiones Apostolicas seu Bullas Singulas Summorum Pontificum* (5 vols. in 2, Venetiis, 1729), in *Constitutione unica Honorii II*, Sectio I, n. 14, p. 277 (hereafter cited as *Commentaria*); Icard, *Prælectiones*, I, 400-401.

[32] Icard, *Prælectiones*, I, 401.

[33] *Loc. cit.*

Within the past century the conciliar institute took on practical significance again. Councils began to be held in a number of countries, so that the law became a part of the *vigens disciplina Ecclesiæ*.[34] Yet the re-birth of the law was none too secure. Icard (1805-1893) insisted that all Catholics were expected to esteem the law which demanded the holding of provincial synods as most useful for the renewal of discipline and for the advancement of the clergy. Yet he also stated that it was left to the prudence of the metropolitan together with his co-bishops to call a provincial council, according to the mind of the Church and the ruling of the Council of Trent, whenever he judged that such a convocation was for the good of the province. Since the law of the Council of Trent was not observed in the last century as completely as it could have been, metropolitans were requested by the Popes, lest discipline suffer harm because of the situation, to make known the reason of the omission of the conciliar celebration to the Roman Pontiff, and to submit to the Pope's judgment the reasonableness of their action in their report on the condition of their churches.[35] This situation remained unchanged until the publication of the Code.

Article 2. Provincial Visitation

The right of provincial visitation on the part of the metropolitans was retained by the Council of Trent. Yet this right could be exercised by them only upon the fulfillment of two conditions. The first condition, which required the metropolitan to visit his own diocese entirely before setting out upon the visitation of the province, was a carryover from Decretal Law.[36] The other condition was placed by the Council itself. The metropolitan could not make the

---

[34] Hinschius, *Kirchenrecht*, II, 18.

[35] *Prælectiones*, I, 401.

[36] C. 1, *de censibus, exactionibus et procurationibus*, III, 20, in VI°; cc. 14, 22, 25, X, *de censibus, exactionibus et procurationibus*, III, 39.

visitation without the consent of the provincial council upon its approval of the reason for the visitation.[37]

Connected with the right of visitation, according to the law of the Decretals, was the power of the metropolitan to punish his suffragan bishops should they prove disobedient to him. This right was not approved by the Council of Trent; in fact, the law regarding this earlier right was changed completely. The metropolitan power of jurisdiction was curtailed by the reservation to the Pope of all major criminal cases in which bishops were involved. The Pope could delegate the cognizance regarding such causes not only to metropolitans but to bishops as well. The definitive sentence, however, was reserved to the Supreme Pontiff in every case.[38] The power to punish minor crimes committed by suffragan bishops was still left to the decision of the provincial council.[39] Even though metropolitans could no longer suspend or excommunicate any of their suffra-

---

[37] Sess. XXIV, *de ref.*, c. 3: "...metropolitani...propriam diœcesim per se ipsos aut, si legitime impediti fuerint, per suum generalem vicarium aut visitatorem, si quotannis totam propter ejus latitudinem visitare non poterunt, saltem majorem ejus partem, ita tamen, ut tota biennio per se vel visitatores suos compleatur, visitare non prætermittant. A metropolitanis vero, etiam post plene visitatam propriam diœcesim, non visitentur cathedrales ecclesiæ, neque diœceses suorum comprovincialium, nisi causa cognita et probata in concilio provinciali." — Schroeder, *Canons and Decrees*, p. 463; p. 193; Reiffenstuel, *Jus Canonicum*, Lib. I, tit. 31, n. 47; Hinschius, *Kirchenrecht*, II, 18; Wernz, *Ius Decretalium*, II, 852.

[38] Sess. XXIV, *de ref.*, c. 5: "Causæ criminales graviores contra episcopos, etiam hæresis, quod absit, quæ depositione aut privatione dignæ sunt, ab ipso tantum summo Romano pontifice cognoscantur et terminentur. Quod si ejusmodi sit causa, quæ necessario extra Romanam curiam sit committenda, nemini prorsus ea committatur, nisi metropolitanis aut episcopis a beatissimo Papa eligendis. Hæc vero commissio et specialis sit et manu ipsius sanctissimi pontificis signata, nec unquam plus his tribuat, quam ut solam facti instructionem sumant processumque conficiant, quem statim ad Romanum pontificem transmittant, reservata eidem Sanctissimo sententia definitiva." — Schroeder, *Canons and Decrees*, p. 466; p. 196.

[39] Sess. XXIV, *de ref.*, c. 5: "Minores vero criminales causæ episcoporum in concilio tantum provinciali cognoscantur et terminentur, vel a deputandis per concilium provinciale." — Schroeder, *Canons and Decrees*, p. 466; p. 196.

gans, it was still possible for them to declare or publicize a censure against any of them once suspension or excommunication was incurred *ipso iure* by any one of them. This was a remnant of Decretal Law.[40]

Some authors[41] held that the Council of Trent did not change the former law concerning the penal power of metropolitans over their suffragans.[42] But such an opinion cannot be held, for it militates against the meaning of c. 5 of Sess. XXIV of the Tridentine Council. Since censures could not be inflicted unless a *cognitio iudicialis* of the crime committed by the bishop preceded the metropolitan action, it was altogether impossible for metropolitans to inflict censures. Their hands were tied with regard to major crimes, because the *cognitio iudicialis* of such was reserved to the Supreme Pontiff, and so also with regard to minor crimes, for the *cognitio iudicialis* of these was reserved to the provincial council. The only conclusion which can be drawn from this reasoning is that after the Council of Trent metropolitans could not inflict any censures on their suffragans.[43]

Since very few provincial councils were held during the three centuries following the Council of Trent, there was little occasion for any problem concerning the exercise of penal jurisdiction over the minor criminal causes of suffragans which demanded a concurrent action of the metropolitan with that of the provincial council. Nevertheless, the problem could have arisen in the middle of the last century

---

[40] C. 1, *de pœnis*, V, 9, in VI°; Kober, *Kirchenbann*, p. 70.

[41] Ferraris, *Prompta Bibliotheca*, I, v. *archiepiscopus*, art. 1, n. 19; Petra, *Commentaria*, I, Const. II Leonis IX, sect. 5, nn. 60-71; Barbosa, *Pastoralis Sollicitudinis, sive de Officio et Potestate Episcopi Tripartita Descriptio* (Lugduni, 1656), Lib. I, tit. 4, n. 11 (hereafter cited as *De Officio et Potestate Episcopi*); De Luca, *Theatrum Veritatis et Iustitiæ sive Decisivi Discursus ad Veritatem Editi in Forensibus Controversiis, Canonicis, et Civilibus* (16 vols. in 8, Coloniæ Agrippinæ: apud Henricum Rommerskirchen, 1706), VIII, 136 (hereafter cited as *Theatrum*).

[42] C. 52, X, *de sententia excommunicationis*, V, 39; c. 1, *de officio ordinarii*, I, 16, in VI°.

[43] Wernz, *Ius Decretalium*, II, 853-854; Bouix, *De Episcopo*, I, 461-463, 469-471, 472-473; Kober, *Kirchenbann*, p. 70; Hinschius, *Kirchenrecht*, II, 19; Schmier, *Jurisprudentia*, Lib. I, tract. 5, cap. 4, n. 2.

when provinical councils had a place in the existing discipline of the Church. As far as this situation was concerned, there would have been nothing contrary to law if metropolitans had renewed the exercise of their visitation rights, inasmuch as the factor of desuetude in this case did not imply an abrogation. The law concerning the visitation rights of metropolitans was retained by the Council of Trent for the express purpose of maintaining Church discipline. Desuetude created a custom to the contrary, but the custom was unlawful in that it infringed upon a law which the Church intended to maintain.[44] Nevertheless, even after the re-introduction of the celebration of provincial councils into Church life, a metropolitan could not inflict any censures in major or minor criminal cases of his suffragans. The only exception to this rule was the metropolitan's declaration of *ipso iure* incurred censures, which right of the metropolitan was mentioned above.

Since the Council of Trent made no mention of cases involving the vicar general and the official of a suffragan, the metropolitan could still proceed against them with suspension and excommunication without delegation from the Holy See and without conciliar concurrence, if either of them had not fulfilled such duties as were subject to the metropolitan's surveillance, or if one or the other directly violated the rights of the metropolitan. The metropolitan could not punish them, however, if their negligence was outside the scope of metropolitan vigilance, or if the rights they violated had no connection with the metropolitan power.[45]

---

[44] Hinschius, *Kirchenrecht*, II, 19; Schulte, *Kirchenrecht*, II, 207, n. 1.

[45] C. 1, *de officio ordinarii*, I, 16, in VI°; c. 1, *de officio vicarii*, I, 13, in VI°. The gloss to the words *rationabili causa* in the latter decretal reads as follows: "...aliter non debet ferri excommunicationis sententia. Quod de sententia excommunicationis cum medicinalis et potuit esse rationabilis causa, cuius officialis episcopi peccat in his quæ sunt iurisdictionis: quia idem est consistorium episcopi et sui officialis; tunc archiepiscopi eos sicut episcopi punire possunt.... Si vero officialis episcopi aliquid possideret vel faceret ut privatus: tunc archiepiscopus eum plus punire non posset, nisi sicut alios subditos episcoporum...."; Barbosa, *De Officio et Potestate Episcopi*, Lib. I, tit. 4, n. 11: "Causas autem rationabiles excommunicandi Vicarium recenset...quando Vicarius

Article 3. Supervision of Province

With regard to the right of supervision over the affairs of the province, the Tridentine Council declared that metropolitans had the right to care for the erection, continuation and direction of seminaries in the episcopal dioceses.[46] Although the metropolitan had the duty to rebuke the bishop sharply and to compel him to comply with the rulings of this law, he himself could also be rebuked and compelled by the provincial council to erect and maintain a diocesan seminary in his own diocese. The second part of this ruling had no practical significance, however, in view of the non-celebration of provincial councils in the post-Tridentine period. If on account of the lack of means not every diocese of the province could afford to build and maintain its own seminary, then the metropolitan in union with the two oldest suffragans had the right to combine several dioceses

---

impedit causam appellationis delatam ad Archiepiscopum, vel si deliquit circa officium commissum, si peccaret in iis, quæ sunt iurisdictionis, si uteretur iurisdictione Episcopi sui excommunicatur [Episcopi sui excommunicati?], si non servat Sedis Apost. privilegia, et fit criminosus, et incorrigibilis. . . . Verum propositio illa quod Archiepiscopus fit Iudex Vicariorum generalium suorum Suffraganeorum, quando delinquunt in officio, non est indistincte accipienda, sed distinguendi sunt duo casus. . . prior est quando Vicarius ita delinquit in officio ut offendat iurisdictionem Metropolitani, veluti si nolit deferre appellationi ad eundem legitime emissæ, vel illius inhibitionem spernat, et tunc fatemur Archiepiscopum posse eum coercere censura ecclesiastica. . . . Alter est si deliqui [delinquit?] in officio præiudicando simpliciter partibus et iustitiæ, et hoc quidem casu nisi propter notorietatem, et gravitatem criminis facta sit devolutio, cognitio, et punitio pertinet ad ipsum Episcopum, qui habet facultatem a Iure, prout quivis alius Magistratus, coercendi Officialem suum appellatione remota. . . ."; Kober, *Kirchenbann*, p. 71; Hinschius, *Kirchenrecht*, II, 19; Wernz, *Ius Decretalium*, II, 854.

[46] Sess. XXIII, *de ref.*, c. 18: "Quod si cathedralium et aliarum majorum ecclesiarum prælati in hac seminarii erectione ejusque conservatione negligentes fuerint, ac suam portionem solvere detrectaverint, episcopum archiepiscopus, archiepiscopum et superiores synodus provincialis acriter corripere, eosque ad omnia supra dicta cogere debeat, et ut quam primum hoc sanctum et pium opus, ubicumque fieri poterit, promoveatur studiose curabit." — Schroeder, *Canons and Decrees*, pp. 448-449; pp. 177-178; Hinschius, *Kirchenrecht*, II, 19; Wernz, *Ius Decretalium*, II, 853; Bouix, *De Episcopo*, I, 468-469.

into a seminary district, and to provide each of these with a seminary, or to erect one institution of learning for the entire province. This right was not exclusive, for the provincial council was also competent in this matter.[47] Again, inasmuch as provincial councils were so rarely held, this right was left almost exclusively in the hands of the metropolitans until such time as these councils would be more frequently held. Both these rights concerning the diocesan seminaries implied new powers for the metropolitan, since this legislation was something altogether new in the Church.

Another right associated with the metropolitan's duty of supervision was that of enforcing the observance of the law of residence on the part of the bishops subject to him.[48] Any bishop who unlawfully absented himself for more than a year was subject to severer penalties than those pre-

---

[47] Sess. XXIII, *de ref.*, c. 18: "Si vero in aliqua provincia ecclesiæ tanta paupertate laborent, ut collegium in aliquibus erigi non possit, synodus provincialis, vel metropolitanus cum duobus antiquioribus suffraganeis, in ecclesia metropolitana vel alia provinciæ ecclesia commodiori unum aut plura collegia, prout opportunum judicabit, ex fructibus duarum aut plurium ecclesiarum, in quibus singulis collegium commode institui non potest, erigenda curabit, ubi pueri illarum ecclesiarum educentur." — Schroeder, *Canons and Decrees*, p. 449; p. 179; Hinschius, *Kirchenrecht*, II, 21.

[48] Sess. VI, *de ref.*, c. 1: "Si quis a...metropolitana seu cathedrali ecclesia, sibi quocumque titulo, causa, nomine seu jure commissa, quacumque ille dignitate, gradu et præeminentia præfulgeat, legitimo impedimento seu justis et rationabilibus causis cessantibus, sex mensibus continuis extra suam diœcesim morando abfuerit, quartæ partis fructuum unius anni, fabricæ ecclesiæ et pauperibus loci per superiorem ecclesiasticum applicandorum, pœnam ipso jure incurrat. Quod si per alios sex menses in hujusmodi absentia perseveraverit, aliam quartam partem fructuum similiter applicandam eo ipso amittat. Crescente vero contumacia, ut severiori sacrorum canonum censuræ subjiciatur, metropolitanus suffraganeos episcopos absentes, metropolitanum vero absentem suffraganeus episcopus antiquior residens sub pœna interdicti ingressus ecclesiæ eo ipso incurrenda infra tres menses per litteras seu nuncium Romano pontifici denunciare teneatur, qui in ipsos absentes, prout cujusque major aut minor contumacia exegerit, suæ supremæ Sedis auctoritate animadvertere et ecclesiis ipsis de pastoribus utilioribus providere poterit, sicut in Domino noverit salubriter expedire." — Schroeder, *Canons and Decrees*, pp. 325- 326; pp. 47-48; Hinschius, *Kirchenrecht*, II, 19; Wernz, *Ius Decretalium*, 852-853; Bouix, *De Episcopo*, I, 470.

scribed in the law, once the metropolitan denounced his contumacious suffragan to the Roman Pontiff. Yet the right of the metropolitan in this regard was not absolute, for the Fathers of the Council made it clear that, should the metropolitan absent himself unlawfully for more than a year, this was to be reported to the Pope by the oldest of the resident suffragan bishops. Whenever Christian charity, urgent necessity, due obedience, and manifest advantage to the Church or commonwealth required or demanded that ecclesiastics be absent at times, the Council of Trent decreed that their lawful absence had to be approved in writing by the Roman Pontiff, or by the metropolitan, or, in his absence, by the oldest resident suffragan bishop, whose duty it was to approve the absence of the metropolitan.[49] This right of the senior suffragan bishop to approve the legitimate absences of the comprovincial bishops in the absence of the metropolitan was reserved to the Apostolic See at a later date.[50]

Certain authors attempted to extend the right of metropolitan supervision to every imaginable affair which concerned suffragan bishops and their dioceses. Barbosa (1589-1649) stated that metropolitans had the right to interdict preaching to some clerics throughout the province,[51] as also the right to command all vagabond and apostate monks and regulars to return to their monasteries after he had issued a previous but inefficacious warning to the suffragan bishops and superiors regular to recall them.[52]

---

[49] Sess. XXIII, *de ref.*, c. 1: "Nam cum Christiana caritas, urgens necessitas, debita obedientia ac evidens ecclesiæ vel reipublicæ utilitas aliquos nonnumquam abesse postulent et exigant, decernit eadem sacrosancta synodus, has legitimæ absentiæ causas a beatissimo Romano pontifice, aut metropolitano vel, eo absente, suffraganeo episcopo antiquiori residente, qui idem metropolitani absentiam probare debebit, in scriptis esse approbandas...." — Schroeder, *Canons and Decrees*, pp. 436-437; pp. 164-165.

[50] Urbanus VIII, const. "*Sancta Synodus*," 12 dec. 1634, § 7 — *Fontes*, n. 215; Benedictus XIV, const. "*Ad universæ*," 3 sept. 1746, § 13 — *Fontes*, n. 371; Wernz, *Ius Decretalium*, II, 854.

[51] *De Officio et Potestate Episcopi*, Lib. I, tit. 4, n. 27; cf. c. 11, X, *de privilegiis*, V, 33.

[52] Barbosa, *loc. cit.*; cf. c. 7, X, *de officio iudicis ordinarii*, I, 37.

Ferraris (+ca. 1763) enumerated a long list of such affairs. This author declared that metropolitans had to enjoin their suffragans to observe the canons which concerned simony, and in the event of non-observance the former could inflict punishments upon the latter.[53] He likewise contended that metropolitans were in duty bound to compel the bishops to constitute rural archpresbyters,[54] that metropolitans had to fulfill the last wills of the subjects of their suffragans if the suffragans neglected to do this,[55] that metropolitans had the right to dispense the subjects of their suffragans from vows and oaths,[56] that they had power to exile delinquents from their own diocese in any and all the dioceses of their province,[57] and that they could commission persons throughout their province to gather alms for the maintenance fund *(fabrica)* of their metropolitan church.[58]

Other writers mentioned such rights as that of eradicating depraved morals *(pravæ consuetudines)*,[59] of instituting benefices throughout the province,[60] of watching that divine services in the cathedrals of their suffragans were celebrated after the manner observed in the metropolitan church,[61] as well as of insisting that the bishops of the province held their annual diocesan synods.[62] But the duty of metropolitan supervision cannot be so extended as to comprise all these cases, for none of these particular norms were intended to serve as general laws. All the cited decretals which permitted the infliction of censures in connection with the exercise of supervision were abrogated by

---

[53] *Prompta Bibliotheca,* I, v. *archiepiscopus,* art. I, n. 10; cf. c. 30, X, *de simonia,* V, 3.

[54] Ferraris, *ibid.,* n. 13; cf. c. 4, X, *de officio archipresbyteri,* I, 24.

[55] *Ibid.,* n. 29; cf. c. 11, X, *de officio iudicis ordinarii,* I, 31.

[56] *Ibid.,* n. 30.

[57] *Ibid.,* n. 41; cf. c. 2, X, *de arbitris,* I, 43; c. 11, X, *de privilegiis,* V, 33.

[58] *Ibid.,* n. 42; cf. c. 1, *de pœnitentiis et remissionibus,* V, 10, in VI°.

[59] C. 18, X, *de filiis presbyterorum ordinandis vel non,* I, 17.

[60] C. 3, X, *de institutionibus,* III, 7.

[61] C. 13, D. XII; cf. *supra,* p. 43, footnotes 82 and 83.

[62] Conc. Trident., sess. XXIV, *de ref.,* c. 2; cf. Schroeder, *Canons and Decrees,* p. 463; p. 193.

the Council of Trent, and thus every means of penal enforcement was lacking for metropolitans in their endeavor to effect the correction of these misdemeanors. The duty of observing in the cathedrals of the suffragans the metropolitan form of cathedral services was found to be altogether impracticable even before the Council of Trent. The metropolitan duty to enforce the celebration of the annual diocesan synods could be carried into effect very weakly, if at all, on the grounds simply of the Tridentine decrees.[63]

One may draw the conclusion that this long litany of applications as derived from the metropolitan right of supervision was mainly a matter of tradition, one author enumerating what he had taken from another. Schulte (1827-1914) put the matter in a very clear light when he remarked that metropolitans had the right and the duty to call in a suffragan to inform him that he had been remiss in his duties, to admonish him to correct his ways, and eventually to denounce him to the Pope. All this was already contained in the nature and the purpose of the metropolitan constitution, so that there was no need of the acknowledgment of the positive law to the same effect. So, too, with the duty on the part of the suffragan to cede this right entirely to his metropolitan.[64] Icard similarly stated that it was the office of the metropolitan to be vigilant lest his suffragans fail in their duties. If the metropolitan knew that some of the suffragans did not reside in their dioceses, according to the ruling of the law, or that they neglected the rule of their dioceses *(cura regiminis)*, or that they offended in some way against the sacredness of the episcopal order, the metropolitan was to admonish his suffragans with fraternal solicitude.[65]

---

[63] Sess. XXIV, *de ref.*, c. 2: "Synodi quoque diœcesanæ quotannis celebrentur....Quod si in his tam metropolitani quam episcopi et alii supra scripti negligentes fuerint, pœnas sacris canonibus sancitas incurrant." — Schroeder, *Canons and Decrees*, p. 463, p. 193; Hinschius, *Kirchenrecht*, II, 19.

[64] *Kirchenrecht*, II, 367.

[65] *Prælectiones*, I, 237.

Article 4. Rights of Instance

The Council of Trent did not at all mention the exercise of metropolitan jurisdiction in the first instance in contentious trials when these concerned suffragan bishops, either when one of them was called to trial by another suffragan or by any other plaintiff, or when one of them accused his own subject before a court. Because of this, some doubts have been raised with regard to this power. Many authors, basing their contention on the fact that c. 5, *de ref.*, of Sess. XXIV of the Tridentine Council reserved criminal trials only, acknowledged that metropolitans could continue to exercise this right. This specification of criminal trials to the utter omission of any mention regarding contentious trials inclined the authors to hold that metropolitans had a *iurisdictio ordinaria* over simple bishops.[66]

But this opinion, notwithstanding the great array of authors defending it either whole-heartedly or perhaps only hesitatingly, had no foundation in the previous law of the Church. Nowhere did the earlier law state that the metropolitan alone, without the concurrence of the provincial councils, was competent to decide the contentious causes in-

[66] Reiffenstuel, *Ius Canonicum*, Lib. I, tit. 31, n. 38: "An archiepiscopus de facto cognoscat de causibus civilibus suffraganei, per proprium subditum coram eo conventi? Dicitur notanter, circa causas horum criminales. Nam loquendo de causis civilibus, adhuc de facto metropolitanus cognoscit de ipsis, quando subditus suffraganei coram ipso convenit proprium episcopum in causa aliqua mere civili. Ratio est, quia circa causas civiles nihil reperitur immutatum in concilio Tridentino, sicque remanet jus antiquum in suo vigore....Atqui de jure antiquo generale est, quod actor debeat sequi forum rei, et hunc convenire coram judice suo ordinario; qualis respectu episcopi est archiepiscopus." Ferraris, *Prompta Bibliotheca*, I, v. *archiepiscopus*, art. I, n. 7: "Est enim archiepiscopus judex ordinarius et competens omnium episcoporum suæ provinciæ, unde quicunque habens actionem contra episcopum, potest illum convenire coram archiepiscopo." Gonzalez-Tellez, *Commentaria*, ad c. 9, X, *de officio iudicis ordinarii*, I, 31: "Archiepiscopi etiam in proprios suffraganeos non inferiorem obtinent auctoritatem; habent enim ordinariam iurisdictionem in Episcopos ipsius provinciæ....Hodie civiles tantum causas definire valent." Barbosa, *De Officio et Potestate Episcopi*, Lib. I, tit. 4, n. 13: "Unde pro declaratione materiæ adverto primo Archiepiscopum de civilibus causis tantum Suffraganeorum cognoscere posse....Archiepiscopus indifferenter cognoscit de causa civili,

volving suffragan bishops. Since the earlier law was not corrected by the Council of Trent except in the reservation of major criminal causes to the Roman Pontiff, it must be concluded that the provincial council was still the competent judge in deciding all minor contentious causes dealing with comprovincial bishops. But by a gradual change of ecclesiastical discipline even these contentious causes of bishops came to be referred in their first instance to the Apostolic See, or they were referred to the secular forum if the causes were purely secular according to concessions made to certain countries in concordats, or if special permission was granted in individual cases.[67]

A few canonists who held the opinion that metropolitans had the right of taking judicial cognizance in first instance in these contentious trials nevertheless considered that it was not expedient for them to carry this right into practice without consulting the Sacred Congregation beforehand.[68]

---

etiamsi subditus Episcopi conveniat Episcopum...secus tamen dicit si Episcopus ageret contra sum subditum, quia non decet, ut Episcopus conveniat eum coram Episcopo, cum Archiepiscopus non fit iudex subditorum Episcopi, neque Episcopus debeat esse iudex in causa propria, et ideo eligi debent arbitri auctoritate iuris, et a sententia arbitrorum appellatur ad Papam omisso medio." Barbosa also makes this same distinction in his *Iuris Ecclesiastici Universi Libri Tres* (3 vols., Lugduni, 1650), Lib. I, tit. 7, n. 46, and Engel (*Collegium Universi Juris Canonici* [9. ed., Beneventi, 1760], Lib. I, tit. 32, n. 28 [hereafter cited as *Collegium*]) stated: "Concilium autem Trident. nec verbo causarum civilium exceptionem fecit; cum ergo tantum causarum criminalium meminerit, potius infertur, quod exceptio de causis criminalibus firmet regulam in causis civilibus non exceptis: neque enim plus de iure veteri censetur correctum, quam expressum." Cf. Schmier, *Jurisprudentia*, Lib. I, tract. 5, cap. 4, n. 28; Phillips, *Kirchenrecht*, VI, 828; Icard, *Prælectiones*, I, 237. Hinschius (*Kirchenrecht*, II, 20) is rather hesitant in his opinion.

[67] S. C. S. Off., 23 ian. 1886 in *Acta Sanctæ Sedis* (41 vols., Romæ, 1865-1908), XVIII (1886), 416 (hereafter cited as *ASS*); Bouix, *De Episcopo*, I, 457-460; Wernz, *Ius Decretalium*, II, 853, footnote 154.

[68] Barbosa was hesitant in his opinion, for he had found a Rescript to the Bishop of Reggio Calabria from the Sacred Congregation of Bishops and Regulars dated the 31st of May, 1588, in which it was stated that archbishops could not act as judges in contentious trials which were instituted against suffragan bishops. Cf. *Iuris Ecclesiastici Universi Libri Tres*, Lib. I, tit. 7, n. 46. Both Engel and Reiffenstuel denied the existence of this rescript. Cf. also Petra, *Commentaria* in II Const.

Hinschius insisted on the correctness of the opinion that metropolitans had the right of taking judicial cognizance in first instance in these contentious trials, since the Decretals expressly granted the power of penal jurisdiction to metropolitans.[69] He argued that, since both the contentious and the criminal trials of bishops were formerly decided by the provincial council, and since the Tridentine Council, and for that matter any other source of legislation, did not reserve the episcopal contentious trial to the Pope, it had to be concluded that metropolitans still possessed jurisdiction in this form of trial.[70] The author closed his argument with the statement that this controversy had no practical significance, since practically everywhere the jurisdiction over the civil trials of bishops was exercised by secular courts.[71] Notwithstanding the opinions of these canonists, the policy of the Church in the contentious trials of bishops created the new discipline of reserving these trials to the Apostolic See. As was stated above, all secular matters were left to the secular courts either by the provision of a concordat or by the express permission of the Holy See.[72]

A right which metropolitans did enjoy after the Council of Trent, and which cannot be contested, was that of changing or confirming the judicial sentences given by suffragans in contentious and criminal causes heard and adjudicated in the first instance.[73] This right could be employed only after the judicial sentence was given in the first instance by the suffragans acting as ordinaries, and only after an appeal was sent to the metropolitan tribunal.[74] Metropoli-

---

Leonis IX, I, sec. V, 158-159; De Luca, *Theatrum*, Discursus LII, *de Jurisdictione;* Ferraris, *Prompta Bibliotheca*, I, v. *archiepiscopus*, art. 1, n. 19.

[69] *Kirchenrecht*, II, 20; cf. c. 52, X, *de sententia excommunicationis*, V, 39; c. 1, *de officio ordinarii*, I, 16, in VI°.

[70] *Loc. cit.;* c. 3, C. VI, q. 4; c. 46, C. XI, q. 1.

[71] *Loc. cit.*

[72] *Supra*, p. 131.

[73] Wernz, *Ius Decretalium*, II, 853.

[74] C. 11, X, *de officio iudicis ordinarii*, I, 31; c. 3, *de appellationibus*, II, 15, in VI°; Benedictus XIV, const. "*Ad militantis*," 30 mart. 1742, § 42 — *Fontes*, n. 326.

tans could also admit a recourse or complaint against the extra-judicial orders given by suffragans, but ordinarily it was accepted with a merely non-suspensive effect.[75] This right was brought under this heading for the sake of showing the metropolitan power over suffragans; it will be taken up again at greater length under the heading of metropolitan rights over the subjects of suffragan bishops.

Article 5. Right of Devolution

With regard to the right deriving through devolution, the Decretal Law held good in all those cases which involved the bestowal of offices.[76] The Council of Trent added two rules. In case a cathedral chapter did not appoint one or more qualified economes for the administration of the diocesan temporalities during the vacancy of a see, the choice of economes devolved to the metropolitan. If the cathedral chapter of a vacant see did not nominate a qualified person as vicar-capitular within eight days, his appointment also devolved to the metropolitan.[77] The Council of Trent by means of this decree abolished the law that the chapter was to administer the diocese *in corpore* during the vacancy of

---

[75] Concilium Provinciæ Remensis (1849), tit. XVII, cap. 2 — *Acta et Decreta Sacrorum Conciliorum Recentiorum, Collectio Lacensis* (7 vols., Friburgi Brisgoviæ: Herder, 1870-1890), IV, 145 (hereafter cited *Coll. Lac.*).

[76] *Supra*, pp. 102-103; Wernz, *Ius Decretalium*, II, 852, footnote 147; Hinschius, *Kirchenrecht*, II, 20; Icard, *Prælectiones*, I, 238-239.

[77] Sess. XXIV, *de ref.*, c. 16: "Capitulum sede vacante, ubi fructuum percipiendorum ei munus incumbit, œconomum unum vel plures fideles ac diligentes decernat, qui rerum ecclesiasticarum et proventuum curam gerant, quorum rationem ei, ad quem pertinebit, sint reddituri. Item officialem seu vicarium infra octo dies post mortem episcopi constituere, vel existentem confirmare omnino teneatur, qui saltem in jure canonico sit doctor vel licentiatus, vel alias, quantum fieri poterit, idoneus. Si secus factum fuerit, ad metropolitanum deputatio hujusmodi devolvatur. Et si ecclesia ipsa metropolitana fuerit aut exempta, capitulumque, ut præfertur, negligens fuerit, tunc antiquior episcopus ex suffraganeis in metropolitana, et propinquior episcopus in exempta œconomum et vicarium idoneos possit constituere." — Schroeder, *Canons and Decrees*, p. 475; p. 206; Bouix, *De Episcopo*, I, 470, 476-477; Hinschius, *Kirchenrecht*, II, 20; Wernz, *Ius Decretalium*, II, 852.

a see, which ruling was possibly still in force until that time.[78] Wernz added another case of devolved right to those already mentioned: the right of instituting those who had been presented by patrons in parochial churches when the suffragans, through negligence, did not execute the canonical institution within two months.[79] But the right of supplying the negligence of suffragans with regard to cases not expressed in law was not to be extended further.[80]

SECTION D

RIGHTS OF METROPOLITANS OVER THE EXEMPT

Article 1. The Office of Preaching in the Diocese

As delegates of the Apostolic See, metropolitans had to watch that abbots and regular prelates *nullius* took care of the office of preacher in the parochial churches subject to their monasteries,[81] and to compel them, if necessary, to the fulfillment of the law with regard to preaching.

Article 2. The Convocation of Congregations

Again, as delegates of the Holy See they were to convoke the congregations or general chapters which were to be

---

[78] C. 4, *de supplenda negligentia prælatorum*, I, 8, in VI°; *supra*, p. 103; Hinschius, *Kirchenrecht*, II, 20, footnote 6.

[79] *Ius Decretalium*, II, 852; Pius V, const. "*In conferendis*," 18 mart. 1567, § 7 — *Fontes*, n. 119.

[80] Bouix, *De Episcopo*, I, 471; Phillips, *Kirchenrecht*, VI, 833.

[81] Sess. V, *de ref.*, c. 2: "Si quæ vero parochiales ecclesiæ reperiantur subjectæ monasteriis in nulla diœcesi exsistentibus, si abbates et regulares prælati in prædictis negligentes fuerint, a metropolitanis, in quorum provinciis diœceses ipsæ sitæ sunt, tamquam quoad hoc Sedis Apostolicæ delegatis compellantur. Neque hujus decreti executionem consuetudo vel exemptio aut appellatio aut reclamatio sive recursus impedire valeat, quousque desuper a competenti judice, qui summarie et sola facti veritate inspecta procedat, cognitum et decisum fuerit." — Schroeder, *Canons and Decrees*, p. 306; p. 27; Wernz, *Ius Decretalium*, II, 856; Hinschius, *Kirchenrecht*, II, 21; Ferraris, *Prompta Bibliotheca*, I, v. *archiepiscopus*, art. I, n. 44.

attended by all such monasteries as were not subject to general chapters or to bishops, but which were governed under the protection and direction of the Apostolic See, if these monasteries neglected to call these congregations or general chapters every three years. If the superiors and visitors failed to make frequent visitations of these monasteries, the metropolitan was to demand that they do so under the sanction that in case of neglect the visitation of all their monasteries was to devolve to the bishops in whose diocese the aforesaid monasteries were situated.[82]

SECTION E

RIGHTS OF METROPOLITANS OVER THE SUBJECTS OF SUFFRAGANS

Article 1. Second Instance

With reference to the rights over the subjects of suffragan bishops, it may be said that metropolitans still had a number of rights over all the subjects of their province.[83]

They remained competent judges in all cases which the subjects of their comprovincial bishops brought to them in second instance,[84] that is to say, which were brought to

[82] Sess. XXV, *de regularibus et monialibus*, c. 8: "Quod si in his negligentes fuerint, liceat metropolitano, in cujus provincia prædicta monasteria sunt, tamquam Sedis Apostolicæ delegato, eos pro prædictis causis convocare.... Quod si etiam metropolitano instante prædicta [visitationem et convocationem congregationum] exsequi non curaverint, episcopis, in quorum diœcesibus loca prædicta sita sunt, tamquam Sedis Apostolicæ delegatis subdantur." — Schroeder, *Canons and Decrees*, pp. 490-491; pp. 222-223; Hinschius, *Kirchenrecht*, II, 21; Wernz, *Ius Decretalium*, II, 856.

[83] Wernz, *Ius Decretalium*, II, 854-856; Phillips, *Kirchenrecht*, VI, 829; Hinschius, *Kirchenrecht*, II, 20.

[84] C. 1, X, *de officio legati*, I, 30; c. 11, X, *de officio iudicis ordinarii*, I, 31; c. 1, *de officio ordinarii*, I, 16, in VI°; Benedict XIV in his Constitution "*Ad militantis*," 30 mart. 1742, set certain limitations in the use of this right — *Fontes*, n. 326. Cf. c. 5, *de officio ordinarii*, I, 16, in VI°; c. 3, *de appellationibus*, II, 15, in VI°; Bouix, *De Episcopo*, I, 478-479.

their tribunals through a legitimate appeal from a sentence which was either really or equivalently definitive, but they could not accept any causes in the first instance even with the consent of the subjects' suffragans.[85] Nor could they remand to themselves the judicial cognizance of causes which were being adjudicated in the first instance before the tribunal of the suffragan, or impede the procedure in such causes, or admit an appeal from a merely interlocutory sentence.[86] But if the cause was not completed in the curia

---

[85] Fagnanus, *Commentaria in Quinque Libros Decretalium* (5 vols. in 3, Venetiis, 1661), in c. 18, X, *de foro competenti*, II, 2, nn. 29-37 (hereafter cited as *Commentaria*). The vicar general of the suffragan, if he proved delinquent in assuming metropolitan jurisdiction, or in discharging the duties of the office which was committed to him as vicar general, had to be judged in first instance by the metropolitan as his competent judge, and not by his own bishop. Cf. *supra*, pp. 123-124. Bouix, *De Episcopo*, I, 473-474; Bouix, *Tractatus de Judiciis Ecclesiasticis* (3. ed., 2 vols., Parisiis, 1884), I, 448-449 (hereafter cited *De Judiciis Ecclesiasticis*); Ferraris, *Prompta Bibliotheca*, I, v. *archiepiscopus*, art. I, n. 22.

[86] Conc. Trident., sess. XIII, *de ref.*, c. 1: "Cum igitur rei criminum plerumque ad evitandas pœnas et episcoporum subterfugienda judicia querelas et gravamina simulent, et appellationis diffugio judicis processum impediant, ne remedio ad innocentiæ præsidium instituto ad iniquitatis defensionem abutantur, atque ut hujusmodi eorum calliditati et tergiversationi occurratur, ita statuit et decrevit: in causis visitationis et correctionis, sive habilitatis et inhabilitatis, necnon criminalibus, ab episcopo seu illius in spiritualibus vicario generali ante definitivam sententiam ab interlocutoria vel alio quocumque gravamine non appelletur, neque episcopus seu vicarius appellationi hujusmodi tamquam frivolæ deferre teneatur, sed ea, ac quacumque inhibitione ab appellationis judice emanata, necnon omni stylo et consuetudine etiam immemorabili contraria non obstante, ad ulteriora valeat procedere, nisi gravamen hujusmodi per definitivam sententiam reparari vel ab ipsa definitiva appellari non possit, quibus casibus sacrorum et antiquorum canonum statuta illibata persistant." — Schroeder, *Canons and Decrees*, p. 358; p. 82; Sess. XXIV, *de ref.*, c. 20: "Causæ omnes ad forum ecclesiasticum quomodolibet pertinentes, etiamsi beneficiales sint, in prima instantia coram ordinariis locorum dumtaxat cognoscantur...nec antea [biennium] aliis committantur, nec avocentur, neque appellationes ab eisdem interpositæ per superiores quoscumque recipiantur, earumve commissio aut inhibitio fiat, nisi a definitiva vel a definitivæ vim habente, et cujus gravamen per appellationem a definitiva reparari nequeat." — Schroeder, *Canons and Decrees*, pp. 479-480; p. 211.

of the suffragan within two years, either party was free to bring the cause to the tribunal of the metropolitan.[87]

The right of judicial cognizance in second instance had a great practical value in the period which followed the Council of Trent because of the rarity, if not the total absence, of the celebration of provincial councils. Somewhere in the middle of the last century, in spite of the limitations of ecclesiastical jurisdiction by secular legislation in many countries, this metropolitan jurisdictional right was very much in use wherever disciplinary jurisdiction over the clergy had been turned over to the Church entirely either explicitly or implicitly.[88]

Article 2. Selection of Arbiters and Delegates

Metropolitans could compel their suffragans to choose arbiters for the latter's subjects, if the suffragans had been rejected as suspect judges by their own subjects.[89]

Metropolitans were not prohibited from constituting the subjects of their suffragans as metropolitan delegates; but these subjects could not be obligated or compelled to accept the delegation either for the sake of executing the metropolitan sentences or for the sake of furnishing testimony in causes which had been brought to the metropolitan tribunal by an appeal in second instance.[90]

---

[87] Conc. Trident., sess. XXIV, *de ref.*, c. 20; "...atque omnino saltem infra biennium a die motæ litis terminentur; alioquin post id spatium liberum sit partibus vel alteri illarum judices superiores, alias tamen competentes, adire, qui causam in eo statu, quo fuerit, assumant et quam primum terminari curent...." — Schroeder, *Canons and Decrees*, p. 479; p. 211.

[88] Cf. Hinschius, *Kirchenrecht*, II, 20.

[89] C. 61, X, *de appellationibus, recusationibus, et relationibus*, II, 28; Bouix, *De Episcopo*, I, 474.

[90] C. 1, *de foro competenti*, II, 2, in VI°; c. 11, X, *de officio iudicis ordinarii*, I, 31.

Article 3. Visitation Rights

Once the reason for a provincial visitation was approved by the provincial councils, and when they had completed the visitation of their own dioceses, metropolitans could visit the dioceses of their suffragans[91] and, either personally or through delegates, preach the Word of God, hear the confessions of the subjects of their suffragans, absolve them even from censures reserved to the suffragans, enjoin salutary penances,[92] punish notorious crimes, leaving the others to the suffragans, inflict punishment befitting these crimes, demand the procuration for their decent sustenance,[93] and finally punish notorious injuries done to themselves, their messengers, or any member of their cortège, if the injury was perpetrated with a view to impeding their jurisdiction during the visitation; otherwise they could not do so unless custom granted them this added right and power.[94]

Article 4. Indulgences, Divine Services, Blessings

Metropolitans could grant a forty days' indulgence in their whole province even outside the time of the canonical visitation.[95]

They were able to celebrate divine services in their pontificals and to bless people with the solemn or simple blessing.[96] But they could not do so even in their own see

---

[91] C. 1, *de censibus, exactionibus et procurationibus*, III, 20, in VI°; Conc. Trident., sess. XXIV, *de ref.*, c. 3; *supra*, pp. 121-123; Reiffenstuel, *Ius Canonicum*, Lib. I, tit. 36, n. 47 in the discussion of the word *visitat;* Barbosa, *Iuris Ecclesiastici Universi Libri Tres*, Cap. VII, n. 89; Icard, *Prælectiones*, I, 239-240; Bouix, *De Episcopo*, I, 477-478.

[92] C. 5, *de censibus, exactionibus et procurationibus*, III, 20, in VI°.

[93] C. 16, X, *de præscriptionibus*, II, 26; c. 1, 5, *de censibus, exactionibus et procurationibus*, III, 20, in VI°.

[94] C. 1, *de pœnis*, V, 9, in VI°; cf. Ferraris, *Prompta Bibliotheca*, I, v. *archiepiscopus*, art. 1, n. 32; Bouix, *De Episcopo*, I, 497-498.

[95] C. 14, 15, X, *de pœnitentiis et remissionibus*, V, 38; c. 1, *de pœnitentiis et remissionibus*, V, 10, in VI°; Hinschius, *Kirchenrecht*, II, 21.

[96] C. 2, *de privilegiis et exactionibus privilegiatorum*, V, 7, in Clem.; Benedictus XIV, ep. "*Exemplis Prædecessorum,*" 19 mart. 1748 — *Fontes*, 386; *Bullarium Romanum Benedicti XIV* (3 vols. in 4, Prati, 1846), II, 340 (hereafter cited as *Bullarium*); Hinschius, *Kirchenrecht*, II, 21.

in the presence of the papal legate, unless the legate permitted it. The nuncio being present, the metropolitan had to ask him for permission, and the nuncio was expected to permit him to do so.[97] Regarding other pontifical functions, such as the conferral of orders in the diocese of his suffragans, the rulings of the Council of Trent declared that the metropolitan needed the permission of his suffragans.[98]

Section F

Delegation of Metropolitan Jurisdiction

Article 1. Limitation of Delegation

The power of delegating metropolitan jurisdiction to a representative was recognized because of the general principle that every *iudex ordinarius* could delegate his faculties. Delegation was possible for the exercise of the rights of judicial cognizance in second instance, and for the acts of supervision and the exercise of devolved rights as determined by the Council of Trent.[99] On the other hand, the metropolitan could not delegate anyone else for the holding of the provincial councils, for while he had the primary right to convoke them according to the express prescription of the Council of Trent, yet, if he was hindered, this right devolved to the oldest suffragan bishop.[100] With regard to the controverted metropolitan right to correct bishops, it hardly seems possible that the historical development of the

---

[97] Ferraris, *Prompta Bibliotheca*, I, v. *archiepiscopus*, art. I, nn. 47, 48; S. R. C., 9 mart. 1593 — *Decreta Authentica Congregationis Sacrorum Rituum ex Actis Eiusdem Collecta Cura et Studio Aloisii Gardellini* (3. ed. prepared by Capalti, 4 vols., Romæ: Typis S. Congregationis De Propaganda Fide, 1856-1858, Vol. I, 1856), I, pp. 15-16, n. 44.

[98] Sess. VI, *de ref.*, c. 5; Sess. XIV, *de ref.*, c. 2 — Schroeder, *Canons and Decrees*, pp. 327, 381-382, 50, 107.

[99] *Supra*, pp. 125-135; Hinschius, *Kirchenrecht*, II, 21-22.

[100] Sess. XXIV, *de ref.*, c. 2, cf. *supra*, pp. 120-121.

problem warranted the delegation of the right.[101] Finally, in cases involving suffragans, the possibility of delegating the imposition or the declaration of censures had been already practically excluded by the Decretal Law, for according to the decretals the *officialis* of the metropolitan could be empowered to impose these punishments only in the absence of the metropolitan.[102]

Article 2. Vicar General of the Metropolitan

Concerning the question whether the vicar general, who represented the metropolitan in matters of episcopal administration, had this power only in the archiepiscopal diocese, or whether he had it in the whole province, it must be said that his power was limited to the diocese of the metropolitan.[103] No special norms of law developed for the substitution of the metropolitan whenever he was impeded. The same rules which were employed when bishops were impeded applied also with reference to the metropolitan.[104]

Article 3. The Cathedral Chapter and the Vicar Capitular

According to Decretal Law, the cathedral chapter of the metropolitan church had control during the vacancy of the see, not only of the administration of the archiepiscopal diocese, but also of the province. One of the decretals granted the metropolitan chapter the right to confirm the election of suffragan bishops during the period of vacancy

---

[101] *Supra*, pp. 122-124. Hinschius (*Kirchenrecht*, II, 22) maintained that it was possible.

[102] C. 1, *de officio ordinarii*, I, 16, in VI°, gloss to the phrase *non attentent:* "licet de iure hoc possunt: quia licet sint minores ordine, sunt maiores iurisdictione: propter eos quorum vices gerunt...tamen inhonestum erat: et ideo Papa hoc prohibuit. Sed quid si excommunicet: nunquid tenet? videtur quod non: quia sufficit legislatorem aliquid prohibuisse: etiam si non adijicat." Cf. Kober, *Kirchenbann*, pp. 74-75; Hinschius, *Kirchenrecht*, II, 22.

[103] Hinschius, *Kirchenrecht*, II, 205-228.

[104] *Op. cit.*, II, 249-261.

in the metropolitan see.[105] But generally these rights were to be transferred to a determined vicar.

The *Antiquitates Magnæ Britanniæ* relate for the year of 1327 that the Prior of the Primatial and Metropolitan Chapter of Canterbury was such a vicar capitular.[106] This principle of appointing a vicar capitular during the vacancy of the metropolitan see was not put aside after the Council of Trent. The cathedral chapter could exercise metropolitan rights with modifications *sede vacante,* but according to the restriction of the Council of Trent it could exercise no rights once the vicar capitular was appointed.[107] The Sacred Congregation of the Council both in 1683 and in 1685 declared that the election of the vicar capitular for a vacant suffragan church which lacked a cathedral chapter devolved to the chapter of the metropolitan see when the latter see was vacant.[108]

---

[105] C. 14, X, *de maioritate et obedientia,* I, 33. Thomassinus (*Ecclesiæ Disciplina,* Pars I, Lib. III, c. 10, n. 10) listed examples of the exercise of metropolitan jurisdiction on the part of cathedral chapters.

[106] "*Hic paucis mensibus omnem illam intermediam jurisdictionem ante intermissam plene exercuit atque renovavit. De clericis ad ecclesiastica beneficia præsentatis et patrononorum jure diligenter inquisivit, electiones confirmavit, intestatorum bona administranda commisit, provocantium appellationes recepit, visitavit, procurationes recepit, synodum celebravit, clerum ex mandato regio ad parlamentum citavit, contumaces et in suam jurisdictionem committentes coercuit, beneficia vacantium sedium contulit, omniaque ad archiepiscopalem jurisdictionem per singulas species tam exquisite exercuit, ut nihil fuerit prætermissum præter episcoporum consecrationem, quam cum sua authoritate peragere non poterat, episcopo Londinensi mandavit et iniunxit, ut suffraganeis congregatis, Menenensem et Pargorensem episcopos tum electos et sua authoritate confirmatos consecraret. Quibus sic consecratis, in testimonium et fidem consecrationis, litteras conventus sigillo sigillatas dedit, excitata hoc modo et agnita Cantuariensis conventus, sede vacante, potestate.*" — Thomassinus, *Ecclesiæ Disciplina,* Pars I, Lib. III, c. 10, n. 10.

[107] Sess. XXIV, *de ref.,* c. 16. Cf. *supra,* pp. 133-134.

[108] Deputatio autem Vicarii Ecclesiæ suffraganeæ vacantis, et Capitulo carentis, spectat ad Metropolitanum, et Metropolitana Ecclesia Pastore viduato, ad illius Capitulum, non obstante consuetudine et Decreto Concilii Provincialis ad favorem Episcopi antiquioris ex comprovincialibus in dubium administrationis Ecclesiarum die 18 augusti 1683 et die 14 aprilis 1685. Cf. Pallottini, XVII, p. 77, n. 17.

Benedict XIV (1740-1758) supported the same ruling in this type of eventuality.[109] Only the right to convoke provincial councils and the right to exercise powers dependent on the provincial councils were taken away from metropolitan chapters.[110] The Sacred Congregation of the Council, in solving a case on the 10th of February, 1624, determined the matter in the same manner.[111] Benedict XIV warned that no other arrangement could be made in such cases.[112]

Section G

Use of Terminology

Finally, with regard to the designations *metropolitanus* and *archiepiscopus* as used within this later period, it must be said that both terms retained their former signification.[113] The term most commonly employed was *archiepis-*

---

[109] *De Synodo Diœcesana* (2 vols., Parmæ, 1764), L. II, c. 9, n. 2: "Si tamen contingat, vacare Ecclesiam suffraganeam, carentem Capitulo, tempore, quo etiam Metropolitana est sua Pastore viduata, in hoc casu, electionem Vicarii non spectare ad antiquiorem ex Suffraganeis, ut nonnulli opinabantur, sed ad Capitulum vacantis Ecclesiæ Metropolitanæ...."

[110] Conc. Trident., sess. XXIV, *de ref.*, c. 2 — Schroeder, *Canons and Decrees*, pp. 462-463; pp. 192-193.

[111] Pallottini, XVI, 612.

[112] *De Synodo Diœcesana*, L. II, c. 9, n. 8: "Cave tamen, ne hanc potestatem Synodum Diœcesanam celebrandi, quam pluribus vindicavimus Vicario Capitulari, ita extendas ad Vicarium vacantis Ecclesiæ Metropolitanæ, ut jus pariter huic adscribas indicendi Synodum Provincialem; nam, cum indecens et absonum visum fuerit tantam jurisdictionem tribuere Vicario Capitulari Metropolitanæ Ecclesiæ, ut valeat ad Synodum compellere totius provinciæ Episcopis, idcirco sancitum est, ut vacante Sede Metropolitana, non ad istius Vicarium, sed antiquiorem Suffraganeum jus pertinet Provincialem Synodum cogendi...."

[113] Conc. Trident., sess. XXIV, *de ref.*, c. 2, 3, 5, 16; sess. XXIII, *de ref.*, c. 18; sess. VI, *de ref.*, c. 1; sess. V, *de ref.*, c. 2; sess. XXV, *de regularibus et monialibus*, c. 8. In all these citations one can find the interchange of both terms. Cf. Hinschius, *Kirchenrecht*, II, 22; Wernz, *Ius Decretalium*, II, 856.

copus. The lists of the members of the various Congregations of the Vatican Council (1869-1870) contain this designation to the complete exclusion of the title *metropolitanus.*[114] The *Annuario Pontificio* from 1792 to our own day enumerates metropolitan sees under the name of *sedi arcivescovili.*[115]

However, it must be stressed that these two terms were never meant to be identical in concept. The word *metropolitanus* insists on the relation the metropolitan derived from his delegated jurisdiction over his entire province, while the word *archiespiscopus,* as formerly, stressed his special position as ecclesiastical superior of his suffragan bishops. For this reason the designation of archbishop was employed as a title of honor more than of jurisdiction.[116] In conclusion it can be said that every metropolitan was an archbishop, but not every archbishop was a metropolitan, inasmuch as certain bishops were independent of a metro-

---

[114] *AAS,* V (1913), 280-281, 286, 313-314, 318.

[115] It was called *Notizie* at the time. During Leo XIII's time, when it was called *Gerarchia Cattolica,* the term *metropolitanus* was in use.

[116] Barbosa, *Iuris Ecclesiastici Universi Libri Tres,* Lib. I, tit. 7, n. 7: "Sed advertere oportet, quod fieri potest ut aliquis Archiepiscopus non fit Metropolitanus, veluti si nullum habuerit Suffraganeum...."; Reiffenstuel, *Ius Canonicum,* I, 31, n. 33: "Potest dari archiepiscopus, qui non sit proprie metropolitanus. Atque hæc procedunt ordinarie loquendo. Contingit enim aliquando, ut quis sit archiepiscopus, et tamen non metropolitanus proprie, ac in præfato sensu; eo quod nullum sub se habent episcopum suffraganeum." Ferraris, *Prompta Bibliotheca,* I, v. *archiepiscopus,* art. 1, n. 4: "Dantur tamen aliqui archiepiscopi, qui proprie juxta datam explicationem non sunt metropolitani, ex quo nullum sub se habeant suffraganeum." Benedict XIV (*De Synodo Diœcesana,* L. XIII, c. 14, n. 4) settled a case concerning an archbishop who had no suffragans with regard to the holding of provincial synods; likewise Benedict XIV, in his Constitution "*Gravissimum ecclesiæ,*" November 26, 1745 (*Opera Omnia* [17 vols., Prati, 1845], XV, 604, n. 5) included the granting of the "facultates assumendi nomen et titulum archiepiscopi, etiamsi pallium quis non habeat" as belonging to the Secretary of Briefs. Cf. Hinschius, *Kirchenrecht,* II, 23; Wernz, *Ius Decretalium,* II, 856-857.

politan by being directly dependent upon the Apostolic See. The Council of Trent acknowledged such a condition.[117]

Concerning the use of the terms *episcopi suffraganei* and *episcopi comprovinciales* it should be noted that the former phrase was used almost to the total exclusion of the latter in the decrees of the Council of Trent. The only time that the Council of Trent used the expression *episcopi comprovinciales* was in Sess. XXIV, *de ref.*, c. 2.[118] The *Annuario Pontificio* throughout all its phases refers to them as *suffraganei.*

[117] Sess. XXIV, *de ref.*, c. 2: "Itidem episcopi, qui nulli archiepiscopo subjiciuntur, aliquem vicinum metropolitanum semel eligant, in cujus synodo provinciali cum aliis interesse debeant, et quæ ibi ordinata fuerint observent ac observari faciant." — Schroeder, *Canons and Decrees*, p. 463; p. 193. This choice of a metropolitan still left them independent in all other matters, and bound them to a particular metropolitan only in the matter of the provincial council.

[118] Schroeder, *Canons and Decrees*, p. 463; p. 193.

Canonical Commentary

CHAPTER VI

GENERAL NORMS OF LEGISLATION ON METROPOLITANS

SECTION A

PRELIMINARY NOTIONS

Article 1. Definition of the Term "Metropolitan"

Canon 272. *Provinciæ ecclesiasticæ præest Metropolita seu Archiepiscopus; quæ dignitas coniuncta est cum sede episcopali a Romano Pontifice determinata vel probata.*

Although the Code of Canon Law does not present a complete definition of the term *metropolitan,* it does give a brief and telling description of the metropolitan institution when it declares in canon 272 that "a metropolitan or archbishop is at the head of an ecclesiastical province, this dignity being conjoined with an episcopal see which has been determined or approved by the Roman Pontiff."

Such commentators as Augustine (1872-1943),[1] Cance,[2] Ferreres (1861-1936),[3] Prümmer (1866-1931),[4] Sipos,[5] Toso,[6] and Woywod (1880-1941)[7] content themselves with a mere re-statement of the descriptive notes given in the

---

[1] *A Commentary on the New Code of Canon Law* (1. ed., 8 vols., St. Louis, Mo.: Herder Book Co., 1918-1922, Vol. II, 6. ed., 1936), II, 288 (hereafter cited as *Commentary*) ; *The Rights and Duties of Ordinaries* (St. Louis, Mo.: Herder Book Co., 1924), p. 57 (hereafter cited as *Ordinaries*).

[2] *Le Code de Droit Canonique* (3 vols., Paris: Librarie Lecoffre, Gabalda et Fils, 1927-1929), I, 280 (hereafter cited as *Le Code*).

[3] *Institutiones Canonicæ* (1. ed., 2 vols., Barcinone, 1918), I, 205 (hereafter cited as *Institutiones*).

[4] *Manuale,* p. 151.

[5] *Enchiridion,* p. 224.

[6] *Ad Codicem Iuris Canonici Commentaria Minora* (5 vols. in 2, Romæ: Marietti, 1921-1927), III, 95 (hereafter cited as *Commentaria*).

[7] *A Practical Commentary on the Code of Canon Law* (4. ed., 2 vols., New York: Joseph Wagner Inc., 1932), I, 105 (hereafter cited as *Commentary*).

Code without making an attempt to define the term *metropolitan.*

The suggestion offered in canon 272 is, however, employed by other canonists for the purpose of drawing up a practical definition of the notion *metropolitan.* Badii (1884-1938) held a metropolitan to be a chief [bishop] to whom are subject bishops of a certain ecclesiastical province who do not have other bishops subject to them.[8] Bargilliat's (1853-1926) definition ran along the same lines as that of Badii.[9] Beste says that a metropolitan is a bishop who is at the head of an ecclesiastical province and has under him other bishops, the so-called suffragans or comprovincials.[10] To Blat, a metropolitan is one who presides with jurisdiction over many other bishops inasmuch as he has obtained a see in some important city to which other inferior episcopal cities are annexed.[11] A metropolitan, according to Cappello, is a prelate who heads an ecclesiastical province and has other bishops as suffragans under him.[12] Chelodi (1880-1922) declared that the name *metropolitan* is a title of office given to a prelate who presides over an ecclesiastical province and has other bishops as suffragans under him.[13] Cocchi says that a metropolitan is so called because he is a chief [bishop] of a metropolis, which is the head of the neighboring cities, and, as such, the metropolitan, chiefly after the Tridentine Council, exercises a certain jurisdiction over the bishops of a province who are called his suffragans.[14] Coronata defines a metropolitan as a bishop who

---

[8] *Institutiones*, I, 187.

[9] *Prælectiones*, I, 409.

[10] *Introductio in Codicem* (2. ed., Collegeville, Minn.: St. John's Abbey Press, 1944), p. 252.

[11] *Commentarium Textus Codicis Iuris Canonici* (5 vols. in 6, Romæ: Apud "Angelicum," 1919-1927; Lib. II, 2. ed., 1921), Lib. II, pars 1, p. 290 (hereafter cited as *Commentarium*).

[12] *Summa Iuris Canonici* (3 vols., Vol. I, 4. ed., Romæ: Apud Aedes Universitatis Gregorianæ, 1945), I, 307 (hereafter cited as *Summa*).

[13] *Ius Canonicum de Personis* (3. ed., curavit Pius Ciprotti, Trento: Libreria Moderna Editrice, 1942), p. 279 (hereafter cited as *Ius Canonicum*).

[14] *Commentarium*, III, 117.

enjoys some jurisdiction over the suffragan bishops of an ecclesiastical province.[15]

De Meester, after explaining the nature of a mother-city [*urbs matrix*], holds the metropolitan to be a ruler who fulfills the episcopacy in a mother-city and who exercises jurisdiction over all the bishops of the province.[16] Raus (1881-1943) stated that the metropolitan is a bishop who is at the head of a certain ecclesiastical province as the chief of the mother-city and has suffragan bishops under him.[17] Regatillo says that he is the bishop of a see which has been determined or approved by the Roman Pontiff and in his office stands at the head of an ecclesiastical province.[18] A metropolitan, according to the view of Vermeersch (1858-1936)-Creusen, is the bishop of a city which, generally taken, is the principal one among other cities of a civil province, and in his office obtains certain rights in the dioceses of an ecclesiastical province. The bishops of these dioceses are called comprovincial or suffragan bishops.[19] To Wernz (1842-1914)-Vidal (1867-1938) he is a prelate who, for the most part, in virtue of his office [*ex officio*] connected with his see, is at the head of the bishops within an ecclesiastical province [eparchy] who do not have other bishops under them.[20]

Throughout this long array of definitions certain characteristic notes occur and recur. When these notes are taken together a good definition of a metropolitan can be formulated. A metropolitan is a bishop who, inasmuch as he occupies a see within a certain ecclesiastical province which is a metropolitan see by pontifical determination or approval, heads that ecclesiastical province, and by reason of his office possesses a certain amount of jurisdiction over

[15] *Institutiones*, I, 432.

[16] *Compendium*, II, 104.

[17] *Institutiones*, p. 174.

[18] *Institutiones Iuris Canonici* (2. ed., 2 vols., Santander-Madrid: Aldus, 1942-1946), I, 234 (hereafter cited as *Institutiones*).

[19] *Epitome*, I, 309.

[20] *Ius Canonicum*, II, 635.

the suffragan bishops who occupy lesser sees within that same ecclesiastical province.

What has been said above concerns the metropolitan of the Latin Discipline. The metropolitan of the Greek Discipline corresponds very closely to the Latin one. He heads a determinate ecclesiastical province and is subject to a patriarch, a *catholicus,* or major archbishop. He has suffragan bishops under him also.[21]

Article 2. Difference Between the Institutes and Terms "Metropolitan" and "Archbishop"

Canon 272. *Provinciæ ecclesiasticæ præest Metropolita seu Archiepiscopus, etc., etc.*

The text of canon 272 draws no clear-cut distinction between a metropolitan and an archbishop. In fact, the employment of the conjunction *seu* seems to confirm the opinion which certain canonists have that these two institutions are altogether identical, and that these two appellations are altogether synonymous. Yet, in reviewing the historical aspects of the growth and decline of metropolitan rights, and, in a careful study of the canons of the Code of Canon Law pertinent to the point at hand, it can be seen that these two institutes and names are different.

Such canonists as Augustine, Ayrinhac (1867-1930), Ferreres and Woywod pass over this problem without a

---

[21] *Statistica, con cenni storici della Gerarchia e dei Fedeli di Rito Orientale* (Sacra Congregazione Orientale, Roma: Tipografia Poliglotta Vaticana, 1932), p. 533, footnote 1 (hereafter cited as *Statistica*). Coussa (*Epitome Prælectionum de Iure Ecclesiastico Orientali* [2 vols., Città del Vaticano: Typis Polyglottis Vaticanis, Vol. I, 1940], I, 110) defines the metropolitan in the same fashion and calls him a *metropolita simpliciter.* The same author defines the institute of *catholicus* in *op. cit.*, pp. 109-110. (Hereafter this work is cited as *Epitome*). An older author, Papp-Szilagyi (*Enchiridion Juris Ecclesiæ Orientalis Catholicæ* [2. ed., Magno-Varadini, 1880], p. 109) stated that metropolitans are bishops who have the title of a metropolis, some of whom do not have suffragans, such as the metropolitan of the Catholic Armenians of Lemberg. (Hereafter this work is cited as *Enchiridion*).

word of comment, hence they shall not be drawn into the controversy.

From the historical standpoint, even before the seventh century the title of *archbishop* generally designated patriarchs and primates without any concern whatsoever about the ruling of a province or the subjection of so-called comprovincial bishops. It was simply a title of honor which gave the patriarchs and the primates no special jurisdiction. Only after the sixth century was the title of archbishop given to metropolitans. The grant of this title to them was again a matter of honor to indicate the prestige of metropolitans who, independently of the title, already enjoyed jurisdiction over comprovincial bishops. From those early centuries until the publication of the Code of Canon Law the traditional distinction was clearly drawn between the two institutions and the two appellations.[22]

But, abstracting from the historical usage of the terminology, one can draw an accurate viewpoint of distinction between metropolitans and archbishops from the opinions of canonists and from the language of the Code itself. In this matter one can discern four schools of thought: (a) there is no difference at all between the two institutes and names; (b) there is a difference only between archbishops (or metropolitans) who have suffragans and archbishops (or metropolitans) who have no suffragans; (c) there is a distinction between residential archbishops (or metropolitans) with suffragans, residential archbishops (or metropolitans) without suffragans and non-residential archbishops (or metropolitans) without suffragans; and (d) there is a difference between metropolitans, residential archbishops and non-residential archbishops.

The first class of canonists which sees no difference between metropolitans and archbishops, and therefore holds the two names synonymous, includes such authors as Bargilliat, De Meester and Prümmer. Bargilliat defined the term *archbishop* with all the usual properties given to the

---

[22] *Supra*, pp. 61-63; pp. 88-89; pp. 142-144.

term *metropolitan*. To him an archbishop is called a metropolitan only because he is the head of the metropolis, that is, the mother-city of the other neighboring cities.[23] The author completely reverses the two concepts and thereby confuses rather than clarifies the issue. De Meester defines the institution through the employment of the term *metropolitan*, yet he makes it clear that according to the present discipline, as well as from the sixth century, the terms *archbishop* and *metropolitan* have the same meaning and are no longer two distinct dignities. He employs his terminology so loosely that he misquotes canon 272 by declaring that an "archbishop or metropolitan" heads an ecclesiastical province.[24] Later, in his running commentary on canons 272-280, he continues to speak of the power of the archbishop rather than of the power of the metropolitan.[25] Prümmer declared that a metropolitan, by force of his name, signifies a bishop of a mother-church. Since the church of a metropolitan is not always a mother-church, but often only a more worthy church, metropolitans are often called archbishops at the present time.[26] Since the author does not differentiate types of archbishops and metropolitans, it must be taken for granted that he considers both institutions identical, even though he uses the term *metropolitan* exclusively in describing the various administrative and judicial rights of the institution. However, he mingles the two names in his delineation of the honorific rights, chiefly in his discussion on the pallium.[27]

Badii and Cocchi belong to that group of canonists which sees a distinction between archbishops (or metropolitans) who have suffragans and archbishops (or metropolitans) who lack suffragan bishops. Although these authors are not inclined to admit a difference between archbishops and metropolitans, they put both institutes into one

---

[23] *Prælectiones*, I, 409.
[24] *Compendium*, II, 104.
[25] *Ibid.*, pp. 108-110.
[26] *Manuale*, p. 151.
[27] *Ibid.*, pp. 151-153.

category and draw a line of demarcation between two types of archbishops (or metropolitans). In speaking of the second type of archbishops, those who do lack suffragans, Badii identifies the two institutes by saying that these archbishops lack suffragans either because the one-time cathedrals of their one-time suffragans are extinct at the present time or because the Popes give the archiespiscopal name, insignia and dignity without archiepiscopal [*sic*] jurisdiction to certain bishops.[28] Nevertheless, he insists that the names *archbishop* and *metropolitan*, as in use today, have the same signification, although they did at one time have a different meaning: the title *archbishop* having been given to those only who presided over greater sees, the name *metropolitan* having been employed to indicate those prelates who headed the bishops of certain ecclesiastical provinces.[29] Cocchi also admits that there are archbishops who have no suffragans. These, he says, are comparable to certain bishops who are subject neither to a metropolitan nor to an archbishop, but are subject directly to the Holy See.[30] But in opposition to Badii, Cocchi declares that the pre-Code distinction still runs true, for, according to him, a metropolitan is very often called an archbishop, not because he is the head of a metropolis, but simply of a more worthy church.[31]

The third opinion, which defends a distinction between residential archbishops (or metropolitans) who have suffragans, residential archbishops (or metropolitans) who have no suffragans and non-residential archbishops (or metropolitans) without suffragans, is held by Toso and Wernz-Vidal. Without alluding to the class of archbishops who have suffragans, Toso proceeds to speak of a few residential archbishops who are immediately subject to the Roman

---

[28] *Institutiones*, I, 187, footnote 3.

[29] *Ibid.*, p. 185.

[30] *Commentarium*, III, 117. The author cites as examples of this type the bishops of Parma, Piacenza and Luni-Sarzana-Brugnato.

[31] *Loc. cit.*

Pontiff and who lack suffragans.[32] Because these archbishops are destitute of metropolitan [*sic*] jurisdiction in fact and in law, they are archbishops only by reason of honor, and hence are called titular archbishops. In reality these prelates, as archbishops, are merely titular, that is, they have only the title and lack altogether all power over bishops. Therefore the pallium, which signifies archiepiscopal power, which they ask for and seek to obtain, they receive by privilege as mere honorific insignia. The author continues by stating that these residential titular archbishops are not to be confused with titular archbishops of ecclesiastical provinces which are already extinct *(in partibus infidelium)*, since these latter enjoy no power by any title, either archiepiscopal or episcopal. These non-residential archbishops, since they lack a territory which is subject to them, are never singled out to receive the pallium even by privilege.[33] Wernz-Vidal distinguish between true *(veri)* residential *(residentiales)* metropolitans, who have other bishops subject to them, and the merely titular *(titulares)* metropolitans, who are exempt bishops with the title of archbishop or non-exempt bishops with the privilege of precedence only by the honorific title of archbishop.[34] All in all, Toso and Wernz-Vidal, in spite of their attempt to clarify the problem, seem only to becloud it the more by their interchange of the two controverted terms.

Such canonists as Beste, Blat, Cance, Cappello, Chelodi, Coronata, Raus, Regatillo, Sipos and Vermeersch-Creusen are advocates of the fourth opinion. These authors hold that the names of *metropolitan* and *archbishop* are not altogether synonymous. They draw a distinction between a metropolitan who, as a residential bishop, heads a province and has suffragans subject to him; an archbishop who, as a residential bishop, simply rules his own see, without any

---

[32] *Commentaria*, III, 95. The author gives a number of such as found in Italy: Aquila, Cosenza, Gaeta, Rossano, Lucca, Ancona, Camerino, Ferrara, Amalfi, Catania, Perugia, Spoleto, and Udine. Cf. Benedict XIV, *De Synodo Diœcesana*, L. II, c. 4, n. 5.

[33] *Loc. cit.*

[34] *Ius Canonicum*, II, 636-637.

suffragans subject to him, having received the title he bears as a honorific privilege; and an archbishop who, as a nonresidential bishop, neither rules a diocese nor has any connection with suffragan bishops, but bears the title of archbishop as a privilege of honor.

Beste holds this distinction between metropolitans and archbishops, and confirms it by declaring clearly that every metropolitan is an archbishop, but that not every archbishop is a metropolitan.[35] Blat does not clearly distinguish the two institutions in his commentary on canon 272, although he does speak of the name under two aspects: as a dignity which is given by reason of honor, and as an office with proper jurisdiction.[36] Only by reviewing his commentary of canons 273-279, where he uses the term *metropolitan* to the exclusion of the term *archbishop*, and of canon 280, where he states that the name of *archbishop* does not carry with itself the right to head suffragans as does the name *metropolitan*, does it become clear that the author wishes to distinguish between the signification of the two terms.[37]

Cance, though not as clear as Beste, can be said to incline toward this fourth opinion. He speaks of archbishops who have no suffragans and who depend directly on the Holy See. The sees of such archbishops can be called archiepiscopal, but they cannot be called metropolitan sees. Evidently the author is speaking of residential archbishops, for in the very next sentence he refers implicitly to nonresidential archbishops when he says that the title of archbishop can be given to a bishop without his see becoming an archdiocese.[38] Furthermore, when the author lists the rights of those mentioned in canons 272-279, he uses the term *metropolitan* exclusively, and when he lists the privileges of honor, he employs the term *archbishop*.[39]

According to Cappello a metropolitan can be called an

---

[35] *Introductio in Codicem*, p. 252.
[36] *Commentarium*, Lib. II, pars 1, p. 291.
[37] *Ibid.*, pp. 291-295.
[38] *Le Code*, I, 281, footnote 1.
[39] *Ibid.*, p. 285.

archbishop. This name however does not belong to a metropolitan exclusively; it can be given to certain bishops by way of honor whether in their rule they be immediately subject to the Holy See, or whether without the government of any territory they be simply titular bishops.[40] Chelodi declared that the title of *metropolitan* is a title of office *(titulus officii)* which belongs to a prelate who heads an ecclesiastical province and has suffragan bishops under him, while the name *archbishop* is given to him, but not exclusively, for, by reason of honor it can also be given to certain bishops who in their rule are subject immediately to the Holy See while not having any suffragans, or also to titular bishops.[41] Evidently the author wished to declare, as does Cappello, that the name *archbishop* is broader than the name *metropolitan,* for he held that the former can include both metropolitans and archbishops. Another conclusion which can be drawn from Chelodi's statement is that the name *metropolitan,* from the standpoint of power, is broader than the name archbishop, which is merely a title of honor.

Coronata speaks as clearly as Beste in this matter. To him, a metropolitan is sometimes called an archbishop also, but he claims that these two appellations are not altogether synonymous. There can be an archbishop even without suffragans, such as an archbishop who is immediately subject to the Holy See, or a titular archbishop, but these are not thereby metropolitans at one and the same time.[42] His definition of a metropolitan does not employ the equivocation *Metropolita seu Archiepiscopus* but simply uses the word *Metropolita.*[43] Raus also defined the term *metropolitan* without employing the equivocating phrase *seu archiepiscopus*. He explained that when a metropolitan is the head not of a metropolis, but simply of a more honored church, he is often [*sic*] called an archbishop. Nevertheless the title of archbishop is given to bishops who have no

[40] *Summa,* I, 308.
[41] *Ius Canonicum,* p. 279.
[42] *Institutiones,* I, 432, footnote 1.
[43] *Ibid.,* p. 432.

suffragan bishops. Hence he concluded that these latter archbishops are not metropolitans in the strict sense.[44]

Although the canonical reason for the distinction as given by Raus is somewhat misleading, he belongs to the proponents of the fourth opinion, for he, too, drew the distinction belonging to it. Regatillo gives his definition of a metropolitan in much the same manner as Coronata. In a separate sentence the author adds that a metropolitan can also be called an archbishop. This deliberate separation can mean only one thing, namely, a distinction between the two institutes. Regatillo further divides archbishops into residential and merely titular archbishops who hold old sees which have been suppressed. Nevertheless, the author enlarges the thought by saying that whenever a residential bishop receives the title of archbishop his see does not become a metropolitan see. Titular archbishops, and those who have no suffragans, are not called metropolitans, nor are they such.[45]

Although Sipos uses the phrase *Metropolita seu Archiepiscopus* in his text, he adds an explanatory footnote in which he clearly states that every metropolitan is an archbishop, but not vice versa. The author amplifies his meaning by stating that a metropolitan always has suffragans under him; there are archbishops who are exempt from metropolitan jurisdiction, but these do not head a province, and hence they are so named only by reason of honor.[46] Finally, Vermeersch-Creusen, in defining a metropolitan do not use the equivocation spoken of above. Only after giving a short historical sketch of the metropolitan institution do the authors add a sentence in which they speak of residential or titular archbishops who are immediately subject to the Roman Pontiff or dependent on a primate.[47] They fortify their implicit distinction between metropolitans and archbishops by speaking of the rights and insignia of a metropolitan without bringing the term *archbishop* into their text.[48]

---

[44] *Institutiones*, p. 174.
[45] *Institutiones*, I, 234.
[46] *Enchiridion*, p. 224, footnote 8.
[47] *Epitome*, I, 309.
[48] *Op. cit.*, I, 309-311.

Unfortunately, the canonists who hold this fourth opinion do not give any canonical proof for their stand.[49] Nevertheless, once the canons of the Code are studied, it can be noted that the two institutions are evidently distinct one from the other. Canon 272 itself, with its equivocating *seu* simply confirms the opinion that every metropolitan is an archbishop. Were the canon phrased "archbishop or metropolitan," as certain canonists openly make the inversion,[50] it would follow that every archbishop is a metropolitan. But the canons do not permit this inversion.

From among the general legal principles given for the proper interpretation of the Code in canons 1-7, canon 6, 2°, is of importance here. This canon states that the Code, for the most part, retains the existing discipline, even though it does enact certain opportune modifications. With regard to these modifications, the canon continues that those canons which restate former laws in their entirety must be interpreted in accordance with the earlier law. Canon 272 restates the former law. Should it be argued that the comprehensive enumeration of metropolitan rights and obligations as given in canon 274 changes the former law, then it can nevertheless be stated that, even if such were the case, there is no justification for identifying the two institutions, since canon 6, 3°, states that those canons which agree only in part with the former law must be interpreted according to the former law, whereas in those parts in which they differ from the earlier law the canons must be interpreted according to the meaning of the words employed. Certainly the complete enumeration of the metropolitan rights and obligations constricts the former legislation as to the rights and obligations, but this constriction does not extend to the meaning of the former metropolitan institution as it is described in canon 272. The institution

[49] Blat (*Commentarium*, Lib. II, pars 1, p. 295) is an exception, for he uses canon 274 to defend his distinction between the two institutions.

[50] Badii, *Institutiones*, I, 187; Bargilliat, *Prælectiones*, I, 409; Claeys Bouuaert-Simenon, *Manuale Juris Canonici* (3 vols., Vol. I, Gandæ et Leodii: De Meester et Fils, 1931), I, 247 (hereafter cited as *Manuale*); De Meester, *Compendium*, II, 104.

as such belongs to the former law, hence this part of the present law which agrees with the former law must be interpreted according to the former law; the limitation of metropolitan rights is part and parcel of the present law, and hence this section must be interpreted according to the meaning of the words employed, as prescribed in canon 18. But, should the argument be carried further, then canon 6, 4°, would still favor the distinction, for it clearly states that in a case of doubt whether some provision of the canons differs from the earlier law, one must adhere to the former law. It is the writer's opinion that canon 272 restates the former law, and hence the principle as established in canon 6, 2°, is to be followed in its entirety.

Another argument can be drawn from the title as found in the Code. The title reads: *De Patriarchis, Primatibus, Metropolitis.* The wording *De Archiepiscopis* is not made part of the title. Evidently the notion of the archiepiscopal institution was not included in the title, for the whole section of the Code of which canons 271-280 form a part treats of the supreme authority of the Church and those who by ecclesiastical law share in it: *De suprema potestate deque iis qui eiusdem sunt ecclesiastico iure participes.* Hence the entire section deals with powers flowing from jurisdiction rather than with powers flowing from orders.

Turning now to those canons in which the Code makes explicit use of the terms *metropolitan* and *archbishop,* one notes that the Code never intended an equivocation which might read: "archbishops or metropolitans." The Code omits the term *archbishop* in canons 273-279, and employs only the word *metropolitan* to define the administrative and judicial rights of metropolitans.[51] Furthermore, other references in the Code with regard to these rights use only the term *metropolitan.* The right to a deliberative vote in a plenary council,[52] the right to convoke and to preside at a

[51] Canon 275 uses the phrase: *potestas archiepiscopalis;* canon 278: *sedes archiepiscopalis.* Cf. canon 284: *sedes archiepiscopalis.* These shall be explained *infra*, p. 162.

[52] Canon 282, § 1.

provincial council,[53] the right to arrange a meeting of suffragan bishops,[54] the right to denounce a bishop who is unlawfully absent from his diocese,[55] the right of visitation in the sees of suffragans,[56] the right to make recourse for a bishop who has been punished by ecclesiastical authority,[57] the right to depute a vicar capitular in vacant sees, abbacies and prelacies *nullius*,[58] the right to appoint a vicar capitular after an invalid election,[59] the right to denounce a bishop who is negligent in the administration of the sacrament of confirmation,[60] and, finally, the right to receive appeals in their courts, as courts of second instance,[61] are given to metropolitans only, for the Code specifies only metropolitans through the exclusive use of the term *metropolita*. All these rights concern the administrative, judicial and special jurisdiction the metropolitans alone have over the subjects and bishops of their provinces.

On the other hand, when the Code wishes to speak of special concessions given to archbishops by law or by the Holy See, or to speak of honorific privileges, it does not use the word *metropolita*. The right to a deliberate vote at an ecumenical council is a concession granted to all archbishops by the law itself.[62] The archiepiscopal pallia are given by the cardinal proto-deacon in the name of the Pope to archbishops. This again is a concession by law.[63] The matter of precedence is a honorific privilege.[64] By special arrangement of the Holy See an archbishop, and even a bishop, may have the right to appoint an administrator for a vacant

[53] Canon 284, 1° and 2°.
[54] Canon 292, § 1.
[55] Canon 338, § 4.
[56] Canon 342, § 3.
[57] Canon 429, § 5.
[58] Canon 432, § 2, § 3.
[59] Canon 434, § 3.
[60] Canon 785, § 4.
[61] Canon 1594, § 1, § 2.
[62] Canon 223, § 1, 2°.
[63] Canon 239, § 3.
[64] Canon 280.

diocese.[65] The right of granting an indulgence on the occasion of consecrating a church or altar is given to archbishops by a grant of the law. The same can be said for the granting of an indulgence on the anniversary of the consecration.[66] The privilege of the canon, as expressed in canon 119, is extended to all archbishops. Anyone who violates the prescription of this canon by laying violent hands on them incurs the penalty of a *latæ sententiæ* excommunication reserved in a special manner to the Apostolic See. This privilege of the canon is a privilege of honor.[67] In all these canons the term *archbishop* is used. Inasmuch as it is a broader term than that of *metropolitan*, all these rights and privileges are also enjoyed by all metropolitans.

Perhaps the best canonical proof for the difference between the two institutions, and hence between the appellations, is found in such canons as 285, 286, § 1, 292, § 2, 347, 429, § 5, and 1594, § 3.

In canon 285 the Code legislates that bishops who are not subject to any metropolitan, such as abbots, prelates *nullius* and archbishops who have no suffragans, are with the previous approval of the Apostolic See to choose once and for all, if they have not already done so before, one of the neighboring metropolitans, whose provincial council they will attend with a view to subjecting themselves to the observance of its decrees. Here the Code itself draws a line of demarcation between metropolitans (taking for granted that they by their very office have suffragans) and archbishops without suffragans. Canon 286, § 1, supplies what is left unmentioned in canon 282, § 1. Canon 282, § 1, accords to metropolitans the right of a deliberative vote in a provincial council; canon 286, § 1, amplifies this legislation by specifying that the archbishops mentioned in canon 285 are also to enjoy a deliberative vote at such a council.

Canon 292, § 2, extends the legislation of § 1 of the same canon when it declares that the archbishops mentioned in

[65] Canon 431, § 2.
[66] Canon 1166, § 3.
[67] Canon 2343, § 3.

canon 285 are also to be called to take part in the meetings of the Ordinaries of the province held every five years, in which meetings ways and means of promoting the cause of religion in the various dioceses are discussed and matters are prepared for the future provincial council. Both terms, *archiepiscopus* and *metropolita,* are used in canon 347 as an amplification of the legislation on precedence as given in canon 106.

Canon 429, § 5, speaks again of the archbishops mentioned in canon 285, this time with reference to the right and obligation a metropolitan has to make recourse for an excommunicated, interdicted or suspended bishop or archbishop within the limits of his province. The insertion of canon 285 in this legislation shows clearly that there is a difference between the two institutions. Finally, canon 1594, § 3, in speaking of the tribunal of second instance, draws the archbishops of canon 285 into the metropolitan's jurisdiction. It hardly seems possible that there should be no difference between metropolitans and archbishops in the face of the distinctions drawn in the above-mentioned canons.

Some objections may be raised with regard to canons 275, 278 and 284, which seem to identify the two institutions. The use of the phrase *potestas archiepiscopalis* in canon 275, and *sedes archiepiscopalis* in canons 278 and 284, does not, however, present any serious difficulty. The phrase in canon 275 is employed with a view to describing the pallium. As will be shown later, the pallium can be given to archbishops. Since this title of honor is a wider term than that of metropolitan, there is nothing peculiar about its usage in this canon which speaks of the obligation to petition the pallium. Again, the phrase used in canons 278 and 284 is clearly intended to describe the see which a metropolitan holds, and not the metropolitan institution. Since a metropolitan is an archbishop, his see is honored with the title of archiepiscopal dignity. Another objection may be raised with regard to the seeming identification of the two terms *metropolitan* and *archbishop* in the Index found at the end of the Code.[68] It must be noted that the Index was never intended to serve as a source of canonical interpretation of the various ecclesiastical institutions. Even if the identification were intended by the author, the most weight that could be acknowledged in relation to this cross-reference would still be one of private authority. The arguments given above should suffice to show that the two institutions and the two appellations are not identical.

Article 3. Types of Metropolitans and Archbishops

Canon 110. *Quamvis Prælati titulo, honoris causa, a Sede Apostolica etiam nonnulli clerici donentur sine ulla iurisdictione, proprio tamen nomine Prælati in iure dicuntur clerici sive sæculares sive religiosi qui iurisdictionem ordinariam in foro externo obtinent.*

In the Latin Discipline there is but one type of metropolitan. As such he is completely independent of any and all forms of intermediary hierarchical jurisdiction between himself and the Holy See, inasmuch as he is immediately dependent on the Roman Pontiff. Wernz-Vidal speak of autocephalous metropolitans. These, they say, are called thus because they are subject to no patriarch, exarch or primate.[69] The authors develop their thought by stating that in this sense almost all the metropolitans of our day are acephalous, since they depend immediately on the Roman Pontiff inasmuch as the somewhat superior jurisdiction of primates and exarchs no longer exists. They conclude that this terminology is not received at least in the Latin Church.[70]

This description of the autocephalous and acephalous metropolitans is purely academic. It tends only to compli-

---

[68] Cardinal Gasparri employed the term *metropolita* as a cross-reference for *archiepiscopus*.

[69] *Ius Canonicum*, II, 637. The authors mention that the metropolitan of Constantia on the Island of Cyprus is an example of this type. Cf. Hinschius, *Kirchenrecht*, I, 578.

[70] *Loc. cit.*

cate the simple statement that there is only one type of metropolitan in the Latin Discipline. Canon 271 clearly declares that the titles of patriarch and primate do not confer any special jurisdiction outside of granting the prerogative of honor and the right of precedence, unless concerning other things a different provision is made in particular law. Should there be any case in the Latin Discipline in which a metropolitan should be dependent upon a patriarch or a primate, or a case in which the former should be made independent of the latter, such exceptions would be ruled by the norms of particular law.

Inasmuch as there exist intermediary positions in the Oriental Discipline there are three types of Oriental metropolitans. The metropolitan, strictly so-called, heads a determinate ecclesiastical province and is subject to a patriarch, *catholicus* or major archbishop. Such a metropolitan has suffragan bishops. Although he corresponds very much to a Latin metropolitan, he is not dependent directly upon the Roman Pontiff, as is the Latin metropolitan, but upon one form or another of the intermediary hierarchical personages within the scheme of the Oriental Church.[71]

The second type of metropolitan in the Oriental Discipline is the autocephalous type. He differs from the simple metropolitan inasmuch as he lacks suffragan bishops, even though he heads a specific eparchy under the authority of a patriarch, *catholicus* or major archbishop. He can be called an honorary metropolitan. This type of metropolitan has no equivalent in the Latin Church. Only the Byzantine Discipline has such metropolitans. These autocephalous metropolitans have increased beyond number among the Greeks, so that almost every bishop is decorated with the title of metropolitan even though he have no suffragans.[72]

Neither *Statistica,* Coussa nor Papp-Szilagyi mention the third type. This type of metropolitan corresponds exactly

[71] *Statistica,* p. 533, footnote 1; Coussa, *Epitome,* I, 110; Papp-Szilagyi, *Enchiridion,* p. 109.

[72] *Statistica,* p. 533, footnote 1; Coussa, *Epitome,* I, 110, Papp-Szilagyi, *Enchiridion,* p. 109.

to the Latin metropolitan, inasmuch as he heads an ecclesiastical province, has suffragans, and is immediately subject to the Supreme Pontiff. The metropolitans of Halicz (Ruthenian), Făgăraş and Alba-Julia (Rumanian), and Ernakulam (Chaldean) are examples of this type.[73]

There are in the Latin Church two types of archbishops: the residential and the titular. To the first class of archbishops belong those bishops who are immediately subject to the Holy See, being thereby exempt from metropolitan jurisdiction. These hold residential sees, which through pontifical arrangement have no suffragan sees attached to them.[74] Such a pontifical arrangement may be governed by historical reasons which the Holy See desires to maintain.

The archdiocese which a certain archbishop occupies may once have been a metropolitan see containing the mother-city which headed an ecclesiastical province, and the Holy See may correspondingly wish to honor the incumbent of the see with the title of archbishop for the sake of the one-time prestige of that city. Then again, it may be that the Holy See simply wishes a certain archiepiscopal see to remain under its immediate jurisdiction for reasons entirely its own. Oesterle gives an example of the first type when he reports that the diocese of Riga was elevated to the rank of an archdiocese without suffragan sees on October 25, 1923, in order to restore the ancient title which Riga had held since the twelfth century.[75] The same author gives an example of the second type when he declares that the see of Trent was raised to the honor of an archiepiscopal see without suffragan sees on June 14, 1929, for the sake of lending

[73] Cf. Appendix B, *infra*, p. 422.

[74] Beste, *Introductio in Codicem*, p. 252; Cappello, *Summa*, I, 308; Chelodi, *Ius Canonicum*, p. 279; Coronata, *Institutiones*, I, 432, footnote 1; Regatillo, *Institutiones*, I, 234; Vermeersch-Creusen, *Epitome*, I, 309. Cance (*Le Code*, I, 281, footnote 1), Raus (*Institutiones*, p. 174) and Sipos (*Enchiridion*, p. 224, footnote 8) do not distinguish between the residential and the titular archbishops, but simply put both in one class. Blat (*Commentarium*, Lib. II, pars 1, pp. 290-295) is not explicit on this point.

[75] *AAS*, XV (1923), 585-586; Oesterle, *Prælectiones*, p. 152.

a certain dignity to the city in which the great Council was held in the sixteenth century.[76]

At the present time, aside from metropolitans, there are no residential archbishops in the Philippine Islands. However, a somewhat unusual arrangement was made in the United States when Washington, D. C., was made an archiepiscopal see in 1939. Although the entire District of Columbia was cut off from the archdiocese of Baltimore, the former was still joined with the latter in a co-ordinate union *(æque principaliter)* and governed by the archbishop of Baltimore.[77] This arrangement was changed near the end of the year 1947 when His Holiness Pope Pius XII disunited the archdiocese of Washington from the province of Baltimore. The archdiocese was made immediately subject to the Holy See and hence, the archbishop of Washington is the only residential archbishop in the United States.

The archdiocese of Winnipeg in Canada is immediately subject to the Holy See. It was erected as such on December 4, 1915.[78] The bishop of this archdiocese is a residential archbishop who has no suffragan bishops subject to him. There are no similar residential archbishops in Newfoundland, Ireland, England and Wales. However, the archbishop of Glasgow, Scotland, is a residential archbishop whose archdiocese is immediately subject to the Holy See. This arrangement was brought about by the Apostolic Letter *Ex Supremo Apostolatus apice,* written by Pope Leo XIII on March 4, 1878.[79] Evidently the Pope was restoring the former honor to Glasgow, since it had been a metropolitan see at one time, having been erected as such by a Bull of Innocent VIII, dated the 9th of January, 1491. Cuba and Mexico have no such residential archbishops at the present writing.

The second class of archbishops consists of titular or honorary archbishops. These are immediately subject to the Holy See and exempt from metropolitan jurisdiction.

---

[76] *AAS,* XXI (1929), 471-472; *Op. cit., loc. cit.*

[77] *AAS,* XXXI (1939), 668-670.

[78] *AAS,* VIII (1916), 89-91. Cf. Appendix A, *infra,* p. 418.

[79] *ASS,* XI (1878), 3-11. Cf. Appendix A, *infra,* p. 419.

They have no residential sees and hence can also be called non-residential archbishops. Their title is simply one of honor for it is derived by pontifical decree from ecclesiastical provinces which are long since extinct *(in partibus infidelium)*. Such titles are usually granted to noteworthy bishops whom the Holy See wishes to reward for special service to the Church, to co-adjutor and auxiliary archbishops, and to legates such as nuncios, internuncios and apostolic delegates. Any number of these can be found in the *Annuario Pontificio* and in the *Official Catholic Directory of the United States.*

Among the Orientals the title of *archbishop* has an altogether different meaning than it has among the Latins. There are two types of Oriental archbishops: the major and the minor. The major archbishop, besides having under him many ecclesiastical provinces over whose metropolitans and suffragans he presides, has his own proper ecclesiastical province with suffragan bishops subject to him. In this sense he is an archbishop (one presiding over many provinces) and a metropolitan, in much the same manner as the Roman Pontiff is the metropolitan of the Roman Province which consists of seven suburbican bishoprics. He can be compared somewhat to the primate of the Latin Discipline, and in reality is equivalent to a patriarch.[80]

The title of *archbishop and metropolitan* which certain Orientals hold at the present time is a matter of relatively recent origin, since its usage does not seem to antedate the eighteenth century.[81] Since the divers metropolitan provinces subject to them have disappeared or never were instituted, they retain the title *archbishop and metropolitan* in order that they may be distinguished from the simple archbish-

[80] *Statistica*, p. 533, footnote 1; Coussa, *Epitome*, I, 111; Papp-Szilagyi, *Enchiridion*, p. 109.

[81] *Statistica*, p. 537. Cf. Appendix B, *infra*, p. 422. An example of this type of archbishop is the metropolitan of Alba-Julia and Făgăraş. The Bull of Erection (1854) does not give the reason for this Oriental terminology, however the city has a historic past, having had a metropolitan in that period. The archbishop of Lemberg, metropolitan of Halicz, is a true major archbishop. The double title of *archbishop and*

ops who lack suffragans and who live in the patriarchates.[82]

The minor archbishop is in reality an autocephalous metropolitan, inferior in hierarchic rank, however. Such minor archbishops are found in the patriarchate of Jerusalem, whether they have an eparchy or not. In the Russian metropolis of Kiev there are two such archbishops: one of Polock and the other of Smolensk.[83] In the West there is no corresponding institute, unless the archbishops without suffragans can be compared to them.

SECTION B

JURIDIC ORIGIN OF METROPOLITAN JURISDICTION

Article 1. Pontifical Determination and Approval of an Ecclesiastical Province

Canon 215. § 1. *Unius supremæ ecclesiasticæ potestatis est provincias ecclesiasticas, diœceses, abbatias vel prælaturas* nullius, *vicariatus apostolicos, præfecturas apostolicas erigere, aliter circumscribere, dividere, unire, supprimere.*

In founding His Church Jesus Christ commended the entire world to the jurisdiction of Peter and his successors.[84] It is therefore by divine right that the Pope holds his eminent position as the spiritual ruler of the entire

---

metropolitan is altogether legitimate, although *de facto* he has only one ecclesiastical province. The archbishop of Ernakulam, India, also carries the double title. Cf. Coussa, *Epitome*, I, 111, footnote 26.

[82] Justinian in his *Novels* raised the episcopal see in which he was born to the archiepiscopal honor according to the custom of his times. The constitution reads: The sacrosanct prelate of Iustiniana Prima not only is a metropolitan but also an archbishop from this time forward, and certain provinces will be under his authority, namely: Dacia Mediterrania, Dacia Ripensis, Maesia Prima, Dardania, Praevalitana, Macedonia Secunda, and part of Pannonia Secunda. *Corpus Iuris Civilis* (3 vols., Vol. III, *Novellæ*, recognovit Rudolfus Schoell, absolvit Gulielmus Kroll, 5. ed., Berolini: Apud Weidmannos, 1928), Nov. 11. Cf. Coussa, *Epitome*, I, 111, footnote 27.

[83] *Statistica*, p. 533, footnote 1; Coussa, *Epitome*, I, 111. Kiev is a true major archiepiscopate separate from the patriarchate of Constantinople.

[84] Matt. XXVIII, 18-19.

Church diffused as it is throughout the entire territorial expanse of the world. Yet Christ in His divine wisdom understood that it would be humanly impossible for one man to attend perfectly to all the tasks such a tremendous responsibility would place on him, and because of this He appointed the Apostles and their successors to aid the Pope in the government of the Church.[85]

Though it must be emphasized that it is by divine right that bishops help to rule the universal Church of God by governing under the dependence of the Supreme Pontiff some portion of the faithful, nevertheless it cannot be said that the territorial division of the Church into specific sections flows directly from a divine command. Christ nowhere specified the extent or limits of the territory which ought to be assigned to individual bishops. Although bishops could aid the Pope in the government of the Church without territorial specifications, order and peaceful relations most assuredly require such convenient delimitations of territory. The most which can be said is that the major or fundamental division of the universal ecclesiastical domain into those broad sections called dioceses is required by divine law only generically, mediately or reductively *(generice, mediate vel reductive)*.

Canonists agree that it would be impossible rightly to govern all society diffused as it is over so great a territory as the world unless some proper division of it would be made. Not even that much can be said for the other territorial divisions mentioned in canon 215, § 1. Ecclesiastical provinces, abbacies and prelacies *nullius*, vicariates apostolic and prefectures apostolic do not depend in any way upon divine law but simply on ecclesiastical law.[86]

---

[85] Acts, XX, 28.

[86] Badii, *Institutiones*, p. 138, p. 139; Bargilliat, *Prælectiones*, I, 396; Claeys Bouuaert-Simenon, *Manuale*, I, 215; Maroto, *Institutiones Iuris Canonici ad Normam Novi Codicis* (2 vols., Vol. I, 2. ed., Vol. II, 1. ed., Romæ, 1919), II, 10 and 111 (hereafter cited as *Institutiones*); Coronata, *Institutiones*, I, 363; Cocchi, *Commentarium*, III, 3-4; Regatillo, *Institutiones*, I, 212; Sipos, *Enchiridion*, pp. 177-178; Wernz-Vidal, *Ius Canonicum*, II, 457-458.

Hence it must be concluded that the Church is divided into those distinct and separate ecclesiastical territorial sections known as provinces only for the sake of convenience or utility. Another conclusion which can be drawn is the dispensable nature of a province or of the whole provincial system. Nevertheless, because it is such a useful arrangement, it seems very unlikely that the Pope would suppress the entire system.

Since canon 272 states that a metropolitan presides over an ecclesiastical province, a clearer notion of the metropolitan institution will evolve from a study of the juridic concept of this major ecclesiastical division of territory. Canon 215, § 1, in enumerating the major ecclesiastical territorial divisions, places the ecclesiastical province at the head of the listing. Inasmuch as the Code of Canon Law nowhere defines the notion of *province*, canonists have supplied this lack by offering definitions which for the most part are identical in wording. A synoptic definition might read: an ecclesiastical province is a major section of Church territory which consists of a number of dioceses, vicariates or prefectures apostolic, one diocese of which, in being the principal episcopal see by pontifical determination or approval, is called the metropolitan see, while the other dioceses, vicariates or prefectures apostolic remain subordinate to it, and hence are called suffragan or comprovincial sees.

Certain authors say that a province is composed of dioceses alone, without any allusion to the inclusion of vicariates and prefectures apostolic.[87] None of these authors add any word of explanation for the omission. It may be that the word *diocese* was intended to include not only abbacies and prelacies *nullius* according to the express wording of canon 215, § 2, but also vicariates and prefectures apostolic,

[87] Badii, *Institutiones*, p. 140. This author insists on using the term *archbishop* instead of *metropolitan* in his definition. Ferreres (*Institutiones*, I, 136) also uses the word *archbishop* instead of *metropolitan*. Maroto, *Institutiones*, II, 136; Prümmer, *Manuale*, p. 126; Regatillo, *Institutiones*, I, 213; Sipos, *Enchiridion*, p. 178; Vermeersch-Creusen, *Epitome*, I, 274; Wernz-Vidal, *Ius Canonicum*, II, 449.

which are ecclesiastical sections of territory in which a prelate presides with episcopal jurisdiction. But it seems unlikely that these canonists would extend the meaning of *diocese* to such proportions. Regatillo is an exception in the case. He states that the hierarchy is said to be normally constituted in a certain region only when there exists this division into provinces, even though it consists of only one province; however, missions are normally constituted when they have their quasi-incipient provinces *(provinciæ quasi-incipientes)*.[88] Beste,[89] and Claeys Bouuaert-Simenon[90] are somewhat more generous, for they state that a province consists of dioceses and vicariates apostolic. It is difficult to understand why these authors mention only the vicariates apostolic without adding prefectures apostolic. It may be that they intended the phrase *vicariate apostolic* to include *prefecture apostolic,* for a vicariate apostolic is only a prefecture apostolic in more evolved state.

A third class of canonists, which includes Blat, Cocchi and Coronata, declare expressly that a province is composed of dioceses, vicariates apostolic and prefectures apostolic.[91] They, too, assign no reason for their opinion. It seems likely that this last opinion is the best of the three when one bears in mind the procedure of the Church in the erection of ecclesiastical provinces.[92]

There is no difficulty concerning abbacies and prelacies *nullius* for the simple reason that canon 215, § 2, clearly states that both of these institutes are included in the term *diocese.* Hence every definition which states that provinces are made up of dioceses implies that abbacies and prelacies

---

[88] *Institutiones,* I, 213.

[89] *Introductio in Codicem,* p. 224.

[90] *Manuale,* I, 215.

[91] Blat, *Commentarium,* Lib. II, pars 1, p. 189; Cocchi, *Commentarium,* III, 6; Coronata, *Institutiones,* I, 366.

[92] See Appendix A, *infra,* p. 414, for the inclusion of the vicariate apostolic of Alaska, in the province of Portland in Oregon; p. 416, of the vicariate apostolic of Lower California in the province of Monterrey; p. 417, of the vicariate apostolic of Grouard and of Mackenzie in the province of Edmonton; etc.

nullius can enter into the composition of an ecclesiastical province.[93]

The ecclesiastical province is considered a non-collegiate moral person in the sense of canon 99. The symbol *etc.* found at the end of the canon indicates that the law does not intend to give an exhaustive enumeration of non-collegiate persons. Hence it must be deduced that there are other ecclesiastical institutes which fall into the non-collegiate group without being explicitly mentioned in canon 99.

That the ecclesiastical province is a non-collegiate moral person can be best understood in the light of the requirements which constitute the nature of moral persons. A moral person can be defined as a juridic entity which is brought into being by public authority as subsisting independently of the individual persons which constitute it and as endowed with competence to acquire and exercise rights and to contract obligations. There are four constitutive elements which enter into the make-up of a moral person: the material element, the end or scope, the means and the formal element.

The material element is that in which the moral person subsists as a subject of law. This may be twofold inasmuch as the substratum of the moral person may consist of a plurality of physical persons or inasmuch as it may consist of a complexity of things. In the former case it is called a collegiate person; in the latter case it is called a non-collegiate person. The ecclesiastical province is a non-collegiate person from the standpoint of the material element, for it subsists in incorporeal things and spiritual objects, and has various offices, benefices and duties which are permanently instituted for the utility of the Church.

The end or scope of a moral non-collegiate person is the principle of union and centralization, the specific reason for its existence. The ecclesiastical province has a religious

---

[93] See Appendix A, *infra*, p. 411, for the inclusion of the *Abbatia Nullius* of Belmont in the province of Baltimore; p. 418, of the abbey of St. Peter, Muenster, in the province of Regina.

goal and scope for its purpose and is conducive and conformable to the supernatural aims of the Church.

The third element constituting a moral person is the means or the rights which it employs to obtain its end or purpose. This element is necessary, since a juridic personality must have a juridic capacity. An ecclesiastical province has spiritual and material means by which it obtains its own purposes and the purposes of the Church.

The formal element of a non-collegiate moral person is its erection by which public authority transmutes the complexity of things and makes of them a juridic entity. The ecclesiastical province is a juridic entity by creation of ecclesiastical law.[94]

Beste[95] and Vermeersch-Creusen[96] hold that an ecclesiastical province falls into the class of non-collegiate moral persons. The ecclesiastical province is that type of non-collegiate moral person which is included implicitly in canon 99 in the word *beneficium*. The Code of Canon Law defines an ecclesiastical benefice as a juridic entity permanently constituted or erected by competent ecclesiastical authority, consisting of a sacred office and of the right to receive revenue from the endowment connected with the office.[97]

Four requirements are necessary to constitute an ecclesiastical benefice: a sacred office, the right to receive revenue from the endowment connected with the office, the erection as a juridic entity, and, finally, perpetuity which is at least objective.[98] In view of these requirements it is more than probable that the ecclesiastical province is an ecclesiastical benefice. It has a sacred office inasmuch as the prelate who

---

[94] Beste, *Introductio in Codicem*, pp. 150-151; Blat, *Commentarium*, Lib. II, pars 1, 35-36; Cappello, *Summa*, I, 172-173; Chelodi, *Ius Canonicum*, pp. 162-164; Cocchi, *Commentarium*, II, 31-34; Coronata, *Institutiones*, II, 157, 161-166; Prümmer, *Manuale*, p. 75; Regatillo, *Institutiones*, I, 129-131; Sipos, *Enchiridion*, pp. 95-96; Vermeersch-Creusen, *Epitome*, I, 189-192; Wernz-Vidal, *Ius Canonicum*, II, 32-36.

[95] *Introductio in Codicem*, p. 224; p. 151.

[96] *Epitome*, I, 274.

[97] Canon 1409.

[98] Cance, *Le Code*, III, 185-186; Coronata, *Institutiones*, II, 357-358; De Meester, *Compendium*, III, pars I, 321-322.

presides over it participates in the power of orders because of his episcopal consecration, and also in the power of jurisdiction because of his metropolitan institution.[99]

The metropolitan has the right of enjoying returns from endowments connected with his office as head of the ecclesiastical province. Authors distinguish in every benefice: the office, the right of revenue, and the revenue itself. The office is something spiritual, the right to revenue is something annexed to the spiritual, and the revenue is something temporal. Because of his office the metropolitan has the right to revenue even though this right may not be carried out into actualization by the enjoyment of the revenue. This right may be in abeyance at times, but it can be insisted on should the metropolitan so insist. If there is no source of revenue a metropolitan could assure himself of it by making certain provisions in keeping with the specifications of the bull of circumscription. The ecclesiastical benefice under consideration is erected as a juridic entity by the competent authority of the Church. The ecclesiastical province is objectively perpetual, that is, once it is erected as a benefice it remains in existence until it is suppressed.

Canonists, however, do not explicitly include the ecclesiastical province among the types of ecclesiastical benefices. Beste in his commentary on canon 1414, § 1, which speaks of the exclusive right of the Apostolic See to erect consistorial benefices, refers to canon 215, § 1, as a practical application of the afore-mentioned canon.[100] Coronata explains that consistorial benefices include not only the episcopate, but also abbacies and prelacies *nullius*, vicariates and prefectures apostolic.[101] It is strange that the author does not also include the ecclesiastical province in his listing of consistorial benefices when he enumerates all the other types of benefices mentioned in canon 215, § 1. He contents himself with the phrase that offices superior to the episcopate are also conferred as consistorial offices. Such canon-

[99] Canons 145, § 1; 197, §1.
[100] *Introductio in Codicem*, p. 699.
[101] *Institutiones*, II, 366.

ists as Blat, Cance, De Meester, Ferreres, Prümmer, Regatillo, Sipos and Vermeersch-Creusen also use the term *episcopate* in giving examples of consistorial offices and benefices.[102] Wernz-Vidal, in speaking of the erection of major offices and benefices, include metropolitans in their listing.[103]

It must be kept in mind that there is a distinction between an ecclesiastical office and an ecclesiastical benefice. An office is very much like the genus and as such is divided into two species: an office which is at the same time a benefice and an office which is not a benefice.[104] In the present legislation no benefice can exist without being at the same time connected with an ecclesiastical office. There are ecclesiastical offices however which are not benefices. Hence whatever the law states generically concerning offices applies specifically also to benefices, but not every specific statement of the law in relation to benefices can be predicated alike of offices in general. The office of metropolitan and the benefice of an ecclesiastical province are bound together by canon 272.

Canon 100, § 1, offers two methods of creating moral persons within the Church, one by the prescription of the law itself and the other by the special concession of a competent ecclesiastical superior by means of a formal decree. This general law on the erection of moral persons is specifically brought into play with regard to ecclesiastical provinces in canon 215, § 1. Through the use of the word *erigere* canon 215, § 1, declares that by its own prescription the supreme authority of the Church alone has the power to

[102] Blat (*Commentarium*, Lib. II, pars 5, p. 436) mentions also certain types of abbacies *nullius;* Cance (*Le Code*, III, 187) gives the examples of abbacies and prelacies *nullius;* De Meester (*Compendium*, III, pars I, 324) speaks of the cardinalate and episcopate; Ferreres (*Institutiones*, II, 165) includes all offices which require episcopal power; Prümmer (*Manuale*, p. 507) adds the cardinalate; Regatillo, *Institutiones*, I, 164; Sipos (*Enchiridion*, p. 770) lists the cardinalate, episcopate and abbacies *nullius;* Vermeersch-Creusen, *Epitome*, II, 524.

[103] *Ius Canonicum*, II, 207-208.

[104] Canons 145; 146; 1409; 1413, § 2. Cf. Coronata, *Institutiones*, II, 241; Sipos, *Enchiridion*, p. 770, footnote 2; Vermeersch-Creusen, *Epitome*, II, 522; Wernz-Vidal, *Ius Canonicum*, II, 196.

erect ecclesiastical provinces. The law does not make it clear that the first method of creation specified in canon 100, § 1, is the one which holds true in the case of ecclesiastical provinces. The second method of creation delineated in canon 100, § 1, that of special concession on the part of an ecclesiastical superior, is employed in the erection of ecclesiastical provinces, since the erection of these major territorial divisions requires the intervention of the Pope himself. By law their erection is made a consistorial affair.[105] Such consistorial matters are never settled by special concessions to any other inferior ecclesiastic, but follow the strict prescript of law.[106]

The erection of ecclesiastical provinces does not depend in any way upon the intervention of civil powers. If in former times the Byzantine emperors in the East[107] and the Visigothic and Frankish Kings in the West[108] actually busied themselves with such affairs, this was done either with the consent of the Roman Pontiff or with real injury to and usurpation of the supreme ecclesiastical authority. From the fifth century onward, when the Faith was propagated in England, Scotland and Germany, quite frequently the immediate intervention of the Roman Pontiff alone in this matter can be noted, for the missionaries to these countries, Patrick, Augustine and Boniface erected provinces by apostolic authority. From the eleventh and twelfth centuries onward, this right over provincial erection was reserved more and more to the Roman Pontiff alone. This right is denied not only to civil authority but also to major prelates and bishops as well. If in the past, patriarchs, metropolitans and provincial councils intervened in the establishment and division of ecclesiastical territory, they did this with at least the tacit consent of the Roman Pontiff.[109]

---

[105] Canons 1411, 1°; 248, § 2.

[106] Canon 1414, § 1.

[107] *Supra*, pp. 6-8.

[108] *Supra*, pp. 39-47.

[109] Badii, *Institutiones*, p. 140; Cocchi *Commentarium*, III, 4-6; Coronata, *Institutiones*, I, 364; Sipos, *Enchiridion*, p. 179; Wernz-Vidal, *Ius Canonicum*, II, 459-460.

However, certain concessions are sometimes granted to major prelates and to civil authorities by the Roman Pontiff if the purposes of the Church can be served better by such arrangements. If certain prelates are better acquainted with the needs of their own territories, and hence are able to aid with more ease and speed the erection and delimitation of ecclesiastical provinces, the Roman Pontiff may allow them to make suggestions and to co-operate in such cases.[110]

But it is always the Roman Pontiff who grants this concession of co-operation, and it is always the Roman Pontiff who has the final word of adaptation or confirmation. In these affairs also the Roman Pontiff can invite the co-operation of those civil states which have diplomatic relations with the Holy See. In such cases the consent and intervention of civil authority may carry with them a more thorough and practical execution of papal plans.[111] Here, too, it must be remembered that it is the Roman Pontiff, and not the civil state, which makes the final decisions in matters concerning the provincial arrangement. This is the *raison d'etre* of the Sacred Congregation for Extraordinary Affairs and the burden of the concordats about which canon 3 speaks.[112]

---

[110] "Quod quidem perpendentes Nos benigne excipiendam duximus petitionem venerabilis Fratris Ioanni Timothei McNicholas, Archiepiscopi Cincinnatensis, qui ab hac Apostolica Sede postulavit ut ecclesiastica sua provincia dismembretur et nova exinde erigatur ecclesiastica provincia...."—*AAS*, XXXVII (1945), 101. Cf. *AAS*, XXVIII (1936), 488-490; *AAS*, XXIX (1937), 391-393; *AAS*, XXX, (1938), 260-262, 258-260, which speak of the suggestion and advice the Roman Pontiffs sought from the Apostolic Delegate to the United States, Amleto Giovanni Cicognani, in the erection of the ecclesiastical provinces of Los Angeles, Detroit, Louisville and Newark.

[111] Cocchi, *Commentarium*, III, 6; Coronata, *Institutiones*, I, 366; Regatillo, *Institutiones*, I, 214; Vermeersch-Creusen, *Epitome*, I, 275; Wernz-Vidal, *Ius Canonicum*, II, 460.

[112] Cf. Plöchl, "Reflections on the Nature and the Status of Concordats"—*The Jurist*, VII (1947), 10-44; cf. Wagnon, *Concordats et Droit International*, Universitas Catholica Lovaniensis Dissertationes ad gradum magistri in Facultate Theologica vel in Facultate Iuris Canonici consequendum conscriptæ, Series II, Vol. XXIX (1935).

The erection of ecclesiastical benefices is carried out by means of a legal document in which the place where the benefice is to be erected is defined and in which the revenue of the benefice and the rights and obligations of the one receiving the benefice are properly delineated.[113] According to Regatillo this document should also carry the name of the one who erects the benefice, the signature of the latter, the date of erection, the actual words of erection.[114] The formal document demanded by canon 100, § 1, is a public ecclesiastical instrument; hence it must be drawn up by competent authority and in authentic form, so that it may carry a probative force in the external forum.[115]

In the erection of new ecclesiastical provinces the territorial limits are always clearly defined. The see which is to be the metropolitan one is explicitly designated and described as to its limits, and all the suffragan sees are enumerated and marked out in their limits.[116] The competent authority for issuing the Bull of Circumscription belongs to the Supreme Pontiff; hence all the specifications demanded by canon 1813, § 1, 1°, will be observed. The Supreme Pontiff issues the Bull of Circumscription through the Apostolic Chancery.[117]

Canon 1418 includes no invalidating clause. Hence the erection of a benefice would be valid even though the one erecting the benefice would not issue the formal document. Canon 11 supports this position.[118] If the Supreme Pontiff would not issue a Bull of Circumscription at the time of the erection of a new ecclesiastical province, the erection would

---

[113] Canon 1418.

[114] *Institutiones*, I, 166.

[115] Canon 1816.

[116] Cf. *AAS*, XXXVIII (1936), 488-490; XXIX (1937), 391-393; XXX (1938), 258-260, 260-262; XXXIV (1942), 192-194; XXXVII (1945), 101-103; XXXVIII (1946), 197-199.

[117] Canon 260, § 1.

[118] Cf. Beste, *Introductio in Codicem*, p. 700; Cappello, *Summa*, II, 516; Coronata, *Institutiones*, II, 369; Regatillo, *Institutiones*, I, 166; Sipos, *Enchiridion*, p. 773; Vermeersch-Creusen, *Epitome*, II, 528. Woywod (*Commentary*, II, 139) stated that this document is necessary for validity.

be valid. However, such an omission seems unlikely in consideration of the untold difficulties which such an omission could provoke.

Usually a canonical cause is present which prompts the erection of new ecclesiastical provinces. The Pope need not guide himself by the rulings of canon 1423, § 1, since this canon legislates for local ordinaries inferior to him, yet he is required to motivate his actions in this connection to fulfill that which is necessary for the Church or that which serves a great and evident utility.[119]

Since in the United States the juridic personalities created by the Church are not recognized by the State, a benefice, to have legal standing before the civil law must be incorporated under the laws of the respective States in which the benefice is found.[120] Hence the formalities required by the States must be followed for the civil incorporation of ecclesiastical provinces should there be a need for civil recognition.

All that has been said concerning the erection of ecclesiastical provinces holds true also in the restoration of extinct provinces, proper allowances being made for the rulings of canon 102, § 1.

Canon 215, § 1, uses the phrase *"aliter circumscribere."* According to the canon it is the right of the supreme ecclesiastical authority, not only to give ecclesiastical provinces their original circumscription at the time of their erection, but also to circumscribe them in any fashion dictated by the need which arises for such changes. It seems that all changes other then division and union are contemplated in the phrase, since the canon explicitly employs the expres-

---

[119] "Nimis amplas ecclesiasticas provincias dividere et aliter circumscribere, novasque exinde provincias constituere, quoties id temporum locorumque adiuncta requirant, omni studio curare debemus...." — *AAS*, XXVIII (1936), 488. "Quo Christifidelium regimen facilius ac salubrius exerceretur, perutilis sane est recta Ecclesiarum circumscriptio quæ temporum et locorum adiunctis aptissime respondere videatur...." — *AAS*, XXX (1938), 260.

[120] Cappello, *Summa*, II, 516; Vermeersch-Creusen, *Epitome*, II, 528; Woywod, *Commentary*, II, 139.

sions "*dividere*" and "*unire.*" In the light of canons 1419-1430, which treat of the union, transfer, division, dismemberment, conversion and suppression of benefices, the phrase "*aliter circumscribere*" evidently seems to embrace transfer, dismemberment and conversion.

According to canon 1421 the *transfer* of a benefice occurs when the seat of a benefice is changed from one place to another. It is possible for such a change to occur should the supreme authority of the Church decide to change the metropolitan see by taking the dignity from one see and giving it to another. Should such a transfer occur, all the rights and obligations, both temporal and spiritual, would be transferred to the newly chosen see.[121] The change need not be as sweeping as the change of an entire see; it may involve only the transfer of the metropolitan dignity from one city to another, or the metropolitan dignity from one church to another.[122]

As in the case which relates to the erection so also in all provincial transfers of a major nature a Bull of Circumscription would have to be issued to that effect by the compentent authority making the transfer. Such a document, however, is not needed for validity. A canonical cause may be present. The Holy See need not bind itself by the common law as enacted in canons 1423-1430. The same method of procedure with regard to all these formalities is followed as in the case of the canonical erection of ecclesiastical provinces.[123] Only the Apostolic See can make such transfers, since they involve a consistorial benefice.[124]

Dismemberment occurs when a part of a territory or of the goods of a benefice is withdrawn and is assigned to another benefice or to a charitable or other ecclesiastical in-

---

[121] Beste, *Introductio in Codicem*, p. 701; Prümmer (*Manuale*, p. 510) adds the note that the benefice itself remains unchanged in nature, even though such a transfer should take place; Sipos, *Enchiridion*, p. 776.

[122] Cf. Blat, *Commentarium*, Lib. III, pars 5, p. 450; Cappello, *Summa*, II, 519.

[123] *Supra*, pp. 177-179.

[124] Sipos, *Enchiridion*, p. 776; Wernz-Vidal, *Ius Canonicum*, II, 218.

stitute.[125] The territorial dismemberment of an ecclesiastical province consists in a partial separation of a territory together with its clergy and people from an ecclesiastical province to which it formerly belonged. This process involves a partial suppression for the original ecclesiastical province and a canonical erection for the new ecclesiastical province. The direct object of such a dismemberment is a part of territory which in the act of being separated carries along with it in relation to the previously extant province a partial diminution of goods and supplies as an accessory element.[126] It happens not infrequently that the Apostolic See dismembers ecclesiastical provinces in order to create new provinces, thereby decreasing the size of a large province or increasing the size of a small province. A number of examples of such dismemberments have occurred in the United States within the past ten years.

To create the ecclesiastical province of Los Angeles, Monterey-Fresno was cut off the ecclesiastical province of San Francisco, while Tucson was taken from the province of Santa Fe.[127] The ecclesiastical province of Detroit was created when the dioceses of Detroit and Grand Rapids were taken from the Cincinnati province, and the diocese of Marquette was cut off from the Milwaukee province.[128] The province of Cincinnati was further dismembered when the dioceses of Louisville, Covington and Nashville were withdrawn from its jurisdiction and territory to form the new province of Louisville.[129] The province of New York was partly dismembered when the new province of Newark was created.[130] When the diocese of Denver was taken away from the province of Santa Fe, this dismemberment brought about the creation of the province of Denver in

---

[125] Canon 1421.

[126] Cf. Beste, *Introductio in Codicem*, p. 701; Cappello, *Summa*, II, 521; Prümmer, *Manuale*, p. 510; Sipos, *Enchiridion*, p. 777; Wernz-Vidal, *Ius Canonicum*, II, 227.

[127] *AAS*, XXVIII (1936), 488-490.

[128] *AAS*, XXIX (1937), 391-393.

[129] *AAS*, XXX (1938), 260-262.

[130] *AAS*, XXX (1938), 258-260.

1941.[131] The province of Cincinnati yielded to still another dismemberment when the new province of Indianapolis was created in 1945.[132] The province of Dubuque was dismembered in 1945 in order to create the province of Omaha.[133]

In all cases of dismemberment the document of circumscription not only makes the territorial changes clear but likewise as an effect incidental to it withdraws the ecclesiastical goods of the dioceses from the limited jurisdiction of the former metropolitan and places them under the limited jurisdiction of the new metropolitan. It belongs to the Supreme Pontiff alone to dismember an ecclesiastical province, for such an action falls within the category of consistorial affairs.[134] The ecclesiastical and civil formalities for dismemberment follow the rulings given for the erection and the transfer of a province.[135]

Canon 1421 speaks of the *conversion* of benefices. Conversion signifies the change of a benefice from one specific category to another. The nature of an ecclesiastical province, following the descriptive notes of canon 1411, is a consistorial, residential, perpetual benefice which has attached to it the care of souls. The use of conversion would involve the change of the nature of an ecclesiastical province; all the descriptive notes, in the opinion of the writer, enter into the essence of the ecclesiastical province.

Canon 215, § 1, employs the word *"dividere."* According to this canon again only the supreme authority of the Church has the right to divide an ecclesiastical province. One form of division is dismemberment which was treated above.[136] Another is the form spoken of in canon 1421. This canon states that a *division* occurs when two or more benefices are made out of one benefice. The Apostolic See has often partitioned ecclesiastical provinces. As an ex-

---

131 *AAS,* XXXIV (1942), 192-194.

132 *AAS,* XXXVII (1945), 101-103.

133 *AAS,* XXXVIII (1946), 197-199.

134 Cappello, *Summa,* II, 521; Sipos, *Enchiridion,* p. 777; Wernz-Vidal, *Ius Canonicum,* II, 221.

135 *Supra,* pp. 177-179; p. 180.

136 *Supra,* pp. 180-182.

ample of the policy of division, the partition of the province of Baltimore into four provinces can be cited here. The enormous tract of territory was split into the provinces of Baltimore, Cincinnati, New Orleans and New York on July 19, 1850.[137] Another example touching more recent times is the division of the province of Westminster into three provinces: Westminster, Birmingham and Liverpool. This occurred on October 28, 1911.[138] Birmingham was divided into still another province, that of Cardiff, which was formed out of the dioceses of Newport and Menevia.[139]

The Apostolic See may also employ the right of internal division. This method does not decrease the territory, but increases the number of suffragan sees within an ecclesiastical province. Examples of this type of circumscription are the recent changes which have taken place in the provinces of Cincinnati and Milwaukee. The new diocese of Steubenville in the province of Cincinnati[140] and the new diocese of Madison in the province of Milwaukee[141] were created only after many adjustments of territory were made within the respective provinces.

The ecclesiastical and civil formalities observed in the division of provinces are similar to the ones employed in the erection of ecclesiastical provinces.[142]

Another right of the supreme authority of the Church is that of effecting the union of ecclesiastical provinces, for canon 215, § 1, expressly employs the word "*unire.*" According to canon 1419 the *union* of benefices can be extinctive *(unio exstinctiva)*, co-ordinative *(unio æque principalis)*, or subordinative *(unio minus principalis)*. If out of two or more ecclesiastical provinces a single new province is created, or if one or several provinces are united to another

[137] Cf. Guilday, *A History of the Councils of Baltimore 1791-1884* (New York: Macmillan Company, 1932), p. 161 (hereafter cited as *Councils of Baltimore*).

[138] *AAS*, III (1911), 553-554.

[139] *AAS*, VIII (1918), 257-259.

[140] *AAS*, XXXVII (1945), 153-155.

[141] *AAS*, XXXVIII (1946), 340-342.

[142] *Supra*, pp. 177-179.

province in such a manner that they cease to exist by enlarging the territory of the province to which they are added, then the union is an *extinctive* one. In accordance with canon 1420, § 1, the new ecclesiastical province thus emerging from the effected union would gain all the rights and obligations of the extinct provinces. Not only canon 215, § 1, but also canon 1422 declares that the effecting of such a union is reserved to the Holy See.

A union is *co-ordinative* if the united benefices remain the same as they were before, so that there does not result any subordination of the one to the other. If ecclesiastical provinces were joined in this manner, each province would preserve its nature, rights and obligations, and in virtue of the union the titles of the united ecclesiastical provinces would be conferred on one and the same metropolitan. Canon 215, § 1, reserves this type of union to the Holy See.

A union is *subordinative* if the various benefices remain the same as they were before the union, but one or more of them are made secondary to another as accessory to the principal benefice. Such a union not only seems unlikely but also inherently inadmissible in the case of ecclesiastical provinces. In this type of union the accessory ecclesiastical province would follow the principal one, so that the metropolitan who would obtain the principal province would also acquire by that union the rights and obligations of both. Canon 215, §1, would of course reserve the effecting of that type of union as the exclusive right of the Apostolic See, were one to grant that the effecting of such a union is within the realm of what exists in the law as admissible.

The principle of union is reflected also in all those cases in which ecclesiastical provinces are enlarged territorially through the addition of one or more dioceses when these are taken away from another ecclesiastical province and made suffragan sees of the enlarged ecclesiastical province. The policy of the Holy See seems to center on the diminution of the territory of provinces, but there can be cases in which a newly effected civil division of territory might prompt the Holy See to enlarge the ecclesiastical province to take in all of the territory of the civil division or region.

Although the Church adopts the civil form of legal prescription as a method of acquiring goods and rights in certain instances, it does not do so in the case of ecclesiastical provinces.[143]

A moral person is by its very nature perpetual, yet it can be suppressed by legitimate authority or it can cease to exist after a period of one hundred years of manifest inactivity.[144] Canon 215, § 1, states that the supreme authority of the Church has the right to suppress ecclesiastical provinces, for the canon employs the word "*supprimere*" in its text. In the meaning of canon 1421 *suppression* implies the complete extinction of a benefice. Canon 1422 confirms the general law found in canon 215, § 1, by declaring that only the Apostolic See can suppress an ecclesiastical province. Through the application of these collated canons any one or all ecclesiastical provinces can be suppressed by the Holy See. In case of suppression, all the spiritual and temporal rights of the ecclesiastical province would also be suppressed.

The other method of extinction mentioned in canon 102, § 1, is the *de facto* existing condition whereby a moral person ceases to exist after a period of one hundred years of manifest inactivity. Canon 215, § 1, states nothing concerning this form of extinction. It is probable that the very nature of this type of extinction is responsible for the omission. This mode of extinction does not depend upon authority but upon the passage of time. Regatillo makes no distinction in the types of benefices when he says that a benefice ceases to exist upon the lapse of a hundred years of inactivity.[145] Beste, Chelodi, Cocchi, Coronata, Prümmer, Sipos, Vermeersch-Creusen and Wernz-Vidal, in commenting on canon 102, § 1, make no exceptions for any type

[143] Canon 1509, 4°.
[144] Canon 102, § 1.
[145] *Institutiones*, I, 170.

of moral person.[146] It hardly seems that such a fate could meet ecclesiastical provinces. It can be taken for granted that the knowledge which the Holy See obtains through the quinquennial reports would prod the Holy See into action before one hundred years of inactivity had elapsed.

The erection, circumscription, division, union and suppression of ecclesiastical provinces are major causes *(causæ maiores)* reserved to the Roman Pontiff. Canon 220 does not furnish an all-inclusive enumeration of these major causes, for certain transactions can become such simply through the fact that the Roman Pontiff has taken such matters in hand.[147] Nevertheless, certain causes in the course of time have become major and are enumerated as such in the Code of Canon Law by the positive wording of its legislation. That the erection, delimitation and suppression of ecclesiastical provinces belong to those administrative causes which are reserved as major causes to the Pope is the opinion held by Beste, Claeys Bouuaert-Simenon, Cance, Cappello, Chelodi, Cocchi, Ferreres, Vermeersch-Creusen and Wernz-Vidal.[148] Blat seems to limit the mean-

[146] Beste, *Introductio in Codicem*, pp. 154-155; Chelodi, *Ius Canonicum*, p. 164; Cocchi, *Commentarium*, II, 37-38; Coronata, *Institutiones*, I, 169; Prümmer, *Manuale*, p. 75; Sipos, *Enchiridion*, p. 97; Vermeersch-Creusen, *Epitome*, I, 195; Wernz-Vidal, *Ius Canonicum*, II, 43-45.

[147] Canon 220. Cf. canons 1557, § 3; 1435, § 1, 4°.

[148] Beste (*Introductio in Codicem*, p. 224) speaks of major causes on pp. 230-231, but does not explicitly include mention of the erection, etc., of provinces; yet his footnote calls attention to canon 215 without indicating any exceptions. Claeys Bouuaert-Simenon (*Manuale*, I, 220-221) implicitly include the erection, etc., of provinces by citing canon 215 when writing of administrative causes. Cance, *Le Code*, I, 227; Cappello (*Summa*, I, 394) gives a broad meaning to the phrase *causa maior* without making any decision whether a matter is such by nature or law; Chelodi (*Ius Canonicum*, pp. 242-243) includes mention of the erection, etc., of provinces implicitly when speaking of the *potestas regiminis* of the Supreme Pontiff; Cocchi (*Commentarium*, III, 24-25) calls attention to canon 1435, which speaks of such reservation with regard to the granting of a benefice. Ferreres (*Institutiones*, I, 140) mentions the erection and suppression of dioceses and of vicariates apostolic as being major causes, and refers the reader to p. 137, n. 38, which includes mention of the erection, etc., of provinces as well as of dioceses and vicariates apostolic; Vermeersch-Creusen (*Epitome*, I, 281) explicitly include the erection and suppression of provinces among

ing of the phrase *causæ maiores* to matters which demand judicial or extra-judicial competence. He does not seem to include doctrinal, administrative or legislative matters among the major causes. Hence one can conclude that in his opinion none of the last-mentioned matters are major causes, since the Pope expedites them through the Roman Congregations or the Tribunals of the Roman Curia.[149] The present writer inclines toward the opinion that the phrase *causæ maiores* has a broad meaning and includes the power of erecting, circumscribing and suppressing provinces among the major causes.

Among the major causes there are some which are and must remain such essentially; there are others which, though they be such essentially, nevertheless can be delegated by the Roman Pontiff for their administration; finally, there are those which are contingently such in view of their actual reservation by the Roman Pontiff. These latter can likewise be delegated to others for their administration.[150] The erection and arrangement of provinces seems best to be considered as belonging to the intermediate type of major causes. Bishops are equal as regards jurisdiction, but the Pope possesses the primacy of jurisdiction. A matter like the provincial arrangement seems from its very nature to belong rather to the Pope in his jurisdictional primacy than to the bishops in their jurisdictional equality. From a practical standpoint, too, there would be no end of controversy if such a matter were left as an ordinary affair of jurisdiction to the decisions of the individual bishops.[151]

Although the erection, modification and suppression of ecclesiastical provinces are reserved to the Roman Pontiff

---

the major causes; Wernz-Vidal (*Ius Canonicum*, II, 459-460) speak clearly of this sort of reservation, however they do not include mention regarding provinces when they speak of the ruling power of the Pope on pp. 494-495, although one could from their former remark under (b) on p. 495 implicitly include these factors among the affairs reserved to the Pope.

[149] Blat, *Commentarium*, II, pars 1, 199-200.

[150] Claeys Bouuaert-Simenon, *Manuale*, I, 220.

[151] Cf. Vermeersch-Creusen, *Epitome*, I, 274.

as major causes, all of these transactions are expedited by the Sacred Consistorial Congregation. Canon 248, § 2, states that this Congregation constitutes new provinces in all those parts of the world which are placed under the common law of the Church.[152] This canon states nothing concerning the modification of provinces, but the fact that this Congregation can do so is to be deduced from the law which gives the Congregation the right to divide already constituted dioceses.[153] Certain authors in commenting on this section of the canon state openly that such is the case.[154] Canon 248, § 2, likewise states nothing about the suppression of provinces, but the very nature of this transaction demands that it be implied in the law. Coronata mentions this in his commentary on this canon.[155] It must be emphasized that the Roman Pontiff himself is the Prefect of the Sacred Consistorial Congregation.[156] This fact is a strong confirmation that the erection, modification and suppression of ecclesiastical provinces are factors which constitute *causæ maiores* reserved to him alone.

Canon 248, § 2, seems to indicate that the Congregation for the Propagation of the Faith is competent to erect, modify and suppress provinces in the missions. Canon 252, §1, shows the wide powers of this Congregation. Nevertheless, as it is not the Sacred Consistorial Congregation itself which makes decisions in such matters for the regions of the common law, so too, it is not the Congregation for the Propagation of the Faith which determines the final policy about provinces in the missions. The Supreme Pontiff alone

---

[152] Canon 248, § 2. Cf. Blat, *Commentarium*, Lib. II, pars 1, 256; Claeys Bouuaert-Simenon, *Manuale*, I, 235; Capello, *Summa*, I, 289; Chelodi, *Ius Canonicum*, p. 261; Coronata, *Institutiones*, II, 409-410; Prümmer, *Manuale*, p. 140; Raus, *Institutiones*, p. 156; Sipos, *Enchiridion*, p. 208; Regatillo, *Institutiones*, I, 229.

[153] Canon 248, § 2.

[154] Cappello, *Summa*, I, 289; Chelodi, *Ius Canonicum*, p. 261; Coronata, *Institutiones*, II, 409-410; Raus, *Institutiones*, p. 156; Regatillo, *Institutiones*, I, 229.

[155] *Institutiones*, II, 409-410.

[156] Canon 248, § 1.

erects, modifies and suppresses provinces in the missions.[157]

If there is question of erecting, circumscribing or suppressing provinces in those states with which the Church has drawn up a concordat, these matters are the concern of the Congregation of Extraordinary Ecclesiastical Affairs.[158] Canon 255, dealing with the competence of the latter Congregation, treats of the constitution and divisions of dioceses, but states nothing concerning provinces. It can be taken for granted that the spirit of canon 215, § 1, pervades this canon, and hence that provinces are included among the affairs settled by this Congregation. The Pope, however, makes the final decisions about provinces in these countries.

The Sacred Congregation for the Oriental Church concerns itself with the erection, delimitation and suppression of provinces within the scope of the Oriental Church.[159] The Roman Pontiff is the Prefect of this Congregation.[160] This specification points to the reservation of such matters as *causæ maiores*.

Such matters as are within the competence of the Sacred Congregation of the Propagation of the Faith for the missions are within the jurisdiction of the Sacred Congregation for the Oriental Church in accordance with the Motu proprio "*Sancta Dei Ecclesia.*" According to Staffa,[161] as often as the civil government must be dealt with in regard to the above named affairs, these matters are referred by the Sacred Congregation for the Oriental Church to the Sacred Congregation for Extraordinary Affairs.

By the Motu proprio "*Sancta Dei Ecclesia*" of Pius XI (1922-1939), given on the 25th of March, 1938, the Congregation for the Oriental Church has full and exclusive jurisdiction in these regions: Egypt, the Peninsula of Sinai, Eritrea, Northern Ethiopia, Southern Albania, Bulgaria,

---

[157] Coronata, *Institutiones*, II, 366; Regatillo, *Institutiones*, I, 213.

[158] Canon 255. Cf. Coronata, *Institutiones*, II, 415; Regatillo, *Institutiones*, I, 213.

[159] Canon 257, § 2.

[160] Canon 257, § 1.

[161] "De Sacræ Congregationis pro Ecclesia Orientali Competentia" — *Apollinaris*, XI (1938), 372.

Cyprus, Greece, the Dodecanese Islands, Iran, Iraq, the Lebanon, Palestine, Syria, Transjordan, Asiatic Turkey and the part of Thrace which is subject to Turkey.[162]

A different arrangement was made for the Russians.[163] If ecclesiastical provinces for the Latin Discipline should be created or modified in Russia, the special pontifical Commission is competent. Action concerning provinces for the Oriental Discipline is a matter of competence for the Sacred Congregation for the Oriental Church. The Supreme Pontiff, however, makes, in either case, the final arrangements and provisions.

There is nothing in the Code of Canon Law which determines the territorial size of ecclesiastical provinces. Such determinations depend solely on the Supreme Pontiff.[164] In a number of cases one province may extend over the limits of an entire country.[165] In other cases the great territorial expanse of a country[166] or the great number of Catholics in

---

[162] *AAS*, XXX (1938), 154-159. Cf. Dziob, *The Sacred Congregation for the Oriental Church*, The Catholic University of America Canon Law Studies, n. 214 (Washington, D. C.: The Catholic University of America Press, 1945), pp. 124-139.

[163] All affairs which concerned Russians were reserved to a pontifical Commission for Russia. This Commission was constituted on June 20, 1925, and annexed to the Sacred Congregation for the Oriental Church by Pope Pius XI. By the Motu proprio "*Inde ab initio*," issued on April 6th, 1930, the same Pope separated it from the above-mentioned Congregation and made it *sui-iuris*, independent of all authority except that of the Pope.—*AAS*, XXII (1930), 153-154. Cf. Oesterle, *Prælectiones*, p. 141. Finally, by means of another Motu proprio ("*Quam sollicita*," issued on December 21, 1934), Pope Pius XI decreed that thenceforth only those matters which referred to Russians of the Latin Discipline, and living in their own country, were to be reserved and entrusted to the pontifical Commission, without prejudice to the authority and rights of the Sacred Congregation for Extraordinary Ecclesiastical Affairs. Cf. Dziob, *The Sacred Congregation for the Oriental Church*, pp. 128-129, footnote 10.

[164] Maroto, *Institutiones*, II, 133.

[165] Lithuania was made to consist of one province. Cf. *AAS*, XIX (1927), 427. For the cases of Newfoundland, Wales and Scotland cf. Appendix A, *infra*, p. 419.

[166] Cf. Appendix A, *infra*, pp. 411-415, for the United States; pp. 417-418, for Canada.

smaller countries[167] may demand a greater number of ecclesiastical provinces.

The primary concern of the Church is the practical advantage of a territorial organization which can best aid it in the administration of ecclesiastical temporalities and spiritualities. If this purpose can be served well with a few provinces, then the Roman Pontiffs content themselves with a few; if, on the contrary, this purpose is thwarted by a small number of them, but can be advanced by a larger number, then the Roman Pontiffs increase the number of ecclesiastical provinces.

Another matter which the Code of Canon Law does not touch is the number of suffragan sees which must enter into the make-up of an ecclesiastical province. This, too, is a matter which is left to the discretion of the Roman Pontiffs.[168] The smallest number of suffragan sees would be one, since the nature of an ecclesiastical province demands the subjection of a diocese. Even one diocese alone is enough to maintain the concept of subjection demanded by the definition of an ecclesiastical province. The province of Cardiff in England, erected on February 7, 1916, has but one diocese, that of Menevia, subject to it.[169] There is no legislation about the greatest number of suffragan sees within the confines of an ecclesiastical province. The *Glossa ordinaria* to c. 2, C. VI, q. 3, which demanded ten or eleven bishops as the number of suffragans needed by a metropolitan for court procedure, had no legal value in early ecclesiastical history, nor does it have any legal value today.[170]

The means employed by the Roman Pontiffs in assigning suffragan sees to a province are the Bulls of Circumscription attendant upon the erection of a new province or

[167] Cf. Appendix A, *infra*, pp. 415-416, for Mexico; p. 419, for England; *AAS*, XVII (1925), 275-276, for Poland; Regatillo, *Institutiones*, I, 214, for Spain.

[168] Maroto, *Institutiones*, II, 133.

[169] *AAS*, VIII (1916), 258.

[170] *Supra*, p. 1, footnote 2.

the delimitation of an older province.[171] These Bulls are issued by the Apostolic Chancery.[172]

The prelates of those sees which are not subject to any metropolitan choose once and for all time a metropolitan, with the approval of the Holy See, for the sake of attending at his provincial councils[173] and for the sake of having a tribunal of second instance,[174] but such sees are not to be considered part and parcel of the ecclesiastical province of the metropolitan so chosen. Such sees are exempt from metropolitan jurisdiction, and are subject immediately to the Roman Pontiff. Hence there is no justification for considering this procedure as an extraordinary means of augmenting the territorial limits of a province.

When the Holy See decides for the erection of an ecclesiastical province, it does not need to model its boundaries on those already drawn up by the civil authority, for to do so could prove altogether impracticable for the purposes of the Church. But the Church can, if it so decides, be directed in its determination of the limits of the province by the geographic divisions already in existence through the arrangement of civil administrative powers. The practice of the Church inclines toward choosing the same boundaries as those determined by the civil powers, or toward recognizing the same ethnic delineations as those already fixed by the civil authority.[175]

A study of the formation of the provincial system in the United States, reveals that the Church is endeavoring more and more to superimpose the provincial institution along the lines of the forty-eight States wherever possible. In answer to Bishop Carroll's request that the Holy See divide the great diocese of Baltimore, Baltimore was made into a

---

[171] Coronata, *Institutiones*, I, 366; Augustine, *Commentary*, II, 205.

[172] Canon 260, § 1.

[173] Canon 285.

[174] Canon 1594, § 3.

[175] "Inter cœtera Nostri Apostolici muneris officia semper curavimus ut provinciæ ecclesiasticæ eosdem fines haberent, quas regiones civiles, vel constitutæ essent iuxta ethnicas rationes." — *AAS*, XVIII (1926), 207.

province, and sees were created at Boston, New York, Philadelphia and Bardstown by the Briefs *Ex debito pastoralis officio* and *Pontificii muneris* of April 8, 1808.[176] As the diocesan structure grew with the expansion of the territory of the United States, Pius IX, by the brief *Universi dominici*, given on the 24th of July, 1846, erected the vast province of Oregon City with the suffragan sees of Nesqually, Walla Walla, Fort Hall, Colville, Vancouver, Princess Charlotte Island and New Caledonia.[177] Very soon after, on July 20, 1847, St. Louis became a province by the brief *Apostolici muneris* with the choice of suffragan sees left to the choice of the next Provincial Council.[178]

Three years later the Holy See erected the provinces of New York, Cincinnati and New Orleans on July 19, 1850. Within another three years the Apostolic See created still another province, that of San Francisco, on July 29, 1853. The provincial division was further developed when Boston, Milwaukee, Philadelphia and Santa Fe became provinces on February 12, 1875. Chicago became a province in 1880.[179] St. Paul received its provincial status on May 4, 1888; Dubuque on June 15, 1893.

After thirty-three years of a fourteen-province arrangement, the Holy See began a rather systematic policy of creating more and more provinces. San Antonio was created a province on August 3, 1926; Los Angeles on July 11, 1936; Detroit on August 3, 1937; Louisville and Newark on December 10, 1937; Denver on November 15, 1941; Indianapolis on December 9, 1944; and, last of all, Omaha on August 7, 1945.[180]

Of the twenty-two provinces in the United States, ten are already limited to one State, namely: Chicago includes all of Illinois, Cincinnati all of Ohio, Detroit all of Michigan, Dubuque all of Iowa, Indianapolis all of Indiana, Milwaukee

---

176 Cf. Guilday, *Councils of Baltimore*, p. 72.
177 Cf. Guilday, *Councils of Baltimore*, p. 154.
178 Cf. Guilday, *Councils of Baltimore*, p. 155.
179 Guilday, *Councils of Baltimore*, pp. 72, 154, 155, 161, 162.
180 Appendix A, *infra*, pp. 411-415.

all of Wisconsin, Newark all of New Jersey, New York all of New York State, Omaha all of Nebraska and Philadelphia all of Pennsylvania. It seems that the policy of the Holy See is an attempt to confine provinces to but one State of the Union wherever feasible.

Much the same seems to be evident in the provincial systems in Canada, Mexico, Cuba, England, Ireland, Scotland and Newfoundland.[181]

The concordats issued after the publication of the Code of Canon Law also give evidence that the Holy See attempts to correlate ecclesiastical provinces with civil boundaries.[182] The Concordat with Poland, signed on February 10, 1925, attempted to divide the country into ecclesiastical provinces in conformity with the civil sections.[183] But Vilno became a bone of contention between Poland and Lithuania.[184] The Concordat with Lithuania, ratified on December 10, 1927, solved the problem of provincial arrangement by declaring in Article IX that the limits of the ecclesiastical province were to conform with the frontiers of the Lithuanian State in accordance with the regulations of the Apostolic Constitution promulgated on April 6, 1926.[185] This Apostolic Constitution established the ecclesiastical province of Lithuania, and specified that it consisted of the metropolitan see of Kaunas and the suffragan sees of Kaišedorys, Panevėžys, Telšiai and Vilkaviškis, with one prelacy *nullius*, that of Klaipėda, which was formerly a part of one of the German ecclesiastical provinces.[186] The Concordat with the German

---

[181] Appendix A, *infra*, pp. 415-419.

[182] Plöchl, "Reflections on the Nature and the Status of Concordats" —*The Jurist*, VII (1947), pp. 14-15; p. 26, footnote, 48. The author gives an extensive bibliography.

[183] *AAS*, XVII (1925), 275. Article IX of the Concordat designated five provinces for the Latin Discipline, one province for the Greek Ruthenians, and one archdiocese for the Armenians.

[184] Cf. Prunskis, *Comparative Law, Ecclesiastical and Civil in Lithuanian Concordat*, The Catholic University of America Canon Law Studies, n. 222 (Washington, D. C.: The Catholic University of America Press, 1945) (hereafter cited as *Lithuanian Concordat*).

[185] *AAS*, XIX (1927), 427.

[186] *AAS*, XVIII (1926), 121-123. Cf. Prunskis, *Lithuanian Concordat*, pp. 38, 40, 83, 84.

Reich, signed on July 20, 1933,[187] and with Austria on June 5, 1933,[188] also make it clear that the Church desires to follow the civil boundaries in its provincial arrangements.

A moral person can be the subject of all rights, just as a physical person, with the exception of those rights which by their nature suppose a physical person. Hence it can possess, acquire, and alienate property, enter into contracts, contract debts, obtain privileges and indults, elect, present candidates, exercise jurisdiction, enact statutes for itself, enjoy the right of precedence, call itself by a fitting name, select distinctive insignia, act as plaintiff or defendant in trials, commit delicts and suffer penalties. Nevertheless, this juridic capacity is not a full one, for by reason of the public good, all moral persons are subject to peculiar limitations in the exercise of their rights.[189] All moral persons, whether collegiate or non-collegiate, are regarded as equivalent to minors when it comes to the exercise and the enjoyment of rights. This means that under the law their right of acting is subject to certain limits, and that their right to enjoy favors follows the rulings extended to minors by the law.[190] The reason back of this legislation is to insure that they may not be deprived of the special protection they need. As minors can suffer harm through the malice or negligence of a tutor or curator, so also can moral persons suffer harm in view of the fact that they are wont to act and to defend themselves through agents alone.[191]

For the reason that an ecclesiastical province is a non-collegiate moral person, it, too, must be regarded as having the equivalent status of minors under the law. All things considered and the proper adjustments made, an ecclesi-

---

[187] *AAS*, XXV (1933), 394.

[188] *AAS*, XXVI (1934), 251-252.

[189] Chelodi, *Ius Canonicum*, pp. 164-165; Cappello, *Summa*, I, 173-174; Coronata, *Institutiones*, I, 168-169; Sipos, *Enchiridion*, p. 96; Wernz-Vidal, *Ius Canonicum*, II, 38-39.

[190] Canon 100, § 3.

[191] Beste, *Introductio in Codicem*, pp. 152-153; Oesterle, *Prælectiones*, p. 63; Prümmer, *Manuale*, p. 75; Vermeersch-Creusen, *Epitome*, I, 192; Wernz-Vidal, *Ius Canonicum*, II, 38-39.

astical province can possess, acquire, and alienate property, enter into contracts, contract debts, obtain privileges and indults, elect and present candidates, exercise jurisdiction, enact statutes for itself, enjoy the right of precedence, select and maintain a fitting name, designate and use distinctive insignia, act as plaintiff or defendant in trials, commit delicts and suffer penalties.[192]

Article 2. Provision of Office: the Episcopal See Determined by the Supreme Pontiff

Canon 147. § 1. *Officium ecclesiasticum nequit sine provisione canonica valide obtineri.*

§ 2. *Nomine* canonicæ provisionis *venit concessio officii ecclesiastici a competente auctoritate ecclesiastica ad normam sacrorum canonum facta.*

An ecclesiastical office in the strict sense is a position firmly constituted either by divine or ecclesiastical law, to be conferred according to the norms of the sacred canons, and carrying with it at least some participation of ecclesiastical power either of orders or of jurisdiction.[193] The metropolitan institution is an ecclesiastical office in the strict sense, for it is a position which is constituted by ecclesiastical law[194] and it embodies a certain participation of ecclesiastical power of orders and of jurisdiction.[195]

Before a cleric can preside over an ecclesiastical province as a metropolitan, and before he can assume the rights and obligations of a metropolitan, he must have the ecclesiastical office conferred on him according to the norms of Canon Law.[196] Without this conferral of office, which is technically called the canonical provision, no cleric can

---

[192] Canons 1499, § 2; 1500; 161-178; 106, 5°; 1649; 1653; 2274, § 1; 2255, § 2; 1687, § 1; 1688, § 2; etc.

[193] Canon 145, § 1.

[194] Canon 272.

[195] Cf. canons 273 and 274. Cf. Cappello, *Summa*, I, 308; Chelodi, *Ius Canonicum*, pp. 279-280; Sipos, *Enchiridion*, p. 224; Wernz-Vidal, *Ius Canonicum*, II, 635. Cf. *infra*, pp. 204-209.

[196] Canon 145, § 1.

validly assume the ecclesiastical office of metropolitan.[197] Canonical provision postulates the concession of an ecclesiastical office by competent ecclesiastical authority made according to the norms of the sacred canons.[198]

The only competent ecclesiastical authority to set a metropolitan at the head of an ecclesiastical province is the Roman Pontiff, who alone also determines or approves the ecclesiastical province over which the metropolitan is to preside.[199] Canon 147, § 2, demands further that the provision of office must be made according to the norms of law. Canon 272 is the fundamental law which determines the method of metropolitan provision. The canon clearly states that the metropolitan dignity is conjoined with an episcopal see which has been so determined or so approved by the Roman Pontiff. In other words, no cleric can become a metropolitan unless he is provided with an episcopal see[200] to which the metropolitan dignity is annexed by pontifical determination or approval. It must be stressed that the metropolitan dignity is not primarily joined with the person of a cleric; it is directly joined with a particular see.[201] As soon as the Roman Pontiff grants an episcopal see which is by dignity a metropolitan see, the cleric upon gaining canonical possession of the see, immediately becomes the metropolitan of the province over which he is to preside, and obtains a limited jurisdiction over the suffragans and their subjects. If the cleric is already a consecrated bishop, he still becomes the metropolitan only after he has taken canonical possession of the metropolitan see. In both cases he assumes the title of metropolitan *ipso facto* with his entering into possession of the see.[202] A bishop ceases to be a

---

[197] Canon 147, § 1.

[198] Canon 147, § 2.

[199] Canon 272. Cf. *supra*, pp. 168-196.

[200] Cf. canon 329, § 1. Cf. canon 248, § 2.

[201] This confirms the opinion given above (*supra*, pp. 158-163) that there is a difference between metropolitans and archbishops. The dignity of archbishop is radically given to the person of a cleric, while the dignity of metropolitan is radically conjoined with a particular episcopal see.

[202] For the assumption of the title of *archbishop* see *infra*, pp. 321-322.

metropolitan if he is transferred to another see which does not carry the metropolitan dignity; the same result would occur if he resigned a metropolitan see, but in such a case he would in all likelihood continue to carry the title of *archbishop*. A bishop would remain a metropolitan if he were transferred from one metropolitan see to another; however, he would lose the metropolitan dignity of his former see altogether, and then gain the metropolitan dignity of his new see completely.[203]

The episcopal see is a metropolitan see either because it has been so determined by the Pope when the ecclesiastical province was created, or because it has been so approved by the Pope after the dignity had become tacitly annexed to an episcopal see.[204]

In filling an ecclesiastical office three distinct acts can be discerned: (a) the designation of a person to hold the office; (b) the actual conferral of the office by a legitimate superior; and (c) the actual taking over of the office by the designated person.[205] These are all included in the term *provision*.

The common law specifies five methods of provision with regard to ecclesiastical offices: (a) free bestowal; (b) institution after presentation by a patron or after nomination; (c) confirmation after election; (d) admission after postulation; and (e) acceptance when confirmation is not necessary after election.[206]

The first method of filling an office consists in its free bestowal by a legitimate superior. Since canon 272 implicitly insists that a metropolitan is a cleric endowed with episcopal orders and jurisdiction, it hearkens to all those

[203] A bishop is granted the honorary title of archbishop by the Roman Pontiff. This title gives him no greater power of orders or jurisdiction. It simply increases his privileges of honor. The archiepiscopal honor can also be joined with a see, namely when a diocese is made an archdiocese; but such an honor in itself does not make the see a metropolitan see. A bishop can cease to be an archbishop by decree of the Roman Pontiff. Cf. *supra*, pp. 163-168.

[204] Blat, *Commentarium*, Lib. II, pars 1, p. 291; Sipos, *Enchiridion*, p. 225.

[205] Wernz-Vidal, *Ius Canonicum*, II, 243-244.

[206] Canon 148, § 1.

canons which speak of the promotion of clerics to the episcopate.[207] Consequently, in accord with these canons, the legitimate superior who can freely bestow the metropolitan office is the Supreme Pontiff alone. As such the Pope is free to choose for episcopal consecration whomsoever he will, without requesting advice from anyone. However, such a free bestowal is fraught with many dangers, especially if unknown clerics, in places at too great a distance from the Holy See, would be chosen for the episcopal and metropolitan dignity.[208] Free bestowal of a metropolitan see is perhaps the best method in those cases wherein a cleric is already a consecrated bishop who has ruled his episcopal see with due credit to the Church and the episcopal dignity. The Roman Pontiff would have first-hand information concerning the capabilities of the metropolitan candidate from many sources. This seems to be the method followed in the filling of the metropolitan sees in the United States.

The second method of provision is institution after presentation by a patron. This method consists in the presentation by a patron of a candidate for the episcopal and metropolitan dignity, or for the metropolitan dignity alone, together with the Pope's institution of that candidate. The candidate for the metropolitan office would have to be designated by someone who possesses the right of patronage, while the act of canonical institution could be effected by the Roman Pontiff alone.[209] The right of patronage itself implies the possession of a number of privileges together with certain obligations which accrue to the founders of churches, chapels and benefices.[210] The Code not only forbids the future establishment of the right of patronage, but

[207] Cf. Canons 329-334.

[208] Cf. canons 153; 154; 330.

[209] Godfrey, *The Right of Patronage According to the Code of Canon Law*, The Catholic University of America Canon Law Studies, n. 21 (Washington, D. C.: The Catholic University of America, 1924); Benko, *The Abbot* Nullius, The Catholic University of America Canon Law Studies, n. 173 (Washington, D. C.: The Catholic University of America Press, 1943), p. 43.

[210] Canon 1448. Cf. *infra*, pp. 218-219.

greatly curtails the privileges inherent in that right wherever it be in existence.[211]

Nevertheless, the Code admits the use of the right of patronage if its possession can be proved. Among the restricted privileges, patrons still enjoy the right to present candidates for vacant benefices. Consequently those who enjoy this right in regard to a metropolitan see may present their candidate for the office to the Supreme Pontiff, who will, if the candidate is acceptable, canonically institute the candidate in the office.[212] This method does not find application in the United States in view of the non-existence of any legitimately established patrons.[213]

The second method of filling offices includes further the process of nomination followed by institution. Nomination is a generic term which means any designation of a person for an office. In the Code of Canon Law, however, the meaning of the word varies.[214] In canon 148 it signifies a right to designate a candidate for an office in view of the possession of a special privilege (excluding the privilege of patronage) or in view of some other rightful claim established in law. It may be that a certain personage, a group of persons, a collegiate or a non-collegiate moral person, has such a special privilege or legal claim to designate a metropolitan. Once the candidate is so nominated for the metropolitan office, it is left to the exclusive jurisdiction of the Supreme Pontiff canonically to institute the one nominated to the office if he be deemed acceptable.[215] According to canon 329, § 2, this is the method employed by the Supreme Pontiff, with this difference from what is said above about institution after presentation by a patron, that he alone nominates or designates the candidate freely for the metropolitan office without intervention on the part of any one. After this free papal nomination, the papal institution fol-

---

[211] Canons 1450; 1454; 1455.

[212] Canons 331, § 2; 332, § 1.

[213] Cf. *infra*, pp. 220-221.

[214] Köstler, *Wörterbuch zum Codex Iuris Canonici* (München: Verlag Josef Kösel und Friedrich Pustet, 1927-1929), s. v. *nominatio*.

[215] Canons 331, § 2; 332, § 1.

lows. Upon closer investigation this is a form of free bestowal.

The third mode of filling offices consists in the act of election followed by the act whereby that election is confirmed by the Supreme Pontiff.[216] In this instance the person is designated by a certain chapter or group which has the right to elect a candidate, but the canonical institution is again carried out by the Roman Pontiff if the candidate be deemed acceptable.[217]

The election must be governed in accordance with the general norms regarding elections as outlined in canons 160-178. Before proceeding to the election all the electors must take an oath that they will elect whomsoever they deem most worthy before God.[218] If in the body of the electors there are clerics eligible for the office, these are to be warned against campaigning either for themselves or for others. Upon the conclusion of the election the candidate who has received the absolute majority of votes[219] is free to accept or refuse the election. If he accepts he acquires an intermediate right *(ius ad rem)*[220] with regard to the office, but he cannot exercise any of the powers of the office before he receives the necessary confirmation of his election.[221]

In the event of the election of a metropolitan, the candidate needs the confirmation of his election from the Holy See,[222] episcopal consecration,[223] and canonical provision as well as canonical possession.[224] Within eight days after a candidate accepts the results of the election, he must apply for the necessary confirmation; otherwise he loses the acquired intermediate right *(ius ad rem)* which accrued to

---

[216] Canon 329, § 3.
[217] Canons 331, § 2; 332, § 1.
[218] Canon 506, § 1.
[219] Canon 329, § 3, cites canon 321 as a requisite for the elections of bishops.
[220] Canon 176, § 2.
[221] Canon 176, § 3.
[222] Canon 329, § 2.
[223] Cf. canons 333; 953.
[224] Canons 332, § 1; 349, § 1 and § 2; 272.

him upon his acceptance of his election.[225] Should there exist such a right of election on the part of any group of persons by way of privilege, or on the part of any civil power in consequence of concordat law, the metropolitan could be so designated.[226] The confirmation of the candidate so elected would depend on the Roman Pontiff.

According to Parsons (1911-1945), "the election of a bishop, which had been the typical canonical election in decretal law, became the rare exception during the period after the Council of Trent."[227] This being the case for bishops, it seems that by analogy the elections of metropolitans by this method likewise became of rare occurrence.

A fourth mode of procedure, which is complementary to the act of election and somewhat similar to it, is admission after postulation.[228] It is used when a candidate whom the electors wish to select is found to lack some specific requirement for holding the office, e.g., when the candidate is illegitimate and the office requires legitimacy for its valid or licit possession. In the process of postulation, which is carried out like a canonical election, "the voters do not elect the candidate; rather, by electoral petition they ask the superior to effect the appointment."[229] A candidate designated by postulation receives the canonical institution through the admission granted by the legitimate superior. This admission depends solely on the good will of the superior, who dispenses from the impediment which bars the postulated candidate from office.

If the postulation is effected by means of a full electoral procedure, the postulation requires a two-thirds majority of votes for its validity.[230]

---

[225] Canon 177, § 1.

[226] Cf. Plöchl, "Reflections on the Nature and Status of Concordats" — *The Jurist*, VII (1947), p. 26 and footnote 48.

[227] *Canonical Elections*, The Catholic University of America Canon Law Studies, n. 118 (Washington, D. C.: The Catholic University of America Press, 1939), pp. 78-79.

[228] Canons 179-182.

[229] Parsons, *Canonical Elections*, p. 4.

[230] Canon 180, § 1.

Should a candidate for the episcopal and metropolitan office be desired by the electors for a sufficient reason though he labors under some impediment keeping him from the office, then postulation could be resorted to.[231] In keeping with what has been said about the rarity of episcopal elections, it can be taken for granted that postulation in such cases must be rarer still. By another analogy, the postulation for metropolitan candidates must be very rarely, if ever, employed.

The fifth method of filling an office is by the simple acceptance of an election which does not need confirmation. This mode of filling an episcopal see does not hold, for canon 329, § 2, states that every bishop needs canonical nomination from the Roman Pontiff, and further, canon 332, § 1, declares that every bishop needs canonical provision or institution by the Roman Pontiff, no matter what method he used in the designation of the candidate. What holds true for bishops, holds true for metropolitans.

In conclusion it can be said that the usual mode of filling metropolitan sees consists in the act of free appointment in keeping with the norm enacted in canon 329, § 2. Institution, either after presentation by a patron or upon nomination by some privileged person or persons, and confirmation after an election obtain quite rarely. In all cases it is the Roman Pontiff who has the right of making the canonical provision or institution of metropolitans.

The second act of filling an ecclesiastical office is the actual conferral of the office by a legitimate superior. This distinct act can be noted in all the above remarks which refer to the papal confirmation of the candidate and the provision or institution in a particular see also made by him. In the case of a metropolitan, the papal provision would concern an episcopal see which is endowed with the metropolitan dignity.

The third act for the filling of an ecclesiastical office is the actual taking over of the office by the person designated

[231] The requirements for the office of metropolitan are the same as those for the office of bishop. Cf. canon 331.

and instituted. This is always required for the filling of a benefice.[232] A residential bishop takes canonical possession of his diocese as soon as in person or by proxy he exhibits to the cathedral chapter, in the presence of the secretary of the chapter or of the chancellor of the curia, and in the diocese for which he has been instituted, the Apostolic Letter of canonical provision. In countries like the United States, where there are no cathedral chapters, the Apostolic Letter of provision must be exhibited to the diocesan consultors. The presence of the secretary or of the chancellor answers to the need of having the act of taking possession duly recorded among the official acts.[233] A metropolitan, inasmuch as he is a residential bishop, takes canonical possession of his metropolitan see in the same fashion.

SECTION C

JURIDIC EXTENT OF METROPOLITAN JURISDICTION

Article 1. Ordinary Proper Power of Metropolitans

Canon 197. § 1. *Potestas iurisdictionis ordinaria ea est quæ ipso iure adnexa est officio; delegata quæ commissa est personæ.*

§ 2. *Potestas ordinaria potest esse sive propria sive vicaria.*

The Roman Pontiff enjoys supreme and full power of jurisdiction over the entire Church not only in matters of faith and morals but also in those matters which pertain to the discipline and government of the Church. The Code of Canon Law simply recapitulates this dogmatic teaching.[234] When canon 218, § 1, states that the papal jurisdiction embraces all matters of faith and morals, it treats of the Pope's power to teach divine truth *(potestas magisterii).*

---

[232] Cf. canon 1443, § 1.

[233] Canon 334, § 3.

[234] Canon 218, § 1.

Because of this right the Pope is the guardian of the deposit of faith and the teacher of morality for the universal Church, so that whenever he teaches *ex cathedra,* either in declaring Catholic doctrine, or in condemning heretical opinions, he is endowed with infallibility. The same canon affirms that the papal jurisdiction reaches out to the matters of discipline as well through the power of administration which he possesses *(potestas ministerii)*. This right entitles the Pope to order and direct all matters which concern divine worship and the ministration of the sacraments and sacramentals. Finally, the canon specifies that the papal jurisdiction includes the right to govern the Church *(potestas imperii vel regiminis)*. Through the employment of this right the Pope governs the universal Church with legislative, judicial, coercive and administrative authority.[235]

Relative to the particular papal right of governing the entire Church *(potestas imperii vel regiminis)*, both Dogmatic Theology and Canon Law place the Pope in a unique position. This universal jurisdiction over the entire Church originates from a divine institution, and therefore the Pope enjoys it by divine right *(iure divino)*. As such it is the foundation of Church authority and thus can become the source of jurisdiction other prelates may possess in the Church.

Bishops have jurisdiction which is subordinate to that of the Pope.[236] This limited jurisdiction by which they preside over certain churches is theirs by divine institution *(iure divino)*. But there is nothing in the divine law which determines the intensity or the scope of this jurisdiction which is both subordinate and limited. Hence it follows that the juridic position of bishops is determined by ecclesiastical law *(iure ecclesiastico)*, always granted, however,

---

[235] Augustine, *Commentary*, II, 209-210; Badii, *Institutiones*, p. 143; Bargilliat, *Prælectiones*, I, 332-337; Beste, *Introductio in Codicem*, pp. 228-229; Blat, *Commentarium*, Lib. II, pars 1, 197-199; Claeys Bouuaert-Simenon, *Manuale*, I, 217; Chelodi, *Ius Canonicum*, p. 243; Coronata, *Institutiones*, I, 372-373; Ferreres, *Institutiones*, I, 139; Sipos, *Enchiridion*, pp. 181-182; Vermeersch-Creusen, *Epitome*, I, 278; Wernz-Vidal, *Ius Canonicum*, II, 488-496.

[236] Canon 329, § 1.

that they are ordinary and immediate shepherds in the dioceses committed to them.[237]

In practice the expeditious care of souls demands that there be other ordinary and immediate pastors besides the Supreme Pontiff. Since divine law specifies only bishops as the helpers of the Pope, it was left to the Church to choose whatever other forms of an intermediary hierarchy it might need to expedite the rule of the faithful. The forms which have been retained in the Latin Discipline are the institutions of the patriarch, the primate and the metropolitan. Speaking generally of these prelates who are constituted members of the intermediary hierarchy between the Roman Pontiff and ordinary bishops, Wernz-Vidal say that they are so constituted that besides having the rule of their own dioceses they are given in perpetuity an ordinary prominence over other bishops in varying degrees by reason of their office *(vi officii)* as well as by reason of their episcopal see and their participation in the pontifical power.[238]

It is important to bear in mind the fundamental principles which underlie the higher position of metropolitans over the bishops of their provinces. Bishops are all equal from the standpoint of the power of orders so long as they exercise them validly.[239] In the hierarchy of episcopal orders, as instituted by Christ, there have not been constituted any divergent degrees substantially distinct one from another; hence all bishops are on a par with the Roman Pontiff himself inasmuch as they, too, have the power of episcopal orders. Hence a gradation, if one exists among bishops, cannot be anything but a contingent one, either by reason of the licit and legitimate use of the power of orders, or because it flows from another source, namely, the power of jurisdiction.

By divine right only the Roman Pontiff is constituted

---

[237] Canons 334, § 1; 335, § 1.

[238] Wernz-Vidal, *Ius Canonicum,* II, 633; cf. Sipos, *Enchiridion,* p. 222; Toso, *Commentaria,* III, 93-94.

[239] Coronata, *Institutiones,* I, 429; Toso, *Commentaria,* III, 94; Wernz-Vidal, *Ius Canonicum,* II, 637.

over all bishops with supreme and full power of jurisdiction. Although the office of bishop rests equally on a divine institution as its basis, yet episcopal jurisdiction is granted to individual bishops by the Roman Pontiff as the proximate cause. Hence no bishop has any superior authority over any other bishop unless he obtains it from the Roman Pontiff.[240]

By divine right all bishops are equal as to jurisdiction. In the hierarchy of jurisdiction there is but one superior grade outside the grade held by bishops; it is the primacy of jurisdiction held by the Roman Pontiff who eminently contains in himself all inferior grades of jurisdiction.[241] The metropolitan institution as part of the intermediary hierarchy between the Supreme Pontiff and the bishops is not of divine origin *(iure divino)*; it is simply of ecclesiastical origin *(iure ecclesiastico)*. Metropolitan jurisdiction has been instituted by merely human law.[242] This is so because metropolitan jurisdiction is a qualified participation in the pontifical power granted to metropolitans either in an express or in a tacit manner.[243]

The II Plenary Council of Baltimore (1866) quoted a decree of the Council of Mount Lebanon (1736) to illustrate these same fundamental principles.[244]

---

[240] Cocchi, *Commentarium,* III, 118; Coronata, *Institutiones,* I, 429; Sipos, *Enchiridion,* p. 222; Toso, *Commentaria,* III, 94; Wernz-Vidal, *Ius Canonicum,* II, 637-638.

[241] Cocchi, *Commentarium,* III, 118; Coronata, *Institutiones,* I, 429; Sipos, *Enchiridion,* p. 222; Wernz-Vidal, *Ius Canonicum,* II, 638.

[242] Raus, *Institutiones,* p. 171; Sipos, *Enchiridion,* p. 222; Wernz-Vidal, *Ius Canonicum,* II, 638.

[243] Coronata, *Institutiones,* I, 429; Sipos, *Enchiridion,* p. 222; Toso, *Commentaria,* III, 93-94, 96; Wernz-Vidal, *Ius Canonicum,* II, 638. Cf. canon 108, § 2, § 3.

[244] "Etsi ratione ordinis omnes episcopi sint æquales, at ratione jurisdictionis nonnulli sunt aliis superiores. Primum autem in ea prælatorum subordinatione locum tenet Romanus Pontifex...alterum locum tenent Patriarchæ; tertium Primates seu Catholici, qui et Exarchæ; quartum Metropolitani, sive Archiepiscopi; ultimum Episcopi simpliciter dicti....Ut autem unus alteri Episcopus subesset, ex eo factum est, quia etsi ab ipsis Ecclesiæ incunabulis, quum exiguus esset credentium numerus, pauci Episcopi reperirentur, iis tamen semper aliquis major Episcopus superpositus fuit, quemadmodum Apostoli præerant illis Episcopis quos ipsi in diversis urbibus consecraverant....re tamen

Metropolitan power of jurisdiction is ordinary, and as such it is variously designated by the authors. It is called "*auctoritas metropolitana*," "*lex metropolitana*," and "*ius metropoliticum*."[245] Metropolitan power is ordinary since it is given *vi officii* in perpetuity and since it is annexed to a certain episcopal see. According to Wernz-Vidal this derived jurisdiction must not be confused with delegated jurisdiction, otherwise the jurisdiction of bishops, and even of the Roman Pontiff, would have to be considered as delegated jurisdiction. Jurisdiction can be derived from one person and given to another *vi officii,* and as such it is conceded as ordinary, or it can be given *vi commissionis,* and as such it is granted as delegated. Metropolitan power is ordinary by reason of the office.[246] From the fact that metropolitan jurisdiction is derived from a participation in pontifical power it cannot be deduced that metropolitan jurisdiction over other bishops is delegated power. It is argued that the Roman Pontiff can concede a participation in his jurisdiction in a permanent manner and can annex to an office the power he thus shares with others.[247] This is what has actually happened in the case of the metropolitan institution. Hence metropolitans have ordinary power. It is further argued that this ordinary metropolitan power is not simply a vicarious power. That statement is maintained on the grounds that the power has been so annexed to the metropolitan office by the Roman Pontiff that he who holds such an office exercises jurisdiction in his own name and not in a vicarious manner.[248]

The corollary which flows from this fundamental principle is that the power of the metropolitan can revert to the source from which it is derived. The Roman Pontiff, on

---

ipsa, potestate atque jurisdictione id unusquisque erat, quod subsequutis temporibus excogitata nomina clarius significarunt...nam qui Episcopus sibi subjectos habebat, Metropolitanus...."—*Acta et Decreta Concilii Plenarii Baltimorensis II*, n. 80, pp. 60-61. Cf. *infra*, p. 395.

[245] Cocchi, *Commentarium*, III, 118; Sipos, *Enchiridion*, p. 222.

[246] Wernz-Vidal, *Ius Canonicum*, II, 638.

[247] Coronata, *Institutiones*, I, 429. Cf. canons 145, § 1; 197, § 1.

[248] *Loc. cit.* Cf. canon 197, § 2.

account of the fulness of his power, can not only increase but he can also decrease metropolitan rights and obligations. The Supreme Pontiff can use the power of increasing and limiting metropolitan jurisdiction in such matters as territory, persons and causes, either by perpetual privileges or transitory dispensations. The Pope can direct the manner in which metropolitan rights are to be exercised. He can suppress all the intermediary grades of the hierarchy completely or partially, for the Pope can govern the universal Church alone with but the aid of the ordinary bishops and without the help of such an intermediary hierarchical institution as that of the metropolitans.

The Roman Pontiff is constituted by divine right above all those canons and customs by which the prerogatives of metropolitans are supported. The suppression, however, of the metropolitan institution seems unlikely in the face of the long history and the great utility of this institute. That the Church wishes to retain it is made clear by the insertion of the chapter entitled "*De Patriarchis, Primatibus, Metropolitis*" in that part of the Code which treats of the supreme power and of all those who participate in it by ecclesiastical law.[249]

In the Latin Church, metropolitans are immediately dependent on the Holy See, except in Hungary where they are constituted under the Primate of Esztergom (Gran). In the Oriental Church, some are immediately dependent on patriarchs, while others are immediately subject to the Holy See.[250] The II Plenary Council of Baltimore (1866) took note of the intermediary position of metropolitans in decree 79.[251]

---

[249] Liber II, *De Personis*, Sectio II, *De Clericis in specie*, Titulus VII, *De suprema potestate deque iis qui eiusdem sunt ecclesiastico iure participes.*

[250] Concerning Hungary see Regatillo, *Institutiones*, I, 234; for the matter of the dependence of Oriental metropolitans see *infra*, pp. 386-397.

[251] "Quemadmodum autem Episcopi cujusvis provinciæ Metropolitano Episcopo subjiciebantur, ita Metropolita ipse Romano Pontifici, sive directe, sive indirecte, interveniente nempe Primate aut Patriarcha, subdebatur. . . ." — *Acta et Decreta Concilii Plenarii Baltimorensis II*, n. 79, p. 60.

Article 2. Full Episcopal Power in Diocese

Canon 273. *Salvo præscripto can. 275-280, Metropolita in propria diœcesi easdem obligationes eademque iura habet quæ Episcopus in sua.*

Canon 273 gives the norm which delineates the extent of jurisdiction the metropolitan has in his own diocese, that is, the see to which the metropolitan dignity is attached. According to this canon a metropolitan has the same obligations and the same rights in his own diocese (archdiocese) as a bishop has in his. The chief obligations a bishop has are the following: the observance of residence,[252] the application of the *Missa pro populo,*[253] the making of the quinquennial report to the Holy See,[254] the instituting of the *ad limina* visit,[255] and the canonical visitation of his diocese.[256] Hence a metropolitan is bound to observe these episcopal obligations in his own archdiocese. The chief rights a bishop has in his own diocese are the ones enumerated in canon 349, § 1, § 2. These episcopal rights are enjoyed by metropolitans in their own archdioceses.

However, even in his own archdiocese, certain obligations and rights of a metropolitan are somewhat different from those of a bishop. The use of the phrase "*salvo præscripto can. 275-280*" in canon 273 brings the exceptional character of the metropolitan power to the fore. Canons 275-280 contain mention of certain rights and of certain specific obligations which the metropolitan must fulfill in order that he may rightly perform in his diocese the duties which are common to all bishops.[257] Canons 275-279 concern the obligation of obtaining the imposition and the use of the pallium. Certain acts of jurisdiction and orders placed by the metropolitan even within his own diocese re-

---

[252] Canon 338.

[253] Canon 339.

[254] Canon 340.

[255] Canons 341; 342.

[256] Canons 343-346.

[257] Toso, *Commentaria,* III, 96.

quire both the imposition and the use of the pallium.[258] Canon 280 refers to the special precedence a metropolitan has in his own diocese.[259]

Article 3. Limited Metropolitan Power in the Suffragan Sees of the Province

Canon 274. *In diœcesibus vero suffraganeis Metropolita potest tantum: etc.*

The phrase *"in diœcesibus vero suffraganeis Metropolita potest tantum"* limits the exercise of the metropolitan power within the suffragan sees of an ecclesiastical province. This is in keeping with the old juridic principle found in c. 9, X, *de officio iudicis ordinarii*, I, 31, which spoke chiefly of patriarchs and primates, but which was later applied to metropolitans: These (patriarchs and primates) have no more rights than do other bishops except to the extent that the canons have conceded them or custom has granted them from former times.[260]

The II Plenary Council of Baltimore quoted the words of the ninth canon of the Council of Antioch (341) in this connection. It did so with a view to showing that the rights of metropolitans as compared with the measure of rights accorded in the older canons had undergone some curtailment. In its decree on the exact number of metropolitan rights, it mentioned only five rights which it considered still in effect.[261]

---

[258] Cf. *infra*, pp. 308-322.

[259] Cf. *infra*, pp. 374-376.

[260] "...nihil iuris præ ceteris Episcopis habere, nisi quantum ss. canones concedunt, vel prisca consuetudo contulit ab antiquo...." Cf. Blat, *Commentarium*, Lib. II, pars 1, p. 291; Cocchi, *Commentarium*, III, 119.

[261] "Varia fuit variis temporibus Metropolitarum jurisdictio; plura enim iis olim jura competebant, quæ nostris temporibus aut desuetudine abrogata, aut positiva Ecclesiæ lege coarctata et certis limitibus circumscripta fuerunt. Ad quinque fere reducuntur jura, quæ ex hodierna Ecclesiæ praxi Metropolita in suffraganeos exercet...." — *Acta et Decreta Concilii Plenarii Baltimorensi II*, nn. 79, 81, pp. 59-61. These five specific metropolitan rights will be taken up by the writer at appropriate points within the following chapters to show whether or not they harmonize with the canons of the Code which treat of these same rights.

Metropolitan rights, as the foregoing quotation shows, were once the outcome not only of written law but also of custom. At the present time these rights are defined by the written law alone. The opening phrase of canon 274 indicates that the enumeration of metropolitan rights is intended as all-inclusive. Because of this complete listing, the opinion which asserts that metropolitan rights once possessed by metropolitans can be recovered by custom cannot be sustained any longer.[262]

Unless particular law rules otherwise, metropolitans no longer have the right to intervene in the election of comprovincial bishops, to confirm their election, and to consecrate them. Canon 329, § 2, declares that the right of free nomination of bishops belongs to the Roman Pontiff. If any college has the right of electing a bishop, it is the exclusive right of the Apostolic See to judge whether or not the candidate is qualified for the office.[263] The canonical provision, according to canon 332, § 1, is the exclusive right of the Roman Pontiff.[264]

---

[262] Bargilliat, *Prælectiones*, I, 432; Claeys Bouuaert-Simenon, *Manuale*, I, 247; Chelodi, *Ius Canonicum*, p. 281; Cocchi, *Commentarium*, III, 118. Cf. canon 5.

[263] Canon 331, § 3.

[264] The metropolitan still figures quite conspicuously in the selection of bishops. In the United States, as in other places, the method of the selection of candidates changed with the growth of the Church. Bishop Carroll by special concession of the Apostolic See was nominated by the clergy of the country. The II Plenary Council of Baltimore listed a number of methods approved by the Holy See for the future selection of bishops. The decree issued by the Congregation for the Propagation of the Faith on March 18, 1834, was changed somewhat by another decree issued on the 10th of August, 1850. Other changes followed in 1856, 1859 and 1861 (*Acta et Decreta Concilii Plenarii Baltimorensis II*, nn. 101-107, pp. 69-75).

The III Plenary Council of Baltimore (1884) indicated another method (*Acta et Decreta Concilii Plenarii Baltimorensis Tertii, A.D. MDCCCXXXIV*, [Baltimoræ: Typis Joannis Murphy Sociorum, 1886], n. 15, pp. 12-13). Some bishops were chosen at the suggestion of their metropolitan and fellow suffragans, and others had their names presented by individual bishops. (Smith, *Elements of Ecclesiastical Law* [3 vols., 1887-1888; Vol. I, 9. ed., 1887, New York: Benziger Brothers],

The consecration of a bishop is reserved by law to the Roman Pontiff in such a way that no bishop is allowed to consecrate anyone a bishop unless he has been so authorized by a pontifical mandate.[265] This pontifical reservation of episcopal consecration is sanctioned by canon 2370, which suspends a consecrating bishop and the assisting bishops or priests who dare to violate the norm of canon 953. Only the Holy See can dispense from this type of suspension. The pontifical mandate usually permits the cleric who is to be consecrated the free choice of bishops who are to consecrate him. The chief requisite for these consecrating bishops is their communion with the Holy See.

The metropolitan no longer has the right to judge any of his suffragans by means of a judicial procedure. This right

---

I, 151-156; Smith, *Notes on the Second Plenary Council of Baltimore* [New York: Benziger Brothers, 1874], pp. 93-94). From 1884 to 1916 the hierarchy of the United States as well as all diocesan consultors and irremovable rectors had the right to recommend candidates according to a mode which was somewhat like an election. (Barrett, *A Comparative Study of the Councils of Baltimore and the Code of Canon Law,* The Catholic University of America Canon Law Studies, n. 83 [Washington, D. C.: The Catholic University of America, 1932], pp. 56-59). This method continued until the decree which indicated the method to be used at the present time was issued by the Sacred Consistorial Congregation (*AAS*, VIII [1916], 400). This is not a method of making appointments of bishops, but rather a method of ascertaining the fitness of a candidate. The method is reflected in the following:

"Every other year at the beginning of Lent each Bishop is to indicate to his Metropolitan one or two priests whom he deems fit for the episcopal office, stating the name, age, origin, residence and position of each. ...When the Metropolitan has received all these names, he adds his own and draws up a general list in alphabetical order. A copy of this he sends to each of his suffragans that they may make opportune investigations....After Easter on a day and a time fixed by the Archbishop, the Bishops meet, without any solemnity to avoid drawing attention, for a serious but moderate discussion of the candidates proposed. After this discussion the Bishops vote on each candidate in alphabetical order....A report of the proceedings is to be sent to the Holy See with whatever information may help in the selection of the best fitted person...." Cf. Barrett, *op. cit.*, pp. 58-59; Parsons, *Canonical Elections*, pp. 79-80. Throughout the new legislation given in 1916, the metropolitan figures prominently, but nowhere does he receive power to elect bishops, as it was his former right to do.

[265] Canon 953.

belongs to the Roman Pontiff.[266] The metropolitan has neither the right to inflict any censures on his comprovincial bishops, nor has he the right to depose any suffragan.[267]

There is no mention in the Code of the right which metropolitans had of demanding a promise of canonical obedience from their suffragans; nor is there any mention of their right to hold suffragans to the obligation of making an appearance in the metropolitan church at stated times outside of times when provincial councils are held. The right of adjudicating criminal and contentious causes which were under the jurisdiction of the suffragans, even though the metropolitans employed members of the tribunals of their suffragans or acted in concert with the rest of the bishops gathered in a provincial council, no longer belongs to metropolitans. The right to receive appeals of all sorts against the decrees and sentences of bishops is no longer as broad as it was before. The metropolitan has no right to receive appeals against decrees. His right to receive appeals against sentences is limited to those causes only which are mentioned in canon 274, 7°.

The right to grant *litteræ formatæ* and licenses for journeys to suffragans leaving their dioceses; to express his consent for the alienation of ecclesiastical goods which suffragans wished to make; to order, at least indirectly, the observance of the liturgy and the celebration of feasts throughout the entire province; and to administer the dioceses of his province during their vacancy — all had fallen into desuetude long before the Council of Trent.

Although the enumeration of the rights and obligations which metropolitans are given by the Code is all-inclusive, the interpretation of the laws referring to these rights and obligations can be as broad as the terms of the canons permit. Toso claims that since metropolitan power is ordinary

---

[266] Canon 1557, § 1, 3°; § 2, 1°.

[267] Cf. canon 430, § 1. Cf. Cappello, *Summa*, I, 308, footnote 2; Chelodi, *Ius Canonicum*, p. 280; Cocchi, *Commentarium*, III, 119; Wernz-Vidal, *Ius Canonicum*, II, 657-658.

and has been given to supply the ordinary power of suffragans, it is not to be interpreted strictly. The author cites canon 200 in support of his view.[268]

Article 4. Relation of Metropolitans to Legates

Canon 269. § 1. *Legati Ordinariis locorum liberum suæ iurisdictionis exercitium relinquant.*

The intermediary position of the metropolitan institution suggests the question of the relation of metropolitans to Apostolic Legates who also enjoy intermediary jurisdiction.

A legate can be defined as an ecclesiastical personage who is sent by the Roman Pontiff to some part of the world with or without ecclesiastical jurisdiction.[269] It is clear from canon 265 that certain legates have jurisdiction while others have not. Those legates who have jurisdiction are: legates *a latere*, nuncios, internuncios, and delegates. The legate *a latere* is a cardinal who is sent by the Roman Pontiff as his *alter ego* to represent him in some major matter. He can do only that which the pontifical mandate of the Supreme Pontiff permits.[270] His jurisdiction is delegated and not ordinary.[271]

The nuncio is a prelate who is sent by the Roman Pontiff to a certain country in order to sustain pontifical authority in that particular country. His relations with the civil government are the official acts of the Holy See. His power of jurisdiction is ordinary, being determined by law, and annexed to his office.[272]

The internuncio is a prelate who is sent by the Roman Pontiff to a place where an apostolic nunciature does not exist. His duties and obligations are the same as those of the nuncio. His power is also ordinary since it is so determined by law and is annexed to his office.[273]

---

[268] *Commentaria*, III, 97.
[269] Cf. canon 265.
[270] Canon 266.
[271] Coronata, *Institutiones*, I, 426; Sipos, *Enchiridion*, p. 221.
[272] Canon 267, § 1, 3°.
[273] Canon 267, § 1, 3°.

Apostolic delegates are prelates sent by the Roman Pontiff to watch over the condition of the Church in a territory assigned to them. They have the duty to inform the Holy See of that condition. They have no official relations with the civil governments of the territories assigned to them. They have ordinary power but are also given certain other powers by the Holy See in the form of delegated faculties.[274]

Usually the three last-mentioned prelates, according to custom, are made titular archbishops.[275]

The Code of Canon Law is clear on the point of jurisdiction. Canon 269, § 1, states that legates are to leave the free exercise of jurisdiction to the local ordinaries.[276] In keeping with this general norm, legates with jurisdiction have no right to impede metropolitans in the exercise of their proper jurisdiction in their archdioceses or within their provinces.

An index of faculties was promulgated by the Holy See not long after the promulgation of the Code. These faculties granted by private letters to all apostolic nuncios, internuncios and delegates must be taken into account in order to determine just how far their jurisdiction extends by way of delegated powers. These one would also have to study in detail in order to see how legates can restrain metropolitans from the exercise of their jurisdiction.[277]

---

[274] Canon 267, § 2.

[275] Cocchi, *Commentarium*, III, 103; Cappello, *Summa*, I, 306; Chelodi, *Ius Canonicum*, p. 277.

[276] "Legati quoque, etiam de latere, nuntii, gubernatores ecclesiastici, aut alii, quarumcumque facultatum vigore, non solum episcopus in prædictis causis impedire, aut aliquo modo eorum iurisdictionem eis præripere, aut turbare non præsumant." — Conc. Trident., sess. XXIV, *de ref.*, c. 20.

[277] Vermeersch-Creusen (*Epitome*, [Appendix I], I, 634-640) furnished a Latin version of these faculties. For an English translation of the same see Bouscaren, *The Canon Law Digest* (2 vols., Milwaukee: Bruce Publishing Co., Vol. I, *Officially Published Documents Affecting the Code of Canon Law 1917-1933*, 4. printing, 1934; Vol. II, *Officially Published Documents Affecting the Code of Canon Law 1933-1942*, 1. printing, 1943), I, 175-187 (hereafter cited as *Digest*).

CHAPTER VII

METROPOLITAN RIGHTS IN THE DIOCESES OF SUFFRAGAN BISHOPS

SECTION A

ADMINISTRATIVE RIGHTS

Article 1. Devolution: Institution in Benefices in the Case of a Suffragan's Negligence

Canon 274. *In diœcesibus vero suffraganeis Metropolita potest tantum:*

1° *A patronis ad beneficia præsentatos instituere, si Suffraganeus intra tempus iure statutum, iusto impedimento non detentus, id facere omiserit.*

The first administrative right which a metropolitan has in the dioceses of his suffragans is that of instituting in benefice those who have been presented by patrons if a suffragan, who is not impeded by any legitimate cause, omits to do so within the time fixed by law.

An ecclesiastical benefice is a juridical entity permanently constituted or erected by competent ecclesiastical authority, consisting of a sacred office and of the right to receive the revenue flowing from the endowment of that office.[1] Ecclesiastical benefices which are free from the right of patronage do not follow the rules of patronage,[2] but follow the rules of free conferral.[3] According to canon 1432, § 1, a local ordinary has a presumptive claim founded in law for the conferral of vacant benefices within his proper territory without the intervention of patrons. If an ordinary has not within six months upon obtaining certain knowledge of their vacancy conferred such non-patronal benefices over which he has the right of free appointment,

[1] Canon 1409.

[2] Canons 1448-1471.

[3] Cf. canons 148, § 1; 152-159; 1431-1447.

the conferral of such benefices devolves to the Apostolic See, with the exception of those benefices which are specified in canon 458.[4]

Formerly metropolitans had the right of conferral by devolution with regard to non-patronal benefices in the case of a suffragan's negligence; the Code of Canon Law grants this right to the Apostolic See.[5] Canon 274, 1°, does not refer to non-patronal benefices, and hence no metropolitan can assume authority to institute anyone in such benefices. Canon 1432, § 3, reserves the devolution of non-patronal benefices to the Apostolic See.

Canon 1448 explains that the right of patronage is the sum total of the privileges which, together with certain duties, are conceded by the Church to Catholic founders of a church, chapel or benefice. This right may be given also to those who have acquired the respective privileges and the duties from the founders.[6] Among the privileges of patrons is that of presenting a cleric for the occupation of a vacant benefice.[7]

Since the act of presentation must precede the act of institution in office,[8] the former must be made to the local ordinary, who has the duty to judge whether or not the person presented is qualified for the occupancy of the benefice.[9] If the cleric has been legitimately presented and found qualified, and accepts the presentation, he has the right to canonical institution. This right of granting canonical institution or conferral of a benefice is vested in the local ordinary.[10] Canonical institution in any benefice, even though no care of souls is attached to it, must be granted within two months from the date of presentation, if no im-

---

[4] Canon 1432, § 3. Cf. Beste, *Introductio in Codicem*, p. 252; Claeys Bouuaert-Simenon, *Manuale*, I, 248; Coronata, *Institutiones*, I, 433; Prümmer, *Manuale*, p. 152, footnote 23; Sipos, *Enchiridion*, p. 225.

[5] Sipos, *Enchiridion*, p. 225, footnote 10.

[6] Cf. canons 1449-1471.

[7] Canon 1455, 1°.

[8] Cf. canon 148, § 1.

[9] Canon 1464, § 1 and § 2. Cf. canon 149.

[10] Canon 1466, § 1, § 2.

pediment justifies a longer delay.[11] It is to this type of benefice, namely the patronal, that canon 274, 1°, has reference.

With the due observance of all the prescripts concerning patronal benefices, the metropolitan can institute in benefice only those who are presented by patrons. This metropolitan right of conferral obtained by devolution depends on two conditions. The first condition is that the suffragan has neglected to institute the presented cleric within the time fixed by the law. The time as determined by the law is two months from the day of presentation: "*intra duos menses ex quo præsentatio facta sit.*"[12] The rules of canon 34, § 3, 1°, and 3°, provide the norms for the reckoning of time in this instance.[13] The months are so reckoned that the fixed time ends at midnight of the day which after two months (taken as found in the calendar) has the same number as the day of the presentation. If the two months go by without the suffragan's instituting the presented cleric, the institution devolves *ipso iure* to the metropolitan.

The second condition is the lack of a just impediment which restrains the suffragan from making the institution. Should a suffragan refrain from the act of institution because of a certain legitimate reason, negligence would not be present and the metropolitan remedy by devolution would not apply.[14] However, in such cases the burden of proof rests on the suffragan. If he cannot prove the existence of a just impediment, the metropolitan can institute the presented cleric in the benefice if he finds him qualified.

Although the canon uses the word *potest* rather than *debet*, it seems that the metropolitan ought to act lest great harm come to the diocese of his suffragan because of the delayed institution. It is for the metropolitan to judge whether the impediment alleged by the suffragan is or is

---

[11] Canon 1467.

[12] Canon 1467.

[13] Blat, *Commentarium*, Lib. II, pars 1, p. 291; Toso, *Commentaria*, III, 97.

[14] Blat, *Commentarium*, Lib. II, pars 1, p. 291; Coronata, *Institutiones*, I, 433, footnote 3.

not just, and likewise to introduce before the Apostolic See the recourse of the suffragan who does not acquiesce in his judgment concerning the impediment. It seems that the effect of the recourse would possess a suspensive force in such cases.[15]

In the United States, according to the II Plenary Council of Baltimore (1866), which confirmed the former decrees of the Provincial Councils of Baltimore, the right of patronage does not exist.[16] For a while, mainly in the first half of the nineteenth century, there was a tendency in many parts of the United States for lay trustees to claim the right of nominating the pastors of their parishes. Besides this claim they also demanded other rights. They based their claims on the fact that they, as trustees, were the representatives of the people who built the church and who maintained it by their common offerings. However, these claims could not be upheld, for the Sacred Congregation of the Council, as early as November 19, 1729, had ruled that no right of patronage could be acquired by a congregation or by its lay representatives if a church had been built, endowed or maintained by the voluntary offerings of the faithful.[17]

When the II Plenary Council of Baltimore made a special provision by which metropolitans were to supply for the negligences of their suffragan bishops, nothing was said concerning the right of devolution with regard to patronal benefices.[18] However, the decree contained the phrase, "*in casibus a jure statutis,*" which was fortified with a footnote containing citations of the older legislation. But an investigation of these citations proves that the Fathers of the Council were positive that the right of patronage was not a matter for legislation in the United States.

---

[15] Toso, *Commentaria*, III, 97-98.

[16] *Acta et Decreta Concilii Plenarii Baltimorensis II*, n. 184, pp. 111-112.

[17] Pallottini, XI, 114. Cf. Woywod, *Commentary*, II, 153.

[18] "Negligentiam suffraganeorum in casibus a jure statutis supplet." — *Acta et Decreta Concilii Plenarii Baltimorensis II*, n. 81, 3, p. 61.

The right of devolution spoken of in canon 274, 1°, does not apply to purely residential archbishops or non-residential archbishops, for the opening clause of this canon uses only the restrictive term "*Metropolita.*" Nevertheless, a metropolitan cannot extend this right to include its exercise outside the dioceses of his province. According to the main clause of the canon, this right is limited to the dioceses of his suffragans. The negligence of bishops who are subject to no metropolitan, of abbots and of prelates *nullius*, and of archbishops without suffragans, all of whom are mentioned in canon 285, is not touched on in canon 274, 1°, in the matter of instituting patronal benefices. It may be that the Holy See reserves the right of supplying for their negligences in this regard to itself. It could be that the metropolitan has the right to notify the Roman Pontiff of such abuses in accord with canon 274, 4°. At most it may be said that canon 20 may be invoked. This canon states that if an express prescription of a general or of a particular law is lacking in a certain matter, the norm for the matter is to be taken from laws enacted in similar cases.

According to the writer's opinion this right of devolution may be licitly exercised by an instituted metropolitan throughout his entire province prior to the imposition of the pallium.[19]

Article 2. Devolution: Deputation of Vicars Capitular in Vacant Suffragan Sees

Canon 274. *In diœcesibus vero suffraganeis Metropolita potest tantum:*

3° *Deputare Vicarium Capitularem ad normam can. 432, § 2.*

During the vacancy of an episcopal see the government of the diocese devolves on the cathedral chapter,[20] unless an apostolic administrator already is in the diocese, or unless

---

[19] *Infra*, pp. 311-315.

[20] Cf. canons 391-422.

the Holy See has otherwise provided.[21] Since the institution of the cathedral chapter does not exist anywhere in the United States, the rules which apply to cathedral chapters for the most part apply to the diocesan consultors.[22] Hence in the United States the rule of a vacant diocese falls to the diocesan consultors.[23]

In a case of the vacancy of an episcopal see, the cathedral chapter must constitute a vicar capitular for the government of the diocese. This must be done within eight days from the accepted notice of the vacancy of the see.[24] It can depute only one vicar capitular, all contrary custom being reprobated. The selection of the vicar capitular must be a capitular action which follows the norms of canons 160-182.[25] Because of the rulings of canons 423 and 427, in the United States the faculty of deputing an administrator who is to rule the diocese during the vacancy belongs to the diocesan consultors.[26]

There is no doubt that the diocesan consultors of the dioceses of the United States have the right to select the administrators for a vacant see. The Commission for the Authentic Interpretation of the Code was asked the following questions by the Apostolic Delegate to the United States: (a) whether the particular provisions of the Council of Baltimore,[27] as to the right to name an administrator of a diocese, are still in effect, or are revoked by the Code; and (b) if the said provisions are not in effect, whether canon

---

[21] Canon 431, § 1. Cf. canons 313-318.

[22] Cf. canons 423-428. Cf. Klekotka, *Diocesan Consultors*, The Catholic University of America Canon Law Studies, n. 8 (Washington, D. C.: The Catholic University of America, 1920).

[23] Canons 423, 427.

[24] Canon 432, § 1.

[25] Canon 433, § 1 and § 2.

[26] Cf. Beste, *Introductio in Codicem*, p. 282. It is proper to note here that the administrator chosen to rule the diocese in place of the diocesan consultors is not to be confused with the apostolic administrator mentioned in canon 431, § 1.

[27] *Acta et Decreta Concilii Plenarii Baltimorensis II*, nn. 96-99, pp. 67-68; *Acta et Decreta Concilii Plenarii Baltimorensis III*, n. 22, p. 16.

427 is to be observed. The Commission replied to the first question in the negative to the first part and in the affirmative to the second part. In answer to the second question it replied in the affirmative, *et ad mentem*. It was the mind of the Commission that inasfar as special circumstances hindered the application, immediately after the publication of the Code of Canon Law, of canon 427 in the United States, the Sacred Consistorial Congregation should issue a set of instructions to be observed temporarily; but the right of bishops to name an administrator of the diocese *mortis causa* was entirely abrogated.

The Holy Father ratified and confirmed these resolutions of the Commission for the Authentic Interpretation of the Code. On the motion, however, of the Cardinal Secretary of the Sacred Consistorial Congregation, in view of the peculiar circumstances existing in the dioceses of the United States, the Roman Pontiff also decreed that in all dioceses in which there are not at least five or six diocesan consultors (without prejudice to the prohibition made by the Commission), the metropolitan or senior suffragan of an ecclesiastical province may provide for the naming of a diocesan administrator during the vacancy of a see, the appointment to be confirmed by the apostolic delegate. This special permission was given for three years, provided that the board of diocesan consultors had not in the meantime been increased to the number indicated above. The answers to the two questions and the instructions were issued by the Sacred Consistorial Congregation on February 22, 1919. The special arrangement giving the metropolitan the right to choose the administrator is no longer in effect since 1922.[28]

The same rule which was enacted for the dioceses of the United States by the Decree of February 22, 1919, as to the appointment of administrators of dioceses, *sede vacante*, was to be in effect for the dioceses of Canada and Newfoundland.[29]

---

[28] *AAS*, XI (1919), 75. Cf. Bouscaren, *Digest*, I, 242-243; Beste, *Introductio in Codicem*, p. 281; Woywod, *Commentary*, I, 155; II, 566.

[29] *AAS*, XI (1919), 233. Cf. Bouscaren, *Digest*, I, 243.

According to canon 274, 3°, the metropolitan has the right to depute a vicar capitular in accordance with canon 432, § 2, only in the dioceses of his suffragans.

This right, however, is not an exclusive metropolitan right. The law gives this right of deputation to the senior suffragan in canons 432, § 2, and 434, § 3. This holds true only when the conditions specified by law are verified. Should the metropolitan see itself be vacant, or if both the metropolitan and a suffragan see of the same ecclesiastical province were vacant, the right of deputation would fall to the senior suffragan bishop within that particular province.[80] To act in such cases, the senior suffragan must see to it that the conditions for the exercise of the right of deputation are present.[81] Canon 432, § 2, does not give the senior suffragan the right to depute a vicar capitular or a diocesan administrator in case the metropolitan neglects to make the deputation.

Furthermore, the metropolitan has the right given him in canon 434, § 3, to appoint a vicar capitular or a diocesan administrator if the cathedral chapter or the diocesan consultors, as the case may be, should invalidly choose a cleric who has not the requirements specified by canon 434, § 1. He can do this as soon as he hears of the invalid choice. Here again the senior suffragan can only act if the metropolitan see is vacant; he cannot assume the right of deputation if the metropolitan refuses or neglects to act in cases of invalid choices.

It is also possible for archbishops and even bishops to have the right of deputation. Canon 431, § 2, declares that by special arrangement of the Holy See an archbishop or a bishop may designate an administrator for a vacant see. Such an administrator has all those, and only those, faculties which a vicar capitular has, and is subject to the same obligations and penalties. This canon makes a distinction.

---

[80] This suffragan is the oldest bishop in the province by reason of promotion to the suffragan see in the province. Cf. canon 284. For a detailed study regarding the senior suffragan bishop see *infra*, pp. 274-275.

[81] *Infra*, pp. 225-227.

It does not call the cleric designated by the archbishop or the bishop a vicar capitular; it calls him an administrator.

Although the devolved right to depute a vicar capitular or an administrator is the right of a metropolitan *par excellence,* as can be seen not only from canon 274, 3°, but also from canons 432, § 2, and 434, § 3, it is not an absolute right. Canon 274 does not give metropolitans this right in the form of an obligation but rather as a choice, since it uses the word *"potest"* only and not the word *"debet."*

Before a metropolitan can exercise the right of deputing a vicar capitular or a diocesan administrator, certain conditions must be verified. The first of these conditions is that the see which is vacant must be a suffragan see. This is clear from the introductory governing clause of canon 274. With regard to the vacant sees of the prelates mentioned in canon 285 a distinction must be made. The sees of bishops who are immediately subject to the Holy See and of archbishops who have no suffragans follow the general ruling of canon 432, § 3. This canon uses the phrase *"Etiam vacante diœcesi...de quibus in can. 285."* Accordingly both types of sees mentioned above are included. It must be taken for granted that the special arrangements of canon 431, § 2, are excluded. Should one or the other of the two special arrangements of canon 431, § 2, hold for the sees of bishops immediately subject to the Holy See or of archbishops without suffragans, the metropolitan has no right to exercise the right of deputation. If neither of these two special provisions is applicable, and the chapter or the consultors neglect within eight days, to select a cleric to rule the see during the time of vacancy, the metropolitan whom they have chosen in accord with canon 285 has the right to make the deputation of the vicar capitular or of the administrator, as the case may be.

With regard to the vacant abbacies and prelacies of abbots and prelates *nullius* who also are mentioned in canon 285, canon 432, § 3, makes a special provision. In a case of the vacancy of an abbacy or prelacy *nullius,* the chapter must within eight days nominate the vicar. If the chapter neglects to do so, the metropolitan of the province who was legitimately chosen in keeping with the ruling of canon 285 has the right to appoint the vicar or the administrator. Yet, the metropolitan's right is not absolute in such cases, for canon 432, § 3, continues with a special norm. If the incumbency in the abbacy or in the prelacy *nullius* belongs to the religious and the constitutions of the religious institute make other provision, then the procedure will follow the specific regulations enacted in the constitutions.

Another condition which must be verified is the vacancy of the see. An episcopal see, abbacy or prelacy *nullius*, becomes vacant upon the death of the bishop, abbot or prelate; on his resignation after it has been accepted by the Roman Pontiff; on his transfer from one see to another; and on his suffering a deprivation of office after it has been made known to him by the Roman Pontiff.[32] The see is not considered vacant if there is present in the diocese a coadjutor bishop who has the right of succession. As soon as the particular church is widowed, the coadjutor bishop immediately becomes the ordinary of the diocese in accordance with canon 355, § 1.

Still another postulated condition is the neglect of the cathedral chapter or of the board of diocesan consultors to choose the vicar capitular or the administrator within eight days from the accepted notice of the vacancy of the episcopal see. Should death bring about the vacancy of a see, the obligation of the cathedral chapter or of the board of diocesan consultors begins at the moment it receives certain notice of the bishop's death. The notification must be given to the entire cathedral chapter or board of diocesan consultors; private and individual notification would not be sufficient.[33]

If a bishop were to resign, the time period for the fulfillment of the chapter's or the diocesan consultors' obligation would begin at the time when the official notice of the Roman Pontiff's acceptance of the resignation would be made

[32] Canon 430, § 1.
[33] Canon 432, § 1. Cf. canons 433, § 2; 160-182.

known to one or the other group, as the case may be.[34] Again, the norms of canons 433, § 2, and 160-182 govern their subsequent action.

If a bishop were to be transferred from one diocese to another, his former diocese would become fully vacant from the day he takes possession of the new diocese.[35] The see would not become vacant at the time that the bishop would receive official word from the Holy See of his transfer, as canon 430, § 1, could seem to imply. Canon 430, § 3, is much too clear to allow such an interpretation. Hence in cases of transfer the obligation of the cathedral chapter or of the board of diocesan consultors begins at the time when they receive notice that their former bishop has taken canonical possession *("capta possessio")* of the new diocese.[36]

If bishops are removed from their sees or deprived of them by the Holy See, the chapters' or the consultors' obligation begins at the time the official notice of deprivation is made known to them by the Roman Pontiff along official channels.[37]

From the *terminus a quo* to the *terminus ad quem,* the law requires that no more than eight days elapse.[38] The time period *"intra octo dies"* is to be reckoned according to the norm given in canon 34, § 3, 1°.[39] According to canon 432, § 2, as soon as the eight day period has run out, the metropolitan has the right to depute the vicar capitular or the administrator of the vacant see. This is in keeping with the norm of canon 274, 3°.

Canon 434, § 3, extends the metropolitan right of deputation to still another case which is not contemplated either in canon 274, 3°, or in canon 432, § 2. If the cathedral chapter or the board of diocesan consultors choose a cleric who

---

[34] Canons 432, § 1; 430, § 1.

[35] Canon 430, § 3.

[36] Canon 432, § 1. Cf. canons 160-182.

[37] Canons 432, § 1; 430, § 1. Cf. canons 160-182.

[38] Canon 432, § 1.

[39] Beste, *Introductio in Codicem,* p. 282; Blat, *Commentarium,* Lib. II, pars 1, p. 467.

does not have the requirements specified by law for the validity of his appointment, the metropolitan may appoint a vicar capitular or an administrator in place of the one chosen as soon as he learns of the invalid choice. It is canon 434, § 1, which insists that a cleric cannot be validly deputed to the office of vicar capitular or of administrator unless he is already a priest, fully thirty years of age, and not elected, nominated or presented as a candidate for the episcopal office of the same see.[40]

The II Plenary Council of Baltimore did not issue any specific decree which covered this type of deputation on the part of metropolitans in its special section on metropolitans. It simply issued the general decree that a metropolitan is to supply the negligence of suffragans in the cases indicated by the law.[41] However, the footnote appended to this general decree refers to one of the laws of the Council of Trent, which stated the duty devolving upon the chapter during the vacancy of an episcopal see. This Tridentine law has been taken over almost verbatim into the Code of Canon Law, and specifies that the deputation of the vicar capitular devolves to the metropolitan if the chapter fails to constitute one within eight days.[42] The II Plenary Council of Baltimore adverted to this metropolitan right of deputation in decrees n. 97 and n. 98, when the Fathers of the Council treated of the communication of faculties in vacant episcopal sees. Even though the treatment is incidental, nevertheless it harmonizes with canon 432, § 1 and § 2, and with canon 274, 3°.[43]

Canon 274, 3°, treats only of the deputation of the vicar capitular or of the administrator; it states nothing concerning the econome. Yet canon 274, 3°, refers to canon 432, § 2,

---

[40] Canon 434, § 3 and § 1. In the United States the diocesan consultors need attend only to the requirements of priesthood and age, since there are no dioceses in which bishops can be elected, nominated or presented.

[41] "Negligentiam suffraganeorum in casibus a jure statutis supplet." —*Acta et Decreta Concilii Plenarii Baltimorensis II*, n. 81, 3, p. 61.

[42] Conc. Trident., sess. XXIV, *de ref.*, c. 16.

[43] *Acta et Decreta Concilii Plenarii Baltimorensis II*, p. 68.

which uses the phrase "*Vicarium aut œconomum.*" It seems that the metropolitan has the right to depute the econome if the cathedral chapter neglects to do this. Canon 432, § 1, states that the cathedral chapter must not only constitute a vicar capitular but must also choose one or more faithful and diligent economes if the office of the vicar capitular has connected with it the obligation of collecting revenues. It seems that if canon 432, § 1, makes this connection between the two offices depend upon the task of administering extant revenue, then canon 432, § 2, makes the same connection. Therefore, wherever the cathedral chapter neglects to constitute one or the other or both of these representatives, the metropolitan has a right to supply their neglect.

In the United States there is no obligation to constitute an econome, for the *mensa episcopalis* does not consist of revenue received from the goods of a church.[44] Bishops are paid salaries, and these are suspended during the vacancy of a diocese. The whole administration of spiritualities and temporalities rests upon the diocesan consultors, and after the legitimate deputation of an administrator the latter takes over the administration in accordance with the norms of the Code.[45]

The right to depute a vicar capitular or an administrator when cathedral chapters or boards of diocesan consultors neglect to make such an institution during the vacancy of an episcopal see does not belong to purely residential archbishops nor to titular archbishops. Canon 274, 3°, gives this right only to metropolitans. This is the usual arrangement. Only by special disposition of the Holy See can par-

---

[44] The econome mentioned in canons 432 and 433 appears only during the vacancy of an episcopal see, and his office ends with the rendering of an account to the new bishop. His office is to take care of the revenues of the *mensa episcopalis*, so that the income which belongs to the bishop may be kept for the successor. If there are no goods to be preserved for the successor, the appointment of an econome appears superfluous. The Code itself in canon 432, § 1, suggests that he is to be appointed only when there are goods to be administered for the benefit of the successor to the episcopal see.

[45] Beste, *Introductio in Codicem*, p. 282.

ticular, individual residential or non-residential archbishops enjoy this right.[46]

In the opinion of the writer the metropolitan can depute vicars capitular and administrators in accord with canon 274, 3°, even before he receives the pallium from the Roman Pontiff.

Article 3. Devolution: Visitation of Suffragan Sees in the Case of a Suffragan's Neglect

Canon 274. *In diœcesibus vero suffraganeis Metropolita potest tantum:*

5° *Canonicam visitationem peragere, causa prius ab Apostolica Sede probata, si eam Suffraganeus neglexerit; tempore autem visitationis, potest prædicare, confessiones audire etiam absolvendo a casibus Episcopo reservatis, de vita et honestate clericorum inquirere, clericos infamia notatos Ordinariis ipsorum, ut eos puniant, denuntiare, notoria crimina, manifestas et notorias offensas tum sibi tum suis forte illatas, iustis pœnis, censuris non exclusis, punire.*

If a suffragan bishop neglects to conduct the canonical visitation of his diocese, the metropolitan of the province is to supply the neglect, but before he does so, the Holy See must first approve the reason for the visitation.

Every residential bishop is bound to make a canonical visitation of his diocese, so that he visits at least a part of his diocese annually so as to cover his entire diocese at least once in five years either in person, or, if legitimately excused, through his vicar general or some other priest.[47] The seriousness of this episcopal obligation can be seen from the wording of canon 343, § 1. The obligation rests on the bishop primarily in such a way that he himself, personally, must conduct the visitation if he is in no way impeded. Furthermore, he cannot completely forego the visitation even if he is legitimately excused from making it

[46] Canon 431, § 2.

[47] Canon 343, § 1.

personally, for the canon states that he must conduct the visitation through his vicar general or some other priest. If the canonical visitation were not of a serious nature, it would be strange to find another reason for the specific detail as to the substitutes of the bishop. Another argument for the seriousness of this episcopal obligation in this regard is the prescription found in canon 343, § 3, which declares that, if a bishop seriously neglects to make the visitation of his diocese, the rulings of canon 274, 4° and 5°, are to be observed. Therefore canon 274, 5°, and 343, § 3, must be collated for a study of the metropolitan right to visit the sees of his suffragans should the suffragans themselves neglect to fulfill their obligation.

Canon 274, 5°, makes it very clear that a metropolitan cannot make the canonical visitation of any of his suffragans' sees without obtaining approval from the Holy See beforehand: "*causa prius ab Apostolica Sede probata.*" No matter how necessary a visitation may be, the conducting of such a visitation by a metropolitan is so serious a wound to the authority of a suffragan because of the interposition of metropolitan power in the affairs of another bishop, that the law demands that the metropolitan should not act on his own authority but upon the authority of the Holy See.[48] It is necessary, therefore, once the metropolitan sees the suffragan's neglect to observe the norms of canon 343, § 1, that he first make known this neglect to the Holy See in keeping with canon 274, 4°.

It is the Holy See alone which reviews the reason or reasons which the metropolitan presents for the necessity of making use of this type of devolution. The metropolitan may show that because of the neglect of the visitation in the suffragan see unhealthy and unorthodox doctrines are being broadcast; that good morals are being undermined; that depravities are not being corrected; that discord is rampant; that purity, piety and discipline of both the laity and clergy is on the wane; that in general the good of reli-

[48] Toso, *Commentaria,* III, 98.

gion is seriously suffering.[49] It would not be enough for the metropolitan to speak of such abuses in a general way; it would be necessary for him to show particular instances of such abuses.

After the Holy See has been informed by the metropolitan of the sad conditions within a suffragan diocese brought about by the neglect of the canonical visitation, he cannot presume that he has fulfilled all the requirements necessary for the exercise of the devolutive power granted him by canon 274, 5°, and accordingly begin the canonical visitation. The canon does not employ the words "*causa prius ab Apostolica Sede cognita,*" but the important word "*probata.*" The metropolitan must wait until the Holy See has approved the reason or reasons he has presented for exercising by devolution this right of visitation.[50] As soon as this approval is obtained, the metropolitan may begin the canonical visitation of the particular suffragan see, for the visitation of which he has received the apostolic approval. He cannot presume that this approval can be extended to all the dioceses of his province, unless the Holy See has approved his reason or reasons for the visitation of all the sees within his province.

Canon 343, § 3, uses the words "*graviter defuerit*" to explain the nature of the neglect on the part of the suffragan; canon 274, 5°, simply uses the word "*neglexerit,*" without making any mention of the type of neglect.[51] Inasmuch as the exercise of this metropolitan right restricts the free exercise of the suffragan's rights, canon 343, § 3, must be interpreted strictly in the spirit of canon 19. The metro-

---

[49] Canon 343, § 1.

[50] According to the Council of Trent (sess. XXIV, *de ref.*, c. 3) a metropolitan could visit the sees of his suffragans only after he had made a complete visitation of his own diocese and only after the cause he had for visiting the suffragan see was known and approved by the provincial council: "*nisi causa cognita et probata in concilio provinciali.*" The Code does not allude to the necessity of presenting reasons to a provincial council or to the need of making the visitation within his own diocese beforehand. Cf. *supra*, pp. 121-122.

[51] Blat, *Commentarium*, Lib. II, pars 1, p. 368.

politan does not have the right to inform the Holy See of each and every item of neglect on the part of the suffragan, but only of those which are serious in nature. Furthermore, the metropolitan cannot report as an abuse the fact that the bishop chooses to make the visitation through his vicar general or some other priest. Nor could the metropolitan inform the Holy See if the bishop visited a part of the diocese and postponed the visitation of the rest of it to a later date. However, it seems that he may inform the Holy See if the suffragan refused to visit personally, or through his vicar general or some other priest, a particular section of his diocese as a matter of policy. There is nothing in the canon which states that the metropolitan has the duty to inform the suffragan of his intention to notify the Holy See of the neglect of which the suffragan is guilty.

Once the reason for the exercise of the visitation-right is approved by the Holy See, the metropolitan receives certain rights over the subjects of the diocese he is to visit. During the actual visitation he may preach, hear confessions and absolve from cases reserved to the bishop, inquire into the life and morals of the clerics, denounce to their ordinary clerics marked by infamy, so that the ordinary may punish them, and punish with just penalties and even with censures all notorious crimes, as well as all manifest and notorious offenses inflicted upon himself or the members of his retinue.[52]

Since persons, things and places of piety within the limits of a diocese are subject to the visitation of a bishop unless it can be proved that a special exemption from the visitation has been granted them by the Apostolic See, the metropolitan has the right to include all these persons, things and places of piety within the itinerary of his legitimate canonical visitation. By law even exempt persons, things and places of piety can be visited by a bishop, so it follows that the metropolitan can do the same.[53] The bishop can visit exempt religious only in cases explicitly stated in

[52] Canon 274, 5°.

[53] Canon 344, § 1.

law. This holds true in a parallel fashion for the metropolitan.[54]

The metropolitan can visit the following religious: the individual houses of congregations of diocesan approval (c. 512); the individual houses of lay congregations of pontifical approval, of men and of women (c. 618); individual monasteries of nuns according to the norms of canon 512; individual houses of clerical congregations of pontifical approval, but only with reference to the church, the sacrarium, the public oratory and the confessional (c. 512). It does not seem that he has the right to visit the churches of religious orders, except to ascertain whether the laws enacted by the bishop with reference to public worship in his territory are observed (c. 1261).[55] In this visitation the metropolitan is to proceed in the same fashion as a bishop. The chief function is investigation rather than punishment; he is to act in a paternal manner and is not allowed to act as a judge.[56]

Even though canon 1337 states that the local ordinary alone concedes the faculty of preaching for his own territory, it is canon 274, 5°, which grants the metropolitan the faculty of preaching throughout the suffragan see during a legitimate visitation, without the need of his getting the consent of the suffragan bishop. Since there is no limiting clause or word in the phrase "*potest prædicare,*" the metropolitan may preach throughout the entire diocese of the suffragan. He may also preach in the churches of the exempt religious, for there is nothing in the Code to the contrary.[57] It is important to remember that the phrase is "*potest prædicare,*" and not "*debet prædicare.*" The faculty is given to the metropolitan alone; he cannot presume that he has the right to grant the same faculty to whomsoever he wills to give it within the diocese of his suffragan.

---

[54] Canon 344, § 2.

[55] Cf. canons 1274; 1338; 1382. Cf. Claeys Bouuaert-Simenon, *Manuale*, I, 272.

[56] Canon 345. Cf. canons 343-346; 274, 1°, 3°, 4°, 5°. Cf. Cappello, *Summa*, I, 308; Chelodi, *Ius Canonicum*, p. 280, footnote 1.

[57] Cf. canons 344, § 2; 512.

According to canon 239, § 1, 3°, cardinals have the faculty granted them by law to preach the Word of God everywhere in the world without the need of asking the consent of any local ordinary. However, a metropolitan who is not at the same time a cardinal has no such general faculty given him by canon 274, 5°. Outside of the time of visitation he is required by canon 1337 to ask for the faculty of preaching within each and every diocese of his province.[58]

This faculty is not given to purely residential archbishops or to non-residential archbishops. These have no legal right to exercise the rights derived by devolution as specified in canon 274, 5°; hence they have no faculties which are connected with a legitimate visitation of a suffragan bishop's see.

The metropolitan has the right to hear confessions during a legitimate visitation of a suffragan see: *"confessiones audire."* Since canon 274, 5°, sets no limitations with regard to the quality of those whose confessions he may hear, it must be understood that he may hear the confessions of all lay people and clerics.[59] There is no mention made concerning the confessions of women religious, hence it can be taken for granted that the metropolitan can hear their confessions as well. Not only may he hear confessions throughout the entire suffragan see, but he may absolve all those who come to him in confession from all cases reserved by the suffragan bishop of the diocese he is canonically visiting: *"etiam absolvendo a casibus Episcopo reservatis."*[60] The sacramental jurisdiction the metropolitan needs is given him by force of this canon.[61]

Canon 274, 5°, explicitly mentions that a metropolitan may absolve from cases reserved by the bishop, but it states nothing about the sin reserved to the Holy See as mentioned in canon 894, nor does it state anything about the sins reserved to the superior general of exempt clerical religious

[58] Blat, *Commentarium*, Lib. II, pars 1, p. 292.
[59] Blat, *loc. cit.*
[60] Canon 893, § 1, § 2. Cf. canons 895 and 897.
[61] Cf. canons 872; 873, § 1; 874, § 1.

congregations or to the abbots of autonomous monasteries. In keeping with canon 19, the metropolitan cannot absolve from any of these sins under the ordinary circumstances of visiting a suffragan's diocese. However, canon 519 grants all religious, even of exempt organizations, the right to go to confession for the peace of conscience to any confessor approved by the ordinary of the place where the confession is made. This extraordinary confessor may validly and licitly absolve the religious even from any sin reserved in the religious organization.[62] In such an extraordinary case the metropolitan may, without the approval of the local ordinary, absolve from a sin reserved by the superior general of an exempt clerical religious institute, or to the abbot of an autonomous monastery. But the right of absolution is granted to a metropolitan by law not for the reason that he is a metropolitan, but for the reason that he is a priest. He can, without the approval of the local ordinary, absolve from these reserved sins like any other priest approved by the ordinary during the time of visitation. There is no such extraordinary remedy given for the sin reserved to the Holy See in canon 894. Hence the metropolitan cannot presume that the right of absolving which he derives from canon 274, 5°, grants him faculties to absolve this sin without recourse to the Holy See for special faculties.

Again, the faculty of absolving and of hearing confessions as granted to metropolitans for the time of the legitimate visitation is not as extensive as that given to cardinals in canon 239, § 1, 1°. The latter may throughout the world hear the confessions of all, including the religious of both sexes, as well as absolve from all sins, even those which are reserved. A metropolitan may not presume to hear confessions outside his own archdiocese, except by legal right in the suffragan sees, and then only during the time of an actual canonical visitation. He may absolve from all non-reserved sins and also from those reserved sins which the particular suffragan bishop has so designated; he may not

---

[62] Cf. canon 522.

absolve from any others. The faculties of cardinals permit them to absolve all persons from all censures, even those which are reserved, except those which are reserved to the Apostolic See in a most special manner and those which are annexed to the revelation of a secret of the Holy Office. There is nothing in canon 274, 5°, which indicates that a metropolitan may absolve any subject of his suffragan from any reserved censure during the canonical visitation. The regular legal channels must be employed for the absolution of these.

The prescript of canon 274, 5°, does not apply to purely residential or non-residential archbishops.

During the visitation the metropolitan has the right to inquire concerning the life and morals of the clerics within the see of the suffragan bishop: *"de vita et honestate clericorum inquirere."* All the matters treated within the section entitled *"De Obligationibus Clericorum,"* from canon 124 to canon 144, can be the object of the metropolitan's inquiry. He can review and examine the interior life, exterior conduct, the frequentation of confession, meditation, visits to the Blessed Sacrament, the recitation of the rosary, the acceptance and the fulfillment of offices assigned to clerics by the bishop, their examination of conscience, retreats, respect and obedience shown the ordinary, the study of the sacred sciences, clergy examinations, diocesan conferences, celibacy, suspicious conduct with women, community life, the recitation of the breviary, clerical garb, the giving of bail or surety, the practice of unbecoming arts or of games of chance, the carrying of weapons, hunting, the visiting of taverns, the practice of medicine or surgery, the holding of public offices, the acceptance of agency for goods and property belonging to lay people, participation in criminal cases in secular courts, competition for secular offices, attendance at theatres, dances and shows, volunteering for military service, participation in business or trading, absence from benefice, office or diocese, and other matters of similar import.

This inquiry is to be a general one. The result of this

general inquiry is to be reported to the Holy See in accordance with canon 274, 4°. The metropolitan has no right to make the special investigation spoken of in canon 1939, §1. The special investigation is to be conducted only in connection with a criminal trial, and as such it is a part of judicial process. The metropolitan has no right to act in first instance trials within the suffragan sees; the only first instance causes he is allowed to take up are those mentioned in canon 274, 8°. But even those which he is permitted to take up are to be settled in his own tribunal.[63]

Purely residential and non-residential archbishops do not have the right by devolution to make inquiry concerning the life and morals of clerics.

The next right which the metropolitan has during the legitimate canonical visitation is that of denouncing to their ordinaries clerics marked with infamy in order that these ordinaries may punish them: *"clericos infamia notatos Ordinariis ipsorum, ut eas puniant, denuntiare."*[64] This metropolitan right is limited to denunciation only; he has no right whatever to punish such clerics himself. This denunciation is to be efficacious, that is to say, if the ordinaries of these clerics do not punish the guilty clerics who have been denounced to them by the metropolitan, the ordinaries are guilty of abusing a strict obligation. The phrase of canon 274, 5°, which reads *"ut eos puniant,"* indicates the legal obligation ordinaries have to inflict punishment upon such clerics should all the specifications of the canon be verified. Furthermore, the metropolitan has the right to notify the Roman Pontiff concerning this abuse in accordance with canon 274, 4°.

The infamy which the metropolitans are to denounce may be either an *infamia iuris* or an *infamia facti.*[65] Infamy of law is that which is determined in common law for specific cases; infamy of fact is contracted when, through

---

[63] Cf. *infra,* pp. 264-269. Cf. Blat, *Commentarium,* Lib. II, pars 1, p. 292.

[64] Canon 274, 5°.

[65] Blat, *Commentarium,* Lib. II, pars 1, p. 292.

the commission of an offense or bad morals, one has lost good repute with upright and serious Catholics; the judgment as to whether infamy of fact exists in a given case is vested in the ordinary.[66]

Infamy of law ceases only after a dispensation is obtained from the Apostolic See.[67] Hence, after the denunciation of a cleric marked by infamy of law is made by the metropolitan, his ordinary must not only punish him in accordance with the canons, but must refrain from attempting to dispense him from the infamy without receiving authorization from the Holy See. Infamy of fact ceases when the ordinary, after considering all the circumstances and especially the prolonged amendment of the guilty cleric, prudently judges that the cleric has regained good repute with righteous and serious Catholics.[68]

The metropolitan has no difficulty in determining whether a cleric is marked by infamy of law, for the law determines the delicts which have this type of infamy attached to them. With regard to infamy of fact, since the ordinary of the guilty cleric has not made the judgment, the right to determine whether or not infamy of fact is present devolves upon the metropolitan.

The clerics to whom the infamy is attached must be known to deserve the infamy, for the canon uses the phrase "*clericos infamia notatos.*"[69] If the infamy of law or of fact flows from a public delict as defined in canon 2197, 1°, and the cleric has not been punished by his ordinary, the metropolitan must proceed to the fulfillment of the right given him in canon 274, 5°. Should the infamy of law or fact develop from a materially or formally occult delict as

---

[66] Canon 2293, § 1; § 2; § 3. The following canons bear reference to infamy. *Infamia iuris:* 2294, § 1; 766, 2°, 796, 3°; 167, § 1, 3°; 765, 2°; 795, 2°; *ipso facto:* 2320; 2328; 2342; 2343, § 2, 2°; 2351, § 2; 2356; 2357, § 1; *declaratione:* 2314, § 1, 2°; 2359, § 2. Some canons refer exclusively to *infamia facti:* e.g., 2294, § 2; 987, 2°; etc.

[67] Canon 2295.

[68] Canon 2295. Cf. canon 672, § 1.

[69] Blat, *Commentarium,* Lib. II, pars 1, p. 292; Toso, *Commentaria,* III, 98.

described in canon 2197, 4°, it seems that the metropolitan does not have the right to denounce the cleric. However, it seems advisable in such cases that the metropolitan report the infamy of fact or of law to the ordinary.

The metropolitan's right is limited to the denunciation of clerics only. Canon 274, 5°, uses the word "*clericos*" only. The omission of a phrase like "*et laicos*" or "*omnes*" restricts the metropolitan right of denunciation. In accordance with canon 19, the norm of canon 274 which treats of this form of denunciation must be interpreted strictly, for in infamy there is question of a penalty. Since the canon does not distinguish between the types of clerics, but simply employs the word "*clericos,*" the metropolitan has the right to denounce all secular and all religious clerics except exempt clerics in accordance with canon 615. However, even exempt religious clerics can be denounced by the metropolitan if they fit into the classes described in canons 616 and 617.[70]

With regard to the ordinary to whom the metropolitan is to make the denunciation, the Code simply uses the phrase "*Ordinariis ipsorum.*" Since the canon does not use the expression *local ordinaries*, the phrase can mean both local ordinaries for all secular clerics and the religious superiors of exempt regulars mentioned in canons 616 and 617. The ordinary and the religious superior must be the proper ordinary or superior of the cleric who is known to be marked with infamy of law or of fact. The proper ordinary or superior alone has the right to punish the guilty cleric for the delict to which the odium of infamy is attached.

The final right which metropolitans have in the legitimate canonical visitation of one of their suffragan sees is that of actually punishing, with just penalties and even censures, notorious crimes as well as manifest and notorious offenses inflicted upon the metropolitan himself or his retinue: "*notoria crimina, manifestas et notorias offensas tum sibi tum suis forte illatas, iustis pœnis, censuris non exclu-*

[70] Blat, *Commentarium*, Lib. II, pars 1, p. 292.

sis, punire."[71] This is the broadest of all the rights which a metropolitan has during the visitation.

The first type of offense which the metropolitan can punish is a notorious crime. Inasmuch as the canon employs not the word *delictum*, but the word "*crimen*," it seems that the genuine meaning to be given to the word "*crimen*" implies an adaptation of the sense which is attached to a delict as defined in canon 2195, § 1. A crime as mentioned in canon 274, 5°, is any external and morally imputable violation of the law, with this exception, however, that it does not necessarily have a canonical penal sanction attached to it. The crime, according to canon 274, 5°, must be notorious. Canon 2197, 2°, 3°, defines notoriety of law and of fact.

The notorious crimes with which canon 274, 5°, deals cannot be those which are such by notoriety of law, for the metropolitan is not allowed to act as judge within the sees of his suffragans. Canon 274, 7°, and 8°, give the only types of judicial causes which the metropolitan can take up in his own tribunal. No other specification is made in canon 274, nor does any other canon of the Code grant the metropolitan the right to institute his own tribunal in the suffragan sees. The notorious crimes spoken of in canon 274, 5°, can be only those which are such by notoriety of fact.[72]

Crimes of this type are publicly known and are committed under such circumstances that they cannot be concealed by any subterfuge or excused by any help of the law. In such crimes both the fact and the imputability must be publicly known.[73] Should an occult crime or a public crime which is not as yet divulged be committed against a metropolitan or any member of his retinue, the metropolitan could not punish such crimes according to the strict interpretation of the norm of canon 274, 5°. Punishment of such a crime would be left to the suffragan bishop.[74]

The second type of wrongdoing which the metropolitan

---

[71] Canon 274, 5°.

[72] Canon 2197, 3°.

[73] Blat, *Commentarium*, Lib. II, pars 1, p. 292.

[74] Sipos, *Enchiridion*, p. 225, footnote 12.

is allowed to punish is reflected in manifest and notorious offenses. This form of wrongdoing could be any word, writing or deed, which would injure the person or dignity of the one against whom it is leveled, in this case against the metropolitan or any one of his retinue. The offense must be manifest in its culpability and notorious with regard to the manner in which it is known. Notoriety of law is excluded on the same grounds as above, hence the notoriety must be one which exists in fact.[75] If one or the other element is missing, either the culpability or the notoriety, the metropolitan would not, in line with the principle of interpretation confirmed in canon 19, be allowed to punish the offense.[76]

It is further postulated that the notorious crimes or the manifest and notorious offenses be inflicted upon the metropolitan during the visitation. However, the law includes those who accompany him throughout the legitimate visitation in such a way that if any injury comes to them, the metropolitan can punish those who have brought about the injury.[77] Canon 274, 5°, does not distinguish between clerics and laymen. Hence the metropolitan can punish both types of offenders. The employment of the conjunctions "*tum... tum*" shows that the crimes and offenses need not be leveled against both the metropolitan and his retinue at one and the same time; it shows that it is sufficient to injure either the metropolitan alone, or any member of the retinue alone, to deserve the punishment.

The metropolitan can punish the notorious crimes as well as the manifest and notorious offenses described above so long as they do not need to be proved or decided on by a judicial trial. If a judicial trial is to be instituted in any such cases, the metropolitan would not be the judge. The cause would have to go through the judicial procedure in the tribunal of the suffragan as required by law.[78] If these crimes or offenses require no judicial procedure, the metro-

---

[75] Canon 2197, 3°.
[76] Blat, *Commentarium*, Lib. II, pars 1, p. 292.
[77] Canon 343, § 2.
[78] Canon 345.

politan may punish those who are guilty with just penalties and with censures. The penalty would be just if it were proportionate to the offense committed. The inflicted censures could take the form of excommunication, suspension or interdict. Since the method of inflicting these penalties and censures is extra-judicial, they would have to be inflicted by way of precept: *"per modum præcepti."* [79]

The metropolitan could inflict these penalties or censures upon each of the guilty individuals either by means of a legitimate document or in the presence of two witnesses. If one or the other method were employed, the precept would bind everywhere, though it could not be enforced judicially, and would not cease with the expiration of the authority of the metropolitan who imposed it.[80] If the metropolitan gave the precept without using a legitimate document or without employing witnesses, the binding force of the precept would cease with the expiration of his authority.

The metropolitan cannot use the right of punishing crimes and offenses except during the legitimate canonical visitation. Should any crimes or offenses be leveled against him or his retinue at any other time, the metropolitan cannot presume to make use of this extraordinary right. Outside the time of visitation, the remedies for crimes and offenses would flow from the regular channels of law.

Toso declares that the enumeration of the metropolitan rights on the occasion of the canonical visitation of suffragan sees is all-inclusive. From a study of canon 274, 5°, and the introductory governing clause of the canon itself, it does not seem to him that the metropolitan has legislative power at any time during the visitation. Hence the metropolitan cannot issue decrees of the kind that are spoken of in canon 345. The pre-Code legislation had already taken away this power from visiting metropolitans.[81]

Furthermore, the Code does not enact any prescription

[79] Canon 1933, § 4. Cf. Blat, *Commentarium*, Lib. II, pars 1, pp. 292-293.

[80] Canon 24.

[81] *Commentaria*, III, 98.

for cases of neglect in which the metropolitan is involved. No canon in the Code allows the senior suffragan to make use of the right by devolution should a metropolitan neglect to make the canonical visitation of his archdiocese.

According to the writer's opinion, the imposition of the pallium is not necessary for the licitness of a legitimate canonical visitation by the metropolitan of suffragan sees.

Both the II and the III Plenary Councils of Baltimore stress the obligation resting on bishops to make the canonical visitation of their dioceses. The former states that it should be made at least once every two years; the latter, at least once every three years. However, nothing was stated in these decrees as to just what was to be done if bishops neglected to fulfill the obligation.[82]

The footnote appended to decree n. 81, 3, of the II Plenary Council of Baltimore, which declares that metropolitans are to supply for the negligences of their suffragans, refers to the legislation of the Council of Trent on the matter.[83] The legislation of the Council of Trent has been changed by the Code. Canon 274, 5°, makes it clear that there must be negligence in this matter on the part of the suffragan, that this negligence must be reported to the Roman Pontiff by the metropolitan, and that the metropolitan cannot proceed with the visitation until the cause has been approved by the Holy See. Such norms as : previous visitation on the part of the metropolitan of his own archdiocese before the visitation of the diocese of his suffragan; the previous cognizance and approval of the cause by the provincial council; the right of the metropolitan in the absence of negligence on the part of the suffragan as grounds for the visitation, are abrogated by the Code. Hence these specifications as adopted by the II Plenary Council of Baltimore are now *contra legem*.[84]

---

[82] *Acta et Decreta Concilii Plenarii Baltimorensis II*, n. 86, p. 65; *Acta et Decreta Concilii Plenarii Baltimorensis III*, n. 14, p. 11.

[83] Conc. Trident., sess, XXIV, *de ref.*, c. 3.

[84] Canon 343, § 3, has extended the period of episcopal visitation from two to five years. But the provisions of both councils are to be considered as simply *præter legem* in the matter of the time period allowed for the total visitation of the diocese.

Article 4. Vigilance

Canon 274. *In diœcesibus vero suffraganeis Metropolita potest tantum:*

4° *Vigilare ut fides ac disciplina ecclesiastica accurate serventur, ac de abusibus Romanum Pontificem certiorem facere.*

One of the broadest rights which metropolitans enjoy over the suffragan sees is that of vigilance. Canon 274, 4°, declares that a metropolitan has the right not only to be vigilant in order that faith and ecclesiastical discipline be accurately observed, but also to furnish information to the Roman Pontiff about the abuses. There is contained in this power of vigilance the power of using all those means which seem necessary or opportune to the conscience and judgment of the metropolitan to obtain the desired effect. According to Toso this power seems to be in accord with the legal principle enunciated in canon 66, § 3: faculties granted by the Holy See include also such other powers as are necessary for their exercise.[85]

The metropolitan right of vigilance is to be exercised from outside suffragan sees, and not from within them. It contains in a sense the rights possessed by devolution as mentioned in canon 274, 1° and 3°, and such rights of canon 274, 5°, as the inquiry into the life and morals of clerics and the denunciation of clerics marked with infamy, so long as the metropolitan does not presume to exercise these rights within the see of the suffragan.

The phrase "*fides ac disciplina ecclesiastica*" is broad enough to include all those matters which are the object of an episcopal visitation. Canon 343, § 1, enumerates these matters in some detail. When canon 274, 4°, states that a metropolitan is to insure that faith and ecclesiastical discipline are preserved, it is with the purpose that he may notify the Roman Pontiff of any abuses flowing from the inaccurate observance of both. The canon employs the

---

[85] *Commentaria*, III, 98.

phrase "*de abusibus.*" Accordingly a metropolitan is not to report all such transgressions of faith and discipline which are apt to occur everywhere in the world, even frequently; if the law wished transgressions of the law to be reported as such, it would not have used the word *abuses*. It is only when transgressions are so serious and so frequent as to disrupt faith and ecclesiastical discipline that they take on the nature of abuses.[86]

The vigilance of the metropolitan extends to other types of abuses besides those mentioned above. Chief among them is the illegitimate absence of bishops from their dioceses. According to canon 338, § 4, if a bishop is absent from his diocese over six months without a legitimate reason, the metropolitan is to denounce him to the Apostolic See. This canon cites 274, 4°.[87] The six month period of absence is to be computed in accordance with the norm given in canon 34, § 2, i.e., "*de momento ad momentum,*" and the months are to be taken as in the calendar.[88]

The absence must be illegitimate. Evidently if a suffragan bishop, in opposition to canon 338, § 2, prolonged his "*ad limina*" visit, or the time needed for attendance at a council or for the performance of civil duties, or his vacation, to more than six months, it is the right of the metropolitan to denounce him to the Roman Pontiff. If, again, a suffragan combined the vacation of two years and overstayed the six month period, or if a newly appointed suffragan delayed to take up his residence in the suffragan see for more than six months, the metropolitan could use his right of denunciation. Under the letter of the law, the metropolitan has no right, however, to denounce a suffragan whose illegitimate absence is in opposition to canon 338, § 3.[89]

The metropolitan has no right to punish suffragans who do not observe the law of residence. His only duty in the matter is to give notice of the abuse to the Roman Pontiff

---

[86] Blat, *Commentarium*, Lib. II, pars 1, p. 292.

[87] Cf. Beste, *Introductio in Codicem*, p. 252.

[88] Cf. Blat, *Commentarium*, Lib. II, pars 1, p. 360.

[89] Blat, *Commentarium*, Lib. II, pars 1, p. 360.

in accord with canon 274, 4°, or as canon 338, § 4, puts it, he is to denounce him to the Apostolic See. Any punitive action on the part of the metropolitan would be an overstepping of his power.

The term "*Episcopum*" used in canon 338, § 4, broadens the meaning of the word *suffraganeus* in the introductory clause of canon 274. Hence it includes not only suffragan bishops in the strict sense, but also all those bishops who are immediately subject to the Holy See, archbishops without suffragans, and abbots and prelates *nullius*, who have chosen a particular metropolitan as their own in accordance with canon 285.[90] The prelates mentioned in canon 285 are included here by analogy of law, for canon 20 states that, if an express prescript of a general or a particular law is lacking, the norm is to be taken from laws enacted in similar things.[91]

The II Plenary Council of Baltimore legislated that a metropolitan was bound to denounce to the Apostolic See a comprovincial bishop who did not observe the law of residence and who was absent contumaciously from his diocese beyond the time granted by the sacred canons. The denunciation was to be made within three months by means of letters or messenger.[92] The conciliar legislation referred to the decrees of the Council of Trent, which tolerated two periods of absence, each lasting six months, before the metropolitan denunciation was to take place.[93] The Code of Canon Law tolerates only one period of six months of illegitimate absence, and it does not specify the three month limitation for the metropolitan denunciation. The conciliar legislation of Baltimore is therefore *contra Codicem,* and accordingly must be regarded as abrogated in accordance with the norm of canon 6, 1°.

---

[90] *Infra,* pp. 278-279.

[91] Blat, *Commentarium,* Lib. II, pars 1, p. 360.

[92] "Comprovincialem Episcopum non residentem, et ultra tempus a sacris canonibus concessum cum contumacia absentem, tenetur intra tres menses per literas seu nuntium Sedi Apostolicæ denuntiare...." — *Acta et Decreta Concilii Plenarii Baltimorensis II,* n. 81, 1, p. 61.

[93] Sess. VI, *de ref.,* c. 1.

Canon 338, § 4, makes provision for the denunciation of an absent metropolitan. Should the metropolitan be illegitimately absent from his own archdiocese for a period longer than six months, the senior suffragan is to denounce him to the Apostolic See. This senior suffragan is the one described in canon 284 as the one who is oldest in promotion to a suffragan church within a province: "*antiquior promotione ad ecclesiam suffraganeam.*" However, there is a slight variation in canon 338, § 4. The canon inserts the word "*residens*" after the phrase "*antiquior Suffraganeus.*" This was done advisedly. It could happen that both the metropolitan and the senior suffragan would be illegitimately absent from their dioceses at one and the same time. In such an eventuality the senior residing suffragan, i.e., the senior suffragan in appointment to a suffragan see who actually observes the law of residence, is to make the denunciation to the Apostolic See. After all, such a bishop could make known in the best manner the truth of the transgression and by his own fidelity to discipline would be in the best position to make the denunciation.[94]

The legislation of the II Plenary Council of Baltimore gave the right of denouncing the absent metropolitan to the senior bishop of the province.[95] The conciliar decree cited the Tridentine legislation in support of its enactment.[96] The law of the Council of Trent made it clear that the senior suffragan thus burdened must be resident. In this it agrees with the Code. However, the denunciation of a metropolitan was allowed only after the passing of two six months' periods. The second six months' period is abrogated by the Code. Hence the decree of the Council of Baltimore is also *contra legem* in this point; the rest of the decree can be said to be in agreement with the Code.

Another abuse which the metropolitan has the right and

[94] Blat, *Commentarium*, Lib. II, pars 1, p. 360.

[95] "...ipsum vero Metropolitam similiter absentem antiquior provinciæ Episcopus denuntiare tenetur." — *Acta et Decreta Concilii Plenarii Baltimorensis II*, n. 81, 1, p. 61.

[96] Sess. VI, *de ref.*, c. 1.

duty to report to the Roman Pontiff is that which has already been treated above, namely, the episcopal neglect to conduct the canonical visitation of his see.[97]

The metropolitan can use this right also when one of his suffragan bishops has fallen into excommunication, interdict, or suspension. This report to the Holy See is to be made not only for the purpose of having provision made for the impeded see, but also for the sake of informing the Roman Pontiff of the unhappy legal condition of his suffragan.[98] Canon 429, § 5, declares further that the metropolitan is to make recourse for the prelates mentioned in canon 285, should these fall into any of the censures mentioned above. Hence it can be said that in their case, too, the metropolitan has the right to inform the Roman Pontiff of the abuses flowing from their excommunication, interdict or suspension. Should the metropolitan himself be excommunicated, interdicted or suspended, the senior suffragan has the right given him by law to notify the Roman Pontiff about the censures which have befallen either the suffragans or the metropolitan respectively.[99]

According to canon 785, § 1, a bishop is bound to administer confirmation to his subjects who legitimately and reasonably ask for it, especially at the time of his visitation of the diocese. Furthermore, this same canon states in § 3 that an ordinary who is prevented by a legitimate reason from administering confirmation, or an ordinary who has no faculty to confirm, must see to it that at least every five years, if possible, this sacrament is administered to his subjects. Finally § 4 of the canon states that if he is gravely negligent in administering confirmation to his subjects, either in person or through another, canon 274, 4°, is to be observed.

Should a suffragan bishop neglect to confirm his sub-

---

[97] Canon 343, § 3. For a fuller treatment of the exercise of this right the reader is referred to pp. 230-244, *supra*. Cf. also Beste, *Introductio in Codicem*, p. 252.

[98] Canon 429, § 5. Cf. Beste, *Introductio in Codicem*, p. 252.

[99] Canon 429, § 5. Cf. Beste, *loc. cit.*

jects *"per se vel per alium"* for a period of over five years, the metropolitan has a right to report the abuse to the Roman Pontiff.[100] The metropolitan could not refer the matter to the Holy See if the suffragan took care of the administration of confirmation through another bishop, or if the persons who asked for confirmation were not subjects of the suffragan. According to the canon the neglect would have to be grave or serious, for it employs the word *"graviter."* The period of five years is to be reckoned according to the norm given in canon 34, § 2.

The metropolitan does not need the pallium for the exercise of the right granted him in canon 274, 4°.

Residential and non-residential archbishops do not enjoy any of the rights of vigilance over the sees of suffragan bishops. This right belongs to the metropolitan, to the exclusion of mere archbishops; the introductory clause of canon 274 makes the point clear.

Section B

Judicial Rights

Article 1. Second Instance Causes

Canon 274. *In diœcesibus vero suffraganeis Metropolita potest tantum:*

7° *Appellationem recipere a sententiis definitivis aut interlocutoriis definitivarum vim habentibus, prolatis in Curiis suffraganeis, ad normam can. 1594, § 1.*

According to the law of the Church, the judge in an ecclesiastical trial who tries a cause in one instance cannot try the same cause in another instance.[101] Hence the law makes provision for courts of appeal to which the tribunals both of suffragans and of metropolitans can send their causes for a second instance decision. The appeal court can

[100] Beste, *Introductio in Codicem*, p. 252.
[101] Canon 1571.

confirm, change, abrogate or declare null and void the decision made in the tribunal of first instance.

Only two types of appeal can be made from the tribunal of the suffragan bishop to the tribunal of his metropolitan: (a) an appeal from a definitive sentence, and (b) an appeal from an interlocutory sentence which has definitive force. Both these types of appeal must be made in accordance with canon 1594, § 1.

According to canon 1879, a party who feels aggrieved over a sentence, and the promoter of justice *(promotor iustitiæ)* or the defender of the bond *(defensor vinculi)* in those causes in which either took part, have the right to appeal from the sentence, that is to say, they may go from the inferior judge who issued the sentence to a superior judge. Regularly the appeal is proposed to an ordinary tribunal which is immediately superior, but appeal to the ordinary tribunal of second instance is not obligatory, for a direct appeal from all adjudicated causes decided by any ordinary in the first instance can always be made directly to the Holy See.[102] Canon 1569, § 1, states that it is the right of any one of the faithful in the whole Catholic world to present his cause, whether it be contentious or criminal, in whatever instance of the trial and in whatever stage of the procedure, to the Holy See for adjudication. The Holy See can accept all causes in their second instance because of the primacy of the Roman Pontiff. This extraordinary manner of making an appeal is described in canon 1599, § 1, 1°, where it is stated that the Sacred Roman Rota has the right to try all causes in the second instance which have already been tried in the first instance in the courts of any of the ordinaries and which are brought to the Holy See by legitimate appeal.

However, the Code of Canon Law legislated that the

---

[102] Roberti, *De Processibus* (2 vols., Romæ: Tip. Soc. Ed. del Libro Italiano, 1941. [Vol. I, *De Actione, De Præsuppositis Processus et Sententiæ de Merito,* 2. ed., 1941]), I, 239-240 (hereafter cited as *De Processibus*).

ordinary means of appeal from the tribunals of suffragan bishops is that which is made to the tribunal of their metropolitan.[103] This designation by law makes the metropolitan the ordinary judge of second instance, i.e., the competent judge of appeals brought to his tribunal from the sentences rendered in the first instance tribunals of his suffragans.[104] Both canon 274, 7°, and canon 1594, § 1, make it clear that the metropolitan can accept these appeals only from the tribunals of his suffragans, that is to say, the curias of those bishops who are his subjects within the ecclesiastical province, since their dioceses are parts of the territory which make up the province. Canon 274, 7°, does not include the tribunals of the prelates of canon 285. Even canon 285 states nothing about the ordinary tribunal of second instance for the causes tried in the first instance in the tribunals of these prelates. It is canon 1594, § 3, which legislates in part for them.

Nevertheless, this norm does not include all the prelates mentioned in canon 285; it mentions only the archbishops who lack suffragans, and local ordinaries who are immediately subject to the Holy See; it is silent about the abbots and prelates *nullius*. Paragraph 4 of canon 1594 makes special provision for the courts of appeal of the religious. It states that causes tried in the first instance by the local abbot are to be taken to the supreme moderator of the monastic congregation. In consequence of this exception in § 4, it seems that canon 1594, § 3, wishes to include all other types of abbots and prelates *nullius* in the phrase "*coram loci Ordinario immediate Sedi Apostolicæ subiecto.*" Canon 198, § 1, states clearly that the term "*Ordinarii*" in law includes the "*Abbas vel Prælatus* nullius," unless an express exception is made.[105] The only exception made in canon 1594, § 4, is that concerning the local abbot. Hence all causes tried in the first instance by the other types of ab-

[103] Canon 1594, § 1.

[104] Cf. Coronata, *Institutiones*, III, 40.

[105] Cf. canons 110 and 319, § 1, in explanation of these terms.

bots and prelates *nullius* can be taken to the tribunal of the metropolitan chosen in accordance with canon 285.[106]

The very definition of an appeal, as given in canon 1879, takes it for granted that a sentence has been rendered by an inferior judge before the grievance is taken to the superior judge. Canon 1868, § 1, defines a sentence as a legitimate pronouncement by which a judge decides a cause proposed by litigants after it has been tried in judicial form. The same canon also clarifies the notion of a sentence by defining the two types of sentences: the definitive, which settles the principal cause, and the interlocutory, which decides an incidental cause. Canon 274, 7°, specifies that a metropolitan can only take an appeal if the sentence pronounced in the tribunals of his suffragans is either definitive or interlocutory with a definitive force.

The definitive sentence presents little difficulty; it is the interlocutory sentence which needs some explanation. The interlocutory sentence is said to have definitive force when, even though it does not interrupt the principal cause in a particular instance, it nevertheless frustrates the settlement of the principal cause.[107] Such interlocutory sentences can be rendered: when a judge declares an appeal to be forbidden by law, or to be *de facto* abandoned; when a judge declares that a minor who requests a *restitutio in integrum* exceeds the age of a minor; when a judge declares himself incompetent in a certain cause; or, when a judge declares that a peremptory exception, which puts an end to the litigation, has been admitted.[108] Interlocutory sentences do not allow appeal except when conjoined with an appeal from a definitive sentence or when they have a definitive force.[109] This is why canon 274, 7°, makes it clear that, to be subject

[106] Wernz-Vidal (*Ius Canonicum*, VI, 109-110) declare that causes tried in their first instance in the tribunals of archbishops lacking suffragans and of bishops immediately subject to the Holy See, according to former law had to be appealed to the Holy See. Canon 1594, § 3, involves therefore, a change of the former law.

[107] Cf. canon 1875.

[108] Cf. canons 1629, § 1; 1737. Cf. Toso, *Commentaria*, III, 99.

[109] Canon 1880, 6°.

to appeal to the metropolitan's tribunal, the interlocutory sentence must have a definitive force.

The general law prescribes certain modes of procedure for particular exigencies. In some cases the presentation of a matter from a lower tribunal to a higher one is clearly an appeal, in others it is simply a recourse. The nature of the action depends on the all-important factor, namely, whether or not the presentation of the controverted point takes place during an actual trial after an interlocutory sentence with a definitive force has been issued by the judge, or at the end of a trial after a definitive sentence has been rendered. Should such a disputed matter be taken to a higher tribunal before a trial begins, it is not an appeal, but rather a petition prior to the inception of the first instance.

Again, should such a matter be presented to a higher tribunal during a trial before the intervention of a sentence by the judge of the first instance, the presentation must be looked on as a recourse, and not as an appeal. Canon 1610, § 3, for example, states that should a judge declare himself incompetent, the party who regards himself aggrieved by this declaration may make an appeal to a higher court within ten days. Evidently the canon refers to an interlocutory sentence with definitive force, for it uses the word *appeal*. The action on the part of the aggrieved party would be an appeal in the sense of canon 274, 7°. However, should the judge declare himself incompetent during the trial by means of a decree, the party could not make an appeal against this decree until after the definitive sentence is rendered by the competent judge who is appointed in place of the incompetent judge. It would have to be conjoined to the definitive sentence and presented in appeal to the superior tribunal for decision.[110]

If the bill of complaint is rejected at the time of its introduction, the party is at liberty to have *recourse* to the higher court. The higher court is to give a hearing to the party and hand down a most prompt ruling on the question

---

[110] Canon 1880, 6°. Cf. Roberti, *De Processibus*, I, 436.

of rejection.[111] Canon 1709, § 3, refers to a matter which takes place before a trial begins, hence it uses the word *recourse*, even though the disputed point is taken to a higher court for a ruling.

It is erroneous, therefore, to insist that all canons which grant a party the right to present disputed points to a higher tribunal for settlement give the metropolitan the right to receive these controversies in the form of an appeal. At most the metropolitan has the right to receive certain disputes into his tribunal in the form of a recourse. Such canons as 1612, § 1, § 2; 1614, § 2; 1615, § 3; 1709, § 3, and 1710 grant the metropolitan the right of settling certain disputed points which come to him from the tribunals of his suffragans. They carefully avoid the use of the term *appellatio*.[112] Canon 274, 7°, must be interpreted in the light of canon 19, which states that all laws which restrict the free exercise of rights must be interpreted strictly. All canons which refer to appeals from a definitive sentence or interlocutory sentence with definitive force point to the permissibility of seeking redress in the metropolitan's tribunal.[113]

There can be no appeal to a metropolitan's tribunal from extra-judicial decrees enacted by suffragans in their particular dioceses. In correct legal terminology, a presentation of such a grievance cannot be called an appeal, for it flows not from a judicial procedure, but from an administrative action of an ordinary. The true nature of such a presentation of grievance demands that it be called a recourse.[114] Such recourses cannot even be made to the Sacred Rota; they must be presented exclusively to the Sacred Congregations.[115]

After summary proceedings arranged for the removal

---

[111] Canon 1709, § 3.
[112] Cf. Roberti, *De Processibus*, I, 224; 225.
[113] Cf. canons 1610, § 3; 1879; 1899; 1991; 1993, § 3.
[114] Coronata, *Institutiones*, I, 434, footnote 3.
[115] Canon 1601.

or transfer of pastors as well as for the punishment of clerics who do not observe the law of residence or who are guilty of concubinage, or of pastors who neglect their pastoral duties, the ordinary issues definitive decrees. There is but one remedy in law against such decrees: recourse to the Holy See. The law expressly takes these cases out of the purely judicial class, and places them among proceedings which partake of an administrative character. This segregation makes appeals inadmissible and makes recourse alone possible.[116] The metropolitan has no power over such definitive decrees. Furthermore, there is no appeal from a decree given "*ex informata conscientia*" by which a suffragan extra-judicially pronounces the penalty of suspension against a cleric, or from a decree by which the latter refuses to advance a cleric to higher orders. Metropolitans cannot accept any grievances against such decrees from the dioceses of his suffragans. Only recourse to the Holy See is possible for the clerics involved.[117]

The II Plenary Council of Baltimore (1866) simply stated that the metropolitan could receive appeals from the sentences rendered by suffragans according to the rules defined by the sacred canons.[118] If the bald statement of the Council that metropolitans had the right to receive appeals from the tribunals of their suffragans is accepted as such, it can be said that the decree is *iuxta Codicem.* But the conciliar legislation did not define the types of sentences from which the appeals could be accepted, except that in a general way it hearkened back to the norms given in the pre-Code law. By the norms of pre-Code law the Plenary Council meant chiefly the decrees of the Council of Trent. According to the Tridentine doctrine in causes relating to

[116] Canon 2146, § 1.

[117] Cf. canons 2186, § 1; 2194. Cf. Bargilliat, *Prælectiones,* I, 411; Beste, *Introductio in Codicem,* p. 252; Claeys Bouuaert-Simenon, *Manuale,* I, 248.

[118] "Appellationes a sententia suffraganeorum, juxta regulas a sanctis canonibus definitas, recipit." — *Acta et Decreta Concilii Plenarii Baltimorensis II,* n. 81, 4, p. 62.

visitation and correction, or to competency or incompetency as also to criminal causes, before a definitive sentence was rendered there was to be no appeal from the bishop or his vicar general in spiritual matters by reason of an interlocutory sentence or because of any other grievance. The bishop or his vicar was not bound to take notice of such an appeal or any restraining act emanating from the judge of appeal, every written statement and custom, even immemorial, to the contrary notwithstanding. This was to hold unless a grievance could not be repaired by a definitive sentence, or if there was no appeal from it.[119]

It follows from a consideration of this text that the Council of Baltimore is in agreement with the Code inasmuch as appeals could not be made before a definitive sentence was rendered in the tribunal of first instance. Since the Council of Trent made no distinction between simple interlocutory sentences and interlocutory sentences with a definitive force, the decree of the II Plenary Council of Baltimore is *contra Codicem* inasmuch as it did not limit appeals to case of interlocutory sentences with a definitive force.

Furthermore, the Council of Trent made special mention of criminal causes. Where an appeal from the sentence of a bishop or his vicar general, authorized for spiritual matters, was warranted in a criminal cause, then, if it happened to be a cause assigned locally to the former's tribunal by apostolic authority, it was to be committed to the metropolitan or to his vicar general, authorized for spiritual matters. If the metropolitan's tribunal was suspect for some reason, or if his court was more than two legal days' journey away, or if his own court was making the appeal, the cause was to be assigned to one of the nearest bishops or the vicars, but not to inferior judges.[120]

The Code makes no distinction between contentious and criminal causes in the matter of appeal. Hence, whatever

---

[119] Conc. Trident., sess. XIII, *de ref.*, c. 1.
[120] Conc. Trident., sess. XIII, *de ref.*, c. 2.

the type of cause, so long as the sentence is either definitive or interlocutory with a definitive force, the metropolitan has the right to accept it. There is no longer any special assignment of criminal causes by apostolic authority. The Code of Canon Law simply declares that all the appeals answering the description of canon 274, 7°, belong to the jurisdiction of the metropolitan. The Code grants the tribunal of second instance in canon 1594, § 1, to the metropolitan only, and there is no mention of his vicar general. Further, the Code no longer gives the right of second instance to the nearest bishops or their vicars in consequence of the exceptions of suspicion or of distance relative to the metropolitan court. If the 81st (4) decree of the II Council of Baltimore is to be understood in the sense that all these specifications are included, the decree must be said to be *contra legem* and must be considered as having no legal force today.

If a controversy as to competence should arise between two or more judges who must look to the same immediately higher tribunal, the conflict must be settled by the higher tribunal which they have in common.[121] Thus, if two suffragans of the same metropolitan have such a conflict, it is the tribunal of the metropolitan which settles it. If the conflict is between tribunals which are under distinct superior tribunals, the conflict is to be settled by the tribunal which is the superior of that court before which the action was first proposed,[122] or to which the petition was first made.[123] Thus, if a conflict arises between the tribunals of suffragans who are subject to different metropolitans, it is settled by the tribunal of the metropolitan of the suffragan before whose tribunal the cause was first proposed. If the conflict is between those who have no superior tribunal, the cause is settled by the legate of the Holy See or by the Apostolic Signatura.[124] Thus, if there is a conflict between two metro-

[121] Canon 1612, § 1.
[122] Canon 1612, § 2.
[123] Canon 1706.
[124] Canon 1612, § 2.

politans, or between a metropolitan and his own suffragan, the norm of canon 1612, § 2, is observed.[125]

The tribunal of second instance for causes tried in their first instance before the metropolitan is the curia of that local ordinary which the metropolitan himself has chosen once and for all time with the approval of the Apostolic See.[126] The metropolitan is not bound by law to select the tribunal of any one of his suffragans as the tribunal of second instance. Canon 1594, § 2, employs the phrase *"ad loci Ordinarium."* Hence the metropolitan is free to choose the tribunal of any local ordinary, even of one outside his own ecclesiastical province. If he does choose the tribunal of one of his suffragans, the metropolitan is not bound by law to choose the closest suffragan. This liberty of choice involves a change from the former law. In pre-Code law a cause having been decided in its first instance before a metropolitan had to be taken in its second instance to the Holy See. From about the year 1884 this practice was reformed through a series of particular concessions and privileges which the Holy See granted.[127] Once the metropolitan makes his choice, the chosen tribunal, by disposition of law, becomes a higher tribunal with a higher grade of jurisdiction for those causes which have been adjudicated in the tribunal of the metropolitan. For these adjudicated causes the tribunal of the metropolitan is subordinate to the tribunal of a suffragan, if the latter is chosen as the tribunal for appeals from his tribunal.[128] Canon 1594, § 2, includes no invalidating clause, hence the approval, to be given by the Apostolic See, of the tribunal of second instance chosen by the metropolitan is not a *conditio sine qua non* for its valid constitution.[129]

---

[125] Cf. Roberti, *De Processibus*, I, 437-439.

[126] Canon 1594, § 2.

[127] Cappello, *Summa*, III, 38; Cocchi, *Commentarium*, VII, 59; Wernz-Vidal, *Ius Canonicum*, VI, 108.

[128] Wernz-Vidal, *Ius Canonicum*, VI, 108.

[129] Cf. canon 11.

The III Plenary Council of Baltimore (1884) decreed that if relative to a sentence given in its first instance in the metropolitan curia an appeal was to be made to another curia, the appeal, by special concession of the Holy See, was to be made to the nearest metropolitan.[130] This provision is now *contra legem,* for it restricts the great freedom given in the matter of choice in canon 1594, § 2. The Code does not insist that the judge of the second instance be a metropolitan; it simply states that a local ordinary may be chosen. The Code likewise states nothing concerning the proximity or distance between the tribunals of the metropolitan and of the local ordinary whose court may be chosen. However, the conciliar expression, *"the nearest metropolitan,"* could be understood in the sense that such a metropolitan could be the local ordinary chosen by the metropolitan exercising his right of selection.

According to the latest listing the following are the tribunals of appeal for the metropolitans of the United States. The names are arranged in such manner that the name of the metropolitan court of first instance is followed by the name of the court of appeal.

Baltimore: St. Louis[131]
Boston: New York[132]
Chicago: Springfield[133]
Cincinnati: Cleveland[134]
Denver: Santa Fe[135]

---

[130] "Quodsi a judicio curiæ metropolitanæ primæ instantiæ ad aliam curiam appellandum sit, appellatio ex speciali concessione S. Sedis... fiet ad Metropolitanum viciniorem." — *Acta et Decreta Concilii Plenarii Baltimorensis III*, n. 316, p. 181.

[131] *AAS*, XII (1920), 14; cf. *Annuario Pontificio* (1947), p. 115.

[132] *AAS*, XII (1920), 163; cf. *Annuario Pontificio* (1947), p. 126.

[133] *AAS*, XXVI (1934), 635; cf. *Annuario Pontificio* (1947), p. 148.

[134] *AAS*, XIX (1927), 348; cf. *Annuario Pontificio* (1947), p. 151.

[135] In a letter dated the 23rd of May, 1947, Rev. David Maloney, Assistant Chancellor of the archdiocese of Denver stated the following: "The tribunal of Santa Fe, New Mexico, has been the court of appeal for the diocese of Denver *ab initio*. When, in 1942, Denver was created an archdiocese, the matter was brought up orally with the authorities

Detroit: Cincinnati[136]
Dubuque: St. Paul (Minnesota)[137]
Indianapolis: Cincinnati[138]
Los Angeles: Monterey-Fresno[139]
Louisville: Cincinnati[140]
Milwaukee: Green Bay[141]
Newark: New York[142]
New Orleans: Oklahoma[143]

---

and approval was given to the proposal that Santa Fe continue to act as the tribunal of second instance for any cases heard by our own marriage court."

[136] The Assistant Chancellor of the archdiocese of Detroit, Rev. Alexander Zaleski, on May 5th, 1947, answered the inquiry of the writer in these words: "...the tribunal of second instance for the archdiocese of Detroit is Cincinnati. This selection was approved by the Sacred Consistorial Congregation on September 1, 1937."

[137] *AAS*, XXVI (1934), 635; cf. *Annuario Pontificio* (1947), p. 170.

[138] The Rev. Henry F. Dugan, Chancellor of the archdiocese of Indianapolis, in a letter written on May 5th, 1947, assured the writer that "the Metropolitan Court of Cincinnati, which was the Court of Appeal of the diocese of Indianapolis, remained the Court of Appeal after Indianapolis was elevated to the status of an archdiocese." Cf. *Annuario Pontificio* (1947), p. 202.

[139] The Rev. Daniel P. Collins, Secretary of the archdiocese of Los Angeles, in his answer to the writer on May 9, 1947, enclosed a copy of the rescript of the Sacred Consistorial Congregation. It reads as follows: "Beatissime Pater, Ioannes G. Cantwell, Archiepiscopus archidiœcesis Angelorum, ad sedis metropolitanæ dignitatem nuper erectæ, cum pro appellatione in secunda instantia semel pro semper designaverit tribunal Ordinarii Montereyensis Fresnensis, humillime implorat ut Sanctitas Vestra hanc designationem benigne approbare dignetur. Et Deus etc." "S. Congregatio Consistorialis, vigore facultatum a SSmo Dño Nostro Pio Div. Prov. PP XI tributarum, præfatam designationem benigne approbavit. Contrariis quibusvis minime obstantibus. Datum Romæ, ex ædibus S. C. Consistorialis die 14 Maii 1947." Cf. *Annuario Pontificio* (1947), p. 229.

[140] *AAS*, XXX (1938), 319; cf. *Annuario Pontificio* (1947), p. 229.

[141] *AAS*, XXIII (1931), 413; cf. *Annuario Pontificio* (1947), p. 244.

[142] In reply to the writer's request, Rev. James A. Hughes, Chancellor of the archdiocese of Newark, wrote the following on May 5th, 1947: "The Consistorial Congregation, under the date of December 1, 1938, and in accordance with the wish of the Most Reverend Archbishop, designated the Tribunal of the archdiocese of New York as the court of second instance for the archdiocese of Newark."

[143] *AAS*, XI (1919), 279; cf. *Annuario Pontificio* (1947), p. 263.

New York: Philadelphia[144]
Omaha: Dubuque[145]
Philadelphia: Baltimore[146]
Portland (Oregon): San Francisco[147]
St. Louis: Kansas City[148]
St. Paul: Dubuque[149]
San Antonio: Galveston[150]
San Francisco: Los Angeles[151]
Santa Fe: Denver[152]

These, for the most part, have been approved by the Sacred Congregation of the Consistory.[153] The metropolitan, because he is a bishop, is always free to appeal to the Holy See directly.[154]

In accordance with canon 1595, the metropolitan tribunal of appeal must be constituted in the same manner as

---

[144] *AAS*, XII (1920), 329; cf. *Annuario Pontificio* (1947), p. 264.

[145] Replying to the writer's question concerning the tribunal of second instance, Msgr. Nicholas Wegner, Chancellor of the archdiocese of Omaha, wrote the following: "Since Omaha was created an archdiocese we have not as yet selected a court of second instance. However, *ceteris paribus*, I think we shall retain the one we had, which is Dubuque." The letter was dated October 29, 1947.

[146] *AAS*, XX (1928), 232; cf. *Annuario Pontificio* (1947), p. 178.

[147] *AAS*, XIX (1927), 348; cf. *Annuario Pontificio* (1947), p. 284.

[148] *AAS*, XII (1920), 14; cf. *Annuario Pontificio* (1947), p. 312.

[149] *AAS*, XXVI (1934), 635; cf. *Annuario Pontificio* (1947), p. 314.

[150] *AAS*, XX (1928), 37; cf. *Annuario Pontificio* (1947), p. 318.

[151] According to *AAS*, XI (1919), 348, Monterey-Los Angeles was chosen to be the tribunal of second instance for the archdiocese of San Francisco. However, since then, the diocese of Monterey (now called Monterey-Fresno) was separated from the archdiocese of Los Angeles and is one of its suffragan sees. Cf. *Annuario Pontificio* (1947), p. 308.

[152] Cf. *Annuario Pontificio* (1947), p. 316.

[153] For a complete listing of the second instance tribunals of metropolitans throughout the world see Roberti, *De Processibus*, I, 226-236. Beste (*Introductio in Codicem*, p. 771) gives a list of those in the United States and Canada with a degree of partial completeness. The third edition of Beste's *Introductio* (1946) is also not altogether complete in its enumeration.

[154] Coronata, *Institutiones*, III, 41.

the court of first instance. The same norms, accommodated to the requisites of procedure in second instance, must be observed in the discussion of the cause. If in the first instance the cause was tried by a collegiate tribunal in the curia of the suffragan, in the second instance it must also be treated by a collegiate tribunal in the curia of the metropolitan. The collegiate tribunal of the court of appeal cannot be composed of a smaller number of judges than the original tribunal of first instance.[155]

The rule of canon 1620 must be observed. The metropolitan must see to it that the judges endeavor to finish the cause before them as a result of an appeal as speedily as possible without prejudice to justice. In particular are the judges bound not to protract the completion of the cause beyond a year. If without the intervention of any impediment no procedural act has been performed in the tribunal of appeal for one year the law-suit abates. In such a case the sentence which is contested in the appeal becomes a *res iudicata*,[156] that is to say, an adjudicated cause from which there is no appeal.[157]

In conclusion it may be said that metropolitans have the right and the obligation to receive appeals from the tribunals of their suffragans; if the appealing litigant insisted on the hearing of the appeal case in the metropolitan court, he does so rightfully, and the court of first instance must abide by his indicated determination. However, suffragans do not have the obligation of sending their appeals exclusively to the tribunal of the metropolitan; they are free to send their appeals to the Holy See. Metropolitans may be relieved of the appellate burden if their tribunals are not equipped sufficiently for the acceptance of appeals.[158]

---

[155] Canon 1596.
[156] Cf. canon 1902.
[157] Canon 1736.
[158] *AAS*, XXIV (1932), 272. Cf. Bouscaren, *Digest*, I, 802-803.

Article 2. First Instance Causes

Canon 274. *In diœcesibus vero suffraganeis Metropolita potest tantum:*

8° *Controversias de quibus in can. 1572, § 2, in prima instantia dirimere.*

Canon 1572. § 2. *Si vero agatur de iuribus aut bonis temporalibus Episcopi aut mensæ vel Curiæ diœcesanæ, controversia dirimenda deferatur vel, Episcopo consentiente, ad diœcesanum tribunal collegiale quod constat officiali et duobus iudicibus synodalibus antiquioribus, vel ad iudicem immediate superiorem.*

The metropolitan has the right to settle only those causes in the first instance which are brought to him from the tribunals of his suffragans in accordance with canon 1572, § 2.[159] According to this canon, if the rights or the temporal goods of a bishop, or of the episcopal *mensa*, or, finally, of the diocesan curia are involved, the bishop may consent to refer any of such causes to a collegiate tribunal of his own diocese consisting of his own *officialis* and two of his own senior synodal judges. What is important here is this, that the bishop may consent to use an alternative method specified in law, namely, to have such causes tried before an immediately superior judge. For a suffragan bishop the immediately superior judge is the metropolitan.[160]

Canon 1572, § 2, does not refer to criminal causes in which bishops may be involved as defendants. The only competent judge in such causes is the Roman Pontiff himself.[161] Canon 1557, § 1, 3°, does not prevent a bishop from using the diocesan tribunal when he stands as plaintiff in a case. If the non-winning of this case as plaintiff in a criminal case would imply a declaration of guilt against the bishop, it seems maintainable that, in keeping with canon

---

[159] Canon 274, 8°.
[160] Canon 1594, § 1.
[161] Canon 1557, § 1, 3°.

1557, § 1, 3°, the only competent judge in such a cause could be the Pope himself. Nor does it refer to contentious trials which involve residential bishops as defendants. Such causes are reserved to the Apostolic See by canon 1557, § 2, 1°, which expressly makes canon 1572, § 2, an exception. Should the bishop act as a plaintiff in a contentious cause, as long as the judge's sentence can involve the bishop in a declaration of his guilt, or in a sentence which constrains him as to the performance of the adjudicated obligation, as liberative of his opponent, but as resting upon the bishop, the intermediate court may not prosecute the case even if the bishop be the plaintiff. Nor does the canon refer to the causes of a bishop's church, i.e., the causes which directly and principally pertain to the diocese.[162] In a word, canon 1572, § 2, does not refer to the person of a bishop or his diocese, but only to causes which can be called fiscal *(fiscales)*. There are only three types of such causes mentioned in the canon, namely, those which concern: (a) temporal rights and goods of a bishop which are strictly personal; (b) temporal rights and goods of a bishop's *mensa;* and (c) temporal rights and goods of an episcopal curia.[163]

The temporal rights and goods of a bishop are those intangible and tangible realities which belong to a bishop personally. This can cover a wide range of possible items, depending upon the variety of the personal belongings of a particular bishop.

The episcopal *mensa* is that mass of goods which serves for the maintenance of the bishop while he rules the diocese. It embraces not only goods but revenues which are set aside for the bishop's personal use. These goods and revenues can include all moneys, properties and pensions due a residential bishop.[164] The bishop, both by the natural and the positive divine law, has the right to a fitting maintenance. This was provided for in the course of history by

---

[162] Wernz-Vidal, *Ius Canonicum,* VI, 78, footnote 5.

[163] Regatillo, *Institutiones,* II, 168.

[164] Beste, *Introductio in Codicem,* p. 272; Regatillo, *Institutiones,* II, 261-262.

various modes. At present the Code states the general principle that the Church has the right, independently of civil powers, to demand from the faithful the necessary means for the decent maintenance of the clergy and other ministers.[165] In keeping with this general norm a residential bishop has the right to demand the *cathedraticum* and the *subsidium caritativum*.[166]

The *cathedraticum* is a moderate tax paid annually to a bishop as a token of submission. All churches and benefices subject to the jurisdiction of a bishop, and all lay confraternities must pay the amount which is determined in accordance with the regulations of canon 1507, § 1, unless it has already been fixed by ancient custom.[167]

The *subsidium caritativum* is an extraordinary small tax imposed on all beneficiaries, both secular and religious, in case some special need of the diocese requires it.[168]

The bishop can help maintain his *mensa* by other means. Although canon 346 forbids bishops and their retinues to accept donations during canonical visitations of their dioceses, it guarantees them and their retinues all living and travelling expenses in accordance with the legitimate customs of the particular dioceses. Another means of support can be a pension imposed on benefices either by the Roman Pontiff or by the grantors of the benefice;[169] or the payment of the *decimæ* and *primitiæ* as regulated by the special laws and laudable customs of a country.[170] Other taxes for the benefit of the diocese may be imposed on churches, benefices and other ecclesiastical institutions subject to a bishop, but only at the time of their foundation.[171] Still another source of revenue can be the fees paid for the various acts of so-called voluntary jurisdiction (the concession of dispensa-

---

[165] Canon 1496.

[166] Cocchi, *Commentarium*, III, 233-234; Vermeersch-Creusen, *Epitome*, I, 348, 210.

[167] Canon 1504.

[168] Canon 1505.

[169] Canon 1429.

[170] Canon 1502.

[171] Canon 1506.

tions and other favors) for the execution of rescripts of the Holy See, or on the occasion of the administration of the sacraments and sacramentals in keeping with canon 1507, § 1. Residential bishops have the right to receive the income of the episcopal *mensa* from the moment they take possession of their see.[172]

According to canon 1483, § 1, a bishop must take care of the administration of the *mensa*. This obligation is a serious one, for what is generally legislated for every beneficiary holds also for every bishop.[173] As beneficiary he must administer the goods and the property of his *mensa* in accord with the rules of Canon Law, and if through neglect or some other fault he injures the benefice, he must repair the damage.[174] Canon 1483, § 2, states that the episcopal residence is to be kept up and must be repaired with the funds of the *mensa*, whenever the burden does not, by special law, rest on others. Furthermore, according to canon 1483, § 3, every bishop must see to it that an exact inventory is prepared of the furniture and movable property pertaining to the episcopal residence and belonging to the *mensa episcopalis*, in order that such property may be transmitted safely and in its entirety to his successor in the bishopric. The *mensa episcopalis* is considered a legal person in Canon Law.

In the United States the bishopric as such is usually not endowed; therefore the bishop gets his salary through the *cathedraticum* and other assessments placed on parishes for diocesan expenditures.[175]

The temporal rights and goods of the episcopal curia also fall in the class of causes treated in canon 1572, § 2. The diocesan curia consists of those persons who aid the bishop, or that person who rules the diocese in place of the bishop, in the government of the diocese.[176] The persons

---

[172] Canon 349, § 2, 1°.
[173] Canon 1476, § 1.
[174] Cf. canon 1476, § 2.
[175] Woywod, *Commentary*, II, 162.
[176] Canon 363, § 1.

composing the curia can be divided into two categories: (a) those who aid the bishop in the exercise of the administrative or so-called voluntary jurisdiction: the vicar general, the chancellor, the notary, the synodal examiners and the parish priest consultors; and (b) those who help the bishop in the exercise of judicial jurisdiction: the *officialis* or judge, the synodal judges, the auditors, the notaries, the promoter of justice, the defender of the bond, the couriers and the apparitors.[177]

Canon 1507, § 2, declares that fees for judicial acts follow the norm set in accordance with the ruling of canon 1909. Canon 1056 states that a small charge can be made for the necessary expenses of the chancery office involved in the granting of dispensations which are not issued *in forma pauperum*. It could be that the cases involved in these two canons, in addition to those mentioned above should be included among the controversial matters spoken of in canon 1572, § 2.

The bishop, according to Beste and Regatillo, is excluded from handling such causes on the grounds that no one can be a judge in his own cause. The presumption is that he has too much interest in the outcome of such personal causes.[178] Sipos says that the jurisdiction of a bishop is limited both territorially and personally. Canons 1636 and 1637 show by implication the territorial limitation of episcopal jurisdiction in judicial matters. The personal restriction flows from the principle that he cannot judge causes in his own favor.[179] Wernz-Vidal say that it is contrary to the natural law for a bishop to act as judge and party in one and the same cause. Such a situation would only throw suspicion on him because of the possibilities of gain or loss and the grave danger of favor as well as of disfavor connected with such causes.[180]

---

177 Canon 363, § 2.

178 Beste, *Introductio in Codicem*, pp. 765-766; Regatillo, *Institutiones*, II, 168.

179 Sipos, *Enchiridion*, p. 855.

180 Wernz-Vidal, *Ius Canonicum*, VI, 78.

It is for these reasons that the law takes these causes out of the jurisdiction of the ordinary diocesan tribunal of a bishop. Of the two extraordinary tribunals mentioned in canon 1572, § 2, only the tribunal which is immediately higher than the ordinary diocesan tribunal is of interest here. Even though it is an immediately higher tribunal, it is nevertheless, for the cases now under consideration, a tribunal of first instance. It is not a tribunal of second instance.[181]

Although canon 1594, § 1, refers only to the tribunal of appeal, it can serve as the norm for the determination of the higher tribunal for the causes mentioned in canon 1572, § 2. The suffragans of the province can apply to the tribunal of the metropolitan who has the right to accept such cases in accordance with canon 274, 8°. The same would hold true for the prelates mentioned in canon 1594, § 3, in view of the norm which canon 20 leaves applicable with reference to them.

Even though metropolitans have the right and the obligation to accept the first instance causes which receive mention in canon 1572, § 2, they cannot force their suffragans to present them to the metropolitan tribunal. Canon 1572, § 2, uses the phrase "*Episcopo consentiente,*" which clearly expresses the freedom of suffragans to choose one or the other of the two methods presented in the canon itself. Besides, canon 1569, § 1, and 1597 give the suffragan the right to present such causes to the Roman Pontiff.

In the writer's opinion the metropolitan does not need the pallium for the licit exercise of the right given him in canon 274, 8°.

The right expressed in this canon does not refer to purely residential and non-residential archbishops. The introductory clause of canon 274 makes it evident that this right is granted to metropolitans only.

---

[181] Beste, *Introductio in Codicem*, p. 224.

CHAPTER VIII

METROPOLITAN OBLIGATIONS IN THE DIOCESES OF SUFFRAGAN BISHOPS

SECTION A

ADMINISTRATIVE OBLIGATIONS

Article 1. Convocation and Presidency of Provincial Councils

Canon 284. *Metropolita, eoque legitime impedito vel sede archiepiscopali vacante, Suffraganeus antiquior promotione ad ecclesiam suffraganeam:*

1° *Locum ad celebrandum Concilium intra provinciæ territorium, auditis omnibus qui assistere debent cum suffragio deliberativo, eligit; cessantibus tamen iustis impedimentis, metropolitana ecclesia ne negligatur;*

2° *Concilium convocat eique præest.*

The Code of Canon Law legislates that in every ecclesiastical province a provincial council is to be held at least every twenty years.[1] A provincial council is a type of particular council in which bishops and other ecclesiastics of a particular province gather under the presidency of their metropolitan in order to discuss and decide such matters as seem opportune for the province and serve to increase faith, guide morals, correct abuses, settle controversies, and promote the observance or the introduction of a uniform discipline.[2]

Canon 281, which speaks of plenary councils, does not hold these to be obligatory in nature, for it uses terminology which does not indicate any form of obligation. The phrase

---

[1] Canon 283.

[2] Canon 290. Cf. Badii, *Institutiones*, p. 201; Bargilliat, *Prælectiones*, I, 531; Cocchi, *Commentarium*, III, 128; Coronata, *Institutiones*, I, 437; Ferreres, *Institutiones*, I, 211; Prümmer, *Manuale*, p. 32; Raus, *Institutiones*, p. 261; Regatillo, *Institutiones*, I, 236; Sipos, *Enchiridion*, p. 230; Vermeersch-Creusen, *Epitome*, I, 313; Wernz-Vidal, *Ius Canonicum*, II, 670.

"convenire possunt" of the canon leaves the calling of plenary councils to the discretion of the Roman Pontiff and of those prelates who may deem such a council advantageous. Canon 283, however, enjoins the convocation of provincial councils through the employment of the word *"celebretur,"* and the specification of time in the phrase *"vicesimo... anno."* Both these expressions make the holding of a provincial council an obligation which rests on the metropolitan who is to call it and on those prelates who are obliged to attend it.[3]

Canon 283 states that such councils should be convoked at least every twenty years. The severity of the law enacted by the Council of Trent, which demanded that provincial councils be held every three years, no longer possesses juridic force.[4] The *de facto* current omission of the celebration of provincial councils evidently prompted the legislator to reduce the frequency of these councils from once every three years to at least once every twenty years. Although the factor of frequency in the celebration of the councils was reduced by the Code of Canon Law, the latter does not intend the abrogation of them. In fact, the Code insists upon the fulfillment of this obligation not only once every twenty years, but oftener if possible. There can be no other explanation for the insertion of the word *"saltem"*

---

[3] Blat, *Commentarium*, Lib. II, pars 1, p. 300; Toso, *Commentaria*, II, 105. Authors generally use the forms, *"celebrandum est, convocandum est,"* in order to indicate the obligation of calling provincial councils. Cf. Chelodi, *Ius Canonicum*, p. 374; Cocchi, *Commentarium*, III, 131; Coronata, *Institutiones*, I, 441; Ferreres, *Institutiones*, I, 211; Raus, *Institutiones*, pp. 262-263; Regatillo, *Institutiones*, I, 236; Sipos, *Enchiridion*, p. 230; Vermeersch-Creusen, *Epitome*, I, 313. Claeys Bouuaert-Simenon (*Manuale*, I, 251) use the phrase *"fieri debet."*

[4] Conc. Trident., sess. XXIV, *de ref.*, c. 2. Cf. *supra*, pp. 119-121. Cf. Cance, *Le Code*, I, 288; Cocchi, *Commentarium*, III, 131; Raus, *Institutiones*, p. 261. Provincial councils were not held in Post-Tridentine times with the three year regularity demanded by the Council of Trent. In many places they were not held even once in fifty years. The Vatican Council tried to remedy the situation by proposing that provincial councils be held every fifth year, but even this seemed impossible in the majority of provinces. Cf. Ferreres, *Institutiones*, I, 211; Wernz-Vidal, *Ius Canonicum*, II, 679, footnote 39.

in canon 283. According to Blat and Chelodi the phrase "at least" shows that the obligation of convoking provincial councils is not to be deferred beyond the period of twenty years, but that the obligation can be fulfilled oftener if the majority of comprovincial bishops give their consent.[5]

The II Plenary Council of Baltimore (1866), which strove to bring the ecclesiastical discipline of the United States into conformity with the universal legislation of the Church, emphasized the duty of metropolitans to call provincial councils every third year.[6] This particular conciliar legislation is not *contra legem,* but *præter legem,* in the sense explained above. The metropolitans in the United States could convoke provincial councils every third year, basing their action on the phrase *"saltem,"* but they have no strict obligation to carry out the decree of the II Plenary Council of Baltimore. Their strict obligation flows from canon 283, and thus they are to convoke provincial councils at least once every twenty years.

By a special decree of the Sacred Consistorial Congregation, given on February 15, 1919, fourteen sections of Italy were exempted from holding provincial councils, but were told to convoke plenary councils instead. However, the time specification for the celebration of these plenary councils is the same as that for provincial councils, namely, every twenty years. It is important to note that in spite of the difficulties connected with the holding of provincial councils in those localities, the Holy See did not exempt these particular sections from holding councils altogether.[7]

---

[5] Blat, *Commentarium,* Lib. II, pars 1, p. 300; Chelodi, *Ius Canonicum,* p. 374.

[6] "Suffraganeos unoquoque saltem triennio ad Concilium Provinciale convocat. . . ." — *Acta et Decreta Concilii Plenarii Baltimorensis II,* n. 81, p. 61.

[7] *AAS,* XI (1919), 72-73. The reader is referred to pp. 337-338, footnote 24, *infra,* for a fuller account of this special arrangement. Cf. Beste, *Introductio in Codicem,* p. 254; Blat, *Commentarium,* Lib. II, pars 1, p. 299; Claeys Bouuaert-Simenon, *Manuale,* I, 251; Chelodi, *Ius Canonicum,* p. 374, footnote 5; Cocchi, *Commentarium,* III, 131; Coronata, *Institutiones,* I, 438, and *ibid.,* footnote 5; Regatillo, *Institutiones,* I, p. 237; Sipos, *Enchiridion,* p. 230; Toso, *Commentaria,* III, 105-106.

According to canon 284 the first right of selecting the place where the provincial council is to be held belongs to the metropolitan. However, this right is not absolute. The law clearly states that his choice must be made only after he has heard all those who have the obligation to attend the council with a deliberative vote. In accordance with the rulings of canon 105, 2°, before the choice of the place is made, the metropolitan must legitimately call all those who have the obligation of assisting with the right of a deliberative vote in a provincial council, that they, thus assembled, may express their minds. The failure to call them does not matter so long as those who were not called were nevertheless present.[8]

Canon 284 uses the expression "*auditis omnibus.*" Accordingly it would suffice for the validity of the choice of the place if the metropolitan did no more than consult those who have the obligation of attending the council with the right of a deliberative vote. He is not obliged to obtain their consent. After consultation, therefore, the metropolitan is not obliged to follow their choice of a place, even if their choice is unanimous. However, he should have a great regard for the unanimous vote of those he hears, and should not, without good reason, of which he is the sole judge, act contrary to their counsel.[9] The metropolitan could not make the choice of the place for the holding of the council before the imposition of the pallium.[10] The choice of the place is very intimately connected with the convocation of a provincial council which by law demands that metropolitans use the pallium. The metropolitan, prior to its imposition, could not delegate this right of choice to others. No one can delegate a right which he himself does not possess.

It may happen that the metropolitan is legitimately impeded or that the archiepiscopal see is vacant at the time

---

[8] Cf. canon 162, § 4.

[9] Canon 105, 1°.

[10] Cocchi, *Commentarium,* III, 132; Sipos, *Enchiridion,* p. 230; Toso, *Commentaria,* III, 106; Wernz-Vidal, *Ius Canonicum,* II, 677, and *ibid.,* footnote 183.

when the provincial council is to be called. Canon 284 takes care of such eventualities by the declaration that the senior suffragan is to select the place where the provincial council is to be held. The right of the senior suffragan to choose the place is, like the metropolitan's, conditioned on a previous hearing of all those who are required to attend the council with a deliberative vote. The law does not oblige the senior suffragan to the previous imposition of the pallium. The rules of canon 105, 1° and 2°, apply as much to the action of the senior suffragan as they do to that of the metropolitan. The II Plenary Council of Baltimore (1866) made the same provision regarding the senior suffragan in case the metropolitan was impeded. However, it made no ruling for the procedure to be followed in case the archiepiscopal see was vacant.[11]

In order to forestall the possibility of confusion, the law defines who the senior suffragan is. According to canon 284 he is the oldest in promotion to one of the suffragan bishoprics within the ecclesiastical province which is to have the provincial council. The canon employs the words: "*Suffraganeus antiquior promotione ad ecclesiam suffraganeam.*" It may happen that a certain suffragan bishop may be the oldest in age among all the suffragans of the province. The matter of age does not enter into the picture, if this suffragan bishop is not at the same time the one who holds a suffragan see longest in the province. An individual suffragan bishop may be the senior with regard to the reception of episcopal orders; if such a suffragan is not at the same time the incumbent of his suffragan see longer than the rest of the other suffragan bishops, he cannot claim the qualified right of choosing the site of the future provincial council.

It may be that one of the suffragan bishops within the province is a residential archbishop. The honorary title of archbishop in itself does not entitle him as a suffragan

[11] "Metropolita autem legitime impedito, coepiscopus antiquior id præstabit." — *Acta et Decreta Concilii Plenarii Baltimorensis II*, n. 81, p. 61.

bishop of the province to name the place of the council. If such an archbishop were in possession of his suffragan see for a longer time than any of the other suffragans, the fact of his seniority in the incumbency would entitle him to name the place of the council. A titular or non-residential archbishop, even though he lives within one of the sees of the province, could not presume to name the place of the council, since he cannot be considered a suffragan in the strict sense. In the writer's opinion, no bishop, abbot *nullius*, prelate *nullius*, or archbishop mentioned in canon 285 can be considered a suffragan in the sense given in canon 284.[12] Hence none of the prelates mentioned in canon 285, though he may be in possession of his particular see longer than any of the suffragan bishops within the province planning the provincial council, may presume to exercise the right of choosing the site of the council. However, every one of these prelates must be called to the meeting where the choice of the site is made, for canon 286 grants them the right of a deliberative vote at the provincial council.[13]

The senior suffragan may exercise this right if the metropolitan is legitimately impeded. The impediment must be of such a nature that it prevents the metropolitan from acting in the manner prescribed by canon 284. Such an impediment could be that of serious illness. A number of authors say that the lack of the pallium is such a legitimate impediment.[14] In such cases the senior suffragan does not need delegation from the metropolitan, for the law specifically gives him the right once a legitimate impediment withholds the metropolitan from making the choice in accordance with canon 284, 1°. The other case in which the senior suffragan can name the place is presented by the vacancy of the metropolitan see. The senior suffragan has the right to name the place even though an apostolic administrator

---

[12] Cf. Coronata, *Institutiones*, I, 441, footnote 6.

[13] Cf. canon 284, 1°.

[14] Cocchi, *Commentarium*, III, 132; Sipos, *Enchiridion*, p. 230; Toso, *Commentaria*, III, 106; Wernz-Vidal, *Ius Canonicum*, II, 677, and *ibid.*, footnote 183. Cf. Blat, *Commentarium*, Lib. II, pars 1, p. 300.

or a vicar capitular endowed with episcopal character be governing the metropolitan see.[15] The law does not grant the apostolic administrator or the vicar capitular this right; it specifically names the senior suffragan. However, the conditions of canon 284, 1°, must be fulfilled in order that the latter may be permitted to act.

Neither the metropolitan nor the senior suffragan has the right to name a place outside the province itself for the holding of the provincial council. Canon 284 implies that the place of the celebration of the council be situated within the territory of the province: "*Locum ad celebrandum Concilium intra provinciæ territorium...eligit.*" Ordinarily the cathedral of the metropolitan should be the place. The reason for the choice of the metropolitan church is the dignity of that cathedral church, in which the metropolitan is wont to pontificate. As long as there are no legitimate impediments and all the advantages are on the side of choosing the metropolitan church, the metropolitan or the senior suffragan must not choose another place. The wording of the law demands that once the legitimate impediments cease, the metropolitan church is not to be passed over.[16] These words can mean only that even though another church is chosen because of certain legitimate, impediments which prove an obstacle to the choice of the metropolitan church, once these impediments are removed, the metropolitan church should have preference.[17] In other words, should there be any legitimate impediment which is an obstacle in the way of choosing the metropolitan church, another church may be chosen temporarily or for the entire council, depending upon the duration of the legitimate impediments.

The metropolitan has the obligation and the right to

---

[15] Blat, *Commentarium*, Lib. II, pars 1, p. 300.

[16] Canon 284, 1°.

[17] Cf. Blat, *Commentarium*, Lib. II, pars 1, p. 300; Cance, *Le Code*, I, 288-289; Chelodi, *Ius Canonicum*, p. 275; Cocchi, *Commentarium*, III, 132; Coronata, *Institutiones*, I, 441; Ferreres, *Institutiones*, I, 211; Raus, *Institutiones*, p. 262; Sipos, *Enchiridion*, p. 230; Toso, *Commentaria*, III, 106; Wernz-Vidal, *Ius Canonicum*, II, 679.

convoke the provincial council.[18] He does not need the approval of the Holy See to make use of this right. Canon 284, 2°, does not contain any clause which resembles the phrase "*petita tamen venia a Romano Pontifice,*" as found in canon 281 concerning the convocation of plenary councils. The metropolitan, however, cannot licitly convoke a provincial council unless the pallium has been imposed upon him.[19] An apostolic indult could permit him to do so licitly apart from the previous imposition of the pallium.[20] The senior suffragan, however, is not bound by this special norm which applies only to metropolitans. Even though he may be a residential archbishop with the honorary privilege of wearing the pallium, canon 276 does not place him under the obligation which it imposes on metropolitans only.

In the convocation of those who are to attend the provincial council, the metropolitan must invite all those within the confines of his province to whom the law grants a deliberative vote, namely: (a) the suffragans of the province, whether they are residential bishops or residential archbishops; (b) residential bishops who are immediately subject to the Holy See who have chosen him as their metropolitan; (c) archbishops without suffragans who have chosen him as their metropolitan; (d) prelates *nullius* who have chosen him as their metropolitan; (e) abbots *nullius* who have chosen him as their metropolitan; (f) apostolic administrators of dioceses within the province; (g) vicars apostolic if there be any in the province; (h) prefects apostolic if there be any in the province; and (i) vicars capitu-

[18] Canon 284, 2°. In the following pages the writer takes it for granted that the metropolitan is not impeded, and that the metropolitan see is not vacant. Should the metropolitan be impeded or the metropolitan see be vacant, whatever is said of the metropolitan refers also to the senior suffragan, unless it is indicated that the senior suffragan is excluded.

[19] Canon 276. "...antequam obtinuit quis Pallium...non licet ei... convocare concilium...." — Pontificale Rom., tit. *De pallio*, n. 5; Benedictus XIV, *De Synodo Diœcesana*, lib. II, c. 5, n. 8. Cf. Cocchi, *Commentarium*, III, 132; Sipos, *Enchiridion*, p. 230; Toso, *Commentaria*, III, 106; Wernz-Vidal, *Ius Canonicum*, II, 677, and *ibid.*, footnote 183.

[20] Canon 276.

lar of any vacant see in the province.[21] This is made clear in canons 286, § 1, and 282, § 1.

If any of these prelates cannot attend, they must prove the impediment which holds them from attendance, and they must send a proxy in their stead. The excusing cause must be made to the metropolitan by letter.[22] The proxy thus chosen enjoys only a consultative vote. If he is one of the Fathers of the council who already has the right of a deliberative vote, his choice as proxy for one of the absent prelates neither deprives him of his original deliberative vote nor gives him a double deliberative vote.[23] In view of the mutually complementary statements contained in canons 282, § 1, and 286, § 1, it is evident that residential bishops, residential archbishops and the metropolitan can send their coadjutor or auxiliary bishop, if they have one, without the necessity of having a cause for absence or without needing to prove the impediment holding them from attendance. In such a case the coadjutor and the auxiliary bishop enjoy a deliberative vote.[24] All these prelates are to be considered true Fathers of the council.

The suffragan bishops are bound to be present once they have received and presented their bulls of canonical provision to the cathedral chapter, or, in this country, to the body of diocesan consultors, in accordance with the rule of canon 334, § 3, even though they may not be consecrated as yet.[25]

Any residential bishop who is immediately subject to the Holy See, any abbot or prelate *nullius* who lives outside the confines of a province or who lives within a province and belongs to none, and any residential archbishop who actually rules a see which has been given archiepiscopal

[21] Letters b, c, d, e, include all the prelates of canon 285 who have with the approval of the Holy See chosen once and for all time a certain metropolitan in order to be present at the provincial council of that particular metropolitan.

[22] Cance, *Le Code*, I, 290; Cocchi, *Commentarium*, III, 134.

[23] Canon 287, § 1, § 2. Cf. canons 286, § 1; 164 and 224, § 1, § 2.

[24] Canon 282, § 1. Cf. Coronata, *Institutiones*, I, 442; Sipos, *Enchiridion*, p. 230.

[25] Beste, *Introductio in Codicem*, p. 254; Sipos, *Enchiridion*, p. 230; Wernz-Vidal, *Ius Canonicum*, II, 677.

dignity, has the duty to choose a neighboring metropolitan to whose provincial council he must be called. Purely titular or non-residential archbishops do not have this duty. A question arises as to the meaning of the phrase "*aliquem viciniorem Metropolitam*" contained in canon 285. Blat says that the determination flows from proximity between the churches of the metropolitan and of the prelate making the choice.[26] This seems to be a very good interpretation of the phrase in consideration of the purpose of the choice. Canon 285 legislates for the presence of these prelates at provincial councils. The uniformity of particular legislation obviously calls for the subjection of such prelates to the metropolitan closest to them in distance if they are outside his province, or to the metropolitan within whose province they reside. The choice of a metropolitan who would be at a greater distance would do little, if anything at all, for the uniformity of legislation within a particular territorial section of the Church.[27]

Beste says that the reason for canon 285 is clear. Without such a limited subjection these ordinaries would be completely independent of the obligation to assist at any provincial council.[28] If the legislator considers the convocation of these councils necessary for the maintenance or the introduction of uniformity of ecclesiastical discipline, it

[26] *Commentarium*, Lib. II, pars 1, p. 301.

[27] The obligation of recourse for the provision of a see impeded by the excommunication, interdict or suspension of its bishop on the part of the metropolitan as demanded by canon 429, § 5, seems to call for a metropolitan who is close at hand. Canon 432, § 3, treats of the right by devolution of the metropolitan to appoint a vicar capitular or an econome in such dioceses, abbacies and prelacies *nullius* as are mentioned in canon 285. Here, too, it seems that the metropolitan who is closest at hand can learn of the vacancy and the unlawful delay in the filling of the vacancy much more quickly than one who is at a considerably greater distance. The ordinary tribunal of second instance for the archbishop who has no suffragans and for the local ordinaries who are immediately subject to the Holy See is the tribunal of the metropolitan of their choice. So legislates canon 1594, § 3. Again proximity seems to afford the best opportunity of expediting second instance cases. Cf. *supra*, pp. 252-253; *infra*, pp. 293-295.

[28] *Introductio in Codicem*, p. 254.

would be strange that certain sees would be altogether out of the line of the Church's plan. Toso argues that such an independence would defraud the subjects of these prelates of many benefits which are apt to accrue from the harmonious deliberations of the Fathers of the council.[29]

Titular bishops (and this includes titular archbishops) who live in the province may be called to the provincial council by the metropolitan. That these be invited, it suffices that they have a quasi-domicile in the province. Inasmuch as it is possible to have domicile or a quasi-domicile in two places, it is possible also for titular bishops and titular archbishops to be invited to two provincial councils.[30] In order to invite them to attend, the metropolitan needs the consent of the majority of all those who attend the provincial council with a deliberative vote. Once it is decided that they are to be called, the titular bishops and titular archbishops have a deliberative vote unless it is stated otherwise in the convocation.[31] If an invited titular bishop or titular archbishop cannot attend in view of being detained by some impediment, he has no right to send a proxy in his stead.

The cathedral chapters or diocesan consultors of the dioceses whose ordinaries are bound to attend the provincial council must be invited by the metropolitan. Once invited they are bound to attend by sending either two capitulars (in the case of cathedral chapters) or two consultors (in the case of diocesan consultors) from each diocese. These delegates must be elected *collegialiter*. They enjoy only a consultative vote.[32]

---

[29] *Commentaria*, III, 107.

[30] Vermeersch-Creusen, *Epitome*, I, 313.

[31] Canon 286, § 2. With regard to the manner of voting for the attendance of these titular bishops see canon 105, 1° and 2°, and canon 162, § 4. Before the Code the unanimous consent was necessary to permit the titular bishops to attend. Cf. Wernz, *Ius Decretalium*, II, 855, footnote 1.

[32] Canon 286, § 3. Certain authors claim that these capitulars or consultors have the obligation to attend and must explain the cause of their absence if they do not attend. Beste, *Introductio in Codicem*, p. 254; Coronata, *Institutiones*, I, 442. Others say that they have no obligation to attend. Cocchi, *Commentarium*, III, 133; Regatillo, *Institutiones*, I, 237; Vermeersch-Creusen, *Epitome*, I, 313-314.

Major superiors of clerical exempt religious institutes and of monastic congregations living in the province must be invited by the metropolitan and are bound to attend. They have a consultative vote only. If they are impeded from attendance, they must make known the impediment to the council.[33]

Other members of the clergy, both secular and religious, may be called by the metropolitan. These have only a consultative vote.[34]

The metropolitan presides at the sessions of the provincial council.[35] As the presiding officer of the council he is not in the same position as the papal legate who presides at plenary councils. The metropolitan does not act in the name and with the authority of the Roman Pontiff; therefore his position is best described as *primus inter pares*. Outside the right to convoke and preside, he comes to the provincial council vested with the authority of a local ordinary of one of the dioceses within the province and fortified with only one deliberative vote. As a consequence, the metropolitan needs the consent of the Fathers of the council to open, transfer, suspend or close the provincial council. He must have the consent of the Fathers of the council in order to determine the order in which the matters under discussion will be examined.[36] He cannot inflict any censures on any of the bishops attending the council, nor can he command any of them to observe silence.[37] Nor does the metropolitan alone give permission to anyone desiring to leave the council

---

[33] Canon 286, § 4.

[34] Canon 286, § 4.

[35] Canon 284, 2°. Cf. *supra*, p. 277, footnote 18, concerning the right of the senior suffragan to preside.

[36] Canon 288. Cf. Blat, *Commentarium*, Lib. II, pars 1, p. 303; Cocchi, *Commentarium*, III, 132, 134; Coronata, *Institutiones*, I, 443. All these matters are decided *collegialiter*. The metropolitan, as the presiding officer, may resolve the tie vote and decide the issue. The vote of the Fathers on given issues need not be unanimous. The metropolitan acts invalidly if he does not obtain the consent of those endowed with the right of a deliberative vote. Cf. Blat, *Commentarium, loc. cit.* Cf. canon 105.

[37] Cocchi, *Commentarium*, III, 132.

before its conclusion. He must act together with the Fathers of the council in approving the just cause for departure.[38]

At the end of the provincial council the metropolitan sends all the acts and decrees to the Holy See. These decrees are not to be promulgated until after the Sacred Congregation of the Council has considered and reviewed them.[39] Although the metropolitan does not designate the manner of the promulgation nor the time at which the decrees are to go into effect after the promulgation, nevertheless, he is the one who promulgates them.[40] The manner of promulgation and the time when the acts and decrees are to go into effect are matters which the Fathers of the council decide.[41] The decrees of the provincial council, after their promulgation, bind all persons in the province and in the territories subject to the prelates mentioned in canon 285, and the local ordinaries cannot dispense from them except in individual cases and for a just cause.[42] The subjects of those prelates who possess a deliberative vote or a consultative vote, although these prelates were absent from the sessions of the provincial council, are bound as much as those whose ordinaries were present. The metropolitan is bound by the provincial decrees as much as the other prelates, since in relation to them he is simply *primus inter pares*.[43]

In a case of the division of a province, the laws made in provincial councils still bind those sections for which the laws were made. The Sacred Consistorial Congregation was asked whether the laws and decrees enacted by the Provincial Councils of Westminster in 1852, 1855, 1859 and 1873, continued in force and were to be observed after the

---

[38] Canon 289.

[39] The acts and decrees of provincial councils held in mission territories must be sent to the Sacred Congregation for the Propagation of the Faith. Cf. canons 250, § 4; 252, § 2; 304, § 2.

[40] Chelodi, *Ius Canonicum*, p. 375; Cocchi, *Commentarium*, III, 136.

[41] Canon 291, § 1.

[42] Canon 291, § 2. Cf. canons 82; 199, § 1; 285.

[43] Cocchi, *Commentarium*, III, 136; Sipos, *Enchiridion*, p. 232; Wernz-Vidal, *Ius Canonicum*, II, 684.

dismemberment of the province through its division into four new provinces. The reply was in the affirmative, with the provision that all decrees to the prejudice of the Code were abrogated.[44]

As a parting word concerning provincial councils it should be stated that the cognizance and the review of the provincial decrees by the Holy See does not give them any specific papal authority. This action on the part of the Holy See is merely a condition for their legitimate promulgation.[45]

Article 2. The Calling of Episcopal Conferences

Canon 292. § 1. *Nisi aliter pro peculiaribus locis a Sede Apostolica provisum fuerit, Metropolita, eoque deficiente, antiquior e Suffraganeis ad normam can. 284, curet ut Ordinarii locorum, saltem quinto quoque anno, stato tempore apud Metropolitam aliumve Episcopum comprovincialem conveniant, ut, collatis consiliis, videant quænam in diœcesibus aganda sint ut bonum religionis promoveatur, eaque præparent de quibus in futuro Concilio provinciali erit agendum.*

§ 2. *Etiam Episcopi aliique de quibus in can. 285, una cum aliis Ordinariis convocari et convenire debent.*

§ 3. *Iidem Ordinarii congregati sedem proximi conventus designent.*

Episcopal conferences are meetings in which the bishops of a certain province gather for the discussion and the settlement of matters pertinent to the province as such.

Since the legislator realized that the period of twenty years is a rather long space of time between the earlier and the later provincial councils, the law which requires that these episcopal conferences be held at specific intervals of

---

[44] *AAS*, X (1918), 365.

[45] *AAS*, XIII (1921), 228. Beste (*Introductio in Codicem*, p. 255) enumerates the different types of revision and recognition given to conciliar decrees.

five years was enacted. Thus there could be assured the holding of three meetings in the twenty year interval.

Canon 292, § 1, states that metropolitans shall see to it that episcopal conferences be arranged. The right to call these meetings is also given by law to the senior suffragan, but only in accordance with the norms given in canon 284. This canon states that the senior suffragan may take over the exercise of this right only if the metropolitan is legitimately impeded or if the metropolitan see is vacant.[46]

The time of these conferences is determined by law, for canon 292, § 1, states that they are to be held at least every five years: *"saltem quinto quoque anno."* The term *"saltem"* permits a more frequent holding of the episcopal conferences. The canon also uses the words *"stato tempore."* The date of these meetings is to be specific. The choice of the date can be made at the previous episcopal conference, or at the previous provincial council. The metropolitan does not determine the date alone; he does so together with all the ordinaries who have the duty to attend these conferences.[47] Coronata says that the metropolitan can select the date of the first episcopal conference which is to begin the series. This he can do, but only upon having consulted with the other prelates.[48]

That the legislator most earnestly desires to see this law fulfilled can be deduced from the phrase, *"nisi aliter pro peculiaribus locis a Sede Apostolica provisum fuerit."* The Holy See may allow others to call these conferences in place of the metropolitan or of the senior suffragan. It may also change the frequency of these meetings for particular localities, making them more frequent or less frequent. It may also change the disposition as to the region or section in which the conferences are to be held by extending it to a number of provinces or by limiting it to particular dioceses. A circular letter of the Sacred Consistorial Congregation to the Bishops of Italy, dated the 22nd of March, 1919, pointed

[46] Cf. *supra*, pp. 274-276.

[47] Chelodi, *Ius Canonicum*, p. 276.

[48] *Institutiones*, I, 444.

out that canon 292, § 1, which provides for the provincial meetings of bishops at least every five years "unless the Holy See has provided otherwise for particular localities," leaves unimpaired the obligation of the Italian bishops to meet every year according to the special provision made for them by the Holy See on August 24, 1889.[49] This provision of the Holy See not only decreed more frequent episcopal conferences, but also broke down the provincial character of these meetings into regional meetings.

The place of these episcopal conferences is not determined as it is in the case of provincial councils. The Code gives a greater freedom in the choice of the place, for it permits these meetings to be held in the presence of the metropolitan or of any one of the comprovincial bishops: "*apud Metropolitam aliumve Episcoporum comprovincialem conveniant.*" This phrase also shows that the metropolitan does not necessarily preside at the gatherings. Furthermore, the words do not include the term "*ecclesia*"; hence these conferences need not be held in any church. Canon 284, 1°, on the other hand, uses the expression "*metropolitana ecclesia.*" From the absence of the word *church* it can be concluded that the solemnities of the provincial council need not be observed.

Those to be called and those who must attend are the local ordinaries who have a deliberative vote in the provincial council. Canon 292, § 1, uses the terms "*Ordinarii locorum.*"[50] The bishops and others mentioned in canon 285 must also be called by the metropolitan according to canon 292, § 2. Once called, these prelates must attend.

The matters taken up in these conferences concern the means to be employed for the sake of promoting the good of religion in the diocese of the province and in the territories of the prelates of canon 285; the preparation of those matters which must be done in the future provincial coun-

---

[49] *AAS*, XI (1919), 175; *AAS*, XXIV (1932), 242. Cf. *supra*, p. 272; *infra*, pp. 337-338, footnote 24.

[50] Cf. canon 282, § 1; canon 286, § 1. Cf. Coronata, *Institutiones*, I, 444.

cil; and, the choice of the place of the next episcopal conference.[51]

The decrees of these episcopal conferences have no juridic force. They are a matter of counsel rather than obligation.[52] However, these decrees could be announced by each bishop to the people of his diocese and promulgated in the form of law.[53]

Article 3. Recourse in Cases of Impeded Sees

Canon 429. § 5. *Si Episcopus in excommunicationem, interdictum vel suspensionem inciderit, Metropolita, eoque deficiente, vel, si de eodem agatur, antiquior inter Suffraganeos ad Sedem Apostolicam illico recurrat, ut ipsa provideat; quod si de diœcesi agatur vel prælatura de quibus in can. 285, Metropolita qui fuit legitime electus, obligatione recurrendi tenetur.*

If a governing prelate is lacking in a diocese or a quasi-diocese, the see can be said to be impeded *(sedes impedita)* or vacant *(sedes vacans)*. Canon 429 speaks of sees which are impeded. A see is impeded when the bishop is prevented from exercising his jurisdiction because of some physical or canonical impediment, even though he still possesses jurisdiction. The first four paragraphs of canon 429 speak of physical impediments; the fifth paragraph treats of canonical impediments. If a bishop incurs excommunication, interdict or suspension, the metropolitan has the obligation of making recourse at once to the Holy See in order that provision may be made for the penalized bishop's see.[54]

The canon does not use the wide term *archiepiscopus;*

---

[51] Canon 292, § 1 and § 3.

[52] Badii, *Institutiones*, p. 202; Claeys Bouuaert-Simenon, *Manuale*, I, 253; Cocchi, *Commentarium*, III, 137; Coronata, *Institutiones*, I, 445; Oesterle, *Prælectiones*, p. 157. Regatillo (*Institutiones*, I, 238) says that certain decrees could be enforced by way of obligation, e.g., judicial and other taxes (cf. canons 1507 and 1909), but not such taxes as are connected with funerals and Masses (canons 831, § 1, and 1234).

[53] Cocchi, *Commentarium*, III, 137; Coronata, *Institutiones*, I, 445; Oesterle, *Prælectiones*, p. 157.

[54] Canon 429, § 5.

hence a residential archbishop who is not at the same time a metropolitan is not obliged to make this form of recourse. Since he has no legal obligation, he has no legal right to assume that he may exercise this form of metropolitan jurisdiction, unless he is the senior suffragan of the province. The canon employs the word *Metropolita.* In consequence of this usage, only those who are at the head of a province have the obligation of making recourse for the proper provision relative to the impeded sees of penalized bishops.

The action on the part of the metropolitan has an administrative character; hence the canon employs the word "*recurrat.*" The action under consideration is not a legal redress against a judicial sentence, known as an appeal. The law does not give metropolitans the obligation of making an appeal for the excommunicated, interdicted or suspended bishops, but obliges them simply to make recourse for the proper provision with reference to their impeded sees.

Since the law uses the word *metropolitan,* the bishop to whom the canon has reference with the term "*Episcopus*" must of necessity be one of the suffragans or comprovincial bishops within the province subject to the metropolitan who is obliged to make the recourse for him. The canon extends the metropolitan's obligation of recourse to the cases which concern the prelates mentioned in canon 285.[55] Therefore the metropolitan is obliged to make recourse not only for the sees of his suffragan bishops within his province who incur the penalties of excommunication, interdict or suspension, but also for the dioceses, abbacies and prelacies of any bishop, abbot *nullius,* or prelate *nullius,* or also for any similarly penalized archbishop without suffragans who has chosen him as the metropolitan of the province in which he must attend the provincial council. The words "*legitime electus*" in canon 429, § 5, relate to the method by which the second class of prelates, as mentioned in canon 285, become subject to their particular metropolitan.[56]

---

[55] Canon 429, § 5.

[56] Oesterle, *Prælectiones,* p. 206.

Negatively, the metropolitan has no obligation to make recourse for the sees of any and every bishop who might be penalized by excommunication, interdict or suspension. No provision is made for purely titular bishops or archbishops in canon 429, § 5, for the entire canon speaks of obstructions impeding the government of dioceses. Titular or non-residential bishops or archbishops do not have a diocese to govern.

The bishop for whose see the recourse must be made must be excommunicated,[57] interdicted[58] or suspended.[59] Once a bishop is excommunicated, interdicted or suspended, his episcopal jurisdiction is suspended.[60] Because of the juridic association of bishop and vicar general, the jurisdiction of the vicar general is suspended concomitantly with that of the bishop.[61] At such times, however, there is still a possibility of delegating jurisdiction, for not every kind of excommunication, interdict and suspension implies a total loss of power.[62] A suspended cleric, for example, can exercise his jurisdiction not invalidly but simply illicitly, and hence, a bishop can also under the same circumstances validly, though not licitly, delegate his possessed jurisdiction to others within the diocese. A penalized bishop can, if such be the case, validly delegate his possessed power because he still possesses power; yet he cannot do so lawfully, since he himself cannot lawfully use it. It is because he cannot do so licitly that the Holy See, upon the recourse made by the metropolitan, undertakes to make provision for the diocese of the excommunicated, interdicted or suspended bishop. Should the excommunication, interdict or suspension imply a total loss of power, delegation would be out of question. There is nothing in law by which there is granted

---

[57] Canons 2257; 2259, § 2; 2261; 2265.

[58] Canons 2268; 2275.

[59] Canons 2278; 2283; 2284.

[60] Cf. Chelodi, *Ius Canonicum*, p. 339; Toso, *Commentaria*, IV, 77-78; Wernz-Vidal, *Ius Canonicum*, II, 897.

[61] Canon 371.

[62] Cf. canon 2265, § 2, for excommunication; canon 2275, 3°, for personal interdict; canon 2284 for suspension.

to bishops, who have lost all their power, the faculty of delegating jurisdiction for the time of their eventual juridic incapacity while they are still in possession of jurisdiction and have not incurred excommunication, interdict or suspension.[63] Nor does the law grant jurisdiction to the chapter or to the diocesan consultors in such circumstances.[64] Because of the impasse created in such an eventuality, the law presents a means of provision for the impeded see. Canon 429, § 5, obliges the metropolitan of the ecclesiastical province in which the impeded see is found to have immediate recourse to the Holy See.

It is evident that the canon treats of an excommunication, interdict or suspension which suspends some or all ecclesiastical jurisdiction but which has not as yet come to the notice of the Holy See. From the very wording of the canon, therefore, all *ferendæ sententiæ* censures must be excluded, for canon 1557, § 1, 3°, conjoined with canon 2227, § 1, makes it clear that only the Roman Pontiff can inflict *ferendæ sententiæ* penalties[65] on bishops. Hence canon 429, § 5, must refer to *latæ sententiæ* censures.[66]

In accordance with canon 2264 any act of jurisdiction placed either in the external or in the internal forum by an excommunicated bishop is illicit, and if a condemnatory or a declaratory sentence of excommunication has been issued against him, the act of jurisdiction is also invalid, without prejudice to canon 2261, § 3. Canon 2227, § 2, declares that bishops do not fall under the *latæ sententiæ* censures of suspension or interdict unless they are expressly mentioned in the law.[67] In the light of these juridical facts it seems that the cases in which bishops would act in only an illicit manner are chiefly cases of *latæ sententiæ* excommunications. Yet canon 2227, § 1, states that only the Roman Pontiff can declare *latæ sententiæ* censures against bishops. The bish-

---

[63] Toso, *Commentaria*, IV, 77.

[64] Sipos, *Enchiridion*, p. 301; Toso, *Commentaria*, IV, 77.

[65] Canon 2217, § 1, 2°.

[66] Canon 2217, § 1, 2°.

[67] Canon 2227, § 2.

op as an offender can be excused from observing the *latæ sententiæ* excommunication in the external forum before a declaratory sentence whenever he cannot observe it without infamy, and no one can demand its observance *in foro externo* unless the delict be notorious.[68] Among the *latæ sententiæ* censures, which are not occult but public, there come into play, as far as the validity of the exercise of jurisdiction is concerned, only such which rest upon the censured bishop *post sententiam declaratoriam*. Since only the Holy See can make such a declaration, the canon under consideration seems to point to the Holy See's concern that the censured bishop should not have occasion to exercise his episcopal authority even then when his incurred censure stands in the way simply of the licit use of his power.

Toso, following Wernz-Vidal, says that a case can scarcely happen in which a bishop can be effectively impeded from the exercise of jurisdiction because of an incurred censure without the matter being taken at once to the Holy See. This is so because an episcopal confessor obtains sacramental jurisdiction *ipso iure* for all reserved censures, except for those which are reserved to the Holy See in a most special manner and for those censures which are connected with the revelation of a secret of the Holy Office.[69]

It is because of the multiplication of difficulties that the law demands the metropolitan to make recourse at once, "*illico*," and in order that the normal sequence of licit and valid acts of episcopal jurisdiction may be resumed. Wernz-Vidal say that as soon as such cases would be reported to the Holy See, it would make immediate provision.[70]

The metropolitan has no right to fill the see nor has he the right to take over the jurisdiction of the particular impeded diocese. He cannot delegate to another the jurisdiction which is necessary in the see. The canon grants him no

---

[68] Canon 2232, § 1.

[69] Canon 349, § 1, 1°, collated with canon 239, § 1, 2°. Cf. Beste, *Introductio in Codicem*, p. 282; Toso, *Commentaria*, IV, 78; Wernz-Vidal, *Ius Canonicum*, II, 897.

[70] *Ius Canonicum*, II, 897.

authority, but reserves the right of provision to the Holy See through the words: "*ut ipsa provideat.*"[71] His only obligation is to make recourse to the Holy See in order to inform it of the necessity of providing for the impeded see.[72]

In the opinion of Coronata, which opinion he leaves open to correction with the phrase "*salvo meliori iudicio,*" if such a case should occur in places so distant from the Holy See that recourse could not be made without the lapse of many days or many weeks while the response is being expected from the Holy See, the chapter or those who are taking its place should take over the provisional administration in the interim.[73]

The law places the obligation of recourse on the senior suffragan as well.[74] The senior suffragan is that suffragan who is mentioned in canons 284 and 292.[75] This is not an absolute obligation, for the canon states that he must make recourse only on condition that the metropolitan does not act. The phrase "*eo deficiente*" is broad enough to include the two specifications given in canon 284, namely: "*eoque legitime impedito*" and "*sede archiepiscopali vacante,*" to which canon 429, § 5, adds a third, "*si de eodem agatur,*" i.e., if the metropolitan himself falls under censure.

The law is clear on two points. The senior suffragan, once the metropolitan does not make the recourse, either because he is legitimately impeded or for the reason that the metropolitan see is vacant, has the obligation of making it for the sake of making provision in the see of an excommunicated, interdicted or suspended suffragan bishop. Then, too, the senior suffragan is obliged by law to make recourse for the see of the metropolitan of the province should the metropolitan himself be under the censure of excommunication, interdict or suspension.

However, the canon is not clear on whether or not the

---

[71] Cf. canons 147 and 148.

[72] Coronata, *Institutiones*, I, 548.

[73] *Institutiones*, I, 548.

[74] Canon 429, § 5.

[75] Blat, *Commentarium*, Lib. II, pars 1, p. 464. Cf. *supra*, p. 274.

senior suffragan has the obligation to make recourse for the dioceses, abbacies or prelacies of which canon 285 speaks. The canon is silent about the senior suffragan; it mentions only the metropolitan.[76] Blat, Cance and Regatillo are of the opinion that in accordance with the principle of canon 20 he has the obligation of making recourse.[77] Blat confirms his opinion by referring to canon 327, § 2, which states that impeded abbacies and prelacies *nullius* are to observe the rulings of canon 429 in their entirety.[78]

SECTION B

JUDICIAL OBLIGATIONS

Article 1. Cases of Second Instance

Canon 274. *In diœcesibus vero suffraganeis Metropolita potest tantum:*

7° *Appellationem recipere a sententiis definitivis aut interlocutoriis definitivarum vim habentibus, prolatis in Curiis suffraganeis, ad normam can. 1594, § 1.*

Canon 1594. §1. *A tribunali Episcopi Suffraganei appellatur ad Metropolitam.*

Canon 274, 7°, enunciates the right which metropolitans have to accept appeals from definitive and interlocutory sentences given in the tribunals of their suffragan bishops.[79] Yet this canon does not bring out into full light that it is the obligation of the metropolitan to accept these cases once they are presented to him. That it is a serious obligation flows from the consideration of a number of canons.

The phrasing of canon 1594, § 1, declares that it is a personal obligation on the part of the metropolitan to receive these appeals. But even this canon is not as clear concerning the obligation as is canon 1608. The latter canon

---

[76] Canon 429, § 5.

[77] Blat, *Commentarium*, Lib. II, pars 1, p. 464; Cance, *Le Code*, I, 389; Regatillo, *Institutiones*, I, 296.

[78] *Commentarium*, Lib. II, pars 1, p. 464.

[79] For a more detailed study of this metropolitan right the reader is advised to see pp. 250-263, *supra*.

brings out in a negative manner the obligation which a competent judge has to accept a case from one who legitimately presents it to him by stating that he is not allowed to refuse his services. The canon is fortified with the citation of canon 1625, § 1, which contains the legal sanction.

In accordance with the prescription of canon 1608, it is clear that a metropolitan is not permitted to refuse to accept an appeal from one who makes it legitimately without the serious risk of deserving the sanction. Once the competency of the metropolitan is certain and evident, and he refuses to try the case in its second instance, he is liable to punishment meted out by the Apostolic See. The proceedings against the metropolitan may be instituted either at the request of the parties or *ex officio*. The penalty is in proportion to the gravity of the guilt, and may even extend to the deprivation of his office.[80]

Since canon 1625, § 1, deals with a penalty, it must be interpreted strictly.[81] As a consequence, the metropolitan can be punished only according to the exact specifications of the law.

Canon 274, 7°, declares that a metropolitan has the right to receive appeals from definitive or interlocutory sentences which have a definitive force. Therefore, the first requirement is that the appeal be made after a sentence has been rendered. According to canon 1868, § 1, a sentence is a legitimate pronouncement by which a judge decides a case proposed by litigants and tried in judicial form. Any action which takes place before an ecclesiastical trial begins is not to be considered a part of the judicial form. A judicial trial begins with the instance of the suit *(litis instantia)*. Canon 1732 declares that the instance begins with the joinder of issue *(litis contestatio)*. The refusal on the part of the metropolitan to accept for decision any unsatisfactory action connected with the introduction of the cause, such as the bill of complaint *(libellus litis)*, the summons *(citatio)*, the joinder of issue *(litis contestatio)* or the an-

[80] Canon 1625, § 1.
[81] Canon 19.

nouncement of the judicial acts *(denuntiatio actorum iudicialium)*, would be contrary to canon 1594, § 1, and could be punished in an extraordinary fashion by the Holy See in keeping with canon 2222, but the norms of canon 1625, § 1, would not apply.

The principle of appeal, as found explained in canon 1879, would have to be involved in all its entirety. Hence it must be a question of a judicial sentence already rendered with which either the litigants or the promoter of justice or the defender of the bond is legitimately dissatisfied. Canon 274, 7°, insists that the metropolitan can receive appeals only. Should he be requested to take up a case before a sentence was rendered in the first tribunal, he would not be taking an appeal, but would be assuming to take a case in its first instance. Canon 1594, § 1, also speaks only of appeals.

The next requirement which must be borne in mind is the nature of the sentence from which the appeal can be made. It must be either an interlocutory or a definitive sentence. According to canon 1868 an interlocutory sentence is one which settles an incidental issue, while a definitive sentence is one which decides the principal issue. These sentences must have definitive force. A decree issued by a judge on some particular point is not an interlocutory or a definitive sentence, and should a metropolitan refuse to accept a complaint against such a decree, the sanction of canon 1625, § 1, would be ineffective.

Finally, the appeals must come to the metropolitan from the courts of his suffragans. By special provision of law, the metropolitan is also required to receive appeals from the tribunals of those archbishops who lack suffragans and of those local ordinaries who are immediately subject to the Holy See, when they have chosen him as their metropolitan in accordance with canon 285.[82] Canon 274, 7°, insists on the suffragan subjection, and so does canon 1594, § 1 and § 3; hence metropolitans are not obliged to receive appeals

[82] Canon 1594, § 3. This canon makes provision for the abbacies and prelacies *nullius* in § 4.

from curias other than those of their suffragans. In fact, it would be unlawful for them to accept extra-provincial appeals, except for the provision made by canon 1594, § 3. The acceptance of a case tried in its first instance in a civil tribunal could not be accepted as a second instance case by a metropolitan. His refusal to accept such a case would not make him liable to the penal sanction of canon 1625, § 1.

The competent judge of second instance cases is the metropolitan or his *officialis*, as can be seen from the wording of both canon 274, 7°, and canon 1594, § 1 and § 3. Any inferior judge in the tribunal of the metropolitan could not without the delegation of the metropolitan assume to accept cases which have been previously tried in the curias of the suffragans. The penal sanction of canon 1625, § 1, affects the metropolitan. Should a delegated judge in the curia of the metropolitan refuse to accept a second instance case without legitimate excusing reasons, he, too, would be liable to the punishment decreed in canon 1625, § 1.

Residential archbishops do not have the right to accept second instance cases; hence they do not have the obligations connected with their acceptance. Since there is no obligation, there cannot be any penal sanction. Purely titular or non-residential archbishops are in the same position as residential archbishops in this regard. Canon 1594, § 2, makes provision for the second instance curias which are to take care of appeals from the tribunals of metropolitans, but these are not necessarily the tribunals of residential archbishops. The choice of the tribunal is left to the metropolitan himself. This choice once made must be approved by the Apostolic See and must be maintained permanently.

The II Plenary Council of Baltimore (1866) made no provision for any penal sanction. It only mentioned the right and the duty of the metropolitan to receive appeals from the tribunals of the suffragan bishops.[83] Should it have intended a sanction by its employment of the phrase

---

[83] "Appellationes a sententia suffraganeorum, juxta regulas a sanctis canonibus definitas, recipit." — *Acta et Decreta Concilii Plenarii Baltimorensis II*, n. 81, p. 62.

"juxta regulas a sanctis canonibus definitas," canon 6, 5°, would apply.

In accordance with the ruling of canon 1595, all the other penalties mentioned in canon 1625 would apply, the proper adjustments being made to fit the guilt of the persons involved in the procedure of second instance.

Article 2. Cases of First Instance

Canon 274. *In diœcesibus vero suffraganeis Metropolita potest tantum:*

8° *Controversias de quibus in can. 1572, § 2, in prima instantia dirimere.*

Canon 1572. § 2. *Si vero agatur de iuribus aut bonis temporalibus Episcopi aut mensæ vel Curiæ diœcesanæ, controversia dirimenda deferatur vel, Episcopo consentiente, ad diœcesanum tribunal collegiale quod constat officiali et duobus iudicibus synodalibus antiquioribus, vel ad iudicem immediate superiorem.*

The metropolitan has the right to settle controversies in the first instance which concern the rights or temporal goods of a bishop or his *mensa,* and those which concern the rights or temporal goods of a diocesan curia, should a bishop decline to submit any such case to a diocesan collegiate tribunal consisting of certain members of his own curia.[84] Once a bishop presents such cases to his metropolitan, the latter has the obligation to accept them for decision in the metropolitan tribunal. This obligation flows from canon 1608. It is canon 274, 8°, which makes the metropolitan the competent judge as soon as a bishop declines to submit these cases to his own tribunal.

Canon 1625, § 1, indicates the legal sanction applicable upon the refusal to accept such cases.[85] It must be stressed that this penal sanction demands a strict interpretation in accordance with canon 19.[86] Canon 274, 8°, speaks of a

[84] The reader will find a fuller account of this metropolitan right, *supra,* pp. 264-269.

[85] *Supra,* pp. 292-293.

[86] *Supra,* p. 293.

metropolitan only, hence the obligation of assuming such cases in the first instance weighs on metropolitans only, and not on residential or non-residential archbishops. The bishop presenting the case must be a suffragan bishop in the strict sense, i.e., a suffragan who resides within the province and is subject to the metropolitan. Canon 274, 8°, is clear on this point. Canon 1572, § 2, even though it does not mention the archbishops without suffragans and the local ordinaries who are immediately subject to the Holy See as included among the prelates mentioned in canon 285, seems to include them implicitly. This canon uses not the restrictive term *suffraganeus*, but the extensive word *Episcopi*. The generic word *bishops*, if connected with the phrase "*ad iudicem immediate superiorem*," seems to indicate a parallelism between canon 1572, § 2, and canon 1594, § 3. This opinion can be fortified in the light of the ruling of canon 20, which states that if a general or particular law does not contain an explicit provision concerning a certain matter, a norm of action is to be taken from laws enacted in similar cases. Abbots and prelates *nullius* would be governed by canon 1594, § 4. Hence it seems to be the obligation of the metropolitan to accept these cases from his own suffragans and from the two types of prelates mentioned in canon 1594, § 3. No other bishops are permitted to present the cases mentioned in canon 1572, § 2, to a metropolitan outside their own province, nor is a metropolitan permitted to receive such cases from non-suffragan bishops.

The suffragan bishop must give his consent to have the case tried in the metropolitan tribunal, for the canon states "*Episcopo consentiente.*" The metropolitan could not be punished if he refused to take up the cases mentioned in canon 1572, § 2, if they be presented by any one except the suffragan bishop. Then, too, he would not be liable to the penal sanction if the cases presented to his tribunal by the suffragan bishops were other than those described in canon 1572, § 2.

CHAPTER IX

METROPOLITAN RIGHTS AND OBLIGATIONS CONNECTED WITH THE PALLIUM

SECTION A

DESCRIPTION AND TYPES OF PALLIUM

Canon 275. *Metropolita obligatione tenetur, intra tres menses a consecratione vel, si iam consecratus fuerit, a provisione canonica in Consistorio, per se vel per procuratorem a Romano Pontifice pallium petendi, quod significat potestatem archiepiscopalem.*

The *pallium* is the chief ensign of a Latin metropolitan. It consists of a circular band of white lamb's wool from which hang two pendants of the same material; when the pallium is worn the one pendant falls over the breast and the other falls over the back. The band as such is about three or four inches wide; the pendants are about a foot long. Six little black crosses are embroidered in silk: four on the circumference of the band and one on each lappet. The pallium is worn over the chasuble, to which it is fastened by three golden pins. The circular band rests upon the shoulders, while the front pendant falls over the center of the breast and the rear pendant falls down from the middle of the back.[1]

The lamb's wool from which the pallia are made is that

[1] Badii, *Institutiones*, p. 189; Bargilliat, *Prælectiones*, I, 412; Beste, *Introductio in Codicem*, p. 252; Blat, *Commentarium*, Lib. II, pars 1, pp. 293-294; Claeys Bouuaert-Simenon, *Manuale*, I, 249; Cance, *Le Code*, I, 282-283; Cappello, *Summa*, I, 309; Chelodi, *Ius Canonicum*, p. 281; Cocchi, *Commentarium*, III, 119; Coronata, *Institutiones*, I, 434; Ferreres, *Institutiones*, I, 207; Nainfa, *Costumes of Prelates of the Catholic Church* (new and revised ed., Baltimore: John Murphy Co., 1926), pp. 13-14 (hereafter cited as *Costumes*); Prümmer, *Manuale*, p. 152; Raus, *Institutiones*, p. 174; Sipos, *Enchiridion*, p. 226; Vermeersch-Creusen, *Epitome*, I, 310; Wernz-Vidal, *Ius Canonicum*, II, 659.

which is sheared from two lambs which the Roman Pontiff blesses every year on the feast of Saint Agnes (January 21). In the Church of Saint Agnes outside the Walls, two white lambs, which are decorated and placed in baskets lined with silk, are placed on the altar after a Pontifical Mass has been offered. Here they are blessed by one of the prelates in attendance. Immediately after this first blessing, the Commission of the Lateran Chapter takes these lambs to the Roman Pontiff for the second blessing mentioned above. Then they are sent to the Benedictine nuns of Saint Cecilia beyond the Tiber, who care for the lambs and make the pallia from the sheared wool mixed with other wool.[2]

On the vigil of the feast of Saints Peter and Paul (June 28), the Roman Pontiff blesses the pallia in the Vatican Basilica. These blessed pallia are then placed in a golden casket and carried to the Confession of Saint Peter, where they are kept close to the body of Saint Peter for at least one day, i.e., the feast of the Apostles itself (June 29). The pallia remain at the tomb of Saint Peter until they are taken from that place by the ranking cardinal-deacon and given to the metropolitans, archbishops and bishops who enjoy the privilege of wearing them.[3] For this reason it is said that the pallia are taken from the body of Saint Peter *"de corpore Beati Petri assumpta."*[4]

There are two types of pallia: the *pallium latinum*, which has just been described, and the *pallium græcum*, also called the omophorion. The omophorion is a much longer and larger ornament or vestment, and it resembles a stole.

---

[2] Regatillo, *Institutiones*, I, 235; Sipos, *Enchiridion*, p. 226, footnote 15.

[3] Canon 239, § 3.

[4] Badii, *Institutiones*, p. 189, footnote 3; Bargilliat, *Prælectiones*, I, 412; Beste, *Introductio in Codicem*, p. 252; Blat, *Commentarium*, Lib. II, pars 1, p. 294; Claeys Bouuaert-Simenon, *Manuale*, I, 249; Cance, *Le Code*, I, 283, footnote 1; Ferreres, *Institutiones*, I, 208; Prümmer, *Manuale*, p. 152; Regatillo, *Institutiones*, I, 235, footnote 2; Sipos, *Enchiridion*, p. 226, footnote 15; Wernz-Vidal, *Ius Canonicum*, II, 664. Cocchi (*Commentarium*, III, 120) says that the pallia are so described because the Roman Pontiff consecrates them at the altar of Saint Peter.

It is marked with a number of red crosses. Only after patriarchs, in union with the Church, receive the Latin pallium from the Roman Pontiff may they grant the omophorion to their metropolitans and to bishops of the more outstanding churches.[5]

Section B

The Significance of the Pallium

Canon 275. *Metropolita obligatione tenetur, intra tres menses a consecratione vel, si iam consecratus fuerit, a provisione canonica in Consistorio, per se vel per procuratorem a Romano Pontifice pallium petendi, quod significat potestatem archiepiscopalem.*

At one time all the bishops in the Orient wore the Greek pallium.[6] They received the omophorion from their metropolitan at the time of their consecration. Metropolitans received theirs from their patriarchs; the patriarchs invested themselves with their omophorions. Hence, among the Orientals, the pallium is nothing more than a symbol of the pastoral office.[7]

In the West, among the Latins, the pallium denotes the

---

[5] Chelodi (*Ius Canonicum*, p. 282), Ferreres (*Institutiones*, I, 207), Sipos (*Enchiridion*, p. 227) and Wernz-Vidal (*Ius Canonicum*, II, 659-660, 664) seem to give this right to all Oriental Catholic patriarchs. The sources are not so generous however. According to a decree given in the Council of Mount Lebanon (1736), the Maronite patriarch was given this right. — Pars III, c. VI, n. 7, XXIII, *Coll. Lac.*, II, 343-344. Coussa (*Epitome*, I, 169), besides mentioning the Maronite patriarch, says that the Armenian patriarch also has this right. Cf. *infra*, pp. 396-397.

[6] Eidenschink, *Election of Bishops*, pp. 107-108; Oesterle, *Prælectiones*, p. 152; Vermeersch-Creusen, *Epitome*, I, 310.

[7] Cance, *Le Code*, I, 282; Chelodi, *Ius Canonicum*, pp. 281-282; Regatillo, *Institutiones*, I, 235; Sipos, *Enchiridion*, p. 226. Coronata (*Institutiones*, I, 434-435) adds the note that patriarchs received their pallia either as a hereditament from their predecessor or at the time of their consecration.

fulness of the pastoral office and power.[8] Hence the Roman Pontiff can wear it at all times and in all places.[9] If the pallium is granted to others, it is as if these prelates were called to share part of his solicitude for the souls of men. As the authors put it, the pallium "*aliis autem quasi in partem sollicitudinis vocatis conceditur.*"[10] Oriental patriarchs receive the Latin pallium in this very sense.[11] Prümmer mentioned that besides patriarchs and archbishops, primates are also given pallia.[12] Sipos and Wernz-Vidal explain that these three types of prelates receive the pallium only because they enjoy true patriarchal, metropolitan or primatial jurisdiction.[13] Merely titular patriarchs, archbishops and primates who have no residential see, have neither the right nor the obligation to request the pallium.[14]

By special privilege certain bishops may also receive the pallium from the Roman Pontiff. These bishops obtain it

---

[8] Beste, *Introductio in Codicem*, p. 252; Cappello, *Summa*, I, 446; Cocchi, *Commentarium*, III, 120; Chelodi, *Ius Canonicum*, p. 281; Oesterle, *Prælectiones*, p. 152; Vermeersch-Creusen, *Epitome*, I, 310; Wernz-Vidal, *Ius Canonicum*, II, 659. Cance (*Le Code*, I, 283) in giving the symbolistic meaning of the pallium declares that it is a sign of pastoral charity or of the solicitude of a shepherd for his sheep. The crosses on the pallium symbolize the compassion the wearer is to have for his brethren, that he may be crucified in his heart rather than give in to the pleasures of this world. The three golden pins symbolize the three nails with which Christ was nailed to the cross. Cocchi (*Commentarium*, III, 120) says that the wool signifies that the wearer of the pallium is an imitator of Christ who searched for the erring sheep and placed it about his shoulders after He had found it. To him the crosses signify the four cardinal virtues. Strange that six crosses should symbolize four virtues! Cf. Thomassinus, *Ecclesiæ Disciplina*, Pars I, Lib. II, cap. 53, n. 1.

[9] Badii, *Institutiones*, p. 190; Claeys Bouuaert-Simenon, *Manuale*, I, 249; Cappello, *Summa*, I, 446; Chelodi, *Ius Canonicum*, p. 281.

[10] Cappello, *Summa*, I, 309; Chelodi, *Ius Canonicum*, p. 281.

[11] *Supra*, pp. 299-300.

[12] *Manuale*, p. 152.

[13] Sipos, *Enchiridion*, p. 227; Wernz-Vidal, *Ius Canonicum*, II, 664.

[14] Bargilliat, *Prælectiones*, I, 413; Beste, *Introductio in Codicem*, p. 252; Cappello, *Summa*, I, 310, footnote 5; Chelodi, *Ius Canonicum*, p. 282; Coronata, *Institutiones*, I, 436; Prümmer, *Manuale*, p. 152; Sipos, *Enchiridion*, p. 227; Wernz-Vidal (*Ius Canonicum*, II, 664) add the note that titular exarchs are also in this same position.

as a reward *(præmium)* for singular merits or as a sign of pontifical benevolence *(benevolentia)* for special reasons.[15] Oesterle gives an example of this by citing the case of Raymond Silva, Bishop of Mérida in West Indies, who received in the year 1923 the pallium *"pro sua persona,"* and who shortly after obtaining this special privilege was named an archbishop.[16] Then again there are certain bishops who receive the pallium by right of their see, *"ex iure Ecclesiarum suarum."*[17] Oesterle cites two such sees in which bishops received the pallium *"pro ipsa sede respectiva,"* namely, the bishop of Tarbes-Lourdes[18] whose see was so honored by Benedict XV, and the bishop of Soissons (France), whose see was so privileged by Pius XI.[19] De Meester says that in France alone there are seven such sees.[20] According to Ferreres and Regatillo the bishop of the see of Barcelona has the privilege of the pallium. The see was so honored by Pius X in 1904.[21] Trombetta reports that at his time there were twenty-two episcopal sees which enjoyed the privilege of the pallium.[22]

---

[15] Badii, *Institutiones*, p. 189, footnote 1; Bargilliat, *Prælectiones*, I, 413; Beste, *Introductio in Codicem*, p. 252; Claeys Bouuaert-Simenon, *Manuale*, I, 250; Chelodi, *Ius Canonicum*, p. 282; Cocchi, *Commentarium*, III, 122; Coronata, *Institutiones*, I, 436; Ferreres, *Institutiones*, I, 209; Oesterle, *Prælectiones*, p. 152; Raus, *Institutiones*, p. 175; Regatillo, *Institutiones*, I, 235; Sipos, *Enchiridion*, p. 227; Vermeersch-Creusen, *Epitome*, I, 310; Wernz-Vidal, *Ius Canonicum*, II, 664.

[16] *Prælectiones*, p. 152.

[17] Bargilliat, *Prælectiones*, I, 413; Coronata, *Institutiones*, I, 413, footnote 8; Oesterle, *Prælectiones*, p. 152; Regatillo, *Institutiones*, I, 235; Vermeersch-Creusen, *Epitome*, I, 310; Wernz-Vidal, *Ius Canonicum*, II, 664.

[18] Tarbes-Lourdes is a combined see, like Savannah-Atlanta. There is but one bishop. He resides at Lourdes from April until November, and at Tarbes from November until April. The bishop has the privilege of the pallium since 1917, but only for Lourdes. Lourdes was united with Tarbes in 1912.

[19] *Prælectiones*, p. 152.

[20] *Compendium*, I, 624.

[21] Ferreres, *Institutiones*, I, 209; Regatillo, *Institutiones*, I, 235.

[22] *De Pallio Archiepiscopali, elubricatio canonico-liturgica-historica* (Surrenti: Ex Typographia Hen. D. Onofrio, 1923), cap. VI (hereafter cited as *De Pallio*).

Whether the pallium is obtained by pontifical privilege extended to the person of a particular bishop or to a particular see held by a bishop, the bishops so honored are not thereby withdrawn from the jurisdiction of their metropolitan. The pallium does not increase their own jurisdiction, nor does it give them the right of precedence over other bishops who do not have the privilege of the pallium. This privilege entitles these bishops to wear the pallium only in the churches of their sees.[23] Before such bishops receive the pallium it is not necessary for them to abstain from acts of episcopal jurisdiction or acts of episcopal orders as is the case with metropolitans according to the interpretation given to canon 276.[24] In the manner of bishops, once they are properly instituted, they may convoke diocesan synods, ordain clerics, consecrate churches and exercise all the other rights of episcopal orders and jurisdiction.[25]

Together with the privilege of wearing the pallium the Roman Pontiff regularly grants the use of the *(ad instar)* cross of metropolitans.[26] This cross may be used by these bishops within their own churches except on occasions when their own metropolitan is present. However, if their metropolitan grants permission for its use, these bishops may also use the cross in his presence.[27]

Notwithstanding the fact that the pallium may be obtained by patriarchs, primates and bishops, the pallium is the chief ensign of metropolitans.[28] It is significant that

---

[23] Badii, *Institutiones*, p. 190, footnote 1; Bargilliat, *Prælectiones*, I, 413; Chelodi, *Ius Canonicum*, p. 282; Cocchi, *Commentarium*, III, 122; Coronata, *Institutiones*, I, 436; Ferreres, *Institutiones*, I, 209; Oesterle, *Prælectiones*, p. 152; Regatillo, *Institutiones*, I, 235; Sipos, *Enchiridion*, p. 227; Vermeersch-Creusen, *Epitome*, I, 310; Wernz-Vidal (*Ius Canonicum*, II, 666) declare that this honor does not subject them immediately to the Holy See.

[24] *Infra*, pp. 311-317.

[25] Wernz-Vidal, *Ius Canonicum*, II, 666.

[26] Badii, *Institutiones*, p. 189, footnote 2; Sipos, *Enchiridion*, p. 227. The metropolitan cross is discussed *infra*, pp. 360-364.

[27] Badii, *Institutiones*, p. 189.

[28] Beste, *Introductio in Codicem*, p. 252; Chelodi, *Ius Canonicum*, p. 281.

the Code of Canon Law employs the term *"Metropolita"* throughout all the canons which treat of the pallium.[29] In giving the significance of the pallium, the Code itself declares that it symbolizes archiepiscopal power.[30] The reason for the use of the broader term *archiepiscopal* instead of the restricted term *metropolitan* is found in canon 276, which includes acts of metropolitan jurisdiction and acts of episcopal orders as effects of the power of a metropolitan. Blat says that the pallium has this significance as such only by ecclesiastical law.[31]

The pallium is given to metropolitans to designate supra-episcopal power. Through the pallium a bishop truly becomes a superior type of bishop, an archbishop, and as such he participates in the primatial power of the Roman Pontiff.[32] This supra-episcopal or archiepiscopal power touches the episcopal power of his suffragan bishops inasmuch as the metropolitan is allowed to place certain acts of episcopal orders throughout his entire province without making any request for permission or delegation from his suffragans, once the pallium has been imposed on his person.[33]

His participation in the primatial power of the Pope extends his episcopal jurisdiction from the mere inclusion of his own diocese to the inclusion of the dioceses which are part and parcel of the ecclesiastical province over which he presides. Through this participation in the pontifical right of jurisdiction he obtains the right to rule over a certain number of bishops in the name of the Roman Pontiff.[34] Prümmer stated that the pallium is not given to metropolitans solely for reasons of elegance, but for the purpose of

---

[29] Canons 275-279.

[30] Canon 275.

[31] *Commentarium*, Lib. II, pars 1, p. 293.

[32] Badii, *Institutiones*, p. 189; Bargilliat, *Prælectiones*, I, 412; Claeys Bouuaert-Simenon, *Manuale*, I, 249; Cocchi, *Commentarium*, III, 119-120; Coronata, *Institutiones*, I, 435; Ferreres, *Institutiones*, I, 207; Regatillo, *Institutiones*, I, 235; Sipos, *Enchiridion*, p. 226.

[33] Canon 276.

[34] Canon 276.

signifying archiepiscopal jurisdiction.[35] Vermeersch-Creusen declare that the pallium is given to archbishops [*sic*] as a sign of jurisdiction over other bishops.[36]

SECTION C

THE OBLIGATION OF PETITIONING FOR THE PALLIUM

Canon 275. *Metropolita obligatione tenetur, intra tres menses a consecratione vel, si iam consecratus fuerit, a provisione canonica in Consistorio, per se vel per procuratorem a Romano Pontifice pallium petendi, quod significat potestatem archiepiscopalem.*

The metropolitan is bound by a strict obligation to petition the Roman Pontiff for the pallium within three months from the time of his consecration, or, if he is already consecrated a bishop, within three months from the time the Sacred Consistory made the canonical provision. He is given a choice of petitioning for it in his own person or through a proxy of his choice. That the petition is of strict obligation flows from the very words of canon 275. The employment of the phrase "*obligatione tenetur*" alone is proof enough. Then, too, the time limit set by the canon emphasizes the strictness of the obligation. The sanction invoked in the following canon, which, in the absence of the pallium, makes certain acts of metropolitan jurisdiction and episcopal orders illicit, shows the strictness of the obligation in the fullest light.

The law requires that the petition be made to the Roman Pontiff alone, for he exclusively can grant supra-episcopal powers of jurisdiction and the extension of the basic powers of episcopal orders as to time and place.[37] This obligation brings to the fore the subjection of metropolitans to the Holy See.[38] Coronata mentions that this obligation was

---

[35] *Manuale*, p. 152.

[36] *Epitome*, I, 310.

[37] Badii, *Institutiones*, p. 190; Sipos, *Enchiridion*, p. 227; Vermeersch-Creusen, *Epitome*, I, 310; Wernz-Vidal, *Ius Canonicum*, II, 664.

[38] Beste, *Introductio in Codicem*, p. 252.

introduced into the practice of the Church in order to strengthen the unity of bishops with the Apostolic See.[39] Certainly such an obligation will do much to forestall the great danger of those efforts toward metropolitan independence from the Holy See as attempted at times in the past.[40]

This petition must be made within three months. The time for the fulfillment of this principal metropolitan obligation is computed according to the norm given in canon 34, § 3, 1° and 3°.[41] Since the time mentioned in canon 275 consists of several months and the starting point is explicitly set (i.e., the day of consecration if the metropolitan is not as yet consecrated, or the day of canonical provision in the Consistory if the metropolitan is already a consecrated bishop), the months are to be taken according to the calendar. Further, since the starting point of the three-month period does not coincide with the beginning of the day, the first day (i.e., the day of consecration or the day of the canonical provision) is not to be counted; the three-month period expires with the end of the day which marks the same date three months later. Should a metropolitan be consecrated a bishop or nominated in the Consistory on the 30th of October, this day would not be counted; the three-month period would start with the beginning of the 31st of October, and would end at midnight on the 30th — 31st of January. Canon 34, § 3, 4°, would apply should a metropolitan be consecrated a bishop or nominated in the Consistory on the 30th of November. Since the month of February lacks the corresponding date, i.e., the 30th, the time period would expire at the end of the last day of the month of February. Canonists, however, stress that even now this strict obligation must be fulfilled "*instanter, instantius, instantissime.*"[42] The prayers for the pallium should be most

[39] *Institutiones*, I, 436.
[40] Claeys Bouuaert-Simenon, *Manuale*, I, 249. Cf. *supra*, pp. 76-84.
[41] Cf. Blat, *Commentarium*, Lib. II, pars 1, p. 293.
[42] C. 2, D. C.

eager in accordance with the spirit of the older law.[43] If the pallium is not asked for, it is not given to the metropolitan.[44]

The pallium can be requested either in person or by proxy. Canon 275 is clear on this point. The metropolitan is to ask for it in person if he is in Rome within the prescribed three-month period.[45] Usually, however, the request is made by proxy.[46] This proxy must be selected by the metropolitan from among the Consistorial advocates.[47]

Section D

The Ceremony and Form of Petition

Canon 239, § 3. *Demum Cardinalis Proto-diaconus pallia Archiepiscopis et Episcopis privilegio fruentibus eorumve procuratoribus, vice Romani Pontificis, imponit....*

If the one who is to be decorated with the pallium is present in the Curia, he makes his appearance in the Consistory before the Roman Pontiff. On the right of the petitioner stands the Consistorial advocate who makes the plea for the prelate to be invested, and on the left of the petitioner stands the Master of Ceremonies. If the prelate to be decorated with the pallium is not present in the Curia, his proxy stands at the right, the Master of Ceremonies stands at the left, while the Consistorial advocate stands in the middle. It is the Consistorial advocate who humbly begs the Pontiff for the granting of the pallium.

---

[43] "...prisca consuetudo obtinuit ut honor pallii...nisi fortiter postulanti dari non debeat." — C. 1, D. C. Cf. Beste, *Introductio in Codicem*, p. 252; Cocchi, *Commentarium*, III, 120; Chelodi, *Ius Canonicum*, p. 282; Coronata, *Institutiones*, I, 436; Sipos, *Enchiridion*, p. 227; Vermeersch-Creusen, *Epitome*, I, 310.

[44] Claeys Bouuaert-Simenon, *Manuale*, I, 249.

[45] Vermeersch-Creusen, *Epitome*, I, 310.

[46] Reg. 68, R. J., in VI°: Potest quis per alium, quod potest facere per seipsum.

[47] Benedictus XIV, *De Synodo Diœcesana*, Lib. XII, cap. 15, n. 18. Cf. Beste, *Introductio in Codicem*, p. 252; Chelodi, *Ius Canonicum*, p. 282; Coronata, *Institutiones*, I, 436; Wernz-Vidal, *Ius Canonicum*, II, 664-665.

The formula of the petition reads: "*Ego N. electus Ecclesiæ N. instanter, instantius, instantissime peto mihi tradi et assignari pallium de corpore Beati Petri sumptum, in quo est plenitudo pontificalis officii.*"[48] Before the pallium is imposed, the prelate who is to receive it recites the oath of fidelity and of obedience to the Holy See, and pays a twentieth part of his annual beneficial revenue *(annatæ)* as a tax. These two rules are observed also if a proxy acts in the name of the metropolitan.[49]

If the prelate receiving the pallium is a cardinal, it is the Pope himself who places the pallium on his shoulders.[50] But if the one receiving the pallium is lower in dignity than a cardinal, the ranking cardinal-deacon places it on the shoulders of the prelate or of the proxy in the name of the Roman Pontiff.[51] According to Regatillo even a bishop may confer the pallium in the name of the Pope if he be chosen in keeping with the norms given by the Holy See.[52]

Section E

The Juridic Necessity of the Pallium

Canon 276. *Quare ante pallii impositionem, excluso speciali indulto apostolico, ipse illicite poneret actus sive iurisdictionis metropolitanæ, sive ordinis episcopalis in quibus, ad normam legum liturgicarum, usus pallii requiritur.*

Canon 276 states the juridic necessity of the metropolitan pallium. Before the imposition of the pallium a metropolitan performs illicitly those acts of metropolitan juris-

---

[48] Oesterle, *Prælectiones*, pp. 152-153.

[49] Bargilliat, *Prælectiones*, I, 413; Coronata, *Institutiones*, I, 436; Raus, *Institutiones*, p. 174; Sipos, *Enchiridion*, p. 227; Wernz-Vidal, *Ius Canonicum*, II, 665.

[50] Coronata, *Institutiones*, I, 436, footnote 3; Ferreres, *Institutiones*, I, 208; Sipos, *Enchiridion*, p. 227; Wernz-Vidal, *Ius Canonicum*, II, 665.

[51] Canon 239, § 3. Cf. Bargilliat, *Prælectiones*, I, 413; Beste, *Introductio in Codicem*, p. 252; Chelodi, *Ius Canonicum*, p. 282; Coronata, *Institutiones*, I, 436; Ferreres, *Institutiones*, I, 208; Sipos, *Enchiridion*, p. 227; Wernz-Vidal, *Ius Canonicum*, II, 665.

[52] *Institutiones*, I, 235.

diction or episcopal orders in which the use of the pallium is prescribed by the norms of liturgical law. Such acts of jurisdiction and episcopal orders which liturgically require the pallium are licit before the imposition of the pallium only if the metropolitan has been so authorized by a special apostolic indult.

The word "*quare*" placed at the beginning of canon 276 seems to betoken a deliberate attempt on the part of the legislator to establish a connection between the canon under consideration and the preceding canon. Canon 275 stresses the metropolitan obligation to request the pallium and specifies the time and method of the petition. Canon 276 flows necessarily from the preceding canon, inasmuch as it declares the sanction of illicitness which attaches to certain acts which metropolitans might perform before the pallium has been imposed on them.[53]

The phrase "*ante pallii impositionem*" makes it clear that the imposition of the pallium must be an accomplished reality to guarantee the licitness of certain acts of metropolitan jurisdiction and episcopal orders. If the metropolitan has applied for the pallium either in person or through a proxy within the prescribed time limit, and the Roman Pontiff has not as yet imposed it, the performance of the proscribed acts would still labor under the sanction of illicitness. Should the time period prescribed in canon 275 run out without a request on the part of the metropolitan, he cannot assume that he is free to perform these acts without the sanction taking effect. Hence a metropolitan cannot licitly perform the proscribed acts until he has had the pallium imposed on him by the Roman Pontiff. So, too, it would not suffice for a metropolitan, when he has received word from Rome that the pallium was imposed on his proxy, to act licitly in those cases wherein the pallium is prescribed by liturgical law. None of the functions can be licitly performed according to liturgical law unless the pallium is actually worn by a metropolitan. Furthermore, he must

---

[53] Toso, *Commentaria*, III, 101.

wear his own pallium and no other, for if canon 279 explicitly forbids all metropolitans to lend or give their own pallium to other prelates, it implicitly forbids all metropolitans to borrow and wear the pallium which belongs to others.

Canon 276 places an exception to the general law by the insertion of the clause "*excluso speciali indulto apostolico.*" Such a special apostolic indult may grant a prorogation, i.e., an extension of time. The time period prescribed by canon 275 is limited to three months; hence such a special apostolic indult could extend the time limit to such a length as the Roman Pontiff may deem necessary in particular cases. An indult granting prorogation does not necessarily imply that a metropolitan is allowed to act licitly in all matters touching metropolitan jurisdiction and episcopal orders; it simply extends the time limit prescribed for the petition of the pallium. However, if the indult should supply, besides prorogation, authorization for the exercise of metropolitan jurisdiction in all matters without the use of the pallium, the metropolitan could act licitly within the scope of metropolitan jurisdiction and episcopal orders. Another type of special apostolic indult may grant authorization for the exercise of metropolitan jurisdiction in all matters without the actual use of the pallium, but without granting prorogation of the time for the petition of the symbolic ornament. In such a case the metropolitan would immediately possess the right licitly to perform all acts of metropolitan jurisdiction and episcopal orders without having to wear the pallium. He would still have the obligation to petition the Roman Pontiff for its imposition according to the norms of canon 275.[54]

No metropolitan is allowed to invoke custom as a defense for the licitness of functions which he performs without the pallium but for which the laws of liturgy require the use of the pallium.[55] Although there is no clause in

[54] Toso, *Commentaria*, III, 101.

[55] Blat, *Commentarium*, Lib. II, pars 1, p. 294.

canon 276 to prohibit future customs in this regard, the phrase "*excluso speciali indulto apostolico*" does not seem to give such attempts to begin a custom enough force to change the present ecclesiastical law. It is difficult to see how a metropolitan custom to act contrary to this law could be in continuous and uninterrupted usage for forty years without being brought to the notice of the Holy See.[56]

Canon 276 refers to metropolitans exclusively, for it employs the pronoun "*ipse*" which refers to the word "*Metropolita*" of canon 275. Hence all other prelates who do not enjoy metropolitan jurisdiction are excluded from its scope even though they may have the privilege of wearing the pallium.[57]

The universal discipline involving the pallium, as well as the metropolitan power signified by it, depend on purely ecclesiastical law; therefore, once natural equity is safeguarded, the Roman Pontiff can do all things in reference to it. As chief legislator of the Church he could restrict or enlarge metropolitan power if he deemed such a move advantageous to the Church. He could cause to be invalid all those acts of metropolitan jurisdiction and even those acts of episcopal orders which depend upon purely ecclesiastical law, should these be performed before the imposition of the pallium, in much the same way as he can by special apostolic indult prorogue its imposition or concede metropolitan jurisdiction with a dispensation from the obligation of using the pallium.

However, the legislator declared the acts mentioned in canon 276 illicit *("illicite")*, and not invalid. Should a metropolitan place the proscribed acts mentioned in canon 276, these would be valid in spite of their illicitness.[58] These acts are illicit only because they have been declared such by ecclesiastical law. The Church declares the per-

---

[56] Canon 27, § 1. Cf. Blat, *Commentarium*, Lib. II, pars 1, p. 294.

[57] *Supra*, pp. 301-303. Cf. Blat, *Commentarium*, Lib. II, pars 1, p. 294.

[58] Blat, *Commentarium*, Lib. II, pars 1, p. 294; Claeys Bouuaert-Simenon, *Manuale*, I, 249; Cocchi, *Commentarium*, III, 120; Sipos, *Enchiridion*, p. 227; Toso, *Commentaria*, III, 100-101.

formance of the acts proscribed in canon 276 illicit, since it holds that the one performing them lacks the right to exercise metropolitan jurisdiction in their regard. The pallium does not give a metropolitan his jurisdiction; it simply releases to the full the use of all the metropolitan powers which he received with his canonical appointment.[59] Hence Badii is not altogether correct when he gives the impression that the one petitioning the pallium receives true power through the concession of the pallium.[60]

The acts of metropolitan jurisdiction and episcopal orders *("actus sive iurisdictionis metropolitanæ, sive ordinis episcopalis")* which cannot be licitly placed without the previous imposition of the pallium are those only in which the use of the pallium is required by the norms of liturgical law. The phrase, *"in quibus, ad normam legum liturgicarum,"* seems to apply in canon 276, to both types of functions: those of metropolitan jurisdiction and those of episcopal orders, and not to the latter only.[61]

If the phrase were considered to apply only to acts of episcopal orders, the law of canon 276 would make all acts of metropolitan jurisdiction illicit without any heed to the question of whether or not they required the liturgical use of the pallium. An interpretation of this kind would constrict the power of a metropolitan to such a degree that, from the time of the canonical appointment to his metropolitan see to the actual imposition of the pallium, he could act only as a bishop. This would mean that he could within the confines of his diocese licitly perform only those acts of episcopal orders which do not require the pallium, and all those acts which concern the exercise of episcopal jurisdiction alone. According to such an interpretation no metropolitan could exercise such rights[62] and obligations[63] as are treated above. He could not grant indulgences,[64] nor could

[59] *Infra*, pp. 313-317.
[60] *Institutiones*, p. 190.
[61] Coronata, *Institutiones*, I, 435.
[62] *Supra*, pp. 217-269.
[63] *Supra*, pp. 270-297.
[64] *Infra*, pp. 353-356.

he attend plenary councils[65] before the imposition of the pallium.

Inasmuch as canon 276 restricts the free exercise of metropolitan rights, the rule of strict interpretation given in canon 19 applies. According to this interpretation, a metropolitan could licitly exercise such administrative rights as those deriving from devolution and vigilance, and such judicial rights as those of first and second instance trials.[66] Further, this interpretation would assure him of the obligation to make recourse for any of his excommunicated, interdicted or suspended suffragan bishops, and to accept such cases of first and second instance as are prescribed by law.[67] According to this opinion he would also have the right to be called to a plenary council and to have a deliberative vote in its proceedings.[68] The only purely metropolitan right of jurisdiction which canon 276 would restrict, in the light of this interpretation, would be that of convoking the provincial council. The basis of this restriction is the inclusion of this right and obligation among the functions which are enumerated by liturgical law as those requiring the use of the pallium.[69]

The Code of Canon Law insists in canon 2 that all liturgical laws retain their own force, unless some of them are expressly corrected in the Code. There is no express correction of any liturgical precept; in fact, there is an insistence that the norms of liturgical law be observed in the very wording of canon 276. Hence the ruling of the Roman Pontifical stands: "*...antequam obtinuit quis Pallium... non licet ei...convocare concilium....*"[70] The metropolitan,

---

[65] *Infra*, pp. 336-343.

[66] *Supra*, pp. 217-269.

[67] *Supra*, pp. 286-297.

[68] *Infra*, pp. 336-343.

[69] *Pontificale Romanum in tres Partes Distributum Clementis VIII ac Urbani VIII auctoritate recognitum, Auctore Josepho Catalano* (nova ed., Parisiis: Apud Mequignon Juniorem, 1850), tit. *De pallio*, n. 5 (hereafter cited as Pontificale Rom.).

[70] Pontificale Rom., tit. *De pallio*, n. 5. Cf. Oesterle, *Prælectiones*, p. 153.

since he must wear the pallium when he celebrates the solemn Mass at the provincial council, cannot, without an apostolic indult, convoke or celebrate a provincial council before the reception of the pallium.[71]

None of the other acts of purely metropolitan jurisdiction are mentioned in the liturgical books in connection with the use of the pallium. Hence all acts of purely metropolitan jurisdiction, except the convocation of the provincial council, do not require the use of the pallium, and because of this can be licitly exercised by the metropolitan within the province assigned to him even before the imposition of the pallium.

Since canon 276 speaks of the licitness only and not of the validity of those acts of metropolitan jurisdiction which require the imposition of the pallium, it seems to the writer that the metropolitan is the head of the ecclesiastical province *de facto* and *de iure* as soon as he takes canonical possession of his see. He has metropolitan power, even though its exercise in its lawful use is suspended with regard to those acts of metropolitan jurisdiction proscribed in canon 276, much in the manner of a bishop who, although, suspended by censure from the exercise of episcopal power, does not cease to be the ordinary of his diocese. It would be different if the law invalidated these acts, for then the metropolitan power of jurisdiction would seem to flow from the imposition of the pallium and not from canonical provision. Even canon 275 is circumspect in this regard. It does not state that the pallium *confers* metropolitan jurisdiction; it simply declares that the pallium *signifies* archiepiscopal power.[72]

Cappello and Chelodi, after enumerating the functions

---

[71] *Cæremoniale Episcoporum in duos libros distributum Clementis VIII et Innocentii X auctoritate recognitum, a Benedicto XIII in multis correctum, cura et studio Josephi Catalani Presbyteri* (nova ed., Parisiis: Sumptibus A. Jouby, Editoris, 1840), lib. I, c. XXXI, n. 6 (hereafter cited as Cæremoniale Episcopor.). Cf. Wernz-Vidal, *Ius Canonicum*, II, 667-668, footnote 183.

[72] Cf. Toso, *Commentaria*, III, 101.

which require the use of the pallium for licitness, state that a metropolitan can licitly place acts of diocesan jurisdiction *and even of metropolitan jurisdiction* in the rest of the acts *("in ceteris negotiis")* which do not depend upon the use of the pallium.[73] According to Coronata only those acts of metropolitan jurisdiction which require the use of the pallium are interdicted for a metropolitan before the imposition of the pallium. The author then gives but one example, namely, the convocation of a provincial council.[74] Wernz-Vidal also state that an archbishop [*sic*], before the imposition of the pallium, is not forbidden to exercise the rights of episcopal orders and jurisdiction, *and even of metropolitan jurisdiction,* which can and must be done without the pallium.[75]

As regards the exercise of episcopal orders, the metropolitan acts illicitly before the imposition of the pallium if he performs any function within his own diocese or province which requires the use of the pallium. According to the *Cæremoniale Episcoporum* the ordination of clerics, and the consecration of bishops, of abbots and of virgins, require the use of the pallium. The list of such acts in the *Pontificale Romanum* is somewhat longer: the consecration of bishops, the blessing of chrism, the dedication of churches, the ordination of clerics, pontifical Mass, and the consecration of virgins.[76]

A concise list reads as follows:

1. Pontifical Mass[77]
2. The ordination of clerics[78]

---

[73] Cappello, *Summa,* I, 310; Chelodi (*Ius Canonicum,* p. 281) uses the phrase *"in reliquis negotiis."* Italics are those of the writer.

[74] *Institutiones,* I, 435.

[75] *Ius Canonicum,* II, 665-666. Italics those of the writer.

[76] Oesterle, *Prælectiones,* p. 153.

[77] Cæremoniale Episcopor., lib. I, c. XVI, n. 3; Pontificale Rom., tit. *De pallio,* n. 9. Not all pontifical Masses require the use of the pallium. A fuller treatment of this point is given on pp. 366-370 *infra.*

[78] Cæremoniale Episcopor., lib. I, c. XVI, n. 4; Pontificale Rom., tit. *De pallio,* n. 5.

3. The consecration of bishops,[79] abbots,[80] and virgins[81]

4. The blessing of chrism[82]

5. The dedication of churches.[83]

The Roman Pontifical itself states nothing concerning the validity of these acts when performed without a pallium; it clearly states, however, that the enumerated acts are illicit if posited without the use of the pallium.[84]

Canon 276 does not expressly change the rulings of liturgical books with regard to the exercise of episcopal orders. Hence, should a metropolitan perform any other act of episcopal orders which does not require the use of the pallium within his own diocese, he acts both validly and licitly.[85] However, any act of episcopal orders which requires the pallium would be valid, but illicit, if placed by the metropolitan even within his own see. These acts are illicit because ecclesiastical law makes them such. The positive law of the Church requires that the metropolitan perform them as an archbishop and not as a bishop.[86]

Furthermore, should the metropolitan place any of the five functions of episcopal orders mentioned above within the dioceses of his suffragans before the imposition of the pallium, he would act illicitly. These acts of episcopal orders take on the nature of metropolitan acts by law, and if performed within the sees of his suffragan bishops would be an unlawful assumption of metropolitan jurisdiction. The delegation of any of these five functions to the metropolitan

---

[79] Cæremoniale Episcopor., lib. I, c. XVI, n. 4; Pontificale Rom., tit. *De pallio*, n. 5, 10.

[80] Cæremoniale Episcopor., lib. I, c. XVI, n. 4.

[81] Cæremoniale Episcopor., lib. I, c. XVI, n. 4; Pontificale Rom., tit. *De pallio*, n. 10.

[82] Pontificale Rom., tit. *De pallio*, n. 5.

[83] Pontificale Rom., tit. *De pallio*, n. 5, 10.

[84] "...antequam obtinuerit quis Pallium...non licet ei Episcopos consecrare...nec chrisma conficere, neque ecclesias dedicare, nec clericis ordinare...." — Pontificale Rom., tit. *De pallio*, n. 5.

[85] Canon 2.

[86] Badii, *Institutiones*, p. 190.

by any of his suffragans would not make the acts licit as long as the imposition of the pallium is lacking.

Again, since canon 276 speaks of licitness and not of validity, acts of episcopal orders which are performed by powers deriving through the divine law are valid whenever performed even when the use of the pallium is a legal requirement.

Canonists speak of certain ways in which metropolitans could circumvent the prescriptions of canon 276. According to Coronata and Sipos there are but two ways of doing this: (a) by delegating the performance of the proscribed acts in his own diocese to another bishop, and (b) by performing them himself in a church outside his own province, but with the permission of the local ordinary of the diocese in which the church is located.[87] These authors say nothing about a metropolitan delegating the performance of the proscribed pontifical acts to suffragan bishops within their own ecclesiastical province.

Beste mentions three methods of thwarting the hindrance set by the law: (a) by committing such acts as require the use of the pallium to another bishop; (b) by performing them himself but outside his own province; and (c) by performing them within his province on days on which the use of the pallium is not permitted.[88]

Ferreres also indicated three methods, but he did not give them a general application to all pontifical functions. According to him, a metropolitan may: (a) perform pontificals on days in which the use of the pallium is not permitted; (b) delegate another bishop to confer orders to the subjects of the metropolitan within the diocese of the

[87] Coronata, *Institutiones*, I, 435; Sipos, *Enchiridion*, p. 227.

[88] The author (*Introductio in Codicem*, p. 253) does not make it clear in case (a) whether a commission of such acts to another bishop holds throughout the province or only in his own diocese; in case (b) he says nothing about the permission which the metropolitan needs from the local ordinary of the diocese in which he performs the pontifical functions; he likewise says nothing about the authorization of suffragans to perform these acts within the province.

metropolitan; and (c) confer orders outside his own province, but with the consent of the local ordinary.[89]

As regards episcopal orders Cappello and Chelodi give four possibilities of circumventing the law: (a) by delegation of these functions to another bishop; (b) by the performance of these acts outside the province; (c) by the exercise of such sacred functions in which the use of the pallium is forbidden; and (d) by the performing of pontificals on days on which the use of the pallium is not permitted.[90]

Wernz-Vidal also point to four methods of circumventing the restrictions set by canon 276: (a) within his own archdiocese an archbishop [*sic*] is not prohibited from delegating certain pontifical acts to another bishop, since the wearing of the pallium is not required for delegation; (b) outside his own province the archbishop [*sic*] himself may perform certain pontifical acts in which the pallium is not used, provided that he has the permission of the local ordinary, for he has no right to wear the pallium outside his own province: (c) before the imposition of the pallium the archbishop [*sic*] is not forbidden to exercise those powers of episcopal orders and jurisdiction, and even of metropolitan jurisdiction, which can and must be done without the use of the pallium; and (d) he is not forbidden to exercise his episcopal orders in the celebration of ponti-

---

[89] *Institutiones*, I, 208. It may be that through the use of "*etc.*" which follows this enumeration the author wishes to include all the other pontifical acts.

[90] Cappello, *Summa*, I, 310; Chelodi, *Ius Canonicum*, p. 281. According to the opinion of these two authors the right to convoke the provincial council is outside the class of possible circumvention, for they make it clear that only that type of metropolitan power can be licitly exercised which is free from the obligation of wearing the pallium. Concerning the acts of episcopal orders, neither Cappello nor Chelodi mentions whether the delegation spoken of in (a) is to be given only within the diocese or can be given within the entire province. They do not make it clear whether the performance of pontificals mentioned in (b) needs the permission of the local ordinary, and whether the functions mentioned in (c) and (d) can be licitly performed only in the see of the metropolitan or throughout his entire province. These authors say nothing concerning the delegation of these acts of suffragans.

fical Mass on those days on which the use of the pallium is interdicted.[91]

It may be said in conclusion that a metropolitan can exercise all the acts of episcopal orders within both his diocese and his province as long as liturgical law does not require the use of the pallium for them. However, he cannot place any act of episcopal orders either within his diocese or within his province for which the laws of liturgy require the use of the pallium. By circumvention, (a) any act of episcopal orders which requires the use of the pallium may be delegated to another bishop by a metropolitan for exercise within the archdiocese alone, even on such days when the liturgy calls for its use.[92] The metropolitan himself can place such acts within his own diocese without the need of delegating another bishop to perform them if (b) he exercises pontificals on those days when the use of the pallium is not required by liturgical law[93] and if (c) he exercises such acts in which the use of the pallium is always forbidden.[94] The metropolitan cannot use any form of circumvention concerning those acts of episcopal orders which require the use of the pallium in order to exercise them within the dioceses of his suffragan bishops, because such a procedure is expressly forbidden by canon 276. Such acts, although they are the effect of episcopal orders, partake of metropolitan jurisdiction. The metropolitan may exercise

---

[91] *Ius Canonicum,* II, 665-666. The two authors make it clear that metropolitans may exercise all those metropolitan rights of jurisdiction, both in their own diocese and in their province, which do not require the use of the pallium. Hence the law which makes the right and the obligation of convoking a provincial council contingent on the previous imposition of the pallium cannot be circumvented.

[92] "Potest etiam hujusmodi consecrationes ante Pallii receptionem alteri committere, dummodo non sit in mora petendi Pallium." — Pontificale Rom., tit. *De pallio,* n. 7.

[93] "Aliis autem diebus in privilegiis non expressis, vel inter prædictos non comprehensis, Archiepiscopus si voluerit in pontificalibus celebrare, uti non debet pallio." — Cæremoniale Episcopor., lib. I, c. XVI, n. 4. "Potest tamen, quando vult, Missam sine Pallio...celebrare." — Pontificale Rom., tit. *De pallio,* n. 6.

[94] "Nec potest...Archiepiscopus uti Pallio...in processionibus, neque in Missis pro defunctis...." — Pontificale Rom., tit. *De pallio,* n. 9.

acts of episcopal orders within the dioceses of his suffragan bishops, which forbid or do not require the use of the pallium, or on days on which the use of the pallium is forbidden or not required. He may (d) with the permission of the local ordinary perform all acts of episcopal orders, even those which require the use of the pallium, outside his province.[95] The following chart should clarify the situation.

PREREQUISITE CONDITIONS PRESUMED

1. Canonical nomination to the metropolitan office
2. Episcopal consecration
3. Canonical possession of archdiocese
4. No apostolic indult
5. No imposition of the pallium
6. The validity of the acts under consideration

I. Within his own archdiocese
- A. Acts of episcopal order
  1. All those are licit which do not require the use of the pallium (c. 276)
  2. All those are illicit which require the use of the pallium (c. 276)
     - a. Exception: These are licit if delegated to another bishop by circumvention of the law (c. 337, § 1)
     - b. Exception: These are licit if performed by circumvention of the law on the part of the metropolitan himself on days on which the use of the pallium is not required (c. 277)
- B. Acts of episcopal jurisdiction

  All acts are licit, since no act of purely diocesan jurisdiction requires the use of the pallium (c. 275)

---

[95] "Pallio autem utitur Archiepiscopus in singulis Ecclesiis provinciæ suæ, non autem extra provinciam...." — Cæremoniale Episcopor., lib. I, c. XVI, n. 3. "Nec potest...Archiepiscopus uti Pallio extra [suam]...provinciam...." — Pontificale Rom., tit. *De pallio*, n. 9.

II. Within the sees of his suffragan bishops

A. Acts of episcopal orders

1. All those are licit which do not require the use of the pallium under the specified conditions of canon 274, 6°
2. All those are illicit which require the use of the pallium; no circumvention possible (c. 274, 6°, and c. 276)

B. Acts of metropolitan jurisdiction

1. All those are licit which do not require the use of the pallium (implicitly contained in c. 276)
2. All those are illicit which require the use of the pallium (explicitly contained in c. 276)

III. Outside his province

A. Acts of episcopal orders

All are licit with the consent of the local ordinary since the pallium can be used only in a metropolitan's own province (c. 337, § 1)

B. Acts of metropolitan jurisdiction

All acts are illicit, since no metropolitan has any jurisdiction outside his own province (c. 272)

Canonists, quite generally, insist that a prelate assigned to an archiepiscopal see is not allowed to assume the name *archbishop* until after the imposition of the pallium. Their claim rests on a fully rigorous interpretation of the law.[96] Oesterle and Wernz-Vidal cite c. 3, X, *de auctoritate et usu pallii,* I, 8, as authority for their opinion.[97] Cocchi, after presenting the problem, does not take any stand in this

---

[96] Badii, *Institutiones,* p. 190; Chelodi, *Ius Canonicum,* p. 281; Oesterle, *Prælectiones,* p. 153; Trombetta, *De Pallio,* cap. 7-8; Wernz-Vidal, *Ius Canonicum,* II, 665.

[97] Oesterle, *Prælectiones,* p. 153; Wernz-Vidal, *Ius Canonicum,* II, 665.

matter.[98] Coronata merely records the opinion of Trombetta.[99]

Blat, on the contrary, thinks that this pre-Code legislation is abrogated. He fortifies his opinion by referring to the omission of this ruling in the Code of Canon Law.[100] In his opinion canon 6, 6°, is applicable in this instance, for there is no mention of this pre-Code discipline in canon 276. In the writer's opinion the pre-Code discipline holds in all its rigor, for canon 6, 6°, clearly makes exception for those disciplinary laws which are to be found in approved liturgical books by using the phrase *"nisi in probatis liturgicis libris reperiatur."* Both the *Cæremoniale Episcoporum* and the *Pontificale Romanum* explicitly declare that one elected to a metropolitan see cannot use the name *archbishop* until after the pallium is imposed.[101] Canon 2 can also be invoked to show that the name cannot be used unless the pallium is imposed. Canon 276 makes no mention of this ruling, for it deals with metropolitan jurisdiction and episcopal orders, and not with archiepiscopal honors.

Oesterle says that those elected to the metropolitan see before the imposition of the pallium are to call themselves *ministers of that specific church* to which they are assigned. He adds the note that they are not to use the seal of a bishop or archbishop; they are to employ merely a ministerial seal.[102] In practice, however, the use of the name *archbishop* should present no difficulty. The papal rescript giving the canonical nomination to a metropolitan see may obviate the law by granting an apostolic indult in this matter.

---

[98] *Commentarium,* III, 121.

[99] *Institutiones,* I, 435, footnote 4.

[100] *Commentarium,* Lib. II, pars 1, p. 295.

[101] "Electi vero ad... metropolitanas Ecclesias, non ante... Archiepiscopi appellari possunt, quam pallium receperunt...." — Cæremoniale Episcopor., lib. I, c. XVI, n. 6. "...antequam obtinuerit quis Pallium, licet sit consecratus, non sortitur nomen... Archiepiscopi...." — Pontificale Rom., tit. *De pallio,* n. 5.

[102] *Prælectiones,* p. 153.

SECTION F

NORMS FOR THE USE OF THE PALLIUM

Canon 277. *Metropolita uti potest pallio intra quamlibet ecclesiam etiam exemptam suæ provinciæ in Missarum sollemnibus, diebus in Pontificali Romano designatis aliisque forte sibi concessis; nullatenus vero extra provinciam, etsi Ordinarii loci consensus accedat.*

Canon 278. *Si Metropolita pallium amittat vel ad aliam sedem archiepiscopalem transferatur, novo indiget pallio.*

Canon 279. *Pallium neque commodari potest neque donari nec in morte alicui relinqui, sed omnia pallia quæ Metropolita obtinuit, cum eodem sunt sepelienda.*

Canon 277 restricts the use of the pallium as to place and time. Since these restrictions are intimately connected with the liturgical rights of metropolitans, they are taken up under that particular heading in the following chapter.[103]

In general it can be said that the use of the pallium is a singular privilege; hence all canons which treat of its use must be interpreted strictly.[104]

There is an intimate connection between the pallium and a particular metropolitan see. Once the pallium is imposed upon a metropolitan it binds him to a specific archiepiscopal see which has metropolitan rights over other dioceses of that particular ecclesiastical province.[105]

There are two ways in which a metropolitan can lose his association with the particular metropolitan see to which he is bound by the pallium: by resignation and by transfer.

The words of canon 278 which read "*pallium amittat*"

---

[103] *Infra*, pp. 364-371.

[104] Canon 67. Cf. Badii, *Institutiones*, p. 190; Toso, *Commentaria*, III, 101; Wernz-Vidal, *Ius Canonicum*, II, 666.

[105] Badii, *Institutiones*, p. 190; Bargilliat, *Prælectiones*, I, 413; Beste, *Introductio in Codicem*, p. 253; Blat, *Commentarium*, Lib. II, pars 1, p. 295; Cappello, *Summa*, I, 309; Chelodi, *Ius Canonicum*, p. 281; Ferreres, *Institutiones*, I, 209; Sipos, *Enchiridion*, p. 227; Toso, *Commentaria*, III, 101.

can be referred to the first way in which a metropolitan can sever his connection with his see, namely, by resignation.[106] Should a metropolitan resign his see, he loses the privilege of wearing the pallium both as to place and time as specified in canon 277. Since the use of the pallium is altogether restricted to a particular province from the very outset, the resigning metropolitan cannot presume to use it outside the province from which he resigns.[107] This is clear from the rulings found in the *Cæremoniale Episcoporum* and the *Pontificale Romanum*.[108]

However it seems narrow to restrict the way in which the pallium can be lost to resignation. After all, canon 278 adds the phrase *"novo indiget pallio."* This clause seems to indicate that even a metropolitan who had not resigned might need a new pallium. One who resigns with no proximate or distant hope of obtaining another metropolitan see certainly does not need to request the Roman Pontiff for a new pallium. In reality he has no right to ask for a new pallium. Should such a resigning metropolitan obtain an episcopal see, he cannot request the new pallium, since that privilege *"de iure"* does not belong to bishops, but only to those who enjoy metropolitan power. However, should such a metropolitan receive another metropolitan see after a lapse of time, this canonical provision would place him under the obligation of petitioning the Roman Pontiff for a new pallium.[109]

To the mind of the writer the phrase *"pallium amittat"* should have a wider and more obvious meaning than the one which connects it solely with the act of resignation. Canonists do not allude to the possibility of actually losing the pallium by carelessness, theft, fire, etc. Ferreres uses the

---

[106] Canon 72, § 1. Cf. canons 183-191.

[107] Canon 277. Cf. Beste, *Introductio in Codicem*, p. 253; Claeys Bouuaert-Simenon, *Manuale*, I, 250; Cocchi, *Commentarium*, III, 121; Wernz-Vidal, *Ius Canonicum*, II, 668.

[108] Cæremoniale Episcopor., lib. I, c. XVI, n. 3; Pontificale Rom., tit. *De pallio*, n. 9.

[109] Toso, *Commentaria*, III, 102; Cocchi, *Commentarium*, III, 101-102.

expression *"aut inutile reddatur,"* which could be another way of losing the pallium, namely, by its becoming useless in consequence of a long continued use of it, so that it appears threadbare or is actually disintegrating in shreds.[110] Although in such cases the metropolitan does not lose his intimate connection with his see, it seems that, in keeping with canon 276, he could not perform any act of episcopal orders or metropolitan jurisdiction which requires the use of the pallium until a new pallium would be obtained from the Roman Pontiff. Canon 279 also forbids the loaning and giving of the pallium; hence the only remedies for the situation would be to have recourse to Rome for a new pallium or for a special apostolic indult which would permit the performance of pontifical functions without the use of the pallium until the new one arrives.

The other way in which a metropolitan severs connection with his see is by transfer.[111] This method is contemplated by the law, for canon 278 employs the phrase *"ad aliam sedem archiepiscopalem transferatur."* In keeping with canon 275, a metropolitan involved in the transfer from one metropolitan see to another metropolitan see would be bound within three months from the canonical provision in the Consistory to ask the Roman Pontiff for a new pallium either *per se* or *per procuratorem*.[112]

He may not use the pallium of his deceased predecessor, nor may he presume to use the pallium he obtained for the metropolitan see from which he has been transferred.[113] He cannot use the pallium of his predecessor, since it symbolized the connection between the predecessor and the province, a connection which was broken by death; the pal-

---

[110] *Institutiones*, I, 209.

[111] Canons 183; 193-195.

[112] "...sed nec translati de una Ecclesia metropolitana ad aliam uti possunt pallio sui prædecessoris defuncti, nec translati, sed opus est, ut iterum pro nova Ecclesia petatur, et habeatur novum pallium...." — Cæremoniale Episcopor., lib. I, c. XVI, n. 6. "...etiamsi Pallium in alia Ecclesia habuisset, cum oporteat petere novum Pallium." — Pontificale Rom., tit. *De pallio*, n. 5.

[113] *Loc. cit.*

lium of a metropolitan's former province is the symbol of jurisdiction in that particular province alone, and it was lost through the transfer to the new metropolitan see. Neither one of these two pallia can become the symbol of metropolitan power in the newly acquired province, and it is for this reason that the canon uses the words *"novo indiget pallio."* It is the new pallium alone which symbolizes the metropolitan power in the newly acquired province.[114]

The metropolitan must take his pallium along to the newly acquired province; he may not leave it behind in the relinquished province in order that his successor may have a pallium.[115] Until the imposition of the new pallium has taken place, the rulings of canons 276 and 277 bind the transferred metropolitan.[116] The *Cæremoniale Episcoporum,* in speaking of those who are elected metropolitans and those who are transferred from one metropolitan see to another, declares that they may not licitly perform any pontifical functions which require the use of the pallium until the imposition of it has taken place: *"nec interim ipsis Electis licet pontificalia munia exercere."*[117] If the metropolitan is transferred to an episcopal see, he loses the right to wear the pallium.[118]

---

[114] Badii (*Institutiones,* p. 190) stated that the new pallium confers jurisdiction in the new province. This opinion is not supported by the statement contained in canon 275. Beste (*Introductio in Codicem,* p. 253) calls the pallium a local ornament which adheres to the see to which it is granted. One can conclude that this author holds that a transfer breaks the adherence of the pallium to a particular see. Blat (*Commentarium,* Lib. II, pars 1, p. 295) and Chelodi (*Ius Canonicum,* p. 281) incline toward Beste's opinion. Cocchi (*Commentarium,* III, 122) and Toso (*Commentaria,* III, 102) hold that a metropolitan needs the new pallium, since it alone can signify the metropolitan power in the newly acquired province.

[115] Prümmer, *Manuale,* p. 152; Sipos, *Enchiridion,* p. 227; Wernz-Vidal, *Ius Canonicum,* II, 668.

[116] Raus, *Institutiones,* p. 175; Toso, *Commentaria,* III, 102.

[117] Lib. I, c. XVI, n. 6.

[118] Cocchi, *Commentarium,* III, 101-102; Toso, *Commentaria,* III, 102.

The pallium is not only an ornament attached to a particular see; it is likewise a personal ornament.[119] Inasmuch as it is intimately bound to the metropolitan's person, he may not alienate it in any way either while he is living or after his death to anyone who has the privilege of wearing it, or to anyone who does not have the privilege. The pallium may not be lent *("commodari")* to another metropolitan or archbishop who perchance has not received his pallium from Rome, or who perhaps may have lost his own.[120]

Likewise the pallium may not be given *("donari")* by a metropolitan to his successor in the province from which he has been transferred, to his coadjutor with the right of succession while the metropolitan is still alive, or to a friend who may not have the privilege of wearing the pallium; in short, it may not be given to anyone.[121] The pallium may not be willed *("in morte alicui relinqui")* to anyone, not even to the metropolitan's successor in the metropolitan see.[122] This rule is in keeping with the principle established in canon 74. The Roman Pontifical is also clear on this point.[123]

After his death a metropolitan is buried with the pallium placed about his shoulders if the burial takes place within the province. If he is buried outside his province

---

[119] Badii, *Institutiones*, p. 190; Bargilliat, *Prælectiones*, I, 413; Beste, *Introductio in Codicem*, p. 253; Blat, *Commentarium*, Lib. II, pars 1, p. 295; Claeys Bouuaert-Simenon, *Manuale*, I, 250; Cance, *Le Code*, I, 284; Cappello, *Summa*, I, 309; Chelodi, *Ius Canonicum*, p. 281; Cocchi, *Commentarium*, III, 121; Prümmer, *Manuale*, p. 152; Sipos, *Enchiridion*, p. 227; Toso, *Commentaria*, III, 102; Wernz-Vidal, *Ius Canonicum*, II, 668.

[120] Blat, *Commentarium*, Lib. II, pars 1, p. 295; Toso, *Commentaria*, III, 102; Wernz-Vidal, *Ius Canonicum*, II, 668.

[121] *Loc. cit.*

[122] Badii, *Institutiones*, p. 190; Bargilliat *Prælectiones*, I, 413; Blat, *Commentarium*, Lib. II, pars 1, p. 295; Toso, *Commentaria*, III, 102; Wernz-Vidal, *Ius Canonicum*, II, 668.

[123] "...et quia Pallium est personale, ideo accommodari non potest, neque in morte alicui relinqui...." — tit. *De pallio*, n. 9. The Code adds the word "*donari*" to this listing.

the pallium is folded and placed under his head.[124] This is a strict obligation; both the *Cæremoniale Episcoporum* and the *Pontificale Romanum* use the word *"debet."* The Code treats of cases in which a metropolitan may have received more than one pallium, for it uses the phrase *"sed omnia pallia quæ Metropolita obtinuit, cum eodem sunt sepelienda."* It is possible for a metropolitan to receive more than one pallium during his lifetime, especially in the eventuality of a transfer from one metropolitan see to another. In such cases, if he is buried in his province, the metropolitan is buried with the last pallium he received placed about his shoulders. All the others he may have received are folded and placed under his head and are buried with his body.[125]

Finally, the pallium may not be worn by any prelate in the presence of the Roman Pontiff or of his legate *a latere*. It is as if the vicarious power which metropolitans received from the Roman Pontiff ceased while the Pope is actually or vicariously present.[126]

---

[124] "Post obitum debent Archiepiscopi cum pallio sepeliri; si quidem sepeliantur in provincia sua, circa humeros supra planetam: si vero extra provinciam, ponendum erit pallium plicatum sub eorum capite." — Cæremoniale Episcopor., lib. I, c. XVI, n. 7. "...et quia Pallium est personale...Archiepiscopus cum eo sepeliri debet." — Pontificale Rom., tit. *De pallio*, n. 9.

[125] Beste, *Introductio in Codicem*, p. 253; Blat, *Commentarium*, Lib. II, pars 1, p. 295; Cance, *Le Code*, I, 285; Cocchi, *Commentarium*, III, 121; Coronata, *Institutiones*, I, 436, footnote 6; Prümmer, *Manuale*, p. 152; Sipos, *Enchiridion*, p. 227; Regatillo, *Institutiones*, I, 235; Toso, *Commentaria*, III, 102; Wernz-Vidal, *Ius Canonicum*, II, 668.

[126] Badii, *Institutiones*, p. 190; Coronata, *Institutiones*, I, 436; Wernz-Vidal, *Ius Canonicum*, II, 668. An exception to this rule is the dean in the college of cardinals when called on to ordain or consecrate the newly elected Pontiff who would still need to receive sacred orders or episcopal consecration. In the absence of the dean the sub-dean would perform this function, and in the latter's absence the oldest of the suburbicarian cardinal bishops, each with the right of wearing the pallium. Cf. canon 239, § 2.

CHAPTER X

ADDITIONAL RIGHTS AND OBLIGATIONS OF METROPOLITANS AND ARCHBISHOPS

SECTION A

SPECIAL RIGHTS AND OBLIGATIONS

Article 1. Attendance and Voting at Ecumenical Councils

Canon 223. § 1. *Vocantur ad Concilium in eoque ius habent suffragii deliberativi:*

2° *Patriarchæ, Primates, Archiepiscopi, Episcopi residentiales, etiam nondum consecrati.*

An ecumenical council is a legitimate gathering of all the bishops of the whole world and also of other prelates who by pontifical privilege obtain the right to attend. It is convoked by the Roman Pontiff. He presides either personally or through one of his legates. At an ecumenical council the universal affairs of the Church are discussed and settled.[1]

According to canon 223, § 1, 2°, archbishops are to be called to an ecumenical council whenever such a council is convoked by the Roman Pontiff. During the sessions of the council they have the right of a deliberative vote. A question arises immediately whether the term "*Archiepiscopi*" which is employed in the canon includes all three types of archbishops, namely: metropolitans, residential archbishops and purely titular or non-residential archbishops, or whether the law is restrictive in any way. At first glance it would seem that the term *archbishop* is used in its widest sense so as to include all three types of prelates; but upon closer study it must be noted that purely titular or non-residential archbishops are excluded.

[1] Claeys Bouuaert-Simenon, *Manuale*, I, 221; Ferreres, *Institutiones*, I, 152.

Canon 18 states that ecclesiastical laws must be understood according to the proper meaning of the words considered in their text and context. The word *"Archiepiscopi"* in canon 223, § 1, 2°, would have the wider meaning except for the contextual word *"residentiales"* which follows thereafter. Canonists link the two words to read *"Archiepiscopi residentiales,"* and conclude that this combination includes only those who are metropolitans and residential archbishops.

Blat, in commenting on canon 223, § 1, 2°, uses the phrase *"quod verbum est distributive sumendum"* in reference to the word *"residentiales,"* thereby declaring that the word *residential* must be applied to each class of prelates mentioned: patriarchs, primates, archbishops, and bishops. This interpretation of the law certainly excludes non-residential or purely titular archbishops from the list of those who are expected to attend the ecumenical council, and *ipso iure* denies them the right of a deliberative vote. According to the author, all residential bishops must be called in consequence of the episcopal office which they possess as successors of the Apostles and on account of the universal nature of the council at which the whole Church is represented through its shepherds.[2] Chelodi followed the same reasoning through the employment of the synthetic phrase *"omnes cuiusque gradus episcopi residentiales."*[3]

So, too, Cocchi declares that all residential bishops (patriarchs, primates, archbishops) of the whole Catholic world who have actual jurisdiction in a determinate diocese must be called to an ecumenical council and have a deliberative vote by a right which is ordinary and proper. The author states the reason for his opinion when he declares that all the above mentioned prelates are by divine right successors of the Apostles and form the Apostolic College. This Apostolic College is endowed with the prerogative of infallibility together with the Roman Pontiff, and represents the universal teaching and ruling Church.[4] Ferreres

[2] *Commentarium*, Lib. II, pars 1, p. 205.
[3] *Ius Canonicum*, p. 370.
[4] *Commentarium*, III, 35.

also includes patriarchs, primates and archbishops in the class of residential bishops by inserting the three types of prelates within a parenthesis which is placed between the two words *"Episcopi"* and *"residentiales."* He gives the same reason for the necessity of their attendance at the council which Cocchi gives.[5]

Oesterle states that the term *"residentiales"* must be referred to all four types of prelates: patriarchs, primates, archbishops and bishops. He fortifies his position by declaring that patriarchs, archbishops and non-residential bishops can be titular bishops.[6] Prümmer stated that only those can cast votes in an ecumenical council who *ex iure divino* or *ex iure ecclesiastico* are endowed with this power. He continued by stating that all Catholic residential bishops in union with the Apostolic See have by divine law, the right to vote in general councils for the Holy Spirit placed bishops in the Church that they may rule over it. He then enumerated all the four classes of prelates given in numbers 1-4 of canon 223, § 1, as having the right to be called to an ecumenical council and the right of a deliberative vote.[7]

Wernz-Vidal also hold the opinion that all residential (archbishops, primates, patriarchs) bishops of the entire Catholic world, who have actual jurisdiction in a determinate diocese, are called to an ecumenical council by ordinary and proper right, and as such have a deliberative vote. These authors say that residential bishops are principally the successors of the Apostles, and together with the Roman Pontiff constitute the College of Bishops, which, through the promises of Christ, is fortified with the prerogative of infallibility and represents the universal teaching and ruling Church. Titular bishops, since they lack jurisdiction, need not be called to an ecumenical council, for the matters of such councils concern the power of jurisdiction and not the power of orders.[8]

---

[5] *Institutiones*, I, 152.
[6] *Prælectiones*, p. 121.
[7] *Manuale*, p. 25.
[8] *Ius Canonicum*, II, 531-532.

Claeys Bouuaert-Simenon and Vermeersch-Creusen, in giving the list of all those who by law must be called to an ecumenical council and who have the right of a deliberative vote, surprisingly omit the word *archbishops*. It seems that these authors include metropolitans and residential archbishops in the phrase *residential bishops*, for they speak of ordinaries with proper jurisdiction.[9]

The whole spirit of § 1 of canon 223 concerns the power of jurisdiction rather than the power of orders. This can be seen in the specific exception made in 1° with regard to cardinals. When the canon declares that they need not be bishops *("etsi non Episcopi")* it explicitly excludes the power of orders as a necessary requisite for attendance at an ecumenical council and for the right of a deliberative vote. Those cardinals who are not bishops are to be called, since with the Roman Pontiff they participate in his supreme power of jurisdiction over the universal Church.[10] Further, the use of the phrase *"etiam nondum consecrati"* in 2° with reference to patriarchs, primates, archbishops and bishops, shows by implication that the reception of episcopal orders is not a prime requisite for attendance and for the possession of a deliberative vote at an ecumenical council. It is the word *"residentiales"* which is important, for it points to episcopal jurisdiction.[11] What is essential for these prelates, even though they are not consecrated bishops, is the canonical possession of the sees with which they are canonically provided.[12] So speak Blat and Toso.[13]

Finally, all the prelates mentioned in 3° and 4° are such as have a specific territory or group of persons under their jurisdiction. This is especially emphasized by the non-inclusion of the supreme moderators of non-exempt reli-

---

[9] Claeys Bouuaert-Simenon, *Manuale*, I, 223; Vermeersch-Creusen, *Epitome*, I, 283.

[10] Canon 230. Cf. Toso, *Commentaria*, III, 20.

[11] Canon 334, § 1.

[12] Canon 334, § 2 and § 3.

[13] Blat, *Commentarium*, Lib. II, pars 1, p. 205; Toso, *Commentaria*, III, 20.

gious who do not have such jurisdiction. Hence the argument that episcopal orders are the deciding factor for attendance at an ecumenical council and for the possession of a deliberative vote falls to the ground. No titular archbishop can use the argument of the possession of episcopal orders in order to assure himself of an invitation to an ecumenical council.

Cardinals who are not bishops are invited to ecumenical councils by reason of their dignity. This is a privilege given them expressly in the law. That is why they are listed separately under 1° in canon 223, § 1. The same does not hold true for patriarchs and primates who are not local ordinaries. Canon 271 clearly enunciates that the title of patriarch or primate carries no special jurisdiction with it; it only gives the prerogatives of honor and the right of precedence. Therefore non-residential patriarchs and primates are not included in 2° of canon 223, § 1. The prescript of law refers only to residential patriarchs and primates. If such is the case for patriarchs and primates, it cannot be otherwise for the archbishops mentioned in 2° of canon 223, § 1. Only residential archbishops must be convoked to ecumenical councils and they alone among archbishops have a deliberative vote. Titular or non-residential archbishops cannot invoke a privilege to justify their attendance at such councils as can the non-residential cardinals.

Even though the argument that canonists are not to distinguish when the law does not distinguish is a valid one in itself, one cannot use it in this connection in order to assure titular archbishops or non-residential archbishops the right which belongs to metropolitans and residential archbishops. Although the word "*Archiepiscopi*" in itself could mean that all classes of archbishops were included by the lawgiver on the grounds that the word "*residentiales*" refers only to the term "*Episcopi*," there is still room for distinguishing between residential and merely titular archbishops in matter of attendance at ecumenical councils. The rules of interpretation call for an examination not only of the text but also of the context of the law. The lawgiver intends a clear distinction between residential and non-residential archbishops by means of the insertion of § 2 in canon 223. It is here that the lawmaker places all forms of titular bishops, no matter what their rank or dignity may be.

The closer one examines the nature of an ecumenical council, the clearer it becomes that titular or non-residential archbishops need not be called to attend them. An ecumenical council discusses and settles the general affairs of the Church. Inasmuch as it does so, only those bishops who have proper jurisdiction within the universal Church need be called to make decisions which concern the universal Church. There can be no denial that metropolitans and residential archbishops are bishops who govern their respective dioceses as ordinaries possessing proper jurisdiction. Titular archbishops are non-residential bishops who lack all jurisdiction. They are only a higher form of titular bishops.[14]

Because of these reasons titular or non-residential archbishops need not be summoned to ecumenical councils, and do not have the *ipso iure* granted deliberative vote enjoyed by the metropolitans and residential archbishops mentioned in canon 223, § 1. At most they can be called, and once they are called, like all titular bishops, they obtain a deliberative vote, unless this is denied them expressly in the act of being convoked.[15]

Should metropolitans and residential archbishops be detained from making their appearance at an ecumenical council by reason of some just impediment, they must send a proxy in their stead and give proof of the existence of the impediment which restrains them from attendance. If the proxy is one of the Fathers of the council, he does not have the right of a double vote; if he is not one of the Fathers of the council, he is allowed to be present only at the public sessions and does not have the right to vote. However, at the completion of the council, the proxy has the

[14] Canon 348, § 1.
[15] Canon 223, § 2.

right to subscribe the acts of the council.[16] Since titular or non-residential archbishops are not included among the prelates mentioned in canon 223, § 1, they do not have the right to send proxies if they are impeded after they have been called to the ecumenical council. However, once they have been summoned, they seem to have the obligation of showing the impediment which restrains them from attendance at the council.[17]

Metropolitans and residential archbishops, since they are considered Fathers of the council, may add other questions to those proposed by the Roman Pontiff. These questions must be previously approved by the prelate who presides at the council.[18] If titular or non-residential archbishops are admitted to the council with a deliberative vote, they too have the right to be called Fathers of the council, and as such may also add other questions for discussion in the same fashion as metropolitans and residential archbishops.

Further, no archbishop is permitted to leave before the council is lawfully concluded, unless the presiding prelate knows and approves the reason for the departure and grants permission for withdrawal. The canon uses the phrase "*Nemini eorum qui Concilio interesse debent*" instead of the phrase "*Patres,*" hence the wider signification includes everyone and anyone who attends the ecumenical council in fulfillment of the norm contained in canon 223.[19] Ferreres gives a twofold reason for this ruling: all are present at the council in virtue of obedience to the law and to the Roman Pontiff; hence only the Pontiff himself or his delegate can release any of those present from this obedience, and the sight of the departure of anyone of those to be present at the council might give scandal to those who might regard it as a sign of rebellion.[20]

---

[16] Canon 224, § 1, § 2; cf. canon 164.

[17] Ferreres, *Institutiones*, I, 154; Toso, *Commentaria*, III, 21.

[18] Canon 226. Cf. canon 222, § 2.

[19] Blat, *Commentarium*, Lib. II, pars 1, p. 206; Cocchi, *Commentarium*, III, 37; Coronata, *Institutiones*, I, 385.

[20] *Institutiones*, I, 154.

The right of a deliberative vote entitles metropolitans and residential archbishops to act as true judges in the handling and discussion of the matters brought before the council and in the giving of the decisions. Because of this intimate connection with all the matters of the council, they are called *Fathers of the council (Patres)* and they append their names to the conciliar decrees under the formula *"Definiens subscripsi."* Should titular or non-residential archbishops enjoy the deliberative vote by the express convocation to the council, they too would be called *Fathers* and would sign the decrees under the same formula as the metropolitans and residential archbishops. Should titular archbishops be denied the deliberative vote, they would not be considered Fathers of the council, and they would sign their names with all those who have only a consultative vote under the formula which reads: *"Consentiens subscripsi."*[21]

The right and the obligation to attend an ecumenical council and the right of a deliberative vote therein is given by law to metropolitans not for the reason that they are the heads of ecclesiastical provinces, but for the reason that they are residential archbishops. Fundamentally residential archbishops have these rights and this obligation not because of the title of archbishop but because of episcopal jurisdiction within a particular residential see or diocese.

Article 2. Attendance and Voting at Plenary Councils

Canon 282. § 1. *Concilio plenario assistere debent cum suffragio deliberativo, præter Legatum Apostolicum, Metropolitæ, Episcopi residentiales, qui sui loco, mittere possunt Coadiutorem vel Auxiliarem, Apostolici diœcesium Administratores, Abbates vel Prælati* nullius, *Vicarii Apostolici, Præfecti Apostolici, Vicarii Capitulares.*

A plenary council is a legitimate gathering in which the local ordinaries of at least several ecclesiastical provinces meet under the presidency of a pontifical legate to discuss

[21] Beste, *Introductio in Codicem*, p. 232.

and settle ecclesiastical matters which pertain to their particular region. The ecclesiastical provinces represented may be those of a certain section within a country, of all the sections of a country, or of a number of states which are geographically close to one another. An example of the first type is the regional council held in Etruria; examples of the second type are the Baltimore Councils held in the United States in 1852, 1866 and 1884 respectively; an example of the third type is the council of the many Latin American Republics which was held in Rome in 1899.[22] After the publication of the Code, a plenary council was held in Shanghai, China, in 1929.

Since there is nothing in the general law of the Church which prescribes the regular convocation of plenary councils, there is no legal obligation to hold them. It is quite evident, however, that such councils have at times a practical purpose in the matter of co-ordinating ecclesiastical discipline for sections of the Church larger than provinces.[23] There is likewise nothing in the common law of the Church which specifies the time or place in which such councils should be held.[24] Councils of this type may be held

---

[22] Cf. Badii, *Institutiones*, p. 201, footnote 3; Bargilliat, *Prælectiones*, I, 530; Beste, *Introductio in Codicem*, pp. 231, 253-254; Blat, *Commentarium*, Lib. II, pars 1, p. 298; Claeys Bouuaert-Simenon, *Manuale*, I, 250; Chelodi, *Ius Canonicum*, p. 373; Cocchi, *Commentarium*, III, 128; Coronata, *Institutiones*, I, 437; Ferreres, *Institutiones*, I, 210; Oesterle, *Prælectiones*, p. 154; Prümmer, *Manuale*, p. 32; Raus, *Institutiones*, p. 257; Regatillo, *Institutiones*, I, 236; Sipos, *Enchiridion*, pp. 228-229; Vermeersch-Creusen, *Epitome*, I, 312; Wernz-Vidal, *Ius Canonicum*, II, 669, 676.

[23] Badii, *Institutiones*, p. 201; Beste, *Introductio in Codicem*, p. 253; Blat, *Commentarium*, Lib. II, pars 1, p. 298; Claeys Bouuaert-Simenon, *Manuale*, I, 250; Chelodi, *Ius Canonicum*, p. 374; Cocchi, *Commentarium*, III, 129; Coronata, *Institutiones*, I, 438; Raus, *Institutiones*, p. 257.

[24] By a particular ruling, fourteen regions of Italy, in which it is very difficult to hold provincial councils, are to hold plenary councils every twenty years in place of the provincial councils in accordance with canons 281, 282, 287. The motives underlying this particular ruling are the following: ethnographic reasons, political disturbances, the complete change of the boundaries of ecclesiastical provinces and dioceses which brought it about that not a few metropolitan sees were de-

whenever the needs of a certain region or country demand attention. They are never held for the sake of settling dogmatic controversies, but are concerned with the promotion of ecclesiastical discipline.[25] Plenary councils may not be called without the permission of the Roman Pontiff, who determines the number of provinces which are to gather and designates the legate who in the name of the Holy Father is to convoke and preside at the council.[26]

It is the special right of metropolitans to be called to plenary councils held in their district and to have a deliberative vote during their sessions.[27] Canon 282, § 1, employs the restrictive term "*Metropolitæ*" and not the phrase "*Archiepiscopi residentiales*" which is used in canon 223, § 1, 2°; hence all the heads of those provinces which have

---

prived of suffragan sees while others retained only one or another see. The decree entitled *Conciliorum Provincialium*, issued on the 15th of February, 1919, by the Sacred Consistorial Congregation (cf. *AAS*, XI [1919], 72-73), re-iterated what was decided by the Sacred Congregation for Bishops and Regulars by a circular letter dated the 24th of August, 1889. This circular letter of 1889 divided Italy into dioceses according to ecclesiastical districts and decreed that the bishops of these districts should meet annually. The decree *Conciliorum Provincialium* added that these bishops should fix the time of the plenary councils when they meet in their quinquennial gathering provided for in canon 292. The fourteen regions which are to hold the plenary councils instead of provincial councils are: Emilia, Romagna, Tuscany, Umbria, the Marches, Abruzzi and Molise, Benevento, Campania, Salerno, Basilicata, Apulia, Calabria, Sicily and Sardinia. Special norms were promised for Latium. The provinces of Venice, Milan, Vercelli, Turin, Genoa and Rome are excluded from this particular ruling, and are to follow the common law with regard to the holding of provincial councils. Cf. Bouscaren, *Digest*, I, 187-188; Beste, *Introductio in Codicem*, p. 254; Blat, *Commentarium*, Lib. II, pars 1, p. 299; Coronata, *Institutiones*, I, 438, footnote 5.

[25] Canon 290.

[26] Canon 281. Cf. canon 220. The convocation of a plenary council is a *causa maior* reserved by its nature and by positive law to the Roman Pontiff alone. Badii, *Institutiones*, p. 201; Bargilliat, *Prælectiones*, I, 530-531; Beste, *Introductio in Codicem*, p. 253; Blat, *Commentarium*, Lib. II, pars 1, p. 298; Claeys Bouuaert-Simenon, *Manuale*, I, 250; Cance, *Le Code*, I, 287-288; Chelodi, *Ius Canonicum*, p. 373; Sipos, *Enchiridion*, p. 229; Vermeersch-Creusen, *Epitome*, I, 312; Wernz-Vidal, *Ius Canonicum*, II, 676.

[27] Canon 282, § 1.

been determined by the Roman Pontiff as entitled to representation at the plenary council have the right and the obligation of attending in virtue of their metropolitan jurisdiction. The right and the obligation of attendance flow from the use, in canon 282, § 1, of the term *"debent"* which follows *"assistere."* Residential archbishops must also attend the plenary councils to which they are summoned. However, their right and their obligation do not flow from the dignity of archiepiscopal title, but rather from their inclusion in the law under the phrase *"Episcopi residentiales"* according to canon 282, § 1. Archbishops with residence come to plenary councils only as the heads of their sees and as endowed with episcopal jurisdiction. But metropolitans not only represent their own episcopal see but their province as well; they come to a plenary council endowed with both episcopal jurisdiction and metropolitan jurisdiction. This of course does not give the metropolitan any greater power of voting over archbishops who are not metropolitans, for the canon specifies only one vote each for all those mentioned in § 1. Canon 287, § 2, also denies a double vote to any of the prelates in attendance at a plenary council.

Although canon 282, § 1, denies all non-residential or purely titular archbishops the right and the obligation of attending a plenary council as well as the *ipso iure* granted deliberative vote, all those living in the territory where such a council is to be held may be called to attend. They may be called only if the instructions given to the apostolic legate by the Roman Pontiff permit their invitation. Once they are called by the pontifical legate they have the right and the obligation of attending and they have also a deliberative vote, unless the document of convocation denies them this right.[28] The employment of the term *"debent"* emphasizes their right and obligation of attending the plenary council.

According to canon 282, § 1, metropolitans and residential bishops (archbishops) have not only the right but also the obligation to attend plenary councils. This obligation

---

[28] Canon 282, § 2.

is a strict one, for if they do not attend in person they must send a proxy in their stead. Canon 282, § 1, gives both metropolitans and residential bishops (archbishops) the option of sending their coadjutor or one of their auxiliary bishops in their stead. According to Blat they may do so without having any cause or impediment as a condition.[29] Coronata also holds this opinion.[30] These coadjutor and auxiliary bishops who serve as proxies of their own metropolitans and residential bishops (archbishops) have a deliberative vote by reason of their inclusion in canon 282, § 1.[31]

The obligation of attendance is re-emphasized in canon 287, § 1, in which it is stated that all those who must attend a plenary council and have a deliberative vote are to send a proxy if they themselves are lawfully impeded, and are to give proof of the impediment which restrains them from attending. Therefore all metropolitans and residential bishops (archbishops) who have no coadjutor or auxiliary bishop, or when having one do not send him as a proxy, are obliged by law to send some other cleric in their stead or to select one of the prelates in attendance as their proxy. The law also demands proof of the lawfulness of the impediment. This type of proxy does not have the deliberate vote; the nature of his vote depends on the specifications of canon 287, § 2. This canon declares that if a proxy be one of the Fathers of the council who already has a deliberative vote, he does not have a double vote; however, if he is not a Father of the council, he has a consultative vote only.[32]

Non-residential or purely titular archbishops are not required by law to attend the plenary councils held in their territory, and hence have no right to send proxies. But once they are invited to such councils, should they be given

---

[29] *Commentarium*, Lib. II, pars 1, p. 298.

[30] *Institutiones*, I, 438.

[31] Blat, *Commentarium*, Lib. II, pars 1, p. 298; Chelodi, *Ius Canonicum*, p. 373; Cocchi, *Commentarium*, III, 130; Coronata, *Institutiones*, I, 438; Prümmer, *Manuale*, p. 32; Regatillo, *Institutiones*, I, 236; Sipos, *Enchiridion*, p. 229; Toso, *Commentaria*, III, 105; Wernz-Vidal, *Ius Canonicum*, II, 676-677.

[32] Cf. canon 164.

a deliberative vote in the convocation, they must attend in person or send a proxy if they are lawfully impeded. In such a case they must prove the licitness of the impediment restraining them from attendance. The proxy has the type of vote specified in canon 287, § 2. If non-residential or purely titular archbishops are called to a plenary council and given only a consultative vote, it seems from the wording of canon 287, § 1, that they need not send a proxy or explain their absence.[33]

The rights of metropolitans with regard to plenary councils include only those of being called and of having a deliberative vote during the proceedings. No individual metropolitan may assume the right to convoke a plenary council or the right to preside at it. The right to convoke a plenary council and to preside at such a gathering belongs exclusively to the Roman Pontiff. Only he can delegate both these rights to a delegate of his own choice.[34] Furthermore, no assumption of these rights is possible, for the episcopal jurisdiction of a metropolitan extends only to the territorial limits of his episcopal see, and the metropolitan jurisdiction he possesses is limited to one particular ecclesiastical province over which he has been appointed the head. Hence, neither his episcopal nor his metropolitan jurisdiction can extend by fact or law over all the bishops and metropolitans of those provinces which are represented in a plenary council. The only manner in which his power could be so extended would be by pontifical delegation to convoke and preside at a plenary council. This is a conclusion which flows from the consideration that all metropolitans, according to the existing discipline, are equal to one another and immediately subject to the Holy See.[35]

No metropolitan can be given the right to convoke a plenary council or to preside during its sessions by the local

---

[33] Blat, *Commentarium*, Lib. II, pars 1, p. 303.

[34] Canon 281.

[35] Bargilliat, *Prælectiones*, I, 531; Cance, *Le Code*, I, 287; Cocchi, *Commentarium*, III, 130; Regatillo, *Institutiones*, I, 236; Sipos, *Enchiridion*, p. 229; Wernz-Vidal, *Ius Canonicum*, II, 676.

ordinaries who might desire to hold such a council in their region. No one local ordinary and no group of local ordinaries may assume authority beyond that which they possess over that particular section of the Church placed under their jurisdiction by papal appointment. Such a choice would postulate the existence of an intermediary jurisdiction between the Roman Pontiff and metropolitans. The common law of the Church knows no such intermediate jurisdiction.[36]

A plenary council is by its nature supra-episcopal and supra-metropolitan, for it legislates in matters which concern a larger circumscription of territory than one diocese or one province; its decrees are made for many dioceses and at least several provinces considered as one region. Since all metropolitans are equal to one another and immediately subject to the Holy See, the needed jurisdiction exceeds episcopal and metropolitan power. Hence only one who is singled out as the special delegate of the Roman Pontiff, in whom all episcopal and metropolitan jurisdiction is concentrated, can authoritatively convoke all the bishops and all the metropolitans of the region to a plenary council to be held in a particular region.[37]

The Roman Pontiff is free to choose any of the local metropolitans as his special legate for the convocation and the presidency of the plenary council. In such a case it would be the delegated papal authority and not metropolitan jurisdiction which would give a particular metropolitan the rights to convoke and preside at a plenary council.[38]

---

[36] Claeys Bouuaert-Simenon, *Manuale*, I, 250.

[37] Bargilliat, *Prælectiones*, I, 530-531; Cocchi, *Commentarium*, III, 130; Regatillo, *Institutiones*, I, 236; Sipos, *Enchiridion*, p. 229; Toso, *Commentaria*, III, 103; Wernz-Vidal, *Ius Canonicum*, II, 676.

[38] According to canon 271 the titles of patriarch and primate are merely honorific and carry no special jurisdiction with them. Hence, in the Latin Discipline, if a patriarch or primate retains certain jurisdiction by particular law, he no longer has the right to convoke plenary councils without the permission of the Holy See. Cf. Wernz-Vidal, *Ius Canonicum*, II, 676, and *ibid.*, footnote 34. According to the decrees of the Synod *Sciarfensis* (1888) and the Synod *Alexandrina* (1898), the right to convoke national councils is attributed to the patriarchs of the Syrians and the Copts respectively. Cf. *loc. cit.*

Should such be the case, according to canon 288, he would determine the order to be observed in the examination of questions; and he would open, transfer, suspend and close the council. As the presiding officer he would not need the consent of the Fathers of the council to do any of these things since he represents the Roman Pontiff.[39] But it must be stressed that a metropolitan could act in this way only if he were chosen as the delegate of the Roman Pontiff.

No metropolitan or residential bishop (archbishop) may leave the plenary council once its sessions have begun, unless he has a just cause and this be approved by the papal legate. Non-residential archbishops, whether they have the deliberative or merely a consultative vote, once they attend the council, may not leave unless they, too, have a just cause which has been approved by the papal legate. Canon 289 makes no distinction between those who attend with a consultative or with a deliberative vote when it employs the phrase *"nemini eorum qui interesse debent."*

At the conclusion of a plenary council the legate of the Roman Pontiff sends all the acts and decrees of the gathering to the Holy See. These decrees cannot be promulgated until the Sacred Congregation of the Council has examined and reviewed them for promulgation.[40] Should a metropolitan be the apostolic legate, it would be his duty to send the acts and decrees of the council to the Holy See. These decrees, once they are promulgated, bind all persons in the respective territory for which they were drawn up, not excluding the metropolitans and bishops. Local ordinaries can dispense from these decrees only in individual cases and only for a just cause.[41]

---

[39] Cf. *Blat, Commentarium*, Lib. II, pars 1, p. 303; Toso, *Commentaria*, III, 109.

[40] Canon 291, § 1. Cf. canon 250, § 4. The acts and decrees of plenary councils held in mission territories would have to be sent to the Sacred Congregation for the Propagation of the Faith. Cf. canons 250, § 4; 252, § 2; 304, § 2.

[41] Canon 291, § 2. Cf. canon 82; canon 199, § 1.

Article 3. Qualified Rights over Certain Prelates

Canon 285. *Episcopi qui nulli Metropolitæ subiiciuntur, Abbates vel Prælati* nullius, *et Archiepiscopi Suffraganeis carentes, aliquem viciniorem Metropolitam, nisi forte iam elegerint, semel pro semper prævia Sedes Apostolicæ approbatione, eligant, cuius Concilio provinciali cum aliis intersint, et quæ ibi ordinata fuerint, observent et observanda curent.*

Metropolitans have certain qualified rights over (a) bishops who are not subject to any metropolitan; (b) abbots and prelates *nullius;* and (c) archbishops who have no suffragans. Metropolitans obtain these rights by the application of law. The afore-mentioned bishops, abbots and prelates *nullius* and archbishops become permanently subject in a limited fashion to a metropolitan only after each of them makes a permanent choice of one of the neighboring metropolitans as his own metropolitan. This must be done with the approval of the Apostolic See.[42] These special rights which metropolitans have over the prelates mentioned in canon 285, once the choice has been made and approved, are limited to five in number.

A metropolitan has the right to call these prelates to a provincial council which he has the duty to convoke. Connected with this metropolitan right is the obligation of the prelates of canon 285 not only to attend the provincial council but also to observe the laws made therein and to see that these are observed in their respective territories.[43]

Another expression of this special right over the prelates listed in canon 285 is connected with the episcopal conferences which the metropolitan is to hold at least once every five years in accordance with the rule expressed in canon 292. The metropolitan has the right to call these prelates

---

[42] Canon 285.

[43] Canon 285. A substantially complete discussion of the provincial council is taken up *supra*, pp. 270-283. Regarding the manner of holding these prelates to the observance of the provincial laws cf. *supra*, p. 282.

to attend the meeting, and they have the obligation to heed his call by taking part in the deliberations.[44]

Still another extension of this right over such prelates as are mentioned in canon 285 is the metropolitan duty to make recourse to the Holy See in order to make provision for the see of such a prelate should he be excommunicated, interdicted or suspended. This is not only a right but an obligation as well which a metropolitan must fulfill in such an emergency.[45]

The next application of this special power over the prelates adverted to in canon 285 concerns the matter of appointment by devolution of an administrator of a vacant diocese. A metropolitan has the right to institute a vicar capitular or diocesan econome if the chapter has not nominated one or the other in a vacant see within eight days. This right extends to a vacant abbacy or prelacy *nullius*.[46]

Finally, the prelates who are archbishops lacking suffragans, or who are local ordinaries immediately subject to the Apostolic See, have the right to appeal to the tribunal of the metropolitan they have chosen. The tribunal of the metropolitan has the obligation to accept these second instance cases.[47]

In all these canons which concern the prelates mentioned in canon 285, the Code uses the word *Metropolita* and not *Archiepiscopus;* hence all these rights and obligations pertain exclusively to metropolitans. Purely residential archbishops and non-residential archbishops cannot claim any of these special powers for themselves on the grounds of their archiepiscopal dignity.

---

[44] Canon 292, § 2. A fuller account of these episcopal conferences can be found *supra*, pp. 283-286.

[45] Canon 429, § 5. A detailed presentation of this metropolitan obligation can be read *supra*, pp. 286-292.

[46] Canon 432, § 3. For a detailed discussion of this power on the part of the metropolitan, see *supra*, pp. 221-230.

[47] Canon 1594, § 3. Abbots and prelates *nullius* have the ordinary tribunal of second instance which is mentioned in canon 1594, § 4. A fuller presentation of this right and obligation can be found *supra*, pp. 250-263; 292-296.

Article 4. The Right of the Privilege of the Canon

Canon 2343. § 3. *Qui [violentas manus iniecerit] in personam Patriarchæ, Archiepiscopi, Episcopi etiam titularis tantum, incurrit in excommunicationem latæ sententiæ Sedi Apostolicæ speciali modo reservatam.*

All archbishops, i.e., metropolitans, residential archbishops and non-residential archbishops enjoy the privilege of the canon.[48] According to the general canon which treats of this clerical privilege all the faithful owe reverence to clerics according to their various ranks and offices, and they defile themselves with the delict of sacrilege if they inflict a real injury on clerics.[49] The common law refers to the latter clause of canon 119 in inflicting the penalty enacted in canon 2343, § 3. The latter canon declares that those who lay violent hands on the person of an archbishop fall automatically *(latæ sententiæ)* into an excommunication which is reserved in a special manner to the Apostolic See.[50]

The term *"Qui"* which heads canon 2343, § 3, is not to be restricted to that one person alone who actually inflicts the real injury on the person of an archbishop. All accomplices described in canon 2209, §§ 1-3, incur the *latæ sententiæ* excommunication reserved in a special manner to the Apostolic See, since canon 2231 expressly states that if several persons concur in the perpetration of an offense, though the law speaks of one only, all accomplices as specified in canon 2209, §§ 1-3, are liable to the same penalty, unless the law explicitly states the contrary. Canon 2343, § 3, states nothing to the contrary; therefore all accomplices mentioned in canon 2209, §§ 1-3, are liable. The other accomplices, such as are described in canon 2209, §§ 4-7, according to canon 2231 do not automatically incur the excommunication enacted in canon 2343, § 3, but can be pun-

[48] Cf. McGrath, *The Privilege of the Canon*, The Catholic University of America Canon Law Studies, n. 242 (Washington, D. C.: The Catholic University of America Press, 1946).

[49] Canon 119.

[50] Canon 2343, § 3.

ished with some other just penalty at the discretion of the superior, since canon 2343, § 3, provides no other special penalty for such accomplices.[51]

According to canonists the clause *"violentas manus in personam iniecerit"* denotes a delict which is a certain external and morally imputable injury.[52] Inasmuch as the injury is inflicted in some fashion upon a privileged person not by means simply of words or of threats, but by means of physical acts, the harmful action connotes a deed which is gravely sinful. This real invasion upon the person of a major prelate is for the most part properly called the crime designated as *læsæ maiestatis*. The act or deed which violates the privilege of the canon is therefore a real and violent laying of hands upon the privileged person. The laying of violent hands can be directed at his body, and can take the form of killing, mutilating, wounding, poisoning, striking, throwing to the ground, casting out of a house by force, etc. Or it may be directed against his liberty, and can assume the shape of casting the prelate into jail or into some other such place even though it may be private in nature, of holding him prisoner in one's own home, or of holding him under guard or under authority. Finally, it may be directed against his dignity by such actions as spitting at him, disfiguring him with mud, throwing stones or sordid things at him, forcefully seizing his crosier or skull-cap, violently stopping his car, tearing his clothes or vestments, pulling his beard, chasing him with a dog, or heaping any other similar contumelious action upon him.

To incur the penalty declared in canon 2343 it is necessary that the injurious action be grave by reason of the delict of sacrilege.[53] The attack upon the person must be

---

[51] Cf. Beste, *Introductio in Codicem*, p. 951; Chelodi, *Ius Canonicum de Delictis et Pœnis* (Trento: Libreria Moderna Editrice, 5. ed. recognita et aucta a Pio Ciprotti, 1943), p. 102 (hereafter cited as *De Delictis et Pœnis*); Cocchi, *Commentarium*, VIII, 286; Coronata, *Institutiones*, IV, p. 444; Sipos, *Enchiridion*, p. 115.

[52] Canon 2195, § 1.

[53] Cf. canons 119 and 2195, § 1.

external. Internally there must be both advertance and intention. It must be noted, however, that the gravity of the malice of the external act must be estimated not only from the material harm done, but especially also from the violation of honor and dignity. This penalty is not incurred by those who do not know that the person they injure comes under the privilege of the canon. Nor are those punished by it who strike a prelate without grave subjective fault, e.g., in legitimate self-defense, in a joke, by chance, through sudden anger in which serious guilt is excluded, in just correction, or in view of the equity of law should the injured cleric be apprehended while committing vile deeds with the mother, sister, daughter or blood-relative of the striker.[54]

It must be noted that the Code employs the term "*Archiepiscopi*" in canon 2343, § 3. Since the Code does not distinguish, the word *archbishops* must be understood in its broad significance; hence it applies to all three types of archbishops.[55] This privilege is conceded to archbishops not in view of their possession of jurisdiction, but on account of their episcopal character, which as an indelible mark inheres in their person, independently of the power of jurisdiction.[56] Archbishops enjoy this privilege from the day of their consecration, and not from the day of their election.[57]

---

[54] Badii, *Institutiones*, p. 98; Beste, *Introductio in Codicem*, p. 176; Blat, *Commentarium*, Lib. II, pars 1, pp. 69-70; Lib. V, pars 3, pp. 236-237; Claeys Bouuaert-Simenon, *Manuale*, I, 161, Cance, *Le Code*, I, 143; Cappello, *Summa*, I, 280; Cappello, *Tractatus Canonico-Moralis de Censuris iuxta Codicem Iuris Canonici* (3. ed., Romæ: Officina Libraria Marietti, 1933) pp. 248-252 (hereafter cited as *De Censuris*); Chelodi, *Ius Canonicum*, p. 180; Chelodi, *De Delictis et Pœnis*, pp. 100-101; Cocchi, *Commentarium*, II, 81-84; VIII, 285; Coronata, *Institutiones*, I, 212; IV, 442-445; Ferreres, *Institutiones*, I, 99; McGrath, *The Privilege of the Canon*, pp. 98-110; Prümmer, *Manuale*, p. 86; Raus, *Institutiones*, p. 106; Regatillo, *Institutiones*, I, 148; II, 412; Sipos, *Enchiridion*, pp. 113-115; Toso, *Commentaria*, II, 73-74; Vermeersch-Creusen, *Epitome*, I, 210-211; Wernz-Vidal, *Ius Canonicum*, II, 104-106; VII, 493.

[55] McGrath, *The Privilege of the Canon*, p. 121.

[56] Cappello, *De Censuris*, p. 251.

[57] *Loc. cit.*

In accordance with the general norms given above, all those who offer injury to an archbishop's person, i.e., to his body, his liberty or his dignity, are *ipso facto* excommunicated. Since the canon uses the phrase "*in personam Archiepiscopi,*" all injurious actions leveled against his property, or against a person who is in some way connected with an archbishop (e.g., a member of his household or a servant) are implicitly excluded.

When a real offense is committed against the person of an archbishop, the excommunication incurred is reserved *speciali modo* to the Holy See. Excommunication, in general, is a censure by which a person is excluded from the communion of the faithful with all the legal consequences mentioned in the Code.[58] The legal consequences of the excommunication incurred through violence perpetrated against the person of an archbishop do not differ in any way from the legal effects of the *specialissimo modo* reserved excommunication incurred through similar violence perpetrated against the person of the Pope. The *speciali modo* reserved excommunication can be considered to be less severe, however, than the latter, to the extent that the power to absolve from an excommunication incurred through violation of the privilege of the canon in the case of an archbishop is more easily obtained and the penances are somewhat mollified.[59]

Special faculties from the Sacred Penitentiary are necessary for the granting of absolution from a censure which is reserved in a special manner. In granting such faculties, the Sacred Penitentiary is less exacting in its demands on the penitent than in cases reserved *specialissimo modo,* but more exacting than in cases reserved *simpliciter.*[60] No other penalties besides this excommunication are incurred when violent hands are laid upon archbishops.

---

[58] Canon 2257, § 1. Canons 2259-2267 speak of the effects.

[59] Regatillo, *Institutiones*, II, 363.

[60] Coronata, *Institutiones*, IV, 170.

Article 5. The Right to Permit Passive Membership in Certain Forbidden Societies

The III Plenary Council of Baltimore (1884) decreed that a Commission be formed of all the archbishops within the provinces of the United States to judge whether or not any given forbidden society was to be considered condemned under censure of excommunication.[61] This mode of action was prescribed lest confusion in discipline cause great scandal to the faithful and a detriment to ecclesiastical authority, since one and the same society might be so condemned in one diocese and be tolerated without censure in another diocese. The Council decreed that no society was to be placed under the ban of excommunication by express mention before an ordinary had presented the case for consideration to the archiepiscopal Commission. If the members of the Commission could not reach an unanimous verdict whether the forbidden society was to be placed under the ban of excommunication, recourse was to be made to the Holy See for a decision in the matter.[62]

The Code of Canon Law presents a series of canons which show the Church's strict discipline with regard to forbidden societies.[63] Outside the clear mention of the Masonic Society, the Code contents itself with a general manner of condemning other societies which are comparable to the Masonic Sect. It uses such phrases as: "*societates ab Ecclesia damnatæ,*" "*secta massonica et aliæ eiusdem generis societates,*" "*societates secretæ ab Ecclesia damnatæ,*" "*secta massonica et aliæ eiusdem generis associationes,*" "*secta massonica et aliæ similes associationes.*" In the light

---

[61] Lest there be a possible assumption that the forbidden society here contemplated is the Masonic Society, it must be noted that there was a papally reserved excommunication in store for those who became Masons. Cf. *Acta et Decreta Concilii Plenarii Baltimorensis III*, Tit. VIII, cap. 3, n. 251, p. 142.

[62] *Acta et Decreta Concilii Plenarii Baltimorensis III*, Tit. VIII, cap. 3, n. 255, pp. 143-144.

[63] Canons 1065, §§ 1, 2; 1240, § 1, 1°; 1241; 2339; 542, 1°; 693, § 1; 1453, §§ 1, 3; 2335; 2336.

of this legislation it seems that the prescription of the III Plenary Council of Baltimore is *præter legem* with regard to the formation of such an archiepiscopal commission which would have as its purpose the decision as to the nature of certain forbidden societies; however, no such commission could attach the censure of excommunication, since the Code of Canon Law implicitly takes care of such condemnations in its employment of the general phrases given above. Finally, the Council's decision to send the matter to the Holy See for a definitive action with regard to a specific banning of any society can be considered *præter legem.*

The Holy Office condemned the joining of such societies as the Knights of Pythias, the Odd Fellows and the Sons of Temperance, under pain of grave sin. This condemnation was issued on August 20, 1894. Not long after, the Holy Office was asked whether members of these three condemned societies could be dispensed from the need of formally withdrawing from these societies and whether such members could be given permission to continue paying their dues. The Holy Office responded on January 19, 1896, that by way of exception they could be permitted passive membership under specific conditions. These conditions were: (a) that they joined the society in good faith before knowing that it was condemned; (b) that no scandal result therefrom, or that it be removed through a declaration that the only reason for the relation of membership was that of escaping material losses, and that meanwhile all communication with the sect be avoided and meetings be not attended; (c) that it be impossible to withdraw without grave loss; and (d) that there be no danger of perversion for the party himself or his family, in particular in the eventuality of sickness or death, and no danger of a non-Catholic funeral.[64] It was added that, in order to secure uniformity

[64] *ASS*, XXVII (1894), 699; cf. Ayrinhac-Lydon, *Penal Legislation in the New Code of Canon Law* (rev. ed., New York: Benziger Brothers, 1936), p. 200 (hereafter cited as *Penal Legislation*); Lydon, *Ready Answers in Canon Law* (2. ed., New York: Benziger Brothers, 1934), p. 482 (hereafter cited as *Ready Answers*).

of practice, all such cases should be referred to the apostolic delegate.[65]

Nearly a score of years later, at the request of Cardinal Gibbons, Archbishop of Baltimore, the Sacred Congregation of the Holy Office, on June 26, 1913, extended the faculty of permitting passive memberships in these three societies to all the metropolitans of the United States. The American bishops had asked the Holy See, through Cardinal Gibbons, that, since it was necessary in nearly every instance to consult the ordinary with regard to the details of such cases happening in his jurisdiction, it would simplify matters if the faculty were extended to all the bishops of the country. The Holy Office compromised by extending the faculty, not to the bishops, but to the metropolitans for their respective provinces.[66]

The faculty to grant passive membership in these three forbidden societies was not granted to archbishops but to metropolitans. Even though the decree uses the phrase *"ad singulos Archiepiscopos,"* it clarifies its own meaning by adding the phrase *"ad unumquemque pro sua respectiva provincia"* immediately after.[67] According to Ayrinhac-Lydon there is no censure attached to membership in these

---

[65] *American Ecclesiastical Review*, Vols. I-XXXII, Philadelphia, 1889-1905; from 1905: *The Ecclesiastical Review*, Vols. XXXIII-CIX, Philadelphia, 1905-1943; from 1944: *The American Ecclesiastical Review*, Washington, D. C., Vol. CX, 1944- . *American Ecclesiastical Review* (Philadelphia, 1889-1905), XIV (1896), 361 (hereafter cited as *AER* or *ER* respectively).

[66] "Firmis manentibus facultatibus Delegati Apostolici, supplicandum Ssmo pro extensione Facultatis ad singulos Archiepiscopos, ad unumquemque pro sua respectiva provincia, servatis prorsus omnibus conditionibus decreti insequenti IV diei 19 Januarii, 1896, onerata eorum conscientia. Et insequenti feria V die 27 ejusdem mensis Junii Sanctitas Sua petitam extensionem juxta Emorum et Rmorum Patrum suffragia benigne concessit."—*ER*, XLIX (1913), 468. Cf. Quigley, *Condemned Societies*, The Catholic University of America Studies in Canon Law, n. 46 (Washington, D. C.: The Catholic University of America, 1927), pp. 122-123.

[67] Cf. Ayrinhac-Lydon, *Penal Legislation*, pp. 200-201; Lydon, *Ready Answers*, pp. 480-482; Quigley, *Condemned Societies*, pp. 201-202. These authors use both words, archbishop and metropolitan, indiscriminately.

three condemned societies at present, but such membership is still forbidden. Purely passive membership may be allowed even today under the above mentioned conditions, but the priest requesting such membership for any one of his faithful must refer the case either to the apostolic delegate or to his metropolitan.[68]

Section B

Liturgical Rights and Obligations

Article 1. Indulgences and Papal Blessings

Canon 274. *In diœcesibus vero suffraganeis Metropolita potest tantum:*

2° *Indulgentias centum dierum, sicuti in propria diœcesi, concedere.*

Canon 274, 2°, declares that a metropolitan can grant an indulgence of one hundred days in the dioceses of his suffragans in the same manner as he can in his own diocese. Most of the canonists simply repeat the wording of the Code without making any comment on this section of the law.[69] However, a few canonists have revised their commentary in accordance with the change made by Pope Pius XII.[70]

In recognition of the solicitude and good wishes which he had received from cardinals and ecclesiastical prelates from all parts of the world on the occasion of the twenty-fifth anniversary of his episcopacy, Pope Pius XII decreed on July 20, 1942, that the faculty given to metropolitans in

[68] *Penal Legislation*, p. 200. See Appendix C for the specimen of the questionnaire to be used in applying for such membership from one's metropolitan, as well as the specimen of the metropolitan rescript.

[69] Badii, *Institutiones*, p. 180; Bargilliat, *Prælectiones*, I, 411; Blat, *Commentarium*, Lib. II, pars 1, p. 291; Claeys Bouuaert-Simenon, *Manuale*, I, 248; Cance, *Le Code*, I, 281; Cappello, *Summa*, I, 445; Chelodi, *Ius Canonicum*, p. 281; Cocchi, *Commentarium*, III, 119; Coronata, *Institutiones*, I, 433; Ferreres, *Institutiones*, I, 205; Prümmer, *Manuale*, p. 151; Raus, *Institutiones*, p. 176; Sipos, *Enchiridion*, p. 225; Toso, *Commentaria*, III, 98; Vermeersch-Creusen, *Epitome*, I, 310.

[70] Regatillo, *Institutiones*, I, 234; Wernz-Vidal, *Ius Canonicum*, II, 658.

canon 274, 2°, is enlarged so that they may grant an indulgence of two hundred days. The grant is to hold *in perpetuum,* apart from all need of sending an Apostolic Brief, all things to the contrary notwithstanding.[71]

There was a time when metropolitans could grant an indulgence of forty days at least at the time of the provincial visitation. By a decree of the Sacred Congregation of Indulgences, given on the 28th of August, 1903, the number of days was increased to one hundred.[72] The Code of Canon Law took over the increased number of days as granted by the Sacred Congregation of Indulgences. Nothing in canon 274, 2°, nor in the enlargement granted by Pope Pius XII, limits the grant of these indulgences to the time of the visitation of a suffragan's diocese. In other words, the granting of the indulgences may take place at any time according to the discretion of the metropolitan.

Canon 274, 2°, however, specifies the manner in which the indulgence is to be granted by the insertion of the words "*sicuti in propria diœcesi, concedere.*" Canon 349, § 2, 2°, indicates the method for bishops when it declares that residential bishops have the right to grant indulgences in the territory of their jurisdiction from the moment they have taken possession of their diocese. By a parallelism, a metropolitan has the right of granting the indulgence only "*a capta possessione*" of his province. Since bishops do not have the right to grant indulgences from the time they receive authenic notification of their canonical provision, as is clear from canon 349, § 1, 1° and 2°, so a metropolitan

[71] "Itemque facultas Indulgentias concedendi... Episcopis residentialibus per can. 349, § 2, 2°, impertita, sic augetur, ut iisdem liceat *Indulgentiam centum dierum concedere.* Facultas autem Archiepiscopis per can. 274, 2°, data, ita pariter adaugetur, ut *ducentorum dierum Indulgentiam* iisdem concedere liceat.... Præsenti in perpetuum valituro absque ulla Apostolicarum Litterarum in forma brevi expeditione, et contrariis quibuslibet non obstantibus." — *AAS,* XXXIV (1942), 240. Cf. Bouscaren, *Digest,* II, 221-222; Sartori, *Enchiridion Canonicum seu Sanctæ Sedis Responsiones* (7. ed., Romæ: Ex Typographia Augustiniana, 1944), p. 67 (hereafter cited as *Enchiridion*); *The Jurist,* III (1943), 157-158.

[72] *ASS,* XXXVI (1903), 518-519; *Fontes,* n. 5137.

does not have the right of granting two hundred days' indulgence *"ab accepta authentica notitia peractæ canonicæ provisionis."* To grant the indulgence before he has taken canonical possession of the province would be an unlawful assumption of metropolitan jurisdiction. Neither canon 274, 2°, nor canon 349, § 2, 2°, specifies the number of times a year the two hundred days' indulgence can be granted.

According to the mind of the writer the power of granting the two hundred days' indulgence is given only to metropolitans, for canon 274 in its entirety refers to metropolitans only. Hence this power is not enjoyed by archbishops as such. The decree issued by the Sacred Penitentiary on the 20th of July, 1942, hearkens to canon 274, 2°, which has no reference to archbishops as such.[73] Archbishops, in the opinion of the writer, enjoy only the right of granting such an indulgence as do residential bishops.[74] Metropolitans must observe the prescriptions of canon 913 in the matter of granting indulgences.

The decree of the Sacred Penitentiary given on July 20, 1942, also enlarged the power of all archbishops and metropolitans, as well as bishops, for it increased the number of times they may exercise the faculty to impart the papal benediction with a plenary indulgence, mentioned in canon 914, from two to three times a year.[75] The decree specifies bishops only, but it certainly intends the inclusion of all those who participate in episcopal orders. Hence all archbishops and metropolitans who have received episcopal consecration are granted the extension of power with regard to the papal benediction. Canon 914 declares that the papal blessing is to be given by bishops in their respective dio-

---

[73] Cf. *supra*, pp. 353-354. Bouscaren (*Digest*, II, 221-222) and Sartori (*Enchiridion*, p. 67) make use of the word *archbishops* in keeping with the decree found in *AAS*, XXXIV (1942), 240.

[74] Canon 349, § 2, 2°. Cf. *supra*, pp. 353-354. *AAS*, XXXIV (1942), 240, enlarges the number from fifty to one hundred days.

[75] "Facultas impertiendi Benedictionem papalem cum Indulgentia plenaria de qua in can. 914 Cod. Iur. Can., ita adaugetur, ut Episcopis ter in anno...eam impertire liceat ad normam eiusdem canonis." — *AAS*, XXXIV (1942), 240.

ceses once on Easter Sunday and again on another solemn feast to be designated by the bishop. This blessing may be given even though the bishop does not say the Mass; it suffices that he have assisted at it. In keeping with these specifications, archbishops can grant the papal benediction only in their own dioceses, and not outside them; metropolitans, as archbishops, can also grant the papal blessing only in their own dioceses, but not in their provinces. Archbishops and metropolitans are to adhere to the ruling of canon 914 as to the determination of the Easter blessing, but are free to choose at will the solemn occasions for the second and third bestowing of the papal blessing. Neither canon 914 nor the decree of the Sacred Penitentiary as given above have determined the occasions of the second and third papal benediction. The archbishops and metropolitans are not obliged to celebrate the Mass on any of the three occasions on which they are allowed to give the papal blessing.

The Code of Canon Law contains still another ruling on the archiepiscopal granting of indulgences. At the time a church or altar is consecrated, the officiating archbishop, though he has no jurisdiction in the territory, can give an indulgence of one year to those who visit the church or the altar on the very day of the consecration, and one hundred days on the anniversary of the consecration.[76]

Article 2. Exercise of Pontificals and Metropolitan Blessings

Canon 274. *In diœcesibus vero suffraganeis Metropolita potest tantum:*

6° *In omnibus ecclesiis, etiam exemptis, Ordinario loci præmonito, si ecclesia sit cathedralis, peragere pontificalia, uti Episcopus in proprio territorio, populo benedicere....*

A metropolitan has the right to exercise pontifical functions according to the limitations set by canon 274, 6°. The

[76] Canon 1166, § 3.

phrase "*peragere pontificalia*" of canon 274, 6°, is parallel to that of "*exercere pontificalia*" as found in canon 337, § 2. In law this phrase denotes the performance of those sacred functions in which by liturgical law the use of the pontifical insignia of crosier and miter is required.[77] Connected with the performance of pontifical functions is the use of the throne and canopy. Once a bishop grants permission for the exercise of pontifical functions in his territory he can also permit the use of the throne and the canopy.[78]

A metropolitan has the right to perform pontifical functions in all the churches within his ecclesiastical province. By express mention of law, he may perform such functions even in those churches within his province which are exempt from his jurisdiction. The only restriction set upon this metropolitan right concerns pontifical functions he may wish to perform in the cathedral churches of his suffragans. He has the right to pontificate in these cathedral churches only after he notifies his suffragan bishops in advance of his desire to exercise this right. Throughout his entire province, too, a metropolitan may set up his throne and canopy in all churches, including exempt and cathedral churches. Once the metropolitan makes known his desire to pontificate in the cathedral church of any one of his suffragans, this previous notification entitles him to the use of the throne and canopy.[79]

The metropolitan right to perform pontifical functions in his province is much greater than that which bishops, abbots and prelates *nullius* have. Bishops are allowed to exercise them in all churches, even those which are exempt, only within their own diocese, but they may not perform them outside their own diocese without the express or at least the reasonably presumed consent of the local ordinary of the diocese in which they may wish to pontificate. They may not pontificate in an exempt church outside their own

---

[77] Canon 337, § 2.

[78] Canon 337, § 3.

[79] Cf. canon 349, § 2, 3°.

diocese without the consent of the religious superior.[80] Abbots and prelates *nullius*, though not possessing episcopal consecration, may use the pontifical insignia only in their own territory along with the use of the throne and canopy. Only in their own jurisdiction may they celebrate liturgical functions according to the pontifical rite.[81] Residential archbishops and non-residential archbishops follow the ruling of canon 337, § 1, since canon 274, 6°, refers to metropolitans only.

The metropolitan right in this regard is not as broad as that given by law to cardinals and legates. Cardinals may perform pontifical functions with the use of the throne and canopy in all the churches of the world outside the City of Rome. The only restriction concerns cathedral churches. As the metropolitan must notify his suffragan before he pontificates in the latter's cathedral, so, too, the cardinal must notify all ordinaries beforehand if he wishes to pontificate in their cathedral churches.[82] The common law gives positive rulings concerning the exercise of pontifical functions in the City of Rome.[83] If legates of the Roman Pontiff are bishops, they may, without the permission of ordinaries, perform liturgical functions of the pontifical rite in all churches, except cathedral churches of the country where they hold papal delegation. They may also use the throne and canopy. They may not, however, perform these functions in cathedral churches without the permission of the ordinary of the diocese in which the cathedral is located.[84]

Should a metropolitan wish to celebrate pontifical functions outside his province, the rule of canon 337, § 1, must be observed. In such a circumstance he needs the express or at least the reasonably presumed consent of the local ordinary of the diocese in which he desires to pontificate,

---

[80] Canon 337, § 1.
[81] Canon 325.
[82] Canon 239, § 1, 15°.
[83] Canon 240, § 3.
[84] Canon 269, § 3.

or, in exempt churches outside his own province, the consent of the religious superior.

Connected with pontifical ceremonies is the metropolitan right to bless people in all the churches of his province, be they non-exempt or exempt. His right to bless people within the cathedral churches of his suffragans depends on his having notified beforehand the suffragan bishop who is the ordinary of the place in which the cathedral is located. The manner of the blessing is described in the Code; he is to bless as a bishop blesses in his own territory.[85] A bishop may bless his people in all the churches of his diocese from the time he receives authentic notification of his canonical appointment.[86]

The legislation of the II Plenary Council of Baltimore was broader in this regard, for it permitted the metropolitan to bless the people of his province in every place. No exception was made for the cathedral churches of his suffragans under the circumstances wherein the Code demands a previous notification be made to the suffragans before the metropolitan can bless people in their cathedrals.[87] Metropolitans of this country must in the present follow the ruling of the Code which are somewhat restrictive in relation to the conciliar legislation. The Code of Canon Law demands that the blessings be restricted to the interior of churches, and that a previous notification be given to the suffragan bishops should the metropolitan desire to bless the people in their cathedrals.

Residential archbishops and non-residential or titular archbishops follow the ruling given in canon 349, § 1, 1°. The metropolitan right is more extensive, for it is not limited to the churches of the diocese he rules, but extends to all the churches of his entire province. However, he may

---

[85] Canon 274, 6°.

[86] Canon 349, § 1, 1°.

[87] "Metropolitæ licet ubicumque per Provinciam...populo benedicere...." — *Acta et Decreta Concilii Plenarii Baltimorensis II*, n. 81, v., p. 62.

not bless the people in the cathedral churches of his suffragans unless he has given them previous notice. From the time he receives authentic notification of his canonical appointment as metropolitan he may bless the people of his province as a bishop does in his own diocese. He does not need to take canonical possession of his metropolitan see to bless the people of his province.[88]

This metropolitan right, though greater than that of bishops, is not as extensive as that of cardinals and legates in this matter. Cardinals have faculties to bless people in any place after the manner of bishops; in the City of Rome, however, only inside churches, holy places, and at meetings of the faithful.[89] Legates, if they are bishops, may, without the permission of the ordinaries, bless people in all the churches of the place of their delegation, except in cathedral churches. They may bless people even in these churches if they have the permission of the ordinary of the place.[90]

Article 3. The Metropolitan Cross

Canon 274. *In diœcesibus vero suffraganeis Metropolita potest tantum:*

6° *In omnibus ecclesiis, etiam exemptis, Ordinario loci præmonito, si ecclesia sit cathedralis...cruce ante se delata incedere....*

Besides the pallium, the "*crux gestatoria*" is another metropolitan ensign.[91] The "metropolitan cross," commonly though improperly called the "archiepiscopal cross," is much like a processional cross inasmuch as it has a corpus of Christ attached to one side of it. This cross is not a

---

[88] Cf. canon 349, § 1, 1°.

[89] Canon 239, § 1, 12°.

[90] Canon 269, § 3.

[91] Badii, *Institutiones*, p. 188; Beste, *Introductio in Codicem*, p. 252; Cocchi, *Commentarium*, III, 122; Prümmer, *Manuale*, p. 152; Raus, *Institutiones*, p. 175; Sipos, *Enchiridion*, p. 226.

double-armed cross.[92] According to law this cross is to be borne before a metropolitan in all the churches of the province, even in those which are exempt from his episcopal and metropolitan jurisdiction. The only exceptions to this ruling are the cathedral churches of his suffragan bishops. Should a metropolitan desire to have this cross carried before his own person in these cathedral churches, all the metropolitan needs to do is to give notification beforehand of this desire to the suffragan bishop who is the ordinary of the place where the cathedral is situated.[93]

The provision of the II Plenary Council of Baltimore permitted the metropolitan to have his metropolitan cross carried before him throughout his province.[94] The term "*ubicumque*" of the conciliar legislation has been restrictively modified in the Code by the insertion of the phrases: "*In omnibus ecclesiis*" and "*Ordinario loci præmonito, si ecclesia sit cathedralis.*" Outside these exceptions the rest of the conciliar legislation stands. In other words, a metropolitan cannot follow the conciliar legislation and have the metropolitan cross carried before his person in all places of his province, but must limit the use of his cross to the interior of churches. He must abide by the common law rul-

---

[92] Formerly the double-armed cross was the proper mark of the patriarchal dignity in heraldry. Archbishops placed an ordinary processional or one-armed cross of gold behind their heraldic shield. Bishops, who did not use a cross in processions and liturgical functions, did not place it in their coats-of-arms. About the seventeenth century, archbishops began to place the double-armed cross in their arms, and bishops began to use the ordinary one-armed cross which had hitherto been employed by archbishops in their bearings. This practice has now become universal. It is to be noted that the double-armed cross with which all archbishops timber their arms is not to be confused with the metropolitan cross. The heraldic double-armed archiepiscopal cross does not bear the figure of Christ, while the metropolitan one-armed cross bears the figure. Cf. Nainfa, *Costumes*, pp. 12-14, 37, 175, 177-178.

[93] Canon 274, 6°. Cf. Badii, *Institutiones*, p. 189; Beste, *Introductio in Codicem*, pp. 252-253; Cance, *Le Code*, I, 285; Cocchi, *Commentarium*, III, 122; Sipos, *Enchiridion*, p. 226.

[94] "Metropolitæ licet ubicumque per Provinciam crucem, jurisdictionis suæ insigne, præ se ferre. . . ." — *Acta et Decreta Concilii Plenarii Baltimorensis II*, n. 81, v., p. 62.

ing concerning the previous notification about its use in the cathedral churches of his suffragan bishops, and cannot claim exemption from the common law on the grounds of the broader ruling of the II Plenary Council of Baltimore.

Whenever the metropolitan cross is in use, it is held or carried by a subdeacon or a member of the metropolitan's household, in such a way that the corpus of the crucifix is turned toward the metropolitan.[95]

The metropolitan cross is a token of metropolitan jurisdiction as much as is the pallium; hence it should never be used outside the province over which the metropolitan has authority.[96] It may not be used until after the pallium has been imposed on the metropolitan.[97] Nor may it be held or carried before a metropolitan in the presence of a cardinal, or a papal legate.[98] The reason for this is evidently the same as that given for the non-use of the pallium in the presence of the Roman Pontiff and papal legates.[99]

Since the metropolitan cross is a symbol of metropolitan jurisdiction, non-residential or titular archbishops have no right to use such a cross, for they possess no provincial jurisdiction.[100] Residential archbishops likewise have no right to use a metropolitan cross in any liturgical function, since their jurisdiction extends simply over a diocese, and not over an ecclesiastical province.[101] However, if non-residential or purely titular archbishops and residential archbishops are granted the pallium *"intuitu personæ vel sedis"*

---

[95] Cæremoniale Episcopor., lib. I, c. II, n. 4; lib. I, c. IV, n. 1; lib. II, c. VIII, n. 27; lib. II, c. XXII, n. 3; lib. I, c. XV, n. 2. Cf. Cance, *Le Code*, I, 285; Nainfa, *Costumes*, p. 14. The cross-bearer of the metropolitan should wear a purple cassock according to Nainfa (*Costumes*, pp. 36-37).

[96] Nainfa, *Costumes*, p. 14.

[97] "Neque ante habitum Pallium potest Electus ante se crucem deferre, sed tantum postea." — Pontificale Rom., tit. *De pallio, n.* 8. Cf. Badii, *Institutiones*, p. 189.

[98] Badii, *Institutiones*, p. 189; Cocchi, *Commentarium*, III, 122; Vermeersch-Creusen, *Epitome*, I, 310.

[99] *Supra*, p. 328.

[100] Nainfa, *Costumes*, p. 14.

[101] Nainfa, *Costumes*, p. 178.

by the Roman Pontiff, the privilege of the cross is usually also granted. In all correctness this cross *"ad instar Metropolitarum"* should be called an archiepiscopal cross, and not a metropolitan cross.[102]

Canon 274, 6°, ends with an important phrase. It reads as follows: *"non autem alia exercere quæ iurisdictionem importent."* If this phrase is collated with the opening phrase of the canon, *"In diœcesibus vero suffraganeis Metropolita potest tantum,"* it is clear that the metropolitan cannot do anything in the churches of his suffragan bishops or in exempt churches which in any way implies jurisdiction at the time he exercises pontifical functions. This "jurisdiction" comprehends not only jurisdiction itself, but, as can be seen, also the exercise on the power of orders. If the metropolitan desires to make use of his jurisdictional authority or episcopal orders at the time he exercises pontifical functions in these churches he needs either apostolic faculties or the consent of the suffragans, if there is question of their churches, or the permission of the exempt superiors, if there is question of their churches.[103] In other words, a metropolitan may perform pontifical functions, may bless the people and have the metropolitan cross borne before himself, in all the churches of his province, even in the exempt churches, apart from the giving of any previous notification either to the suffragans or to the exempt superiors. Only cathedral churches are exceptions to this general rule. Should the metropolitan wish to pontificate, or to bless people, or to have the metropolitan cross borne before him, in the cathedrals of his suffragans, he must notify the suffragan beforehand of his intention with regard to these three acts. The law broadens this restriction when it adds the phrase quoted above; hence, outside the act of canonical

---

[102] *Supra*, p. 303. In the Oriental Church the torch *(fax)* is carried before patriarchs, which by way of privilege was also granted to the archbishops of Bulgaria and of the Island of Cyprus. Cf. Badii, *Institutiones*, p. 189, footnote 2.

[103] Blat, *Commentarium*, Lib. II, pars 1, p. 293; Toso, *Commentaria*, II, 99.

visitation, a metropolitan could not preach or hear confessions in any of the churches within the confines of his suffragan's see without an apostolic indult which permits him to do so, or without the consent of the suffragan. The same would hold for exempt churches.[104]

Even though the pallium has been imposed upon a metropolitan, he may not presume within the sees of his suffragans, to ordain clerics who are not his own subjects, but who are the subjects of his suffragans or of exempt superiors.[105] Outside his own metropolitan see he may not even ordain his own subjects, or those who are members of non-exempt and exempt religious institutes within his diocese, apart from the permission of the ordinary of the place where the ordinations are to take place.[106] Therefore, only the three specific actions mentioned in canon 274, 6°, can be performed by the metropolitan in the churches of the province according to the specifications of the canon; no other action which entails the use of the power of jurisdiction or of orders may be exercised by the metropolitan according to the restrictive phrase *"non autem alia exercere quæ iurisdictionem importent."*

Article 4. The Pallium as a Liturgical Vestment

Canon 277. *Metropolita uti potest pallio intra quamlibet ecclesiam etiam exemptam suæ provinciæ in Missarum sollemnibus, diebus in Pontificali Romano designatis aliisque forte sibi concessis; nullatenus vero extra provinciam etsi Ordinarii loci consensus accedat.*

The pallium can not only be considered as a symbol of metropolitan jurisdiction,[107] but it can be viewed also as a liturgical vestment. The Code of Canon Law is not a collection of rules for the carrying out of liturgical rites and

---

[104] Cf. canons 1327, § 1; 1328; 1337; 1338; 1343; 872; 873, § 1 and § 2; 2366.

[105] Cf. canons 955-957; 962; 964-967.

[106] Canon 1008.

[107] *Supra*, pp. 304-305.

ceremonies; yet it does touch upon certain liturgical laws.[108] It does so in canon 277, where it speaks of the rules which govern the use of the pallium with regard to the place where it may be worn. The metropolitan may use the pallium in every church of his province, both non-exempt and exempt, during solemn Masses, on the days designated in the Roman Pontifical and other days on which its use may have been conceded to him. He may not use it at all outside his own province, even though he may have obtained the consent of the local ordinary.[109]

The pallium, like the metropolitan cross, can be used only in churches. The phrase *"intra quamlibet ecclesiam"* makes this point clear. The law does not permit the pallium to be worn outside a church, e.g., during a solemn Mass celebrated outdoors, commonly known as a field-Mass. Since the wearing of a pallium is a privilege, and privileges are not to be extended beyond the terms of their concession, a strict interpretation would not permit the pallium to be worn during field-Masses.[110] Furthermore, the metropolitan may wear it in all the churches of his province, both the non-exempt and the exempt.[111] This ruling is different from that given in canon 274, 6°, which refers to the metropolitan cross. The restriction given in the afore-mentioned canon in the phrase *"Ordinario loci præmonito, si ecclesia sit cathedralis"* is missing in canon 277. However, the phrase is implicitly contained in the fact that the pallium is worn at Mass, which is a pontifical function. Once the metropolitan gives previous notification to the local ordinary that he desires to pontificate in his cathedral, this previous notification contains the implicit right for him to wear the pallium during the solemn Mass without the need of notifying his suffragan that he will wear it.

---

[108] Canon 2. Cf. canon 276.

[109] Canon 277.

[110] Canon 67. Cf. Wernz-Vidal, *Ius Canonicum*, II, 666.

[111] "Pallio autem utitur Archiepiscopus in singulis Ecclesiis provinciæ suæ. . . ." — Cæremoniale Episcópor., lib. I, c. XVI, n. 3. ". . . Archiepiscopus uti Pallio . . . tantum in ecclesiis. . . ." — Pontificale Rom., tit. *De pallio*, n. 9.

The truly liturgical character of the pallium is brought out in the fact that it can be worn only during the celebration of solemn Mass: *"in Missarum sollemnibus."*[112] A pontifical Mass would not be licitly said without the pallium if the wearing of it were prescribed by liturgical law for a certain feast day.[113] The pallium is not to be worn at all during the celebration of Masses which are not solemn, for the Code of Canon Law, the Ceremonial of Bishops, and the Roman Pontifical, specify that the Mass must be solemn. The pallium may not be worn during requiem Masses, even though these may be solemn, for the Roman Pontifical proscribes such a usage.[114] It may not be worn in processions, in the administration of the sacrament of confirmation, or in the celebration of a diocesan synod.[115] Again the principle concerning privileges applies. The pallium may be worn only according to the specifications given in the law; the privilege of its use cannot be extended beyond the terms of the law.[116]

The pallium cannot and must not be worn at all solemn Masses; it may be worn only during those which are designated in the Roman Pontifical: *"diebus in Pontificali Romano designatis,"* and on other days on which its use may have been conceded to a particular metropolitan: *"aliisque forte sibi concessis."* The days designated in the Roman Pontifical follow:

1. Nativity of Our Lord — December 25

---

[112] "Pallio autem utitur Archiepiscopus...dumtaxat dum Missam solemnem celebrat...." — Cæremoniale Episcopor., lib. I, c. XVI, n. 3. "...Archiepiscopus uti Pallio...non omni tempore, sed tantum...in Missarum solemniis...." — Pontificale Rom., tit. *De pallio*, n. 9.

[113] Cappello, *Summa*, I, 310.

[114] "...Archiepiscopus uti Pallio...non omni tempore...neque in Missis pro defunctis...." — Pontificale Rom., tit. *De pallio*, n. 9.

[115] "...Archiepiscopus uti Pallio...non omni tempore, non in processionibus...." — Pontificale Rom., tit. *De pallio*, n. 9; Benedictus XIV, *De Synodo Diœcesana*, lib. II, c. 5, n. 8; lib. III, c. 2, nn. 5, 6, 7; C. 1, X, *de auctoritate et usu pallii*, I, 8; cf. Beste, *Introductio in Codicem*, p. 253; Claeys Bouuaert-Simenon, *Manuale*, I, 250; Sipos, *Enchiridion*, p. 227; Wernz-Vidal, *Ius Canonicum*, II, 667-668.

[116] Canon 67. Cf. Wernz-Vidal, *Ius Canonicum*, II, 666.

2. St. Stephen, Protomartyr — December 26
3. St. John, Apostle and Evangelist — December 27
4. Circumcision of Our Lord — January 1
5. Epiphany of Our Lord — January 6
6. Purification of the Blessed Virgin — February 2
7. St. Matthias, Apostle — February 24
8. St. Joseph — March 19
9. Annunciation of the Blessed Virgin — March 25
10. SS. Philip and James, Apostles — May 1
11. Nativity of St. John the Baptist — June 24
12. SS. Peter and Paul, Apostles — June 29
13. St. James, Apostle — July 25
14. Assumption of the Blessed Virgin — August 15
15. St. Bartholomew, Apostle — August 24
16. Nativity of the Blessed Virgin — September 8
17. St. Matthew, Apostle — September 21
18. SS. Simon and Jude, Apostles — October 28
19. All Saints' Day — November 1
20. St. Andrew, Apostle — November 30
21. Immaculate Conception of the Blessed Virgin — December 8
22. St. Thomas, Apostle — December 21
23. Palm Sunday
24. Holy Thursday
25. Holy Saturday
26. Easter Sunday
27. Easter Monday
28. Easter Tuesday
29. Low Sunday

30. Ascension of Our Lord
31. Pentecost Sunday
32. Corpus Christi
33. Anniversary of the dedication of the metropolitan church
34. Anniversary of the consecration of the metropolitan
35. Principal feasts of the metropolitan church
36. Dedication of churches
37. Ordination of clerics
38. Consecration of bishops, abbots and virgins
39. Convocation of provincial councils
40. Blessing of chrism.[117]

The Code of Canon Law states nothing about the listing of the days on which the pallium must be worn according to the *Cæremoniale Episcoporum*.[118] Beste mentions that both these listings hold.[119] There is a slight difference be-

[117] "Dies, quibus Pallio uti potest...Archiepiscopus, hi sunt: Nativitas Domini nostri Jesu Christi, Sancti Stephani Protomartyris, S. Joannis Apostoli et Evangelistæ, Circumcisio Domini, Epiphania Domini, Dominica in Palmis, Feria Quinta in Cœna Domini, Sabbatum Sanctum, Dominica Resurrectionis cum duobus sequentibus diebus, Dominica in Albis, Ascensio Domini, Dominica Pentecostes, Festum Corporis Christi, Festivitates quinque beatæ Mariæ semper Virginis, Purificationis, Annunciationis, Assumptionis, Nativitatis et Immac. Conceptionis, Nativitas S. Joannis Baptistæ, Festum S. Joseph, 19 martii, Festum omnium Sanctorum, Festivitates omnium Apostolorum, Dedicationis ecclesiarum, Principales Festivitates ecclesiæ suæ, Ordinationes Clericorum, Consecrationes Episcoporum, Abbatum et Virginum, Dies anniversarius Dedicationis Ecclesiæ, et Consecrationis suæ." — *Pontificale Romanum Summorum Pontificum jussu editum, a Benedicto XIV et Leone XIII recognitum et castigatum* (Mechliniæ: H. Dessain, 1895), tit. *De pallio*, p. 124 (hereafter cited as Pontificale Romanum [1895 ed.]). "...antequam obtinuerit quis Pallium...non licet ei Episcopos consecrare, nec convocare Concilium, nec Chrisma conficere, neque Ecclesias dedicare, nec Clericos ordinare...." — Pontificale Romanum (1895 ed.), p. 123.

[118] Lib. I, c. XVI, n. 4.

[119] *Introductio in Codicem*, p. 253.

tween the listing in the *Roman Pontifical* and in the *Ceremonial of Bishops;* the latter uses the phrase "*duodecim Apostolorum festivitatibus*" instead of the words "*festivitates omnium Apostolorum.*" Since the Code makes it clear in canon 2 that it does not intend to make any changes in liturgical law except in an express manner, these phrases must be reconciled on a liturgical rather than a canonical plane.

The *Cæremoniale Episcoporum* makes the phrase "*aliisque forte sibi concessis*" clear. It states that a metropolitan may use the pallium on other days besides those given in its listing, but only if these days are specified for his church by way of express privilege.[120] Otherwise he must not use the pallium in the celebrations of pontifical functions. The strong expression "*uti non debet Pallio*" precludes any other conclusion. The Roman Pontifical is not as clear on this point as the Ceremonial of Bishops.[121] Canonists agree that the number of days for the wearing of the pallium can be increased only by way of an express privilege.[122] Such an opinion is in keeping with the pre-Code law.[123] The opinion that custom can extend the use of the pallium to other days beyond the enumeration given in the liturgical books seems hardly in keeping with the wording of the liturgical laws

---

[120] "Pallio autem utitur Archiepiscopus...præscriptis quibusdam diebus, qui in privilegiis Ecclesiæ metropolitanæ exprimi solent." — Cæremoniale Episcopor., lib. I, c. XVI, n. 3. "Quod si non reperiantur expressi, recurrendum erit ad communem consuetudinem, quæ est, ut eo utatur diebus infrascriptis....Aliis autem diebus in privilegiis non expressis, vel inter prædictos non comprehensis, Archiepiscopus si voluerit in pontificalibus celebrare, uti non debet pallio." — *Ibid.*, n. 4.

[121] "Nec potest...Archiepiscopus uti Pallio...sed tantum...in festis præcipuis...." — Pontificale Rom., tit. *De pallio*, n. 9.

[122] Cappello, *Summa*, I, 309, footnote 4; Chelodi, *Ius Canonicum*, p. 281, footnote 1; Wernz-Vidal, *Ius Canonicum*, II, 667.

[123] C. 6, X, *de auctoritate et usu pallii*, I, 8: "Ubicunque fueris in missarum celebrationibus constitutus, diebus solennibus usum pallii... poteris liberius exercere."; c. 7, X, *de auctoritate et usu pallii*, I, 8: "...tam in tua quam in aliena diœcesi potes sine pallio et sandaliis celebrare, qui utique in tua diœcesi non debes semper celebrare cum pallio, sed diebus illis dumtaxat, qui in ecclesiæ tuæ privilegiis sunt expressi."

or of the Code, or in consideration of the fact that the wearing of the pallium is a privilege.[124]

Finally, canon 277 states that a metropolitan may not use the pallium outside his own province, even though the ordinary of the place gives his consent: *"nullatenus vero extra provinciam, etsi Ordinarii loci consensus accedat."*[125] This legislation is based on the pre-Code law.[126] Cocchi declares that a custom to the contrary of this section of canon 277 is a *"corruptela legis."*[127] Coronata and Wernz-Vidal state that no custom can change the law; the only thing which could make the use of the pallium outside the province licit would be an express concession of this privilege on the part of the Roman Pontiff.[128] The juridic reason back of this strict proscription is that the metropolitan has metropolitan authority only in his own province and not beyond it.[129]

The II Plenary Council of Baltimore legislated that a metropolitan is allowed to use the pallium throughout his province as often as he could use it in his own metropolitan

---

[124] Coronata, *Institutiones*, I, 436, footnote 4. Cf. canon 67.

[125] "Pallio autem utitur Archiepiscopus in singulis Ecclesiis provinciæ suæ, non autem extra provinciam...."—Cæremoniale Episcopor., lib. I, c. XVI, n. 3. "Nec potest...Archiepiscopus uti Pallio extra [suam]...provinciam...."—Pontificale Rom., tit. *De pallio*, n. 9.

[126] C. 4, X, *de auctoritate et usu pallii*, I, 8: "Sane solus Romanus Pontifex in missarum solenniis pallio semper utitur et ubique, quoniam assumptus est in plenitudinem ecclesiasticæ potestatis, quæ per pallium significatur; alii autem eo nec semper, nec ubique, sed in ecclesia sua, in qua iurisdictionem ecclesiasticam acceperunt, certis debent uti diebus, quoniam vocati sunt in partem sollicitudinis, non in plenitudinem potestatis." C. 5, X, *de auctoritate et usu pallii*, I, 8: "Consuetudo... quod archiespiscopi extra suas provincias pallio indifferenter utantur ...*usus huiusmodi sit abusus*, et talis consuetudo dicenda sit potius corruptela, *et ii graviter offendere dignoscantur qui utuntur palliis extra suas provincias absque licentia sedis apostolicæ speciali....*"

[127] *Commentarium*, III, 121. Cf. canon 5.

[128] Coronata, *Institutiones*, I, 436, footnote 4; Wernz-Vidal, *Ius Canonicum*, II, 667.

[129] Badii, *Institutiones*, 190; Cappello, *Summa*, I, 309; Toso, *Commentaria*, III, 101.

church.[130] This positive affirmation is in keeping with the Code. Nevertheless, inasmuch as the conciliar decree does not have the restrictive clause of canon 274, 6°, which is implicitly contained in canon 277, it must be considered abrogated by the Code. The council is silent about the use of the pallium outside the province.

Even from a liturgical standpoint canon 277 does not stand alone. In order to appreciate fully the juridic use of the pallium, one must link canon 277 with canon 274, 6°, which speaks of the performance of pontifical functions and the use of the metropolitan cross;[131] with canon 275, which treats of the obligation of the imposition of the pallium;[132] with canon 276, which measures the licitness of acts in relation to its use in the exercise of metropolitan jurisdiction and episcopal orders;[133] and with canons 278 and 279, which relate to the use of the pallium as to time and person.[134]

It must always be borne in mind that this commentary of canon 277 relates only to metropolitans. The canon itself uses only the term *Metropolita.* Should residential archbishops be given the pallium by way of privilege, these rules do not apply to them. In general it may be said that they are allowed to wear the pallium only in the churches of their diocese during solemn Masses on the days designated by the Roman Pontifical, and on those days which have been expressly conceded to them. They may not wear the pallium outside their dioceses, even though the ordinary of the place grants them leave to do so.

Metropolitans may use the *mozetta*[135] and the uncovered *rochetto*[136] throughout their entire province, except in the

---

[130] "Metropolitæ licet ubicumque per Provinciam. . .Pallio uti, quotiescumque in Ecclesia Metropolitana illo uti posset." — *Acta et Decreta Concilii Plenarii Baltimorensis II*, n. 81, v., p. 62.

[131] *Supra*, pp. 356-359.

[132] *Supra*, pp. 305-307.

[133] *Supra*, pp. 309-321.

[134] *Supra*, pp. 323-328.

[135] Nainfa, *Costumes*, pp. 73-78.

[136] *Op. cit.*, pp. 67-72.

presence of an apostolic legate or cardinal.[137] The prelatial hat with ten tassels on each side disposed in four rows, all of which are green in color, is a symbol of archiepiscopal dignity in heraldry.[138]

SECTION C

HONORIFIC RIGHTS

Article 1. Reverence

Canon 119. *Omnes fideles debent clericis, pro diversis eorum gradibus et muneribus, reventiam, seque sacrilegii delicto commaculant, si quando clericis realem iniuriam intulerint.*

The prerogative whereby clerics are entitled to special reverence and respect from the faithful is known as the privilege of the canon. The principles of this privilege are enunciated in canon 119. It must be noted here that the positive obligation of reverence[139] varies in accordance with the rank of the cleric in the hierarchy of orders or of jurisdiction. Hence it is that there is no obligation on the part of the laity to extend equal reverence to all clerics.[140]

First, all clerics have the right to be held in high esteem by the laity. Furthermore, a clergyman of higher rank is entitled to respect from lesser clerics. In keeping with this principle all archbishops deserve esteem from both the laity

---

[137] Badii, *Institutiones*, p. 189; Cocchi, *Commentarium*, III, 122; Raus, *Institutiones*, p. 174.

[138] Beste, *Introductio in Codicem*, p. 253; Cance, *Le Code*, I, 285; Nainfa, *Costumes*, p. 179.

[139] The negative aspect of the privilege of the canon can be found treated *supra*, pp. 346-349.

[140] Badii, *Institutiones*, p. 98; Beste, *Introductio in Codicem*, p. 176; Blat, *Commentarium*, Lib. II, pars 1, pp. 68-69; Claeys Bouuaert-Simenon, *Manuale*, I, 161; Cappello, *Summa*, I, 280; Chelodi, *Ius Canonicum*, pp. 186-187; Cocchi, *Commentarium*, II, 76-78; Coronata, *Institutiones*, I, 212; McGrath, *The Privilege of the Canon*, pp. 47-49; Raus, *Institutiones*, p. 105; Regatillo, *Institutiones*, I, 147; Sipos, *Enchiridion*, pp. 112-113; Toso, *Commentaria*, II, 72; Vermeersch-Creusen, *Epitome*, I, 210.

and the clergy. The clerical state and the reception of episcopal orders guarantee them this especial regard. Residential archbishops and metropolitans deserve proportionately more because of their rank in hierarchical jurisdiction: the residential archbishop chiefly in his diocese and the metropolitan primarily in his province.

Secondly, all clerics deserve to have a more honorable place in the church than the laity. The higher the rank of orders or of jurisdiction, the more honorable the place reserved for the cleric. Archbishops should, following this principle, have a more distinguished place than bishops.

Thirdly, those clerics who are endowed with jurisdiction have the right to canonical obedience. The greater the scope of jurisdiction, the greater should be the duty of obedience. A residential archbishop has a rightful claim on the obedience of the laity and of clerics within his diocese. A metropolitan deserves obedience as a local ordinary within his diocese from all the lay and clerical members of the church within his see, and that obedience from his suffragans and provincial subjects which is vindicated for him by law. Purely titular or non-residential archbishops cannot claim canonical obedience in the same measure as can residential archbishops and metropolitans, for they lack the latter's jurisdiction.

Fourthly, clerics may receive certain honorary titles.[141]

Lastly, the clergy has a right of precedence in ecclesiastical processions and meetings.[142]

Article 2. Title

Pope Pius XI, by a decree given on December 11, 1930, decided that the title "*Most Reverend Excellency*" should be given to archbishops, whether residential or titular. This decree was issued by the Sacred Congregation of Cere-

---

[141] With regard to the titles of archbishops see *infra*, pp. 373-374.

[142] See *infra* on the precedence rights of archbishops, pp. 374-376.

monies on December 31, 1930.[143] Up to the time of this decree all archbishops were titled "*Your Grace.*"

Article 3. Precedence

Canon 280. *Patriarcha præcedit Primati, Primas Archiepiscopo, hic Episcopis, salvo præscripto can. 347.*

Canon 347. *In suo territorio Episcopus præcedit omnibus Archiepiscopis et Episcopis, exceptis Cardinalibus, Legatis Pontificiis et proprio Metropolita; extra territorium serventur normæ traditæ in can. 106.*

The norm given in canon 106 states that all physical persons are bound to observe the precedence it prescribes for them except in those cases wherein special regulations given in the Code of Canon Law prescribe otherwise. The general norm given in canon 106, 2°, of this canon can be applied to the metropolitan, for it declares that he who has authority over physical or moral persons has the right of precedence over such persons. Since a metropolitan has authority over the suffragans of his province and over the moral personality of the province as such, he has the right of precedence over his suffragans throughout his entire province.

Considered as a bishop within his own diocese, a metropolitan precedes all archbishops and bishops, whether residential or titular, within the confines of his diocese. Only a cardinal or a papal legate has precedence over him within his own see.[144]

In his province a metropolitan precedes all bishops, whether or not these are his suffragans. He has precedence over the particular suffragan bishop in whose see the procession or meeting is held.[145] It seems that the metropolitan precedes all other archbishops within his province in

---

[143] *AAS*, XXIII (1931), 131. Cf. Bouscaren, *Digest*, I, 210; Beste, *Introductio in Codicem*, p. 253; Regatillo, *Institutiones*, I, 236.

[144] Canon 347.

[145] Canon 347.

keeping with the spirit of canon 347. The presence of a metropolitan in his own province could certainly be accepted as convertible with the phrase "*in suo territorio*." Cardinals and pontifical legates, however, would still precede him in his own province.[146]

Outside his province, a metropolitan is considered only in the light of his archiepiscopal dignity. Therefore the norms of canon 280 hold.[147] Hence in every diocese outside his own province his place is after patriarchs and primates and before bishops. The only time a bishop can precede him is when the bishop is in his own territory.[148]

Canon 280 does not apply exclusively to metropolitans, for the canon uses not the word *metropolitan* but the term *archbishop*. In consequence all three types of archbishops have the same right of precedence, whether they are metropolitans, residential or non-residential archbishops. When the Commission for the Authentic Interpretation of the Code of Canon Law was asked whether under the Code (canons 106, 3°; 272; 280; 285; 347) a metropolitan archbishop as such outside his province had precedence over an archbishop who was not a metropolitan, that is, one who had no suffragan bishops, the answer was in the negative.[149]

The precise order of precedence within the class of archbishops follows the general norms of canon 106, 3°. Canon 280 is to be regarded as including mention of the metropoli-

---

[146] Cf. Cappello, *Summa*, I, 445; Chelodi, *Ius Canonicum*, p. 280; Prümmer, *Manuale*, p. 152; Raus, *Institutiones*, p. 176; Sipos, *Enchiridion*, p. 226.

[147] Cf. Badii, *Institutiones*, p. 188; Blat, *Commentarium*, Lib. II, pars 1, p. 295.

[148] Cf. canon 347. Cf. Cance, *Le Code*, I, 285; Cocchi, *Commentarium*, III, 122; Raus, *Institutiones*, p. 176; Regatillo, *Institutiones*, I, 235; Toso, *Commentaria*, III, 102; Vermeersch-Creusen (*Epitome*, I, 311) say that bishops in their own territory precede even patriarchs and primates so long as one of these is not their metropolitan.

[149] *AAS*, XXXIII (1941), 378. Cf. Bouscaren, *Digest*, II, 119; Sartori, *Enchiridion*, p. 27; Blat, *Commentarium*, Lib. II, pars 1, p. 295; Chelodi, *Ius Canonicum*, p. 280, footnote 2; Regatillo, *Institutiones*, I, 235-236.

tans and archbishops of the Oriental Church.[150] The general norm of canon 106, 4°, declares that the diversity of Rites is given no consideration in the matter of precedence.

Article 4. Civil Honors

According to the 21st Article of the Constitution of Spain, issued in 1876, all Spanish archbishops were given the rank of senator.[151]

Sipos states that the acknowledgment of civil powers had accorded to archbishops honorific titles, rights of precedence, senatorships and other civil duties in his country. Before World War II, in Hungary, the archbishop of Esztergom (Gran) was a prince, and all archbishops were members of the Upper House.[152] Wernz-Vidal add that in Austria-Hungary, before the end of World War I (1918), six archbishops were given the title of *prince,* namely those of Görz (Italian: Gorizia; Slovenian: Gorsica), Olmütz (Czechoslovakian: Olomauc), Prague (German: Prag; Czechoslovakian: Praha), Salzburg, Esztergom (German: Gran; *Diœcesis Strigoniensis: Strigonia* is an old traditional form to designate the Kingdom of Hungary, Esztergom being its ranking see), and Vienna. All archbishops in Austria, by force of their office, were members of the Upper Houses of the dual monarchy. In the Empire of the Turks, patriarchs and metropolitans were given quite a bit of civil jurisdiction.[153]

The policy of the separation of Church and State in the United States does not permit such civil honors and duties to be given to archbishops and metropolitans.

---

[150] Canon 1.
[151] Ferreres, *Institutiones*, I, 207.
[152] *Enchiridion*, p. 228.
[153] *Ius Canonicum*, II, 668-669.

CHAPTER XI

RIGHTS AND OBLIGATIONS OF ORIENTAL CATHOLIC METROPOLITANS

SECTION A

PRELIMINARY NOTIONS

Article 1. Historical Note

Canon 1. *Licet in Codice iuris canonici Ecclesiæ quoque Orientalis disciplina sæpe referatur, ipse tamen unam respicit Latinam Ecclesiam, neque Orientalem obligat, nisi de iis agatur, quæ ex ipsa rei natura etiam Orientalem afficiunt.*

In the West the rights and obligations of metropolitans steadily grew to great proportions until these were curtailed through decretal legislation which was provoked by abuses actually or purportedly brought on by the metropolitans. This restrictive process continued until the time of the Council of Trent (1545-1563). Its ultimate culmination is now reflected in the all-inclusive enumeration of metropolitan rights as delineated in the Code of Canon Law (1918).[1]

In the East the rights and obligations of metropolitans continued growing until a little after the IV Council of Constantinople (869-870).[2] Restrictions were placed on the further growth of the institute not so much by papal decretals as by the increasing privileges of the Oriental patriarchs. But even greater restrictive influences arose from the frequent wars with infidels, and from the invasions conducted by the Arabs and the Turks. These wars and invasions so reduced the number of Christians in the East

[1] Cf. *supra*, pp. 1-144.

[2] Cf. *supra*, pp. 1-68.

that they slowly effected the transfer of metropolitan rights to the patriarchs.[3]

Article 2. Intermediary Position of Oriental Catholic Metropolitans

Canon 108, § 3, determines the origin of the various hierarchical grades in the Latin Church when it declares that by divine institution the sacred hierarchy of orders consists of bishops, of priests and of other ministers, that the hierarchy of jurisdiction consists of the Supreme Pontificate and of the subordinate episcopate, and that other degrees have been added by ecclesiastical institution. In keeping with this legal principle the metropolitan institute of the Latin Discipline is an intermediary grade or rank within the hierarchical arrangement as effected by ecclesiastical institution.

Both the Latin and the Oriental Disciplines look to history for the origin of the supra-episcopal grades of the sacred hierarchy. Hence the origin of the metropolitan institute in the Oriental Church, as one of the supra-episcopal grades of the hierarchy, is not of divine origin but, as in the Western Church, also of ecclesiastical institution. However, there is a difference between the intermediary positions of the Latin and of the Oriental metropolitans.

The specific arrangement of the hierarchy of the Oriental Church which distinguishes it from that of the Latin Church lies chiefly in this that it has patriarchal churches and non-patriarchal churches.

The patriarchal churches are governed by patriarchs who are chosen by bishops gathered together in synods. Once a patriarch is elected he enjoys the fullest power throughout his entire patriarchate over bishops, clerics and the faithful in accordance with the norms of the canons of the Oriental Church. Juridically, then, every metropolitan within a patriarchate is subject to his patriarch who has the right to exercise a certain authority over him.

---

[3] Coussa, *Epitome*, I, 168.

The non-patriarchal churches are either immediately subject to the Holy See or to a metropolitan see. Should a certain church be a non-patriarchal metropolitan church, the metropolitan would not be subject to any patriarch, but would be subject immediately to the Holy See. Examples of this type are the metropolitan sees of the Rumanians in Rumania, of the Ruthenians in Poland and of the Chaldeans in India.

This arrangement exists among the Catholics of the Oriental Discipline today. However, both juridically and factually *(de iure et de facto)* there are other hierarchical grades among the Dissidents.[4]

Article 3. Patriarchates, Disciplines and Rites

To evaluate properly the rights and obligations of present-day metropolitans in the Oriental Catholic Church, one must keep in mind certain distinctions. The first major consideration is that of the patriarchates. It is all-important to remember whether or not the metropolitan whose see is the subject of study belongs to a particular patriarchate.

In the early Church the faithful were divided into patriarchates according to the geographical position of their race. Each patriarch had a geographical territory over whose inhabitants he reigned. The one great patriarchate of the West was that of Rome, with the Pope as the Patriarch of the entire Western Church; the four great patriarchates of the East were: Constantinople, Alexandria, Antioch and Jerusalem, each having a patriarch at its head.[5]

At the present time the six Catholic Patriarchates in the East do not correspond to the old Eastern patriarchates. In addition to the patriarchates of Constantinople, Alexan-

---

[4] Coussa, *Epitome*, I, 105.

[5] Fortescue (*The Orthodox Eastern Church* [London: Catholic Truth Society, 1907], pp. 5-50) gives a history of these five patriarchates and of the patriarchate of Cyprus. A map delineating the boundaries of the five patriarchates in the 5th century is found in Fortescue, *op. cit.*, p. 49.

dria, Antioch and Jerusalem, *Statistica* enumerates the Armenian and the Chaldean patriarchates.[6] The old idea that the rite follows the patriarchate has given way to its direct opposite: the patriarchate follows the rite.

The next distinction one must bear in mind is that which concerns the five Oriental Catholic Disciplines with their various subordinate rites.

In the earliest period of Christianity there were diversities of local rite and custom in each country, almost in each diocese or local church. Gradually and almost imperceptibly a certain uniformity began to appear throughout each patriarchate. This was most probably due to the fact that priests began to follow the rite of their bishop, bishops began to follow the rite of their metropolitan, who in turn followed the rite of his patriarch. This principle did not seem to go further than this. The patriarchates were too extensive, too distant, and too much separated by language and custom from Rome to adopt the rite of the first Patriarch.[7] Even though uniformity of rite throughout the whole Church did not become a reality at any one time, neither did it become completely so in the patriarchates themselves. The course of history shows the differences of rite which grew up to the present time. *Statistica* lists the following Disciplines and Rites:

I. Alexandrian Discipline:

1. Copts[8]

---

[6] Cf. pp. 534-536. According to Attwater (*The Catholic Eastern Churches* [2. ed., Milwaukee: Bruce Publishing Co., 1937], p. 205), Pope Benedict XIV established a patriarchal see for the Armenians in 1742. It was established in Asia Minor, at Kraim in the Lebanon, with the title of Cilicia. The same author (Attwater, *op. cit.*, pp. 229-231) gives a short history of the turbulent beginnings of the Chaldean patriarchate. For a complete view of the hierarchical arrangement of the patriarchates, see Appendix B, *infra*, pp. 420-422.

[7] Fortescue, *The Uniate Eastern Churches* (ed. G. Smith, London: Burns, Oates and Washbourne, 1923), p. 12.

[8] *Statistica*, pp. 3-37; Attwater, *The Catholic Eastern Churches*, pp. 135-138; Fortescue, *The Lesser Eastern Churches* (London: Catholic Truth Society, 1913), pp. 163-290.

2. Ethiopians (Abyssinians)[9]

II. Antiochene or Syrian Discipline:
1. Malankars (Syro-Malankars)[10]
2. Maronites[11]
3. Pure Syrians (Syrians or Western Syrians)[12]

III. Armenian Discipline (Armenians)[13]

IV. Slav-Byzantine or Greek Discipline:
1. Albanians[14]
2. Bulgarians (Catholic Bulgarians)[15]
3. Georgians[16]
4. Greeks (Pure Greeks)[17]
5. Italo-Albanians (Italo-Greeks)[18]
6. Jugoslavs[19]

---

[9] *Statistica*, pp. 41-45; Attwater, *The Catholic Eastern Churches*, pp. 150-154; Fortescue, *The Lesser Eastern Churches*, pp. 293-322.

[10] *Statistica*, pp. 49-52; Attwater, *The Catholic Eastern Churches*, pp. 196-199.

[11] *Statistica*, pp. 54-56; Attwater, *The Catholic Eastern Churches*, pp. 180-188; Marbach, *Marriage Legislation for the Catholics of the Oriental Rites in the United States and Canada*, The Catholic University of America Canon Law Studies, n. 243 (Washington, D. C.: The Catholic University of America Press, 1946), pp. 50-51; 81-84; 123-125; 150-151; 202 (hereafter cited as *Marriage Legislation*).

[12] *Statistica*, pp. 64-67; Attwater, *The Catholic Eastern Churches*, pp. 163-168; Fortescue, *The Lesser Eastern Churches*, pp. 323-336; Marbach, *Marriage Legislation*, pp. 45-46; 80-81; 118-119; 150.

[13] *Statistica*, pp. 77-82; Attwater, *The Catholic Eastern Churches*, pp. 203-210; Fortescue, *The Lesser Eastern Churches*, pp. 383-445; Marbach, *Marriage Legislation*, pp. 30-31; 76-77; 115-116; 141-142; 203.

[14] *Statistica*, pp. 96-98; Attwater, *The Catholic Eastern Churches*, p. 130.

[15] *Statistica*, pp. 99-103; Attwater, *The Catholic Eastern Churches*, pp. 121-124.

[16] Attwater, *The Catholic Eastern Churches*, pp. 130-131.

[17] *Statistica*, pp. 106-113; Attwater, *The Catholic Eastern Churches*, pp. 117-120.

[18] *Statistica*, pp. 116-122; Attwater, *The Catholic Eastern Churches*, pp. 69-74; Fortescue, *The Uniate Eastern Churches*, pp. 47-145; Marbach, *Marriage Legislation*, pp. 72-74, 108-110; 138-139; 184-185; 203.

[19] *Statistica*, pp. 125-132; Attwater, *The Catholic Eastern Churches*, pp. 98-99.

7. Melkites[20]
8. Rumanians[21]
9. Russians[22]
10. Ruthenians[23]
11. Hungarians (Greek Hungarians)[24]

V. Chaldean Discipline:

1. Chaldeans[25]
2. Malabars[26]

SECTION B

METROPOLITAN RIGHTS AND OBLIGATIONS IN THE PATRIARCHATES

Article 1. Juridic Status

Papp-Szilagyi drew no distinction between the metropolitans who are within patriarchates and the metropolitans who are outside patriarchates; hence it is difficult to state whether the rights which the author attributed to metro-

[20] *Statistica*, pp. 134-141; Attwater, *The Catholic Eastern Churches*, pp. 106-115; Fortescue, *The Uniate Eastern Churches*, pp. 185-233; Marbach, *Marriage Legislation*, pp. 61-62; 93-94; 125; 160-161; 201-202.

[21] *Statistica*, pp. 152-161; Attwater, *The Catholic Eastern Churches*, pp. 100-105; Marbach, *Marriage Legislation*, pp. 70-72; 105-108; 131-132; 184; 203; Plöchl, "The Church Laws for Orientals of the Austrian Monarchy in the 'Age of Enlightenment' " — *Quarterly Bulletin of the Polish Institute of Arts and Sciences in America*, II (1944), 711-756.

[22] *Statistica*, pp. 171-174; Attwater, *The Catholic Eastern Churches*, pp. 125-129; Marbach, *Marriage Legislation*, pp. 74-75; 112-114; 139-140; 189-192; 203.

[23] *Statistica*, pp. 169-220; Attwater, *The Catholic Eastern Churches*, pp. 76-95; Marbach, *Marriage Legislation*, pp. 63-67; 94-99; 127-128; 164-171; 195-198; Plöchl, "The Church Laws for Orientals of the Austrian Monarchy in the 'Age of Enlightenment' " — *Quarterly Bulletin of the Polish Institute of Arts and Sciences in America*, II (1944), 711-756.

[24] *Statistica*, pp. 221-226; Attwater, *The Catholic Eastern Churches*, pp. 96-97.

[25] *Statistica*, pp. 229-238; Attwater, *The Catholic Eastern Churches*, pp. 227-241; Fortescue, *The Lesser Eastern Church*, pp. 199-202; Marbach, *Marriage Legislation*, pp. 37-38; 77-78; 116-117; 148-149; 203.

[26] *Statistica*, pp. 247-253; Attwater, *The Catholic Eastern Churches*, pp. 243-249; Fortescue, *The Lesser Eastern Churches*, pp. 353-379.

politans belong to both classes or simply to one or the other class.

In writing of the general rights of metropolitans, Papp-Szilagyi quoted canon 34 of the *Canones Apostolorum.*[27] The author then quoted Zonaras' commentary on this canon. Zonaras (12th century), after expounding the necessity of a presiding head for the general welfare of a society, declared that the metropolitan was to be held as the head of the bishops of the province in such a way that the latter could not do anything which concerned the common good of the province without his consent and aid. Among the affairs which needed the intervention of the metropolitan were: the settling of dogmatic questions and the making of dispositions concerning those who were in error with regard to these questions and to pontifical constitutions. Bishops were to consult with the metropolitan regarding such matters, and he was to determine what seemed best for all concerned. Even though he had the right to administer certain matters of his suffragan bishops and of their subjects, at no time was the metropolitan to abuse his jurisdiction by assuming dominion of the respective sees of his suffragan bishops.[28]

According to Papp-Szilagyi certain metropolitan rights were consequences of the 34th canon of the *Canones Apostolorum.* The metropolitan has the right (a) to convoke the bishops of the province to a synod in order to discuss and decide matters which are common to the entire ecclesiastical province, such as faith, morals and discipline; (b) to confirm and to consecrate his suffragan bishops, elected by the bishops of the province at synods at which the metropolitans need not be present, this right being dependent upon the consent of the patriarch who is the metropolitan of metropolitans; and (c) to receive appeals from the sentences of bishops.[29]

---

[27] *Enchiridion,* p. 109.
[28] *Op. cit.,* pp. 109-110.
[29] *Op. cit.,* p. 110.

The author stated that other writers also included among metropolitan rights: the prerogative of a metropolitan to summon to his tribunal the bishops of his province who are negligent in the fulfillment of their duties. Papp-Szilagyi did not agree with this opinion, on the grounds namely that this right belongs to the Supreme Pontiff, who alone is the ordinary judge of bishops. The author made it clear that the metropolitan had no jurisdiction in the sees of his suffragans. He conceded that if it should happen that a metropolitan must celebrate the Liturgy in the regions of a subaltern bishop, this could be handled by arrangement. Except in his own metropolitan see, the name of the metropolitan is not to be commemorated in the sacred Liturgy throughout the province. This is a privilege reserved to the patriarch and the Supreme Pontiff. However, if an episcopal see of a province is vacant, the metropolitan must be commemorated in the Liturgy of that particular episcopal see.[30]

Since this author wrote his *Enchiridion* in 1880, his opinions are rather outdated. The chief fault lies in the fact that the patriarchal and non-patriarchal distinction was not drawn by him. Coussa clarifies the position of Oriental Catholic metropolitans by his fine distinction between the two types of metropolitans.

From a purely legal standpoint *(de iure)*, the metropolitan institution is still retained in the patriarchates. The juridic status of metropolitan churches, as well as the rights, obligations and privileges which were associated with them in ancient times, has not been changed and has not been abrogated in any way whatsoever. According to Coussa the whole metropolitan institute remains unimpaired.[31] The author bases his opinion on three arguments: (a) all metropolitan rights, obligations, and privileges have been recognized, confirmed and even at times instituted in the ecumenical and topical (provincial) councils; (b) these

---

[30] *Loc. cit.*

[31] *Epitome*, I, 168.

rights, obligations and privileges were not suppressed by any council; and (c) these rights, obligations and privileges juridically exist at the present time and are to be fully restored at a future opportune time.[32]

The ancient discipline included such metropolitan rights as: (a) the direction of elections conducted for the filling of the vacant episcopal sees of the province, as well as the confirmation and consecration of the newly elected bishop;[33] (b) the convocation of the bishops of the province to meetings held during the year with the right to preside at these provincial councils,[34] and even to punish those who did not attend;[35] (c) the granting of permission to the bishops of the province should these wish to travel;[36] (d) the direction of the common ecclesiastical affairs of the province;[37] (e) the implied right of visitation of the sees of suffragan

---

[32] *Op. cit.*, p. 169.

[33] Canon 4 of the I Council of Nicæa (325) — cf. *Codificazione Canonica Orientale, Fonti* (Serie I, 16 Fascicoli, Città del Vaticano: Tipografia Poliglotta Vaticana, 1930- , Fascicolo IX, *Disciplina Generale Antica Sec. II-IX*, 1933), Serie I, fasc. IX, n. 763 (hereafter cited as *Fonti*); Pitra, *Iuris Ecclesiastici Græcorum Historia et Monumenta* (2 vols., Romæ, Vol. I, 1864; Vol. II, 1868), I, 429 (hereafter cited as *Historia et Monumenta*); *supra*, pp. 5, 15. Canon 6 of the I Council of Nicæa — cf. *Fonti*, Serie I, fasc. IX, n. 758; Pitra, *Historia et Monumenta*, I, 430; *supra*, pp. 9, 15. Canon 12 of the Council of Carthage 387 or 390) — cf. *Fonti*, Serie I, fasc. IX, n. 363; *supra*, p. 36.

[34] Canon 16 of the Council of Antioch (341) — cf. *Fonti*, Serie I, fasc. IX, n. 836; Pitra, *Historia et Monumenta*, I, 462; *supra*, p. 26. Canon 20 of the Council of Antioch — cf. *Fonti*, Serie I, fasc. IX, n. 855; Pitra, *Historia et Monumenta*, I, 463; *supra*, p. 26. Canon 19 of the Council of Chalcedon (451) — cf. *Fonti*, Serie I, fasc. IX, n. 852; Pitra, *Historia et Monumenta*, I, 529; *supra*, p. 27. Canon 6 of the II Council of Nicæa (787) — cf. *Fonti*, Serie I, fasc. IX, n. 854; Pitra, *Historia et Monumenta*, II, 109-110; *supra*, pp. 27-28.

[35] Canon 8 of the Council in Trullo — cf. *Fonti*, Serie I, fasc. IX, n. 856; Pitra, *Historia et Monumenta*, II, 28.

[36] Canon 28 of the Council of Carthage — cf. *Fonti*, Serie I, fasc. IX, n. 392.

[37] Canon 9 of the Council of Antioch (341) — cf. *Fonti*, Serie I, fasc. IX, n. 759; Pitra, *Historia et Monumenta*, I, 459; *supra*, pp. 34-35. *Canones Apostolorum*, c. 34 — cf. *Fonti*, Serie I, fasc. IX, n. 762; Pitra, *Historia et Monumenta*, I, c. 35, p. 20; *supra*, p. 17.

bishops;[38] (f) the acceptance of recourses and appeals from the subjects of his suffragan bishops;[39] and the rendering of decisions and sentences after reviewing these with other bishops.[40] From a juridic standpoint, in view of the arguments advanced by Coussa, these rights still belong to the Oriental metropolitans within the various patriarchates.

Article 2. Factual Status

However the factual *(de facto)* situation must be considered for a true picture of metropolitan rights and obligations within the patriarchates.

The metropolitans of the Copts (Alexandrian Discipline) enjoy rights in keeping with the old canons. According to the decrees of the Council held in Cairo, Egypt (1898), the following are the rights and obligations of a Coptic metropolitan: (a) he must be vigilant that his suffragan bishops fulfill all their duties rightly and faithfully; (b) he has the right to call a provincial council, to preside at it and together with the other bishops to examine the minor criminal causes of his suffragans; (c) he has the right to receive appeals from the judgments made by his suffragans except in "*ex informata conscientia*" cases; (d) he has the right to make a visitation of a suffragan see to supply the negligences of his suffragan bishops; and (e) during the time of the visitation he has the right to ab-

[38] Canon 19 of the IV Council of Constantinople — cf. *Fonti*, Serie I, fasc. IX, n. 597; Pitra, *Historia et Monumenta*, II, p. XLIII; *supra*, pp. 66-67.

[39] Canon 26 of the IV Council of Constantinople — cf. *Fonti*, Serie I, fasc. IX, n. 327; Pitra, *Historia et Monumenta*, II, p. XLIV; *supra*, p. 65.

[40] Canon 26 of the IV Council of Constantinople — cf. *Fonti*, Serie I, fasc. IX, n. 593; Pitra, *Historia et Monumenta*, II, p. XLIV. Capitulum 89 of the Council of Carthage — cf. *Fonti*, Serie I, fasc. IX, n. 547; *supra*, p. 37.

solve from cases reserved by the suffragan to himself.[41] These rights differ from those given to Latin metropolitans by the Code of Canon Law.[42]

The Syrians (Antiochene Discipline) held a provincial council at a monastery at Sharfeh on Mount Lebanon in the year 1888. The decrees clearly delineate the extent of metropolitan power. The metropolitan has the right (a) to choose his own suffragan bishops during a synod of bishops, and to consecrate them after their election; (b) to convoke a provincial council for the bishops subject to him; (c) to make a pastoral visitation of his suffragan sees; and finally, (d) to receive appeals from the sentences rendered by his

---

[41] Art. IV, *De Metropolitæ Iurisdictione:* "Metropolita iura et officia hæc sunt: 1. Invigilare debet ut Episcopi suffraganei omnia officia sua recte et fideliter adimpleant. 2. Ius habet convocandi synodum provinciæ eique præsidendi atque ad eam deferendi causas criminales minores suorum suffraganeorum. 3. Ius ei competit acceptandi appellationes a iudiciis suffraganeorum suorum, excepto casu quo suffraganeus iuxta facultatem a canonibus concessam iudicaverit ex informata conscientia, quo in casu recursus fieri debet ad Sanctam Sedem. 4. Occurente alicuius suffraganei negligentia, Metropolita, ad eam supplendam, ius habet eius Diœcesim visitandi. 5. A casibus suffraganeis reservatis absolvere potest solo visitationis tempore." — *Synodus Alexandrina Coptorum habita Cairi in Aegypto anno MDCCCXCVIII* (Romæ: S. C. de Propaganda Fide, 1899), pp. 184-185 (hereafter cited as *Synodus Alexandrina Coptorum*).

[42] Decree (a) is in keeping with canon 274, 4°, except that it says nothing concerning the report of abuses to the Roman Pontiff. Decree (b) corresponds to canon 284, 2°; however, since canon 1557, § 1, 3°, reserves the adjudication of all criminal causes involving bishops to the Roman Pontiff, this decree assures Coptic metropolitans and bishops greater power than that given to Latin metropolitans and bishops. Decree (c) can be linked with canon 274, 7°, except that it is much broader in its scope than the canon which specifies the types of sentences from which appeals can be made. It is in keeping with canon 1594, § 1, also. Canons 2186 and 2194 can be collated with decree (c) touching the "*ex informata conscientia*" cases; however, canon 2189, § 2, allows a suspended cleric to have recourse to an immediately higher superior for an increase of pension, which the decree does not take into account. Decree (d) agrees generally with canon 274, 5°; nevertheless the canon restricts the types of affairs which a Latin metropolitan can settle. Canon 274, 4°, insists that a Latin metropolitan refer all abuses to the Roman Pontiff. The decree has a much broader scope in the field of rights derived by devolution. Decree (e) agrees with canon 274, 5°, in its entirety.

suffragan bishops.[43] These rights agree somewhat with those given to Latin metropolitans.[44]

Generally considered however, the rights and obligations of metropolitans have been assumed by the patriarchs in spite of legal specification. The underlying reason for this assumption of power lies in the fact that the metropolitan institute has been absorbed by the patriarchal institute. This absorption is clearly declared in the legislation of the most recent councils, even in those councils which have been approved by the Apostolic See.

The Maronite Council of Mount Lebanon (Antiochene Discipline), held at the Monastery of Saidat al-Luaizek in 1736, after declaring that the ancient provincial division in which metropolitan sees were placed at the head of episcopal sees was not feasible because of the great devastation wrought by the infidels, decreed that the patriarchal institute alone was to contain in itself all patriarchal, primatial and metropolitan jurisdiction. The arrangement was not to be permanent; it was to last until the primatial and metropolitan sees were restored to their pristine splendor

---

[43] Art. IV, *De Metropolita:* "Metropolita pluribus prærogativis et iuribus gaudebat. Quorum hæc præcipua: 1. quod in synodo episcoporum eligebat suos suffraganeos episcopos ac ordinabat; 2. quod synodum provincialem ex suis episcopis habebat; pastoralem visitationem peragebat in diœcesibus suffraganeis; denique quod appellationem recipiebat a iudiciis episcoporum suffraganeorum." — *Synodus Sciarfensis Syrorum in Monte Libano celebrata in anno 1880* (Romæ: S. C. de Propaganda Fide, 1896), p. 215 (hereafter cited as *Synodus Sciarfensis*).

[44] Decree (a) sustains a right which no longer holds in the Latin Discipline. Canon 329, § 2, reserves the nomination of bishops to the Roman Pontiff; the pontifical mandate appointing a bishop usually delegates the papal right of episcopal consecration to any bishops chosen by the new bishop, so long as those chosen are in communion with the Holy See. Decree (b) is in keeping with canon 284, 2°. Even though decree (c) is in harmony with canon 274, 5°, it does not set any limitation of metropolitan rights throughout the visitation. The lack of delimitation assures the Syrian metropolitans of broad powers. Decree (d) is in keeping with canon 274, 7°, and 1594, § 1, except that the power of Syrian metropolitans is broader than that of Latin metropolitans inasmuch as no limitation is set in the decree.

once peace returned to the Orient.[45] Before making this decree the Council enumerated the rights which formerly the metropolitan enjoyed: (a) the right to constitute, in conjunction with the bishops of a synod, the suffragan bishops of his province, and to consecrate the new bishops; (b) the right to decide the causes and controversies of bishops, and to call those causes and controversies which had been decided in an episcopal synod for re-examination in a metropolitan synod; (c) the right to convoke provincial councils; (d) the right to watch over the faith and morals throughout the dioceses of the bishops subject to him; (e) the right to grant commendatory letters to all clerics and priests who were leaving their dioceses to approach the Roman Pontiff, their patriarch or their primate; and (f) the right to preside over the province in such a way that nothing of major importance could be done without his permission.[46] In a

---

[45] "Quum devastatis per infideles antiocheni throni diœcesibus, non amplius servetur antiqua provinciarum divisio, nec supersint Metropolitani, qui subiectas Episcoporum provincias, ut supra dictum est, regant et administrent; sed solus Reverendissimus Dominus Patriarcha omnibus sue Patriarchatus et Nationis Metropolitis et Episcopis præsit, in eosque patriarchiam, primatialem, et metropoliticam iurisdictionem exerceat, Metropolitanus autem nil aliud supra Episcopos concedatur, nisi honoris titulus, et in concessibus primus locus: idcirco decernimus, et statuimus ut, quæcumque de Metropolitanis supra allegata sunt, et infra producentur, ad solum Reverendissimum Dominum Patriarcham restricta sint, donec restituta Orienti pace sedes primatiales et metropoliticæ in suum pristinum splendorem, Deo favente, restituantur."—*Fonti* (Serie I, Fascicolo XII, *Disciplina Antiochena: Maroniti, Ius Particulare Maronitarum* [Tipografia Poliglotta Vaticana, 1933]), Serie I, fasc. XII, n. 1135; Synodus Montis Libani (1736), Pars III, cap. IV, n. 14, *Coll. Lac.*, II, 300; Mansi, XXXVIII, 186.

[46] "Metropolitanorum iura in subiectos provinciæ suæ Episcopos, hæc olim erant: 1. Episcopos Provinciæ suæ in Synodo constituebant et ordinabant; 2. Causas et controversias eorumdem Episcoporum decidebant, et quæ in Synodo Episcopi definitæ fuerant, eas iterum vocabant ad examen in Synodo Metropolitana; 3. Conciliorum provincialium seu metropoliticorum, quæ ex Episcopis totius provinciæ constabant, celebratio penes Metropolitanos erat; 4. Tanquam custodes in specula positi invigilabant, ne fides aut disciplina quippiam detrimenti in diœcesibus subiectorum Episcoporum pateretur; 5. Clericis et Episcopis extra diœcesim ad Sanctissimum Romanum Pontificem aut Patriarcham vel Primatem suum proficiscentibus concedebant litteras commendatitias,

later decree within the same Council, the Maronite patriarch is assured that all these rights, obligations and privileges are his so long as he embraces the true faith of the Church of Rome and holds the Roman Pontiff as his superior.[47]

The metropolitan institution of the Armenians (Armenian Discipline) was restored by a decree issued on November 27, 1893, by the Sacred Congregation for the Propagation of the Faith. The following were to be metropolitan sees: Erzerum in Greater Armenia (Erzurum, Turkey), Diarbekr in Mesopotamia (Diỳarbekir, Turkey), Angara in Asia Minor (Ankara, Turkey), Sivas in Lesser Armenia (Sivas, Turkey), Aleppo for Syria and Cilicia (Alep, Syria).[48] This decree, however, did not take effect on account of the troubled conditions in the patriarchate. Hence the Armenian hierarchy drew up a similar proviso for the absorption of the metropolitan rights by the patriarchal institute in canon 184 of the Synod held in Rome in 1911.[49]

---

quas formatas vocant; quarum virtute apud dissitas nationes communione ecclesiastica, seu quæ suo ordini responderet, fruerentur. Eisdem respective privilegiis gaudebant Primates quoad subditos Metropolitanos et Episcopos." — *Fonti*, Serie I, fasc. XII, n. 1135, footnote 1; cf. Synodus Montis Libani (1736), Pars III, cap. IV, n. 11, *Coll. Lac.*, II, 299; Mansi, XXXVIII, 185. "Quod etiam in unaquaque provincia Episcopis Metropolitanus præesse debeat, et nihil magni momenti sine ejus sententia Episcopis aggredi liceat. . . ." — Synodus Montis Libani (1736), Pars III, cap. IV, n. 13, *Coll. Lac.*, II, 300; Mansi, XXXVIII, 184-185.

[47] "Hæc omnia, quæ modo enumeravimus, Rmo D. Patriarcho nostro tum ex sacris canonibus, tum ex consuetudine immemorabili et expressa vel tacita Romanorum Pontificum concessione competere nos omnes Metropolitani et Episcopi declaramus et profitemur, eique tamquam capiti et principi nostro perfectam obedientiam atque subjectionem promittimus, salva semper Summi Romani Pontificis potestate et primatu. . . . Honoramus itaque Patriarchum nostrum, eique subjacemus dummodo ipse orthodoxam Romanam fidem colat et Ssmum Romanum Pontificem, Christi D. in terris vicarium, tamquam suum superiorem et magistrum atque patrem honoret. . . ." — Synodus Montis Libani (1736), Pars III, cap. VI, n. 3, *Coll. Lac.*, II, 336-337; Mansi, XXXVIII, 213-214.

[48] Cf. Coussa, *Epitome*, I, 169.

[49] "Quoniam vero Patriarcha noster, prout res hactenus se habent, est etiam metropolitanus, plane consequitur, eumdem metropolitanorum iuribus gaudere, donec provinciæ ecclesiasticæ apud nos restitutæ fuerint." — Cf. *Statistica*, p. 84.

The Melkites (Slav-Byzantine Discipline) also declared in their Synod held in Jerusalem in 1849 that the patriarch is to exercise all the rights and obligations of the metropolitan.[50] This Synod was not approved by the Holy See.[51] Legislation along this same vein was repeated in the Synod of Ain-Traz in the Lebanon held in 1909.[52]

Two rights, well entrenched in the Oriental Church, were those of metropolitan participation in the elections of their suffragan bishops and of the subsequent ordination of them by their metropolitans. The ancient legislation insisted that the election of a suffragan bishop without the consent of the metropolitan was null and void.[53] Such commentators as Zonaras,[54] Aristenus[55] and Balsamon,[56] who flourished in the twelfth century, were in agreement with the ancient law concerning this metropolitan right.

---

[50] "La maggior parte dei venticinque privilegi sopradetti sono originali e necessariamente annessi alla dignità patriarcale fino dai primi secoli della chiesa; gli altri poi sono attribuiti alla potestà patriarcale per essere i privilegi dei cattolici (primati), esarchi, arcivescovi e metropolitani, coll' andar dei tempi successivamente cessati secondo le discipline degli ultimi secoli della chiesa, e sono di poi restretti nella persona di monsignori partriarca. Perciò questo nostro santo sinodo li accetta di nuovo e rende ferma la loro osservanza alla persona di sua beatitudine senza la minima trasgressione; siccome che sua beatitudine si servirà di questi privilegi secondo lo spirito dei medesimi sagri canoni ed osserverà ai suoi vescovi i loro canonici diritti che hanno nelle loro diocesi intatti senza lesione." — Mansi, XLVI, 1083.

[51] Cf. Marbach, *Marriage Legislation*, p. 125.

[52] N. 122. Cf. Coussa, *Epitome*, I, 143, footnote 124.

[53] Cf. Canon 4 of Nicæa — *Fonti*, Serie I, fasc. IX, n. 763; *supra*, p. 385. Canon 6 of Nicæa — *Fonti*, Serie I, fasc. IX, n. 758; *supra*, p. 385.

[54] "Etsi olim populi suffragiis episcopi in urbibus eligerentur, adhuc tamen post suffragium integra res ad metropolitanum deferebatur, ab eoque confirmabatur electio, et quem ille approbasset, is demum manuum impositione creabatur." — *Fonti* (Serie II, Fascicolo V, *Textus Selecti ex Operibus Commentatorum Byzantinorum Iuris Ecclesiastici* [ed. Isidorus Croce, Typis Polyglottis Vaticanis, 1939]), Serie II, fasc. V, n. 151.

[55] ". . . verumtamen debent et qui absunt [a synodo] sua præsentibus episcopis et electionem facientibus suffragia ferre: post factam autem electionem, potestatem habet metropolitanus ut unum e tribus electis quem ipse præfert, eligat." — *Fonti*, Serie II, fasc. V, n. 148.

[56] *Fonti*, Serie II, fasc. V, n. 149.

Canon 4 of the Council of Nicæa, which treated of the election of comprovincial bishops, required at least three bishops for the ordination of a new bishop.[57] The term *ordination (chirotonia)* had a broader meaning than the word *consecration*. In the ancient law of the Oriental Church it was often understood to mean both the canonical appointment and the actual conferral of episcopal consecration. Zonaras in commenting on Canon 1 of the *Canones Apostolorum* made this meaning clear.[58]

Since the patriarchs absorbed the rights of the metropolitans, as has been shown above, these rights of episcopal confirmation and ordination should have become the juridical and factual rights of patriarchs. Yet this has not happened in practice for the most part. Among the Copts,[59] the Syrians,[60] the Armenians[61] and Chaldeans[62] the confirma-

---

[57] Cf. *supra*, p. 385.

[58] "...antiquitus vero ipsa electio quondam nominata est chirotonia: nam cum urbium multitudinibus liceret eligere episcopos, conveniebant ipsæ multitudines, et alii quidem hunc eligebant, alii vero illum. Ut autem plurim suffragium vinceret, eligentes ferunt solitos extendere manus; et per illas numeratas esse, qui vel hunc, vel illum delegissent. A pluribus vero electum summo sacerdotio præfecere...." — *Fonti*, Serie II, fasc. V, n. 15. Cf. *ibid.*, nn. 16, 81, 251.

[59] "Electo conceditur unius mensis spatium ad præbendum suum consensum Patriarchæ, atque obtenta ab Apostolica Sede confirmatione proceditur ad consecrationem." — *Synodus Alexandrina Coptorum*, p. 193, n. 10.

[60] "Obtenta pontifica confirmatione, electus consecrationem episcopalem recipiat...." — *Synodus Sciarfensis*, p. 224.

[61] *Acta et Decreta Concilii Nationis Armenorum Romæ habiti ad Sancti Nicolai Tolentinatis anno MDCCCCXI* (Romæ: Typis Polyglottis Vaticanis, 1913), n. 242 (hereafter cited *Synodus Romana Armenorum*). Cf. Coussa, *Epitome*, I, 178.

[62] Pius IX, *Cum ecclesiastica disciplina*, 31 aug. 1869, n. VI: "Quoties aliquam diocesim memorati Patriarchatus vacare continget, Patriarcha quamprimum synodum indicat universorum Episcoporum eiusdem Patriarchatus; quo facto, ab eodem Patriarcha et ab Episcopis synodaliter congregatis, tres idonei ecclesiastici viri, collatis consiliis, Rom. Pontifici pro tempore existenti proponatur, ut ex illis digniorem et magis idoneum eligere, et vacanti episcopali sedi providere possit....Hanc vero methodum in electione omnium et quorumcumque Episcoporum in Babylonensi Chaldaici ritus Patriarchatu perpetuis futuris temporibus omnino servari debet." — *ASS*, V (1869), 618-619.

tion of episcopal elections must be obtained from the Roman Pontiff. The Maronites[63] and the Melkites,[64] however, only need to notify the Roman Pontiff about the completed episcopal election. Already during the times of Benedict XV, the Sacred Congregation for the Affairs of the Oriental Church, in reporting in the *Acta Apostolicæ Sedis* on the elections held among the Maronites and Melkites, began to say that the Roman Pontiff "held as valid the election conducted by the Synod of N. N. for the Eparchy N."; whereas, for the others, i.e., the Copts, Syrians, Armenians and Chaldeans, the Congregation used the other expression: "*electionem confirmavit Romanus Pontifex.*"[65]

According to Balsamon, the election of a metropolitan in the ancient law was left to the metropolitans of the other provinces. It was the patriarch who either confirmed the election of the episcopal candidate or selected one of a number of candidates presented to him.[66] This method, according to the same commentator, was a deviation from that which was observed before the time of the Council of Chalcedon (451).[67]

The right of the patriarch to consecrate the legitimately elected metropolitans of his patriarchate is a very old one.

---

[63] "Ad Reverendissimum igitur Dominum Patriarcham solum iure præsenti spectat Metropolitanorum et Episcoporum electio et consecratio, requisito tamen consilio et assensu Synodi Episcoporum et Metropolitarum, non ad alios. . . ." —*Fonti*, Serie I, fasc. V, n. 570; cf. Synodus Montis Libani (1736), Pars III, c. IV, n. 15, *Coll. Lac.*, II, 300; Mansi, XXXVIII, 186.

[64] Coussa (*Epitome*, I, 178, footnote 286) declares that this is a patriarchal right by reason of the canons and custom.

[65] *AAS*, XIII (1921), 525; XIV (1922), 620; XVIII (1926), 253.

[66] "Metropoleon electiones a metropolitanis de more fieri, et quod factum est ab illis ad patriarcham referri, ut eius examinatione ex tribus electis unus ordinetur." —*Fonti*, Serie II, fasc. V, n. 173.

[67] ". . .ante vicesimum octavum canonem Chalcedonensis synodi metropolitani fiebant ab episcopis, et non a Constantinopolitano pro tempore patriarcha, ut nunc fit; dicit canon [sextus sardicen.], quod si sit processura electio metropolitani, non fiat a solis provincialibus episcopis; sed etiam omnino accerseri oportet episcopos vicinarum regionum, propter metropolitani magnitudinem, quem exarchum provinciæ nominat. Sic enim ab omni mala suspicione libera erit electio, ut quæ a pluribus antistitibus facta sit." —*Fonti*, Serie II, fasc. V, n. 269.

Innocent I (401-417), in a letter written in 415 to Patriarch Alexander of Antioch, confirmed this patriarchal right.[68] Patriarchs retain this right to the present day within their patriarchates. The patriarch of the Copts,[69] the Maronites[70] and of the Armenians[71] are assured of this right by law. It can be well imagined that the other patriarchs enjoy this right by reason of the ancient canons and custom.

Although the metropolitans have been deprived of their rights and obligations in the patriarchates, they still retain the right of precedence over other bishops who are not endowed with metropolitan dignity. Among the Maronites, by custom, the metropolitan actually has precedence only according to the priority of consecration, even though the

---

[68] "Itaque arbitramus, Frater charissime, ut sicut Metropolitanos auctoritate ordinas singulari, sic et ceteros non sine permissu et conscientia tua sinas Episcopos procreari. In quibus hinc modum recte servabis, ut longe positos literis datis ordinari censeas ab his, qui nunc eos suo tantum ordinant arbitratu. Quorum enim tua te maxime exspectat cura, præcipue tuum debent mereri judicium." — *MPG*, XX, 548. Cf. *Corpus Iuris Civilis* (3 vols., Vol. II, *Codex Iustinianus* recognovit et rectractavit Paulus Krueger, 10. ed., Berolini: Apud Weidmannos, 1929), (1.4) (29.12); (1.4) (34.6); *Novellæ* (recognovit Rudolfus Schoell, absolvit Gulielmus Kroll, 5. ed., Berolini: Apud Weidmannos, 1928), (7.1).

[69] "In electione ad sedem metropolitanam verificatio chirographorum fieri debet in electione patriarchali, sed devolvitur nunc ad Patriarcham et decanum." — *Synodus Alexandrina Coptorum*, p. 193, n. 8.

[70] "Patriarchæ igitur privilegia sunt: 6°. Metropolitanos et Primates suo Patriarchatui subiectos, vel per se, vel per subdelegatos Episcopos consecrare eisque Pallium largiri." — *Fonti*, Serie I, fasc. XII, n. 1127. Cf. Synodus Montis Libani (1736), Pars III, cap. VI, n. 2, VI, *Coll. Lac.*, II, 334; Mansi, XXXVIII, 212.

[71] "...diœceseos suæ Metropolitanos ordinare; quod ius post sæculum quartum Patriarchis omnibus passim quæsitum est, etenim prioribus sæculis metropolitani a provincialibus episcopis ordinabantur. Primus autem Antiochenus antistes Metropolitanos ordinare cœpit, isque solus eo iure quinto ineunte sæculo fruebatur; eum enim auctoritate sigulari, hoc est iure ipsi soli proprio, Metropolitanos ordinare, ait Innocentius I. Deinceps ius ordinandi metropolitam patriarchicum evasit. Hinc simul cum patriarchica dignitate potestas ordinandi metropolitas in diœcesibus Asiana, Pontica et Thracica Constantinopolitano antistiti tributa est." — *Synodus Romana Armenorum*, n. 183, 2°: cf. Coussa, *Epitome*, I, 148.

Council of Mount Lebanon (1736) prescribed that precedence should follow the priority of the hierarchical order.[72] Among the Melkites it can be noted that, in such official acts as the subscription of decrees and in the listings of all bishops, priority of title holds true on certain occasions, and the priority of consecration on other occasions.[73]

As far as the pallium is concerned, it is the patriarch who, for the most part, enjoys the right to impose it upon metropolitans. Once he receives his pallium from the Roman Pontiff,[74] he has the privilege of granting a pallium to each

---

[72] "Etsi ratione Ordinis omnes Episcopi sint æquales, at ratione iurisdictionis nonnulli sunt aliis superiores. Primum autem in ea Prælatorum subordinatione locum tenet Pontifex Romanus, utpote Christi Domini ac Dei Nostri in terris Vicarius, et Petri Apostolorum Principis in potestate super universam Ecclesiam eiusque Prælatos successor; alterum locum tenent Patriarchæ; tertium Primates seu Catholici, qui et Exarchi; quartum Metropolitani sive Archiepiscopi; ultimum Episcopi simpliciter dicti." — *Fonti*, Serie I, fasc. XII, n. 1191; cf. Synodus Montis Libani (1736), Pars III, cap. IV, n. 4, *Coll. Lac.*, II, 289; Mansi, XXXVIII, 177.

[73] Cf. Coussa, *Epitome*, I, 169.

[74] The pallium is strictly personal. "Et quia Pallium istud est personale, ideo commodari non potest; neque in morte alicui relinqui, sed Patriarcha cum eo sepeliri debet." — *Fonti*, Serie I, fasc. XII, n. 1058; Synodus Montis Libani (1736), Pars III, cap. VI, n. 7, XXIII, *Coll. Lac.*, II, 344; Mansi, XXXVIII, 219. Cf. canon 279.

The patriarch cannot use the Roman pallium outside his own patiarchate, but only in churches during the solemnities of the divine liturgy on the chief feast-days. He cannot use it in processions or in Masses for the dead. "Illo vero (Pallio), quod Romanus Pontifex concedit, non potest uti extra suum Patriarchatum, et non omni tempore, sed tantum in ecclesiis, in Missarum solemniis, in festis præcipuis, non in processionibus, neque in Missis pro defunctis." — *Fonti*, Serie I, fasc. XII, n. 1067; Synodus Montis Libani (1736), Pars III, cap. VI, n. 7, XXIII, *Coll. Lac.*, II, 344; Mansi, XXXVIII, 219. "Præ certis nostræ rationis pontificibus distinguitur Pallio quod ei a Summo Pontifice gratiose confertur iuxta consuetudinem vigentem; eo induitur in solemnitatibus certorum dierum." — *Synodus Sciarfensis*, p. 212, n. 1.

The days for the use of the pallium are indicated in pontifical documents given to patriarchs or in the respective law of each rite. Cf. Innocent III, *Quia divinæ*, 3 ian. 1215 — *Fontes* (Series III, Vol. II, *Acta Innocentii PP. III (1198-1216)* [ed. Theodosius Haluščynskyj, Typis Polyglottis Vaticanis, 1944]), Series III, Vol. II, p. 460; Pius IX, *Cum ecclesiastica disciplina*, 31 aug. 1869, n. IV — *ASS*, V (1869), 618.

of the metropolitans who are subject to his jurisdiction.[75] This privilege is reduced to the imposition of the ritual omōphorion alone, and not to the imposition of the Latin pallium.[76] This right of imposing the pallium is chiefly exercised by the Maronite patriarch[77] and the Armenian patri-

---

[75] Benedictus XIV, *Neminem vestrum*, 1754: "Nobis notum est Orientales Patriarchas, post receptum a Nobis pallium, potiri privilegio illud concedendi metropolitanis suæ iurisdictioni subiectis, iuxta Decretalem Innocentii III, in Cap. *Antiqua, de privilegiis* (c. 23, X, *de privilegiis et excessibus privilegiatorum*, V, 33) et etiam insigniorum Ecclesiarum Episcopis, iuxta consuetudinem....Concedendi prædictis usum pallii restrictum est ad pallium largius et longius, crucibus rubris et plurimum distinctum, quod est pallium græcum, nec se extendit ad pallium latinum, quod ipse a Nobis recepturus est: hoc enim ipse solus uti potest diebus et locis præscriptis, nec eius usum ulli alii concedere valet, cum pallii latini concessio soli Romano Pontifici reservata sit." —*Fonti*, Serie I, Fascicolo I, *Testi Vari di Diritto Nuovo (1550-1902)* (Tipografia Poliglotta Vaticana, 1930, ristampa 1933), p. 327.

[76] *Loc. cit.*

[77] Synodus Montis Libani (1736), Pars III, cap. VI, n. 7, XXIII: "Duplex est patriarchæ pallium, quod omophorion, epitrachelion seu superhumerale dicitur. Alterum brevius ex lana alba contextum et crucibus nigris ornatum, quod a Summo Pontifice novo patriarchæ vel archiepiscopo traditur de corpore beati Petri sumptum, in quo est plenitudo pontificalis officii, ut illo utatur intra ecclesiam suam certis diebus, qui exprimuntur in privilegiis ab Apostolica Sede concessis. Alterum largius et longius, in modum stolæ magnæ pontificiæ ex serico confectum, phrygio etiam opere ornatum et crucibus ut plurimum rubeis distinctum. Isto utitur patriarcha statim a sua consecratione; est enim unum ex indumentis patriarchalibus, in omnibus sacris functionibus adhibendum, quotiescumque patriarcha paramentis pontificiis induitur, et alterum pallium non adhibet. Illo vero, quod Romanus Pontifex concedit, non potest uti extra suum patriarchatum, et non omni tempore, sed tantum in ecclesiis, in missarum solemniis, in festis præcipuis, non in processionibus, neque in missis pro defunctis; et quia pallium istud est personale, ideo commodari non potest, neque in morte alicui relinqui, sed patriarcha cum eo sepeliri debet. Postquam autem istud a Summo Pontifice obtinuerit, poterit et ipse patriarcha suis suffraganeis pallium largiri, illud scilicet largius et longius, quod in ecclesia orientali metropolitanis tantum, vel insigniorum ecclesiarum episcopis conceditur, certis item diebus intra ecclesiam suam adhibendum, sic tamen ut monasticum schema ab omnibus retineatur, quemadmodum præcepit sacrosancta VIII Synodus [Constantinop. IV, an. 870, can. 2]." —*Coll. Lac.*, II, 343-344. Cf. *Fonti*, Serie I, fasc. XII, n. 1127, *supra*, p. 394, footnote 70. *Fonti*, Serie I, fasc. XII, n. 1061, quotes the last sentence of this long passage. Mansi, XXXVIII, 219.

arch. In other rites metropolitans do not have a special omophorion which can be given to mere titular bishops.[78]

In Russia, metropolitans, outside of those of Kiev and especially of Moscow, are equivalent in all things to bishops. In the Balkan Peninsula, among the Greeks and the Bulgarians, all the bishops of the Dissidents have the title of metropolitan.

SECTION C

RIGHTS AND OBLIGATIONS OF METROPOLITANS OUTSIDE OF PATRIARCHATES

Article 1. Metropolitan Sees of the Rumanians, Ruthenians and Malabars

The Rumanians (Slav-Byzantine Discipline) have a metropolitan see which is not connected with any patriarchate. This metropolitan see of Făgăraş and Alba-Julia was restored by Pius IX on the 6th of December, 1853.[79] At present it has four suffragan sees namely: Cluj-Gherla (Kalozsvár-Szamos-Ujvár, in Hungary), Oradea Mare (Nagy-Várad, Gran Varadino, Grosswardein, in Hungary), Lugoj (Lugas, in Rumania) and Maramureş (Nagy-Bánya, Baia Mare, in Hungary).[80] The Ruthenians (Slav-Byzantine Discipline) had Kiev as their metropolitan see from 1596 to 1807, although the metropolitans could not always reside there.[81] The Bull of Pius VII entitled "*In universalis Ecclesiæ regimine*" (February 22, 1807) raised the episcopal see of Lemberg (Lwów) to the archiepiscopal dignity and con-

---

[78] *Synodus Sciarfensis*, p. 213, n. 7. Cf. *supra*, p. 300, footnote 5.

[79] Bulla "*Ecclesiam Christi*," — Mansi, XLII, 620-626.

[80] *Statistica*, pp. 165-168.

[81] *Statistica*, p. 178. Cf. *Fonti*, Serie I, fasc. XI, n. 436.

joined it to the metropolitan see of Halicz.[82] From that time it has been known as the metropolitan see of Halicz. The Ruthenians received the prescripts of the Council of Trent, hence they have accepted all the decrees enacted by it on metropolitans.[83] Ruthenians of the Oriental Church are dispersed throughout the world,[84] yet, in spite of this, the metropolitan of Halicz enjoys jurisdiction only over two suffragan eparchies (dioceses), namely, Przemyśl and Stanislawów in Poland.[85] The other bishops of the Ruthenian Discipline are immediately subject to the Apostolic See.

The Malabars (Chaldean Discipline), who do not have any written law since they were converted by Latin missionaries, use the Latin Discipline in almost everything but their rite.[86] Their metropolitan see is that of Ernakulam,

---

[82] *Statistica*, pp. 191-192. Cf. *Fonti*, Serie I, fasc. XI, nn. 433 and 435. The metropolitan see of Halicz is united to the archiepiscopal see of Lemberg, even though the name *Halicz* could lead one to think that it is completely independent. During the 1596-1807 period, dissident metropolitans also resided in Kiev alongside with the Catholic metropolitans. Between 1806 and 1838 there was also a Catholic metropolitan in czarist Russia. This metropolitan see was suppressed in 1839. Cf. *Statistica*, p. 184.

[83] "Porro licet iura metropolitica antiqua supra recensita a Clemente PP. VIII concessa, atque a Pio VII confirmata fuerint, attamen eo quod regimen præsens Ecclesiarum etiam nostrarum ferme ad Concilii Tridentini normam redactum fuerit, ideo etiam iura Metropolitæ Haliciensis plus minusve eadem sunt, quæ de communi iure omnibus metropolitis competunt, hoc uno excepto, quo usque nunc Metropolita Haliciensis utitur, nempe Sedis Apostolicæ nomine confirmandi atque instituendi Episcopum Præmisliensem eique munus consecrationis conferendi, atque ex novissima S. Sedis concessione etiam relate ad Episcopum Stanislaopolitanum." —*Fonti*, Serie I, Fascicolo XI, *Ius Particulare Ruthenorum* (Tipografia Poliglotta Vaticana, 1933), n. 433. Cf. *Acts and Decrees of the Ukrainian Provincial Synod of Galicia, Lemberg, 1891* (Lemberg: Stavropihiskoho Instituta, 1896), Tit. VII, cap. II, n. 3, pp. 193-194 (hereafter cited as *Synodus Leopolitana*). Since this latter work is in the Ukranian language, the writer will simply make pertinent citations rather than quotations from the work.

[84] Cf. Coussa, *Epitome*, I, 21-23. *Statistica* (pp. 169-220) records that Ruthenians are found in Prussia, Austria, Russia, Poland, Czechoslovakia, Rumania, the United States of America, Canada, the Argentine and Brazil. However this listing is outdated, and they can now be found in many other countries.

[85] *Statistica*, pp. 195-197.

[86] Coussa, *Epitome*, I, 39-41.

erected on December 21, 1923, and it has three suffragan sees: Changanacherry, Trichur, Kottayam.[87]

Article 2. Rights and Obligations in Conformity with the Latin Code

In general, the Rumanian, the Ruthenian and Malabar metropolitans, who hold the metropolitan sees treated above, are bound by canons 272-280 of the Latin Code which refer to metropolitans.

The rights of Latin metropolitans are specified in canon 274. The metropolitans of the Rumanian, Ruthenian and Malabar rites have only certain of these rights. Canon 274, 1°, speaks of the metropolitan right to institute those who are presented for institution in patronal benefices should the suffragan neglect to do so. The Concordat entered into between the Holy See and Rumania on the 10th of May, 1927, cancelled the right of patronage.[88] No such cancellation of the right of patronage is found in the Concordat drawn between the Holy See and the Republic of Poland. Hence it seems that the Ruthenian metropolitan may follow the prescript of canon 274, 1°. The same can be said for the Malabar metropolitan.

The Rumanian metropolitan has the right of vigilance mentioned in canon 274, 4°, for it was granted to him by the I Council of Alba-Julia and Făgăraş (1872).[89] It is greater

---

[87] *Statistica*, pp. 254-256.

[88] Art. XV: "Les droits et les obligations de patronat de toute catégorie sont et restent abolis sans aucun indemnité." — Perugini, *Concordata Vigentia, Notis Historicis et Iuridicis Declarata* (Romæ: Apud Custodiam Librariam Pont. Instituti Utriusque Iuris, 1934), p. 153 (hereafter cited as *Concordata Vigentia*). Cf. canons 1450; 1451; 1571, § 1.

[89] Tit. II, c. III, n. 6: "Metropolita qua caput totius Provinciæ ius habet fidei integritati, morum puritati, ss. canonum observantiæ, cultusque divini uniformitati invigilandi. Ad abusus vero hisce sub respectibus occurentes tollendos, casu necessitatis in Synodo provinciali comprobatas visitationes quoque canonicas instituendi." — *Fonti*, Serie I, Fascicolo X, *Disciplina Bizantina: Rumeni, Testi di Diritto Particolare dei Rumeni* (Tipografia Poliglotta Vaticana, 1933), n. 793; cf. Mansi, XLII, 514.

than that which Latin metropolitans have inasmuch, since he does not need to report abuses to the Roman Pontiff.

Canon 274, 5°, treats of the canonical visitation of suffragan sees in cases in which the suffragan bishop neglects to do so. This right is given to all three metropolitans outside of the patriarchates by the general law enunciated in canon 19 of IV Council of Constantinople. The exercise of this right requires necessity and the approval of the provincial council.[90]

The Rumanian metropolitan has the right to receive appeals from the definitive sentences rendered by his suffragans in keeping with canon 274, 7°. The I Council of Alba-Julia and Făgăraş (1872) gives him this right.[91] The Lemberg Synod (1891) gave this right to the Ruthenian metropolitan.[92]

Canons 275-279 treat of the rights and obligations connected with the pallium. The Rumanian metropolitan has the right to ask for the pallium from the Roman Pontiff, nevertheless, the I Council of Alba-Julia and Făgăraş did not determine the time within which the metropolitan is obliged to ask for it.[93] The Ruthenian metropolitan has the same obligation of asking for the Latin pallium.[94] Both the Rumanian and the Ruthenian metropolitans must follow the rulings of the Latin Code concerning the use of the pallium. Like the Latin metropolitans they can use it during

---

[90] Cf. *Fonti,* Serie I, fasc. IX, n. 597; *supra,* pp. 385-386. Cf. *Fonti,* Serie II, fasc. V, nn. 77, 78, 460.

[91] Tit. II, c. III, n. 4: "Metropolita ius habet in omnibus causis ecclesiasticis appellationes a foris episcopalibus recipiendi." — *Fonti,* Serie I, fasc. X, n. 791. Cf. Mansi, XLV, 766. The II Council of Alba-Julia (1882) adds a bit more to this legislation. Cf. Tit. V, c. III, n. 60: "A foris protopopabilibus in archidiœcesi fiunt appellationes ad consistorium archiepiscopale qua forum II instantiæ. A consistorio archidiœcesano vero promoventur appellationes ad ipsam apostolicam sedem." — Mansi, XLV, 766.

[92] *Synodus Leopolitana,* Tit. XIII, n. 3, p. 253.

[93] Tit. II, c. III, n. 7: "Metropolita ius habet...pallium de corpore S. Petri acceptum veluti iurisdictionis archiepiscopalis insigne gestandi." — *Fonti,* Serie I, fasc. X, n. 876; Mansi, XLII, 514.

[94] *Synodus Leopolitana* (1891), Tit. VII, c. II, n. 4, p. 194.

the solemnities of the Liturgy within all the churches of their province, even those churches which are exempt. They cannot use it outside their provinces, even though they may have the consent of the local ordinary. This is in keeping with canon 277.

The rights conferred by canon 284 concerning the convocation of provincial synods and the right to preside at them are enjoyed by both the Rumanian and the Ruthenian metropolitans. The I Council of Alba-Julia and Făgăraş granted this right to the Rumanian metropolitan in no uncertain terms.[95] The Zamość Council (1720) gave this right to the Ruthenian metropolitan.[96]

Article 3. Rights and Obligations Outside the Scope of the Latin Code

The Rumanian and Ruthenian metropolitans have certain other attributes accorded them by their respective councils. These attributes regard their election, commemoration in the divine Liturgy, the confirmation of the election of their suffragans, and the consecration of their comprovincial bishops.

The Rumanian metropolitan of Făgăraş and Alba-Julia is chosen by the Roman Pontiff from among those presented to him by a group of electors. This group of electors con-

---

[95] Tit. III, c. III, n. 3: "Synodus provincialis est congregatio episcoporum unius provinciæ ecclesiasticæ sub metropolitani præsidio in negotiis ecclesiasticis bonum totius provinciæ respectibus habita.... Synodum provincialium convocatio est exclusivum metropolitani ius, qui iisdem et præest. Locum ac tempus celebrationis synodi provincialis quam singulis trienniis celebrari optandum esset, metropolita defigit." — Mansi, XLII, 532, 534. Tit. II, c. III, n. 3: "Metropolita qua caput provinciæ ius habet Synodos provinciales, ubi ipse satius duxerit, convocandi, iisdem præsidendi, agendorum ordinem dirigendi, fraterneque illos corripiendi, qui absque legitima causa non convenirent." — *Fonti*, Serie I, fasc. X, n. 361; cf. Mansi, XLII, 514.

[96] Tit. V: "In hoc autem potissimum incumbat, ut decreta hujus Synodi observentur in tota provincia, eaque de causa, et post necessariam Sanctæ Sedis approbationem, statim suffraganeis innotescant, et in tota provincia promulgentur." — *Coll. Lac.*, II, 46; cf. Mansi, XXXV B, 1506; *Fonti*, Serie I, fasc. XI, n. 438.

sists of the suffragan bishops, the canons of the metropolitan church, and certain deputed persons from each of the eparchies. The I Council of Alba-Julia and Făgăraş (1872) gives the ruling on this point.[97] Recently the number of electors, that is of those having the right to vote, has been reduced to one hundred by the Sacred Congregation of the Oriental Church.[98]

The Rumanian metropolitan has the right to be commemorated in the divine Liturgy and the divine office immediately after the Roman Pontiff. This is specified by one of the decrees of the I Council of Alba-Julia and Făgăraş.[99] The Ruthenian metropolitan has this right also. It was given him by the Lemberg Synod (1891).[100]

---

[97] Tit. II, c. III, n. 3: "...sede episcopali metropolitana in vacantiam deveniente, senior Episcoporum Suffraganeorum, collatis cum Ordinariatu metropolitano cæterisque comprovincialibus Episcopis consiliis, sollicitudinem impendere tenetur, ut sedes metropolitana compleatur, ipse actum electionis seu designationis moderando, examinat candidatorum habilitatem, propositionemque pro sede vacante metropolitana [complenda] substernit." — *Fonti*, Serie I, fasc. X, n. 798; cf. Mansi, XLII, 514. Cf. The text in *Fonti* does not include the word "*complenda*," whereas Mansi uses it.

[98] Cf. Coussa, *Epitome*, I, 170. The Rumanian Dissidents have a patriarch for all of Rumania, who is at the same time the metropolitan of the province of Bucharest (Bucureşti) and of the following metropolitans: Sibiu, Jaşi, Chişinău and Cernăuţi, to which the new metropolis of Curtea de Argeş was added in 1939. Cf. *op. cit.*, *ibid.*, footnote 226. *Statistica* (p. 168) mentions that the patriarch has three metropolitans subject to him: Jaşi, Cernăuţi and Chişinău. It does not include Sibiu. It has nothing to say about this dissident patriarch as a superior type of metropolitan who heads other metropolitans.

[99] Tit. II, c. III, n. 1: "Metropolita habet ius ut ab Episcopis prout et clero in Sacra Liturgia aliisque publicis precibus commemoretur." — *Fonti*, Serie I, fasc. X, n. 328; cf. Mansi, XLII, 518. Cf. Tit. II, c. IV, n. 3: "Episcopi denique iuribus quoque honorificis gaudent...exigendi ab universo clero, qui post Romani Pontificis et Metropolitæ commemorationem obligatur Episcopi nomen in S. Liturgia aliisque publicis precibus referre." — *Fonti*, Serie I, fasc. X, n. 327; cf. Mansi, XLII, 518. Cf. Tit. II, c. IX, n. 1: "Parochi iure pollent...presbyteris peregrinis facultatem concedendi, ut in ecclesia parochiali sacram Liturgiam celebrare sive aliam quamcumque functionem peragere possint, qui tamen in precibus Romanum Pontificem, Metropolitam, atque diœcesis Episcopum commemorare obligati sunt." — *Fonti*, Serie I, fasc. X, n. 329; cf. Mansi, XLII, 527, 528.

[100] *Synodus Leopolitana*, Tit. VII, c. II, n. 4, p. 194.

Both metropolitans have the right to arrange the election of bishops and to examine those elected together with the suffragan bishops in accord with the canons, as well as the obligation to report the election to the Roman Pontiff. The I Council of Alba-Julia and Făgăraş made this provision for the Rumanian metropolitan.[101] The nomination of the Rumanian bishops is reserved to the Apostolic See in accordance with canon 329, § 2. The same arrangement holds for the Ruthenian bishops with the special provision made in the Concordat drawn up between the Holy See and the Republic of Poland on June 2, 1925, that the nominated candidate obtain a political *"nihil obstat"* from the president of the country.[102]

By the decree of the I Council of Alba-Julia and Făgăraş (1872), the Rumanian metropolitan has the right to consecrate and to enthrone the bishops who have been nominated by the Roman Pontiff. He may exercise this right only after the elected bishop has received pontifical institution and the mandate for his consecration.[103]

Further, the Rumanian metropolitan has the right to

[101] Tit. II, c. III, n. 3: "Metropolita qua caput provinciæ ius habet... Episcoporum electiones, ubi usus tenet, moderandi, una cum Episcopis suffraganeis promovendorum scientiam et habilitatem examinandi, de eoque sibi persuasionem procurandi...." — *Fonti*, Serie I, fasc. X, n. 789; cf. Mansi, XLII, 514. Cf. Coussa (*Epitome*, I, 170, footnote 229) says that the metropolitan proposes the names of the candidates to the nuncio of the Holy See. The clergy of the vacant eparchy have no right to make the presentation.

[102] Art. XI: "Le choix des Archevêques et des Evêques appartient au Saint-Siège. Sa Sainteté consent à s' adresser au Président de la République, avant de nommer les Archevêques et les Evêques diocésains, les coadjuteurs *cum iure successionis*, de même que l' Evêque d'Armée, pour s' assurer que le Président n'a pas de raisons de caractère politique à soulever contre ces choix." — Perugini, *Concordata Vigentia*, p. 38. Art. IX gives the enumeration and circumscription of the Oriental province, archdioceses and dioceses. Cf. *op. cit.*, pp. 36-37. The unsettled condition of Poland today hardly warrants the statement that these conditions hold at present.

[103] Tit. II, c. III, n. 3: "Metropolita qua caput provinciæ ius habet... electum [Episcopum] consecrandi postquam electus canonicam institutionem a Romano Pontifice, et Apostolicum suæ consecrationis mandatum receperit." — *Fonti*, Serie I, fasc. X, n. 538; cf. Mansi, XLII, 514.

compel bishops to return to residence if they are absent without a canonical cause. The I Council of Alba-Julia and Făgăraş clearly specifies this.[104] The metropolitan of the Ruthenians has wider power, namely that of supplying the defects of suffragans in the administration of the eparchy; of admonishing them in a paternal fashion concerning their office, and even of urging that they fulfill his admonition or of referring the matter to the Holy See. The Council of Zamość (1720) made provision for all these rights in its 5th decree.[105] He has the right to constitute a chancellor in a suffragan see if the comprovincial bishop neglects to make a choice.[106]

The Rumanian metropolitan has the right to take care of the vacant episcopal churches and by reason of devolved right to nominate the vicar capitular. This is in keeping with one of the decrees of the I Council of Alba-Julia and Făgăraş.[107] Among the Ruthenians, once a suffragan see is vacant, the chapter is to elect two vicars: one for the administration of the spiritualities of the eparchy, and the other for the administration of the goods of the *mensa episcopalis*. The metropolitan has the right to confirm the elected vicars.[108] If there is no chapter, the Ruthenian metro-

---

[104] Tit. II, c. III, n. 5: "Metropolita ius habet provinciæ Episcopos absque causis canonicis absentes ad residendum compellendi." — *Fonti*, Serie I, fasc. X, n. 559; cf. Mansi, XLII, 514.

[105] "Cum metropolitanus respectu suorum suffraganeorum pastor sit ac dicatur, eoque nomine mediatam totius provinciæ curam gerat, sedulo curare debet, ut eorum defectus, si qui sunt in administratione diœcesis, ipse suppleat, eos officii sui paterne moneat ac etiam ad illud recte obeundum aliquando cogat, aut ad Sedem Apostolicam deferat." — *Coll. Lac.*, II, 46; cf. Mansi, XXXV B, 1506; *Fonti*, Serie I, fasc. XI, n. 438.

[106] Tit. VIII: "Quia præter officialem Episcopo summe necessarius est cancellarius sive notarius, statuit Synodus, ut quilibet ipsum assumat post duos menses a promulgatione horum decretorum, alias pro negligentibus a Metropolitano constituatur." — *Coll. Lac.*, II, 52; cf. Mansi, XXXV B, 1512.

[107] Tit. II, c. III, n. 5: "Metropolita habet ius... Ecclesiarum episcopalium vacantium curam gerendi, devolutionisque ius circa Vicarii Capitularis electionem exercendi." — *Fonti*, Serie I, fasc. X, n. 788; cf. Mansi, XLII, 514.

[108] *Synodus Leopolitana* (1891), Tit. VII, c. II, n. 5: "Cæterum vigentibus adhuc dispositionibus Synodi Zamosciensis quoad obligationes Metropolitarum, modificatio facienda venit solummodo circa adminis-

politan administers the vacant eparchy personally or through one of the neighboring bishops. The administrator, whoever he may be, is bound to render a most exact account of his stewardship to the future bishop of the vacant eparchy.[109]

Among the Malabars, once an episcopal see is vacant, the metropolitan enjoys the right of presiding at the gathering of the consultors of the suffragan eparchies, called for the election of an administrator of the vacant eparchy.[110] Concerning the institution of the administrator, there is no fixed or certain law among the Malabars. Within eight days from the reception of the notice that the see is vacant, the eparchal council is to be called by the metropolitan, or by the oldest suffragan if it is the metropoltan see which is vacant. With the metropolitan as presiding officer, the council chooses the administrator in accordance with the norms of election. If the votes are equal, the tie is broken by the vote of the presiding officer.[111]

---

trationem Diœcesium sede vacante in illis Capitulis, quæ confirmationem suam nec non statutorum suorum approbationem a S. Sede obtinuerunt, quoad duos Vicarios, quorum nempe unum eadem Capitula statim post Episcopi obitum pro administratione spirituali Diœceseos, alterum vero pro administratione temporalium seu bonorum ad mensam episcopalem spectantium eligere tenentur. Horum autem Vicariorum confirmatio a Metropolita petenda est." — *Fonti*, Serie I, fasc. XI, n. 437.

[109] Council of Zamość (1720), Tit. V: "Cum vacaverit aliqua sedes episcopalis, Metropolitanus, vel per se ipsum, vel per Episcopum viciniorem, Ecclesiam administret tam in spiritualibus, quam in temporalibus; si vero sedes ipsa metropolitana vacaverit, antequam administrator a Sancta Sede constituatur, vicinior Episcopus, scilicet, Archiepiscopus Polocensis, eamdem tam quoad spiritualia, quam quoad temporalia regat. Aliam autem Ecclesiam, si quam præter metropolitana, prout fieri solet, obtinebat, vicinior Episcopus administrabit, ita tamen, ut administrator, quicumque is fuerit, exactissimam rationem futuro Episcopo reddere teneatur." — *Fonti*, Serie I, fasc. XI, n. 434; cf. *Coll. Lac.*, II, 46; Mansi, XXXV B, 1506.

[110] The one deputed to administer the vacant eparchy is called an eparchal administrator and not a vicar capitular, for the Malabars do not have the institute of vicar capitular.

[111] Coussa, *Epitome*, I, 172. No law enumerates the rights and the duties of the administrator. In general, it seems that these are the same as those of a vicar capitular. The business of the eparchy is taken care of by the vicar general, or if such a one is lacking, by the oldest of the consultors, until such a time as the administrator is elected. Cf. *op. cit.*, *ibid.*, footnote 237.

Both the Rumanian and the Ruthenian metropolitans have the right to approve for use in the entire province the liturgical books, composed, in accordance with the editions approved by the Holy See, by commissions of learned priests chosen for this task by the respective metropolitans. The metropolitans give the necessary permission that these may be printed. The Rumanian metropolitan received this right in the III Council of Alba-Julia (1900);[112] the Ruthenian metropolitan in the Lemberg Council (1891).[113]

They also have the right to become acquainted with the major affairs of the province and to expedite them together with their suffragans. The I Council of Alba-Julia and Fărăgaş (1872) made this ruling for the Rumanian metropolitan.[114] The Council of Zamość (1720) guaranteed this right to the Ruthenian metropolitan in Title V of its decrees.[115]

The Ruthenian metropolitan has the right to see to it that the rules of monastic life are strictly observed in practice.[116]

---

[112] Tit. III, c. I, n. 1: "...in usu liturgico solummodo libri adhibeantur, quos Ordinariatus Metropolitanus Alba-Iuliensis et Fagarasiensis approbaverit et Apostolica Sedes legitimos recognoverit." — *Fonti*, Serie I, fasc. X, n. 712. Cf. I Council of Alba-Julia and Făgăraş (1872), Tit. VI, c. VI — Mansi, XLII, 568, 570.

[113] *Synodus Leopolitana*, Tit. II, pp. 91-104; Tit. IV, c. III, n. 4, p. 119.

[114] Tit. II, c. III, n. 2: "Metropolita ius habet exigendi, ut Episcopi nihil magni momenti, bonumque totius Provinciæ respiciens absque scitu et cooperatione Metropolitæ adgrediantur." — *Fonti*, Serie I, fasc. X, n. 557; cf. Mansi, XLII, 514. Cf. III Council of Alba-Julia (1900), Tit. II, c. II, n. 4; the 9th canon of the Council of Antioch (341): *Fonti*, Serie I, fasc. IX, n. 759, *supra*, p. 385; canon 34 of the *Canones Apostolorum: Fonti*, Serie I, fasc. IX, n. 762. Aristenus comments in this regard: "Nec episcopi, nec metropolitæ sine sententia primatis sui debent aliquid magni momenti facere, ut episcopos eligere, in nova dogmata quærere, vel alienationes ecclesiasticorum ullorum facere, sed tantum ea quæ spectant ad cuiusque parœciam, et ad loca sibi subiecta. Sed nec primus absque eorum sententia potest aliquid eiusmodi facere. Sic enim concordiæ terminus conservabitur." — *Fonti*, Serie II, fasc. V, n. 73. Cf. *ibid.*, nn. 74, 75. Cf. *supra*, p. 383.

[115] Cf. *Coll. Lac.*, II, 46; Mansi, XXXV B, 1506; cf. *supra*, p. 401.

[116] *Synodus Leopolitana* (1891), Tit. X, n. 3, p. 239.

CONCLUSIONS

As a result of this study the following conclusions are offered:

1. The metropolitan institution antedated the Council of Nicæa (325) since canons 4 and 6 of the aforesaid Council already spoke of it in the terms of a stabilized intermediary grade of the Catholic hierarchy. A combination of ecclesiastical and civil causes brought the metropolitan institution into being.

2. The metropolitan institution was considered a practical intermediary hierarchical grade in the Eastern Church, and as a consequence its power was allowed to grow juridically through progressive conciliar legislation up to the 10th century. The breakdown of the metropolitan institution in the Western Church during this same period of history proves that the utility of this institution was not recognized, except by the Popes who endeavored not only to maintain it but to stabilize its power.

3. The False Decretals, in their attempt to weaken the position of metropolitans, did much to strengthen the juridic position of the papacy and of the episcopacy, and contributed thereby in no small measure to the pre-Code stabilization of metropolitan power in the Latin Discipline. The growth of patriarchal power in the Eastern Discipline of the Catholic Church, together with other historical factors, did all but destroy the metropolitan institution within the Oriental patriarchates.

4. The inclusion of canons 271-280 in the Latin Code speaks for the maintenance of the metropolitan grade within the hierarchy of the Latin Church. The synodal legislation, old and new, gives the assurance that the metropolitan institute in the Oriental Catholic Church, now absorbed by that of the patriarchal one, will be revived in the patriarchates when civil and ecclesiastical conditions will have been ameliorated in the East.

5. The terms and institutes *metropolitan* and *archbishop* are not altogether synonymous in the Western Church: every metropolitan is an archbishop, but not every archbishop is a metropolitan. Canons 272-279 refer to metropolitans, and not to archbishops.

6. An ecclesiastical province, over which a metropolitan presides, includes not only dioceses, but abbacies and prelacies *nullius*, vicariates and prefectures apostolic. An ecclesiastical province is a non-collegiate moral person which must be described as an ecclesiastical benefice. The erection and circumscription of such is a *causa maior*, reserved to the Supreme Pontiff.

7. Once a bishop is consecrated, he becomes a metropolitan in the Latin Discipline immediately upon taking canonical possession of the metropolitan see to which he has been canonically appointed by the Roman Pontiff. The special provisions of synodal legislation and patriarchal privilege make different arrangements for the confirmation, and at times also for the actual nomination of metropolitans in the Oriental Discipline.

8. The Latin pallium is a symbol of archiepiscopal dignity; it does not actually confer metropolitan power. The Greek pallium, called the omophorion, is only a liturgical vestment.

9. The metropolitan of the Latin Church can exercise all forms of episcopal and metropolitan jurisdiction within his archdiocese and province respectively immediately after taking canonical possession of his metropolitan see, even before the imposition of the pallium. Only those acts of metropolitan jurisdiction and episcopal orders are illicit before the imposition of the pallium for which the liturgical laws require its use. The exercise of these acts for which liturgical law requires the use of the pallium would be valid but not licit in case the pallium were not canonically imposed, or if imposed, it were not worn.

10. Canon 274 of the Latin Code offers a comprehensive enumeration of the administrative and judicial rights and

obligations of Latin metropolitans. Custom cannot increase their number, although the specifications listed in Concordats drawn up between the Holy See and States can do so. The nature of the rights and obligations of the Oriental metropolitans depends upon their intra- or extra-patriarchal status, the general legislation of the Oriental Discipline, and the particular laws of each Rite.

11. Inasmuch as canon 274 limits the metropolitan's rights and obligations through its all-inclusive enumeration of them, the interpretation of each norm within the canon must be strict, i.e., all must interfere as little as possible with the metropolitan's rights.

12. In keeping with the correct interpretation of canon 274, a metropolitan, no longer has the right: (a) to correct abuses in the dioceses of his suffragans; (b) to punish any cleric subject to his suffragans, except during a visitation if some manifest and notorious offenses should be directed against him or any member of his retinue; (c) to accept all cases of appeal, but he may accept only those which follow a definitive sentence or an interlocutory sentence with a definitive effect rendered in the tribunals of suffragans; and (d) to accept any first instance causes coming from the dioceses of his suffragans, except the controversies mentioned in canon 1572, § 2.

APPENDIX A

Provincial Arrangement in the United States

PROVINCE OF BALTIMORE
(April 8, 1808)

Includes the States of Maryland, Delaware, Virginia, West Virginia, North Carolina, South Carolina, Georgia, and the Eastern part of Florida

Archdiocese of Baltimore, Maryland

Diocese of Charleston, South Carolina
Diocese of Raleigh, North Carolina
Diocese of Richmond, Virginia
Diocese of St. Augustine, Florida
Diocese of Savannah-Atlanta, Georgia
Diocese of Wheeling, West Virginia
Diocese of Wilmington, Delaware
Abbacy *Nullius* of Belmont, North Carolina

Archdiocese of Washington, D. C. *(Immediately subject to the Holy See)*

PROVINCE OF BOSTON
(February 12, 1875)

Includes the New England States

Archdiocese of Boston, Massachusetts

Diocese of Burlington, Vermont
Diocese of Fall River, Massachusetts
Diocese of Hartford, Connecticut
Diocese of Manchester, New Hampshire
Diocese of Portland, Maine
Diocese of Providence, Rhode Island
Diocese of Springfield, Massachusetts

PROVINCE OF CHICAGO
(September 10, 1880)

Includes the State of Illinois

Archdiocese of Chicago, Illinois

Diocese of Belleville, Illinois
Diocese of Peoria, Illinois
Diocese of Rockford, Illinois
Diocese of Springfield, Illinois

PROVINCE OF CINCINNATI
(July 19, 1850)

Includes the State of Ohio
Archdiocese of Cincinnati, Ohio
Diocese of Cleveland, Ohio
Diocese of Columbus, Ohio
Diocese of Steubenville, Ohio
Diocese of Toledo, Ohio
Diocese of Youngstown, Ohio

PROVINCE OF DENVER
(November 15, 1941)

Includes the States of Colorado and Wyoming
Archdiocese of Denver, Colorado
Diocese of Cheyenne, Wyoming
Diocese of Pueblo, Colorado

PROVINCE OF DETROIT
(May 22, 1937)

Includes the State of Michigan
Archdiocese of Detroit, Michigan
Diocese of Grand Rapids, Michigan
Diocese of Lansing, Michigan
Diocese of Marquette, Michigan
Diocese of Saginaw, Michigan

PROVINCE OF DUBUQUE
(June 15, 1893)

Includes the State of Iowa
Archdiocese of Dubuque, Iowa
Diocese of Davenport, Iowa
Diocese of Des Moines, Iowa
Diocese of Sioux City, Iowa

PROVINCE OF INDIANAPOLIS
(December 19, 1944)

Includes the State of Indiana
Archdiocese of Indianapolis, Indiana
Diocese of Evansville, Indiana
Diocese of Fort Wayne, Indiana
Diocese of Lafayette, Indiana

PROVINCE OF LOS ANGELES
(July 11, 1936)

Includes Southern California and Southern Arizona
Archdiocese of Los Angeles, California
Diocese of Monterey-Fresno, California
Diocese of San Diego, California
Diocese of Tucson, Arizona

PROVINCE OF LOUISVILLE
(December 10, 1937)

Includes the States of Kentucky and Tennessee
Archdiocese of Louisville, Kentucky
Diocese of Covington, Kentucky
Diocese of Nashville, Tennessee
Diocese of Owensboro, Kentucky

PROVINCE OF MILWAUKEE
(February 12, 1875)

Includes the State of Wisconsin
Archdiocese of Milwaukee, Wisconsin
Diocese of Green Bay, Wisconsin
Diocese of La Crosse, Wisconsin
Diocese of Madison, Wisconsin
Diocese of Superior, Wisconsin

PROVINCE OF NEWARK
(December 10, 1937)

Includes the State of New Jersey
Archdiocese of Newark, New Jersey
Diocese of Camden, New Jersey
Diocese of Paterson, New Jersey
Diocese of Trenton, New Jersey

PROVINCE OF NEW ORLEANS
(July 19, 1850)

Includes the States of Louisiana, Alabama, Mississippi, Arkansas, and the Western part of Florida
Archdiocese of New Orleans, Louisiana
Diocese of Alexandria, Louisiana
Diocese of Lafayette, Louisiana
Diocese of Little Rock, Arkansas
Diocese of Mobile, Alabama
Diocese of Natchez, Mississippi

PROVINCE OF NEW YORK
(July 19, 1850)

Includes the State of New York
Archdiocese of New York, New York
Diocese of Albany, New York
Diocese of Brooklyn, New York
Diocese of Buffalo, New York
Diocese of Ogdensburg, New York
Diocese of Rochester, New York
Diocese of Syracuse, New York

PROVINCE OF OMAHA
(August 7, 1945)

Includes the State of Nebraska

Archdiocese of Omaha, Nebraska

Diocese of Grand Island, Nebraska
Diocese of Lincoln, Nebraska

PROVINCE OF PHILADELPHIA
(February 12, 1875)

Includes the State of Pennsylvania

Archdiocese of Philadelphia, Pennsylvania

Diocese of Altoona, Pennsylvania
Diocese of Erie, Pennsylvania
Diocese of Harrisburg, Pennsylvania
Diocese of Pittsburgh, Pennsylvania
Diocese of Scranton, Pennsylvania

PROVINCE OF PORTLAND IN OREGON
(July 24, 1846)

Includes the States of Oregon, Washington, Idaho, Montana and the Territory of Alaska

Archdiocese of Portland, Oregon

Diocese of Baker City, Oregon
Diocese of Boise, Idaho
Diocese of Great Falls, Montana
Diocese of Helena, Montana
Diocese of Seattle, Washington
Diocese of Spokane, Washington
Vicariate Apostolic of Alaska

PROVINCE OF ST. LOUIS
(July 20, 1847)

Includes the States of Missouri and Kansas

Archdiocese of St. Louis, Missouri

Diocese of Kansas City, Kansas
Diocese of Kansas City, Missouri
Diocese of St. Joseph, Missouri
Diocese of Salina, Kansas
Diocese of Wichita, Kansas

PROVINCE OF ST. PAUL
(May 4, 1888)

Includes the States of Minnesota, South Dakota and North Dakota

Archdiocese of St. Paul, Minnesota

Diocese of Bismarck, North Dakota
Diocese of Crookston, Minnesota
Diocese of Duluth, Minnesota

Diocese of Fargo, North Dakota
Diocese of Rapid City, South Dakota
Diocese of St. Cloud, Minnesota
Diocese of Sioux Falls, South Dakota
Diocese of Winona, Minnesota

PROVINCE OF SAN ANTONIO
(August 3, 1926)

Includes the States of Texas (except the Diocese of El Paso) and Oklahoma

Archdiocese of San Antonio, Texas
Diocese of Amarillo, Texas
Diocese of Austin, Texas
Diocese of Corpus Christi, Texas
Diocese of Dallas, Texas
Diocese of Galveston, Texas
Diocese of Oklahoma and Tulsa

PROVINCE OF SAN FRANCISCO
(July 29, 1853)

Includes Northern California, the States of Nevada and Utah, and the Diocese of Honolulu, comprising the Hawaiian Islands and the Islands of Palmyra, Washington, Fanning and Christmas

Archdiocese of San Francisco, California
Diocese of Reno, Nevada
Diocese of Sacramento, California
Diocese of Salt Lake City, Utah
Diocese of Honolulu, Hawaii

PROVINCE OF SANTA FE
(February 12, 1875)

Includes the State of New Mexico, Northern Arizona, and the Diocese of El Paso, Texas

Archdiocese of Santa Fe, New Mexico
Diocese of El Paso, Texas
Diocese of Gallup, New Mexico

IN THE UNITED STATES OF MEXICO

PROVINCE OF MEXICO CITY
(February 12, 1546)

Archdiocese of Mexico City
Diocese of Chilapa
Diocese of Cuernavaca
Diocese of Tulancingo
Diocese of Veracruz

PROVINCE OF MORELLA
(March 19, 1863)

Archdiocese of Morella
- Diocese of Queretaro
- Diocese of Leon
- Diocese of Zamora
- Diocese of Tacambaro

PROVINCE OF GUADALAJARA
(March 19, 1863)

Archdiocese of Guadalajara
- Diocese of Aquas Calientes
- Diocese of Colima
- Diocese of Tepic
- Diocese of Zacatecas

PROVINCE OF ANTEQUERA OR OAXACA
(June 23, 1891)

Archdiocese of Antequera or Oaxaca
- Diocese of Chiapas
- Diocese of Tehuantepec

PROVINCE OF LA PUEBLA DE LOS ANGELES
(August 11, 1906)

Archdiocese of La Puebla de Los Angeles
- Diocese of Huajuapam de Leon
- Diocese of Huejutla
- Diocese of Papantla

PROVINCE OF YUCATAN
(November 11, 1906)

Archdiocese of Yucatan
- Diocese of Campeche
- Diocese of Tabasco

PROVINCE OF DURANGO
(June 23, 1891)

Archdiocese of Durango
- Diocese of Chihuahua
- Diocese of Sinaloa
- Diocese of Sonora

PROVINCE OF MONTERREY
(June 23, 1891)

Archdiocese of Monterrey
- Diocese of San Luis Potosi
- Diocese of Saltillo
- Diocese of Tamaulipas
- Vicariate Apostolic of Lower California

CUBA

PROVINCE OF HAVANA
(December 7, 1925)

Archdiocese of Havana
- Diocese of Matanzas
- Diocese of Pinar del Rio

PROVINCE OF SANTIAGO DE CUBA
(November 24, 1803)

Archdiocese of Santiago de Cuba
- Diocese of Cienfuegos
- Diocese of Camagüey

CANADA

PROVINCE OF EDMONTON
(November 30, 1912)

Archdiocese of Edmonton, Alberta
- Diocese of Calgary
- Vicariate Apostolic of Grouard
- Vicariate Apostolic of Mackenzie

PROVINCE OF HALIFAX
(May 4, 1852)

Archdiocese of Halifax, Nová Scotia
- Diocese of Antigonish
- Diocese of Charlottetown

PROVINCE OF KINGSTON
(December 28, 1889)

Archdiocese of Kingston, Ontario
- Diocese of Alexandria
- Diocese of Peterborough
- Diocese of Sault Ste Marie

PROVINCE OF MONTREAL
(June 8, 1886)

Archdiocese of Montreal, Quebec
- Diocese of Joliette
- Diocese of St. Hyacinthe
- Diocese of Saint-Jean-de-Quebec
- Diocese of Sherbrooke
- Diocese of Valleyfield

PROVINCE OF MONCTON
(February 22, 1936)

Archdiocese of Moncton, New Brunswick
- Diocese of Edmundston
- Diocese of Bathurst
- Diocese of St. John

PROVINCE OF OTTAWA
(June 8, 1886)

Archdiocese of Ottawa, Ontario
- Diocese of Timmins
- Diocese of Mont-Laurier
- Diocese of Pembroke
- Diocese of Hearst
- Vicariate Apostolic of James Bay

PROVINCE OF QUEBEC
(January 12, 1819)

Archdiocese of Quebec, Quebec
- Diocese of Chicoutimi
- Diocese of Gaspé
- Diocese of Nicolet
- Diocese of Rimouski
- Diocese of Trois Rivieres
- Diocese of Amos
- Diocese of the Gulf of St. Lawrence

PROVINCE OF REGINA
(December 4, 1915)

Archdiocese of Regina, Saskatchewan
- Diocese of Prince Albert
- Diocese of Gravelbourg
- Diocese of Saskatoon
- Abbacy *Nullius* of St. Peter, Muenster

PROVINCE OF ST. BONIFACE
(September 22, 1871)

Archdiocese of St. Boniface, Manitoba
- Vicariate Apostolic of Keewatin
- Vicariate Apostolic of Hudson Bay

PROVINCE OF TORONTO
(March 18, 1870)

Archdiocese of Toronto, Ontario
- Diocese of Hamilton
- Diocese of London

PROVINCE OF VANCOUVER
(September 7, 1908)

Archdiocese of Vancouver, British Columbia
- Diocese of Nelson
- Diocese of Victoria
- Vicariate Apostolic of Prince Rupert
- Vicariate Apostolic of Whitehorse (Yukon)

Archdiocese of Winnipeg, Manitoba *(Immediately subject to the Holy See)*

NEWFOUNDLAND

PROVINCE OF ST. JOHN'S, NEWFOUNDLAND
(February 18, 1904)

Archdiocese of St. John's, Newfoundland
- Diocese of Harbor Grace
- Diocese of St. George's

ENGLAND

PROVINCE OF WESTMINSTER
(October 28, 1911)

Archdiocese of Westminster
- Diocese of Brentwood
- Diocese of Northhampton
- Diocese of Nottingham
- Diocese of Portsmouth
- Diocese of Southwark

PROVINCE OF BIRMINGHAM
(October 28, 1911)

Archdiocese of Birmingham
- Diocese of Clifton
- Diocese of Plymough
- Diocese of Shewsbury

PROVINCE OF LIVERPOOL
(October 28, 1911)

Archdiocese of Liverpool
- Diocese of Hexham and Newcastle
- Diocese of Lancaster
- Diocese of Leeds
- Diocese of Middlesborough
- Diocese of Salford

PROVINCE OF CARDIFF
(February 7, 1916)

Archdiocese of Cardiff, Wales
- Diocese of Menevia

SCOTLAND

PROVINCE OF ST. ANDREWS AND EDINBURGH

Archdiocese of St. Andrews and Edinburgh
- Diocese of Aberdeen
- Diocese of Argyll and the Isles
- Diocese of Dunkeld
- Diocese of Galloway

Archdiocese of Glasgow *(Immediately subject to the Holy See)*

APPENDIX B

Provincial Arrangement in the Oriental Catholic Church[1]

I. Oriental Communities in the Proper Territory of the Patriarchate of Rome which are not conjoined with Oriental Patriarchates

- A. The Armenian Discipline
  1. Ordinariate for the Armenians of Greece (Athens)
  2. Administratorship Apostolic for the Armenians of Rumania (Gherla)
- B. The Slav-Byzantine or Greek Discipline
  1. Italo-Greek Diocese of Lungro (Calabria)
  2. Administratorship Apostolic for the parishes of the diocese of Mukačevo (Munkács, with residence at Ungvár [Uzharad]) situated in Hungary and Prešav (Prjašev, Eperjes), situated in Czechoslovakia (Miskalc)
  3. Administratorship Apostolic for the Bulgarians of Byzantine Discipline (Sophia)
  4. Ordinariate for the Ruthenians of the United States who derive from Galicia (Philadelphia)
  5. Ordinariate for the Ruthenians of the United States who derive from Podcarpathia (Homestead)
  6. Ordinariate for the Ruthenians of Canada (Winnipeg)

II. Patriarchate of Constantinople

Ordinariate for the Greek Catholics of the Byzantine Discipline in Turkey and Greece (Constantinople and Athens)

III. Patriarchate of Alexandria

- A. The Alexandrian Discipline
  1. Patriarchate of Alexandria for the Copts (Alexandria)
     Suffragans: Thebes or Luxor (residence at Tahta), Hermopolis Major (residence at Minieh)
- B. The Antiochene Discipline
  Maronite Patriarchal Vicariate of Syria (Cairo)
- C. The Byzantine Discipline
  Melkite Patriarchal Vicariate of Egypt (Cairo)
- D. The Chaldean Discipline
  Patriarchal Vicariate (Cairo)

IV. Patriarchate of Antioch

- A. The Antiochene Discipline
  1. Patriarchate of Antioch for the Maronites (Bekerké=Bikorkī: the residence is at Bekerké in the winter; at Gedaidat — Kannubin in the summer)

---

[1] *Statistica*, pp. 534-537.

Suffragan sees: Gibail and Batrum (patriarchal eparchies: the dioceses of the patriarchate, each administered by a titular archbishop). Aleppo, Baalbek, Beirut, Cyprus, Damascus, Sidon, Tyre, Tripoli

2. Patriarchate of Antioch for the Syrians (Beirut)
   Suffragan sees:
   Metropolitans without suffragans: Homṣ, Mardin-Diarbekir
   Archiepiscopal sees: Bagdad, Mosul, Aleppo
   Episcopal sees: Gezira, Beirut

B. The Byzantine Discipline

1. Patriarchate of Antioch (Damascus)
   Suffragan sees:
   Metropolitan of Tyre (protothrone of the patriarchate) with the episcopal sees of Acri, Sidon, Paneas, Tripoli of Syria
   Metropolitan of Aleppo without suffragans (considered as the second metropolitan see of the patriarchate by tradition)
   Metropolitan of Boṣra
   Metropolitan of Damascus (a patriarchal diocese with the episcopal sees of Baalbek, Zaḥleh)
   Autocephalous metropolitan of Beirut and Homṣ

V. Patriarchate of Jerusalem

A. The Antiochene Discipline
   Maronite Patriarchal Vicariate of Syria (Jerusalem)

B. The Byzantine Discipline
   Melkite Patriarchal Vicariate (Jerusalem)

VI. Armenian Patriarchate

Patriarchate of Cilicia for the Armenians (Beirut)
   Suffragan sees:
   Archiepiscopal sees of Aleppo, Constantinople, Mardin, Sebaste (Sivas)
   Episcopal sees of Alexandria of Egypt, Ispahan (Isfahan), Beirut (patriarchal eparchy), Adana (Seyhan), Di[y]arbekir, Angara (Ankara), Artvin, Prusa (Bursa), Cæsarea of Cappadocia (Kayseri), Erzerum (Erzurum), Kharput (Harput), Maraş, Melitene (Malatya), Trebizond (Trabzon)
   Patriarchal Vicariate of Jerusalem

VII. Chaldean Patriarchate

Patriarchate of Babylonia of the Chaldeans (Mosul)
   Suffragan sees of the patriarchal province:
   Episcopal sees of Kerkūk (Kirkuk), Akra (Aqra), Amadia, Zākhō
   The suffragans of the metropolis of Nisibis (Nusaybin)
   Episcopal sees of Gezira (Cizre), Siirt, Diyarbekir, Mardin

The metropolitans of [Urmyā] Rezayyeh with the episcopal see of Salmas (Shahpur)
The metropolitan of Sena (Sinneh) who has no suffragans
The Patriarchal Vicariate of Basra (Bassorah-Aššār): in Syria (Aleppo), in Egypt (Cairo), in Palestine (Jerusalem)

VIII. Archiepiscopal Sees Separated from the Ecclesiastical Provvinces of Oriental Patriarchs
- A. The Antiochene Discipline
  Malankarese Ordinariate (Trivandrum, Tiruvalla)
- B. The Armenian Discipline
  Archiepiscopal see of Lemberg (without suffragans)
- C. The Byzantine Rite
  1. Archiepiscopal see of Lemberg for the Ruthenians (to which the metropolitan title of Halicz is united) with its suffragan episcopal sees of Przemyśl and Stanisławów
  2. Archiepiscopal see (and metropolitan see) of Făgăraş and Alba-Julia for the Rumanians, with its suffragan episcopal sees of Cluj-Gherla (Kalozsvár-Szamas-Ujvár), Oradea Mare (Nagy-Várad, Gran Varadino, Grasswardein), Lagaj (Lugas) and Maramureş (Nagy-Bánya, Baia Mare)
- D. The Chaldean Discipline
  Archiepiscopal see (and metropolitan of Ernakulam with its suffragan sees of Changanacherry, Trichur, Kotayam

IX. Suffragan Episcopal Sees Subject to Latin Metropolitans (all of the Byzantine Discipline)
- A. Subject to the Primatial Metropolitan See of Strigonia (Esztergom, Gran):
  The Ruthenian episcopal sees of Mukačevo (Munkács) and Prešav (Prjašev) from Podcarpathia (Czechoslovakia)
  The Hungarian episcopal see of Hajdudorog
- B. Subject to the Metropolitan See of Zagreb (Agram)
  The Jugoslav episcopal see of Križevci

APPENDIX C

Questionnaire and Rescript for Membership in Forbidden Societies[1]

1. Questionnaire

1. Give full name and surname ....
2. Give the name of the prohibited Society ....
3. Give the date of entrance into said Society ....
4. Did you enter the Society in good faith? ....
5. Is there any scandal in your remaining in said Society as a passive member? ....
6. Give financial loss consequent upon withdrawal from said Society ....
7. Will you abstain from all communication with, and never assist at any meetings of, said Society? ....
8. Is there any danger of perversion from Catholic faith and practice for yourself or family, from your remaining in it? ....
9. Will you make provision that, in case of death, you will be buried with the rites of the Catholic Church only? ....

N. B. If the Society was entered after the condemnation, a sworn statement, made in the presence of the priest, attesting to the good faith of the petitioner at the time of entrance, is required.

2. Rescript of the Archbishop

Having carefully considered the application of Mr. .... to retain passive membership in the ...., a condemned Society, in virtue of the faculties granted to archbishops by the indult of the Holy Office, June 16, 1913, We grant power to Rev. .... to permit the said petitioner to leave his name on the rolls, and to continue to pay his taxes or debts to the said Society, provided that the circumstances of the case have been truthfully stated, and under the following conditions:

[1] Lydon, *Ready Answers*, pp. 481-482

1. That there be no cause of scandal, or that such scandal be removed by a timely declaration that said passive membership is retained only in order that the benefits to which the petitioner is entitled be not lost to him.
2. That at the same time the petitioner refrain from all communication with, and even from any material intervention in, the affairs of the Society.
3. That there be no danger of perversion to the petitioner, or to his family, especially in the event of sickness, or death, and that there shall be in the funeral services nothing which is not in accordance with the rubrics of the Catholic Church.
4. That the payment of the taxes or debts be acquitted through the intermediary of another person, or by mail, so that the petitioner will, in no way, assist at any meeting of said Society.

N. N.

____

Archbishop of ____________________________

BIBLIOGRAPHY

Sources

Acta Apostolicæ Sedis, Commentarium Officiale, Romæ, 1909- .

Acts and Decrees of the Ukrainian Provincial Synod of Galicia, Lemberg, 1891, Lemberg: Stavropihiskoho Instituta, 1896 (Ukranian).

Acta et Decreta Concilii Nationis Armenorum Romæ habiti ad Sancti Nicolai Tolentinatis anno MDCCCCXI, Romæ: Typis Polyglottis Vaticanis, 1913.

Acta et Decreta Concilii Plenarii Baltimorensis Tertii, A.D. MDCCCXXXIV, Baltimoræ: Typis Joannis Murphy Sociorum, 1886.

Acta et Decreta Sacrorum Conciliorum Recentiorum, Collectio Lacensis, 7 vols., Friburgi Brisgoviæ: Herder, 1870-1890.

Acta Sanctæ Sedis, 41 vols., Romæ, 1865-1908.

Annuario Pontificio, Roma: Tipografia Poliglotta Vaticana, 1912- . Formerly entitled *Notizie,* 1716 (?)-1858; *Annuario Pontificio,* 1860-1871; *La Gerarchia Cattolica,* 1872-1911; and again *Annuario Pontificio* from 1912 onwards. None was published for 1813-1814, 1848-1850, 1859 (?).

Benedicti XIV Romanum Bullarium, 3 vols. in 4, Prati, 1846.

Bouscaren, T. Lincoln, *The Canon Law Digest,* 2 vols., Milwaukee: Bruce Publishing Co., Vol. I, *Officially Published Documents Affecting the Code of Canon Law 1917-1933,* 4. printing, 1934; Vol. II, *Officially Published Documents Affecting the Code of Canon Law 1933-1942,* 1943.

Bruns, Hermann T., *Canones Apostolorum et Conciliorum Sæculorum IV-VII,* 2 vols., Berolini, 1839.

Cæremoniale Episcoporum in duos libros distributum, Clementis VIII et Innocentii X auctoritate recognitum, a Benedicto XIII in multis correctum, cura et studio Josephi Catalani Presbyteri, nova ed., Parisiis: Sumptibus A. Jouby, Editoris, 1840.

Codex Iuris Canonici Pii X Pontificis Maximi iussu digestus Benedicti Papæ XV auctoritate promulgatus, Romæ: Typis Polyglottis Vaticanis, 1917.

Codicis Iuris Canonici Fontes, cura Emi Petri Card. Gasparri editi, 9 vols., Romæ (postea Civitate Vaticana): Typis Polyglottis Vaticanis, 1923-1939. (Vols. VII, VIII, IX, ed. cura et studio Emi Iustiniani Card. Serédi).

Codificazione Canonica Orientale, Fonti, Serie I, 16 Fascicoli; Serie II, Fascicoli; Series III, *Fontes,* volumes, Città del Vaticano: Tipografia Poliglotta Vaticana, 1930- .

Fonti, Serie I, Fascicolo I, *Testi Vari di Diritto Nuovo (1550-1902),* Tipografia Poliglotta Vaticana, 1930, ristampa 1933.

Fonti, Serie I, Fascicolo IX, *Disciplina Generale Antica, Sec. II-IX*, Tipografia Poliglotta Vaticana, 1933.

Fonti, Serie I, Fascicolo X, *Disciplina Bizantina: Rumeni, Testi di Diritto Particolare dei Rumeni*, Tipografia Poliglotta Vaticana, 1933.

Fonti, Serie I, Fascicolo XI, *Ius Particulare Ruthenorum*, Tipografia Poliglotta Vaticana, 1933.

Fonti, Serie I, Fascicolo XII, *Disciplina Antiochena: Maroniti, Ius Particulare Maronitarum*, Tipografia Poliglotta Vaticana, 1933.

Fonti, Serie II, Fascicolo V, *Textus Selecti ex Operibus Commentatorum Byzantinorum Iuris Ecclesiastici*, ed. Isidorus Croce, Typis Polyglottis Vaticanis, 1939.

Fontes, Series III, Vol. II, *Acta Innocentii PP. III (1198-1216)*, ed. Theodosius Haluščynskyj, Typis Polyglottis Vaticanis, 1944.

Concilii Plenarii Baltimorensis II, in Ecclesia Metropolitana Baltimorensi, a die VII ad diem XXI Octobris, A.D. MDCCCLXVI, Habiti, et a Sede Apostolica Recogniti, Acta et Decreta, 2. ed., Baltimoræ: John Murphy, 1880.

Corpus Iuris Canonici, editio Lipsiensis secunda post Aemilii Ludovici Richteri curas ad librorum manu scriptorum et editionis Romanæ fidem recognovit et adnotatione critica instruxit Aemilius Friedberg, 2 vols., Lipsiæ: Ex Officina Bernhardi Tauchnitz, 1879-1881. Editio anastatice repetita, Lipsiæ: Tauchnitz, 1928.

Corpus Iuris Civilis, 3 vols., Vol. II, *Codex Iustinianus*, recognovit et retractavit Paulus Krueger, 10. ed.; Vol. III, *Novellæ*, recognovit Rudolfus Schoell, absolvit Gulielmus Kroll, 5. ed., Berolini: Apud Weidmannos, 1928.

Decreta Authentica Congregationis Sacrorum Rituum ex Actis Eiusdem Collecta Cura et Studio Aloisii Gardellini, 3. ed. prepared by Capalti, 4 vols., Romæ: Typis S. Congregationis De Propaganda Fide, 1856-1858, Vol. I, 1856.

Decretales D. Gregorii Papæ IX, una cum glossis restitutæ, Romæ, 1582.

Decretum Gratiani Emendatum et Notationibus Illustratum una cum Glossis, Romæ, 1582.

Gallia Christiana in Provinciis Ecclesiasticis Distributa, 16 vols., Parisiis: Venit apud Firmin Didot Fratres, Filiosque Sociosque, Vol. XVI, ed. J. B. Haureau, 1865.

Hardouin, Jean, *Conciliorum Collectio Regia Maxima*, 12 vols., Parisiis, 1714-1715.

Jaffé, Phillipus, *Bibliotheca Rerum Germanicarum*, 6 vols., Berolini: apud Weidmannos, Vol. III, *Monumenta Moguntina*, 1866; Vol. IV, *Monumenta Carolina*, 1867; Vol. V, *Monumenta Gregoriana*, 1868.

———, *Regesta Pontificum Romanorum, ab condita Ecclesia ad annum post Christum natum MCXCVIII*, 2. ed., correctam et auctam auspiciis Gulielmi Wattenbach curaverunt F. Kaltenbrunner (ad annum DXC), P. Ewald (DXC-DCCCLXXXII), S. Loewenfeld (DCCCLXXXII-MCXCVIII), 2 vols. in 1, Lipsiæ, 1885-1888.

Mansi, Ioannes, *Sacrorum Conciliorum Nova et Amplissima Collectio*, 53 vols. in 60, Paris, Arnhem, Leipzig, 1901-1927.

Monumenta Germaniæ Historica, edidit Societas aperiendis fontibus rerum germanicarum medii ævi, Berlin: apud Weidmannos; Hannover: Hahn; Leipzig: Karl W. Hiersemann, 1824- .

Epistolæ, Tom. I, pars 1, *Gregorii I Papæ registrum epistolarum*, Libri I-IV, ed. Paulus Ewald, Berolini: apud Weidmannos, 1887; Tom. I, pars 2, *Gregorii I Papæ registrum epistolarum*, Libri V-VII, post Pauli Ewaldi obitum ed. L. M. Hartmann, Berolini: apud Weidmannos, 1891; Tom. II, pars 1, *Gregorii I Papæ registrum epistolarum*, Libri VIII-IX, post Pauli Ewaldi obitum ed. L. M. Hartmann, Berolini: apud Weidmannos, 1893; Tom. II, pars 2, *Gregorii I Papæ registrum epistolarum*, Libri X-XIV, post Pauli Ewaldi obitum ed. L. M. Hartmann, Berolini: apud Weidmannos, 1895.

Epistolæ, Tom. VI, *Epistolæ Karolini Aevi*, 6 vols., ed. Ernestus Perels, Vol. IV, 1925, Berolini: apud Weidmannos.

Epistolæ selectæ, Tom. I, *S. Bonifacii et Lulli Epistolæ*, ed. M. Tangl, Berolini: apud Weidmannos, 1916; Tom. II, fasc. 1, *Gregorii VII registrum*, ed. E. Caspar, pars 1, Libri I-IV, 1920; pars 2, Libri V-IX, 1923; Tom. II, fasc. 2, *Gregorii VII registrum*, ed. E. Caspar, 1923.

Leges, 5 vols., ed. G. Pertz, G. Waitz, H. Brunner, Hannoveræ: Hahn, 1835-1889, 2. unveränderter Neudruck, Leipzig: Verlag K. W. Hiersemann, 1925.

Leges, Sect. II, *Capitularia Regum Francorum*, Tom. I, ed. A. Boretius, 1883, Tom. II, ed. A. Boretius et Victor Krause, 1897; Sect. III, *Concilia*, Tom. I, *Concilia ævi Merovingici*, rec. F. Maassen, 1893, Tom. II, *Concilia ævi Karolini I*, rec. Albertus Werminghoff, pars 1, 1904-1906, pars 2, 1904-1908.

Scriptores, 30 vols. in 31, ed. G. Pertz, G. Waitz, H. Brunner, Hannoveræ: Impensis Bibliopolii Hahniani, 1826-1892, unveränderter Neudruck, Leipzig: Verlag K. W. Hiersemann, Vol. VIII, 1925; Vol. XIII, 1925.

Scriptores rerum merovingivarum, Tom. I: *Gregorii Turonensis opera*, ed. W. Arndt et B. Krusch, 1884.

Muratori, Ludovico Antonio, *Rerum Italicarum Scriptores*, 25 vols., Milan, 1723-1751.

Pallottini, Salvator, *Collectio Omnium Conclusionum et Resolutionum quæ apud Sacram Congregationem Cardinalium S. Concilii Tridentini Interpretum prodierunt ab eius institutione anno MDLXIV ad annum MDCCCLX, distinctis titulis alphabetico ordine per materias digestas*, 18 vols., Romæ: Typis S. Congregationis De Propaganda Fide, 1868-1895.

Pitra, Joannes, *Iuris Ecclesiastici Græcorum Historia et Monumenta*, 2 vols., Romæ, Vol. I, 1864; Vol. II, 1868.

Pontificale Romanum in tres Partes Distributum, Clementis VIII ac Urbani VIII auctoritate recognitum, Auctore Josepho Catalano, nova ed., Parisiis: Apud Mequignon Juniorem, 1850.

Pontificale Romanum Summorum Pontificum jussu editum, a Benedicto XIV et Leone XIII recognitum et castigatum, Mechliniæ: H. Dessain, 1895.

Potthast, Augustus, *Regesta Pontificum Romanorum inde ab anno post Christum natum MCXCVIII ad annum MCCCIV*, 2 vols. in 1, Berolini, 1874-1875.

Sartori, Cosmas, *Enchiridion Canonicum seu Sanctæ Sedis Responsiones*, 7. ed., Romæ: Ex Typographia Augustiniana, 1944.

Schroeder, H. J., *Canons and Decrees of the Council of Trent*, St. Louis: Herder, 1941.

———, *Disciplinary Decrees of the General Councils: Text, Translation and Commentary*, St. Louis: Herder, 1937.

Silva-Tarouca, C., *Textus et Documenta in usum exercitationum et prælectionum academicarum Epistolarum Romanorum Pontificum ad Vicarios per Illyricum Aliosque Episcopos, Collectio Thessalonicensis*, Series Theologica, n. 23, Romæ: apud ædes Pont. Universitatis Gregorianæ, 1937.

Statistica, con cenni storici della Gerarchia e dei Fedeli di Rito Orientale, Sacra Congregazione Orientale, Roma: Tipografia Poliglotta Vaticana, 1932.

Thiel, Andreas, *Epistolæ Romanorum Pontificum Genuinæ a S. Hilario usque ad Pelagium II*, Vol. I, Brunsbergæ, 1868.

Turner, Cuthbert Hamilton, *Ecclesiæ Occidentalis Monumenta Iuris Antiquissima Canonum et Conciliorum Græcorum Interpretationes Latinæ*, 2 vols. in 6, Oxonii: e Typographeo Clarendoniano, 1899-1930, Tomus I, 1930.

Synodus Alexandrina Coptorum habita Cairi in Aegypto anno MDCCCXCVIII, Romæ: S. C. de Propaganda Fide, 1899.

Synodus Sciarfensis Syrorum in Monte Libano celebrata in anno 1880, Romæ: S. C. de Propaganda Fide, 1896.

Reference Works

Attwater, Donald, *The Catholic Eastern Churches*, 2. ed., Milwaukee: Bruce Publishing Co., 1937.

Augustine, Charles, *A Commentary on the New Code of Canon Law*, 8 vols., St. Louis: Herder Book Co., 1918-1922. Vol. II, 6. ed., 1936.

———, *The Rights and Duties of Ordinaries*, St. Louis: Herder Book Co., 1924.

Ayrinhac, H. A. - Lydon, P. J., *Penal Legislation in the New Code of Canon Law*, rev. ed., New York: Benziger Brothers, 1936.

Badii, Caesar, *Institutiones Iuris Canonici*, 3. ed., 2 vols., Florentiæ: Libreria Editrice Florentina, 1921-1922.

Barbosa, Augustinus, *Iuris Ecclesiastici Universi Libri Tres*, 3 vols., Lugduni, 1650.

———, *Pastoralis Sollicitudinis sive de Officio et Potestate Episcopi Tripartita Descriptio*, 4 part. in 2 vols., Lugduni, 1656.

Bargilliat, M., *Prælectiones Juris Canonici*, 2 vols., Parisiis: apud Baston, Berche et Pagis, Vol. I, 37. ed., 1923.

Baronius, Caesar, *Annales Ecclesiastici*, 37 vols., ed. A. Theiner, Vols. I-XXVIII, Barri-Ducis, 1864-1875; Vols. XXIX-XXXVII, Parisiis, 1876-1883.

Barrett, John, *A Comparative Study of the Councils of Baltimore and the Code of Canon Law*, The Catholic University of America Canon Law Studies, n. 83, Washington, D. C.: The Catholic University of America, 1932.

Benedictus XIV, *De Synodo Diœcesana*, 2 vols., Parmæ, 1764.

———, *Opera Omnia*, 17 vols., Prati, 1845.

Benko, Matthew, *The Abbot* Nullius, The Catholic University of America Canon Law Studies, n. 173, Washington, D. C.: The Catholic University of America Press, 1943.

Berardi, Carlo, *De rebus ad canonicam scientiam pertinentibus commentaria in ius ecclesiasticum universum*, 4 vols., Taurini, 1766.

Beste, Uldalricus, *Introductio in Codicem*, 2. ed., Collegeville, Minn.: St. John's Abbey Press, 1944.

Blat, Albertus, *Commentarium Textus Codicis Iuris Canonici*, 5 vols. in 6, Romæ: Apud "Angelico," 1919-1927. Lib. II, 2. ed., 1921.

Bouix, Dominique, *Institutiones Juris Canonici in Varios Tractatus Divisæ: Tractatus de Episcopo ubi et de Synodo Diœcesana*, 2. ed., 2 vols., Parisiis, 1873.

———, *Tractatus de Judiciis Ecclesiasticis*, 3. ed., 2 vols., Parisiis, 1884.

Bury, John Bagnell, *History of the later Roman Empire from the death of Theodosius I to the death of Justinian (A.D. 395 to A.D. 565)*, 2 vols., London: Macmillan and Co., 1923.

Cambridge Ancient History, 12 vols., Cambridge: University Press, 1928-1939. Vol. X, ed. Cook, Adcock, Charlesworth, 1934.

Cance, Adrien, *Le Code de Droit Canonique*, 3 vols., Paris: Librarie Lecoffre, Gabalda et Fils, 1927-1929.

Cappello, Felix, *Summa Iuris Canonici*, 3 vols., Vol. I, 4. ed., Romae: Apud Aedes Universitatis Gregorianæ, 1945.

———, *Tractatus Canonico-Moralis de Censuris iuxta Codicem Iuris Canonici*, 3. ed., Romæ: Officina Libraria Marietti, 1933.

Chelodi, Joannes, *Ius Canonicum de Delictis et Pœnis*, 5. ed. recognita et aucta a Pio Ciprotti, Trento: Libreria Moderna Editrice, 1943.

———, *Ius Canonicum de Personis*, 3. ed. curavit Pius Ciprotti, Trento: Libreria Moderna Editrice, 1942.

Claeys Bouuaert, F. - Simenon, G., *Manuale Juris Canonici*, 3 vols., Vol. I, Gandæ et Leodii: De Meester et Fils, 1931.

Cocchi, Guidus, *Commentarium in Codicem Iuris Canonici ad Usum Scholarum*, 8 vols. in 5, Vol. II, 4. ed., 1937; Vol. III, 4. ed., 1940; Vol. VII, 3. ed., 1940; Vol. VIII, 4. ed., 1938; Taurinorum Augustæ: Marietti.

Coronata, Matthaeus Conte a, *Institutiones Iuris Canonici*, 5 vols., Vols. I-II, 2. ed., 1939; Vol. III, 2. ed., 1941; Vol. IV, 2. ed., 1945; Vol. V, 1936; Taurini: Marietti.

Coussa, Acacius, *Epitome Prælectionum de Iure Ecclesiastico Orientali*, 2 vols., Vol. I, Città del Vaticano: Typis Polyglottis Vaticanis, 1940.

De Clercq, C., *La Legislation Religieuse Franque de Clovis à Charlemagne (507-814)*, Paris: Librairie du Recueil Sirey S. A., 1936.

De Luca, Joannes, *Theatrum Veritatis et Justitiæ sive Decisivi Discursus ad Veritatem Editi in Forensibus Controversiis, Canonicis, et Civilibus*, 16 vols. in 8, Coloniæ Agrippæ: apud Henricum Rommerskirchen, 1706.

De Meester, Alphonsus, *Juris Canonici et Juris Canonico-civilis Compendium*, nova ed., 3 vols. in 4, Brugis: Desclée, 1921-1928.

Dudden, F. H., *Gregory the Great, His Place in History and Thought*, 2 vols., London: Longmans, Green and Co., 1905.

Dümmler, E., *Geschichte des ostfrankischen Reiches*, 2. ed., Leipzig: Dunker und Humblot, 1887-1888.

Dziob, Michael, *The Sacred Congregation for the Oriental Church*, The Catholic University of America Canon Law Studies, n. 214, Washington, D. C.: The Catholic University of America Press, 1945.

Eidenschink, John, *The Election of Bishops in the Letters of Gregory the Great*, The Catholic University of America Canon Law Studies, n. 215, Washington, D. C.: The Catholic University of America Press, 1945.

Engel, Ludovicus, *Collegium Universi Juris Canonici*, 9. ed., Beneventi, 1760.

Fagnanus, Prosper, *Commentaria in Quinque Libros Decretalium*, 5 vols. in 3, Venetiis, 1661.

Ferraris, Lucius, *Prompta Bibliotheca Canonica, Iuridica, Moralis, Theologica, nec non Ascetica, Polemica, Rubricistica, Historica*, 9 vols., Romæ, 1885-1899. Vol. IX prepared by I. Bucceroni.

Ferreres, Joannes, *Institutiones Canonicæ*, 1. ed., 2 vols., Barcinone, 1918.

Fortescue, Adrian, *The Lesser Eastern Churches*, London: Catholic Truth Society, 1913.

———, *The Orthodox Eastern Church*, London: Catholic Truth Society, 1907.

———, *The Uniate Eastern Churches*, ed. G. Smith, London: Burns, Oates and Washbourne, 1923.

Flórez, Enrique, *España Sagrada. Theatro Geographico-Historico de la Iglesia de España*, 54 vols., Madrid. Vol. IV, 1749.

Fournier, P. - Le Bras, G., *Histoire des Collections Canoniques en Occident*, 2 vols., Paris: Recueil Sirey, 1931-1932.

Garcia-Villada, Zacharias, *Historia Eclesiastica de España*, 1 vol. in 2, Madrid: Compañía Ibero-Americana de Publicaciones S. A. Libreria Fernando Fe, 1929.

Godfrey, John, *The Right of Patronage According to the Code of Canon Law*, The Catholic University of America Canon Law Studies, n. 21, Washington, D. C.: The Catholic University of America, 1924.

Gonzalez-Tellez, Emmanuel, *Commentaria Perpetua in Singulos Textus Quinque Librorum Decretalium Gregorii IX*, 5 vols. in 4, Venetiis, 1699.

Guilday, Peter, *A History of the Councils of Baltimore 1791-1884*, New York: Macmillan Company, 1932.

Haring, Johann, *Grundzüge des catholischen Kirchenrechts*, 3. ed., 1 vol. in 2, Graz: Ulrich Moser - J. Mayerhoff, 1924.

Hefele, Carl, et Leclercq, Henri, *Histoire des Conciles*, 10 vols. in 19, Paris: Letouzey et Ané, 1907-1938.

Hergenroether, Joseph, *Photius, Patriarch von Constantinopel*, 2 vols., Regensburg, 1867.

Hinschius, Paul, *Das Kirchenrecht der Katholiken und Protestanten in Deutschland*, 6 vols., Berlin, 1869-1897. Vols. I-IV, System des katholischen Kirchenrechts, 1869-1888.

———, *Decretales Pseudo-Isidorianæ et Capitula Angilramni*, Lipsiæ: Ex Officina Bernhardi Tauchnitz, 1863.

Hostiensis (Henricus de Segusio), *Summa Aurea*, Venetiis: Ad candentis Salamandræ Isigne, 1570.

Icard, H., *Prælectiones Iuris Canonici Habitæ in Seminario Sancti Sulpitii*, 6. ed., 3 vols., Parisiis: apud Lecoffre Filium et Socios, 1886.

Kehr, Paulus Fridolin, *Papsturkunden in Spanien*, 2 vols., Berlin: Weidmann'sche Buchhandlung, 1928.

———, *Regesta Pontificum Romanorum, Italia Pontificia*, 8 vols. in 10, Berolini: apud Weidmannos, 1906-1925. Vol. V, 1911.

King, Archdale, *Notes on the Catholic Liturgies*, London: Longmans, Green and Company, 1930.

Klekotka, Peter, *Diocesan Consultors*, The Catholic University of America Canon Law Studies, n. 8, Washington, D. C.: The Catholic University of America, 1920.

Kober, F., *Deposition und Degradation*, Tübingen, 1867.

———, *Kirchenbann nach den Grundsätzen des canonischen Rechts*, Tübingen, 1863.

Köstler, R., *Wörterbuch zum Codex Iuris Canonici*, München: Verlag Josef Kösel & Friedrich Pustet, 1927-1929.

Lanzoni, Francesco, *Le Origini delle Diocesi Antiche d'Italia*, Studi e Testi, n. 35, Romæ: Tipografia Poliglotta Vaticana, 1923.

Lydon, P. J., *Ready Answers in Canon Law*, 2. ed., New York: Benziger Brothers, 1934.

Makée, P., *Institutiones Juris Ecclesiasticæ tum Publici tum Privati*, 2 vols., Parisiis: apud Roger et Chernovitz, 1897.

Marbach, Joseph, *Marriage Legislation for the Catholics of the Oriental Rites in the United States and Canada*, The Catholic

University of America Canon Law Studies, n. 243, Washington, D. C.: The Catholic University of America Press, 1946.

Mast, J., *Dogmatisch-historische Abhandlung über die rechtliche Stellung der Erzbishcöfe in der katholischen Kirche*, Freiburg, 1847.

Maroto, Philippus, *Institutiones Iuris Canonici ad Normam Novi Codicis*, 2 vols., Romæ, 1919.

McGrath, James, *The Privilege of the Canon*, The Catholic University of America Canon Law Studies, n. 242, Washington, D. C.: The Catholic University of America Press, 1946.

Migne, J. P., *Patrologiæ Cursus Completus — Series Latina*, 221 vols., Parisiis, 1884-1885; —*Series Græca*, 161 vols., Parisiis, 1857-1866.

Nainfa, John, *Costumes of Prelates of the Catholic Church*, new and revised ed., Baltimore: John Murphy Co., 1926.

Oesterle, Gerardus, *Prælectiones Iuris Canonici*, Vol. I, Romæ: in Collegio Sancti Anselmi, 1931.

Ottaviani, Alaphiridus, *Institutiones Iuris Publici Ecclesiastici*, 2. ed., 2 vols., Romæ: Typis Polyglottis Vaticanis, 1935-1936.

Papp-Szilagyi, Joseph, *Enchiridion Juris Ecclesiæ Orientalis Catholicæ*, 2. ed., Magno-Varadini, 1880.

Parsons, Anscar, *Canonical Elections*, The Catholic University of America Canon Law Studies, n. 118, Washington, D. C.: The Catholic University of America Press, 1939.

Perugini, Angelus, *Concordata Vigentia, Notis Historicis et Iuridicis Declarata*, Romæ: Apud Custodiam Librariam Pont. Instituti Utriusque Iuris, 1934.

Petra, Vincentius, *Commentaria ad Constitutiones Apostolicas seu Bullas Singulas Summorum Pontificum*, 5 vols. in 2, Venetiis, 1729.

Phillips, Georg, *Kirchenrecht*, 7 vols., Regensburg: Druck und Verlag von Georg Joseph Many, 1845-1872. Vol. VI, 1864.

Plummer, C., *Venerabilis Bædæ Opera Historica*, 2 vols., Oxonii: e Typographeo Clarendoniano, 1896.

Poulet, Charles, *A History of the Catholic Church*, trans. and adapt. from the 4. French ed. by Sidney Raemers, 2 vols., St. Louis, Mo.: Herder Book Co., Vol. I, 1945.

Prümmer, Dominicus, *Manuale Iuris Canonici in Usum Scholarum*, 6. ed., Friburgi Brisgoviæ: Herder, 1933.

Prunskis, Joseph, *Comparative Law, Ecclesiastical and Civil, in Lithuanian Concordat*, The Catholic University of America Canon Law Studies, n. 222, Washington, D. C.: The Catholic University of America Press, 1945.

Quigley, Joseph, *Condemned Societies*, The Catholic University of America Canon Law Studies, n. 46, Washington, D. C.: The Catholic University of America, 1927.

Raus, J. B., *Institutiones Canonicæ iuxta Novum Codicem Iuris*, ed. altera, Lugduni-Parisiis: Typis Emmanuelis Vitte, 1931.

Regatillo, E., *Institutiones Iuris Canonici*, 2. ed., 2 vols., Santander-Madrid: Aldus, 1942-1946.

Reiffenstuel, Anacletus, *Ius Canonicum Universum*, 5 vols., Parisiis, 1864-1870.

Roberti, Franciscus, *De Processibus*, 2 vols., Romæ: Tip. Soc. Ed. del Libro Italiano, 1941. Vol. I, *De Actione, De Præsuppositis Processus et Sententiæ de Merito*, 2. ed., 1941.

Saegmüller, Johannes Baptist, *Lehrbuch des katholischen Kirchenrechts*, 4. ed., Freiburg im Breisgau: Herder, 1925-1934.

Schmalzgrueber, Franciscus, *Jus Ecclesiasticum Universum*, 5 vols. in 12, Romæ, 1843-1845.

Schmier, Franciscus, *Jurisprudentia canonico civilis seu ius canonicum universum iuxta quinque libros Decretalium*, Salisburgi, 1716.

Schrörs, Heinrich, *Hinkmar, Erzbischof von Reims*, Freiberg: Herder'sche Verlagshandlung, 1884.

Schulte, J. F., *Lehrbuch des katholischen und evangelischen Kirchenrechts*, 4. Auflage des katholischen, 1. Auflage des evangelischen Kirchenrechts, 2 vols., Giesen: E. Roth, 1886.

Sipos, Stephanus, *Enchiridion Iuris Canonici*, 4. ed., Pécs: Ex Typographia "Haladás R. T.," 1940.

Slafkosky, Andrew, *The Canonical Episcopal Visitation of the Diocese*, The Catholic University of America Canon Law Studies, n. 142, Washington, D. C.: The Catholic University of America Press, 1941.

Smith, S. B., *Elements of Ecclesiastical Law*, 3 vols., 1887-1888; Vol. I, 9. ed., 1887, New York: Benziger Brothers.

———, *Notes on the Second Plenary Council of Baltimore*, New York: Benziger Brothers, 1874.

Thomassinus, Ludovicus, *Vetus et Nova Ecclesiæ disciplina circa beneficia et beneficiarios*, 10 vols., Magontiaci, 1787.

Toso, Albertus, *Ad Codicem Iuris Canonici Commentaria Minora*, 5 vols. in 2, Romæ, 1921-1927. Vol. II, Romæ: Marietti, 1922; Vol. III, Romæ: Cura Ephemeridis Jus Pontificium, 1923; Vol. IV, Romæ: Jus Pontificium, 1925.

Trombetta, A., *De Pallio Archiepiscopali, elubricatio canonica-liturgica-historica*, Surrenti: Ex Typographia Hen. D. Onofrio, 1923.

Van Hove, A., *Commentarium Lovaniense in Codicem Iuris Canonici*, Vol. I, Tom. I, *Prolegomena ad Codicem Iuris Canonici*, 2. ed., Mechliniæ-Romæ: H. Dessain, 1945.

Van Espen, Zegerus Bernardus, *Ius Ecclesiasticum Universum*, 5 vols., Lovanii, 1753.

Vermeersch, A., et Creusen, J., *Epitome Iuris Canonici*, 3 vols., Mechliniæ-Romæ: H. Dessain, Vol. I, 6. ed., 1937; Vol. II, 6. ed., 1940; Vol. III, 6. ed., 1946.

Wenger, Leopold, *Institutes of the Roman Law of Civil Procedure*, revised ed. translated by Otis Harrison Fisk, New York: Veritas Press, 1940.

Wagnon, H., *Concordats et Droit International*, Universitas Catholica Lovaniensis Dissertationes ad gradum magistri in Facultate Theologica vel in Facultate Iuris Canonici consequendum conscriptæ, Series II, Vol. XXIX, 1935.

Wernz, Franciscus, *Ius Decretalium*, 2. ed., 6 vols., Romæ et Prati, 1906-1913.

Wernz, Franciscus,-Vidal, Petrus, *Ius Canonicum ad Codicis Normam Exactum*, 7 vols. in 8, 1923-1938; Vol. II, *Ius de Personis*, 3. ed., 1943; Vol. VI, *De Processibus*, 1. ed., 1927-1928, Romæ: Apud Aedes Universitatis Gregorianæ.

Woywod, Stanislaus, *A Practical Commentary on the Code of Canon Law*, 4. ed., 2 vols., New York: Joseph Wagner Inc., 1932.

Articles

Kuttner, Stephan, "Decretalistica: Die Novellen Papst Innocenz' IV und die Literatur zu den Novellen Innocenz' IV," — *Zeitschrift der Savigny-Stiftung für Rechtsgeschichte* (Weimar: Hermann Böhlaus Nachfolger), Kan. Abt., XXVI (1937), 436-470.

Duchesne, L., "L'Illyricum ecclesiastique," — *Byzantinische Zeitschrift* (Leipzig: Druck und Verlag von B. G. Traubner, 1892-), I (1892), 531-550.

Greenslade, J. B., "The Illyrian Churches and the Vicariate of Thessalonica, 378-395," — *The Journal of Theological Studies* (Oxford: Clarendon Press, 1899-), XLVI (1945), 17-30.

Plöchl, Willibald, "The Church Laws for Orientals of the Austrian Monarchy in the 'Age of Enlightenment,'" — *Quarterly Bulletin of the Polish Institute of Arts and Sciences in America*, II (1944), 711-756.

———, "Reflections on the Nature and the Status of Concordats," — *The Jurist*, VII (1947), 10-44.

Staffa, D., "De Sacræ Congregationis pro Ecclesia Orientali Competentia," — *Apollinaris*, XI (1938), 358-376.

Streichhan, F., "Die Anfänge des Vikariates von Thessalonike," — *Zeitschrift der Savigny-Stiftung für Rechtsgeschichte* (Weimar: Herman Böhlaus Nachfolger), Kan. Abt., XII (1922), 330 ff.

Periodicals

American Ecclesiastical Review, Vols. I-XXXII, Philadelphia, 1889-1905; from 1905: *The Ecclesiastical Review*, Vols. XXXIII-CIX, Philadelphia, 1905-1943; from 1944: *The American Ecclesiastical Review*, Washington, D. C., Vol. CX, 1944- .

Apollinaris, Romæ, 1928- .

Byzantinische Zeitschrift, Leipzig: Druck und Verlag von B. G. Traubner, 1892- .

Journal of Theological Studies, The, Oxford: Clarendon Press, 1899- .

Jurist, The, Washington, D. C., 1941- .

Quarterly Bulletin of the Polish Institute of Arts and Sciences in America, New York, 1942- .

Zeitschrift der Savigny-Stiftung für Rechtsgeschichte, Weimar. Rom. Abt., 1880- ; Kan. Abt., 1911- .

ABBREVIATIONS

AAS — *Acta Apostolicæ Sedis.*
AER or *ER* — *American Ecclesiastical Review* or *Ecclesiastical Review.*
ASS — *Acta Sanctæ Sedis.*
Bruns — *Canones Apostolorum et Conciliorum Sæculorum IV-VII.*
Coll. Lac. — *Collectio Lacensis.*
Fontes — *Codicis Iuris Canonici Fontes cura...Gasparri editi.*
Fonti — *Codificazione Canonica Orientale, Fonti.*
Hardouin — *Conciliorum Collectio Regia Maxima.*
Jaffé — *Regesta Pontificum Romanorum,* etc.
Mansi — *Sacrorum Conciliorum Nova et Amplissima Collectio.*
MGH — *Monumenta Germaniæ Historica.*
MGH: LL — *Monumenta Germaniæ Historica: Leges.*
MGH: SS — *Monumenta Germaniæ Historica: Scriptores.*
MPG — *Migne, Patrologia Series Græca.*
MPL — *Migne, Patrologia Series Latina.*
Pallottini — *Collectio omnium Conclusionum et Resolutionum,* etc.
Potthast — *Regesta Pontificum Romanorum,* etc.

INDEX

BIOGRAPHICAL NOTE

ALPHONSE SYLVESTER POPEK was born on December 9, 1913, in Milwaukee, Wisconsin. He received his elementary education in the parochial school of St. Adalbert in the same city. In 1927 he entered Saint Bonaventure Minor Seminary, Sturtevant, Wisconsin, where he obtained his high school training. In 1931 he entered the Seminary of Saint Francis de Sales at St. Francis, Wisconsin, where he received the degrees of Bachelor of Arts in 1936 and of Master of Arts in 1939. He was ordained to the priesthood on June 3, 1939. After five years of parish work in the diocese, he was assigned by his Ordinary to pursue a course of studies in the School of Canon Law at the Catholic University of America, where he received the degree of the Baccalaureate in Canon Law in May, 1945, and the degree of the Licentiate in Canon Law in June, 1946.

CANON LAW STUDIES[1]

1. FRERIKS, REV. CELESTINE A., C.PP.S., J.C.D., Religious Congregations in Their External Relations, 121 pp., 1916.
2. GALLIHER, REV. DANIEL M., O.P., J.C.D., Canonical Elections, 117 pp., 1917.
3. BORKOWSKI, REV. AURELIUS L., O.F.M., J.C.D., De Confraternitatibus Ecclesiasticis, 136 pp., 1918.
4. CASTILLO, REV. CAYO, J.C.D., Disertacion Historico-Canonica sobre la Potestad del Cabildo en Sede Vacante o Impedida del Vicario Capitular, 99 pp., 1919 (1918).
5. KUBELBECK, REV. WILLIAM J., S.T.B., J.C.D., The Sacred Penitentiaria and Its Relation to Faculties of Ordinaries and Priests, 129 pp., 1918.
6. PETROVITS, REV. JOSEPH J. C., S.T.D., J.C.D., The New Church Law on Matrimony, X-461 pp., 1919.
7. HICKEY, REV. JOHN J., S.T.B., J.C.D., Irregularities and Simple Impediments in the New Code of Canon Law, 100 pp., 1920.
8. KLEKOTKA, REV. PETER J., S.T.B., J.C.D., Diocesan Consultors, 179 pp., 1920.
9. WANENMACHER, REV. FRANCIS, J.C.D., The Evidence in Ecclesiastical Procedure Affecting the Marriage Bond, 1920 (Printed 1935).
10. GOLDEN, REV. HENRY FRANCIS, J.C.D., Parochial Benefices in the New Code, IV-119 pp., 1921 (Printed 1925).
11. KOUDELKA, REV. CHARLES J., J.C.D., Pastors, Their Rights and Duties According to the New Code of Canon Law, 211 pp., 1921.
12. MELO, REV. ANTONIUS, O.F.M., J.C.D., De Exemptione Regularium, X-188 pp., 1921.
13. SCHAAF, REV. VALENTINE THEODORE, O.F.M., S.T.B., J.C.D., The Cloister, X-180 pp., 1921.
14. BURKE, REV. THOMAS JOSEPH, S.T.D., J.C.D., Competence in Ecclesiastical Tribunals, IV-117 pp., 1922.
15. LEECH, REV. GEORGE LEO, J.C.D., A Comparative Study of the Constitution "Apostolicæ Sedis" and the "Codex Juris Canonici," 179 pp., 1922.
16. MOTRY, REV. HUBERT LOUIS, S.T.D., J.C.D., Diocesan Faculties According to the Code of Canon Law, II-167 pp., 1922.
17. MURPHY, REV. GEORGE LAWRENCE, J.C.D., Delinquencies and Penalties in the Administration and the Reception of the Sacraments, IV-121 pp., 1923.
18. O'REILLY, REV. JOHN ANTHONY, S.T.B., J.C.D., Ecclesiastical Sepulture in the New Code of Canon Law, II-129 pp., 1923.
19. MICHALICKA, REV. WENCESLAUS CYRILL, O.S.B., J.C.D., Judicial Procedure in Dismissal of Clerical Exempt Religious, 107 pp., 1923.

[1] From the list as here presented the following numbers are no longer available: 1-114, 116, 118, 120, 122, 123, 136, 162 and 198.

20. DARGIN, REV. EDWARD VINCENT, S.T.B., J.C.D., Reserved Cases According to the Code of Canon Law, IV-103 pp., 1924.
21. GODFREY, REV. JOHN A., S.T.B., J.C.D., The Right of Patronage According to the Code of Canon Law, 153 pp., 1924.
22. HAGEDORN, REV. FRANCIS EDWARD, J.C.D., General Legislation on Indulgences, II-154 pp., 1924.
23. KING, REV. JAMES IGNATIUS, J.C.D., The Administration of the Sacraments to Dying Non-Catholics, V-141 pp., 1924.
24. WINSLOW, REV. FRANCIS JOSEPH, M.M., J.C.D., Vicars and Prefects Apostolic, IV-149 pp., 1924.
25. CORREA, REV. JOSE SERVELION, S.T.L., J.C.D., La Potestad Legislativa de la Iglesia Catolica, IV-127 pp., 1925.
26. DUGAN, REV. HENRY FRANCIS, A.M., J.C.D., The Judiciary Department of the Diocesan Curia, 87 pp., 1925.
27. KELLER, REV. CHARLES FREDERICK, S.T.B., J.C.D., Mass Stipends, 167 pp., 1925.
28. PASCHANG, REV. JOHN LINUS, J.C.D., The Sacramentals According to the Code of Canon Law, 129 pp., 1925.
29. PIONTEK, REV. CYRILLUS, O.F.M., S.T.B., J.C.D., De Indulto Exclaustrationis necnon Sæcularizationis, XIII-289 pp., 1925.
30. KEARNEY, REV. RICHARD JOSEPH, S.T.B., J.C.D., Sponsors at Baptism According to the Code of Canon Law, IV-127 pp., 1925.
31. BARTLETT, REV. CHESTER JOSEPH, A.M., LL.B., J.C.D., The Tenure of Parochial Property in the United States of America, V-108 pp., 1926.
32. KILKER, REV. ADRIAN JEROME, J.C.D., Extreme Unction, V-425 pp., 1926.
33. MCCORMICK, REV. ROBERT EMMETT, J.C.D., Confessors of Religious, VIII-266 pp., 1926.
34. MILLER, REV. NEWTON THOMAS, J.C.D., Founded Masses According to the Code of Canon Law, VII-93 pp., 1926.
35. ROELKER, REV. EDWARD G., S.T.D., J.C.D., Principles of Privilege According to the Code of Canon Law, XI-166 pp., 1926.
36. BAKALARCZYK, REV. RICHARDUS, M.I.C., J.U.D., De Novitiatu, VIII-208 pp., 1927.
37. PIZZUTI, REV. LAWRENCE, O.F.M., J.U.L., De Parochis Religiosis, 1927. (Not Printed.)
38. BLILEY, REV. NICHOLAS MARTIN, O.S.B., J.C.D., Altars According to the Code of Canon Law, XIX-132 pp., 1927.
39. BROWN, MR. BRENDAN FRANCIS, A.B., LL.M., J.U.D., The Canonical Juristic Personality with Special Reference to its Status in the United States of America, V-212 pp., 1927.
40. CAVANAUGH, REV. WILLIAM THOMAS, C.P., J.U.D., The Reservation of the Blessed Sacrament, VIII-101 pp., 1927.
41. DOHENY, REV. WILLIAM J., C.S.C., A.B., J.U.D., Church Property: Modes of Acquisition, X-118 pp., 1927.
42. FELDHAUS, REV. ALOYSIUS H., C.PP.S., J.C.D., Oratories, IX-141 pp., 1927.
43. KELLY, REV. JAMES PATRICK, A.B., J.C.D., The Jurisdiction of the Simple Confessor, X-208 pp., 1927.

44. NEUBERGER, REV. NICHOLAS J., J.C.D., Canon 6 or the Relation of the Codex Juris Canonici to the Preceding Legislation, V-95 pp., 1927.
45. O'KEEFE, REV. GERALD MICHAEL, J.C.D., Matrimonial Dispensations, Powers of Bishops, Priests, and Confessors, VIII-232 pp., 1927.
46. QUIGLEY, REV. JOSEPH A. M., A.B., J.C.D., Condemned Societies, 139 pp., 1927.
47. ZAPLOTNIK, REV. JOHANNES LEO, J.C.D., De Vicariis Foraneis, X-142 pp., 1927.
48. DUSKIE, REV. JOHN ALOYSIUS, A.B., J.C.D., The Canonical Status of the Orientals in the United States, VIII-196 pp., 1928.
49. HYLAND, REV. FRANCIS EDWARD, J.C.D., Excommunication, Its Nature, Historical Development and Effects, VII-181 pp., 1928.
50. REINMANN, REV. GERALD JOSEPH, O.M.C., J.C.D., The Third Order Secular of Saint Francis, 201 pp., 1928.
51. SCHENK, REV. FRANCIS J., J.C.D., The Matrimonial Impediments of Mixed Religion and Disparity of Cult, XVI-318 pp., 1929.
52. COADY, REV. JOHN JOSEPH, S.T.D., J.U.D., A.M., The Appointment of Pastors, VIII-150 pp., 1929.
53. KAY, REV. THOMAS HENRY, J.C.D., Competence in Matrimonial Procedure, VIII-164 pp., 1929.
54. TURNER, REV. SIDNEY JOSEPH, C.P., J.U.D., The Vow of Poverty, XLIX-217 pp., 1929.
55. KEARNEY, REV. RAYMOND A., A.B., S.T.D., J.C.D., The Principles of Delegation, VII-149 pp., 1929.
56. CONRAN, REV. EDWARD JAMES, A.B., J.C.D., The Interdict, V-163 pp., 1930.
57. O'NEILL, REV. WILLIAM H., J.C.D., Papal Rescripts of Favor, VII-218 pp., 1930.
58. BASTNAGEL, REV. CLEMENT VINCENT, J.U.D., The Appointment of Parochial Adjutants and Assistants, XV-257 pp., 1930.
59. FERRY, REV. WILLIAM A., A.B., J.C.D., Stole Fees, V-136 pp., 1930.
60. COSTELLO, REV. JOHN MICHAEL, A.B., J.C.D., Domicile and Quasi-Domicile, VII-201 pp., 1930.
61. KREMER, REV. MICHAEL NICHOLAS, A.B., S.T.B., J.C.D., Church Support in the United States, VI-136 pp., 1930.
62. ANGULO, REV. LUIS, C.M., J.C.D., Legislation de la Iglesia sobre la intencion en la application de la Santa Misa, VII-104 pp., 1931.
63. FREY, REV. WOLFGANG NORBERT, O.S.B., A.B., J.C.D., The Act of Religious Profession, VIII-174 pp., 1931.
64. ROBERTS, REV. JAMES BRENDAN, A.B., J.C.D., The Banns of Marriage, XIV-140 pp., 1931.
65. RYDER, REV. RAYMOND ALOYSIUS, A.B., J.C.D., Simony, IX-151 pp., 1931.
66. CAMPAGNA, REV. ANGELO, PH.D., J.U.D., Il Vicario Generale del Vescovo, VII-205 pp., 1931.
67. COX, REV. JOSEPH GODFREY, A.B., J.C.D., The Administration of Seminaries, VI-124 pp., 1931.

68. GREGORY, REV. DONALD J., J.U.D., The Pauline Privilege, XV-165 pp., 1931.
69. DONOHUE, REV. JOHN F., J.C.D., The Impediment of Crime, VII-110 pp., 1931.
70. DOOLEY, REV. EUGENE A., O.M.I., J.C.D., Church Law on Sacred Relics, IX-143 pp., 1931.
71. ORTH, REV. CLEMENT RAYMOND, O.M.C., J.C.D., The Approbation of Religious Institutes, 171 pp., 1931.
72. PERNICONE, REV. JOSEPH M., A.B., J.C.D., The Ecclesiastical Prohibition of Books, XII-267 pp., 1932.
73. CLINTON, REV. CONNELL, A.B., J.C.D., The Paschal Precept, IX-108 pp., 1932.
74. DONNELLY, REV. FRANCIS B., A.M., S.T.L., J.C.D., The Diocesan Synod, VIII-125 pp., 1932.
75. TORRENTE, REV. CAMILO, C.M.F., J.C.D., Las Procesiones Sagradas, V-145 pp., 1932.
76. MURPHY, REV. EDWIN J., C.PP.S., J.C.D., Suspension Ex Informata Conscientia, XI-122 pp., 1932.
77. MACKENZIE, REV. ERIC F., A.M., S.T.L., J.C.D., The Delict of Heresy in its Commission, Penalization, Absoluton, VII-124 pp., 1932.
78. LYONS, REV. AVITUS E., S.T.B., J.C.D., The Collegiate Tribunal of First Instance, XI-147 pp., 1932.
79. CONNOLLY, REV. THOMAS A., J.C.D., Appeals, XI-195 pp., 1932.
80. SANGMEISTER, REV. JOSEPH V., A.B., J.C.D., Force and Fear as Precluding Matrimonial Consent, V-211 pp., 1932.
81. JAEGER, REV. LEO A., A.B., J.C.D., The Administration of Vacant and Quasi-Vacant Episcopal Sees in the United States, IX-229 pp., 1932.
82. RIMLINGER, REV. HERBERT T., J.C.D., Error Invalidating Matrimonial Consent, VII-79 pp., 1932.
83. BARRETT, REV. JOHN D. M., S.S., J.C.D., A Comparative Study of the Councils of Baltimore and the Code of Canon Law, X-223 pp., 1932.
84. CARBERRY, REV. JOHN J., PH.D., S.T.D., J.C.D., The Juridical Form of Marriage, X-177 pp., 1934.
85. DOLAN, REV. JOHN L., A.B., J.C.D., The Defensor Vinculi, XII-157 pp., 1934.
86. HANNAN, REV. JEROME D., A.M., S.T.D., LL.B., J.C.D., The Canon Law of Wills, IX-517 pp., 1934.
87. LEMIEUX, REV. DELISE A., A.M., J.C.D., The Sentence in Ecclesiastical Procedure, IX-131 pp., 1934.
88. O'ROURKE, REV. JAMES J., A.B., J.C.D., Parish Registers, VII-109 pp., 1934.
89. TIMLIN, REV. BARTHOLOMEW, O.F.M., A.M., J.C.D., Conditional Matrimonial Consent, X-381 pp., 1934.
90. WAHL, REV. FRANCIS X., A.B., J.C.D., The Matrimonial Impediments of Consanguinity and Affinity, VI-125 pp., 1934.
91. WHITE, REV. ROBERT J., A.B., LL.B., S.T.B., J.C.D., Canonical Ante-Nuptial Promises and the Civil Law, VI-152 pp., 1934.

92. Herrera, Rev. Antonio Parra, O.C.D., J.C.D., Legislacion Ecclesiastica sobra el Ayuno y la Abstinencia, XI-191 pp., 1935.
93. Kennedy, Rev. Edwin J., J.C.D., The Special Matrimonial Process in Cases of Evident Nullity, X-165 pp., 1935.
94. Manning, Rev. John J., A.B., J.C.D., Presumption of Law in Matrimonial Procedure, XI-111 pp., 1935.
95. Moeder, Rev. John M., J.C.D., The Proper Bishop for Ordination and Dimissorial Letters, VII-135 pp., 1935.
96. O'Mara, Rev. William A., A.B., J.C.D., Canonical Causes for Matrimonial Dispensations, IX-155 pp., 1935.
97. Reilly, Rev. Peter, J.C.D., Residence of Pastors, IX-81 pp., 1935.
98. Smith, Rev. Mariner T., O.P., S.T.Lr., J.C.D., The Penal Law for Religious, VIII-169 pp., 1935.
99. Whalen, Rev. Donald W., A.M., J.C.D., The Value of Testimonial Evidence in Matrimonial Procedure, XIII-297 pp., 1935.
100. Cleary, Rev. Joseph F., J.C.D., Canonical Limitations on the Alienation of Church Property, VIII-141 pp., 1936.
101. Glynn, Rev. John C., J.C.D., The Promoter of Justice, XX-337 pp., 1936.
102. Brennan, Rev. James H., S.S., M.A., S.T.B., J.C.D., The Simple Convalidation of Marriage, VI-135 pp., 1937.
103. Brunini, Rev. Joseph Bernard, J.C.D., The Clerical Obligations of Canons 139 and 142, X-121 pp., 1937.
104. Connor, Rev. Maurice, A.B., J.C.D., The Administrative Removal of Pastors, VIII-159 pp., 1937.
105. Guilfoyle, Rev. Merlin Joseph, J.C.D., Custom, XI-144 pp., 1937.
106. Hughes, Rev. James Austin, A.B., A.M., J.C.D., Witnesses in Criminal Trials of Clerics, IX-140 pp., 1937.
107. Jansen, Rev. Raymond J., A.B., S.T.L., J.C.D., Canonical Provisions for Catechetical Instruction, VII-153 pp., 1937.
108. Kealy, Rev. John James, A.B., J.C.D., The Introductory Libellus in Church Court Procedure, XI-121 pp., 1937.
109. McManus, Rev. James Edward, C.SS.R., J.C.D., The Administration of Temporal Goods in Religious Institutes, XVI-196 pp., 1937.
110. Moriarty, Rev. Eugene James, J.C.D., Oaths in Ecclesiastical Courts, X-115 pp., 1937.
111. Rainer, Rev. Eligius George, C.SS.R., J.C.D., Suspension of Clerics, XVII-249 pp., 1937.
112. Reilly, Rev. Thomas F., C.SS.R., J.C.D., Visitation of Religious, VI-195 pp., 1938.
113. Moriarty, Rev. Francis E., C.SS.R., J.C.D., The Extraordinary Absolution from Censures, XV-334 pp., 1938.
114. Connolly, Rev. Nicholas P., J.C.D., The Canonical Erection of Parishes, X-132 pp., 1938.
115. Donovan, Rev. James Joseph, J.C.D., The Pastor's Obligation in Prenuptial Investigation, XII-322 pp., 1938.

116. HARRIGAN, REV. ROBERT J., M.A., S.T.B., J.C.D., The Radical Sanation of Invalid Marriages, VIII-208 pp., 1938.
117. BOFFA, REV. CONRAD HUMBERT, J.C.D., Canonical Provisions for Catholic Schools, VII-211 pp., 1939.
118. PARSONS, REV. ANSCAR JOHN, O.M.CAP., J.C.D., Canonical Elections, XII-236 pp., 1939.
119. REILLY, REV. EDWARD MICHAEL, A.B., J.C.D., The General Norms of Dispensation, XII-156 pp., 1939.
120. RYAN, REV. GERALD ALOYSIUS, A.B., J.C.D., Principles of Episcopal Jurisdiction, XII-172 pp., 1939.
121. BURTON, REV. FRANCIS JAMES, C.S.C., A.B., J.C.D., A Commentary on Canon 1125, X-222 pp., 1940.
122. MIASKIEWICZ, REV. FRANCIS SIGISMUND, J.C.D., Supplied Jurisdiction According to Canon 209, XII-340 pp., 1940.
123. RICE, REV. PARTICK WILLIAM, A.B., J.C.D., Proof of Death in Prenuptial Investigation, VIII-156 pp., 1940.
124. ANGLIN, REV. THOMAS FRANCIS, M.S., J.C.D., The Eucharistic Fast, VIII-183 pp., 1941.
125. COLEMAN, REV. JOHN JEROME, J.C.D., The Minister of Confirmation, VI-153 pp., 1941.
126. DOWNS, REV. JOSEPH EMMANUEL, A.B., J.C.D., The Concept of Clerical Immunity, XI-163 pp., 1941.
127. ESSWEIN, REV. ANTHONY ALBERT, J.C.D., Extrajudicial Penal Powers of Ecclesiastical Superiors, X-144 pp., 1941.
128. FARRELL, REV. BENJAMIN FRANCIS, M.A., S.T.L., J.C.D., The Rights and Duties of the Local Ordinary Regarding Congregations of Women Religious of Pontifical Approval, V-195 pp., 1941.
129. FEENEY, REV. THOMAS JOHN, A.B., S.T.L., J.C.D., Restitutio in Integrum, VI-169 pp., 1941.
130. FINDLAY, REV. STEPHEN WILLIAM, O.S.B., A.B., J.C.D., Canonical Norms Governing the Deposition and Degradation of Clerics, XVII-279 pp., 1941.
131. GOODWINE, REV. JOHN, A.B., S.T.L., J.C.D., The Right of the Church to Acquire Property, VIII-119 pp., 1941.
132. HESTON, REV. EDWARD LOUIS, C.S.C., PH.D., S.T.D., J.C.D., The Alienation of Church Property in the United States, XII-222 pp., 1941.
133. HOGAN, REV. JAMES JOHN, A.B., S.T.L., J.C.D., Judicial Advocates and Procurators, XIII-200 pp., 1941.
134. KEALY, REV. THOMAS M., A.B., LITT.B., J.C.D., Dowry of Women Religious, IX-152 pp., 1941.
135. KEENE, REV. MICHAEL JAMES, O.S.B., J.C.D., Religious Ordinaries and Canon 198, V-164 pp., 1942.
136. KERIN, REV. CHARLES A., S.S., M.A., S.T.B., J.C.D., The Privation of Christian Burial, XVI-279 pp., 1941.
137. LOUIS, REV. WILLIAM FRANCIS, M.A., J.C.D., Diocesan Archives, X-101 pp., 1941.
138. McDEVITT, REV. GILBERT JOSEPH, A.B., J.C.D., Legitimacy and Legitimation, X-247 pp., 1941.

139. McDonough, Rev. Thomas Joseph, A.B., J.C.D., Apostolic Administrators, X-217 pp., 1941.
140. Meier, Rev. Carl Anthony, A.B., J.C.D., Penal Administrative Procedure Against Negligent Pastors, XI-240 pp., 1941.
141. Schmidt, Rev. John Rogg, A.B., J.C.D., The Principles of Authentic Interpretation in Canon 17 of the Code of Canon Law, XII-331 pp., 1941.
142. Slafkosky, Rev. Andrew Leonard, A.B., J.C.D., The Canonical Episcopal Visitations of the Diocese, X-197 pp., 1941.
143. Swoboda, Rev. Innocent Robert, O.F.M., J.C.D., Ignorance in Relation to the Imputability of Delicts, IX-271 pp., 1941.
144. Dube, Rev. Arthur Joseph, A.B., J.C.D., The General Principles for the Reckoning of Time in Canon Law, VIII-299 pp., 1941.
145. McBride, Rev. James T., A.B., J.C.D., Incardination and Excardination of Seculars, XX-585 pp., 1941.
146. Krol, Rev. John T., J.C.D., The Defendant in Ecclesiastical Trials, XII-207 pp., 1942.
147. Comyns, Rev. Joseph J., C.SS.R., A.B., J.C.D., Papal and Episcopal Administration of Church Property, XIV-155 pp., 1942.
148. Barry, Rev. Garrett Francis, O.M.I., J.C.D., Violation of the Cloister, XII-260 pp., 1942.
149. Bolduc, Rev. Gatien, C.S.V., A.B., S.T.L., J.C.D., Les Etudes dans les Religions Cléricales, VIII-155 pp., 1942.
150. Boyle, Rev. David John, M.A., J.C.D., The Juridic Effects of Moral Certitude on Pre-Nuptial Guarantees, XII-188 pp., 1942.
151. Canavan, Rev. Walter Joseph, M.A., Litt.D., J.C.D., The Profession of Faith, XII-143 pp., 1942.
152. Desrochers, Rev. Bruno, A.B., Ph.L., S.T.B., J.C.D., Le Premier Concile Plénier de Québec et le Code de Droit Canonique, XIV-186 pp., 1942.
153. Dillon, Rev. Robert Edward, A.B., J.C.D., Common Law Marriage, X-148 pp., 1942.
154. Dodwell, Rev. Edward John, Ph.D., S.T.B., J.C.D., The Time and Place for the Celebration of Marriage, X-156 pp., 1942.
155. Donnellan, Rev. Thomas Andrew, A.B., J.C.D., The Obligation of the Missa pro Populo, VII-131 pp., 1942.
156. Eltz, Rev. Louis Anthony, A.B., J.C.D., Coöperation in Crime, XII-208 pp., 1942.
157. Gass, Rev. Sylvester Francis, M.A., J.C.D., Ecclesiastical Pensions, XI-206 pp., 1942.
158. Guiniven, Rev. John Joseph, C.SS.R., J.C.D., The Precept of Hearing Mass, XIV-188 pp., 1942.
159. Gulczynski, Rev. John Theophilus, J.C.D., The Desecration and Violation of Churches, X-126 pp., 1942.
160. Hammill, Rev. John Leo, M.A., J.C.D., The Obligations of the Traveler According to Canon 14, VIII-204 pp., 1942.
161. Haydt, Rev. John Joseph, A.B., J.C.D., Reserved Benefices, XI-148 pp., 1942.
162. Huser, Rev. Roger John, O.F.M., A.B., J.C.D., The Crime of Abortion in Canon Law, XII-187 pp., 1942.

163. KEARNEY, REV. FRANCIS PATRICK, A.B., S.T.L., J.C.D., The Principles of Canon 1127, X-162 pp., 1942.
164. LINAHEN, REV. LEO JAMES, S.T.L., J.C.D., De Absolutione Complicis In Peccato Turpi, 114 pp., 1942.
165. McCLOSKEY, REV. JOSEPH ALOYSIUS, A.B., J.C.D., The Subject of Ecclesiastical Law According to Canon 12, XVII-246 pp., 1942.
166. O'NEILL, REV. FRANCIS JOSEPH, C.SS.R., J.C.D., The Dismissal of Religious in Temporary Vows, XIII-220 pp., 1942.
167. PRINCE, REV. JOHN EDWARD, A.B., S.T.D., J.C.D., The Diocesan Chancellor, X-136 pp., 1942.
168. RIESNER, REV. ALBERT JOSEPH, C.SS.R., J.C.D., Apostates and Fugitives from Religious Institutes, IX-168 pp., 1942.
169. STENGER, REV. JOSEPH BERNARD, J.C.D., The Mortgaging of Church Property, 186 pp., 1942.
170. WALDRON, REV. JOSEPH FRANCIS, A.B., J.C.D., The Minister of Baptism, XII-197 pp., 1942.
171. WILLETT, REV. ROBERT ALBERT, J.C.D., The Probative Value of Documents in Ecclesiastical Trials, X-124 pp., 1942.
172. WOEBER, REV. EDWARD MARTIN, M.A., J.C.D., The Interpellations, XII-161 pp., 1942.
173. BENKO, REV. MATTHEW ALOYSIUS, O.S.B., M.A., J.C.D., The Abbot *Nullius*, XVI-148 pp., 1943.
174. CHRIST, REV. JOSEPH JAMES, M.A., S.T.L., J.C.D., Dispensation from Vindicative Penalties, XIII-285 pp., 1943.
175. CLANCY, REV. PATRICK M. J., O.P., A.B., S.T.LR., J.C.D., The Local Religious Superior, X-229 pp., 1943.
176. CLARKE, REV. THOMAS JAMES, J.C.D., Parish Societies, XII-147 pp., 1943.
177. CONNOLLY, REV. JOHN PATRICK, S.T.L., J.C.D., Synodal Examiners, and Parish Priest Consultors, X-223 pp., 1943.
178. DRUMM, REV. WILLIAM MARTIN, A.B., J.C.D., Hospital Chaplains, XII-175 pp., 1943.
179. FLANAGAN, REV. BERNARD JOSEPH, A.B., S.T.L., J.C.D., The Canonical Erection of Religious Houses, X-147 pp., 1943.
180. KELLEHER, REV. STEPHEN JOSEPH, A.B., S.T.B., J.C.D., Discussions with Non-Catholics: Canonical Legislation, X-93 pp., 1943.
181. LEWIS, REV. GORDIAN, C.P., J.C.D., Chapters in Religious Institutes, XII-169 pp., 1943.
182. MARX, REV. ADOLPH, J.C.D., The Declaration of Nullity of Marriages Contracted Outside the Church, X-151 pp., 1943.
183. MATULENAS, REV. RAYMOND ANTHONY, O.S.B., A.B., J.C.D., Communication, a Source of Privileges, XII-225 pp., 1943.
184. O'LEARY, REV. CHARLES GERARD, C.SS.R., J.C.D., Religious Dismissed After Perpetual Profession, X-213 pp., 1943.
185. POWER, REV. CORNELIUS MICHAEL, J.C.D., The Blessing of Cemeteries, XII-231 pp., 1943.
186. SHUHLER, REV. RALPH VINCENT, O.S.A., J.C.D., Privileges of Religious to Absolve and Dispense, XII-195 pp., 1943.

187. Ziolkowski, Rev. Thaddeus Stanislaus, A.B., J.C.D., The Consecration and Blessing of Churches, XII-151 pp., 1943.
188. Heneghan, Rev. John Joseph, S.T.D., J.C.D., The Marriages of Unworthy Catholics: Canons 1065 and 1066, XVI-213 pp., 1944.
189. Carroll, Rev. Coleman Francis, M.A., S.T.L., J.C.L., Charitable Institutions.
190. Ciesluk, Rev. Joseph Edward, Ph.B., S.T.L., J.C.D., National Parishes in the United States, VI-178 pp., 1944.
191. Coburn, Rev. Vincent Paul, A.B., J.C.D., Marriages of Conscience, XII-172 pp., 1944.
192. Connors, Rev. Charles Paul, C.S.Sp., A.B., J.C.D., Extra-Judicial Procurators in the Code of Canon Law, X-94 pp., 1944.
193. Coyle, Rev. Paul Raymond, A.B., J.C.D., Judicial Exceptions, IX-142 pp., 1944.
194. Fair, Rev. Bartholomew Francis, A.B., S.T.L., J.C.D., The Impediment of Abduction, XII-122 pp., 1944.
195. Gallagher, Rev. Thomas Raphael, O.P., A.B., S.T.Lr., J.C.D., The Examination of the Qualities of the Ordinand, X-166 pp., 1944.
196. Gannon, Rev. John Mark, S.T.L., J.C.D., The Interstices Required for the Promotion to Orders, VII-100 pp., 1944.
197. Goldsmith, Rev. J. William, B.C.S., S.T.L., J.C.D., The Competence of Church and State Over Marriage — Disputed Points, X-128 pp., 1944.
198. Goodwine, Rev. Joseph Gerard, A.B., S.T.B., J.C.D., The Reception of Converts, XIV-326 pp., 1944.
199. Kowalski, Rev. Romuald Eugene, O.F.M., A.B., J.C.D., Sustenance of Religious Houses of Regulars, X-174 pp., 1944.
200. McCoy, Rev. Alan Edward, O.F.M., J.C.D., Force and Fear in Relation to Delictual Imputability and Penal Responsibility, XII-160 pp., 1944.
201. McDevitt, Rev. Vincent John, Ph.B., S.T.L., J.C.L., Perjury.
202. Martin, Rev. Thomas Owen, Ph.D., S.T.D., J.C.D., Adverse Possession, Prescription and Limitation of Actions: The Canonical "Præscriptio," XX-208 pp., 1944.
203. Miklosovic, Rev. Paul John, A.B., J.C.L., Attempted Marriages and Their Consequent Juridic Effects.
204. Mundy, Rev. Thomas Maurice, A.B., S.T.L., J.C.D., The Union of Parishes, X-164 pp., 1944.
205. O'Dea, Rev. John Coyle, A.B., J.C.D., The Matrimonial Impediment of Nonage, VIII-126 pp., 1944.
206. Olalia, Rev. Alexander Ayson, S.T.L., J.C.D., A Comparative Study of the Christian Constitution of States and the Constitution of the Philippine Commonwealth, XII-136 pp., 1944.
207. Poisson, Rev. Pierre-Marie, C.S.C., A.B., Ph.L., Th.L., J.C.L., Droits Patrimoniaux des Maisons et des Eglises Religieuses.
208. Stadalnikas, Rev. Casimir Joseph, M.I.C., J.C.D., Reservation of Censures, X-141 pp., 1944.

209. SULLIVAN, REV. EUGENE HENRY, S.T.L., J.C.D., Proof of the Reception of the Sacraments, X-165 pp., 1944.
210. VAUGHAN, REV. WILLIAM EDWARD, J.C.D., Constitutions for Diocesan Courts, X-210 pp., 1944.
211. PARO, REV. GINO, S.T.D., J.C.L., The Right of Apostolic Delegation.
212. BALZER, REV. RALPH FRANCIS, C.P., J.C.D., The Computation of Time in a Canonical Novitiate, X-227 pp., 1945.
213. DOUGHERTY, REV. JOHN WHELAN, A.B., S.T.L., J.C.D., De Inquisitione Speciali, XII-195 pp., 1945.
214. DZIOB, REV. MICHAEL WALTER, J.C.D., The Sacred Congregation for the Oriental Church, XII-181 pp., 1945.
215. EIDENSCHINK, REV. JOHN ALBERT, O.S.B., B.A., J.C.D., The Election of Bishops in the Letters of Pope Gregory the Great, VII-200 pp., 1945.
216. GILL, REV. NICHOLAS, C.P., J.C.D., The Spiritual Prefect in Clerical Religious Houses of Study, X-140 pp., 1945.
217. HYNES, REV. HARRY GERARD, S.T.L., J.C.D., The Privileges of Cardinals, XII-183 pp., 1945.
218. MCDEVITT, REV. GERARD VINCENT, S.T.L., J.C.D., The Renunciation of an Ecclesiastical Office, XIV-179 pp., 1945.
219. MANNING, REV. JOSEPH LEROY, J.C.D., The Free Conferral of Offices, VIII-116 pp., 1945.
220. MEYER, REV. LOUIS G., O.S.B., A.B., S.T.B., J.C.D., Alms-gathering by Religious, XII-163 pp., 1945.
221. O'DONNELL, REV. CLETUS FRANCIS, M.A., J.C.D., The Marriage of Minors, XII-268 pp., 1945.
222. PRUNSKIS, REV. JOSEPH, J.C.D., Comparative Law, Ecclesiastical and Civil, in Lithuanian Concordat, X-161 pp., 1945.
223. SWEENEY, REV. FRANCIS PATRICK, C.SS.R., J.C.D., The Reduction of Clerics to the Lay State, X-199 pp., 1945.
224. VOGELPOHL, REV. HENRY JOHN, J.C.D., The Simple Impediments to Holy Orders, XVI-190 pp., 1945.
225. BROCKHAUS, REV. THOMAS AQUINAS, O.S.B., J.C.D., Religious Who Are Known as *Conversi*, X-127 pp., 1945.
226. GRIESE, REV. N. ORVILLE, S.T.D., J.C.D., The Marriage Contract and the Procreation of Offspring, XVI-224 pp., 1946.
227. BOUDREAUX, REV. WARREN LOUIS, J.C.D., The "*ab acatholicis nati*" of Canon 1099, § 2, XII-110 pp., 1946.
228. BOWE, REV. THOMAS JOSEPH, A.B., J.C.D., Religious Superioresses, VIII-206 pp., 1946.
229. DIEDERICHS, REV. MICHAEL FERDINAND, S.C.J., J.C.D., The Jurisdiction of the Latin Ordinaries Over Their Oriental Subjects, XIV-153 pp., 1946.
230. DINGMAN, REV. MAURICE JOHN, A.B., S.T.L., J.C.L., The Plaintiff in Contentious Trials.
231. FRISON, REV. BASIL, C.M.F., M.MUS., J.C.D., The Retroactivity of Law, X-221 pp., 1946.
232. GALVIN, REV. WILLIAM ANTHONY, M.A., J.C.D., The Administrative Transfer of Pastors, XII-288 pp., 1946.

233. GORACY, REV. JOSEPH C., J.C.L., The Diriment Matrimonial Impediment of Major Orders.
234. HALE, REV. JOSEPH FRANCIS, M.A., S.T.L., J.C.L., The Pastor of Burial.
235. HENRY, REV. JOSEPH ARTHUR, A.B., J.C.D., The Mass and Holy Communion: Inter-Ritual Law, XII-138 pp., 1946.
236. LINENBERGER, REV. HERBERT, C.PP.S., J.C.L., The False Denunciation of an Innocent Confessor.
237. LOWRY, REV. JAMES MARTIN, A.B., J.C.D., Dispensation from Private Vows, XII-266 pp., 1946.
238. LYNCH, REV. GEORGE EDWARD, A.B., S.T.L., J.C.D., Coadjutors and Auxiliaries of Bishops, X-107 pp., 1947.
239. LYNCH, REV. TIMOTHY, M.S.SS.T., J.C.D., Contracts Between Bishops and Religious Congregations, XIV-232 pp., 1946.
240. MCCLUNN, REV. JUSTIN DAVID, A.B., S.T.L., J.C.D., Administrative Recourse, VII-142 pp., 1946.
241. LOHMULLER, REV. MARTIN NICHOLAS, A.B., J.C.D., The Promulgation of Law, XII-140 pp., 1947.
242. MCGRATH, REV. JAMES, A.B., J.C.D., The Privilege of the Canon, XII-156 pp., 1946.
243. MARBACH, REV. JOSEPH FRANCIS, A.B., J.C.D., Marriage Legislation for the Catholics of the Oriental Rites in the United States and Canada, XIV-314 pp., 1946.
244. SHIMKUS, REV. BERNARD ALOYSIUS, A.B., J.C.L., The Determination and Transfer of Rite.
245. SMITH, REV. VINCENT MICHAEL, A.B., S.T.L., J.C.L., Ignorance Affecting Matrimonial Consent.
246. WACHTRLE, REV. PAUL ANTHONY, A.B., J.C.L., The Baptism of of the Children of Non-Catholics.
247. CROTTY, REV. MATTHEW MICHAEL, J.C.L., The Recipient of First Holy Communion.
248. EAGLETON, REV. GEORGE, J.C.L., The Quinquennial Faculties, Formula IV.
249. GIBBONS, REV. MARION LEO, C.M., LL.B., J.C.L., Domicile of the Wife Unlawfully Separated from Her Husband.
250. KELLY, REV. BERNARD MATTHEW, S.T.L., J.C.L., The Functions Reserved to Pastors.
251. KILCULLEN, REV. THOMAS JOHN, LL.M., J.C.L., The Collegiate Moral Person as Party Litigant.
252. LAFONTAINE, REV. GERMAIN JOSEPH, W.F., J.C.L., Relations Canoniques entre le Missionnaire et Ses Superieurs.
253. LANE, REV. LORAS THOMAS, A.B., S.T.L., J.C.L., Matrimonial Procedure in the Ordinary Court of Second Instance.
254. LOVER, REV. JAMES FRANCIS, C.SS.R., J.C.L., The Master of Novices.
255. MCNICHOLAS, REV. TIMOTHY JOSEPH, J.C.L., The *Septimæ Manus* Witness.
256. MAROSITZ, REV. JOSEPH JOHN, M.S.C., J.C.L., Obligations and Privileges of Religious Promoted to the Episcopal or Cardinalitial Dignities.

257. MURPHY, REV. FRANCIS JOSEPH, A.B., J.C.L., Legislative Powers of the Provincial Council.
258. O'BRIEN, REV. ROMAEUS WILLIAM, O.CARM., J.C.L., The Provincial Superior in Religious Orders of Men.
259. PFALLER, REV. BENEDICT AUGUSTINE, O.S.B., J.C.L., The *Ipso Facto* Effected Dismissal of Religious.
260. POPEK, REV. ALPHONSE SYLVESTER, M.A., J.C.L., The Rights and Obligations of Metropolitans.
261. RISTUCCIA, REV. BERNARD JOSEPH, C.M., J.C.L., Quasi-Religious.
262. SONNTAG, REV. NATHANIEL LOUIS, O.F.M.CAP., J.C.L., Censorship of Special Classes of Books.
263. STADLER, REV. JOSEPH NICHOLAS, J.C.L., Frequent Holy Communion.
264. SZAL, REV. IGNATIUS JOSEPH, J.C.L., The Communication of Catholics with Schismatics.
265. WAGNER, REV. URBAN STANLEY, O.F.M.CONV., J.C.L., Parochial Substitute Vicars and Supplying Priests.

www.ingramcontent.com/pod-product-compliance
Lightning Source LLC
LaVergne TN
LVHW050301080826
844660LV00012B/667
9780813224381